PHILOSOPHIC INQUIRY

LEWIS WHITE BECK
ROBERT L. HOLMES

SECOND EDITION

Prentice-Hall, Inc., Englewood Cliffs, New Jersey

PHILOSOPHIC INQUIRY

AN INTRODUCTION TO PHILOSOPHY

SECOND EDITION **PHILOSOPHIC INQUIRY**

LEWIS WHITE BECK

ROBERT L. HOLMES

© 1952, 1968 by Prentice-Hall, Inc.
Englewood Cliffs, New Jersey

Printed in the United States of America

Library of Congress Catalog Number: 68-10653

Current printing (last number):
10 9 8 7 6 5 4 3 2 1

PRENTICE-HALL INTERNATIONAL, INC.,
London

PRENTICE-HALL OF AUSTRALIA, PTY. LTD.,
Sydney

PRENTICE-HALL OF CANADA, LTD.,
Toronto

PRENTICE-HALL OF INDIA PRIVATE LTD.,
New Delhi

PRENTICE-HALL OF JAPAN, INC.,
Tokyo

. . . this first, and in one sense this sole, rule of reason:

Do not block the way of inquiry.
CHARLES SAUNDERS PEIRCE

PREFACE

"The problems of philosophy are the most natural, the most human, and the most perennially perplexing problems that confront thinking people. Philosophy is a persistent attempt to think things through. Only secondarily is it a study of the writings of philosophers, or a technical field with an obscure terminology. Philosophy is not the exclusive concern of professors of philosophy, but is the rigorous and responsible effort of intelligent men and women to examine their life, the universe, and their place in it.

"The writings of great philosophers of the past and of today are important in carrying through that examination of life without which, Socrates said, life is not worthy of man. But the basic problems of philosophy do not grow out of disputes among philosophers; they grow out of the bafflement and confusion that every intelligent person experiences when he wonders what man is, why he is here, and what his destiny is. Though answers to these questions may be demanded of that group of extraordinary men we call great philosophers, the questions themselves emerge in daily life, in science, in religion, in art, in morals, in politics, and in other deeply felt concerns of men."

These sentences drawn from the Preface to the first edition are as indicative of the basic conception of the second as they were of the first. Yet in the sixteen years that have passed since the first edition was published, there have been changes in the temper of life which have subtly affected the formulation of some questions for philosophic inquiry, and much more obvious changes in the style of philosophy itself. Although the first edition was by no means unaffected by those interests commonly referred to now as existential, analytic, and linguistic, these interests themselves were not subjected to much detailed philosophic inquiry or scrutiny. The techniques of linguistic analysis were used but seldom mentioned. Two decades of philosophizing have made the analytic and linguistic styles in philosophy better known to a wider public than they were then. They have spread into neighboring fields, so that now students' anticipations of what philosophy is and how it is to be practiced are somewhat different from what they were then. On the one hand, the thought and writings of existentialists have perhaps deepened the seriousness of some philosophic issues in the minds of the students of the '60's, and on the other hand, the degree of their analytic and linguistic sophistication has been heightened. The new edition takes into account these trends, and we believe and hope that it will be as acceptable as the first edition was, which was addressed to a different academic generation. Those who found the first edition to express the substance or spirit of their own philosophic commitments will find, we hope, that the large revisions we have made are in step with the revisions they themselves have made in their own thought.

The second edition is the result of a harmonious collaboration between the two authors. Although large amounts of the text of the first edition have been taken over into the second, no chapter has been left without extensive changes, and a few chapters (viz., Chapters 3, 7, 9, 10, 16) have been almost completely rewritten. Each author stands behind the book as a whole, and each has contributed to every chapter. But Mr. Beck has been primarily responsible for the rewriting of Chapters 8, 9, 10, and 12 and Mr. Holmes for the rewriting of the remaining chapters.

The authors are grateful to their colleague Professor R. James Kaufmann for judicious advice.

L.W.B.

R.L.H.

CONTENTS

9 THE LAWS OF NATURE AND HUMAN
FREEDOM 211

10 EXPLANATION AS A GOAL OF INQUIRY 242

11 METAPHYSICS AS HYPOTHESIS 269

12 NATURALISM I—MATERIALISM 288

13 NATURALISM II—CRITICAL NATURALISM 318

PHILOSOPHIC INQUIRY

PART ONE WHY PHILOSOPHY?

Philosophy is primarily a theoretical discipline but it may and, it is to be hoped, sometimes does have direct practical bearing in that its purpose is to increase our understanding of ourselves and the world. It is an extension of the type of thinking in which everyone engages whenever seriously questioning the meaning of life and man's place in the world. The philosopher also questions, but systematically and, as a rule, with greater rigor than the man on the street. The philosopher has an advantage—familiarity with a long tradition in which previous philosophers have attempted to answer the questions men have found most perplexing—and by careful attention to their efforts, he profits from their mistakes as well as from their insights.

Although philosophy is not easily defined, for philosophers have different conceptions of it, it possesses certain distinctive traits. Foremost among these is that it springs from an inquiring attitude that seeks to penetrate beyond the limits of settled, accepted knowledge. We illustrate this by two fairly simple but subtle questions: Is morality based upon theology? and Does man have a free will?

Philosophy's importance is its ability to provide a satisfactory method for arriving at sound beliefs; therefore it is important to understand some common modes of thought that it criticizes and to which it poses an alternative. Chapter 2 considers three of these—common sense, the appeal to faith, and the appeal to authority—each of which may be regarded as a substitute for disciplined inquiry. Each of these substitutes for inquiry contains pitfalls, and anyone seriously intent upon providing a solid foundation for his beliefs must be alert to them. A discussion of the limitations of these modes of thought provides an introduction to the epistemological and metaphysical problems in Part Two.

In addition to disclosing problems and inconsistencies in uncritical thinking, the following discussions will reveal how philosophy may have a clear, if not always immediately obvious, bearing upon many issues of human concern.

1 PHILOSOPHY AND PHILOSOPHIZING

"If a college student's mother died, his girl got pregnant, he acquired a loathesome disease, or he decided to become a conscientious objector, would he go to his philosophy professor for advice?" The writer who posed this question hardly wanted an answer. "Philosophy today," he continued, "is a complicated method of avoiding all the important problems of life."[1] This is not a new criticism. Plato reports that Thales, the father of western philosophy, having once stumbled into a well while studying the stars, was reproached for being so entranced with the heavens that he was unaware of what lay at his feet; and Plato added, prophetically, that anyone who becomes a philosopher is open to such mockery.

With the present world problems of poverty, civil rights, war, and the threat of nuclear war, what is the point of studying philosophy? Does not the immediacy of these problems make philosophy, by comparison, appear to be just a way of avoiding life's problems? Present day philosophy seems so to many people because they picture the philosopher as an elderly sage dispensing Confucian gems of wisdom, a man who not only should be infinitely wise but who should have at his disposal a ready-made set of directives for the resolution of all life's problems. Discovering that the contemporary philosopher is an ordinary person like themselves, that he disclaims privileged access to infallible knowledge, and that his work contains few directives for the ordinary man and in large part is scarcely comprehensible to him, they are disillusioned and conclude that he has betrayed his profession and sacrificed profundity for a factitious preoccupation with minutiae.

However, philosophy does not pretend to have answers to all the problems of men. The essence of philosophy is in the *search* for understanding—a better understanding of the world and the nature of man and his place in

---

[1]Kenneth Rexroth, "The 'Meditations' of Marcus Aurelius," *The Saturday Review*, January 29, 1966. Quoted by permission of The Saturday Review Inc.

the world. History records centuries of persistent attempts to further such understanding, attempts that have resulted in diverse and often conflicting accounts. A review of history can, of course, only disappoint those who expect philosophy to yield final answers intellectually satisfying to all men. As the etymology of the word suggests, it is a *love* of *wisdom* as distinguished from a love of knowledge. Wisdom consists of insight, soundness of perspective, and balance and proportion in judgment. A man who possesses a great many facts has knowledge; this can be had by anyone with good memory, dedication, and a modicum of intelligence. But as the presocratic philosopher Heraclitus once said, and as every college student knows who has ever complained that all he gets from his courses is spoon-fed facts, "much learning does not teach understanding."

Still, in seeking the sort of understanding that the philosopher does, one may thereby achieve a better understanding of some more pressing practical problems of life. A tradition dating back to the ancient Greeks holds that to illuminate the problems of conduct is ultimately the chief function of philosophy. For them, the study of the nature of reality had as its chief purpose the aim of enabling men to understand better how they should live. Accordingly, they distinguished the theoretical and the practical uses of reason: the former to understand the world, the latter to guide conduct. The attainment of excellence in each of these respects endowed a man with both theoretical and practical wisdom, traits that exemplified the highest excellence of man.

There was little agreement, however, concerning the correct account of reality, and different conceptions developed according to the various cultural, philosophical, political, and literary influences upon the speculations of different philosophers. Philosophical ideas are not spontaneous generations of the intellect in isolation both from its surrounding and from the personal temperament of its possessor. "Pretend what we may," the American pragmatist William James once wrote, "the whole man within us is at work when we form our philosophical opinions."[2] It has sometimes been said that the philosopher is the man whose intellect is attuned to reality. Also, different philosophers are, so to speak, tuned in on different wave lengths. What each one conveys to us of his listenings is inevitably influenced both by his personality and by the world around him. In this way a philosopher's thought reflects the spirit and temper of his time.

Plato (428?–347 B.C.), for whom a prime motive was to meet the challenge of the sophists, conceived reality in such a way as to provide an unshakable foundation for the values for guiding conduct. This led him to postulate a higher-order, supersensible realm of being apprehended solely through the intellect. By endowing such notions as Justice and Goodness with reality and enshrining them in this realm, he thought he had so consecrated the

[2]*Essays in Pragmatism* (New York: Hafner Publishing Co., Inc., 1965), p. 24.

foundations of human conduct as to preserve them for all time from those who would make moral values relative to desire, preference, and convention.

Epicurus (342–270 B.C.), on the other hand, was deeply influenced by a conception of the world derived from the presocratic philosophers Democritus and Leucippus. They believed that all reality consists of matter in the form of tiny atoms and that it is knowable only through sense-experience. Unlike Plato, Epicurus made an accomodation with the physical world and tailored his views about conduct accordingly. Sound guidance in life, he thought, issues from understanding man's limitations, the nature of his desires, and his place in a wholly material world holding no promise of an after-life.

However, even where philosophy strives to provide guidance for human conduct and supports its efforts with a whole theory about the nature of reality, it carries no guarantee to give answers to practical problems in all their particularity. The twentieth-century American pragmatist John Dewey, who throughout a lifetime emphasized the practical bearing of philosophy upon conduct, wrote that moral theory, a branch of philosophy dealing directly with conduct, can:

> ... render personal reflection more systematic and enlightened, suggesting alternatives that might otherwise be overlooked, and stimulating greater consistency in judgment. But it does not offer a table of commandments in a catechism in which answers are as definite as are the questions which are asked. It can render personal choice more intelligent, but it cannot take the place of personal decision.[3]

More recently the existentialists, who characteristically address themselves to problems of the human predicament, have stressed even more forcibly that each individual must assume full responsibility for making his *own* decisions. Neither philosophical, political, nor ecclesiastical authority can answer the most vital of life's problems—a realization that must come to anyone who is to achieve authentic existence. In this vein the French existentialist Simone de Beauvoir writes:

> The fact is that no behavior is ever authorized to begin with, and one of the concrete consequences of existentialist ethics is the rejection of all the previous justifications which might be drawn from the civilization, the age, and the culture; it is the rejection of every principle of authority.
> Freedom is the source from which all significations and all values spring. It is the original condition of all justification of existence.[4]

Whether or not one agrees with what they say, the truth in existentialism and pragmatism alike is that responsible human action must issue from autonomous personal choice. Philosophy, for which intellectual freedom and

---

[3] *Theory of the Moral Life* (New York: Holt, Rinehart & Winston, Inc., 1960), pp. 7f. Quoted by permission of the publisher.

[4] *The Ethics of Ambiguity* (New York: The Citadel Press, 1962), pp. 24, 142. Quoted by permission of The Philosophical Library, Inc.

integrity are the highest ideals, betrays itself if it tries to dictate in advance what such choices shall be.

Much of contemporary philosophy refrains from issuing practical injunctions for conduct; it successfully avoids having any practical bearing whatsoever. But there is no reason why it need have such bearing. As Bertrand Russell writes:

We must . . . renounce the hope that philosophy can promise satisfaction to our mundane desires. What it can do . . . is to help us to understand the general aspects of the world and the logical analysis of familiar but complex things. Through this achievement, by the suggestion of fruitful hypotheses, it may be indirectly useful in other sciences, notably mathematics, physics, and psychology. But a genuinely scientific philosophy cannot hope to appeal to any except those who have the wish to understand, to escape from intellectual bewilderment.[5]

The point here is that the justification of philosophy is not to be found in any practical application but rather in its capacity to satisfy the intellect. Herein lies the justification not only of philosophy but of liberal education itself. Neither poetry, medieval history, nor classical archaeology answer many of the practical problems of life; but they are not, or ought not to be, deprecated for that reason. If one is enriched by the study of a particular subject matter, that is justification enough for devoting his time to it or making the study of it his profession. This does not mean that one can *totally* neglect everything else in lieu of his chosen pursuit, for each individual has responsibilities as a person and a citizen that cannot conscionably be ignored. The American philosopher Arthur E. Murphy observes:

As a "whole man," or in other social relations, [the philosopher] of course has other social responsibilities. He may be called on in a crisis to help put out fires, or minister to the sick, or sign petitions for good causes, if he knows them to be good. If he also has the gift of prophecy, or of speaking with tongues, for that matter, by all means let him use it for the public weal. But let him not confuse these gifts, or these responsibilities, with the business of philosophy, or suppose himself qualified as a philosopher to give orders to the fire brigade or as a fire fighter to propound an axiology in which the quenching of conflagrations is set up as the overriding goal of human life. That kind of activity puts out few fires and is, at best, a very dubious approach to philosophic wisdom.[6]

What this means is that philosophy may, depending upon one's personality and where one's philosophical inquiries lead him, illuminate many of life's problems but to do so is not its sole or even its first business. Its first business is to deepen man's understanding of himself and the world, without which understanding practical deliberation will lack direction.

---

[5]*Our Knowledge of the External World* (New York: Mentor Books, 1960), p. 22. Quoted by permission of George Allen & Unwin, Ltd.

[6]W. H. Hay, M. G. Singer, and A. E. Murphy, eds., *Reason and the Common Good* (Englewood Cliffs: Prentice-Hall, Inc., 1963), p. 384.

WHAT IS PHILOSOPHY?

We have been talking *about* philosophy and its bearing upon conduct but the question at issue cannot be fully answered without first understanding *what* philosophy is. Such understanding does not come easily; philosophy cannot be summarized in a few words. Nonetheless, there are some general traits that characterize most of philosophy.

An Inquiring Attitude

Philosophy, first of all, is more an attitude or way of approaching diverse problems than it is a specifiable set of beliefs or doctrines. Essential ingredients in this attitude are inquisitiveness, imagination, and a capacity to see through the immediate and familiar to underlying complexities. Only the person who is capable of experiencing perplexity about the meaning of his life, his relationship to others, and the nature of the world about him and who desires to understand more about these matters than can be learned from history books or in the science laboratory will ever embark in more than cursory fashion upon inquiry that is distinctively philosophical.

An Outgrowth of Ordinary Reflection

For all of its specialization in recent years, philosophy is still basically continuous in spirit with reflection of the sort we all engage in when we are faced with great problems and try to trace out their ramifications in our lives as a whole. But the philosopher goes about this process more seriously, more persistently, and more skillfully than most of us who save our best effort for dealing with more immediate problems.

Every man has opinions on the most basic subjects that the philosopher investigates—hence, the important link of philosophy to the common man but also the chief difference between him and the technically trained philosopher. Most of us, for example, give some thought to the type of life we desire and ideals to which we aspire; but our deliberations upon these matters usually fall short of the meticulous concern for clarity that characterizes the best efforts of the philosopher. As a contemporary moral philosopher puts this:

... the clarification of ideals and the clarification of the terms by means of which they are articulated is a single process, and ... in a humble way, every attempt to determine what sort of life one really wants to live involves essentially the same painful process of analyzing and clarifying the meanings and uses of words to which the analytical philosopher devotes himself professionally. The difference between them is not so much a difference in method as a difference in the thoroughness and sensitivity with which it is applied.[7]

[7]Henry D. Aiken, *Reason and Conduct* (New York: Alfred A. Knopf, Inc., 1962), p. 30. Quoted by permission of the publisher.

Both the philosopher and the common man would like to know whether there is an ideal of justice binding on every man and on every state. Both want to know what, if any, are the limits of human knowledge. Both believe in, disbelieve in, or have doubts about the existence of God. Both speculate on the question of freedom of the will and on the limits of human responsibility. Both think they have, or are looking for, some satisfactory answer to the question of what man is and what is his place in the scheme of things. Most of our ideas on such matters, however, are seldom thought out clearly and systematically and rarely hang together well. But they are important to us. "The philosophy of the common man," Santayana once said, "is an old wife that gives him no pleasure, yet he cannot live without her, and resents any aspersions that strangers may cast on her character."[8]

The common man dislikes theories, but someone has aptly described him as "that wildest of all possible theorists," for he has *many* theories. Rather than having *one* theory to help us answer the above, and still other, questions, most of us hold a separate opinion about each one resulting in a perhaps incompatible aggregate. The theories he has, to be sure, are not usually *labeled* theories; they are regarded simply as opinions, attitudes, or beliefs. He has formed them from his parents, his church, books, newspapers, friends, and enemies. Many a man, had he the wit of Dean Acheson, could rightly say, "All I know I have learned at my mother's knee, or some other joint."

It is not surprising that such beliefs do not usually hang together very well. The unity they have, such as it is, is not a logical unity, with one belief implying or strengthening the others. Their unity is that they are the beliefs that are congenial to a given man—beliefs that fit his own character, sentiments, and needs. Taken together, this complex of beliefs and attitudes is usually called one's "philosophy of life." "Tell me what your philosophy is," the German philosopher Fichte once said, "and I shall tell you the sort of man you are."

Philosophical Questions Are Critical

Philosophy, as the preceding suggests, is, in part, a critical analysis and assessment of conceptions and meanings. These are often taken for granted in some field of endeavor. Every field of experience—science as much as religion—bases its attitudes and inquiries on assumptions that are accepted as starting points. They are accepted on faith and generally used without much critical examination. One of the principal tasks of the philosopher is to examine and evaluate them, to make their meaning explicit, to determine the limits of their application, and to see the grounds on which they may be justified.

This concern is not a new one; it provided the point of departure for even Socrates and Plato. They believed, just as we said of philosophy itself, that

---

[8]George Santayana, *Scepticism and Animal Faith* (New York: Dover Publications, Inc., 1955), p. 11. Quoted by permission of Dover Publications, Inc.

before one could learn very much *about* a given subject he first had to understand clearly *what* it was he was talking about. Such understanding was to be sought by attempting to provide definitions for key concepts. Thus Plato's dialogues often developed around such questions as "What is knowledge?" "What is justice?" and "What is virtue?" Basically this same aim, to get clear in our thinking, though it often receives different expression and involves a different methodology, underlies contemporary as well as traditional philosophy.

Moritz Schlick, an Austrian philosopher who believed that criticism was the whole duty of philosophy, emphasized the bearing of philosophy on the concepts and presuppositions of other intellectual pursuits when he wrote:

There are not specific "philosophical" truths which would contain the solution of specific "philosophical" problems, but philosophy has the task of finding the meaning of all problems and [of] their solutions. It must be defined as *the activity of finding meaning.*[9]

Many of the greatest philosophers of the past are remembered not so much for the great systems and world views that they propounded as for their painstaking analysis of problems and of techniques of solving them. David Hume's analysis of the concept of cause, for instance, to be examined in Chapter 9, is a permanent part of philosophical analysis, acknowledged to be such even by those who disagree with Hume's conclusions. Philosophers have made some very important contributions when they first discerned an assumption or learned to ask a new question that had been overlooked by their predecessors. Their questions were frequently more important than the answers they were able to give.

We shall see many illustrations of philosophical criticism of accepted but vague meanings; the discussion of common sense in Chapter 2 is such an analysis. We cannot answer a question such as "Is common sense dependable?" or consider the common philosophical question, "Has life any meaning?" until we know what each means. Surely everyone's philosophy of life has some answer to the meaning of life, but rather than attempting to tag an answer to such a vague question the philosopher first analyzes the question. Such questions must be made precise, or they cannot be intelligently discussed at all. Spinoza and Hegel and Augustine tried to answer the question of the meaning of life only after they had inquired into what the question itself meant, whereas the same question asked by Job was not a precise question so much as an expression of puzzlement or intellectual bafflement. The man who asks the question usually wants consolation or some message that will satisfy him and either justify or still his rebellion against things. The philosopher quietly begins, "What do you mean by 'meaning'?"

The world has changed much since many accepted ideas were formulated.

---

[9]"The Future of Philosophy," *The University of the Pacific Philosophy Institute Publications in Philosophy*, 1932, p. 58.

It may well be, as many people believe, that the ideas they and their fellows have are becoming useless for making the modern world really intelligible and for guiding us through its complexities. Copernicus upset more than astronomy; he changed men's ways of looking at "everything," and one task of philosophy from his time until the end of the seventeenth century was to repair the damage that he had done to older views of life. But the damage was repaired by changing men's views, not by attacking the astronomers. The formulation of Darwin's theory of evolution in 1859 delivered another profound shock, from which many institutions and the minds of many men have not yet fully recovered. Similar revolutions in thought have been started by Freud and by Einstein. Because intellectual revolutions are slow and seldom complete, the minds of many men are filled with inconsistent ideas. Some of these ideas go back thousands of years, others a few hundred, and a few, challenging all the rest, come from contemporary movements in religion, the arts, science, and politics.

Alfred North Whitehead has defined the function of philosophy with reference to this incongruity: "Philosophy is an attitude of mind towards doctrines ignorantly entertained."[10] Self-examination and the examination of society are human necessities; the study of philosophy and the earnest attempt to philosophize provide an opportunity for and a challenge to personal and social examination.

Philosophic inquiry, in short, aims to uproot outworn ideas, to show where they are inconsistent and why they lack rational support. This can be disturbing to the initiate or student, who may feel that he is witness to the destruction of theory upon theory without being offerred a substantial replacement. But as the American philosopher Morris R. Cohen is said to have replied to a student who objected to having his beliefs criticized without being given alternatives, "Hercules was required to clean the Augean stables; it is not said that he had to refill them."

Philosophical Questions Are Speculative

Philosophy traditionally has been freely speculative but it has become less so in recent years. An increasing number of philosophers, partly under the influence of science and partly as the result of internal evolution within philosophy itself, have come to think that the main task of philosophy, in the spirit of Schlick, is criticism: logical critique and linguistic analysis. But its critical and analytical roles, always an integral part of philosophy, are unlikely ever to be regarded by all philosophers as its sole business.

A complete account of why this is so would almost require the development of a philosophy of philosophy. There is, however, one consideration that is highly relevant to the understanding of both critical and speculative philosophy. This consideration is that philosophy's problems do not, as a rule, admit of conclusive resolution; its claims are rarely verifiable in the manner

[10]*Modes of Thought* (New York: The Macmillan Company, 1938), p. 233.

of typical scientific claims. If they were, their underlying problems, for the most part, would not be distinctively philosophical and would belong, instead, to some other area of inquiry. On this, Bertrand Russell says:

> If you ask a mathematician, a mineralogist, a historian, or any other man of learning, what definite body of truths has been ascertained by his science, his answer will last as long as you are willing to listen. But if you put the same question to a philosopher, he will, if he is candid, have to confess that his study has not achieved positive results such as have been achieved by other sciences. . . . As soon as definite knowledge concerning any subject becomes possible, this subject ceases to be called philosophy, and becomes a separate science. The whole study of the heavens, which now belongs to astronomy, was once included in philosophy; Newton's great work was called "the mathematical principles of natural philosophy." Similarly, the study of the human mind, which was a part of philosophy, has now . . . become the science of psychology.[11]

This suggests that, traditionally, the questions asked by philosophers have pushed past the established limits of knowledge, speculating about what might lie beyond. By the very nature of such questions they were not capable, at the time they were asked or perhaps in principle, of conclusive verification in experience.

Indeed, philosophers have made some of their most important contributions by making intelligent guesses about what lies beyond the knowledge of their time. Democritus suggested the existence of atoms long before there was clinching scientific evidence for accepting their existence; Empedocles, another presocratic philosopher, suggested some kind of evolution long before biologists came to similar conclusions based on much greater knowledge; many scientific discoveries in psychology and sociology vindicate suggestions made previously by philosophers.

The philosopher of science Karl Popper asserts of the presocratic philosophers that "there is the most perfect possible continuity of thought between their theories and the later developments in physics."[12] Anaximander's theory that the earth is freely suspended in space, Popper says, "cleared the way for the theories of Aristarchus, Copernicus, Kepler, and Galileo." The presocratics typically gave explanations of reality in terms of one or more of what they regarded as the four basis elements of the world—fire, air, water, and earth. One of the most famous of them, Heraclitus, maintained that fire is the underlying substance of reality, that all things in the world are manifestations of it, and that it accounts for all change in the world. Despite the seeming oddity of such a claim, the physicist Werner Heisenberg has written that:

> . . . modern physics is in some way extremely near to the doctrines of Heraclitus. If we replace the word "fire" by the word "energy" we can almost repeat his state-

---

[11]*The Problems of Philosophy* (Oxford: Oxford University Press, 1954), pp. 154f.
[12]*Conjectures and Refutations* (New York: Basic Books, Inc., 1962), p. 141.

ments word for word from our modern point of view. Energy is in fact that substance from which all elementary particles, all atoms and therefore all things are made, and energy is that which moves. Energy is a substance, since its total amount does not change, and the elementary particles can actually be made from this substance as is seen from many experiments on the creation of elementary particles. Energy can be changed into motion, into heat, into light and into tension. Energy may be called the fundamental cause for all change in the world.[13]

It is true, of course, that for all those conjectures of philosophers that have subsequently been verified by science, an even larger number have been refuted by the further accumulation of facts. But because the critical scientist usually accomplished more by staying fairly close to the level of what he can observe, and rightly hesitates before making broad generalizations and seeking hypotheses, he is often helped by remembering the freer speculations of philosophers.

This suggests that philosophy not only is continuous with what the ordinary person does in his most careful reflections but that it is also continuous with the spirit that motivates science. Indeed, it has been said that, "Science and Philosophy are merely different aspects of one great enterprise of the human mind."[14] This enterprise is the attempt to understand the world better, to widen our perspective, and to put in rational form what previously may have been incoherent and perplexing. Philosophy as well as science has its starting point in an article of faith, and for philosophy this starting point is the most basic one possible. It presupposes what William James called "the widest postulate of rationality," that is, "that the world *is* rationally intelligible throughout, after the pattern of *some* ideal system. The whole war of the philosophies is over that point of faith."[15]

Philosophical Questions Are Related to Decisions About Values

This is, perhaps, another way of saying that philosophy is a search for wisdom instead of information about facts (knowledge). Wisdom is an attitude of valuing and weighing courses of action so that they will fit into a reasonable interpretation of the human situation. Arthur E. Murphy has said:

The subject matter of philosophy is the thing that men take seriously, not for limited purposes, but in the basic commitments which determine, on the whole, what they make of their lives and of the world they live in.[16]

Except within very narrow limits, science does not tell men what they

[13]*Physics and Philosophy* (New York: Harper Torchbook, 1962), p. 63. Quoted by permission of Harper & Row, Publishers.
[14]Alfred North Whitehead, *Adventures of Ideas* (New York: Mentor Books, 1955), p. 143. Quoted by permission of The Macmillan Company.
[15]*The Principles of Psychology*, II (New York: Dover Publications, Inc., 1950), p. 677.
[16]*The Uses of Reason* (New York: The Macmillan Company, 1943), p. 288. Quoted by permission of The Macmillan Company.

should do. Granting that certain ends are desirable, science can, in many cases, tell them what they must do in order to achieve these goals. Science tells us that hydrogen cyanide is a very good poison and that penicillin is a very good germ-killer, but science alone cannot tell the scientist or anyone else whether euthanasia is morally justified or not. By virtue of science alone, we do not know whether we ought to use the penicillin or the cyanide.

What the ordinary man is interested in is not just knowledge of how to accomplish a certain purpose, important as that knowledge is. He wants to know what purpose to choose from among those open to him. The ultimate ends and purposes to be chosen usually stem, directly or indirectly, from religion. The religious answer, rightly or wrongly, now satisfies fewer people than heretofore. Many people in our society have doubts about the truths claimed by religion. These people are not sure that the standards of conduct that religious teachers set up long ago are applicable for conduct today. Others grant the truth of these teachings but do not see how they can be applied in our complex society. It is not our place here—although it is one of the most important of philosophical inquiries—to examine and evaluate these doubts and hesitancies; but they do exist, and they demand resolution.

One of the purposes of philosophy is to evaluate this kind of doubt. Philosophers do discuss questions of ultimate value, and most philosophical questions raise, either explicitly or implicitly, the issue of the nature of values. Philosophical conclusions about the universe and the place of ideals and values within it eventually lead to decisions as to which of our conflicting ideals are most worthy of pursuit. Even philosophical discussions that are not explicitly about values have a bearing on the value decisions we make. For instance, how one answers the question, "Does God exist?" may determine his answer to questions concerning the standards to be used in judging conduct and guiding choices. Similarly, questions about the relationship of the mind to the body or of the best ways of knowing will, when answered one way or another, suggest attitudes and theories about values and about the obligations of men.

TWO TYPICAL PHILOSOPHICAL PROBLEMS

Given this general characterization of the nature of philosophy, where does philosophic inquiry lead? What problems does it raise, and what insights does it disclose? The whole of this book will be an attempt to answer these questions in detail. Nonetheless, two brief examples from antiquity strikingly illustrate how even relatively uncomplicated but incisive inquiry can disclose problems that concern us all but to which we ordinarily give little attention.

The first is recorded by Plato in his dialogue, *Euthyphro*, in which he describes how Socrates encounters the young Euthyphro about to prosecute his own father for murder. Euthyphro is sure of himself and dogmatically convinced that what he is doing is "pious" and right. Socrates, however, proceeds to question him about the nature of this piety of which is so assured, only to discover that despite his certainty, Euthyphro is unable to provide an adequate definition of the notion about which he has such confidence.

Among the definitions he proposes (all proved inadequate by Socrates) is the following: that piety is what is loved by all the gods. To this Socrates responds by asking a seemingly simple, but highly important, question, namely, (a) whether the gods love piety because it is pious, or (b) whether it is pious because they love it. Euthyphro hesitantly asserts the former. What he does not realize, but what Socrates promptly points out to him, is that the assertion of (a) is inconsistent with his definition. If the gods love piety *because* it is pious, then *piety* and *being loved by the gods* cannot logically be one and the same thing.

Putting the example into more familiar terms, suppose that someone holds that "right" means, or can be defined as, "commanded by God." Many people no doubt subscribe to such a view, if only implicitly. Suppose further that, like Euthyphro, this person also believes that God commands his actions *because* they are right. In the light of Socrates' reasoning, this person can then be shown to harbor a confusion. For if he subscribes to the definition in question, then he is committed to saying that whatever God commands is thereby *made right*, since rightness consists in nothing more than being commanded by God. If this is so, then God cannot command anything because it is right, for the rightness of any action does not antecede God's command. To say, for example, that God commands promise-keeping because it is right would be only to say that God commands it because he commands its, which is trivially uninformative.

Further difficulties follow this one. Suppose that rather than to give up the definition, this person affirms that what is right is right because God commands it (hence opting for the analogue of alternative [b] in Euthyphro's case). He then should realize that, to be consistent, he must be prepared in advance to call *anything* right that is commanded by God, even, for example, murder and theft. For we must remember that on this view, it is God's command alone that makes something right. One cannot avoid this consequence by replying that, by His nature, God is good and hence would never command such wicked acts. For if such acts are not wrong prior to God's prohibition of them, it would not detract in any way from His goodness if He should command them. The acts themselves are completely neutral until God commands or forbids them. Even if He had previously forbidden them—hence making them wrong—the moment He commands the acts they become right.

If, on the other hand, one surrenders the definition and asserts that God commands what is right because it is right, then God is no longer the creator of all things; for then there exist certain standards of right and wrong to which He is beholden no less than everyone else. There is, in other words, something independent of His will that imposes obligations upon Him and limits the range of permissible acts for Him as well as for ordinary human beings, and this, it seems, detracts from the nature of a deity who is thought to be perfect.[17]

Our second example comes from the Stoic philosophers, most probably Chrysippus, who lived in the third century B.C. The Stoics were pantheists —they believed God and the world to be one. Moreover, they believed that the whole operation of the universe is a manifestation of God's will, hence that the universe is rational and governed according to unchangeable laws. This led them to the view called *determinism*: a belief that every event in nature has a cause. *Determinism* is sometimes thought to deny human freedom, and a logical argument employed by the stoics seems to lead to this very conclusion.

They first pointed out that every proposition is either true or false—a statement that is sometimes called the Law of Excluded Middle. On the surface this seems unproblematic enough. If we consider such statements as "this grass is green" or "Columbus discovered America," we should all agree that they must be either true of false, that there is no "middle ground" between these alternatives. Also, the Stoics reasoned, the same is true of propositions about the future. For example, the proposition "It will rain tomorrow" must likewise be either true or false. But what are the implications of this? A moment's reflection shows that they are far-reaching. On the one hand, if that proposition is true *here and now*, then it must be the case that it *will* rain tomorrow, no matter what; that is, that particular state of affairs must necessarily come about. On the other hand, if the proposition is false *here and now*, then it will *not* rain tomorrow—necessarily and irrespective of what happens in the meantime. This does not mean that we know at the moment that the proposition is true or that it is false; the most we can do is look at the sky or consult the weatherman. But this is not the point. The point is that since the proposition must be either true or false, then it is determined, fated, or necessitated here and now that one particular state of affairs rather than another must come into existence tomorrow.

This reasoning has a singularly untoward consequence when applied to human actions, for they, no less than rainfalls, are events that take place in the world. Consider the proposition "You will be married tomorrow." Must not this also be either true or false? If it is true, then it follows that you *will* be married tomorrow, whether you had planned to be or not. On the other hand, if the proposition is false, then you will *not* be married tomorrow, although the date may have been set for months, the announcement made, and friends from afar in town for the occasion.

---

[17]Lest it be thought that Euthyphro's problem is far-fetched, it should be noted that it was debated by the Scholastics of the late Middle Ages. Some, to emphasize God's will as the foundation of all things, argued that God could command man to hate Him, and then the hatred of God would be right.

If a similar line of reasoning can be applied to all human actions, then how can we be said to be free? Are not all our acts determined in advance, and is not our conviction since childhood that we are free to determine the course of our lives an illusion? Certainly we do not *know* exactly what course our lives will take, and it does seem to us that we are free in our actions: but unless the above reasoning can be proved fallacious, this cannot be so.

Thus we have two fairly simple, but nonetheless exceedingly subtle, examples of philosophic inquiry exposing problems to which few of us have given serious attention. Yet to the extent that we are unaware of such problems or their solutions we also lack understanding of ourselves and of the world. Indeed, what could bear more importantly upon our lives, if we believe in God, than whether such belief can provide a rational basis for moral conduct; or, irrespective of our beliefs about God, what could be more important than whether we are free to determine the course of our own lives? One can go through life without ever dealing with such problems; most people do. But, if a person is really to understand himself and the world, he must confront such problems and find solutions, or, as the case may be, at least satisfy himself that they are incapable of solution. Probings of this type, into the unexamined aspects of our existence, are the heart of philosophic inquiry.

THE SCOPE OF PHILOSOPHIC INQUIRY

As an inquiring attitude bred of curiosity, philosophy is virtually unrestricted in scope and subject matter. It cannot, for example be catalogued as a separate and distinct subject apart from science, religion, morality, politics, law, art and so forth. Rather, it cross-cuts all these and, indeed, the whole spectrum of human activities, disciplines, and institutions. Its problems are not those of some special branch of learning but the problems of men, whatever they may be, approached from an impartial and objective attitude and pressed to the limits of understanding.

There is, accordingly, a philosophy of science, a philosophy of religion, moral philosophy (or ethics), philosophy of law, philosophy of language, social and political philosophy, philosophy of art, philosophy of history, and so on. What distinguishes philosophy from the various disciplines and institutions that it examines is the initial attitude, mode of inquiry, and spirit in which its questions are asked. The philosopher of science, for example, may be concerned with causality or the notion of scientific law. But unlike the scientist he does not (*qua* philosopher at least) set about to determine what are the causes of different phenomena or to determine what are the particular scientific laws. He probes to understand what the very concepts of *causality* or *scientific law* themselves mean; whether, and to what extent, they are capable of analysis and clarification. Similarly, the philosopher who studies ethics is not (*qua* philosopher, although he may, and certainly should be, as a person) concerned with whether particular acts are right, wrong, or obligatory; his concern is to understand better what we mean by such concepts and whether or not it is possible to justify the particular judgments in which they occur. The philosopher of art does not himself create works of art, unless of course he happens to have talent as well as philosophical ability; he sets about, rather, to understand such things as the nature of artistic creation, the criteria relevant to assessing works of art, and the role of the artist in society.

The exigencies of everyday life prevent most of us from dwelling for very long upon questions of this sort. Daily pressures compel us to confine ourselves largely to those questions having immediate practical importance. The average lawyer is too busy arguing cases to contemplate seriously the nature and justification of law itself; the average politician is too busy campaigning for office to study political philosophy; and the ordinary person is too busy trying to decide what he ought or ought not do to address himself to the question of the nature of morality and its claim upon the individual. The philosopher is simply the person who is so intrigued by such questions that he devotes his life to exploring them; he is the person for whom the problems concerning human existence are a source of limitless fascination.

Metaphysics and Epistemology

Underlying the various branches of philosophy that we have mentioned are two most basic branches—metaphysics and epistemology. The former is literally a "going-beyond" physics in the study of the world. Metaphysics has traditionally embraced two major areas: ontology, or the study of the nature of reality or being per se, and cosmology, the study of the structure of the universe and such concepts (for example, space and time) as are necessary for understanding its operation. Epistemology (or theory of knowledge) is concerned with questioning the possibility, structure, and limits of knowledge itself. If we think of philosophy as a tree, metaphysics constitutes its roots, epistemology its trunk, and the various other areas such as ethics, aesthetics, and religion, its branches. Just as the life-blood of a tree travels from the roots up through the trunk to the branches, so metaphysics and epistemology feed into all the other areas and problems of philosophy.

Plato very early characterized the most basic metaphysical issue as a battle between gods and giants;[18] between idealists who believe that reality can ultimately be understood only in immaterial terms, through such categories as mind and spirit, and materialists who hold that only the tangible objects of the physical world are actually real, with such central categories as matter and physical substance. This division characterizes virtually the

---

[18] *The Sophist*, Steph. pagination, 246.

whole history of philosophy. The recent British philosopher G. E. Moore explains these polarized attitudes, claiming that common sense recognizes essentially two classes of things in the world: material objects and acts of consciousness.[19] Metaphysical speculation, therefore, in some cases explains the whole of reality in terms of one or the other of these categories and in other cases recognizes the essentially dualistic nature of the world.

As this suggests, it has been in the area of metaphysics that philosophy has been most speculative. Partly for this reason, metaphysical treatises have often seemed to be tangled webs of impenetrable obscurity, and hence metaphysics itself, as C. S. Peirce once put it, to be "a subject much more curious than useful, the knowledge of which, like that of sunken reef, serves chiefly to enable us to keep clear of it."[20] Although one may pursue metaphysics in a more or a less disciplined and rigorous way, one cannot do much philosophy without employing, or at least presupposing, some metaphysics. Even Peirce devoted a large part of his efforts to a type of metaphysics that is just as obscure as any. Moreover, it was Whitehead's view that no one could even do science without presupposing metaphysics. As he said:

... in the absence of some understanding of the final nature of things, and thus of the sorts of backgrounds presupposed in ... abstract statements, all science suffers from the vice that it may be combining various propositions which tacitly presuppose inconsistent backgrounds. No science can be more secure than the unconscious metaphysics which tacitly it pressupposes.[21]

In any event, metaphysics has survived many withering attacks, particularly in the twentieth century, and it continues to command respect and attention from serious philosophers. We will primarily be concerned with metaphysics and epistemology in Parts Two and Three.

Where does one begin, with metaphysics or epistemology? If we try to assign priority to one, we encounter a paradox. If we start with epistemology and ask "What is knowledge?" or "Is there such a thing as genuine knowledge?" it makes sense to ask "Knowledge of what?" Knowledge does not just exist in itself, in majestic isolation; it is always knowledge of something. When we try to describe what it is that constitutes the object or objects of knowledge, we are venturing into metaphysics, and thus it seems that the asking of the most basic epistemological questions presupposes some answer, however partial and incomplete, to certain metaphysical questions. On the other hand, if we start with metaphysics and ask the most comprehensive of its questions "What is reality?" this appears to be a quest for knowledge. If so, then it seems to presuppose that there *is* such a thing as knowledge,

[19]*Some Main Problems of Philosophy* (New York: Collier Books, 1962), p. 27.

[20]Charles Hartshorne and Paul Weiss, eds., *Collected Papers of Charles Sanders Peirce* (Cambridge, Mass.: Harvard University Press, 1935), p. 270.

[21]*Adventures of Ideas* (New York: The Macmillan Company, 1933), p. 158. Reprinted with permission of The Macmillan Company.

and presumably that we have some understanding of what it is—something that belongs in the domain of epistemology.

Plato (as we shall see in Chap. 3) made the possibility of genuine knowledge contingent upon certain views about the nature of reality, thereby assigning at least a methodological priority to metaphysics. He thought that in order for there to be a real difference between knowledge and mere opinion or belief even if true, there must be a higher order of reality beyond what is known through sense experience, which constitutes the proper "object" of knowledge. The absolute idealists, on the other hand (as we shall see in Chap. 6), thought that reality itself was ultimately to be defined by reference to knowledge, that is, as the object of true knowledge. The difference, a matter of emphasis, is important. For Plato, the understanding of what knowledge is presupposes an account of the nature of reality; for the absolute idealist, the understanding of reality pressupposes an account of the nature of knowledge. Accordingly, "knowledge" and "reality" acquire different priorities in their respective philosophies.

The Paradox of Inquiry

What Plato once called the paradox of inquiry is applicable here. He asked, in his dialogue the *Meno*, how inquiry is possible at all. Unless we have some prior knowledge of what we are inquiring about, we will never know if we discover it; yet if we possess such knowledge in advance, there is no need of inquiry in the first place.

Unfortunately there is no solution to this problem for the person intent upon starting "at the beginning," and proceeding systematically to answer all the main questions of philosophy. These questions, particularly when posed in such general terms, interlock in such a way that they cannot be handled in complete independence of one another. Philosophical inquiry does not proceed by putting together piece by piece separate links to form a chain—one that would constitute the finished business of philosophy. Rather, it is more akin to the imaginative and creative work of the artist ever searching for deeper satisfactions; except our search leads to intellectual, not aesthetic, satisfaction. This is a work never completed. One can only begin with those problems that arouse his curiosity most and turn to others as they become relevant.

We will, in Part Two, turn our attention to certain basic epistemological and metaphysical problems to see how they emerge in the philosophical speculations of Plato. Our general concern will be with what can be characterized as the problem of our knowledge of the external world. We will then proceed in Chapters 4 and 5 to consider what transmutations the problem undergoes when a few of its underlying assumptions are altered. In Chapters 6 and 7 we will examine several radically different approaches to the problem. One will be that of the absolute idealist, which we mentioned earlier; the others will be theories of recent philosophers who challenge the basic assumptions of virtually all the preceding discussions of the problem. In Part Three we will consider the role of science in providing an alternative mode of inquiry—one that although not strictly philosophical, suggests a highly useful methodology for the prosecution of philosophical inquiry. Against this background we will return in Chapters 11 and 12 to the area of metaphysics, applying to a number of different problems the general methodology embodied in scientific inquiry. Finally we will conclude in Part Four by discussing two areas of philosophy, religion and ethics, that are capable of only limited treatment from a scientific standpoint.

Returning to our beginning question, "What is the point of studying philosophy?" we saw that this could be answered only by acquiring some understanding of what philosophy is; and this is best summarized by saying that philosophy is an attitude of patient and open-minded inquiry in a serious, disciplined, and ambitious effort to find the general traits of reality, the significance of human experience, and the place of man in the universe as a whole. Philosophy is a vigorous attempt to think about the ultimate questions that are usually "answered" by our emotions and vague hopes and fears. It is a reasoned effort to see facts and ideals, emotions and truths, and man and the universe in such a way that they will yield a satisfying total theory.

In the last analysis, however, a true understanding of philosophy defies verbal communication. It cannot even be taught in the same way that skills and even some knowledge are imparted; as Kant once said, "I cannot teach philosophy, I can only teach philosophizing." It comes only from studying and doing philosophy. Whether one profits from such study by finding a better understanding of life's problems will depend upon what sort of person he is, whether his intellect is the sort in which philosophical ideas take root and flourish, and whether he is capable of finding perspectives in philosophy from which to view his life as a whole. For in addition to what we have already said, philosophy is an intensely personal thing. It is constructed out of a person's own experience and what he can learn from others, and it is aimed at rendering intelligible the problems that beset him as a man. Each man sees the world from his own perspective, is confronted by his own perplexities, and makes his own demands for meaningfulness. Each person, by the necessities of his own nature, must be his own philosopher.

BIBLIOGRAPHY

Baldwin, Robert C., and James A. S. McPeak, *An Introduction to Philosophy Through Literature*, Chap. 1. New York: The Ronald Press Company, 1950.

Cohen, J. W., "The Role of Philosophy in General Education," *Journal of Philosophy*, XLIV, No. 18 (August 28, 1947), 477–85.

Dewey, John, *Philosophy and Civilization* (1931). New York: Capricorn Books, 1963.

James, William, "The Sentiment of Rationality," in *The Will to Believe and Other Essays in Popular Philosophy* (1897). New York: Dover Publications, Inc.,

1956. (Also included in *Essays in Pragmatism*, ed., Alburey Castell. New York: Hafner Publishing Co., Inc., 1948.)

Johnstone, Henry W., Jr., *What Is Philosophy?* New York: The Macmillan Company, 1965.

Kaplan, Abraham, *The New World of Philosophy*. New York: Random House, 1961.

Moore, G. E., *Some Main Problems of Philosophy* (1953). New York: Collier Books, 1962.

Murphy, Arthur E., *Reason and the Common Good*, Englewood Cliffs, N. J.: Prentice-Hall, Inc., 1963.

Russell, Bertrand, *The Problems of Philosophy* (1912). New York: Galaxy Books, 1959.

Santayana, George, *Reason in Common Sense* (1922). New York: Collier Books, 1962.

Selsam, Howard, *What Is Philosophy? A Marxist Interpretation* (1938). New York: International Publishers, 1962.

Sprague, Elmer, *What Is Philosophy?* New York: Oxford University Press, Inc., 1961.

Virtue, Charles F. S., "Hast Any Philosophy in Thee, Shepherd?" *Bulletin of the American Association of University Professors*, XXXV, No. 4 (Winter, 1949), 698–706.

Whitehead, Alfred North, *The Aims of Education*, Chaps. 1 and 8. New York: New American Library Mentor Books, 1950.

QUESTIONS FOR REVIEW AND DISCUSSION

1. What topics do you think a philosopher should deal with? Which of them seem to you most important? Do answers to any of them presuppose answers to others? In what order do you think they might best be studied?
2. Explain the difference between a philosophical and a psychological inquiry into beliefs and standards of value. What contributions, if any, would one of these inquiries make to the other?
3. What are some important and controversial uses of scientific and technological achievements that presuppose judgments of value?
4. Explain what you think is meant by a "postulate of rationality" in the quotation from William James on page 12. Do you agree that science as well as philosophy presupposes such an article of faith? Why? In what ways does such a faith differ from religious faith?
5. Do you think that the "paradox of inquiry" (p. 19) poses a greater problem for philosophy than for any other discipline? Why? Can you suggest a solution to the paradox?

2 SOME SUBSTITUTES FOR INQUIRY

Disciplined and responsible inquiry as a way toward knowing the truth and deciding among conflicting ideals is laborious and often irksome. Men who genuinely desire the truth are frequently unwilling to exert themselves in a persistent attempt to think through their problems, and they fall back upon some supposed substitute for inquiry, tacitly asserting that they already know the truth or that there is some easy way to its discovery.

This chapter will evaluate three ways of knowing that are uncritical—their use requires little thinking or careful weighing of evidence. These three ways of knowing are: the appeal to common sense, the appeal to private faith, and the appeal to authority. They are commonly employed in many of the practical affairs of daily life, and they cannot be wholly avoided in any serious attempt at deciding which of our beliefs are dependable and which should be held in suspicion. But they are not without weaknesses and even dangers, and they may lead men astray as often as they guide them correctly.

By a "way of knowing" is meant a method or a procedure. It has psychological roots that can be explained by the scientist. We are concerned with each method, however, not simply as a psychological phenomenon, but from the standpoint of (a) how dependable it is as a *source* of knowledge about the world, and (b) how trustworthy it is as a *criterion* for deciding which beliefs we have about the world are true.

THE APPEAL TO COMMON SENSE

Common sense is sometimes facetiously thought of as a power or faculty that *we* have, but that most other people unfortunately seem to lack. Many men readily admit that they are ignorant of history or higher mathematics, but few, if any, will concede that they do not have their full share of common sense. Countless jokes on long-haired professors and intellectuals turn on the assumption that these people, in spite of their learning, lack that one precious capacity for using common sense that the most ignorant man may have.

"Common sense" is not easy to define, but three kinds of beliefs or attitudes can be tagged with this name. Common sense may mean beliefs we have as a result of the nature and constitution of the mind itself, which therefore can be expected to be found in every normal mind regardless of its lack of special training and experience. Common sense may also mean a common "turn of mind"—not the *content* of beliefs that are universally held, but a "way of thinking" all minds follow by their very nature. Last, common sense may mean the shared beliefs of men, or a group of men, without implying that these beliefs are "born" in their minds or are present in every man's mind.

Common Sense as Beliefs Belonging to the Nature of the Mind

According to the first meaning of the word, common sense comprises all those beliefs that men have "by nature." Some philosophers have believed that in addition to the ideas we get from our experience (the idea of red, for instance) and the ideas we form in our own mind by combining such ideas (as the idea of a winged horse is constructed by the imagination from the experience we have of horses and wings) there are yet other ideas that are *innate*. Some philosophers have argued that these ideas are placed in the mind by an act of God; other philosophers have argued that they are inherited from our ancestors, who discovered them by experience. Plato, in the *Meno*, suggests that they are remembered from a previous life of the soul. Still other philosophers, not caring to indulge in such speculation, say simply that certain ideas, principles, or beliefs are present in all minds because they are a part of the mind's intrinsic nature. In each of these theories, such ideas are deemed especially trustworthy, since they are due either to faith in God as a being who would not deceive His creatures by giving them false beliefs or to a conviction of our dependence upon the past experience of the race or to what is regarded as the self-evidence of the principles that the mind is able to intuit or apprehend immediately.

Inasmuch as it is extremely doubtful if any ideas or beliefs (in contrast to *abilities* of the organism) are inherited or if the soul existed prior to birth or if there is a God who put certain ideas in our mind, let us concentrate on the view that the mind, by its nature, immediately apprehends self-evident principles. Sometimes the term "common sense" is used to refer to the mind's *ability to grasp self-evident principles*, and sometimes it is used to refer to the *self-evident principles themselves*, which the mind possesses by nature. (The ability and the kind of knowledge seem to imply each other, and accepting one requires accepting the other; but it is well to be aware of this dual meaning and to make sure in which of the two meanings "common sense" is being employed in any particular argument.)

A leading contemporary French philosopher Jacques Maritain says there are

... certainties which arise spontaneously in the mind when we first come to the use of reason [and] are thus the work of nature in us, and may therefore be called an endowment of nature as proceeding from the natural perception, consent, instinct, or natural sense of the intellect. Since their source is human nature itself, they will be found in all men alike; in other words, they are common to all men. They may therefore be said to belong to the common perception, consent, or instinct, or to the *common sense* of mankind.[1]

Among the principles that Maritain says are part of common sense are: "the data of the senses" (for example, "that bodies possess length, breadth, and height"); "self-evident axioms" (such as, "every event has a cause"); consequences immediately deducible from these axioms (like the theorems of geometry, which depend upon the axioms of geometry); and finally, "the great truths without which man's moral life is impossible" (for example, "knowledge of God's existence, the freedom of the will, etc.").

If it is true that *all* men inevitably accept these beliefs or principles, it might be argued that they are more likely to be true than beliefs or principles accepted only by *some* men. Of course, it is possible to find some people who do not understand and accept these principles—infants, unlettered primitive peoples, and so on. The important point is that these principles are invariably accepted by minds that are sufficiently intelligent to understand these principles and their alternatives and to accept the former and reject the latter. It is reasonable to suppose that the principles on which all competent men agree are more dependable than those still disputed among men of understanding and knowledge.

Even so, it is hard to find principles that meet the requirement. For instance, mathematicians and physicists are not now quite so sure as they once were that bodies can be adequately described as three-dimensional. In many problems in physics and astronomy, there are theoretical reasons for considering Euclidean three-dimensional geometry as only a "first approximation" to the geometry of the real world.[2] One cannot say dogmatically that the principles claimed by Maritain as belonging to common sense are *wrong*, but these disputes suffice to show that they are not quite so indubitable as his statement might lead one to suppose.

This is even clearer with respect to the last of the common sense principles mentioned, namely, the existence of God. It is by no means certain that without knowledge of the existence of God the moral life is impossible, unless we *define* the moral life in such a way that belief in the existence of God is *itself* a moral principle. But this seems to be an arbitrary way of considering the "moral life," since many men have lived what is regarded as a "moral

[1]Jacques Maritain, *An Introduction to Philosophy* (New York: David Mckay Co., Inc., 1931), p. 134. Used by permission of the David McKay Company.
[2]The question of geometry is introduced here only to illustrate views that are incompatible with Maritain's examples. It is to be discussed in its own terms later (pp. 90–95).

life" and have had acute awareness of their duties but have doubted or denied that God exists. Such men are too numerous for us to say that it is self-evident that a particular theological principle *must* be accepted as a basis for morality.

Maritain, of course, is aware that there are men who do not share his belief that God's existence is indubitable. So he says, "All men, unless spoiled by a faulty education or by some intellectual vice, possess a natural certainty of these truths."[3] But, we may ask, how are we to decide whether one's education is "faulty," and who it is that is guilty of "intellectual vice"? These are terms of abuse, not of description. Some philosophers have argued that belief in God is the *result* of a "faulty education." Unless one believes in some way that God *does* exist, he might think that the education teaching that God does exist is the education that is faulty.

Let us grant, for the sake of the argument, that *most* men, but not *all*, who seem to be competent, who are suffering from no obvious "intellectual vice," and who have had what seems to be an adequate education do accept the principles that Maritain claims are directly apprehended as self-evident. Does this show that they are true? Or that they belong to the nature of the mind instead of to the "climate of opinion" in which they are accepted? It does not. The history of thought is full of incidents where almost everybody—including those considered at the time to be most competent and best educated—accepted a given belief or principle, and only a few persons held the opposite belief; yet the few have subsequently been found right and the others wrong. For instance, Galileo was forced to renounce the doctrine that the earth moves. In view of such incidents, the appeal to the common sense of mankind (now watered down to an appeal to the opinion of most men who have a "good education" and no "intellectual vice") is not likely to be very effective in evaluating the disputed beliefs.

For these reasons, we may doubt whether any of the principles Maritain cites are self-evident and come to us as an "endowment of nature." This does not imply, of course, that there are not some irrefragable principles; it only suggests that we cannot be sure *what* principles are irrefragable. Every system of knowledge, from geometry to theology, is based upon some unproved assumptions *taken to be* true. Within the framework of that knowledge, they are both indemonstrable and indubitable. But the certainty and necessity we ascribe to these principles is relative to the system they support and to the degree of credence we give to that system as a whole. If one claims to know anything or any truth, however recondite, with absolute certainty but does not claim that it is indubitably self-evident, eventually he must assume that some other truths are self-evident and are evidence for the truth he accepts as certain but not *self*-evident. But just what these other truths taken as evidence are must be a matter of dispute among men working in different systems of ideas that they claim as knowledge. In other words, fundamental

[3]Maritain, *op. cit.*, p. 135.

truths seem to be discoverable, if at all, by examining the position of principles within a related body of statements that one takes to be knowledge; they are not found by inspecting principles in isolation or by studying the nature of the mind that knows them. Because different men of equal competence do accept diverse and incompatible systems of statements as constituting their own "best knowledge," it is not likely that disputes between them can be resolved by putting forth any indubitable principles that they must all accept.

There is one exception to this. There is, indeed, one class of propositions that are indubitable and used in the construction of all consistent systems of propositions, principles, and beliefs. These propositions are like: "*a* is *a*," "if $a = b$, $b = a$," "every effect (*not* every event) has a cause," "every wife has a husband," and so on. These are sometimes called *necessary propositions*, because they cannot possibly be false. There are two types of necessary propositions: those that are true by virtue of their form alone and those that are true by virtue of their meanings (see Chap. 7). Without adherence to the underlying principles of consistency that they express, no coherent thought or communication is possible. People sometimes carelessly violate them even though they do not object to or deny them, but to violate them is to contradict oneself and thereby to vitiate any arguments or claims to knowledge that one may be propounding.

A more serious objection to considering them to be a natural guarantee of knowledge is that, singly or collectively, they cannot serve as sufficient foundation for any knowledge of the real world. They are empty. They do not lead beyond themselves. They do not tell us anything specific about the world, for they apply equally to every thinkable thing, real or unreal. When we know indubitably that "a rose is a rose," we know not a bit more about reality than we know indubitably (as we do) that "a snark is a snark." When we know indubitably that "every wife has a husband," we know a truth that would remain true even if men and women were to become extinct.

We cannot have knowledge of the world made up exclusively of this kind of statement or depending upon it alone. But such statements, *when combined with propositions about the real world*, do give us further knowledge as valid consequences of the propositions about the real world. Any body of factual knowledge must contain some propositions that are not empty in the sense in which the above are empty. Factual knowledge must refer to objects, events, causal relations, and so forth, and the necessary propositions *taken by themselves* do not do this. Rather, they express relationships among concepts without regard to whether the latter have application to real things. Whether or not there are any propositions that are similar to necessary propositions in being necessarily true but that *do* refer to the real world is one of the central issues between empiricism and rationalism. (The issue will be presented in Parts Two and Three.)

It is the business of logic to deal with the relationships among propositions without regard to their content; logic does not in itself tell us anything about what does or does not exist. Yet logic is instrumental to our learning and communicating about the world, since it makes explicit the criteria which must be adhered to if knowledge and communication are to be possible. Specifically, it provides criteria for evaluating arguments—that is, trains of reasoning in which one or more propositions (called conclusions) are supported by appeal to other propositions (called premises). It says that deductive argument is *valid* if and only if it is impossible for the premise to be true and the conclusion false. This, notice, does not in itself tell us whether the premises and conclusion are true; to determine that requires appeal to the facts of the case. That an argument is valid means only that *if* the premises are true, then the conclusion *must* be true. An argument known to be valid whose premises have been established as true is said to be a *sound* argument. Thus although a sound argument will always be a valid argument, a valid argument need not be sound. The self-evident propositions that hold in logic are necessary for *valid* arguments, but they do not thereby establish the truth of the conclusions. For that, some propositions true of matters of fact are necessary; and it is these that the theory of common sense tries, but fails, to establish. Hence, the fact that there are some self-evident propositions in logic contributes nothing to make the theory of common sense plausible.

Common Sense as a Common "Turn of Mind"

That the minds of most men, or perhaps even of all sane men, act in more or less the same way is hardly disputable. Although we might cavil at the "more or less," which can cover a very great variety of differences, it nevertheless seems reasonable to suppose that our minds, like our bodies, have a tendency to behave in much the same way under similar conditions. If we follow this assumption, we need not say that all men hold the same specific beliefs irrespective of their experience and education, but we can say that the "normal" human being is likely to think and behave like other "normal" human beings and to draw similar conclusions from similar experiences. Indeed, this is one of the principal features used in defining what is "normal."

Through the advances of comparative anthropology, even this may appear to some to be an extravagant claim. Primitive peoples who believe in magic, we are told, neither think the same thoughts nor think the same way as we, whose minds have been to some extent formed by science. "Patterns of thought," it seems, vary with the "patterns of culture." It has even been argued that different races have different "ways of thinking." If these arguments are correct, then there is no such thing as common sense in the second meaning of the word.

But let it be assumed that there are patterns or turns of thought that are universal throughout mankind. Would that recommend them as ways of thought that can be depended upon to give us true beliefs? That the commonness or universality of a turn of mind does not guarantee that it will produce correct beliefs is argued by Francis Bacon (1561-1626) in his *Novum Organum*, which is sometimes said to have ushered in the modern age by challenging medieval modes of thinking.

Bacon asks us to consider the "idols and false notions which are now in possession of the human understanding and have taken deep root therein." Among the idols he finds those that he calls the "Idols of the Tribe," which "have their foundation in human nature itself, and in the tribe or race of mankind." They seem to be precisely what was just called common turns of mind. He gives a list of these idols, which although widespread or common to all men, nevertheless lead us astray in the search for truth:

The human understanding is of its own nature prone to suppose the existence of more order and regularity in the world than it finds. . . . Hence the fiction that all celestial bodies move in perfect circles.

The human understanding when it has once adopted an opinion . . . draws all things else to support and agree with it. And though there be a greater number and weight of instances to be found on the other side, yet these it either neglects and despises, or else by some distinction sets aside and rejects.

The human understanding is moved by those things most which strike and enter the mind simultaneously and suddenly, and so fill the imagination; and then it feigns and supposes all other things to be somehow, although it cannot see how, similar to those few things by which it is surrounded.

The human understanding is unquiet; it cannot stop or rest, and still presses onward, but in vain. Therefore it is that we cannot conceive of any end or limit to the world; but always as of necessity it occurs to us that there is something beyond.

The human understanding is no dry light, but receives an infusion from the will and affections.

But by far the greatest hindrance and aberration of the human understanding proceeds from the dullness, incompetency, and deceptions of the senses; in that things which strike the sense outweigh things which do not immediately strike it, though they be more important.

The human understanding is of its own nature prone to abstractions and gives a substance and reality to things which are fleeting.[4]

Bacon points unmistakably at fallacies that are as natural and common now as in his own day. "We feign more order and regularity. . . ." Is that not the basis of much of the unwillingness to believe that physics must give up the principle of "same cause, same effect" in its subatomic research?[5] We are all certainly guilty of adopting an opinion and then neglecting evidence against it. This is known in logic as the fallacy of "neglect of negative instances," and we commit this fallacy whenever we make a judgment such as "All Germans are militaristic," or "All Chow dogs are vicious." The third of the turns of mind on Bacon's list is still among us, as witness the enthusiasm for the strange, the new, and the spectacular in popular science, politics,

[4]Francis Bacon, *Novum Organum* (1620), Aphorisms 45–51. *Bacon Selections*, ed., Mathew Thompson McClure (New York: Charles Scribner's Sons, 1928), pp. 290–94.
[5]See pages 229f.

and religion. Propagandists especially profit from this common fallacy by frightening us into agreement with them. The next of the idols is the one that misleads us when we demand or claim detailed knowledge beyond the scope of our experience, when, for instance, we demand or claim the same kind and degree of certainty in matters of history or politics as we find in mathematics or science. The "infusion from the will and affections" gives rise to what is commonly done, but universally condemned, under the name of "wishful thinking." The last of the idols mentioned by Bacon is present whenever we think, for instance, that a body falls to the earth because of "gravity" instead of saying that the law of gravity is the name we give to the generalization that bodies do attract each other. This is known in logic as the "fallacy of reification," which means confusing a concept with a real object or cause. We commit this fallacy whenever we confuse an abstraction with a reality—thus the success of propaganda, by which we are skillfully seduced into taking words for realities.

If our argument is valid, then, we cannot say that a belief is correct simply because it is a consequence of some common or universal turn of mind or natural tendency of thought. For it is just as natural and common for the mind to fall into error as it is for it to discover true beliefs; the only difference, perhaps, is that it is harder to discover the errors that most of our fellows make just as naturally as we do. But if the truth is hard to find, would we not be more likely to discover it by exercising unusual and uncommon discipline in our search for it, rather than by just depending upon our "human nature" to lead us all to it by an easy path?[6]

Common Sense as Shared Belief

In spite of the fact that our inquiry has not brought to light any universally held beliefs or given us any reason to believe that a common turn of mind is more likely to lead to truth than to error, it may be said that there *is* such a thing as common sense, that we all depend upon it, and that generally it does not lead us astray. This is undoubtedly true if common sense is something much more modest than Maritain suggests. Let us call common sense those beliefs, however they arise and whether they are true or false, that are shared by a group of men in intellectual and practical intercourse with one another. Common sense will then contain the beliefs that people do not have to be formally taught; our common sense beliefs are those that we get almost by a process of "social osmosis." We "absorb" beliefs in all our dealings with our fellows. We all believe that the earth goes around the sun; but it might be hard for many of us to give any very cogent reasons for this belief; after we "learned" it, we forgot the reasons and remembered only the fact. Similarly, most people in our society say they believe in some sort of God, but

[6]See "On Truth," in *The Works of Francis Bacon*, XII, eds., James Spedding, R. L. Ellis, and D. D. Heath (Boston: Brown and Taggard, 1860), pp. 81–84.

they would have considerable difficulty in describing their belief or in showing that it is justified.

We would say, "These beliefs are just a part of common sense; you don't
have to be an expert, or have any special college degree, to know that sort
of thing." The reason we accept such beliefs without knowing or remembering the reasons for them is that they are not ordinarily challenged; the
people we talk with share them, and they do not ask us why we believe just
as they do.

Such beliefs as this are often quite useful. Without such a community of
opinion, practical agreements could not be reached. Like Archimedes, who
said, "Give me a place to stand and I can lift the earth," so also we need a
"place to stand," a set of opinions we do not have constantly to defend, so
that we can go about our practical concerns or get some special knowledge
that is *not* shared by our fellows. These common beliefs have been called the
"emotional cement" that holds society together in spite of differences of
opinion about more specific questions of science, politics, religion, and morality.[7] The man who lacks common sense, in this ordinary meaning, is the man
whose ideas and beliefs on these everyday matters diverge so widely from
those of the majority of his fellows that he is not able easily to cooperate
with them and to share their common hopes, truths, and illusions.

In his own field, dealing with rather poorly defined and unspecific questions of considerable practical importance, there is much to be said for the
man of common sense. He is perhaps wise in not setting up his own experience against what is sometimes called the "wisdom of his race." His acceptance of the common standards of morality, without personal experimentation
to see if, for instance, honesty *is* the best policy, is almost essential for the
existence of a harmonious society of cooperating individuals.

But there are dangers present in too facile an appeal to common sense,
especially when it is backed by the authority of public opinion and the
threat of ostracism for those who disagree. In his famous essay *On Liberty*,
John Stuart Mill emphasized the danger that lies in *any* kind of interference
with freedom of individual thought. Even though we are especially cognizant
of the threat from some powerful agency like a totalitarian state, even in
a democracy there is an insidious but pervasive interference with the freedom
of thought and inquiry. It is the force of public opinion against the man
who seriously questions the common sense, the basic assumptions and con-
ventions, of his society. Some brave thinkers will resist this force, and a few
of them, at great personal cost, will finally convince the public or posterity
that their views are correct. But common sense too often lays the dead
hand of tradition on the individual's mind and prevents him from even
entertaining original ideas. Such a mind is held in invisible bonds by

[7]For descriptions of American common sense, see Robert S. Lynd and Helen M. Lynd,
Middletown, Chapter 20 (New York: Harcourt, Brace & World, Inc., 1929).

dogmatism; common sense is often only a polite name for the dogmatism of ignorant minds that will not listen to argument. It takes originality and rare courage to go against the social pressure of common sense, even when this pressure is not expressed through "thought police." But advance in knowledge and civilization depends upon the possibility that unpopular ideas will be thought of and will gain a hearing. That is why freedom of thought, speech, and religion is not merely a luxury for the individual who enjoys it, but, in the long run, a necessity for the welfare of the society itself. Mill says:

If all mankind minus one, were of one opinion, and only one person were of the contrary opinion, mankind would be no more justified in silencing that one person, than he, if he had the power, would be justified in silencing mankind. . . . The peculiar evil of silencing the expression of an opinion is, that it is robbing the human race.[8]

We have spoken of the social uses and dangers of shared beliefs. What of their truth? Is a belief any more likely to be *true* because our fellows share it with us? Here we must make a distinction between the proper sphere of common sense and what lies beyond its scope—although often in specific cases, this is difficult. Common sense is in its sphere when it deals with decisions of a fairly immediate practical nature: It is right to feed the hungry, to heal the sick, to clothe the naked; it is right to treat a man as innocent until he is proved guilty, and the like. But is common sense a recommendation for the widespread belief that war is inevitable because man is naturally aggressive? That paintings ought to look like the things they are paintings of? That God created the world? That everything has a cause, even if some physicists seem to doubt it? That we can do nothing about improving the human race? That the soul is immortal? These are matters where the common, shared opinions may very well be wrong, if still (although perhaps only in the short run) quite useful for the harmonious relationships among men is a particular society. Common-sense beliefs are those that fit the lowest common denominator of the minds in a society; but if truth is difficult to find, we cannot expect to hear it on every street corner.

There are other reasons for questioning common sense as the touchstone of truth. The most obvious objection is that common sense varies from time to time and from place to place, from one culture to another, and even from one social class to another. Previously we alluded to the earth's movement as a matter of common sense, because among us it is a shared belief not dependent upon expert knowledge or special education; but three hundred years ago a man was punished for teaching it, and certainly the crowd was against him. If it was common sense in 1616 that the earth is stationary and common sense today that it moves, common sense certainly exhibits a vari-

[8]*On Liberty* (1859), ed., Alburey Castell (New York: Appleton-Century-Crofts, 1947), p. 16.

ability that we do not expect the truth to show. I may believe that the earth moves because everyone I know believes it; I may just passively accept the beliefs of my fellows. But if I have a *good* reason for believing it, it cannot be merely that the majority believes it—for the majority has often been as wrong as it was in 1633 when it punished Galileo.

John Stuart Mill, in discussing the way in which men appeal to the "collective authority" of their fellows to support their own beliefs, concludes by saying:

It is as evident in itself, as any amount of argumentation can make it, that ages are no more infallible than individuals; every age having held many opinions which subsequent ages have deemed not only false but absurd; and it is as certain that many opinions, now general, will be rejected by future ages, as it is that many, once general, are rejected by the present.[9]

Again, common sense varies from country to country; a common sense view in America concerning the function of government would be condemned by the Russian government and by the common sense of the Russian people. But what sort of criterion of true belief is it that sanctions one answer here and another there? Certainly not a trustworthy one.

In spite of all this, we may be warned, "Don't lose your common sense." Indeed, it is wise not to lose any sense we have, common or uncommon. But there is probably more danger in taking common sense too seriously than in losing it altogether. Its effects on our thoughts are pervasive even when unnoticed. The following is a sound maxim in trying to judge the claims of our common-sense beliefs: Do not make it a principle to ask at every point, "How does this view conform to common sense?" This question will usually have been tacitly and favorably answered before we ever seriously entertain the new belief, and the danger of being too far "off base" is not nearly so great as the danger of never leaving the base.

THE APPEAL TO PRIVATE FAITH

Suppose a man has believed all his life that absolutely unrestrained economic competition is characteristic of American capitalism or that the sun goes around the earth or that men are by nature evil, and someone shows him reasons to doubt his belief. If his appeal to common sense does not satisfy his need to justify his beliefs, or if he is unable to find common sense agreement with his views, he may respond, "Well, I can't prove it is true, but I know it is, all the same," or "If you don't agree, so much the worse for you. I just feel it in my bones that I am right." In such a case, he is appealing to his own feelings as a source and warrant of true belief. He is depending on

[9]*Ibid.*, p. 18.

a private faith. (Of course many other people may have the same faith, but that is not here the reason for his certainty; he has the touchstone of truth, he believes, in himself.) Something similar to this appeal to faith is found in a woman's intuition that a man is in love with her or a man's hunch that a certain horse will win.

Usually such an appeal is made only for beliefs that involve our emotions. A person is not likely to "feel it in his bones" that water consists of oxygen and hydrogen, although indeed he may do so if his fame and reputation depends upon his answer to a scientific question. But wherever this kind of appeal is made, the person who makes it is retreating from the public forum or laboratory where beliefs can be impartially examined and is claiming that he, and perhaps he alone, possesses the standard of truth. He behaves in this way to avoid the inconvenience and pain of doubt. By insulating himself from criticism and from the danger of having to admit that he is wrong, he preserves his peace of mind. Charles S. Peirce says it cannot be denied

... that a steady and immovable faith yields great peace of mind. It may, indeed, give rise to inconveniences, as if a man should resolutely continue to believe that fire would not burn him, or that he should be eternally damned if he received his *ingesta* otherwise than through a stomach-pump. But then the man who adopts this method will not allow that its inconveniences are greater than its advantages. He will say, "I hold steadfastly to the truth, and the truth is always wholesome." And in many cases it may very well be that the pleasure he derives from his calm faith overbalances any inconveniences resulting from its deceptive character.... When an ostrich buries its head in the sand as danger approaches, it very likely takes the happiest course. It hides the danger, and then calmly says there is no danger; and, if it feels perfectly sure there is none, why should it raise its head to see?[10]

But beliefs held for no better reason than emotional need are by no means guaranteed to be true. False beliefs have been held as tenaciously as true beliefs; the unfortunate patient in the mental hospital, who tenaciously believes he is Henry of Navarre and who preserves this illusion by regarding the doctors and nurses as his courtiers, does not make his belief one bit truer by the profundity of his faith.

Bacon, in the work already quoted, calls such beliefs arising from the "peculiar constitution, mental or bodily, of each individual, and also in education, habit, and accident," the "Idols of the Cave." (The name comes from the famous "Myth of the Cave" in the seventh book of Plato's *Republic*, which is an account of man's errors in his judgments of what is real.) Because each one of us loves his own little idol so dearly that he does not examine it ("Love is blind," as Chaucer and Shakespeare noted), many false beliefs are established that would not stand the cold light of criticism. So far is

---

[10]"The Fixation of Belief" (1878), *Collected Papers of Charles Sanders Peirce*, eds., Charles Hartshorne and Paul Weiss (Cambridge, Mass.: The Belknap Press of Harvard University Press, 1935), pp. 234–235. Reprinted by permission of the publisher.

private faith from being a warrant for a belief that Bacon argues we ought to be especially critical of our dearest beliefs.

Let every student of nature take this as a rule—that whatever his mind seizes and dwells upon with peculiar satisfaction is to be held in suspicion, and that so much the more care is to be taken in dealing with such questions to keep the understanding even and clear.[11]

Recognizing and Checking Tenacious Beliefs

Such caution as Bacon recommends is difficult; frequently we do not even know what our most deep-seated beliefs are, or at least we do not recognize them as our own private beliefs but think that they are so obviously true that everyone should grant them without question. Psychoanalysis has thrown much light on the deep emotional needs that are manifest to consciousness as fixed ideas, obsessions, systematized delusions, and fanatically held religious, political, and moral beliefs. According to the teachings of psychoanalysis, our childhood desires are so thwarted and repressed that they are driven from consciousness, only to appear again in disguised but acceptable form as tenacious belief or compulsive action, having only a symbolical relation to the underlying need.

Whether one accepts the views of the psychoanalysis or not, it is now commonly recognized that much of our thinking is determined by our emotional needs and that frequently we are not aware of the extent to which the wish is father to the thought. To discover the emotional foundation of many beliefs, a carefully conducted psychoanalysis may be necessary. But much of our wishful thinking can be controlled and disciplined by less drastic measures.

There are four steps (short of a psychiatric treatment) involved in examining and, if necessary, correcting our tenaciously held beliefs.

1. *We must find out specifically what our prejudices or tenaciously held beliefs are*— It does not suffice to be just "against prejudices" any more than to be "against sin." It is necessary to know *specifically* what our prejudices are; they do not come before us labeled "prejudice," but they are accepted as truths.

One way of identifying our prejudices is by observing our "emotional temperature." Does someone's saying, "All races are equally good and intelligent" make our blood boil? Do we have a warm glow of satisfaction when someone says, "My country, right or wrong!" Do we feel a cold anger when someone says, "God does not exist"? These emotional reactions show that something more than an intellectual judgment is being challenged.

2. *We must try to find out why we hold the beliefs with such emotional fervor*— Sometimes this can be done only by psychoanalysis; but it can frequently be done by mere self-observation. Is one an ardent Republican because his

---

[11] *Novum Organum* (1620), Aphorism 58. *Bacon Selections*, ed., Mathew Thompson McClure (New York: Charles Scribner's Sons, 1928), p. 297.

family has always been Republican? Does one earnestly believe in God because, as a child, reciting a prayer kept him from being afraid of the dark?

To recognize the source of the emotional "kick" in our beliefs is a great step toward lessening it, so that the belief can be examined. Just as the electrician cuts off the current before he examines a defective socket, so also we need to cut off some of the emotional current before we can safely examine our beliefs.

3. *We must determine the alternatives to our tenaciously held beliefs*—Strong emotional commitments are usually made as if there were only one alternative to our belief: *either* capitalism *or* communism, *either* belief in the literal truth of the Bible *or* absolute atheism, *either* white *or* black, with nothing in between. Such sharp dichotomies, however, are gross oversimplifications. Between one extreme and another there may be many intermediates, and recognizing their existence will give more opinions to choose among: our rejection of atheism, for instance, might not then force us into fundamentalism, or our hatred of communism might no longer blind us to the faults in capitalism. Getting rid of the habit of thinking in simple black and white terms may make the consequences of modifying our beliefs not nearly so fatal as they would be if we had to choose only between two extremes.

4. *We must try to weigh the evidence for and against each belief, so that we can choose among them; and then we must begin to act on the best belief as if we believed it*—Sooner or later we may substitute an intelligently examined and intellectually valid belief for a prejudice.

THE APPEAL TO AUTHORITY

No man is sufficient unto himself, no matter how strong his faith in his own beliefs. Man's experience is too limited for anyone to be able to test every one of his beliefs by first-hand experience. Because human beings have language, they are able to profit by the experience of their predecessors and contemporaries, and the man who attempted to find out *everything* for himself without listening to the testimony of others would put himself almost on the level of the animals, each generation of which has to begin not where the preceding generation left off, but almost where it began. Only because we learn by our own experience and by that of others can human experience be cumulative from generation to generation.

Of course, no man believes everything that he is told. He selects, perhaps unconsciously and unintentionally, the authorities whose opinions he will accept. Each of us tends to believe more of what he reads in one newspaper than of what he reads in another; many have their favorite encyclopedias, favorite radio commentators, favorite preachers, and favorite professors; they accept their favorites' opinions as true and pattern their own beliefs after those of authorities they admire. The child begins on this path when he asks his parents his first questions, and to a great extent, even the most skeptical man continues on the path throughout his life.

We all make use of authorities every time we look at a map, find the pronunciation of a word in a dictionary, or check the atomic weight of some element in a chemical handbook. This use of authority is sensible and unavoidable, but the appeal to authority easily abused. If the authority I appeal to is not competent, the appeal spreads error instead of truth. If I believe whatever I am told by some authority I respect, I may often gain true beliefs; but it is certain that my gullibility will often lead me astray. If I do not form an opinion until I know what decision has been reached by some editorial writer, what shall I do when he does not decide for me? How shall I decide when two authorities to whom I ordinarily defer contradict each other? These are serious questions for anyone who believes that the wisest course is to put his faith in the opinions of some authority.

Since we all depend upon authorities for many of our beliefs, since authorities may disagree with each other, and since each individual cannot make himself an authority on all disputed subjects, it would be well to have some kind of test for deciding which alleged authorities are most dependable. If we do not have and apply such a test, we shall be confused by opposing authorities and experts, and we shall certainly be victimized by some of them if we are not on our guard.

Tests for Putative Authorities

In a court of law, expert testimony is accepted as authoritative only if the man who is offering it is able to meet certain requirements; if he cannot do so, he is not allowed to testify as an expert witness. Similarly, the authority we appeal to in matters of science, politics, religion, or morality might well be subjected to searching questions that would establish his competency or incompetency. There are four questions that may suitably be asked of any man or institution claiming such authority that one is tempted to give up his private judgment and accept the judgment of the "expert."

1. *Does the alleged authority have any credentials as an expert on the matter in question?* Credentials are not necessarily diplomas or college degrees. We are asking: Has the authority any "preeminent right" to his opinion on this special subject? If it is a scientific question, has the man been trained in science? If it is a religious question, has the man thought deeply and critically along these difficult lines?

It is surprising how many so-called authorities do not pass this test. A great scientist expressing an opinion on politics or religion may not himself claim that he is authority on these matters, but the general public and the editors of magazines and newspapers frequently treat his pronouncements on these subjects with the same respect that they would properly accord to his scientific opinions. A spokesman for a church may speak with authority on the doctrines of his church, but he may also pronounce opinions on non-religious matters. How many of his listeners draw the distinction between the sphere where he speaks with authority and the many spheres where his competence to speak is open to question?

Certainly the right to an opinion on any subject should not be taken from one man just because he is an eminent scientist, or from another because he is a respected theologian. The public should be on guard not to confuse a man's authority in one field with his competence to deal with quite different questions. When a theologian speaks on scientific subjects, or a scientist on religious subjects, each is speaking as a private citizen to whom we may well listen; but to neither is due the respect we owe to an authority. If we do not remember this, we have only ourselves to blame, but propaganda and an authority's very human love of dogmatizing may contribute to our forgetting it. Press agents advertise a new book on religion by "a great mathematician," a political treatise by "a great logician," a philosophy of science by "the distinguished theologian and divine, the Rev.———." These are effective advertising devices, giving the authors an aura of authority they do not have in the subject matter of their books. And human beings *do* love to dogmatize. If you accept my opinion on historical matters as authoritative, it may not be long before I try to influence you to accept my religion, my politics, or my morals.

Remember, then, in applying this first test: There are only experts or authorities on special subjects; do not let an authority in one field pose as an authority in all the others.

2. *Does the authority attempt to persuade you by appeals to your reason and to acknowledged facts, or by emotional and propagandistic appeals?* Men are often not rational animals, and an appeal only to men's reason probably would not sell many cigarettes or a particular kind of soap, or get thousands of people to vote for Senator X in an election. That is a regrettable fact about human nature, and it is fully exploited in propaganda. We are trying to find out whether certain beliefs or opinions are *true*. I want to know, for instance, whether there is going to be a depression. The man who answers my question with charts and graphs and statistics may be wrong, may even be intentionally fooling me, but other things being equal, at least he seems more dependable than one who appeals to my vanity and fear or abuses the government.

Men are not always guided by reason, and hence, to get a good idea widely accepted it is sometimes—indeed usually—necessary to enlist their emotions. But the inquiring mind should not confuse an emotional appeal, made for a false belief as well as for a true one, with a reasoned argument that bears on the subject at hand.

3. *Does the authority permit examination of his reasons and disagreement with his decisions, or does he condemn and punish those who dare to question?* An argument may be won by a big boy who tells a little fellow, "Believe me, or I'll

pound you soft." This kind of argument, known in logic as the *argumentum ad baculum* ("appeal to the big stick") may win by quieting opposition and forbidding disagreement; but it does not decide the truth of the matter. It can be used just as well to gain a reluctant acceptance for a false belief as for a true one; indeed, its use raises a serious suspicion in the mind of an observer that perhaps the belief enforced in this way is not true and can be established *only* through appealing to force.

One reason why we are usually ready to accept the statements in science made by an authority is that the scientist does not publish just his conclusions but also his reasons for holding his opinions. By describing his experiments and calculations, he invites others to check his conclusions; this gives us more confidence in him than if he merely announced his results.

A belief is more dependable if it can be checked in an atmosphere of free-dom—when it appeals to our knowledge and good sense and not merely to our blind loyalty to some great name. Only in the open market of ideas where different beliefs are offered for comparison and examination, can we have confidence in those who are reputed to be authoritative or expert.

4. *Does the alleged authority stand to gain by my believing him?* In other words, is he an impartial witness to the truth? It may be true that everyone gains something by being believed; a scientist will receive more promotions, and a historian may sell more of his books, if his conclusions are believed than if they are disregarded or doubted. But this is not sufficient to impugn their objectivity, for their beliefs can be checked (question 3, above) and a mistake may cause them to lose their standing. One may very rightly doubt some of the assertions a politician makes in the heat of a campaign, for he stands to gain from our believing what he says.

Often a man does not claim authority in his own name, but in the name of some great book (say, the Bible), great man (for example, Jefferson), or great insitution (for instance, a church, a political party). In these cases we should apply our questions to the man who claims to speak for the authority, as well as to the authority itself. One of the most tragic instances of the prosti-tution of authority is found in the late medieval attitude toward Aristotle. Bacon calls error made by an uncritical acceptance of authority the "Idols of the Theatre."[12] Most of the errors he opposes under this rubric derive from a blind acquiescence to the philosophy and science of Aristotle. Certain-ly, there were many errors in Aristotle (although perhaps not so many as we are led to believe by the modern revolt of thought against him), but Aristotle was not himself an authoritarian dogmatist. The real *bête noire* of Bacon was not Aristotle—they were in many respects comparable figures—but the Aristotelians, who regarded Aristotle as "the master of those who know" and consulted only his books for authority. Aristotle would successfully have passed

---

[12]Bacon, *Novum Organum* (1620), Aphorisms 44, 61–63. *Bacon Selections*, ed., Mathew Thompson McClure (New York: Charles Scribner's Sons, 1928), pp. 290, 300–302.

our four tests, but the same cannot be said for some of the disciples whose blind subservience to Aristotle was an obstacle in the search for truth.

Dangers in the Appeal to Authority

Because so many "authorities" do not pass the above tests, there is often a prima facie case against acceptance of their decrees. Sometimes an authority meets these tests; should we then accept his conclusions as true? The answer is often that we should, for none of us can have first-hand knowledge of everything he needs to know.

But even where authority is justified, a passive acceptance of it may be dangerous. There are three reasons for this. Authorities, even the "best" authorities, often disagree with one another. Second, authorities, especially in religious, moral, and political questions, are likely to be revered now simply because they have been revered for a long time. It is easier to think of great men of the past as having some distinction and preeminence over those of the present—political writers are more likely to cite Jefferson than Roosevelt, religious writers more likely to appeal to the authority of Luther or Thomas Aquinas than to the leading theologians of today. The reason for this lies partly in the fact that the thought of these men has survived a long time; their writings are "classic." But this attitude neglects the valid discoveries and insights of a later day. For this reason, the appeal to authority is often hidebound and frequently out of touch with present-day problems. An instructive illustration of this is seen in legal disputes, where the conservative calls for a "strict interpretation" of the authority of the Constitution and is opposed by the progressive, who argues that legal thinking should take into account present-day views in science, economics, sociology, and psychology.

But perhaps the greatest danger in unbounded respect for and dependence upon authority is its effect upon character. The man who always appeals to authority does not, and finally cannot, think for himself. He loses his originality, initiative, and intellectual courage. John Stuart Mill well said:

The price paid for this sort of intellectual pacification, is the sacrifice of the entire moral courage of the human mind. . . . No one can be a great thinker who does not recognize, that as a thinker it is his first duty to follow his intellect to whatever conclusions it may lead. Truth gains more even by the errors of one who, with due study and preparation, thinks for himself, than by the true opinions of those who only hold them because they do not suffer themselves to think.[13]

The Social Setting of the Appeal to Authority

The appeal to authority is a social necessity in a highly diversified and specialized society like our own. A society with complex industrial, social, scientific, and governmental tasks, each of which requires expert training

[13]Mill, *op. cit.*, pp. 32–33.

and knowledge, could not function without respect for expert authority. One may hope to become an authority whose judgement in a fairly narrow field is justified, respected, and accepted; but the specialization that enables one to become such an authority requires that he accept the authority of others trained in other fields. The day of the "scientist" is almost past; the day of psychologists, chemists, geologists, botanists, physicists is passing, and each of these scientific fields, is becoming still further fragmented. There are even those who wish to turn government over to specialists or who think this step is inevitable.[14]

One of the chief aims of a liberal education, including the study of philosophy, is to keep this splintering of the intellectual life from disrupting society itself. In addition to knowing a specialty required in his vocation, each of us, if he is to be a good citizen, needs to have some synoptic view of the whole. A danger of the appeal to authority, we have said, is that it will weaken the intellectual fiber of the man who constantly makes this appeal. A liberal or general education frees each of us from the narrow bounds of his own specialty and gives him at least some intelligent insight into other specialties and their bearing on one another. Mutual respect, not blind subservience to the voice of some authority, is one of the fruits of an educational system that does not try to produce more and more men who know more and more about less and less, so that while their knowledge grows along one line their ignorance in all others makes them victims of the unjustifiable claims of unscrupulous "authorities."

Authority over men's minds brings with it great power over their entire life. The blind appeal to and acceptance of authority, therefore, always entails a threat to freedom. Obviously it threatens freedom of thought. But equally certainly it threatens welfare and life itself. Peirce says:

Wherever there is an aristocracy, or a guild, or any association of a class of men whose interests depend, or are supposed to depend, on certain propositions [beliefs] ... cruelties always accompany this system; and when it is consistently carried out, they become atrocities of the most horrible kind in the eyes of any rational man.[15]

Peirce wrote this in 1877; the events of this century have tragically confirmed his words. To think our own thoughts and to put them forth in an atmosphere of freedom for intelligent criticism and evaluation is the first line of defense of everything that reasonable men hold dear. Reasonable men should be aware of all the forces in their own society and in the world that threaten "the first freedom."[16]

In advancing our knowledge and welfare and wisdom, *there is no substitute for inquiry.*

[14]See James Burnham, *The Managerial Revolution* (New York: The John Day Company, Inc., 1941).

[15]Peirce, *op. cit.*, p. 236.

[16]For an account of some of the less obvious but insidious threats to freedom of thought, see Morris L. Ernst, *The First Freedom* (New York: The Macmillan Co., 1946).

BIBLIOGRAPHY

Bury, John, *A History of Freedom of Thought*. New York: Oxford University Press, Inc., 1913.

Commission on Freedom of the Press, *A Free and Responsible Press*. Chicago: University of Chicago Press, 1947.

Dewey, John, "Philosophies of Freedom," in *Experience, Nature and Freedom*, ed., R. J. Bernstein. New York: Liberal Arts Press, 1960.

Hook, Sidney, *The Paradoxes of Freedom* (1962). Berkeley and Los Angeles: University of California Press, 1964.

Lippmann, Walter, *Public Opinion*. New York: The Macmillan Company, 1927.

Meiklejohn, Alexander, *Political Freedom* (1948). New York: Galaxy Books, 1965.

Milton, John, *Areopagitica*. Many editions.

Murphy, Arthur E., *Reason and the Common Good*, Chaps. 22–26. Englewood Cliffs, N. J.: Prentice-Hall, Inc., 1963.

Plato, *The Apology*. Many editions.

Santayana, George, *Reason in Society* (1922), Chaps. 5–8. New York: The Crowell-Collier Publishing Co., 1962.

Stebbing, L. S., *Thinking to Some Purpose* (1939). London: Penguin Books, 1948.

QUESTIONS FOR REVIEW AND DISCUSSION

1. Contrast the "common sense" of our own society with that of a foreign country or with that of some primitive tribe described in books on anthropology.
2. To what extent, if at all, can a false belief be psychologically useful to a person? Is its being useful a justification for holding it? Why?
3. Are the authors of this book guilty of an illicit appeal to authority in quoting Bacon against the appeal to authority?
4. What types of appeal to belief are most common in advertising? In propaganda?
5. Examine your own basic convictions on matters of religion, politics, and philosophy. Why do you accept them?
6. Are there any beliefs that you once held tenaciously but that you have now given up? Why did you surrender them?
7. What are some of the outstanding social forces that make impartial thought difficult?

PART TWO THE PROBLEM OF KNOWLEDGE

This section focuses upon epistemological questions and the metaphysical problems that are directly applicable to them; the theories of empiricism and rationalism provide the key issues for discussing the problem of knowledge of the external world. The rationalists are Parmenides and Plato (Chap. 3) and Descartes (Chap. 4). Plato's two criteria of knowledge—(1) that it be infallible and (2) that it have reality as its object—require the construction of an elaborate system of metaphysics in which reality is neither spatial nor temporal. This leads to serious complications; therefore Descartes modifies Plato's *second* criterion so that material objects qualify as genuinely real. In doing so, his views about experience and perception lead him to the problem of how we know that an external world exists independently of our experience. Descartes' solution is to say that we can prove the existence of such a world a priori—by purely rational processes. But closer examination of his criterion of infallibility and of recent developments in mathematics, shows his solution to be untenable. Against this background we examine some major attempts by empiricists, who reject *both* of Plato's criteria, to solve this problem (see Chap. 5).

John Locke asserts that a causal relationship exists between the data of sense experience (ideas) and externally existing material substances, on the basis of which the existence of the latter can be inferred from the former. But as an empiricist he has rejected the appeal to a priori knowledge, and he is unable to verify the existence of this connection. George Berkeley cites this loophole and argues that since nothing can be known to exist that is not an object of actual or possible experience there are no grounds for belief in material substances as conceived by Descartes and Locke. The proper understanding of the world of nature, he says, is in terms of the relationships among the data of experience: "To be," for physical objects, "is to be perceived," if not by man at least by God.

R. B. Perry, a neorealist, agrees with Berkeley—that nothing can be known without thereby entering into some kind of cognitive relationship to a perceiving mind—but counters that, in this sense, we can never get "outside" our experiences. This egocentric predicament provides no warrant for concluding that nothing exists independently of being perceived. But the inability of neorealism to account for error and illusion leads the critical realists to return to the epistemological dualism of the earlier realists. A chief advocate of this approach, George Santayana, concedes, however, that there is no way we can know that an external world exists; belief in its existence is an article of faith that springs from our biological rather than from our religious nature.

The conclusion is that neither empiricism nor rationalism, so long as they operate within the generally shared assumptions of realism and idealism, can produce a convincing solution to the problem. Is there a convincing solution? *Absolute idealism, pluralistic idealism,* and *phenomenalism* revise one or more of the faulty assumptions of empiricism and rationalism, but each encounters serious difficulties of its own—the idealists because of their highly speculative metaphysics, the phenomenalist because of technical difficulties in carrying through his proposals. The logical positivists, whose criterion is that a proposition has meaning if, and only if, it is verifiable by acceptable scientific techniques, declare that metaphysics is not simply false but meaningless. The job of philosophy, they say, is logical analysis.

The positivist A. J. Ayer provides an example of such analysis in his defense of phenomenalism. From a standpoint otherwise close to Berkeley's, he dispenses with God and shifts the whole problem of the external world to a linguistic level. He argues, not that physical objects are composed of ideas, but that statements about physical objects are translatable or reducible into statements about sense data. The success of such a "reduction" would show the physical objects to be *logical constructions* out of sense data. However, the phenomenalist encounters the objection that his proposed translation can never be followed through. For this, and other reasons, it appears that the phenomenalist meets with little more success than do traditional theorists.

Among recent writers, the American pragmatist John Dewey and Oxford philosophers Gilbert Ryle and John Austin charge that the whole problem of the external world is essentially artifical. Dewey sees the problem as part of a general "quest for certainty," characteristic of western philosophy from the time of ancient Greece. Specifically, it arises from a mistaken, and unempirical, preconception of experience as an intrinsically private phenomenon. This view must be rejected, he says, and both rationalism and traditional empiricism superseded by a genuinely empiricistic reconstruction of philosophy in the context of science. Ryle and Austin trace the problem to conceptual confusions engendered by the abuse of ordinary language. Once these are exposed, they believe, the problem is seen to be artificial.

By rejecting one or more of the assumptions necessary to formulating the problem of the external world, Dewey, Ryle, and Austin each break with tradition. In different ways and for different reasons, each says that when properly understood the problem disappears. Cautioning that these conclusions are controversial and subject to review, we conclude this discussion of the problem of the external world by raising the question of the legitimate bearing of scientific method upon philosophic inquiry.

3 PLATO'S THEORY OF KNOWLEDGE

Man's earliest theoretical speculations concerned the world he could see around him and consisted of attempts to explain unusual phenomena like lightning and thunder and such commonplace facts as change, growth and decay, life and death. Many men gave explanations that sprang from superstition and ascribed the occurrences of nature to mysterious powers and forces. Others were more intellectual, and instead of yielding to fears and emotions, strove for rigor, system, and unity. The latter group attempted to discern rational order in a world of complexity and diversity and thus initiated scientific and philosophic inquiry. In this respect, the early Greek philosophers, the intellectual forefathers of western philosophy, were as much physicists (and often mathematicians and astronomers as well) as they were philosophers. All areas of inquiry, now divided into separate disciplines, were treated by them as parts of a single enterprise to understand the world.

The study of nature, as that of any subject matter, requires a conscious intelligence with a capacity for understanding. This means that in any inquiry, whether it be in physics, philosophy, language, or literature, we can distinguish the subject (or inquirer) from the object (or that which is inquired into). Correspondingly, when knowledge issues from inquiry we can distinguish the subject of knowledge (or knower) from the object of knowledge (or known). This is true even if the subject and object are one, as when a person inquires about his own past or probes into his motives for something he has done. Oneself *qua* inquirer must still be distinguished from that aspect of oneself, say, biographical or psychological, constituting the object of inquiry. This in itself does not tell us what the subject is (except by implication that it must be a conscious intelligence), but it indicates that these two terms—subject and object—are essential to the concept of inquiry.

With the recognition of this distinction, three questions are immediately suggested: (1) What is the nature of the subject of knowledge? (2) What is the nature of the object of knowledge? and (3) What is the nature of the knowing relationship between the two? The first two are metaphysical questions and the third, epistemological; but all three are integrally related. Virtually all the central problems of philosophy emerge from attempts to answer one or more of these questions. Although man's initial concern was an outward one—the surrounding world—the development of reflection soon led to speculation about his own nature. What is man? What is a person? Is he a physical thing composed exclusively of the elements? If so, how do we account for consciousness and intelligence? Is he essentially an immaterial, spiritual being who only temporarily inhabits a physical body? How then do we explain the interaction between his immaterial self (or soul) and material body? Such questions are no less metaphysical than those we mentioned in Chapter 1. The answers to these questions bear closely upon the answers to other questions, such as whether, in any sense, man is immortal. If he is a wholly material being, this cannot be so, since all material things are subject to dissolution. If, however, he is in essence a spiritual being, then perhaps he does survive his mortal life.

Asking these questions one is led to the borders of those areas of philosophy that deal primarily with the *place* of man in the scheme of things, that is, religion and ethics. However, the epistemological question will be our chief concern in the next four chapters, although we will unavoidably be doing some metaphysics as well, particularly in considering answers to question 2.

BASIC QUESTIONS OF EPISTEMOLOGY

Recognition of the subject-object distinction and explaining the relationship between them sets the stage for formulating related questions. There is no one problem of epistemology, but rather a cluster of related problems. Those that interest us most are:

1. What is knowledge?
2. Is genuine knowledge possible?
3. What is the source of knowledge?
4. What are the kinds of knowledge?
5. How is knowledge distinguished from true belief?
6. What are the limits of knowledge?

These interrelate so that a complete answer to any one question would yield answers to each of the others; for this reason no one question can be discussed in complete isolation from the others.

Question 1 has priority, because some understanding of what knowledge is will normally be presupposed in asking the other questions. Question 2 is second in importance, since if it is not answered affiirmatively, there is little point in asking the other questions (although, one could still ask what is the source of putative knowledge, how is *putative* knowledge distinguished from true belief, etc.). The person who answers question 2 negatively is called an epistemological skeptic, for he denies that we can ever know anything about the world (although not necessarily that we should ever believe anything). An account of the source of knowledge, in answer to 3, leads directly to an answer to question 4, about the kinds of knowledge, and helps distinguish knowledge from true belief, in answer to 5. These answers will determine one's stand on the question of the limits of knowledge.

Answers to these questions rarely develop in a neat order of priority, however, and for that reason we shall deal with them as they become relevant. In this chapter we will examine Plato's theory of knowledge. Although his philosophy implicitly contains answers to all these question, we shall deal principally with what he has to say about questions 1, 2, 3, and 5. We shall examine some of the weaknesses of his theory and then proceed to consider whether alternatives constitute an improvement (see Chap. 4).

TWO SUGGESTED SOURCES OF KNOWLEDGE

In order to understand better the philosophical setting in which Plato's views take shape, it will be helpful to consider certain key philosophical developments antedating him. These concern the origin, or source, of knowledge and are relevant to the problems he considers.

What do we mean by the source of knowledge? Superficially what we call "knowledge" has many sources: books, newspapers, radio, television, and so forth—all the sources of belief mentioned in Chapter 2. But where *particular* items of alleged knowledge originate is of little interest to the epistemologist; he is interested in whether *all* our knowledge has a common source. What might be such a source?

Consider, first, that we have five senses; sight, touch, hearing, taste, and smell. During waking life at least the first three are generally in operation and sometimes all five at once. This is necessary to our being able to get around, do things, and communicate with others in the world, and varying degrees of incapacitation result from the loss or impairment of any one of these senses. Furthermore, when we are challenged on any matter about which we claim to have knowledge, we naturally tend to appeal to sense experience. If asked how you know that your neighbor's house is on fire, you are likely to reply that you just saw it burning or that you just heard it from a friend or that it was just broadcast over the radio—in some way referring to your experience. This suggests the possibility that, despite the superficial plurality of the sources of knowledge, ultimately, there is only one and that all our knowledge about the world originates in sense experience.

Suppose, on the other hand, that you are now asked how you know that the area of a triangle equals 1/2 *ba.* You may reply that you have proven it as a theorem of Euclidean geometry and proceed to explain the steps by which, given certain definitions and assumptions, it follows logically and necessarily that, "If T is a triangle whose base is represented by a number b and whose altitude by a number a, then the area of T is represented by a number $= 1/2 \ ba$." In giving your demonstration you obviously will be relying upon sense experience, since you will be speaking to your questioner, perhaps drawing an illustrative triangle on a blackboard, and so forth; otherwise, you could not communicate with him. But the fact that you claim to know is neither one you have seen, as you may have seen your neighbor's house burning, nor one that you have heard, smelled, touched, or tasted. Rather, it is one that requires for its discovery the use of your intellect. Indeed, one might say that the real source of what you claim to know is not sense experience at all but *reason*. This raises the question of whether all our knowledge about the world may not similarly have its origin in reason. Here is a second possibility to explore.

Two general positions therefore suggest themselves with regard to our knowledge about the world. The person who holds that our knowledge about the world derives from, and is tested by, experience is called an *empiricist*, and the person who holds that our knowledge about the world originates in, and is tested by, reason is called an *extreme rationalist*. Few philosophers believe that *all* our knowledge comes from reason. One might grant that our knowledge of such things as mathematics and logic originates in reason, as the above example shows, but still maintain that only through the senses can we know anything about the world. No amount of mental calculation alone will tell you how many dandelions are in your front yard, whether it is raining outside, or whether your dog needs a bath. On these matters one has to consult experience. A philosopher who recognizes this but who insists that *some* knowledge about the world comes from reason alone is called a *rationalist*. Few philosophers have been extreme rationalists, but many have been rationalists.

Despite the initial plausibility of this reply to the extreme rationalist, the view that *all* our knowledge of the world comes from sense experience faces serious problems. Experience can mislead us, for example, when we mistake a mirage for an oasis. This raises the question whether it may not always mislead us, even concerning those matters that seem most certain. Also, what we "know" through sense experience sometimes conflicts with what we "know" through reason, in which case, if the conflict cannot be resolved and we are to avoid skepticism, priority must be assigned to one or the other. This conflict will be explored in this chapter.

APPEARANCE AND REALITY

Reason and experience provided the Greek philosophers the main options in explaining knowledge, and the tension between these alternatives is clearly felt in Plato's writings. But the conflict had been brought to head before

Plato's time by Parmenides (540–470 B.C.) and Zeno (b. 489 B.C.), who were called Eleatics after the city in southern Italy from which they came.

Parmenides believed that one must choose between two opposing modes of inquiry, the Way of Opinion and the Way of Truth. The Way of Opinion is rooted in custom, tradition, and sense experience (belonging to it are the various ways of forming belief considered in the previous chapter). The Way of Truth is the way of reason. It reveals that some of our most deeply entrenched beliefs about the world—for example, that it contains motion, change, and diversity—are mistaken; in fact, the very terms for expressing such beliefs are meaningless. His reasoning centers upon his analysis of the notion of "Not-Being."

The crucial stage of his argument, in abbreviated form, is:

1. Only what can be thought can be real (or have being).
2. Not-Being cannot be thought.
3. Therefore, Not-Being cannot be real.

The argument so stated is valid, which means that if the premises are true, then the conclusion must be true. Therefore let us examine Parmenides' reasons for thinking that the premises are true.

By premise 1 he means: Only what can be thought consistently or without contradiction can be real. We can, for example, think of unicorns without any inconsistency; the concept is simple, being basically that of a horse with a horn in the center of its forehead. Unicorns do not, of course, exist, but it is conceivable that they should exist. On the other hand, compare the concept of a square circle. It signifies something that not only does not exist but that could not even *conceivably* exist because the very notion involves a contradiction. The properties that make up a square preclude absolutely and in principle that anything square could also be circular, and vice versa. We do not have to look around the world in order to determine that such things do not and could not exist; it is enough to reflect upon the nature of the concept itself. Although not everything that can be "thought" need exist, only those things that can be thought *can* exist.

How does this affect the notion of Not-Being? Obviously, it cannot be thought; thought requires an object and Not-Being cannot, in any sense, be an object. How could we adopt, as an object of our rational deliberations, that which is without being (or reality)? We can surely think of things that do not exist, for example, unicorns. But unicorns can, at least, be conceptualized; we can describe their properties and differentiate them from other things real and imaginary and imagine what it would be like if they did exist. Not-Being, on the other hand, cannot even be conceptualized. It is not a "thing" to which properties can be ascribed even imaginatively; for to try to do so is immediately to think of *something*, and that something is no longer nothing—Not-Being. Therefore, if only what can be thought is real, and Not-Being cannot be thought, then it follows that Not-Being cannot be real.

This may seem a curious way of belaboring the obvious. Who, we may ask, would seriously dispute that Not-Being—utter nothingness—has no being or reality whatsoever? Is it not precisely the opposite of what is real? However trivial it may seem, Parmenides thought it important to establish this conclusion securely, for it is a crucial step in the rational inquiry toward knowledge, the Way of Truth.

His conclusions are stunning. He argues: If there is no such thing as Not-Being, then there is no change, motion, or plurality in the world; because these presuppose Not-Being. To demonstrate the unreality of Not-Being is to demonstrate the unreality of all those things to which it is necessary.

There can be no plurality in the world; in order for there to be *many* things, *each* thing must be separate and numerically distinguishable. But if things are to be separate and distinguishable, there must be spaces between them—spaces more or less densely filled than those that things occupy. But if there is no such thing as Not-Being, then there is no empty space, that is, no area not already "occupied" by Being. Contrary to appearances, Reality or Being must be exactly the same in one place as in any other. (Here and throughout we become entangled in our language, for strictly speaking on Parmenides' view, there are no "places.") Thus Being (or what Parmenides calls the One) is continuous and indivisible.

Morevoer, the One is eternal. It can never have come into being, because to do so it would have had to come from either *nothing* (which is impossible, since there is no such thing) or *something else* (which is equally impossible, because there is nothing else). It is immovable, there is no "empty space" into which it could conceivably move, and there is nothing that could conceivably cause it to change. Every part of it is continuous with every other part, making it an indivisible whole. It is necessarily indestructible. If destroyed, it would have to cease to be, therefore implying the subsequent reality of Not-Being. It cannot extend in one direction more than in any other, so Parmenides likens the One to an impenetrable and perfect sphere. The whole of reality is one eternal, immovable, indestructible, unchanging, indivisible Being.

All this contrasts strikingly with experience and common sense. We do believe in diversity, change, and motion and could hardly go about our daily business if we believed otherwise. But for Parmenides, these notions are simply "names" with no intelligible significance. He does not deny that to our senses and our ordinary way of looking at things—the Way of Opinion —there *seem* to be motion, change, and diversity; but these phenomena are all "appearances," irreconcilable with the conclusions reached through reason. They presuppose that there *is* such a thing as Not-Being, which he contends is impossible. Having found a radical conflict between reason and experience, Parmenides says "Let reason be your guide."

Zeno supports these conclusions indirectly by means of *reductio ad absurdum* arguments, that is, by showing that the position of those who would deny Parmenides' conclusions leads to absurdities. The best known of Zeno's arguments, against the possibility of motion, have perplexed philosophers to the present day.

The first of his four arguments concerns the motion of a single object. Suppose that you are setting out to travel a certain distance, the width of a room. If we designate your starting point as X and your destination as Y, it seems clear that before you can get from X to Y you must first pass through the mid-point, m. But once this is granted, we discover that this same line of reasoning has other applications. For now we can say, with equal correctness it seems, that before you can reach the mid-point, m, between X and Y, you must first reach the mid-point between X and m, that is, m_1.

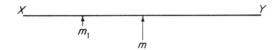

But now the same holds true of X and m_1; before you can get from one to the other you must first pass through their mid-point, m_2. Before that, you must pass through the mid-point between X and m_2, m_3 and so on ad infinitum. Since in principle there will *always* be a mid-point between X and whatever other point we specify, however infinitesimal may be the distance between it and X, it appears that you can never reach your destination. In fact, you never even get started! Therefore, motion of this type is impossible.

Zeno's second example deals with motion involving two objects. Imagine a race between Achilles and a tortoise, and the tortoise has a headstart. The racecourse extends from X to Y, with Achilles starting at point X and the tortoise at headstart point P. The gong sounds, and the race begins. Now, before Achilles can overtake and pass the tortoise, he must first reach point P. By the time Achilles reaches P, however, the tortoise will have advanced some distance beyond (not a great distance, of course, since he is slower than Achilles) to P_1. Achilles must now reach P_1 to overtake and pass the tortoise. This he soon does, since the tortoise has not advanced very far.

But then again it seems that to win the race he must first reach the point where the tortoise is *now*, P_2. And no matter how fast Achilles runs, so long as the tortoise perseveres, it will, by the time Achilles reaches any point through which it has already passed, have advanced some distance beyond. This means that Achilles must pass through an infinite number of points before overtaking the tortoise. Even with his speed, he can never do this and, hence, can never overtake the tortoise.

Third, consider the apparent flight of an arrow through space. At any given instant, the arrow occupies a space *precisely* equal to itself. When an object is in this state we should say that it is at rest. Hence if at any and every instant in time the arrow is at rest, then obviously, contrary to appearances, it cannot be moving.

Fourth, suppose there are three columns of marching men, *A*, *B*, and *C*. *A* remains stationary while *B* and *C* march past it in opposite directions at the same speed.

Starting Position

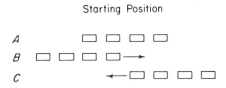

When columns *B* and *C* have moved at a speed sufficient to pass just one man in column *A*, the lead man in column *B* will have passed *two* men in column *C*, and vice versa.

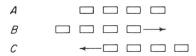

By the time the lead men in *B* and *C* have passed two men in column *A*, they will have passed *four* men in the other moving column.

The men in columns *B* and *C*, therefore, pass one another in half the time it takes them to pass the men in column A. Thus it seem they are moving at two different speeds—one speed being half of the other.[1]

Therefore, Zeno concludes that there can be no such thing as motion; the very concept leads to absurdities. Although it certainly *seems* that we move from place to place, that some objects overtake and pass others, and so forth, this is all only "appearance." If we are to be guided by reason, we must conclude that "reality" is of the nature of Parmenides' One.

Thus develops a headlong conflict between what we "know" through sense experience and what we "know" through reason. If the claims of Parmenides and Zeno based upon reason are correct, then the testimony of our senses must be incorrect. Unless we reject both the claims of reason and the testimony of our senses, one of them must yield.

It is against this background of the conflicting claims of reason and experience that Plato's thought develops. A deep mistrust of experience was engrained in much philosophical thinking, because a distinction between

---

[1] See John Burnet, *Early Greek Philosophy* (Cleveland; Meridian Books, 1961), pp. 310–20.

"appearance" and "reality" had been clearly recognized. Although along with Parmenides and Zeno Plato gives primacy to reason, the theory of knowledge he develops nonetheless marks a move in the direction of giving an account of, not ignoring, the empirical world.

PLATO

Plato, one of the greatest of the Greek philosophers, wrote his works as dialogues. His dialogues are really little dramas of ideas with plots and climaxes. In most of the dialogues, including the one we are about to study, the chief speaker is Plato's teacher, Socrates. Some of the dialogues as we have them probably never took place exactly as Plato describes them, and Socrates is probably used primarily as the spokesman for Plato's own views. But Plato was a great writer, and all through the dialogues, he is able to show the character and personality of his teacher and his associates. Sometimes these personal glimpses of them and of the life around them are among the most interesting parts of his works, and they lend color and impact to the most technical discussions.

That is true of the *Theaetetus*.[2] Theaetetus is a young Athenian who shows great promise as a mathematician, and his teacher wants Socrates to talk with him. Socrates says that he has no knowledge; therefore he cannot teach Theaetetus anything. He compares himself to a barren midwife who delivers another woman's child, then examines the infant, and (according to the Greek custom) destroys it if it is weak and deformed. Hence, instead of telling Theaetetus what he himself might believe, he helps Theaetetus to bring his own ideas to birth. The method he uses is question-and-answer, a type of intellectual midwifery known today as the Socratic method of instruction.

His question to Theaetetus is: *What is knowledge?* This is a crucial philosophical question in the light of Parmenides' and Zeno's arguments, which challenged the claims of experience to yield knowledge, and it is a significant historical question. Plato lived in the period after the Peloponnesian War in which Athens was defeated and the old order was disrupted. Men were confused by the variety of beliefs offered by the sciences, religion, morality, and politics of the day. Believing that sound knowledge was the only valid basis for conduct and that the popular myths and conflicting ideologies were inadequate as a foundation for intelligent behavior, Socrates' circle was anxious to determine what knowledge itself is. This reflects a premise mentioned in Chapter 1: Before one can learn much *about* a given subject matter, he first has to know what it is he is inquiring about. Such understanding, in Plato's view, was to be achieved by the formulation

---

[2]There are many editions. Perhaps the most convenient is that of F. M. Cornford (New York: Liberal Arts Press, 1957). Citations for this and other Platonic dialogues are made to the standard Stephanus pagination, which is the same for all good editions.

of appropriate definitions. The definitions he was seeking, however, could not be found in dictionaries nor asked of people. He sought to determine what concepts *really* stand for, rather than what they are *thought* to represent. This required painstaking inquiry by means of a dialectical method (patterned after the question-and-answer method of Socrates) of stating and testing hypotheses. Having achieved satisfactory definitions, he believed, one would then know what properties belonged essentially to all, and only, those things to which a term applied.

Two specific requirements guide Plato's search for a definition of knowledge: (1) knowledge must be infallible and (2) knowledge must have reality as its object. An adequate definition must meet these two conditions.

Plato does not explain what is meant by saying knowledge is infallible, but this claim can be interpreted in at least three ways. The first, and least controversial, interpretation is that if one has knowledge, then what he *knows* cannot be false. If someone says, for example, that next week's midterm examination has been postponed, then in order for one to be said to know this, it must be true that the examination *has* been postponed; he could not *know* it if it were false. If upon questioning it developed that this person's sole basis for the assertion was a dream, then even if he were right, it could not be said that he was speaking from knowledge.

Second, that knowledge is infallible might be interpreted to mean a person can claim to have knowledge only if he knows that his claim to knowledge is correct. This suggests that genuine knowledge carries an unmistakable guarantee and that one's state of mind when he is in possession of such knowledge certifies to him that he has knowledge.

Third, it might be claimed that when one knows, he has complete certainty about that which he knows. This means that a person is not said to know something if he is vague and unsure about it. Having a hunch—even if it is correct—is not having knowledge. This must be distinguished from the obviously false claim that *whenever* one is certain he then has knowledge; some people are most certain about matters of which they are totally uninformed. However, a strong degree of assurance, not vagueness, seems ingredient in the notion of knowledge.

Plato certainly held the first of these views, and it is possible that he held all three. In any event, these interpretations will be useful in considering his use of infallibility as a requirement for a valid definition of knowledge.

The full import of criterion 2, knowledge must have reality as its object, depends upon one's concept of reality. For Plato, this means, as we pointed out in Chapter 1, that an account of knowledge presupposes a particular conception of reality; hence, answering this epistemological question requires answering first the basic metaphysical question. Parmenides' influence is felt here for Plato shares his conviction that reality must be permanent and unchanging—a fact that he thinks must be reflected by any adequate account of knowledge. If reality were not unchanging, Plato believes, there would be no fixed natures of things to which our language could refer. The meanings of words would change with the permutations of the physical things described by them. Discourse would be impossible. Bearing this in mind, let us examine Plato's assessment of specific proposals.

Definitions of Knowledge

The central proposals that Plato discusses in the *Theaetetus* are: (a) knowledge is perception; (b) knowledge is true belief; and (c) knowledge is true belief accompanied by an account. The first of these receives the most thorough treatment.

It is understandable that Theaetetus should propose that knowledge is perception when we remember the historical context—endless disputes concerning the existence of the gods, the opposing political ideas, and the structure of the universe. Theaetetus is denouncing vain theorizers; he will accept only what his senses show him and will ignore speculations and theories on things he cannot see. This means that he rejects the whole rationalist conception of knowledge implicit in Parmenides and Zeno in favor of thorough-going empiricism.

At first, Socrates seems to believe this answer is plausible, but then he asks: Are the qualities that we perceive in things qualities that belong to them absolutely or only relatively, given to them by us? "Is the wind, regarded not in relation to us, but absolutely, cold or not?" Remembering that some will feel the wind as cold and others will feel it as warm, according to their own bodily state, Theaetetus answers that the wind does not have a quality intrinsically or absolutely, but only relatively to the person who perceives it. In other words, he grants that we perceive things not as they are but as they appear to us. "Appear to us" means exactly the same thing as "we perceive."

Socrates now shows that this is the doctrine of another Greek philosopher, Protagoras, who affirmed that we cannot know anything absolutely, but only in relation to ourselves. Protagoras said, "Man is the measure of all things." In other words, the test of the quality of thing is simply whether you observe that quality, and as different people observe different qualities in the wind, each must be the judge himself. This doctrine, sometimes called the theory of *homo mensura* ("man the measure") and sometimes epistemological relativism (truth is relative to the individual), is expressed in the following argument:

Whatever I perceive is relative to me (to my warmth or cold, whether I am color-blind or not, my illness or health, and so on).
But knowledge is perception (by definition).
Therefore knowledge is relative to me or to the man who has it, and there is no objective knowledge the same for all men.

This argument seems plausible to Theaetetus, and he says, "My perception is true to me, and is always a part of my being; and, as Protagoras says, to myself I am the judge of what is and what is not to me" (*Theaetetus*, Steph. 160).

Although it is certainly true that perception varies from person to person and even from moment to moment for the same person, difficulties arise if we say the same thing about knowledge. If each man's sensing is the sole evidence for the existence or the qualities of a thing, according as he perceives it or does not perceive it, how shall we ever say, as we do, that one man's knowledge is better or more accurate than another's? If both have perceptions, as they do, and if perception is knowledge, why do we accept one man's report on the qualities a thing has but reject another's? Why accept the judgment of a physician instead of that of the patient? After all, the patient is probably having a more vivid experience of pain than the physician has. Why, indeed, let man instead of a baboon be the measure of all things? For each species of animal has its own pattern and mode of perception.

Moreover, if, as Protagoras is also represented as holding, each man is the measure and test of all his beliefs and judgments in the sense that whatever each man judges to be true *is* true, then how can Protagoras consistently profess to be a teacher of others? The very notion of teaching seems to presuppose that some men are better measures of truth and falsity than are others. (Protagoras was a sophist, that is, a professional teacher.) And if Protagoras' thesis is correct, does it not follow (according to the thesis itself) that those who deny it are correct—in which case the thesis is incorrect? If so, then to uphold the thesis is to commit oneself, paradoxically, to denying it if someone else denies it.

Whenever Theaetetus' common sense makes him draw a distinction between truth and error, he implicitly admits there is some difference between mere perceiving and knowing; for the man who is making a mistake and therefore lacks knowledge is nonetheless having perceptions about which he judges. Unless knowledge is something more than mere perception, we could not make a distinction between knowledge and ignorance. A mirage is perceived just as surely as a real lake is perceived. Nonetheless, our belief that it *is* a real lake is false and, hence, cannot constitute knowledge.

In short, knowledge and perception cannot be one and the same. Whenever I state a belief or a sentence that I think is true of the real world or an object, I am stating more than I perceive. "I believe this wine is sweet," or "This wine is sweet," says more than "This wine tastes sweet to me," or "I perceive a sweet taste when I drink this wine." Indeed, in stating our beliefs we sometimes have to go against what we do perceive. I may rightly say, "This is a sweet wine, but because I've just eaten some candy it tastes rather bitter to me." I may say of a stick partly submerged in the water that it is a straight stick even though it appears bent to me at the moment.

Even though Plato rejects claim (a), that knowledge is perception, he nonetheless thinks that perception meets the first of his two criteria. It is infallible. If you say in earnest that this wine "tastes" bitter, there is apparently no way in which you can be mistaken. You are reporting your immediate experience, how things "seem" to you, and by the nature of the case, your testimony cannot fail to be authoritative. No one can be more certain of how things "seem" to him than he himself. This has led some philosophers to characterize as "basic" those propositions reporting such experiences. Among propositions about the world, they seem to enjoy a privileged status in that they cannot be doubted by a person who sincerely asserts them.

Thus perception easily passes the first requirement for knowledge, but it founders on the second. What we immediately perceive is not permanent and unchanging; hence, it does not qualify as genuinely real. To the contrary, perceptions are fleeting and variable; indeed, this is one of their most marked characteristics. The wind that feels warm at a brisk walk acquires a chill when you sit; the partly submerged stick that appears bent in the water looks straight when you withdraw it; the house that looks small at a distance appears larger as you approach, and so on. Our perceptual world is in continuous flux.

In emphasizing this, Plato reflects the influence of another presocratic philosopher Heraclitus (544–484 B.C.), who held that everything is in flux; that continual change and process characterize all reality. This view is directly opposed to that of Parmenides. Yet it also is given a place in Plato's philosophy, because he thinks that it is an accurate description of our perceptual world. But because he shares with Parmenides the view that genuine reality must be unchanging, Plato does not equate the objects of perception with the objects of knowledge. Even though it is infallible, perception fails to constitute knowledge.

Plato also rejects the second and third proposals, (b) that knowledge is true belief and (c) that it is true belief accompanied by an account. But they mark an advance over the first claim; by incorporating the notion of belief (or judgment, as the expression of belief), they reflect the recognition that knowledge must go beyond mere perception. Although we may entertain beliefs and make judgments about our perceptions, for the most part our beliefs and judgments range beyond our immediate experience. It is in this "beyond" that knowledge must be found.

Knowledge cannot, however, be identified with belief or judgment per se, since these obviously are not infallible; people hold mistaken beliefs and make mistaken judgments. "True belief" (or "true judgment"), on the other hand, is by definition correct. The reason why *it* cannot be identified with knowledge is that a person may entertain a correct belief or make a correct judgment without any warrant for what he believes or judges. His only grounds may be hearsay or surmise or, as in the case cited earlier, something he dreamed. Although true belief is infallible in the first sense mentioned on page 55—that it cannot be mistaken— it is not infallible in either of the other two senses; one may have true belief without knowing that he knows and without even being certain about that which he believes.

True belief fails to qualify as knowledge, but Plato nonetheless thinks that it is important and that from a purely practical standpoint and for limited purposes it serves just as well as knowledge. If you want to reach a certain destination, you will get there just as surely if given clear and accurate directions as if you know the way yourself—that is, by acting solely upon true belief. Indeed, Plato believes that most people who are virtuous in this world, those who live moral lives, are so not because they possess knowledge about right and wrong but simply because they have right opinion. Such people are gifted in distinguishing right from wrong; but if asked to explain *why* certain things are right or wrong or to give an account of what rightness and wrongness themselves are, they would be at a loss or would give conflicting answers.

The major consequence of the fallibility of true belief is that a person who has only it, and not knowledge, is susceptible to persuasion; he may be talked out of his belief and influenced to accept what is false. This points up another danger in belief, opposing the one considered in Chapter 2: People sometimes hold tenaciously to beliefs that have no foundation and thereby ignore evidence that might lead them to modify and strengthen their beliefs. If after having got correct directions you meet a person who insists that your first directions were incorrect and who then proceeds to give you mistaken directions, you may be persuaded to exchange a true belief for a false one. Unlike knowledge, mere belief—whether true or false—is not anchored, as Plato puts it, and can often easily be dislodged. The broader implication of this is that the less knowledge people have the more they are prey to rhetoricians, propagandists, false advertisers, and others who have perfected the devices for controlling people's opinions.

Alternative (c), on the other hand, by requiring that true belief be accompanied by an account of the grounds of one's belief, opens the way to reinforcing true belief in just the area in which it is weak—that of understanding. For this reason it promises a vastly strengthened definition of knowledge. Yet Plato, in the *Theaetetus*, rejects even this definition for the lack of a satisfactory explanation of what constitutes an "account" (or logos). In the absence of such an explanation, this definition fails to remedy the deficiency of alternative (b), for it also fails to account for the infallibility of knowledge. It is likely, however, that this definition best expresses the view that Plato endorses, and later we shall see what he may have meant by an "account" in this context.

Thus far Plato agrees with Parmenides that our knowledge about the world cannot be equated with either perception or belief. But Parmenides, we recall, propounded much more than this. His view of reality holds that our ordinary beliefs about the world are not even *true*, much less constitutive of knowledge. The whole edifice of beliefs and convictions founded upon the senses must be rejected. As the next step toward understanding his theory of knowledge, we must ask how Plato makes allowance for true belief.

The key to Plato's answer to this question is found in the earlier and best known of his dialogues, the *Republic,* where he asserts that knowledge and belief can be distinguished according to their respective states of mind and according to their objects (*Republic,* 476). This means that if knowledge has the perfectly real (whatever that is) as its object, then mere belief or opinion must have as its object something different.[3] We also know that the totally unreal—Parmenides' Not-Being—cannot be the object of belief any more than it can be the object of knowledge, since it is not an "object" in any sense whatever. Plato concludes, therefore, that belief has as its object something *intermediate* between the perfectly real and the totally unreal, something that exists between Being and Not-Being.

Here Plato finds a place for the physical world. Although he agrees with Parmenides that it cannot qualify as the ultimate reality, he disagrees in thinking that it is not totally unreal. What it has is a lower-order, secondary reality; it is, as he names it to emphasize its continual change and diversity, a world of "becoming." He thinks that Heraclitus' view—everything is in flux—applies to our perceptual world and, though to a less extreme degree, to the physical world as well. It is this world and the things in it, which we "know" through sense experience, that constitute the "object" of belief and opinion.

This means that in Plato's view true belief is possible. But it also means that not only does true belief fail to meet the first criterion of knowledge, it also fails to meet the second, since it does not have reality as its object. None of what we "know" about the world through physics, biology, chemistry, and so forth, insofar as it is grounded in observation, experiment, and generalization about experience, qualifies as genuine knowledge. On the one hand, it is characteristic of our "knowledge" about the physical world that it is fallible. No matter how infallible certain scientific hypotheses may seem, there is always the possibility that new facts will disprove them. On the other hand, the world that science investigates changes continually. Everything living comes into being, develops to maturity, and eventually dies away. Day changes into night and night into day, the seasons come and go, and even the most substantial inanimate objects, like rocks and minerals, yield eventually to the effects of time and weather. Nothing in the physical world is impervious to change. Given Plato's criteria, therefore, it is understandable why our beliefs about the world, even when they are true and grounded in scientific inquiry, cannot be genuine knowledge.

But where does this leave us? Plato has rejected both perception and experience as possible sources of knowledge. If genuine knowledge is possible,

---

[3]This does not mean that one cannot have beliefs or opinions about reality; it means the usual or normal object of opinion differs from the true object of knowledge.

there must be something that fits his characterization of reality, i.e., something eternal and unchanging, which is capable of being apprehended other than through the senses. His solution to this problem lies in his doctrine of Forms or Ideas.

The Doctrine of Forms

This is the central metaphysical doctrine in Plato's philosophy and one of the most important and controversial metaphysical theses in the history of philosophy.[4] Since Plato's views about the possibility of knowledge depend upon his concept of reality, it is necessary to understand this doctrine. Without it, the distinction between knowledge and true belief, as he conceives it, cannot be sustained; this doctrine contains the key to understanding the "account" that is necessary to transform true belief into knowledge. But what does Plato mean by the Forms, and why does he think there are Forms? The following illustrations should elucidate these questions.

Suppose that we could enumerate all the red things in the world. An extensive but finite list of varied things would include, for example, roses, ripe apples, certain wines, lipstick, an occasional sunset, and so forth. These things would differ so radically in physical makeup that it is likely they would have nothing in common *except* their redness. Yet it seems clear that they do have redness in common, else we would have had no criterion by which to single them out from the vast multiplicity of things in the world, and would have no criterion by which to add to our list subsequent things we might encounter in experience.

But what is this redness they have in common? A moment's reflection shows that it cannot be identified with the *particular* red of any one of the objects or even of any combination of them, since many different shades and hues will be represented in our list: scarlet, pink, maroon, rust, ruby. Our language bears this out. The adjective "red" does not even mean the same as the noun "redness." "Red" characterizes particular things; "redness" signifies the color *itself* that such things are said to share. Even if all these things were of the same hue and shade, we could hardly identify the redness they have in common with the particular red of any one of them; this would be saying that redness is located in one place (in its entirety) and in many places at once. This particular rose is growing here in this particular garden, whereas the other red things are scattered about the world. Moreover, all these things are changeable. Not only will their color eventually change, but each of them came into existence at some point in time and someday will cease to exist. But can we say that *redness itself* ceases to exist after the sun sets, the apple is eaten, or the rose fades? It seems clear, therefore, that the redness these things have in common cannot be identical with the particular red of any one of them.

---

[4]See the discussion of realism and nominalism in Chapter 9, pages 216–19.

Similarly, consider all the things in the world possessing beauty. These, too, will constitute a varied collection, including again the rose and certain sunsets, as well as symphonies, poems, paintings, young ladies, an occasional building, or such things as mathematical proofs, institutions, and systems of law. But just as in the previous case, these things differ so greatly that it is unlikely that they have anything in common except their beauty. What, for example, does Beethoven's Fifth Symphony have in common with the Mona Lisa, except that each in its own way possesses beauty? And again, we cannot identify what they have in common with the particular beauty of any one of them, because that would lead us to the same predicament of stating that beauty can be in one place in its entirety and in many places at the same time.

What then is the nature of beauty and redness? It seems to Plato that there must be such things, since we all understand what they are. Yet the qualities redness and beauty cannot be isolated and identified apart from other things in the world. For example, we never see redness just in itself; we see its manifestation in this or that particular red thing. And search as we may, we never discover in the world anything other than particular beautiful things. Redness and beauty are not found singularly in sense experience.

If redness and beauty are real yet do not exist in the spatio-temporal realm, then it seems we must recognize another dimension to reality over and above the reality of our experience. Plato does precisely this. Redness and beauty abide in an invisible, timeless, unchanging realm of being. They are eternal Essences (Forms or Ideas) of which particular things of the physical world are exemplifications. Because they are not in space or time, they are impervious to the forces that cause change and degeneration in physical things and thus are not, even in principle, susceptible to alteration. Reality, in short, encompasses both a realm of existence known to the senses and a realm of being. The latter, Plato believes, is disclosed only to reason.

The Ideas, Forms, or Essences of this realm should not be confused with what we call ideas in our mind, which presumably exist *only* in our mind and can be located temporally if not spatially. What these latter have is "existence," which connotes being in space or time or both. The Ideas Plato is talking about are independent of anything in the physical world of becoming and independent of our thoughts about them. Moreover, because they are eternal and unchanging, they exactly fit his characterization of perfect reality.

How extensive is this realm of Forms? Plato never completely answers this question, but he thinks there are Forms of Beauty, Justice, Virtue, and Knowledge, as well as, presumably, of types of physical things such as men, dogs, cats, trees, and so forth. That is, for each class of entity, whether we are speaking about properties of things (like redness) or properties of actions (like rightness) or substantial things themselves (like men and dogs), there will be a single Form, an Essence exemplified in many particulars. He even speaks at times as though there may be Forms of actions such as walking and running. Whereas individual dogs may have long or short tails, shaggy or neat coats, the Essence of Doghood is the same in each of them. Likewise, particular men may be short or tall, fat or skinny, black or white, but the Essence of Humanity is the same in each of them.

It is clear that one and the same particular may "participate," as Plato puts it, in more than one Form. A short brown dog participates in Shortness and Brownness as well as Doghood; a fat, bald man, in Fatness and Baldness as well as Humanity. There is, in other words, a complex set of relationships between things in the physical world and the Forms in the realm of being.

Moreover, Plato believes that Forms bear important relationships to one another as well as to physical things. There will be separate Forms of Beagle, Bloodhound, and Basset, but each of these will characterize, or blend with, the Form of Dog; this is why we can intelligibly and correctly speak of these as species of dog. Likewise the Forms of Dog, Man, and Cat all characterize the Form of Animal. This suggests that there is a hierarchy of Forms structured according to how encompassing they are. Eventually one comes to such Forms as Being, Sameness, and Difference, which are all-pervading in the sense that everything else, Form and object alike, participates (or in the case of Forms, blends) with them (*Sophist*, 254–55). Everything has some degree of reality, hence participates in Being; everything is the same as (or identical with) itself, hence participates in Sameness; and everything is different from everything else, hence participates in Difference.

However, for Plato there is one supreme Form at the apex of this hierarchy, which he say is the cause of all knowledge and truth, the ultimate end and final value of the whole of reality (*Republic*, 508). It stands to knowledge and the Forms as the sun stands to vision and physical objects, for only through its illumination can anything be known. It is what he calls the Idea of the Good.

The Idea of the Good

The Idea of the Good is the most important and most difficult notion in Plato's philosophy. He never gives a detailed account of it and probably thought that none could be given. When in the *Republic* (506) Socrates is asked to do so, he replies that it is beyond his powers, and he proceeds to characterize it through simile and allegory. Probably Plato believed that only long and arduous philosophical training such as that he prescribes for the philosopher-king would enable one—assuming that he had the requisite intellectual abilities to begin with—to apprehend the true nature of the Good. With the attainment of such understanding, one would then understand what is right and wrong in human conduct and would have attained the highest excellence of which man is capable.

Let us attempt to gain some understanding of what Plato means by this notion. First we should notice that it is part of his view of the world that everything has a specific purpose, the realization of which constitutes that thing's particular virtue or excellence. The excellence of a race horse, for example, would be judged by its speed, that of a cobbler by his fine shoes, and that of a shipbuilder by his sound ships. The same is true of the parts and organs of the body. The eyes have as their purpose or end to enable us to see, the ears to enable us to hear, the legs to enable us to walk, and so forth. Each of these has a specific function and is a means to an end that has some value.

But now each of these ends itself serves as a means to other ends; seeing, hearing, and walking cooperate as means to the still further end of enabling the organism to adapt to its environement, seek food, and avoid danger. Even this, however, is not valued solely for itself, and it serves in turn as a means to still further ends. In the case of human beings, their adaptability to the environment enables them to live in society with one another, to communicate, cooperate, and perform the tasks necessary to social living. And this serves as a means to the still higher end of providing the conditions that will better enable each individual in society to live a just life.[5] And this, Plato believes, is the unique purpose of man—to live justly—and in the attainment of this end lies his particular excellence. Those persons and *only* those persons who achieve this excellence will find happiness.

The whole of human activities, therefore, and indeed the whole of reality, is pervaded with purposes and values. The notions of good and bad, better and worse, desirable and undesirable are essential to our understanding of the world and to the very workings of intelligence, which continually involves the projection and adoption of ends and the search for means to realize them. Every voluntary, intelligent human action has some purpose or end, which at least for that person at that time has some value. But unless something is valued just *for itself* and not as a means to other things—unless there is some ultimate end and final value—this network of means and ends will continue indefinitely. Therefore, Plato says, there must be an ultimate end and final value for the whole of reality, an end that is eternal and unchanging and supremely good in itself. This is the Idea of the Good.

How can this supreme Idea have any bearing upon human conduct? One of Aristotle's criticisms of Plato was that it could not. But let us see how Plato may have envisaged the connection.

We have seen thus far that the notion of means and ends is continually involved in our daily conduct. Often, however, we adopt improper means for the achievement of our desired ends, and often the ends we have projected do not, when attained, have the value we thought. A prize fighter may desire

---

[5]Actually, for Plato, there is a mutual interdependence between justice and the conditions for social living. Even though the latter are necessary to provide optimum conditions for the former, he also thinks that without some degree of justice men cannot even begin to act and to cooperate.

to be champion, a bank clerk to be wealthy, and a politician to be elected to office. But they have adopted improper means to these ends if they pursue them respectively through bribery, embezzlement, and invalid elections. Even if the means to these ends were effective, it might result (and Plato thinks it will result) that these ends do not have the anticipated value, particularly in the way of bringing happiness. Wisdom in one's conduct, therefore, entails the ability both to adopt sound ends and to choose proper means to them, that is, the ability to distinguish what merely promises to be from what actually will be—good.

Moreover, Plato believes that *every man desires the Good* and will pursue it if he knows what it is. This means that when a person acts wrongly, it is ultimately from ignorance of what is really of value. If the bank clerk fully understood that embezzling is not good, even in the sense of bringing him happiness, then he would not pursue it. The same is true in all our conduct; all wrongdoing is from ignorance. Man's basic desire, Plato says in the *Symposium* (206), is for the everlasting possession of the Good, and insofar as a person knows what it is, he will pursue it.[6]

In desiring the Good, however, men cannot physically possess it as they can possess an automobile, a new hat, or a pair of skis; the Good does not even belong to the spatio-temporal realm. To possess the Good, rather, is to actualize goodness (and its aspects: beauty, proportion, and harmony) in one's soul, one's conduct, and so far as possible in the world around one. Just as there are manifestations of the Forms of Redness, Humanity, and Doghood throughout the world, so it is possible for one to act in such a way as to make his character and actions manifest the Form of Goodness. This is precisely what one does when he lives justly, fulfilling well his specific function to the best of his abilities. The man who lives the well-ordered rational life achieves a definite harmony and proportion within himself by bringing his desires and passions under the superintendence of reason. The very actualization of this state within his soul, as well as the outward conduct that issues from it, is a realization and a possession of the Good in this world. As such it also constitutes a fulfillment of that aspect of the desire for the Good most evident in human affairs—the desire for happiness.

Although everyone desires the Good, not everyone knows what it is and how to realize it in his daily affairs. Here the person who lacks knowledge, as Plato no doubt thought most of us do, will have to live with "right opinion." Ideally, the few persons who are able to know the Good directly are best suited to be rulers and to guide those who lack such knowledge. For with knowledge of the Good comes a new perspective on man and his activities in the world at large, in which everything is seen in its proper place and it becomes clear what is best in the way of individual and social living, economic principles, laws, and institutions.

[6]For further discussion of this in relation to the theory of value, see Chapter 16, pages 415–18.

This perspective will be as different from the ordinary man's as the chess master's is from the child's. What to the child is a haphazard shifting about of odd-shaped pieces on a checkered board with no apparent design or purpose has deep significance to the master who knows the specific function and value of each piece, the ultimate goal of the game, the means by which it is best attained, and the underlying principles by which it is to be pursued. To him it is a complex but orderly working-out of means to an ultimate end, one in which the concept of value is essential. So, too, is the world as a whole to the person who has knowledge of the Good.

It is the realm of Ideas that constitutes the most perfect reality and therefore the proper object of knowledge. He who has knowledge of the Forms, particularly the Idea of the Good, will be possessed of something vastly superior to true belief. His beliefs and judgments will indeed be true, but also he will have understanding of that which he believes and will be able to give an account of it in terms of the relationships among Forms and the relationships between Forms and particulars. The physical world is a reflection of the perfect reality of the realm of being. What is possible in this world is determined by actual relationships among Forms, and what *ought to be* in this world is determined by what will maximize goodness. The ability to give an "account," which is necessary to transform true belief into knowledge and which was lacking in the *Theaetetus,* follows from this awareness of the Forms. Because the knowledge one then possesses has perfect reality as its object, and reality is permanent and unchanging, one's knowledge will therefore have a permanence not guaranteed by mere belief. Such knowledge will be infallible in that not only will what one believes be true, but one will know that he knows and be justifiably certain. Thus knowledge of the Forms meets both criteria of genuine knowledge.

We now have before us the essentials of Plato's answers to four of the original questions. To the question, What is knowledge? his answer is that it is true belief accompanied by the ability to give an account—where such ability follows upon one's apprehension of the Forms. This answers question 5 as well, concerning the distinction between true belief and knowledge, for it is the ability to give an account that transforms true belief into knowledge and gives it the foundation lacked by mere belief, whether true or false. To the question, Is genuine knowledge possible? Plato's answer is that it is providing there is a realm of Forms, since only it has the reality required by the criteria for knowledge.

Finally, this highlights Plato's answer to question 3, concerning the source of knowledge. Here he agrees with Parmenides in maintaining that our knowledge of reality originates in reason. Sense experience, he thinks, is totally unreliable. Where he differs from Parmenides is in his conception of reality. Although both of them take reality to be eternal and unchangeable, for Parmenides it is *One* whereas for Plato it contains diversity. The Forms are many; yet each of them in its eternality and simplicity has some of the essential features of Parmenides' One.

Moreover, for Plato, but not for Parmenides, the physical world, though one of change and appearance, nonetheless has a second-order reality of its own. Rather than deny it altogether, Plato tries to help us better understand the physical world and to point the direction for guidance about how best to live in it. By enlarging our perspective to take in the realm of Forms, we may emerge as from a cave into sunlight, to experience for the first time a world of unimagined beauty and richness; and by comparison, the world of sense experience is like one of shadowy darkness. This new world will be as foreign to the senses as music to the deaf or color to the blind. Only the intellect, in Plato's view, has eyes for the brilliance of perfection and to it alone is such a world revealed.

Two Problems for Plato's Theory

Of the many intriguing issues suggested by Plato's analysis, we shall take account of two that relate closely to the epistemological problems with which we are concerned. As we have seen, his account of knowledge presupposes a particular metaphysical theory about the nature of reality, the basis of which is the doctrine of Forms. If this doctrine can be challenged, then his particular theory of knowledge can be challenged. The first problem is an objection directed specifically against the doctrine of Forms, the second relates more generally to the problem of basing a theory of knowledge upon such a doctrine.

The first problem has become known as the Third Man Argument and is calculated to accentuate the difficulty in clarifying the relationship between Forms and particulars. Interestingly, Plato himself was aware of this problem and discusses it specifically in his dialogue the *Parmenides* (132), where he represents Socrates as defending, and Parmenides as criticizing, the doctrine of Forms. Parmenides advances a number of arguments, but the best known follows.

Given that in Plato's view all things of a particular type (such as men, dogs, red objects, and so forth) are what they are because they "participate" in the appropriate Forms, Parmenides then poses the following problem. Suppose we say that all large things are large in virtue of their participation in the Form Largeness, which itself is a single thing having a reality of its own. If we then consider the class of all particular large things *plus* the Form Largeness itself, we find that we must postulate a second Form, Largeness$_1$, because all the things in the new class are large. Similarly, if we then think of Largeness$_1$ together with the first Form and the original particulars, we shall then be compelled to postulate a third Form, Largeness$_2$ because all things in *this* class are large. The same reasoning that leads us to postulate the first Form will compel us to continue postulating Forms ad infinitum, for there will always be a class of large things requiring another Form of Largeness. Thus it appears that the doctrine of Forms as Plato conceives it leads to an infinite regress.

This argument makes a crucial assumption: Forms themselves exhibit (or can have predicated of them) that property or characteristic of which they are the essence. This has come to be known as the Self-Predication Assumption,[7] and without it the argument does not work. For if there is no reason to suppose that the Form Largeness is itself large, then there is no principle of collection requiring that Largeness together with large things must be included under a second Form of Largeness to account for their unity. If we need not postulate any other such Form, then the regress is forestalled.

Plato apparently did make this assumption, at least with respect to some Forms. He maintains in the *Symposium* (210–12), for example, that the Idea of Beauty, an aspect of the Good, is itself beautiful; and presumably he thought that the Idea of the Good is itself good. However, the implications of extending this assumption to all Forms are so absurd that it is difficult to believe Plato would have endorsed it. For then we would have to say that the Form of Motion is itself in motion, Redness itself red, and so on. In the absence of compelling evidence to the contrary, it seems best to assume that he did not subscribe to this as a general thesis about all the Forms; although the criticism may be directed against certain of the Forms, it does not vitiate his theory as a whole. But the objection does seem to apply to the most important of the Forms, and it constitutes a formidable attack upon Plato's theory and cannot be ignored in any thorough defense of it.[8]

The Third Man Argument, in its most general form, is a cogent argument that any rationalist must face. It points out the difficulty of explaining how the proper objects of true rational knowledge—eternal, unchanging, non-spatial essences—and the objects of sense perception—changing, spatial, and temporal things—are related to each other. How are numbers, which are known by reason but which do not "exist," related to the things of sense, which we count and measure? How is thought, which for the rationalist discloses eternal truths, related to the changing perceptions of everyday experience? How do immutable moral laws relate to the concrete situations in which moral dilemmas arise and in which choices must be made? The rationalist, in attempting to answer these and similar questions, is confronted with the difficulty of bridging a gap between two apparently exclusive domains.

The second objection attacks the core of Plato's theory by questioning the necessity even to postulate a doctrine of Forms. It opts for the primacy of sense experience over reason and denies that we do or can know of a realm of being containing peculiar entities that can be neither seen, heard, smelled, tasted, nor touched. All that exists is the multiplicity of particulars we find

---

[7]See Gregory Vlastos, "The Third Man Argument in the *Parmenides*," *Philosophical Review*, LXIII (1954), 319–49.

[8]The argument also presupposes what has been called the Nonidentity Assumption: that by virtue of which a thing possesses a certain property is not identical with the thing itself. If either of these assumptions can be shown not to be presupposed by Plato's theory, then this argument against him fails.

in this world. This is not to deny that we understand such universal notions as redness, justice, truth, and beauty; there is simply no need to postulate a unique realm of being to explain them. Our understanding of redness, for example, is conceived by first experiencing a great many red things and then abstracting intellectually what they have in common. In this way we are able to form a concept of redness and to speak about it in the abstract without postulating an *entity* redness independent of red things and independent of the concept we have in our mind. Indeed, if there were such an entity, it would be just the sort of thing of which we could have no knowledge and hence which could have no possible bearing upon human affairs.

These contentions would, of course, have to be argued at greater length if they were to be supposed to refute Plato conclusively. But if they are correct, as many philosophers have thought that basically they are, then Plato's doctrine of the Forms is indefensible. If that is the case, then the following dilemma takes shape: On the one hand, if Plato's (as well as Parmenides' and Zeno's) critique of experience is sound, then experience does not yield genuine knowledge. On the other hand, if there are no Forms, then knowledge cannot derive from reason either, at least not in the manner Plato supposes. Is genuine knowledge possible at all, and if so, what is it? Unless some way is found out of this dilemma, philosophic inquiry reaches an impasse.

It would be hasty to concede to the skeptic that there really is no genuine knowledge, for there are several promising avenues to explore in attempting to escape from this dilemma. One is to defend either reason or experience and to try to meet the difficulties attending the claims made on behalf of it. Another is to challenge the basic assumptions underlying Plato's approach to the problem, particularly as contained in his criteria for knowledge. In the next chapter we shall consider alternative approaches to knowledge that involve re-examination of the respective claims on behalf of reason and experience and that modify Plato's way of viewing the problem.

BIBLIOGRAPHY

Burnet, J., *Early Greek Philosophy* (1892). Cleveland: World Publishing Co., 1961.
————, *Greek Philosophy from Thales to Plato* (1914). London: Macmillan & Co., Ltd., 1955.
Cornford, F. M., *From Religion to Philosophy* (1912). London: Macmillan & Co., Ltd., 1955.
————, *Plato's Theory of Knowledge* (1934). New York: Liberal Arts Press, 1957. (Translation of and commentary on *Theaetetus* and *Sophist*.)
Cross, R. C., and A. D. Woozley, *Commentary on Plato's Republic*. London: Macmillan & Co., Ltd., 1964.
Field, G. C., *The Philosophy of Plato*. London: Oxford University Press, 1949.
Grube, G. M. A., *Plato's Thought* (1935). Boston: Beacon Press, 1958.
Nahm, Milton C., *Selections from Early Greek Philosophy* (4th ed.) New York: Appleton-Century-Crofts, 1964.

Nettleship R. L., *Lectures on the Republic of Plato* (1897). London: Macmillan & Co., Ltd., 1961.

Robinson, Richard, *Plato's Earlier Dialectic*, 2nd ed., Chaps. 1 and 5. Oxford: Clarendon Press, 1953.

Ross, Sir David, *Plato's Theory of Ideas*. Oxford: Clarendon Press, 1951.

Taylor, A. E., *Plato: The Man and His Work* (7th ed.). London: Methuen & Co., Ltd., 1960.

——, *The Mind of Plato* (1922). Ann Arbor: University of Michigan Press, 1960.

——, *Socrates: The Man and His Thought* (1933). New York: Doubleday & Co., Inc., 1954.

QUESTIONS FOR REVIEW AND DISCUSSION

1. Would it be a fair objection to Parmenides and Zeno to point out that the language in which they frame their arguments against plurality and motion already presupposes plurality and motion; and that in order to speak intelligibly, they must concede the point at issue?

2. Evaluate the objection that because Plato's criterion of infallibility would prevent most of our scientific learning from qualifying as knowledge, it must for that reason be mistaken.

3. Do you agree with Plato's assumption that permanence is a mark of reality and that what is more enduring is more real? Why? Do you think it is possible to delineate any general traits of reality as a whole? If not, what significance does the word "reality" have?

4. Granting that to be said to know something one must believe it and be certain of it, what further conditions can you suggest (in addition to, or instead of, Plato's requirement of the ability to give a *logos*) as being necessary for knowledge?

5. Do you agree with Plato that all wrongdoing is from ignorance? Why? What relevance would philosophical, psychological, and sociological inquiries have in answering this question? What implications does his view carry for the administration of punishment in society? Can you suggest ways of clarifying the concepts of *knowledge* and *action* so as to elucidate the relationship between the two?

6. Do you think that Plato's theory of Forms is more, less, or equally plausible when applied to abstract notions like beauty and justice as when applied to physical things like men and animals? Why?

Note on Terminology SOME "ISMS"

OF

EPISTEMOLOGY

The technical vocabulary of the theory of knowledge can be puzzling and confusing. It will clarify matters in the following chapters to state clearly the most important distinctions. Fixing labels is not the same as philosophizing; each of the terms will have more significance after the following chapters are studied. But this schematic presentation may help give a sense of direction in the discussions to follow.

In the next two chapters and occasionally in later chapter, four great traditions in epistemology are compared. They are: rationalism, empiricism, idealism, and realism. Everyone knows that rationalism is the view that knowledge comes from reason, that empiricism is the doctrine that knowledge comes from experience, that idealists say that knowledge is in some sense subjective, and that realists hold that what we know is real. But such rough distinctions are certain to be misleading, for centuries of philosophic inquiry have made the issues much more precise than indicated by these approximate definitions.

Three central epistemological problems are discussed:

1. What are the respective roles of reason and experience in knowledge?
2. What relationship exists between that which we perceive and the real things in the world?
3. What is the relationship between the mind and the objects that it professes to know?

ANSWERS TO QUESTION 1: EMPIRICISM AND RATIONALISM

To define empiricism and rationalism, we need to define some other terms.

In a declarative sentence such as "There is not a skeleton in every dark closet," we can distinguish two kinds of expressions: those that have a meaning taken by themselves (such as "skeleton," "dark," and "closet") and those that do not convey a meaning by themselves (such as "There is," "not," "a," "in," and "every"). The former are called *designators* or *categorematic expressions*; the latter are called *syncategorematic expressions*. The concepts signified by each are called, respectively, *categorematic* and *syncategorematic concepts*. We shall be concerned only with categorematic concepts, and for the sake of simplicity, we shall refer to them simply as "concepts."

A concept, represented by such common nouns as "skeleton," "closet," "cause," and "mind" or by such adjectives as "dark," "physical," and "eternal," is called an empirical concept if, and only if, it originates in our sense experience or can be exhibited in such experience. It seems obvious that some concepts are empirical in one or both of these senses; no philosopher, with the possible exception of Parmenides (p. 50) has ever disputed the fact. But are they all, without exception, empirical concepts? On this question there has been and is much dispute, and the possible answers are:

a. Concept-empiricism: All concepts are empirical.
b. Concept-rationalism: Some concepts are not empirical.

Concepts that are not empirical are said to be a priori. The concept-empiricist, therefore, denies that there are any a priori concepts, and the concept-rationalist asserts that some concepts are a priori concepts.

Knowledge is called empirical knowledge if, and only if, it either reports on or is testable (can be shown to be true) by some reference to sense experience. (The knowledge that it is now raining is empirical knowledge in the first sense because I looked out of the window and saw the rain; the knowledge [more properly: knowledge-claim] that there are bacteria in this water is empirical in the second sense because I can put water under a microscope and see whether there are bacteria in it or not.) If there is any knowledge that is not empirical, either in the sense of originating in or being testable by experience, it is called *a priori knowledge*.

Knowledge is called *factual knowledge* if it is knowledge of things, events, or states of affairs. Knowledge is called *conceptual knowledge* if it is knowledge only of relationships among concepts and is based upon concepts (whether empirical or a priori concepts). (It is factual knowledge that John Doe is a bachelor; it is conceptual knowledge that all bachelors are unmarried.)

Everyone grants that some or all conceptual knowledge is a priori;[1] no philosopher has disputed that. The questions is: Is any factual knowledge a priori? Answers to this question are:

c. Epistemic empiricism: All factual knowledge is empirical.
d. Epistemic rationalism: At least some factual knowledge is a priori.

It will readily be seen that (a) and (b) are contradictory and that (c)

---

[1]The conceptual knowledge that is universally agreed to be *a priori* is expressed in *analytic judgments*, *logical truths*, and *tautologies*. For the important distinction between analytic and synthetic judgments, see pages 156–59.

and (d) are contradictory. But various combinations of (a) or (b) with (c) or (d) are possible.

Parmenides (p. 50) defends (b) and (d) in an extreme form. That is, he reads (b) as "No concepts are empirical" and (d) as "*All* factual knowledge is a priori." He may, therefore, be called an extreme rationalist. Plato (p. 54) and Descartes (p. 83) defend the combination of (b) and (d), and they are called simply *rationalists*. Theaetetus (p. 56), Locke (p. 97), Berkeley (p. 104), Hume (p. 221), and the logical positivists (p. 152) combine (a) with (c) and are called *empiricists*.

Other combinations are possible. For example, Kant (p. 237) accepts (b) and (c), and some Aristotelian scholastics defend (a) and (d); hence, it is very misleading to refer to them as either empiricists or rationalists.

ANSWERS TO QUESTION 2 : EPISTEMOLOGICAL MONISM AND EPISTEMOLOGICAL DUALISM

When I perceive an object, such as a star, do I perceive it exactly as it is and as it truly exists? When I perceive it, do I perceive it as it would be even if I did not perceive it? Or do I directly apprehend something else that stands for it, represents it, is a sign of it, and serves as my evidence for its existence? If the answer to the last question is affirmative, I am said merely to apprehend its appearances (*Theaetetus*, p. 56), to have an idea of it (Locke, p. 98), or to have sense data (p. 78).

Answers to the question whether I know an independent object as it is in reality or know only something else that stands for or represents it are given in two theories:

e. *Epistemological monism*: The object of empirical knowledge and what others call sense data (and so forth) are identical when the object is perceived; or, if it is asserted that there are sense data (etc.), sense data (etc.) are the only objects of empirical knowledge.
f. *Epistemological dualism*: There are sense data (etc.), and they are not identical with the object of empirical knowledge.

Defenses of epistemological monism are given by Berkeley (p. 105), Perry (p. 120), and phenomenalists like Ayer (p. 160). Epistemological dualism is defended by Descartes[2] (p. 86), Locke (p. 99), and Santayana (p. 122).

ANSWERS TO QUESTION 3 : EPISTEMOLOGICAL REALISM AND EPISTEMOLOGICAL IDEALISM

Whether one says he knows the object directly, (e), or indirectly, (f), the question of the nature of the object remains. Is it dependent for its ex-

---

[2]Epistemological dualism must not be confused with psychophysical dualism (= Cartesian dualism, p. 273), which is also defended by Descartes.

istence upon the mind that knows it?[3] There are two answers to these questions:

g. *Epistemological realism*: The object of empirical knowledge exists independently of the knower.
h. *Epistemological idealism*: The object of empirical knowledge is dependent upon the knower and does not exist except as known.

Among the epistemological realists are Plato,[4] Descartes, Perry, Santayana, and the phenomenalists. Epistemological idealism is represented by Berkeley.

Whereas (e) and (f) are contradictories of each other, and (g) and (h) are contradictories, various combinations of (e) or (f) with (g) or (h) are possible. Descartes, Locke, and Santayana combine (f), dualism, with (g), realism, and are called *representative realists* because the sense data (etc.) represent the independent object. Berkeley combines (e) with (h), monism with idealism. Perry combines (e) with (g), monism with realism (and his theory is sometimes called *neorealism* or *direct realism* or *naïve realism* on the assumption that this is the theory held by the naïve man of common sense). The phenomenalists also combine (e) with (g), but whereas Perry tends to deny that there are sense data, the phenomenalists assert that there are sense data and regard the physical object as a construction (see p. 160) from sense data; but they deny that sense data are mind-dependent. In this respect they diverge from Berkeley, who asserts that ideas are mind-dependent.

Special care should be taken not to confuse Berkeley's idealism with absolute idealism (p. 126) and pluralistic idealism (p. 138). Pluralistic idealism, in its epistemological theory, is a combination of (f) with (g)—epistemological dualism with epistemological realism. Absolute idealism does not fit very well into any of the rubrics since it is little concerned with the analysis of perceptual knowledge.

The table in Chapter 13 (p. 325) summarizes various theories of perception, including one (objective relativism) that is not discussed in the next chapters.

SUMMARY AND PROSPECTUS

Not all the views on each of these questions held by each philosopher will be presented in the following chapters. Most of the philosophers were primarily concerned with only one or two of our three questions, and we do not always know how they regarded the others. Having dealt with Parmenides, Theaetetus, and Plato, we shall now consider some particular

---

[3]For the distinction between qualities sometimes thought to be independent and those thought to be dependent upon mind (the distinction between primary and secondary qualities), see page 99.

[4]Platonic realism (the theory that Forms are real; see pp. 61, 217) is an extreme form of epistemological realism.

combinations of theses that have been found most viable in modern philosophy. They are the theories of Descartes, Locke, Berkeley, the neo-realists (such as Perry), the critical realists (such as Santayana), and the phenomenalists (such as Ayer).

There are $8^2 = 64$ possible answers to our complex of questions; no combinations of answers have succeeded in defending themselves against all criticisms from the authors of other combinations. Perhaps, it has been suggested, they all rest on certain unexamined presuppositions that have infected them with irremediable errors; therefore, a quite different approach to epistemology is called for. In Chapter 9 (p. 164) we shall examine three such radical proposals—those of John Dewey, J. L. Austin, and Gilbert Ryle.

4 A RATIONALIST'S PROPOSAL

Starting with such rigorous criteria of knowledge, Plato was led to postulate a higher-order realm of Being in order to satisfy these criteria. But, ironically, a realm of Forms beyond space and time and undiscoverable by the senses has seemed to many philosophers to be just the sort of thing of which we do not and cannot have knowledge. The very entities assumed in order to insure the possibility of knowledge make knowledge, in fact, unattainable. This highlights a problem not only for Plato but for metaphysics generally, which for centuries has drawn fire for allegedly ranging beyond the limits of possible knowledge. It is the problem of the proper scope and, indeed, of the very legitimacy of metaphysical speculation. Few issues in philosophy have been more vigorously contested.

This gives special importance to the epistemological question concerning the limits of knowledge. If we clearly understood the limits of what, in fact, is known (or taken as knowledge) and of what, in principle, *can be* known, we could then judge when philosophic inquiry has transgressed such limits. Wildly speculative metaphysical theories would be exposed as attempted excursions into an abyss where if anything exists it is unfathomable to the human intellect. For all their poetic and imaginative value, such theories would not command the attention of those determined to clarify the nature of reality.

The need for more exact guidelines for philosophic inquiry was expressed by the seventeenth-century British philosopher John Locke (1632–1704), who described his own approach to philosophy:

For I thought that the first step toward satisfying several inquiries the mind of man was very apt to run into, was, to take a survey of our own understandings, examine our own powers, and see to what things they were adapted. Till that was done I suspected we began at the wrong end, and in vain sought for satisfaction in a quiet and sure possession of truths that most concerned us, whilst we let loose our thoughts into the vast ocean of Being; as if all that boundless extent were the natural and undoubted possession of our understandings, wherein there was nothing exempt from its decisions, or that escaped its comprehension. Thus men, extending their inquiries beyond their capacities, and letting their thoughts wander into those depths where they can find no sure footing, it is no wonder that they raise questions and multiply disputes, which, never coming to any clear resolution, are proper only to continue and increase their doubts, and to confirm them at last in perfect skepticism. Whereas, were the capacities of our understandings well considered, the extent of our knowledge once discovered, and the horizon found which sets the bounds between the enlightened and dark parts of things; between what is and what is not comprehensible by us, men would perhaps with less scruple acquiesce in the avowed ignorance of the one, and employ their thoughts and discourse with more advantage and satisfaction in the other.[1]

Locke recognizes the need for greater self-discipline in inquiry, the achievement of which would mark a further refinement of the critical attitude we saw to be central to philosophy.

What course would be open to someone who wanted to put philosophy on a surer footing and who agreed with Plato about the infallibility of knowledge but demurred at accepting the doctrine of Forms? One course would be to compromise and say that although knowledge must indeed be infallible and have reality as its object, reality need not be construed as eternal and unchanging. It was this quasi-Parmenidean concept of reality that pre-empted the physical world from being the object of knowledge and thereby caused Plato to formulate the doctrine of Forms. Such a course would represent a significant modification of Plato's criteria, for although one could still say that knowledge must have reality as its object, the material world would not thereby be precluded from being called real.

The way would then be open to a theory of knowledge oriented about the material world and our relationship to it. Even if we should agree with Plato that it is not the ultimate reality and our "knowledge" of it not genuine, it is important to establish as precisely as possible our actual relationship to the world around us. This would require greater attention to the nature of perception (which for Plato, we recall, meets the requirement of infallibility), because it is through it that we have our only awareness of things around us. Moreover, such an inquiry might provide clues both to the limits of knowledge and to the proper scope of metaphysics.

PERCEPTION AND THE LIMITS OF KNOWLEDGE

Earlier we mentioned our senses of sight, hearing, touch, taste, and smell. Let us now ask *what* it is that we sense or perceive when our different sense organs are in operation. To common sense this is a curious question. When

[1]John Locke, *An Essay Concerning Human Understanding* (1690), I. (New York: Dover Publications, Inc., 1959), pp. 31f.

I look across my office or out the window do I not perceive the books on the shelf and the tree in the square? Such answers suffice for common sense, but let us consider the matter further.

Suppose that you are an astronomer focusing through a telescope upon a distant star. It is common sense to say that you see a star; it is the immediate object of your sense experience. But suppose that this star is some 900 light-years away, which means that the light emitted by it requires 900 years traveling at 186,000 miles per second to reach the earth and strike the retina of your eye. This would mean that you see the star only as it was 900 years ago, not as it is today. In fact, the star itself may no longer exist. Had it disintegrated yesterday in a steller explosion, for example, observers on earth would not know this for another 900 years. Thus, in one ordinary sense what you perceive is the star, and in another sense it is not because you have no assurance that the star even exists. And one does not properly say that he sees things that do not exist.

If what you directly perceive is not the star but something else, then what is it? Let us call it an image or impression caused by the impact of light from the star upon the retina of your eye, resulting in the stimulation of the optic nerve and the transmission of certain impulses to your brain. Many philosophers have thought that whatever this image is it is obviously non-identical with the star. It exists here and now as a tiny speck of light, and it ceases to exist as soon as you take your eye away from the telescope. The star itself, assuming that it still exists, is a physical object 900 light-years away, is thousands of times larger than the earth and more brilliant than the sun, and will continue to exist whether you look through the telescope or not. What we directly perceive—the immediate content of our visual sense experience—seems to be distinguishable from the object we "see." In fact, it seems we never directly perceive the star itself; we know of it only what can be inferred from data provided by our senses. This suggests that in situations of this sort we must recognize a third term in addition to the subject and object of inquiry—the data of sense experience intermediate between the two. Even though we quite properly say that we see the star, its apprehension is mediated by directly perceived sense data.

Let us return now to the more commonplace example of the tree in the quad. Does not the same situation obtain here? Again many philosophers have thought that it does, saying that what we *directly* perceive is merely an image or impression caused by the stimulus of certain light waves upon the retina of the eye. True, but in this case the light does not emanate from the tree as it does from the star; it is radiated from the sun and only reflected from the tree. But the basic fact, supported by a vast body of scientific knowledge and theory, remains the same: It takes the light a certain length of time to travel from the tree to your eye, and your visual experience is caused by what then takes place when the light strikes your eyes and activates your nervous system. Because of the proximity of subject and object, the length of time involved in this case will be almost incalculably small in comparison with that of the star; but this is only a difference in degree dependent upon the accidental fact of the different locations of the two objects vis-à-vis the perceiving subject. As long as we assume that light has a finite velocity, there will be a time gap in each instance. If so, and if our visual experience is caused by the action of light on our sense organs, then it seems here, as in the example of the star, that what we immediately perceive is an image or impression caused (in part) by, but nonidentical with, the object. Hence, we must recognize an intermediate datum or content between (not necessarily spatially) subject and object. We *see* the tree directly (as opposed to indirectly, say through mirrors) but directly *perceive* only the data of our immediate experience. The data of immediate experience are now called sense data.

What is the status of such sense data? Perhaps their most marked characteristic, by contrast with objects of the type just mentioned, is that they are subjective, their existence depending upon the perceiving subject. They depend upon such factors as that you are conscious, have a nervous system, and are in possession of properly functioning sense organs. Very slight changes in the state of your mind or body, such as closing your eyes, sleeping, or simply looking in a different direction, may cause this image to cease to exist, for the light reflected from the tree or emitted by the star will then no longer strike the retina of your eye and create the image. The tree itself, however, continues to exist whether or not you close your eyes, go to sleep, or look in another direction. Common sense would say that it would continue to exist even if all percipient beings completely disappeared. The conditions necessary for its existence are independent of the bodily and mental states of actual and possible perceivers. But if percipient beings suddenly disappeared, there would be no more images or impressions of the type described since they exist only in and for such beings. In an important sense, therefore, they are subjective.

It this is correct we seem forced to the conclusion that we never *visually* perceive any objects directly, because the analysis given will apply equally to any other objects. What we directly perceive are sense data that vary from person to person and from time to time for one person. Looked at from different angles a coin successively appears circular, elliptical, and straight and will appear as all three of these at once to different people differently situated. Even looked at from the same angle an object creates different impressions at different times according to the interplay of light and shadow upon it—a fact of which the artist is more keenly aware than the ordinary person (witness Monet's paintings of the Rouen Cathedral as it receives the sunlight at various hours of the day). In each of these cases, changing conditions affecting the relationship of subject and object create different data. It was such facts that led Plato to characterize our perceptual world as one of continuous flux.

So far we have discussed only visual perception. We should now ask whether what we perceive through our other senses, hearing, touch, taste, and smell, are similarly subjective. It has often been assumed that they are. Even though we cannot detail all the arguments of philosophers who have held this view,[2] let us try to understand the argument that led them to this conclusion.

Suppose we ask, What do I directly perceive when I hear the library bells ringing? Here we can verify that a certain physical event occurs before I hear anything: The striking of metal against the side of the bell causes vibrations that are then transmitted through the air (at a speed very much slower than that of light) until they strike my eardrum and give rise to auditory sensations. Again, we may say with perfect propriety from the standpoint of common sense that what I hear is the library bells ringing. Although it would be unusual, it even makes sense to say that I hear this directly if my intention is to signify that I am not hearing an echo, a recording, or a radio broadcast. Notice, however, that the event in the library tower takes place a fraction of a second before the sound in my ears commences. The time lapse between the one and the other is the time required for the disturbance in the air created by the vibration of the bell to travel the distance between the tower and me. In this respect, the situation is parallel to that of visual perception; I do not hear anything until *after* the event in the tower has taken place, or at least commenced. This suggests that what I directly perceive is distinct from what causes my experience. The sensation in my ears is nonidentical both with the event in the tower and with the waves produced by it. And just as in the case of visual perception, its existence depends upon the state of my mind and body. If my ears are defective or dinned by the stereo, I will fail to hear the bells even though the same event is occurring in the tower as when I do hear them. This event might occur even if there were no percipient beings, although in that case there surely would exist no sensations of sound. Thus, it seems that what I directly perceive in auditory experience is no less subjective than what I perceive in visual experience.

Many people may concede this analysis for our visual, auditory, and even olfactory sensations but argue that with touch and taste we directly perceive objects and substances without the mediation of numerically distinct sense data. Here there is no time gap required for the transmission of energy through space. Am I not in direct contact with the desk when I feel its smoothness or with the wine when I taste its sweetness? These cases are more complex and difficult.

---

[2]In the next chapter we shall further consider some of these arguments in connection with the philosophy of George Berkeley.

Let us consider taste first, recalling Plato's point in the *Theaetetus* that how a thing tastes to a person depends upon many factors directly relative to him. If one is not feeling well, a sweet wine may taste bitter, or if one has a bad cold, a delicate food may not taste at all. As Plato recognized, one's experiences depend not only upon the state of the substance tasted but also upon the state of the person tasting; Socrates, he says, is not precisely the same person (meaning the state of his body is not the same) when he is ill as when he is well, and his condition will determine what he experiences when he tastes the wine. But it is one and the same wine that tastes sweet to me and bitter to you. Its existence is not dependent upon you (unless you made it), whereas the bitterness of its taste is dependent upon you; it is a subjective datum of experience just as the image perceived when one looks through the telescope is a subjective datum. This seems to be true of all our taste sensations. Therefore, if the various substances we taste do *not*, at the time they are perceived, depend upon us, or any percipient organism, for their existence, then it seems we must distinguish these "objects" from the directly perceived data generated by our response to them, which are so dependent.

Finally, consider our tactual sensations. Here let us use an example similar to one used by Bishop Berkeley, the eighteenth-century British philosopher. It involves the notion of heat, which we are likely to think of as a property of directly perceived objects no less than smoothness or roughness.

Imagine what happens if you place your hand near the surface of a hot stove. You soon experience warmth as the heat from the stove warms the surrounding air and it, in turn, warms your hand. If you move your hand closer to the stove until you finally touch it, the initial warmth will transform itself to severe pain, and you will no longer be able to distinguish the heat from the pain. Rather than having two perceptions, one of heat (supposedly in the stove) and another of pain (in your hand), you will then have only one sensation—pain. Surely the pain you now perceive cannot be a property of the stove because it is an inanimate object with no feelings. But if the pain is in you and the heat and the pain are indistinguishable, then is not the heat also in you? Does it not depend for its existence upon you no less than your visual percepts do? If, for example, through injury you had lost all feeling in your hand, no sensations of heat or pain would be experienced, even though the other conditions remained the same.

The physical condition that we call heat is the violent motion of molecules in a physical body and the surrounding air, just as the physical condition that we call sound is a vibration in the metallic body and the air. The heat we directly experience is as different from the physical heat as the sound we directly experience is different from a wave motion in the air.

Similar arguments can be developed for all of the various qualities experienced tactually that point to the same conclusion: We do not directly perceive objects and substances but only intermediate subjective data.

EPISTEMOLOGICAL DUALISM AND REALISM

Such considerations have led many philosophers to suppose that we *never* perceive the physical world directly; that all we are ever directly aware of through the senses are subjective impressions. This means that in our experience of the world there are *always* data, or sense contents, intermediate between subject and object. Recognition of the ubiquity of this third term gives rise to three central problems for epistemology. They concern:

1. the relationship between subject and object,
2. the relationship between data and object,
3. the relationship between subject and data.

We have been assuming the common-sense answer to 1—that the subject and object are independently existing realities; that trees, bells, wines, and flowers exist independently of being seen, heard, tasted, and smelled. We also have seen reasons for answering 2 by saying that the immediate data of perception are nonidentical with the objects of the world and for answering 3 by saying that these data are subjective impressions, existing only in the perceiver's mind or consciousness. Certain key epistemological theories take shape in accordance with the answers to these equstions, and two of these theories will be introduced now. They concern the relationships referred to in 1 and 2. The person who holds that the object of knowledge exists independently of a perceiving or cognizant subject is an *epistemological realist*. The person who holds that the data of perception are nonidentical with the object is an *epistemological dualist*. Plato was a realist in this sense; he believed that the objects of knowledge (the Forms) in no way depend for their reality upon the existence of a subject who may know or perceive them. And although we did not approach his theory of knowledge from the standpoint of answering 2, much of his discussion of perception suggests that he may have also been an epistemological dualist.

Epistemological realism captures an important part of our common-sense view of the world, because we do believe that objects exist independently of whether anyone knows or perceives them. Epistemological dualism has the virtue of enabling us to explain such phenomena as error and illusion. When a partly submerged stick appears bent, we can explain this by saying that the refraction of light as it passes from a medium of one density (water) to that of another (air) causes it to create a retinal image different from that observed if the stick were out of water. But since the image and the stick are two distinct things, we can say consistently that the stick is very different in reality (straight) from how it appears (bent). Someone unaware of such phenomena might be led to judge erroneously that the stick is *in fact* bent.

This explanatory power comes at a cost, however, for the combination of assumptions we have been dealing with—that there are sharply distinguishable subjects and objects and that we as subjects directly perceive only subjective intermediaries between the two—conspire to generate one of the most vexing problems in the history of epistemology. This is the problem of our knowledge of the external world. If what we perceive is *always* subjective and private and we *never* perceive objects directly, how can we ever be sure what such objects are really like? How can we even know for certain that objects exist and, hence, that there is an external world?

This is precisely the problem confronting the person who seeks an alternative to Plato by trying to reinstate the material world as an object of knowledge but who is persuaded by the line of reasoning just considered that we never directly perceive this world. The problem lacked urgency for Plato, of course, because he was not committed to saying that we have real knowledge of the material world. But it must be confronted by anyone who would be both a realist and a dualist in his epistemology and who would maintain that it is the independent existence of a material world that is known.

The problem's implications are far-reaching. Unless a person who accepts this line of reasoning can explain how knowledge extends beyond our perceptual field he will be committed either to *solipsism*—nothing exists beyond my own immediate experiences—or to a *skepticism* that says that we cannot know there is an external world. Moreover, if such a person were to agree with Plato that even perception fails to qualify as knowledge, then in the absence of any other mode of knowing he would be on the brink of a radical skepticism about the possibility of knowing anything at all.

We see now why the problem of perception is so crucial to our initial question concerning the limits of knowledge. Unless there is some way to avoid the predicament to which epistemological dualism leads, the limits of knowledge will be fixed by the range of actual and possible subjective sense experiences. If it should, in principle, be impossible for knowledge to extend beyond these limits, then metaphysical theories like Plato's will have been shown to be aimless wanderings in that "boundless extent" of which Locke spoke, where the understanding is incapable of following. They would purport to convey knowledge of a sort that even in principle cannot be had. The problem of knowledge of the external world must therefore be taken seriously, and it will occupy our attention through the next two chapters.

THE CARTESIAN PROOF OF AN EXTERNAL WORLD

This was a central problem for the seventeenth-century French philosopher René Descartes (1596–1650), whose theory of knowledge provides an alternative to Plato's. He believes that knowledge is infallible and has reality as its object, but he allows the material world to qualify as genuinely real and hence as a possible object of knowledge.

Descartes' proposed solution to the problem takes shape in accordance with his assumption, shared by Plato and Parmenides, that the source of knowledge is *reason*. We recall from the previous chapter (p. 48) that our example to illustrate knowledge arrived at through reason was drawn from geometry. In abstract disciplines such as mathematics and logic we have the clearest cases of a priori knowledge. Descartes was a mathematician as well as a philosopher, and he thought the type of reasoning found in mathematics was the ideal of knowledge. By adapting the procedures of mathematics to the study of nature, the mind, and God, he believed that the endless disputes of philosophers and theologians could be settled.

Descartes' *Discourse on the Method of Rightly Conducting the Reason and Seeking for Truth in the Sciences* was published in 1637. It describes a method by which "I can gradually augment my understanding, and raise it, bit by bit, to the highest point which the mediocrity of my mind and the short duration of my life will allow" (p. 5). He discovered this method after he had become disillusioned with the study of philosophy, which seemed never to settle any of its questions, and of the sciences, which, he said, took their first principles from the speculations of philosophers. His personal life also brought him to search for a new method; he traveled widely and discovered such a variety of opinions tenaciously held by different peoples that he could not "choose anyone whose opinions were preferable to those of others, and I found myself forced to undertake to guide myself" (p. 15).

Mathematics, in which he had already distinguished himself, provided Descartes with the guide he needed in thinking for himself.

These long chains of reasoning, so simple and easy, which the geometers customarily used in order to arrive at their most difficult demonstrations, had given me occasion to imagine that all things that can be understood by men follow from one another in the same way, and that, provided only that we abstain from accepting as true anything which is not, and always follow the order that is necessary to deduce each from the other, there can be none so remote that we cannot eventually come upon it, or so hidden that we cannot discover it. And I did not have very much trouble looking for the ones with which I had to begin, for I already knew that it must be with the simplest and easiest to know.[3]

Imitating the mathematician, he set up four rules of method for himself.

The first was never to accept anything as true that I did not know evidently to be such; that is to say, carefully to avoid haste and bias, and to include nothing more in my judgments than that which presented itself to my mind so clearly and so distinctly that I had no occasion to place it in doubt.

The second was to divide each of the difficulties that I examined into as many

[3]From René Descartes: *Discourse on Method, Optics, Geometry and Meteorology*, trans. Paul J. Olscamp, copyright © 1965 by the Bobbs-Merrill Company, Inc., reprinted by permission of The Liberal Arts Press Division of The Bobbs-Merrill Company, Inc. See p. 16.

parts as possible, and according as such division would be required for the better solution of the problems.

The third was to direct my thinking in an orderly way, by beginning with the objects that were simplest and easiest to understand, in order to climb little by little, gradually, to the knowledge of the most complex; and even for this purpose assuming an order among those objects which do not naturally precede each other.

And the last was at all times to make enumerations so complete, and reviews so general, that I would be sure of omitting nothing.[4]

The second rule tells us simply to analyze complex questions into simpler ones; the fourth tells us to review our work to make *sure* that nothing has been omitted and that we have not been guilty of any error in reasoning. But the really original and distinctive parts of Descartes' method are given in the first and third of these rules.

The first is the really decisive one. "Clearness and distinctness" are the marks of a true idea. A clear idea is one that is indubitable to an attentive mind, such as the idea that a three-sided figure has three angles. A distinct idea is one that an attentive mind will not confuse with any other idea, such as the idea of a triangle in contrast to the idea of a square. Descartes called our immediate knowledge of clear and distinct ideas *intuition*. Intuition is the immediate and indubitable knowledge of a clear and distinct idea.

This gives us Descartes' answer to the question "What is knowledge?" Knowledge is what is either clearly and distinctly intuited or demonstrable from premises that are so intuited. This criterion of clearness and distinctness implies that knowledge is infallible; a person who has a clear and distinct intuitive apprehension of something cannot be mistaken, and he will be certain that he knows it. Unlike Plato, Descartes believes that *whatever* passes this test constitutes knowledge; knowledge does not have to meet the further test of having eternal and unchanging reality as its object. Rather than what counts as knowledge being determined by whether it has reality as its object, what counts as real is determined by whether it is an object of knowledge. In this way Descartes does not prejudge, as Plato did, the question whether the material world can be an object of knowledge. Indeed, he believes that the existence of such a world can be known because it can be demonstrated by correct reasoning in the same way that one can prove a theorem of geometry.

The attainment of the same degree of certainty in science and philosophy that has been reached in mathematics will be possible only if there are axioms or simple, clear, and distinct ideas from which we can draw certain conclusions a priori. Descartes, therefore, begins to search for clear and distinct ideas outside the field of mathematics. Initially, he thinks like a skeptic, following a method of doubting every idea that can be doubted. His purpose is to doubt every idea that *can* be doubted even though no sane man *would* seriously doubt it; he is trying to find ideas that are not merely not dubious

[4]*Ibid.*, p. 16.

but indubitable. He finds that he can doubt what is ordinarily considered common sense, and he can doubt authorities; he can doubt his sense experience and memories; he can doubt the sciences, which are based upon them; he can, in fact, doubt everything except the fact that he is doubting. There is at least one indubitable truth: *Cogito, ergo sum*—I think, therefore I am. This "was so firm and well assured that all the most extravagant suppositions of the skeptics were incapable of shaking it" (p. 28). This, then, was the sought-for axiom, and whatever could be deduced from it would be as certain as the axiom itself. (Actually, in his demonstrations Descartes also used other axioms that he regarded as clear and distinct, such as the causal principle that everything must have a cause that is at least as real and perfect as its effect.)

With his indubitable axiom, Descartes then proceeds to prove some of the other beliefs that he had previously found dubitable. He gives several proofs for the existence of God and demonstrates the existence of the external world corresponding to his clear and distinct sense perceptions of it. In this way he believes that he can establish a priori knowledge in both theology and science. The first of his arguments for God is summarized as follows:

I have an idea of God, that is, of a perfect being. This idea may be false; at least its truth can be doubted. But the existence of the idea, whether true or not, cannot be doubted and is not, in fact, disputed even by atheists. Now, by the second axiom, this idea must have a cause, and the cause must be as perfect or real as the effect; hence, the idea of perfection must have a perfect cause. But I am not the cause of this idea, for I am imperfect; I have doubts instead of knowledge. Therefore, a being outside me that is perfect must cause this idea. And a perfect being is God, by definition. Hence, God exists.

At this point in his argument Descartes has moved beyond both skepticism and solipsism although not very far beyond. He *knows* the existence of only two things, himself and God, and in knowing that God exists he knows one thing exists *beyond* the contents of his private experience. But now what of the external world? While Descartes was applying his skeptical method he was, of course, aware of impressions or ideas—what we have called sense data. As he says,

... I am the same being which perceives—that is, which observes certain objects as though by means of the sense organs, because I do really see light, hear noises, feel heat. Will it be said that these appearances are false and that I am sleeping? Let it be so; yet at the very least it is certain that it seems to me that I see light, hear noises, and feel heat. This much cannot be false, and it is this, properly considered, which in my nature is called perceiving, and that, again speaking precisely, is nothing else but thinking.[5]

[5]From René Descartes: *Meditations*, trans. Laurence J. La Fleur, copyright © 1951, 1960, by The Liberal Arts Press, Inc., reprinted by permission of The Liberal Arts Press Division of The Bobbs-Merrill Company, Inc. See pp. 25f.

His point is that it is possible to doubt whether any of the colors, shapes, sounds, and so forth of which we are immediately aware represent actually existing things. Just as we can look through the telescope and speculate whether there still exists an actual star corresponding to the image we perceive, so Descartes thinks it makes sense to ask concerning the totality of our sense impressions whether *anything* corresponds to them. But, for Descartes, the question is not whether external things *continue* to exist after having caused certain sense impressions in us but whether such things *ever* existed. My experience yields impressions of certain colors, shape, and size when I look at what I take to be a tree. But if all these impressions are subjective, what reason can there be to suppose that an actually existing tree—an independent external object—causes them?

Descartes believes this question can be answered by correct reasoning employing the truths he has already established about his own and God's existence. Now, he apprehends clearly and distinctly that he exists and that he has a capacity for sensing—receiving ideas, images, or impressions. But what is the cause of these ideas? It must be either himself or something external to him. However, he knows that he is not the cause; first, because he is, in essence, a thinking being and this cause does not presuppose intellect; second, because these ideas often intrude upon his consciousness against his will. Therefore the cause must lie beyond himself.

If the cause lies outside him, he believes there are only three possibilities: (a) that material objects are the cause, (b) that God is the cause, and (c) that something greater than material objects but lesser than God is the cause. But neither b nor c can be the answer for the following reasons. First, Descartes has no faculty by which he could know that this is so (that is, that God or some other thing is the cause), and second, he has a strong natural inclination to believe that material objects are the cause. If this natural inclination were incorrect, then Descartes would be grossly deceived—not just occasionally but continuously—about the cause of his ideas; and he would be unequipped with any compensating faculty for correcting this deception. God, his creator, constituted him to have this natural inclination; so if it is incorrect and the cause is either God Himself or something other than material objects, God is a deceiver. But because God is perfect—hence perfectly good—He would not deceive. Therefore, Descartes' ideas must *actually* be caused by independently existing material objects. Therefore, an external world exists.

We should note, however, that God guarantees the external existence of only those characteristics of objects of which Descartes has clear and distinct apprehension. Of these there is only one, that is, that they have extension in width, breadth, and depth (hence that they have shape) and relatedly that they have substance, location, motion, duration, and number. Indeed, he takes extension (spatiality) to be the essence of material objects, just as it is his essence to think. Ideas like color, sound, taste, heat, and the like are adventitious and variable. Because they are only confusedly apprehended as properties of objects and hence are uncertified by God, they may or may not accurately represent external objects. What we do know and can prove with the exactitude of a geometrical theorem is that material objects exist and have extension.

In summary, Descartes, distrusting authority, common sense, and the testimony of his senses, tries to model philosophy after mathematics and to take mathematics as the ideal for all knowledge. He searches for indubitable first principles or axioms that can be known intuitively or directly to be true. From these he makes demonstrations independent of sense experience; experience serves only to pose the problem and is referred to again only in the final stage (fourth rule) in order to make sure that no aspect of the problem has been overlooked. The results will be: (a) beliefs that are not self-evidently true can be shown to be true if they can be deduced from those that are self-evident; (b) beliefs can be shown to be false if their contradictories can be deduced from the axioms; (c) beliefs can be shown to be unfounded, so that a prudent man will withhold his judgment, if neither they nor their opposites can be deduced. In a word, all beliefs we can rightly be confident about will be either self-evident, or demonstrably evident, by virtue of being deduced from those that are self-evident. When this program of searching for self-evident principles and then deducing their consequences is rigorously and exhaustively pursued, all knowledge will approach the certainty and rigor of mathematics.

By this method the existence of an external world can be demonstrated by reason employing truths that are self-evident or that are derived from other self-evident truths. Thus, although Descartes does appeal to certain eternal truths (such as that the cause of an idea must be at least as great as the reality represented by the idea), he does not limit reality to eternal unchanging entities in a realm of Being as Plato does. The material world is a real one and can be conclusively known to exist.

PROBLEMS FOR THE RATIONALIST CONCEPTION OF KNOWLEDGE

Having seen the difficulties attached to Plato's requirement that knowledge must have reality as its object, let us now examine more closely the requirement of infallibility, because it is essential to both Plato's and Descartes' theories. Three objections in particular will concern us.

The first was formulated by the ancient Greek skeptics who denied that genuine knowledge is possible at all. Their argument bears directly upon Descartes' whole theory of knowledge; it attacks the general claim that knowledge can be derived from reason.[6] We may reconstruct and amplify it in the following way.

[6]Diogenes Laertius, *Lives of the Eminent Philosophers*, II, trans., R. D. Hicks (Cambridge: Harvard University Press, 1958), pp. 501f.

It seems that if anything is known through reason, then it is either demonstrable (provable) or indemonstrable (unprovable). If it is demonstrable, then the premises from which it is derived are either demonstrable or indemonstrable. If they are demonstrable, then we must ask whether the premises from which *they* are derived are demonstrable. And if they are demonstrable, the same question must be asked of their premises, and so on; therefore, if we seek justification of our initial item of knowledge by continually appealing to premises that require a demonstration for their justification, we will be led to an infinite regress. No matter how far back we carry our inquiry we will always be confronted with some proposition that itself requires to be proved. Thus, it seems that if we have knowledge through reason it cannot be by demonstration from premises all of which, and all of whose antecedent premises, themselves require demonstration.

Suppose, on the other hand, that what is known is indemonstrable—self-evident or intuitive. We must then ask how we know *this*, specifically whether this fact is itself demonstrable or indemonstrable. If we say that it is demonstrable, then unless somewhere in the demonstration, or presupposed by it, there is a premise that is indemonstrable, we will have the same regress as the prior alternative. If, on the other hand, we say that this fact is indemonstrable, then we must ask how *that* is known—whether it is self-evident or in need of demonstration. At this point the whole problem is generated anew. If we say that it is demonstrable, we are led to an infinite series of demonstrations, each of whose premises require proof; if we say that it is indemonstrable, we are led to an infinite sequence of knowledge claims, each of which poses the original problem. Thus, the claims of reason are neither demonstrable nor self-evident. But if they are neither demonstrable nor self-evident, they can hardly be said to yield knowledge. Therefore, the skeptics concluded, knowledge does not have its source in reason.

The second objection is closely related to the first and focuses specifically upon the interpretation of infallibility that requires one to know that he knows. Consider some specific item of information one might claim to know, such as that it is raining outside, that a game is scheduled for Saturday, or with Descartes that material objects exist. Designating this as *P*, the claim will be expressible as follows.

1. I know *P*.

According to the criterion under consideration, in order for this claim to be correct it must not only be the case that it is not mistaken (that is, *P* must actually be the case) and that one is certain of it but that one knows that he knows. That is, the following claim must also be correct:

2. I know *that I know P*,

in which the truth of the first claim is the item putatively known. But if the requirement in question is not to be trivial, 2 must express a claim different from 1; in which case if it is to be correct, it also, must meet the requirement. This means that in order for 2 to be correct, which is a condition of 1 being correct, the following must also be correct:

3. I know (that I know *that I know P*),

where all that is parenthesized is claimed to be known. This in turn must meet the requirement that one knows that he knows it, and so on to infinity. Unless at some point we revert to a different sense of "know" or suspend the initial criterion for knowledge, enforcement of this requirement leads to an infinite regress.

Such problems have led many philosophers to abandon the view that our knowledge about reality is infallible, in the sense that there is something about our state of mind when we have it that guarantees to us *that* we have knowledge. Insofar as this criterion of infallibility and all that it implies are shown to be misconceived or suspect, the whole edifice of a priori knowledge built upon it and the metaphysical systems of Plato and Descartes are called into question.

Descartes and Plato might reply at this point that even if these objections cannot be met, they would at best show that metaphysics is no more adequate—nor any less adequate—than mathematics. The two must stand or fall together. Although metaphysics is in the same boat as mathematics, and the boat has a few leaks, still there is no better boat to be in; mathematics is the most trustworthy ally philosophy can have. If through its methods we can prove (if not to the satisfaction of the skeptic) two important things— that there is a God and an external world—that is justification enough for adopting it as our model.

The final objection to be considered provides a rejoinder to such a reply by citing developments in the evolution of mathematics that have the effect of enriching mathematics at the expense of impoverishing the rationalist, like Descartes, who appeals to it as the model for our knowledge about the world. Let us consider this in greater detail.

IMPLICATIONS OF NEWER VIEWS OF MATHEMATICS

Mathematics, for centuries before and after Descartes, was considered to be the most certain knowledge available. Beginning with self-evident principles that could not be denied and proceeding by logical inferences that could be checked and rechecked, it seemed to lead to indisputable results.

But in the nineteenth century, a new view of mathematics appeared. Mathematicians found that an assumption that Euclid had made could be replaced by alternative and incompatible assumptions, with the result that a whole family of new geometries, called non-Euclidean, could be constructed. Each of them is as logically cogent as Euclid's, but there are some theorems that are incompatible with some of Euclid's theorems because they are based on a different assumption.

Euclid states as a postulate, or unproved assumption, that in the following figure if the angle α is smaller than the angle β, the lines a and b will meet if extended on the same side of line c as the angle α; and from this it follows that if angle α is equal to angle β, the lines a and b are parallel—they will not meet if extended infinitely in either direction. Lobachevski and Riemann, in the nineteenth century, denied that this assumption was logically necessary or self-evident and constructed systems of geometrical propositions in which it was not true. In Riemann's geometry there are *no* parallel lines. Many theorems that are true within the Euclidean system of geometry are therefore not true within the Riemannian. For instance, the sum of the interior angles of a triangle is not, for Riemann, equal to two right angles, for if the lines do meet when angle α = angle β, then $\alpha + (180° - \beta)$ $= 180°$ while there is still to be counted the angle between lines a and b, which is necessary if they are to be legs of a triangle.

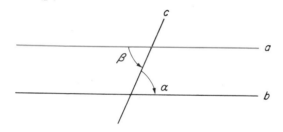

Such a non-Euclidean geometry was regarded for a long time as merely a mathematical curiosity, its rules being no more applicable to reality than are, say, the rules of chess. Non-Euclidean geometry was a harmless but difficult mathematical game, although no one doubted that Euclid's geometry was the geometry of the real world.

Some mathematicians and philosophers, however, began to doubt this. After all, they said, the physical world does not contain absolutely straight lines, and the most accurate measurements we can make with a protractor do not give the sum of the angles of a triangle as absolutely equal to two right angles. Even Euclidean geometry seems to apply only approximately to the world of observation; and even though we may think that any slight divergences from it are due to errors of observation and measurement, we cannot be absolutely sure that greater and greater accuracy in measurement will confirm this belief. The differences in the consequences between Euclidean and non-Euclidean geometries for the measurement of things in the real world would be so slight that they probably could not be discovered by any observations that we might make. Hence, one of the non-Euclidean geometries might apply to our observations with as much accuracy as

Euclidean geometry, and the only reason we would have for preferring Euclid's geometry would be that it is simpler and more familiar to us.

Early in this century, Einstein gave reasons for believing that the facts of astronomy were more conveniently described in terms of a non-Euclidean geometry. Some very careful observations by others and a great deal of theorizing by him led to the belief that very large triangles, such as those whose base line is a ray of light going from one star to another, are triangles whose measurable properties are those of non-Euclidean triangles instead of those of triangles dealt with by Euclid.

Be that as it may, at least one conclusion of philosophical importance followed from the startling scientific innovation: *some statements may be mathematically true, yet not apply to the real world or the world we experience and observe.* From this it can be reasonably argued that the physical truth of mathematical propositions cannot be guaranteed by their self-evidence or "clearness and distinctness," as Descartes believed. They are, on the contrary, a priori simply because they are the logically necessary consequences of assumptions that the mathematician has made. "Mathematically true" means merely "logically implied by a set of mathematical assumptions or postulates." Just as I can logically infer that "If today is Sunday, tomorrow must be Monday," in accordance with the rules of the calendar and definitions of days of the week, whether today *is* Sunday or not, so also I can logically conclude from the rules of non-Euclidean geometry that the sum of the angles of a triangle is not equal to two right angles, whether the real world of physical objects is really non-Euclidean or not. The mathematician makes assumptions that are internally consistent and draws logical inferences from them; but it is no part of mathematics to show that these conclusions will apply to objects in the real world or whether the assumptions describe what actually exists.

It is at this point that the modern interpretation of mathematical knowledge differs most markedly from that of Descartes. Descartes believed that principles he took as axiomatic were not just useful or interesting assumptions that could be logically elaborated into interesting theorems; he believed that they were *true*, accurately describing the real world. Recent philosophy of mathematics, particularly the work of Einstein, is not objecting to the *mathematics* of Descartes but to the assumption he makes about the relationship of mathematics to physical reality. It says, in effect, that the question of the applicability of a set of mathematical principles to physical reality is an *empirical* question: are physical objects of such a character that they can most conveniently be described, or their behavior best computed, in terms of mathematics based on Euclid's axioms or in terms of some other axioms? For everyone, mathematics itself remains purely rational; but the applicability of any particular set of mathematical principles is an empirical matter.

This theory of mathematical knowledge has had wide repercussions in the study of epistemology and the philosophy of science. If we cannot be sure that specific axioms of mathematics apply to the real world, how much less certain can we be that self-evident principles like "Same cause, same effect" apply to it! Encouraged by this theory of mathematics, many scientists and philosophers have claimed the right to assume quite different principles in place of those used by Descartes. It is not a question of which assumptions are self-evidently true; they are interested in which ones—whether self-evident or highly recondite and artificial—will give them a basis for drawing "interesting" or "useful" conclusions in their study of nature.

If reason cannot decide even these questions, how can we meet the views of peoples in different cultures who make quite different assumptions from ours on which they base their conduct? The communists argue that the assumptions one makes are determined not by reason but by the economic factors of society or class; the Nazis used to say that the assumptions were determined by race; some evolutionists say that they are due to instinct, habit, or "inherited modes of thought."

If this is the whole story, it seems that reason is unable to save us from a skepticism even more profound than that implied in Theaetetus' relativism; for he relativized only our sense experience, and this view relativizes our reasoning itself. But fortunately, the existence of alternative mathematical systems does not imply that reasoning is merely a process of arbitrary assumption, although it does suggest that reason is not a superpsychological factor able by only its own power to discover eternal verities. There is still a great difference between reasoning arbitrarily and reasoning responsibly.

Reason is not able to discover eternal truths about reality simply by thinking its own clear and distinct thoughts. Its function is to organize our experience in such a way that it hangs together and makes sense, to interpret it in such a way that we can distinguish within it the true from the false and the basic, pervasive patterns from the trivial and the accidental. When experience is so organized that this is possible, we cannot but think that we have knowledge. However arbitrary or daring some of the assumptions may seem to be, we check them by reference to how they help us to understand what we observe. Sometimes we have to reject the assumptions or principles if experience doggedly stands against them, but sometimes we modify our specific beliefs about what we have observed to make them congruent with the reasonable principles that have satisfactorily served this organizing function.

Reasoning performs two tasks in knowing. First, it is concerned with drawing logical inferences from statements we make on whatever grounds, regardless of whether they are true or assumed to be true. It is the task of reason, not of sensing, to show us that "If T is a Euclidean triangle, the sum of its angles must be equal to two right angles," "If there is a God, then there is some necessary being," or "If today is Sunday, tomorrow must be Monday." But reasoning does not tell us whether the premises are true or not and hence does not tell us whether the conclusions are true. Although these examples of the inferences that reasoning permits us to draw are simple and straightforward, the real work of reason in establishing complex logical relations among propositions is intricate and requires much ingenuity. This work of reason in establishing logical relations among assumed propositions is called the "formal mode of thought," and it is studied in logic and mathematics.

The other task of reason is to elicit propositions from our experience (and imagination) that—although not known indubitably and not demonstrable simply by reference to the rules of formal thought—are capable of explaining what we observe. Observation and imagination give rise to many "ideas" or "hunches" concerning the explanation of things. We can formulate them as propositions, and by logical inference from them we can predict what else we should expect to observe if these propositions are true. Propositions that function in this way are called hypotheses[7] or postulates, not indubitable and self-evident axioms. Reason alone would never discover or demonstrate them, but without reasoning we should never be able to formulate, test, and organize them.

These considerations provide strong grounds for concluding that we cannot demonstrate factual truths about the world from self-evident principles in the manner Descartes thought. Mathematical reasoning merely provides us with conceptual knowledge and says nothing about what does or does not exist, is or is not real. Thus, even if one were to insist that metaphysics and mathematics are "in the same boat" from the standpoint of certainty and infallibility, it still would not follow that metaphysics is capable of yielding substantive knowledge about the world. This means that the limits of knowledge are not definable by reference to our capacity to intuit clearly and distinctly, as Descartes thought; therefore, metaphysics cannot be circumscribed by reference to such limits.

With the whole rationalist enterprise questioned from several aspects, it is understandable, in retrospect, why Descartes' solution to the problem of the external world was viewed with suspicion. There was dissatisfaction with it even before the new mathematics appeared. But if one concedes to Descartes that all we directly perceive are our own ideas and then denies that we can rationally demonstrate the existence of anything beyond these ideas, how can he establish the existence of an external world any more successfully than Descartes did? The considerations that generate the problem have nothing specifically to do with rationslism. They arise from a systematic exploration of the problems of perception, and they constitute a problem for the person who rejects the Platonic-Cartesian theory of knowledge just as they do for one who accepts it. In the next chapter we examine some of the major efforts

---

[7]We shall discuss the role of hypotheses in detail in Part Three.

of philosophers who reject both of Plato's criteria for knowledge to grapple with this problem. These philosophers are called empiricists.

BIBLIOGRAPHY

Ayer, A. J., *The Problem of Knowledge*, Chaps. 1–3. Baltimore: Penguin Books, Inc., 1956.

Chisholm, R. M., *Theory of Knowledge*. Englewood Cliffs, N. J.: Prentice-Hall, Inc., 1966.

Descartes, R., *Descartes Selections*, ed., R. M. Eaton. New York: Charles Scribner's Sons, 1927.

Feigl, H., and W. Sellars, eds., *Readings in Philosophical Analysis*, Section III. New York: Appleton-Century-Crofts, 1949.

Lovejoy, A. O., *The Revolt Against Dualism*, Chap. 1. LaSalle, Ill.: Open Court Publishing Co., 1960.

Moore, G. E., *Some Main Problems of Philosophy*, Chap. 2. New York: Collier Books, 1962.

Price, H. H., *Perception*. London: Methuen & Co., Ltd., 1932.

Reichenbach, H., *The Rise of Scientific Philosophy*, Chaps. 3 and 8. Berkeley and Los Angeles: University of California Press, 1951.

Russell, B., *The Problems of Philosophy*, Chaps 1, 2, 7, and 8. London: Oxford University Press, 1954.

Spinoza, B., "The Principles of the Philosophy of Descartes," in *Earlier Philosophical Writings*, trans., F. A. Hayes. New York: Library of Liberal Arts, 1963.

Whittaker, E., *From Euclid to Eddington*, Part I, Sections 1–16. New York: Dover Publications, Inc., 1958.

Yolton, J. W., ed., *Theory of Knowledge*. New York: The Macmillan Company, 1965.

QUESTIONS FOR REVIEW AND DISCUSSION

1. Evaluate the claim that sense data are subjective. Does the claim presuppose any particular concept of mind or consciousness? Explain.

2. It has been said that, for Descartes, ideas are guilty until proved innocent. Explain. Does this suggest a fault in his methodology? If so, why? If not, why not?

3. Can you really doubt that you have a body or that material objects exist? Suppose that some people can doubt these things and others cannot; would this vitiate Descartes' methodology by making certainty relative? Why?

4. Descartes needs divine certification of his clear and distinct ideas to foreclose the possibility that he is being deceived. Yet, he must know some things clearly and distinctly *before* he can even prove the existence of a God who will provide such certification. Can you suggest any solutions to this predicament?

5. Do you agree with Descartes about the indubitability of "I think, there-

fore I am"? Or is it possible to doubt even this? Would the argument "I walk, therefore I am" do just as well? Why?

6. Evaluate the objection: Unless Descartes knows in advance that material objects exist, he cannot be certain that there is any such thing as a causal relationship between them and ideas; in which case he cannot appeal to causality to argue for the existence of such objects.

7. Comment on Einstein's statement: "As far as the laws of mathematics refer to reality, they are not certain; and as far as they are certain, they do not refer to reality."

5 SOME EMPIRICISTS' PROPOSALS

We have seen how inquiry into the nature of perception leads to the problem of our knowledge of the external world: If it can plausibly be argued that we directly perceive only subjective sense data, then how can we know that anything exists beyond our own experience? Descartes' answer was to say that we can give an a priori demonstration of the existence of an external world in much the same way that we can prove a theorem in geometry. This appeal to reason aligned him with the tradition of Parmenides and Plato. But many other philosophers, because of their dissatisfaction with the rationalist conception of knowledge, maintained that all our knowledge—including that of the existence of an external world — originates in and must be tested by experience. As empiricists, they sought a different solution to the problem.

LOCKEAN EMPIRICISM

One of the pioneers of modern empiricism was the British philosopher John Locke (1632–1704). Locke was one of the most important of the English political thinkers; his views on government profoundly affected the fathers of this country and the development of constitutional monarchy in England. In 1690 he published his influential *Essay Concerning Human Understanding*,[1] which had as its purpose to "inquire into the original, certainty, and extent of human knowledge together with the grounds and degrees of belief, opinion, and assent."[2] Locke's reason for undertaking this investigation was not merely his curiosity about epistemological matters; in addition, he had a very practical political interest in determining the sources and validity of men's

[1]The most convenient abridgment is in Sterling P. Lamprecht, ed., *Locke Selections* (New York: Charles Scribner's Sons, 1928). Page references are to this volume.

[2] Locke, *ibid.*, p. 90.

beliefs that brought them into conflict with each other. He believed that if he could find how men's ideas had their source in diverse experiences, it could be a great step toward mutual understanding and tolerance, which was hindered by the dogmatic conviction of most men that their own beliefs (say, their belief in the divine right of kings) were true because they came from God and should not be subjected to critical questioning.

Instead of imagining that we have true beliefs from birth, Locke asks us to trace our ideas to the experience that engendered them, for it is his doctrine that there is nothing in the intellect that was not first in the senses.

Let us suppose the mind to be, as we say, white paper, void of all characters, without any ideas; how comes it to be furnished? Whence comes it by that vast store which the busy and boundless fancy of man has painted on it, with an almost endless variety? Whence has it all the materials of reason and knowledge? To this I answer, in one word, from experience; in that all our knowledge is founded, and from that it ultimately derives itself.[3]

Unlike Parmenides, Plato, and Descartes, Locke believes that all our knowledge about the world originates in experience. This means that we have a priori *conceptual* knowledge, but our *factual* knowledge about states of affairs in the world is empirical.

We have, Locke says, two kinds of experience, each of which furnishes us with a specific kind of idea. Our senses are "conversant about particular sensible objects," and they give us the ideas of yellow, white, cold, heat, shape, and the like. These he calls the "sensible qualities" that we perceive by our external senses, and the ideas of them he calls "ideas of sensation." We also have an internal sense, which gives us awareness of the operations of our mind when it perceives, thinks, doubts, wills, believes, abstracts, and so on. Our ideas of the operations of our mind, performed on the data of the senses, he calls "ideas of reflection." All that we have in our minds, then, are perceptions or ideas of these two kinds, "having ideas and perception being the same thing."

Our minds are able to abstract, separate, compare, and recombine in the same or a different order the ideas that come from the senses. If the mind retains the combinations in which the ideas first arrived, we call them memories; if it separates and recombines them in a different order, we are imagining. Locke then proceeds to show that every idea in our consciousness can be derived from one or the other of the two sources, although the combinations may vary. For instance, our idea of horse is made up of ideas of sensations of color, shape, size, smell, touch, and so on, combined with the idea of reflection caused by the belief that such a thing exists; our idea of a unicorn, on the other hand, is made up of many of the same ideas of sensation, combined with another idea of sensation (a single horn) and with the reflec-

---

[3]*Ibid.*, p. 111.

tive idea of disbelief. In neither case, however, is there any new, simple idea that does not come from one of the two sources: sensing and reflecting on our own mental operations.

How our ideas relate to reality—The mind combines and separates its ideas. It associates them together so that when one idea occurs, we normally expect that other ideas that have occurred together with them in the past will reappear (association of ideas). For example, I have the idea of white, granular, and solid, and I expect to have the idea of sweet; in this way I suppose that these ideas refer to or mean sugar.

Why do my ideas hang together in this way? Locke tells us that our idea of sugar is a "complication of many ideas together; because . . . not imagining how these simple ideas can subsist by themselves, we accustom ourselves to suppose some substratum, wherein they do subsist, and from which they do result."[4] The thing that causes us to have these ideas and that, we suppose, has the qualities of sweetness, solidity, and whiteness is the real sugar. Locke calls it a *substance*. We do not really know or perceive substances but refer our ideas, which we do perceive, to them as their cause. A substance is merely a "something, I know not what," or "the unknown cause of my sensations."

We infer what the substance is from its effects on us. Locke believes that some of the ideas caused in us by a substance resemble the qualities of the substance itself. Those qualities in a substance that create ideas resembling them he calls the *primary qualities*. They are its shape, size, number, and motion or rest. In other words, they are "physical properties" of the thing, without which it would not exist as a physical thing. We also have other ideas—ideas of the sweetness of sugar or the yellow we sense when we say, "I see a piece of gold," which do not resemble the qualities of the objects but are merely the effects of the object on our senses and mind. "Yellow" is not really a property of gold, but there is a "power" in gold to produce a sensation of yellow. This power is nothing but the "bulk, figure, texture, and motion" of the insensible parts (for example, atoms) of the gold.[5] These qualities, which we attribute to the object but which do not inhere in it, he calls *secondary qualities*.

Locke is here saying that the colors, odors, sounds, and tastes of a thing exist as qualities only in the mind. Like Theaetetus, he says that they depend primarily on the sense organs and the mind and not merely on the substance itself. Most modern psychologists and physicists agree with Locke and Theaetetus in this opinion. Nowadays, we say that the object consists of molecules that we do not see but whose existence we infer from what we do see; the molecules have chemical and physical (that is, primary) qualities, but no color, taste, or odor; but the chemical and physical properties of the

[4]*Ibid.*, p. 176.
[5]*Ibid.*, p. 206.

object have the power to produce an effect on us that we experience as a color or taste or odor. Locke and modern physics and psychology accept the doctrine of epistemological relativism (see page 93) with respect to the secondary qualities, but not with respect to the primary qualities. Locke argued so well and with such great influence that this belief has come to be almost "common sense"; almost everyone who has studied a little physics or psychology will now say, with Locke, that a tree falling in a forest where no one can hear it does not make a sound.

It is clear, however, that Locke's solution to the problem of knowledge of the external world is no more satisfactory than Descartes'. Having agreed that all we directly perceive are our own ideas, he is unable to explain how we can justifiably conclude that objects exist apart from and independent of our experiences. His appeal to causation is of little help, because his view that knowledge derives from experience means that causal connections must be capable of empirical confirmation (Descartes believed that at least some such connections could be established a priori). How can we empirically verify a causal relationship between objects and ideas when, unless we know first that the relationship holds, we cannot know that there are any such things as external objects? Locke needs to verify this relationship in order to infer the existence of an external world, but in order to verify this relation he must first know that there *is* an external world. Even if he could establish its existence, it would be very unlike our experiences of it; because only our ideas of primary qualities would actually represent external things— the secondary qualities are merely subjective. In such a view, that with which we are directly acquainted would have no independent existence, and the world thought to exist independently would be unperceived and unknowable. The consequence is that here Locke founders upon a skepticism concerning our knowledge of both the existence of and the nature of an external world.[6]

One of the most challenging developments in the history of philosophy resulted from the effort of another British empiricist, George Berkeley (1685-1753), an Irish-born bishop of the Church of England, to solve this problem. Because of his daring speculation, his inimitable literary style, his active life, and his attractive personality, Berkeley is one of the most interesting figures in the history of philosophy. He is especially interesting to Americans because he came to this country in 1729 with "the prospect of planting arts and learning in America." He was the first philosophical representative of what we call modern idealism.

---

[6]In addition, the conclusions to which Locke's position leads are incompatible with natural theology. Locke believed that the existence of God could be inferred from a study of nature (not proved a priori as Descartes thought). But in order to advance such an argument he has to establish that there is an orderly arrangement of nature, which is precisely what his theory of knowledge is unable to do.

IDEALISM

Idealism has many facets. Ordinarily, we describe a person as an idealist if he professes and follows high ideals and is not deterred from their pursuit by very real difficulties in attaining them and by the obvious frailty of human nature. Every fortunate person, if really fortunate, knows such persons. Every person with courage, patience, and fortitude has at least a little of this type of idealism in his make-up. The best parts of history are composed of the acts of such idealists: in art, Michelangelo, Beethoven, Van Gogh; in religion, St. Paul, St. Francis; in science, Pasteur and the men with Dr. Walter Reed; in social and spiritual reform, George Fox, Florence Nightingale, Susan B. Anthony, Gandhi; and great heroes from Joan of Arc to the countless, nameless men who "serve beyond the call of duty." In literature, where we always find the best exemplars of the various human types, the world has been made better, at least indirectly, by Antigone, Faust (in Part II of Goethe's poem), Alyosha in *The Brothers Karamazov*, Christian Wahnschaffe in Wassermann's *The World's Illusion*, Dinah Morris in *Adam Bede*, Thackeray's Colonel Newcome, Hans Castorp in *The Magic Mountain*, and their like.

Sometimes we use the word in an opprobrious sense to refer to an unrealistic and Utopian attitude stultified by impatience with the very practical matter of means for attaining the ideal. The idealist in this sense has been described as "a person with both feet firmly planted on a cloud." If placed in power and endowed with influence over others, the good or evil done by such uncompromising and fanatical idealists can be very great; in the literary examples of such character, we sympathize or are annoyed with the fatuity of Don Quixote, Richard Feverel's father, Père Goriot, Mr. Dombey, and others.

Philosophical Idealism

Idealism also represents a number of technical philosophical theses, one or more of which have been held by such philosphers as Berkeley, Leibniz, Hegel, Emerson, Bradley, Royce, Croce, and others. Some of the current unpopularity of the word "idealism" has infected philosophical opinion, and for the past fifty or sixty years the number of philosophers who call themselves idealists has gradually diminished so that idealism has few defenders today. Nonetheless, in its various forms it has made some most important and challenging contributions to philosophy, and the arguments of its defenders deserve careful study.

There is, of course, a reason why the same word, "idealism," is used as a name both for the personal attitudes we have mentioned and for a system of technical philosophy. Philosophical idealists do emphasize the role of high ideals in conduct; they stress the creative role of ideals in the history of culture; they believe that ideals are not subjective human illusions or inventions but are based upon and give evidence of some profound trait of reality itself. But the philosophical idealists are not the only philosophers who insist upon these points. What is essential to philosophical idealism is not a view of *ideals*, but of *ideas*.

"Idea" and "Ideal"

Both etymologically and philosophically, there is a very close connection between these words. We have seen, in Chapter 3, how Plato asserted that the ultimate explanation of things is to be found in universal realities—eternal and perfect—that he called ideas. These ideas are, for Plato, not only principles of explanation but also principles and causes of value. Perhaps it would have been better if the world *ideal* had been used as a translation of the Greek term by which Plato referred to these objective and universal realities, values, and purposes. Plato believed, of course, that the mind could apprehend them through a long process of dialectic; but he did not regard them as "in the mind" and subject to psychological explanation. Plato was a realist[7] in his theories of ideas or universals, whereas in modern times we tend to use the word "idea" in a more nominalistic sense, as something that exists as a content of consciousness and is dependent upon mind.

When Plato is referred to as the "father of idealism," or idealism is called the "Platonic tradition in philosophy," one should not forget that there is a profound difference between his theory of ideas and the metaphysics of modern idealism. Although modern idealism may be compared to Platonism in its concern for "eternal values" that cannot be explained in terms of nature, it places much more emphasis than did Plato upon the concept of mind as the ultimate reality.

The Emphasis Upon Mind

The most important concept in modern idealism is neither "idea" nor "ideal" but *mind*. R. F. A. Hoernlé, a leading idealist of the twentieth century, has said, "Mind is, in some sense, the hero of every idealistic story."

The root *metaphor* of the idealist is that reality is mind, experience, or consciousness. The idealist takes the fact that we do have experiences as the *central* fact. He regards the fact that we *have* experiences (or that reality is so constituted that experiences occur within it) as more important and revelatory of reality than are the things that we happen to experience. Instead of explaining how we experience things in terms of stimuli and responses and the behavior of the nervous system (which he admits to be an important and valid task of science, but not adequate for metaphysics), the

---

[7]For this meaning of realism (Platonic realism), see page 216. This kind of realism is not necessarily incompatible with some forms of idealism and should be contrasted with those forms of realism that are reactions against idealism; see pages 120ff.

idealist takes the fact of experience itself as basic. He points out that all the facts of science are included in experience and must be understood as parts of experience. He takes consciousness of fact and of value as explanatory of fact and value; he holds that fact and value taken alone are mere abstractions from the true reality, which is always concrete *experience* of facts and value. The idealist, therefore, believes that he alone can gain a truly synoptic philosophy; he believes that he alone does not try the impossible in considering facts in utter isolation from the mind that experiences them and gives them their meaning and significance. All other philosophers, he believes, omit or ignore or de-emphasize the most important and obvious fact about every experience—every fact or value is a fact or value only in and for an experiencing, conscious mind. It is for this reason that the idealist sometimes says that the world is best described as an idea or system of ideas:

"The world is my idea:"—this is a truth which holds good for everything that lives and knows, though man alone can bring it into reflective and abstract consciousness. If he really does this, he has attained to philosophical wisdom. . . . If any truth can be asserted a priori, it is this: for it is the expression of the most general form of all possible and thinkable experience: a form which is more general than time, or space, or causality, for they all presuppose it. . . . No truth therefore is more certain, more independent of all others, and less in need of proof than this, that all that exists for knowledge, and therefore this whole world, is only object in relation to subject, perception of a perceiver, in a word, idea.[8]

The basic analogy that the idealist takes as a guide in metaphysics can be expressed in various ways. He sometimes emphasizes the relationship of mind to its objects, in which objects come to have meaning only within consciousness and are to be explained only as aspects of experience. Sometimes the basic analogy is between a deductive logical system and the world itself considered as a synoptic and systematic whole, in which each part functions so as to contribute to the development of the whole. Sometimes it is found in the experience of value—the moral agent grows more self-sufficient and independent of outward things, endowing them with value only as they contribute to the realization of the potentialities of the self. Sometimes it is found in artistic experience, in which the dominance of the creative mind over the material at hand is perhaps most unmistakable. But whatever be the analogy, the idealist thinks reality is a meaningful, intelligible, and valuable whole in which the highest human ideals achieve realization.

Three Theses of Philosophical Idealism

Let us now turn from this general characterization of philosophical idealism to a more specific statement of its theses as they relate to Berkeley.

[8]Arthur Schopenhauer, *The World as Will and Idea*, I, trans., R. B. Haldane and J. Kemp (London: Kegan Paul, Trench, Trubner, Ltd., 1891), p. 3.

This will enable us to focus more sharply upon those aspects of his philosophy directly relevant to his solution of the problem of the external world.

We should note, first of all, that Berkeley is an idealist in both his epistemology and his metaphysics. Descartes and Locke maintain that objects exist independently of perceiving subjects; that is, they are both epistemological realists (which means that both rationalists and empiricists can be realists). Berkeley denies this. He claims rather that the objects of knowledge depend upon the existence of conscious beings who experience them— they do *not* exist independently of all perceiving subjects. This doctrine, which contrasts with realism, is called *epistemological idealism*.

In his metaphysics, Berkeley is an *ontological idealist*. This doctrine opposes materialism and asserts that all reality, consisting of minds (which Berkeley regards as immaterial substances) and their ideas, is spiritual in nature. There is no such thing, in Berkeley's view, as matter in the sense in which Descartes and Locke thought. Ontologically, the latter were dualists (to be distinguished from their epistemological dualism) because they each believed that there are basically two kinds of substance: the material substance of physical objects and the immaterial substance of minds or souls. Although epistemological and ontological idealism frequently go together, as they do in Berkeley, they are logically independent theses; one might be an idealist in one sense and not in the other.

These senses of idealism should be distinguished from both *absolute idealism* and *pluralistic idealism*, explained in the next chapter. The latter, in many of its forms, is a refinement of Berkeleian idealism. Absolute idealism, on the other hand, ordinarily embraces each of the above two theses but goes much farther. One may be both an epistemological and an ontological idealist without being an absolute idealist. This is Berkeley's position. Although we will comment upon his ontological idealism, our chief concern will be to examine his arguments for epistemological idealism and to see their bearing upon the problem of knowledge of the external world. These arguments develop within the general framework of Locke's empiricism, with which Berkeley essentially agreed. Their development is the main purpose of Berkeley's books: *An Essay Towards a New Theory of Vision* (1709), *A Treatise Concering the Principles of Human Knowledge* (1710), and *Three Dialogues between Hylas and Philonous* (1713).[9]

First Stage of Berkeley's Argument

Berkeley's strategy is to argue that if an external world as Descartes and Locke described is unknowable, as he maintains it is, then belief in an

[9]All references are to the following editions of Berkeley's works, edited by Colin M. Turbayne: *Principles, Dialogues and Correspondence* (New York: Bobbs-Merrill Company, Inc., 1965); *Three Dialogues Between Hylas and Philonous* (New York: Bobbs-Merrill Company, Inc., 1954); *Works on Vision* (New York: Bobbs-Merrill Company, Inc., 1963).

external world *in that sense* should be abandoned. If all that anyone directly perceives is subjective ideas, then rather than undertake the impossible task of trying to show that objects exist independently of these ideas, we should realize that objects are properly understood *as* ideas.[10] This reconstitution of the notion of a physical object, dissociating it from the idea of an unknowable material substance, has the effect of making the objects of knowledge dependent upon perceiving subjects; indeed, the central thesis of his philosophy is: "To be is to be perceived," which means that to be is to be *experienced.* At the same time, it eliminates the problem of explaining the connection between the data of perception (for Berkeley, "ideas") and objects, since in Berkeley's view there is no longer a gap between the two. It was Descartes and Locke's inability to provide a satisfactory account of this connection that proved to be the stumbling block for their theories. In addition to being an idealist where Descartes and Locke are realists, Berkeley is an *epistemological monist* where they are dualists; he holds that the data and object in perception are numerically identical.

Although to say that objects do not exist independently of perceiving beings seems to violate common sense, Berkeley maintains that when properly understood, his view really accords with common sense. At first, his argument is one long criticism of the distinction between primary and secondary qualities.[11] He accepts Locke's arguments, which, like those of Protagoras and Theaetetus, were designed to show that qualities like color are subjective and dependent upon the perceiver. But then he goes one step further: He tries to show that if these qualities are subjective, then the primary qualities are subjective also. From this he concludes that if all the properties attributed to the object are only in the mind, there can be no object apart from the mind. Let us briefly recapitulate his arguments.

1. *The distance and size of an object are not directly apprehended*—We see nothing

[10]Berkeley seeks to avoid some of the oddness of this assertion by insisting that "I am not for changing things into ideas but rather ideas into things, since those immediate objects of perception . . . I take to be the real things themselves." Berkeley, *Dialogues*, p. 92.

[11]Locke says that the secondary quality is a "power in the object" to produce an effect on us, such as the idea of color, which does not resemble the power in the object, since the power is only a modification of the primary qualities of the microscopic particles in the object. Berkeley, on the contrary, understands by secondary quality, the quality *of the idea*, which does not resemble anything in the object. Thus Berkeley speaks as if it were admitted that secondary qualities are subjective, and he is often charged, therefore, with having misunderstood Locke's distinction. Perhaps he did, and modern terminology often follows his misunderstanding rather than Locke's own definitions. But if we substitute "sensible qualities" for "secondary qualities" in the arguments we are about to examine, the validity of the argument is not affected. To conform to modern usage, however, we shall speak of secondary qualities as Berkeley did—they are qualities of experienced ideas assumed to resemble nothing independent of the mind and to be subjective; and such qualities are experienced as colors, odors, tastes, sounds, pleasures, pains, and so on. See Gregory D. Walcott, "Primary and Secondary Qualities," *Philosophical Review*, XXXV, No. 5 (September, 1926), 462–72; Reginald Jackson, "Locke's Distinction between Primary and Secondary Qualities," *Mind*, n.s., XXXVIII, No. 149 (January, 1929), 56–76; and Winston H. F. Barnes, "Did Berkeley Misunderstand Locke?" *Mind*, n.s., LXIX, No. 193 (January, 1940), 52–57.

but patterns of color and light and shade; every other characteristic we attribute to an object is an interpretation of these, associated with the remembrance of past experiences in which we have found that a certain feeling of strain in focusing the eyes has accompanied a certain degree of effort in reaching so as to get a sensation of touch from the object. (Many of the principles found in modern books on the psychology of perception of distance were clearly formulated by Berkeley.) But Berkeley was not merely interested in the psychology of the perception of size and distance; he wanted also to draw a philosophical conclusion from it. This was his conclusion: The apprehension of primary qualities depends on, and is psychologically and physiologically more complex than, the perception of secondary qualities; hence, if it be supposed that the secondary qualities are not in the object, we have no good reason for believing that the primary qualities are in the object. There is no more reason to believe that the *perceived* shape of an object (the *image's* shape) is like the *real* shape of the object than to believe that the perceived color resembles some unperceived physical characteristic of the real object.

2. *Primary qualities are not conceivable apart from their relation to the perceiver*—Just as color varies with the eye of the perceiver, so also the size we perceive varies with distance from the perceiver; motion is fast or slow only with respect to the expectations and stream of consciousness of the perceiver. Now variability with respect to the perceiver was one of the reasons why Locke had located the same qualities in the mind; but exactly the same kind of variability attaches to the experience of primary qualities. Hence, to be consistent, they also should be considered as not existing without a perceiver.

3. *Primary qualities attributed to an external object are unthinkable in isolation from qualities that are granted to exist only in the idea*—We cannot frame a conception of an object having size or shape but no quality (like color or hardness) by virtue of which the size or shape could be distinguished from its surroundings. If I am to think of an object that has shape, I must also think of a difference of quality between the inside and the outside of the boundary of its shape. But if all qualities except size, shape, figure, and motion are in the mind, they are neither within nor without the boundary of the supposedly real external object. Hence, if the secondary qualities are subjective and the primary qualities are assumed to be objective, then the shape of the object is the disembodied shape of an airy nothing.

4. *Primary qualities are never perceived in isolation from the secondary qualities*—The size we perceive is a size of tangible body with a certain degree of hardness, or of a colored expanse. We never see secondary qualities that do not have shape, but neither do we see shapes that are not colored or shaded in some way. Now to take the shape of such a figure and imagine that it is in the real world, yet leaving the color in the mind, is like trying to imagine the smile of a Cheshire cat without the cat. It is to commit the fallacy of

"reifying an abstraction." All our ideas appear in experiences, in which we find them in a relationship of "togetherness" and mutual modification; the shapes are shapes of colors, and the colors are colors of shapes. To separate them is to take an abstraction and treat is as capable of existing in isolation.[12]

5. *The conception of a material object having only primary qualities is useless*— Why was it formulated? Only to explain how ideas arise in the mind. But, says Berkeley, it does not help to explain the origin of our ideas. We have not the least conception of how an idea could arise in the mind from something having only physical qualities; and in terms of Locke's philosophy, we are not likely to discover it, since by hypothesis the cause is unknown. Locke's theory that ideas arise as the effect on us of an unknown object is a case of explaining the obscure by something even more obscure.

But, though we might possibly have all our sensations without them, perhaps it may be thought easier to conceive and explain the manner of their production by supposing external bodies in their likeness rather than otherwise; and so it might be at least probable there are such things as bodies that excite their ideas in our minds. But neither can this be said, for, though we give the materialists their external bodies, they by their own confession are never the nearer knowing how our ideas are produced, since they own themselves unable to comprehend in what manner body can act upon spirit, or how it is possible it should imprint any idea in the mind.[13] Hence it is evident the production of ideas or sensations in our minds, can be no reason why we should suppose matter or corporeal substances, since that is acknowledged to remain equally inexplicable with or without this supposition. If therefore it were possible for bodies to exist without the mind, yet to hold they do so, must needs be a very precarious opinion, since it is to suppose, without any reason at all, that God has created innumerable beings that are entirely useless and serve to no manner of purpose.

In short, if there were external bodies, it is impossible that we should ever come to know it; and if there were not, we might have the very same reasons to think there were that we have now.[14]

So much for the argument against an unknown cause of my sensations. Granting that the five preceding arguments have shown the difficulty of the conception that there is a material substance lying wholly outside our experience and having only primary qualities and powers to produce secondary qualities in our minds, we have two questions. How did the conception of an unknown object's existence arise? What is the proper meaning of the statement, "An object exists"?

[12]See Berkeley, *Principles*, §10. Here we see Berkeley's nominalism. Actually he went much further and denied that there are any abstract ideas even in the mind. He was surely wrong in this, but the argument as given in the text is independent of his untenably extreme form of nominalism. For a discussion of nominalism and realism, see Chapter 9.

[13]See Locke's admission of this in S. P. Lamprecht, ed., *op. cit.*, p. 188. (Note that Berkeley calls Locke a materialist because he believes in the existence of matter. Locke is not a materialist in the strict sense of the word, because he does not hold that mind is "reducible" to matter.)

[14]Berkeley, *Principles*, §§19 and 20.

a. *What is the origin of the conception of an unknown object?*—Locke has already answered this question (see p. 99). We find that some of our ideas are so regularly associated with others that we believe they are causally related. But one idea cannot be the cause of another idea;[15] so we suppose that there is something else that is not an idea but is the cause or substratum of our ideas. Common sense, when it gives up the naive belief that things are always exactly as they appear, accepts this conception of the unknown thing behind its appearances.

But if, as Berkeley believes, there cannot be an object having only primary qualities and the power to produce secondary qualities in our ideas, this common notion of an independent material substratum must be in error. If, then, there are no objects independent of the mind, what can we mean when we say an object exists?

b. *What does it mean to say, "Something exists"?*—All the evidence that we have of the existence of a thing is that we experience it. This is obviously the case when we are speaking of the qualities of a thing; we know that sugar is sweet because we have a sweet taste when we put it into our mouth; we know that snow is white by looking. But what is the sugar, or the sun, or the snow? It is a complex of qualities, each one of which is in our experience or can be anticipated to be given in some future experience. Each of these qualities, whether primary or secondary, is a quality of an idea, dependent for its nature and its existence upon its being given to consciousness. (For what is a color that cannot be seen? Or an odor that cannot be smelled? Or a sound that we cannot hear?—Nothing.) Consider, Berkeley tells us, an object like a cherry:

I see this cherry, I feel it, I taste it, and I am sure *nothing* cannot be seen or felt or tasted; it is therefore *real*. Take away the sensations of softness, moisture, redness, tartness, and you take away the cherry. Since it is not a being distinct from sensations, a cherry, I say, is nothing but a congeries of sensible impressions, or ideas perceived by various senses, which ideas are united into one thing (or have one name given them) by the mind because they are observed to attend each other. Thus, when the palate is affected with such a particular taste, the sight is affected with a red color, the touch with roundness, softness, and so on. Hence, when I see and feel and taste in sundry certain manners, I am sure the cherry exists or is real, its reality being in my opinion nothing abstracted from those sensations. But if by the word "cherry" you mean an unknown nature distinct from all those sensible qualities, and by its its "existence" something distinct from its being perceived, then, indeed, I own neither you nor I, nor anyone else, can be sure it exists.[16]

If there is nothing in the whole that we call an object except the congeries of qualities and if the qualities are dependent upon experience, it follows, according to Berkeley, that the thing itself is dependent upon experience. The *evidence* we have for the existence of a thing is found not only in the fact

---

[15]Locke, Berkeley, and Hume agree on this.
[16]Berkeley, *Dialogues*, p. 97.

that we perceive it; its very existence itself is nothing but its givenness in experience. If the "being of a color" means its being perceived and the "being of a sound" means its being heard and so on for all the other qualities, it follows that the complex of all qualities that we call an object owes its being to the joint perception of some or all of its qualities.

Thus Berkeley comes to his famous thesis: "To be is to be perceived;" "*Esse* is *percipi*." Whether there are things unperceived or not makes not the slightest difference to what we do perceive; we have no empirical right to assume the existence of things for which we can have no evidence; unperceived and unperceivable matter explains nothing and is a vacuous concept to which we can attach no properties. It is to be rejected as a poor and false hypothesis.

Transition from First to Second Stage of Argument

If Berkeley had stopped his argument at this point, it would have been one of those philosophical arguments that seem to be logical enough but that no one in his right mind could possibly accept. Consider three conclusions that seem to follow from it.

1. *Assuming "To be is to be perceived," it would follow as its converse that "To be perceived is to be"*— But the converse[17] statement is obviously false. I press my eyeball and perceive two lights where previously I perceived only one; but that does not mean there *are* two lights. Or a man in delirium sees pink rats; this is a vivid perception, although no one else believes that the pink rats really exist, and he will not believe it when he recovers. Hence the theory as it now stands cannot account for error or the illusions of the senses. (This was also a fatal objection to the argument as Theaetetus left it.)

2. *Assuming "To be is to be perceived," it would follow that "What is not perceived does not exist"*—This is the contrapositive implied by the original statement, and Berkeley uses it against the conception of an unknown and unperceivable substratum or cause for our ideas. But no one can really believe that when we leave this room everything in it will cease to exist; to be sure, everything in it will "disappear" in the sense of not being a part of anyone's perceptual consciousness, but that does not make us think it ceases to be. No one seriously maintains that things unperceived *ipso facto* do not exist, although in the nature of the case, no direct or unexceptionable empirical proof can be given that they do exist. The hypothesis of the uniformity and continuity of nature says that they must continue to exist even when not perceived; Neptune must have existed before astronomers observed it; and so on. A theory that implies that things do not exist simply because they are not perceived is absurd, even though logically irrefutable.

---

[17]This is the converse of the original judgment, for the original judgment does not mean that "All that is is perceived" in the sense that some unreal things might also be perceived. The Berkeleian statement is a definition, in which "to be" is asserted to be a synonym of "to be perceived."

3. *What about other persons?*—Does a person cease to exist when no one perceives him? Or, to go still further, how do I know that anyone exists when I myself do not perceive him? How do I know that you are not just an idea in my mind? You may protest that you are not willing to be just an idea in my mind; but I perceive even this protest as an idea in my own consciousness. How do I know that my idea corresponds to anything independent of my own imagination? This is solipsism—all that exists is merely the content of my own consciousness. Even though no sane person would seriously entertain such a belief, it seems to follow from "To be is to be perceived."

Berkeley was as sane as the next man, and he had his full share of the common sense for which the Irish are justly famous. The second stage of his argument shows how he met these questions.

Second Stage of Argument

The second stage of Berkeley's argument involves three steps. The first shows that Locke's statement—all we know is ideas—is too simple; the second is an analogical argument by which Berkeley seeks to find the real cause of our ideas; and the third points out an ambiguity in the word "perceived" in the thesis, "To be is to be perceived."

1. *Consciousness consists of more than ideas*—Locke believed that we have ideas of the operations of our own mind, which resemble but are not identical with these operations themselves. Locke and Berkeley agree that our ideas "are visibly inactive—there is nothing of power or agency included in them."[18] Berkeley concludes that we cannot have an idea of a will or understanding that resembles them, if we believe that our understanding or will are powers that can act. But we do have some feeling, or what Berkeley calls a "notion," of our own activity. Although Berkeley is often accused of inconsistency in admitting this, he is putting his finger on a very important aspect of consciousness, an aspect that common sense has never denied. We feel our own tendencies, impulses, powers, and activity. When we *analyze* this feeling, perhaps only sensations "that are visibly inactive" remain; but there is an air of artificiality about a conception that leaves out all the active tendencies we inwardly experience. Berkeley is perhaps being faithful to the facts of introspection when he says,

So far as I can see, the words "will," "soul," "spirit" do not stand for different ideas or, in truth, for any idea at all, but for something which is very different from ideas, and which, being an agent, cannot be like unto, or represented by, any idea whatsoever. Though it must be owned at the same time that we have some notion of soul, spirit, and the operations of the mind, such as willing, loving, hating—inasmuch as we know or understand the meaning of those words.[19]

[18]Berkeley, *Principles*, §25.
[19]*Ibid.*, §27.

Included in our awareness of ourselves—perhaps constituting it—is the feeling of active spontaneity, of control over the appearance of some ideas in our consciousness.

I find I can excite ideas in my mind at pleasure, and vary and shift the scene as oft as I think fit. It is no more than willing, and straightway this or that idea arises in my fancy; and by the same power it is obliterated and makes way for another. This making and unmaking of ideas does very properly denominate the mind active.[20]

Berkeley is saying that we know ourselves, considered as minds or spirits, without the intervention of an idea that might veil reality from our consciousness. If everything experienced exists only as an idea in a mind, then certainly minds must also be real. Thus, in addition to the thesis "To be is *to be perceived*," Berkeley also subscribes to the thesis "*To perceive* is to be." This theory of self-awareness provides a basis for the analogy that constitutes the next step in his argument.

2. *By analogy, mind causes all ideas*—As we have just seen, I know that I, a spirit or mind, can generate some ideas. At the same time, however, I know that I am not the cause of many of my ideas; if my eyes are open, I see the tree, and I hear sounds. Where, then, do the ideas originate that I am not the author of? There are three possible hypotheses: (a) from something wholly unlike myself, namely, a material cause having only primary qualities. But the first stage of Berkeley's argument was designed to show that this is untenable; (b) in other ideas. But this is impossible, for one idea does not cause another, as Berkeley and Locke agree; or (c) from something like me, namely, another active mind.

Berkeley chooses the third answer because of the following analogy:

My mind is to ideas of my imagination as x is to ideas over which I have no control. From this analogy, he determines what characteristics x must have. It must be a mind; it must be more powerful than my own so as to force ideas upon me against my own will; it must be permanent in order to account for the existence of things that I do not now perceive; it must be internally coherent and create its ideas in regular and uniform ways in order to account for what men call the "uniformity of nature." In short, it must be a perfect and divine mind.

The mind of God is the external source of the ideas that we do not spontaneously generate. God is the guarantor and support of the common, permanent ideas we call the external world. Taking the existence of the world as described by science or experienced in our every-day consciousness as his premise and rejecting the first two hypotheses as inadequate to explain it, Berkeley infers the existence of God:

It is therefore plain that nothing can be more evident to anyone that is capable of the least reflexion than the existence of God, or a Spirit who is intimately present to

---

[20]*Ibid.*, §28.

our minds, producing in them all that variety of ideas or sensations which continually affect us, on whom we have an absolute and entire dependence, in short "in whom we live, and move, and have our being."[21]

3. *The word "perceived" is ambiguous*—Berkeley is now able to uncover an ambiguity in the word "perceived" that led to the untenable and absurd conclusions on pages 109–10. If by "perceived" we mean "perceived by man," then, "To be is to be perceived" denies a difference between error and true perception and leads to a discontinuous world that ceases to exist when I close my eyes and to solipsism. But "perceived," in the thesis, "To be is to be perceived," does not have primary reference to human perception; human perception is at most evidence of existence, not the essence of existence. "To be" means ultimately to be an idea in a supreme mind, a mind permanent, eternal, omniscient, and omnipotent.

The ambiguity in the concept of perception is very well brought out in two famous limericks on Berkeley:

> There once was a man who said, "God
> Must think it exceedingly odd
> If he finds that this tree
> Continues to be
> When there's no one about in the Quad."

> "Dear Sir: Your astonishment's odd,
> *I* am always about in the Quad
> And that's why the tree
> Will continue to be,
> Since observed by Yours faithfully, God."

Berkeley's Defense of His Conclusions

Because the ambiguity in the word "perceived" is often overlooked, Berkeley's philosophy is sometimes thought of as downright silly. It seems so far removed from credibility as to be patently absurd, or at most, an amusing tour de force. Boswell says that Dr. Johnson praised Berkeley as a "profound scholar, as well as a man of fine imagination," but he must nevertheless have thought Berkeley singularly obtuse to the most common facts. For, Boswell writes,

After we came out of the church, we stood talking for sometime together of Bishop Berkeley's ingenious sophistry to prove the nonexistence of matter, and that everything in the universe is merely ideal. I observed, that though we are satisfied his doctrine is not true, it is impossible to refute it. I never shall forget the alacrity with which Johnson answered, striking his foot with mighty force against a large stone, till he rebounded from it—"I refute it thus."[22]

[21]*Ibid.*, §149.
[22]James Boswell, *Life of Samuel Johnson, LL.D.* (New York: Random House, Modern Library edition, n.d.), p. 285.

Johnson argued in this way in spite of Berkeley's having asked rhetorically, just fifty years earlier: "Do I not know this to be a real stone that I stand on . . . ?"[23]

Berkeley, in fact, anticipated many of the objections that have been naively made to his views, and in this section we shall glance at a few of them and his answers.

1. *Berkeley's philosophy reduces everything to an illusion*—Berkeley answers,

It were a mistake to think that what is here said derogates in the least from the reality of things. It is acknowledged, on the received principles, that extension, motion, and in a word all sensible qualities, have need of a support, as not being able to subsist by themselves. But the objects perceived by sense are allowed to be nothing but combinations of those qualities, and consequently cannot subsist by themselves. Thus far it is agreed on all hands. So that in denying the things perceived by sense an existence independent of a substance or support wherein they may exist, we detract nothing from the received opinion of their *reality*, and are guilty of no innovation in that respect. All the difference is that, according to us, the unthinking beings perceived by sense have no existence distinct from being perceived, and cannot therefore exist in any other substance than those unextended indivisible substances or *spirits*, which act and think and perceive them.[24]

2. *Berkeley's philosophy is impractical; it does not recognize the "hard facts" that we have to take into account*—Berkeley, on the contrary, recognizes that real things in the world do not depend upon *our* perception and even less on our wishful thinking. Only experience can tell us what is real, so that we can deal practically with objective ideas and ignore those that are only subjective:

The set rules or established methods wherein the mind we depend on excites in us the ideas of sense are called "the laws of nature"; and these we learn by experience, which teaches us that such and such ideas are attended with such and such other ideas in the ordinary course of things.

This gives us a sort of foresight, which enables us to regulate our actions for the benefit of life. And without this we should be eternally at a loss; we could not know how to act anything that might procure us the least pleasure or remove the least pain of sense.[25]

3. *Berkeley, in reducing the reality of everything to experience, cannot distinguish truth from error*—Not at all, answers the philosopher. "By whatever method you distinguish *things* from *chimeras* on your scheme, the same, it is evident, will hold also upon mine."[26]

Berkeley distinguishes between real and illusory things, or what he calls chimeras, in two ways. First, there is the vividness of the experiences of "real things," whereby we find that ideas of "real things" are "more strong,

[23]Berkeley, *Dialogues*, p. 73.
[24]Berkeley, *Principles*, §91.
[25]Berkeley, *Principles*, §§30 and 31.
[26]Berkeley, *Dialogues*, p. 82.

lively, and distinct than those of the imagination."[27] Common sense tends to use this criterion, although it is often led into error in so doing, for hallucinatory and illusory ideas can be just as vivid as ideas of real objects. Second, there is the regular order and connection of the ideas that we take as evidence for objects, in contrast to the lack of consistency among our mere fanciful ideas. We distinguish dreams from waking consciousness by the greater orderliness of the latter, even though the dream may be intensely vivid; it is in this way that we decide that an idea of water in a desert is a mirage and not a true perception.

Though [illusory ideas] should happen to be never so lively and natural, yet, by their not being connected and of a piece with the preceding and subsequent transactions of our lives, they might easily be distinguished from realities.[28]

4. *Berkeley's philosophy would make science impossible*—Berkeley is one of the first philosophers to formulate a positivistic theory of science. Positivism restricts scientific knowledge to knowledge of the correlations among perceptions and does not admit any explanation in terms of hypothetical entities that we might suppose exist "behind" the phenomena as their cause. Although there are serious objections to such a view, one should certainly not say dogmatically that a theory like that of Berkeley or the modern positivists would render science impossible. Berkeley gives excellent arguments that scientific objects are really intellectual constructions or syntheses of perceptions; he points out very clearly that scientific explanation is not in terms of unknown and unknowable causes but in terms of correlations among observables.

. . . You will say there have been a great many things explained by matter and motion; take away these and you destroy the whole corpuscular [atomic] philosophy [science] and undermine those mechanical principles which have been applied with so much success to account for the phenomena. In short, whatever advances have been made, either by ancient or modern philosophers, in the study of nature do all proceed on the supposition that corporeal substance of matter does really exist. To this I answer that there is not any one phenomenon explained on that supposition which may not as well be explained without it, as might easily be made appear by an induction of particulars. To explain the phenomena is all one as to show why, upon such and such occasions, we are affected with such and such ideas.[29]

If therefore we consider the difference there is betwixt natural philosophers and other men with regard to their knowledge of the phenomena, we shall find it consists not in an exacter knowledge of the efficient cause that produces them—for that can be no other than the *will of a spirit*—but only in a greater largeness of comprehension, whereby analogies, harmonies, and agreements are discovered in the works of nature, and the particular effects explained, that is, reduced to general rules . . . which rules, grounded on the analogy and uniformness observed in the production of natural

---

[27]Berkeley, *Principles*, §30.
[28]Berkeley, *Dialogues*, p. 82.
[29]Berkeley, *Prinoiples*, §50.

effects, are most agreeable and sought after by the mind; for that they extend our prospect beyond what is present and near to us, and enable us to make very probable conjectures touching things that may have happened at very great distances of time and place, as well as to predict things to come.[30]

5. *Berkeley's philosophy reduces all sciences to psychology, because it deals with the relations among ideas instead of among things—*

... It will upon this be demanded whether it does not seem absurd to take away natural causes and ascribe everything to the immediate operation of spirits? We must no longer say, upon these principles, that fire heats, or water cools, but that a spirit heats, and so forth. Would not a man be deservedly laughed at who should talk after this manner? I answer, he would so; in such things we ought to "think with the learned, and speak with the vulgar." They who by demonstration are convinced of the truth of the Copernican system do nevertheless say "the sun rises," "the sun sets," or "comes to the meridian"; and if they affected a contrary style in common talk it would without doubt appear very ridiculous. A little reflection on what is here said will make it manifest that the common use of language would receive no manner of alteration or disturbance from the admission of our tenets.[31]

This objection is based upon the common usage of "idea" as antonym of "object," but Berkeley, in his technical writings, identifies them.

6. *Berkeley's philosophy is skeptical*—This charge is perhaps the one that Berkeley is most interested in refuting, and he returns to it again and again. Philonous ("lover of mind"), who represents Berkeley in the *Dialogues*, answers this charge from Hylas (from the Greek *hyle*, "matter").

I am of a vulgar cast, simple enough to believe my senses and leave things as I find them. To be plain, it is my opinion that the real things are those very things I see and feel, and perceive by my senses. These I know and, finding they answer all the necessities and purposes of life, have no reason to be solicitous about any other unknown beings. ... Wood, stones, fire, water, flesh, iron, and the like things, which I name and discourse of, are things that I know. And I should not have known them but that I perceived them by my senses; and things perceived by the senses are immediately perceived; and things immediately perceived are ideas; and ideas cannot exist without the mind; their existence therefore consists in being perceived; when, therefore, they are actually perceived, there can be no doubt of their existence. Away then with all that skepticism, all those ridiculous philosophical doubts. What a jest is it for a philosopher to question the existence of sensible things till he has it proved to him from the veracity of God,[32] or to pretend our knowledge in this point falls short of intuition and demonstration![33] I might as well doubt of my own being as of the being of those things I actually see and feel.[34]

Thus, Berkeley carries Locke's empiricism to what he regards as its logical conclusion, reasoning that if a material world independent of our ideas

---

[30]*Ibid.*, §105.
[31]*Ibid.*, §51.
[32]The allusion is to Descartes; see text, page 87.
[33]The allusion is to Locke; see text, page 98.
[34]Berkeley, *Dialogues*, pp. 76f.

cannot even in principle be known, then the notion of such a world is best discarded.[35] This does not imply that tables, chairs, trees, and other things do not exist; it implies that their existence can be understood only in terms of our experiences of them. As Descartes and Locke failed to take us to the external world, Berkeley brings the external world to us.

Realistic and Linguistic Criticisms of Berkeley

Berkeley, however, did not succeed in convincing philosophers that realism per se must be abandoned. Two particularly important subsequent defenses of realism were designed, not only to provide an alternative to idealism but also to provide an alternative to the representative realism of Descartes and Locke. Before considering them, let us examine three more recent objections to Berkeley; the second objection is one of the most important. All three are directed against the thesis "To be is to be perceived." The first two are advanced by the prominent American philosopher Ralph Barton Perry (1876–1957); if correct, they show not that epistemological idealism is false but that there is no reason to believe that it is true.[36]

1. *Definition by initial predication*—Berkeley truly argues that it is an initial predicate of anything that I perceive *that* I perceive it. But this does not suffice to establish the conclusion unless it means, "A thing I perceive *must* be perceived by me." That is, "To be is to be perceived," does not follow unless the initial predicate is taken as a defining predicate[37]—the thing perceived is unthinkable and unreal apart from this predicate.

To see whether this is plausible, consider a simple analogy. Mrs. John Doe is the wife of John Doe, by definition. Although in relation to Mr. Doe she is defined as "wife," Mrs. Doe may stand in other relationships to other people, such as "customer" to Mr. Roe and "bridge partner" to Mrs. Roe. Now if we suppose that Mr. Doe knows her *only* as his wife and calls her a name that indicates this relationship it still does not follow that her *existence* depends on Mr. Doe; only the name that he gives her, or the name

[35]Actually, the Scottish philosopher David Hume (1711–1776) carries Locke's empiricism even further. He not only argues as Berkeley did that there is no such thing as material substance but that there is no such thing as immaterial substance. When we introspect we do not find a spiritual "self" as Berkeley thought; we find only impressions or ideas of an internal sort. As he says, "what we call a *mind*, is nothing but a heap or collection of different perceptions, united together by certain relations, and suppos'd, tho' falsely, to be endow'd with a perfect simplicity and identity." Although agreeing with Berkeley that the object of knowledge can be understood only in terms of our impressions or ideas (but rejecting Berkeley's appeal to God as the cause of these ideas), Hume then goes beyond Berkeley by drawing the same conclusion about the subject of knowledge. See David Hume, *A Treatise of Human Nature*, ed., L. A. Selby-Bigge (Oxford: Oxford University Press, 1958), p. 207.

[36]See his "The Egocentric Predicament," in *The Development of American Philosophy* (2nd ed.), eds. W. G. Muelder, L. Sears, and A. V. Schlabach (Cambridge, Mass.: Houghton Mifflin Company, 1960), pp. 331–37; and his *Present Philosophical Tendencies* (New York: David McKay Co., Inc., 1912), pp. 126–32.

[37]A defining predicate is one that applies to every instance of the thing being defined and to only the thing defined.

others give her because she is married to him, depends upon her relationship to him.

Now, apply this analogy to mind (Mr. Doe) and its object (Mrs. Doe). I think I know the table on which I am writing; the table is then, by Locke's and Berkeley's definition, my "idea," because it is a part of my experience. But that does not in the least imply that the existence of the table itself depends upon my experience, for the initial predicate (the predicate "known by me") is not a defining predicate. It only implies a tautology—that I cannot experience a table except as a table I experience, that is, as an idea. But just as there may be many things about Mrs. Doe that Mr. Doe does not know and that do not depend upon him, the same is true for the table. Its being an idea depends upon my experience, and I can experience it *only* as my idea; but that does not mean that it is nothing apart from my experience.

2. *The egocentric predicament*—The second of Perry's arguments is a powerful one with far-reaching implications. He characterizes idealism as asserting that whatever exists does so by virtue of standing in a particular relationship, which he designates *Rc*, to some ego or subject. This relationship is that of being an object of consciousness (where "consciousness" includes perceiving, remembering, desiring, willing, and so forth). In broadest terms this is the import of "To be is to be perceived."

Now suppose that this thesis is challenged, and someone insists that it is common sense to say that an object, say, a tree in the quad, continues to exist when no one is perceiving it. The idealist will respond by asking him how he knows this. The critic will then be confronted by the following problem: Whatever evidence he cites for claiming to know that the tree exists independently of being perceived will inevitably require presupposing that the tree *is* perceived. It will not do, for example, to turn away and glance back quickly to try to catch a glimpse of it unperceived or to steal back in the dead of night to see if it is still there; for you will succeed only in perceiving it under different circumstances, thereby re-establishing the very relationship held to be essential to its existence. Nor will it do to argue that although you cannot see the tree existing unperceived, you can imagine or conceive it to exist; even to "think about" the tree is at that instant to institute some species of the relationship in question to it.[38] The only conditions

---

[38]Although "imagine" is roughly synonymous with "conceive" in some of the latter's senses, it is important not to confuse the two. It is a criticism of Berkeley that although one cannot imagine an object to exist without its thereby entering into one's consciousness, nonetheless it is *conceivable* that it should exist unperceived, in the special sense that its existence is logically possible (that is, not self-contradictory). A Berkeleian might reply to this by saying, first, that if by "object" his critic means what *he* means—a congeries of directly perceived ideas—then it *is* self-contradictory to say that such things exist unperceived. If, on the other hand, the critic means by "object" something that is unperceived and unperceivable (like Lockean substance), then the Berkeleian need not deny that it is conceivable (logically possible) that such a thing should *exist* unperceived; he denies only that it is conceivable that we should ever *know* that it so exists.

that could allow you to *know* that an object exists would also bring that object in relationship to your consciousness, hence signifying that it is experienced.

This fact, to which this argument calls attention, Perry says, must be acknowledged by anyone; indeed, it "is one of the most important original discoveries that philosophy has made." It is the discovery that "no thinker to whom one may appeal is able to mention a thing that is not an idea, for the obvious and simple reason that in mentioning it he makes it an idea."[39] This, Perry contends, is a methodological problem for any inquiry; as soon as we select and examine, study, or even just think about any thing, problem, or subject-matter, we immediately institute some form of the relationship *Rc* to it. This circumstance he calls the *egocentric predicament*.

But now, Perry says, this fact does not, as it might seem, support idealism. It does not follow that because a thing must stand in this relationship in order to be *known* that it must stand in this relationship in order to *exist*. That is, it does not follow from the truth of the proposition

1. Nothing can ever be perceived (observed, thought, etc.) to exist unperceived (observed, thought, etc.),

which is all that is shown by the egocentric predicament, that the following proposition is also true:

2. Nothing exists unperceived.

And it is the truth of proposition 2, Perry maintains, that the idealist must show if he is to establish his theory. That is, from the admitted fact that for every entity experienced there is an experiencer for whom the entity is an idea, Berkeley cannot validly infer the conclusion that there are no entities that are not ideas. Let it be granted for the sake of argument that there *are* entities that are not experienced; by hypothesis, we should not know them. Hence, Berkeley's *evidence* is just the same whether his "To be is to be perceived" is true or false. "To be is to be perceived" is, therefore, a poor hypothesis, for there can be no *conceivable* evidence against it. Any evidence that could *conceivably* be against it is unavailable by the conditions inherent in the empirical test, namely, that what I experience is what I experience, that is, by *definition* an idea.

To carry this argument further, we could point out that rather than supporting the idealist, the egocentric predicament can actually be used against him. There is no conceivable way to show that a thing, *T*, *depends* for its existence upon being perceived, because we can never examine *T* when it is *not* in this relationship—which, it seems, is just what we should have to do to be sure that the relationship is necessary to its existence. That is, the only

[39]Perry, *Present Philosophical Tendencies*, p. 129.

way we could know that T's having the property Rc makes any difference to T—much less so great a difference as whether or not T even exists—would be to compare instances of T when it is in this relationship with instances of T when it is not. But this is precisely what cannot be done. To attempt to examine T outside this relationship is to institute the relationship anew. Therefore, the very fact the idealist appeals to makes it, in principle, impossible to establish the truth of his thesis.

3. *A linguistic confusion*—The final objection comes from a contemporary philosopher, G. J. Warnock.[40] He argues that Berkeley blurs the distinction between appearance and reality by confusing statements of different logical types. The meaning of "logical types" is illustrated by an analogy. The job of a jury, he points out, is to pronounce a verdict of guilty or not guilty on the basis of evidence. But however much evidence the jury may have of the guilt of a person, a statement of that evidence, or of the convictions of the jury, does not substitute for the decided verdict. The jury cannot return from its deliberations and tell the court that "It seems to us that the evidence weighs heavily against this man" or that "It appears conclusive on the basis of the evidence that this person committed the crime." Its job is to *pronounce* the man guilty or not guilty. Giving a verdict, in other words, is a type of thing logically different from citing evidence or reporting convictions.

Similarly, Warnock argues, to say that something *is* the case is different from describing how it *seems* (or appears); or in Berkeley's terms, statements about ideas are of a different logical type from statements about things. How things seem may be the *reason* for statements about how they are; but just as giving the reasons for a verdict is not to give the verdict, so also to state the reasons for saying that something is the case is not, logically, to state *that* the thing is the case. As Warnock says,

> . . . there is an essential logical difference between saying how things seem and how they are—a difference which cannot be removed by assembling more and more reports of how things seem. If we go on talking only of how things seem, we shall never arrive at a statement of how things are.[41]

In short, statements about perception are not equivalent to statements about things (reality); hence "to be" does *not* mean "to be perceived." The two are of different logical types.

Moreover, Warnock charges that

> Berkeley's view is in fact exceedingly paradoxical. For normally, the whole point of talking about "my own impressions," or about anyone else's impressions, is precisely to leave room for the possibility that my and their impressions were mistaken or misleading. The essential function of the language of "seeming" is that it is *noncommittal* as to the actual facts. . . . [Berkeley] is maintaining that statements of the

---

[40]G. J. Warnock, *Berkeley* (Baltimore: Penguin Books, Inc., 1953). Quoted by permission of Penguin Books, Ltd.

[41]*Ibid.*, p. 186.

form "It seems as if . . . ," statements about "our own ideas," really can amount to saying exactly what they are normally used to *avoid* saying, namely, "There is. . . ." . . . The whole vocabulary which he recommends is that which we normally employ in order to *avoid* saying what is really the case.[42]

SOME MODERN DEFENSES OF REALISM

Neorealism

The problem for the realist who rejects both representative realism and Berkeleian idealism is to develop a theory that is both faithful to the essentials of realism and avoids their respective weaknesses. One theory, of which Perry was a proponent, which was thought to do this, combines certain features of each of the other theories. It is called neorealism.[43]

The neorealists agree with Descartes and Locke that objects exist apart from and independent of perceivers, but they disagree that these objects are not directly perceived. That is, they reject the view that the subject and object are always mediated by sense data numerically distinct from the object. Here, they are in agreement with Berkeley. Although they reject his claim that what is real depends upon being perceived (that is his idealism), they support his assertion that real things are directly perceived. In short, whereas the earlier realists were dualists, the neorealists, like Berkeley, are typically *epistemological monists*.

According to the neorealists,[44] some of whom were among the most influential American philosophers in the first quarter of this century, the object I see before me is a physical object, existing in a network of spatial, temporal, and causal relations. I am directly aware of the physical object and not of a mental duplicate or poor copy of it. The object itself is in my consciousness as it actually is; being in or out of consciousness makes no difference to its properties or its being. It is, when I know it, "in" my consciousness, but it is not "in" my consciousness as a picture is in an album; consciousness is not a kind of "receptacle" that can hold only one kind of thing, namely, ideas. Rather, consciousness might be compared to a searchlight, illuminating objects without making a photograph of them that it substitutes for the real thing. We should not allow the spatial term "in" to suggest that consciousness is a kind of "place" for a certain kind of thing we call idea. The neorealists say that objects can be "in the mind" or "in consciousness" in the very ordinary sense of the words said to someone, "I have kept you in mind."

The problem of error—Locke's theory leads to skepticism because it cannot demonstrate or even show the need of an unknown substratum or cause of

---

[42]*Ibid.*

[43]Realism as a theory of perception is different from Platonic realism (p. 216) in the assertion of the reality of Forms or universals.

[44]See the collaborative volume, *The New Realism* (New York: The Macmillan Company, 1912).

ideas. And Berkeley's proposal to abandon the belief in such a substratum leads to the egocentric predicament. If, therefore, neorealism were defensible, we could at once avoid the problems of dualism and vindicate the common sense belief in the independent existence of objects. However, neorealism founders on the same problem that dualistic theories were best equipped to handle, that of explaining how error or illusion is possible.

What, for example, is the status of the after-image I see when I close my eyes, if the realist is correct that what I see exists independently of the perceiving of it? What is the explanation of my reporting that I see a bent stick when a straight stick is put into water at an angle? The question is not *how* we know that these experiences are illusory if taken to be accurate perceptions of ordinary physical things; it is rather *what* is the nature of the thing that we are experiencing when we are having an illusory perception. It seems fairly simple to say, with Locke, that illusory ideas are ideas in the mind that do not correspond to anything in external reality. But if this is so, one can conclude, with Berkeley, that *everything* is in the mind, even the things that we suppose we correctly perceive. The neorealists refuse to accept Locke's answer, for it would lead either to skepticism or to Berkeley's idealism. They assert that illusory objects are not in a realm of mind but in the realm of nonmental being, as are objects of correct perception.

Being, they say, is made up of two kinds of entities: subsistent entities and existent entities. A subsistent entity is anything conceivable, imaginable, or mentionable but not existing, that is, not having a particular position in space and time or at least not having a position unliable to challenge. Such subsistent entities are universals or imaginary objects, such as a unicorn, a square circle, the seacoast of Bohemia, the number *i*, and so on. An existent entity is one that has a status in space and time and stands in causal relationships to others. Thus a horse exists, whereas a unicorn only subsists. When I see a horse, I see an existent entity; if I think I see a unicorn, I am not seeing a "complex of ideas," as Locke would say, but a subsistent entity. Perception is awareness of existent objects; illusion is awareness of merely subsistent entities as though they were existent.

Most philosophers now believe that this is only a verbal solution to the problem of illusion. It gives a name to the contents of illusory experience, but it leaves most questions about the occurrence of illusory perceptions unanswered. It immensely complicates the conception of being, by attributing subsistent being to some entitites that could not have any place in the world of science or common sense; in this, the theory opens itself to similar objections that were brought against Plato's doctrine of the Forms. Problems of this nature proved to be the undoing of neorealism.

Critical Realism

The failure of neorealism to provide a convincing account of our knowledge of the external world limits the options of those who still believe that realism is the most plausible theory of perception. Such persons are confronted with three choices: the first leads to skepticism and the second to idealism. The third, although it is the way of realism, contains the pitfalls of representative realism and neorealism. Yet, to some philosophers the wisest course is to persevere with realism and to try to solve the problems that it had been unable to solve. This was the course of the critical realists.

Although the critical realists rejected representative realism, they believed that it was essentially correct in one crucial respect: its dualism. The failure of neorealism to provide an adequate account of error was instructive in pointing up what seemed to be insuperable problems in combining realism with epistemological monism. Descartes and Locke's insight, they thought, had been in recognizing that what is immediately perceived is nonidentical with the independently existing objects of the world. But the critical realists did not return full circle to the older realism, because they could not endorse its explanations of our knowledge of the external world. Although they were dualists and in some cases even acknowledged that there is causal mediation between objects and the contents of perception, they nonetheless denied that our knowledge of objects is indirect and inferential. Thus, their problem was to reconcile the assertion of the existence of an external world, which is never directly perceived, with the admission that its existence can neither be proved a priori (as Descartes thought) nor inferred from causal connections (as Locke thought).

Different attacks were made upon the problem: that our judgments about the external world are simply instinctual, occasioned by the presence of certain data to consciousness; that it is a postulate of knowledge that the structures, relationships, and powers of objects are somehow revealed—in a sense never fully explained—in the contents of perception; that actually the existence of an external world is simply the most rational hypothesis to cover the perceptual situation. But to many philosophers no alternative provided a really viable solution to the problem. They avoided the difficulties of neorealism but were unable to offer a plausible solution to the very problem that had led initially to the abandonment of representative realism— that concerning the connection between the data and object.

Perhaps the critical realist who faced the whole issue most squarely was George Santayana (1863–1952), the Spanish-born, American philosopher who taught at Harvard during the days of William James and Josiah Royce. He concedes that there is *no way* in which we can establish, either with certainty or probability, the existence of an external world.[45] Our belief in its existence is ultimately an act of "animal faith." That is, we are so constituted biologically that we just naturally believe in the existence of such a world and—except the philosopher during his meditations—cannot do otherwise. This is a bit reminiscent of Descartes' claim that we have a strong natural inclination to believe that our ideas are produced by material objects. But

[45]See his *Skepticism and Animal Faith* (New York: Dover Publications, Inc., 1955).

Santayana does not believe in God and therefore cannot claim, as Descartes did, divine certification of the truth of such a belief. Only faith can bridge the gap between what we directly intuit in experience (sense data, ideas, impressions, and what Santayana calls "essences") and the physical objects that we believe have independent existence. This is at once a concession to skepticism, in acknowledging that we cannot *know* that an external world exists, and a reaffirmation of the common sense view that external objects do exist.

The deeper significance of Santayana's theory, however, is its tacit admission that the problem of the external world is insoluble and that inquiry here runs into a dead end from which the only escape is a belief with no rational foundation. Santayana willingly embraced this conclusion. But for all its forthrightness, his position was not calculated to satisfy those philosophers for whom the tradition we have been discussing posed a problem requiring a rational (but not necessarily rationalist) solution.

What alternatives are open to them? Both epistemological idealism and the various forms of realism encounter difficulties in the egocentric predicament. If we can never know, perceive, observe, contemplate, and so on, anything without instituting some kind of cognitive relationship to it, then although Perry is right that the idealist cannot infer the truth of his theory from this fact, it also follows that the realist can never establish the truth of his theory. If we can never get "outside" our own experiences and thoughts, how can we ever show that anything exists beyond them? The very predicament that Perry painstakingly argues cannot be used to support idealism also prevents the realist from ever establishing the truth of his theory.[46]

The egocentric predicament reveals the impasse inquiry encounters in attempting to resolve the problem of our knowledge of the external world. Neither the rationalist nor the empiricist is able to offer a convincing solution to the problem, given the assumptions of their approches. These include the view that there are sharply distinguishable subjects and objects, that experience is a subjective apprehending of private sense data, which Descartes, Locke, Berkeley, and some of the later realists say takes place in an immaterial soul, and that only on the basis of what is given in such experience can we know anything about the external world.[47] It is against this background that we shall examine in the next chapter new approaches to the problem.

[46]Although Perry recognizes this objection and attempts to meet it, it is doubtful that his handling of the problem really faces the issue as he himself has posed it.

[47]Some of the later realists do question and modify some of these assumptions, for example, by revising the concept of mind in such a way as to provide an alternative to the Cartesian immaterial-substance theory. But, as John Dewey observes, they nonetheless "admit the reality of the problem; denying only this particular solution, they try to find some other way out, which will still preserve intact the notion of knowledge as a relationship of a general sort between subject and object." Richard J. Bernstein, ed., *On Experience, Nature and Freedom* (New York: The Liberal Arts Press, 1960), p. 44.

BIBLIOGRAPHY

Broad, C. D., "Berkeley's Denial of Material Substance," *Philosophical Review*, Vol. 63 (1954), 155–81.

Hume, D., *A Treatise of Human Nature*, Book I, Part IV, section 2, ed., L. A. Selby-Bigge. Oxford: Oxford University Press, 1958.

Locke, J., *Essay Concerning Human Understanding* (1690), especially Books II and IV. Many editions.

Lovejoy, A. O., *The Revolt Against Dualism*. LaSalle, Ill.: Open Court Publishing Co., 1960.

The Monist, Vol. 51, No. 2 (April, 1967), is devoted entirely to studies of neo-realism and critical realism.

Montague, W. P., "The Story of American Realism," in *The Development of American Philosophy* (2nd ed.), pp. 479–89, eds., W. G. Muelder, L. Sears, and A. V. Schlabach. Cambridge, Mass.: Houghton Mifflin Company, 1960.

Morris, C. R., *Locke, Berkeley, and Hume*. London: Oxford University Press, 1946.

Perry, R. B., *Present Philosophical Tendencies*. New York: George Braziller, Inc., 1955.

———, *et al.*, *The New Realism: Cooperative Studies in Philosophy*. New York: The Macmillan Company, 1912.

Russell, B., *Our Knowledge of the External World*. New York: Mentor Books, 1960.

Santayana, G., *et al.*, *Essays in Critical Realism*. New York: Peter Smith, Publisher, 1941.

———, *Skepticism and Animal Faith*. New York: Dover Publications, Inc., 1955.

Stace, W. T., "The Refutation of Realism" in *Readings in Philosophical Analysis*, pp. 364–72, eds., Herbert Feigl and Wilfrid Sellars. New York: Appleton-Century-Crofts, Inc., 1949.

Steinkraus, W. E., ed., *New Studies in Berkeley's Philosophy*. New York: Holt, Rinehart & Winston, Inc., 1966.

Turbayne, C. M., "The Influence of Berkeley's Science on His Metaphysics," *Philosophy and Phenomenological Research*, Vol. 16 (1955–56), 476–87.

Warnock, G. J., *Berkeley*. Baltimore: Penguin Books, Inc., 1953.

QUESTIONS FOR REVIEW AND DISCUSSION

1. Do you accept the statement made in the text that Locke's theory of knowledge has come to be accepted as common sense? If so, how does common sense overcome the objections Berkeley made against it?
2. Physical properties of objects, such as their chemical and electrical properties, are sometimes now considered to be "primary qualities." Could Berkeley's arguments be modernized so as to show that even these instances of primary qualities are not independent of mind?
3. Does Berkeley prove the existence of God by an argument based on the existence of nature? Or does he, like Descartes (Chap. 4), prove that the external world exists as a consequence of a *premise* that God exists?
4. Is Berkeley's theory of the cause of our ideas (that is, that they are caused by a mind) able to stand up against Hume's analysis of the concept of cause (Chap. 9)?
5. Read an account of Hume's theory of the self. Compare his criticism of

the concept of self with Berkeley's criticism of the concept of material substance.

6. Evaluate the objection that Berkeley is inconsistent in claiming that although we cannot know that unperceived material substance causes our ideas, we *can* know that an unperceived God causes them.

7. Suppose an automatic camera were placed in the quad to photograph the tree at a time when no one was perceiving it. Would the resultant photograph disprove Berkeley's thesis that "to be is to be perceived"? Why or why not?

8. Contrast the conceptions of consciousness in Berkeley and the neorealists. Whose do you think is most nearly correct? For what reasons?

6 MODERN IDEALISM

ABSOLUTE IDEALISM

The metaphysical theory known as absolute idealism was first formulated by the German philosoper Georg Wilhelm Friedrich Hegel (1770-1831). In discussing absolute idealism, it might seem reasonable to give an exposition of the thought of its founder, as we did in the case of Berkeleian idealism. But Hegel lacks the clarity and conciseness of Berkeley; his system is so complex and subtle and his terminology so opaque that this is not a suitable way to introduce the philosophy of absolute idealism. It might be reasonable to turn to the thought of one of his greatest followers; but this poses a difficulty. Hegel's philosophy was so complex and rich that it was interpreted in different ways by different philosophers, and if we were to take any single man—F. H. Bradley, Bernard Bosanquet, John or Edward Caird, Andrew Seth Pringle-Pattison, Josiah Royce, James Edwin Creighton, or Benedetto Croce—and give an exposition of his views, we should have to neglect others equally important who disagree with him. For these reasons we shall give a composite picture of absolute idealism, taking sometimes one man's formulation and sometimes another's. Any loss in historical precision will be offset by a gain in clarity and generality.

Differences Between Berkeley's Idealism and Absolute Idealism

There are two central differences between Berkeley's idealism and absolute idealism. They concern the content of knowledge and the awareness of the self or mind.

Berkeley was an empiricist, who saw in sense experience the source of all knowledge. The absolute idealists, however, take a less restricted view of experience. Experience is much more varied than the empiricists considered it to be. It includes our moral concerns and struggles as well as the perception of Dr. Johnson's stone, our aesthetic reaction to music as well as our hearing the sensations "in our ears," the march of events in history as well as the

126

association of our ideas. In fact, experience is an all-comprehensive term; everything in any way able to be experienced, whether perceived by the senses or not, is comprised within it. The absolute idealist takes it as he finds it without trying to compress it into an awareness of ideas of sensation and reflection.

Berkeley, you will remember, distinguished between ideas and notions. He thought that notions were a pre-eminent kind of knowledge of a particular reality, namely, our own minds or spirits. He believed that ideas are passive and owe their reality to their being perceived; the notions we have of ourselves, on the contrary, give us a direct apprehension of the activity of our own minds. This dichotomy between idea and notion is inconsistent with the definition of the content of experience introduced by Locke and usually accepted by Berkeley. There is some internal evidence in Berkeley's writings that it was introduced as an afterthought. Although it saved Berkeley from skepticism and solipsism, it has always appeared to be an inconsistent part of his system.

In Berkeley's philosophy, ideas presuppose a mind for which they are ideas, but mind presupposes no ideas; it is known directly by intuitive notions. The absolute idealists are in fundamental disagreement with him here, because they assert as one of their principal theses the *mutual* presupposition of mind and object. They hold that neither is conceivable without the other. According to them, we do not first know the mind and only subsequently see how it gets its ideas; rather, we first have experiences of feelings, things, volitions, images, and so on, and from this complex whole we gradually segregate and distinguish two poles—a subjective mental pole and an objective public component we call the object. The Berkeleian conception is that of a mind that, at least in principle, is isolable from its experiences and capable of being known by introspection. The absolute idealistic view is that the mind is not an isolable entity or thing and cannot be known except in contrast and tension with what is not subjective. We do not have minds sharply distinguished from everything else in reality; the mind is not a crystal with sharp edges. We are, says Bosanquet, "individuals with tattered edges," and it is impossible to say exactly where mind ends and the things it does or experiences begin. We find the full content and function of mind only in the whole of experience.

Here the absolute idealist challenges two assumptions underlying the problem of our knowledge of the external world: first, that there is an irreducible distinction between subject and object; second, that experience is a private phenomenon yielding impressionistic data from which the subject must infer or construct an external world. As the American idealist, Josiah Royce, puts it, "neither the external world nor the individual thinker has any *such* reality as traditional popular beliefs, together with most metaphysical schools, have desired us to assume."[1] Accordingly, the idea of a

[1]Josiah Royce, *The Religious Aspect of Philosophy* (New York: Harper Torchbook, 1958), p. 233.

mysterious connection between the two, the explanation of which constitutes an insoluble problem about how to transcend the apparent limits of knowledge, is a "metaphysical figment." For the absolute idealist, Berkeley did not go far enough. Although he was an idealist about the material world, he remained essentially a realist about individual minds, which he believed existed independently of one another.[2] According to the absolute idealist, it is *within* experience that the subject-object distinction emerges; experience is to begin with a richer, more expansive phenomenon than Berkeley (or Descartes or Locke) thought. But, asks the absolute idealist, how can we distinguish *within* experience what is merely subjective from what is objectively true about the world?

The Growth of Experience

Every experience, the absolute idealist says, is partially objective and partially subjective. It is subjective because it is "from a standpoint," but it is objective because in its meaning it "transcends" this limited perspective and adumbrates or suggests what is not included in the momentary consciousness. In its subjective aspect, it is always partial and to some extent distorted. Its partiality, however, entails a growth to larger experience that complements its fragmentariness by covering broader reaches of the objective. The mere fact that we know our consciousness is at any time limited and partial means that we already, in principle, have transcended these limits; otherwise, we should not know that our experience was limited. Some idealists reason from this fact that there must be another mind, an Absolute Mind, in which our own limited minds are imbedded and that when we look upon our ordinary consciousness as finite and limited, we are already participating in the Absolute Mind.

More cautious absolute idealists are unwilling to make such a leap from our experience to an Absolute Mind. They hold that the slow progress of our consciousness to more and more comprehensive knowledge of objects shadows forth the kind of reality we would reach *if* we could see things from the standpoint of experience made completely synoptic. Let us see, then, how experience grows so that, by extrapolation, we can conceive of the perfect experience or absolute knowledge.

Any experience a subject or a mind has is always partial. The simplest statement, such as, "There is a tree," calls for supplementation before it becomes clear and "really" true. For what does "there" mean? As I turn my head, "there" changes its meaning, and what was true a moment ago that, "There is a tree," yields to a new truth, "There is a house." These two statements are both partially true, but because they contradict each other,

---

[2]See Josiah Royce, *The World and the Individual*, second series (New York: Dover Publications, Inc., 1959), pp. 234f. Royce also contends that Berkeley is a realist in his conception of the relationship of individual minds to God. See *The World and the Individual*, first series, p. 247.

the absolute idealist argues that they are partially false; and we must define what we mean by "there" in order to remove this contradiction. We must state the objective conditions under which the two sentences are true, and these objective conditions—stated in terms of time, direction, latitude, and longitude—are far more elaborate than the simple empirical statement I made when I said, "There is a tree."

This simple, almost trivial illustration is taken from Hegel's great work, *The Phenomenology of Mind*. Simple as it is, however, it includes an important truth. Knowledge grows by transcending any particular moment of experience, by referring to still more experience that will be less subjective and less contingent upon the particular point of view or "state of mind" than the original experience was. The transcendence involves "saving the appearances" by finding the additional experiences that make our partial report on our experience true, yet prevent us from thinking that it is the whole truth. When we transcend the experience in which we say, "There is a tree," we do not render this statement wholly false; it retains its truth by becoming imbedded in a context of experience. Also, "There is a house," and "There is a dog," can be true without contradiction.

Searching for these additional conditions is the process of dialectic. We saw earlier (Chap. 3, p. 54) how dialectic for Socrates was essentially a process of question and answer designed to lead progressively to the truth, and how this conversational technique was adapted by Plato to philosophical thinking generally so as to provide the model for philosophic inquiry itself. Hegel and the absolute idealists magnify the dialectic process so that is it no longer merely the structure of philosophical conversation and inquiry—it is for them a real, objective process in the world itself, as it reveals itself in experience. Thus Hegel believed that any sentence, any thought, any historical movement or institution—in fact, anything we experience—contains the seed of its own dissolution. Each thing and each truth is unstable, true, or real only within a specific and limited context of experience. The changes in our own experiences, in conceptual thought, and in objects follow a dialectical pattern in which any partial truth or reality (*thesis*) develops its own opposite (*antithesis*) and then produces a new *synthesis* in which both the thing and its opposite are seen to be partially true or real. According to Hegel and most absolute idealists, this dialectical process goes on forever, or until some experience or reality in experience is found in which all the opposing theses and antitheses are reconciled in one comprehensive and synoptic system. Only then is *the* truth attained; according to Hegel, "Truth is the whole."

The dialectic process is a central conception in all absolute idealism. This is true even though F. H. Bradley called Hegel's dialectic "an unearthly ballet of bloodless categories." And there is much artificiality in some of the applications that Hegel made of it, but Hegel did not employ it in the mechanical, uniform manner often attributed to him. As a general account of the way, in thought and in the world we think about, partiality or partisanship generates opposing partiality or partisanship, with which it is later to be reconciled in a "larger harmony," it does have great merit in exhibiting some aspects of the process and structure of experience and of the world.

From the central conception of dialectic, three other closely connected, partially overlapping, principles of absolute idealism are derived. They are: the coherence criterion of truth, the rational conception of reality, and the theory of degrees of reality.

The Coherence Criterion of Truth

A criterion of truth is a statement of the general character of knowledge by virtue of which true knowledge can be distinguished from error. It is commonly said that a true proposition is one that "corresponds to reality" or to "fact." "It is raining" is true if and only if it *is* raining, for in some way the sentence designates the state of affairs when rain is falling, and it is true if that state of affairs actually exists. This conception of a "correspondence" between a proposition and a fact is difficult or impossible to analyze into any simpler terms; "correspondence" is perhaps an underived, basic concept, and if one understands what is meant by "true," he has some grasp of what is meant by "corresponds," and vice versa.

Although it seems very simple and obvious to say, "Truth is correspondence of thought (belief, judgment, proposition, or the like) to what is actually the case," such an assertion nevertheless involves a metaphysical assumption —that there is a fact, object, or state of affairs, independent of our knowledge to which our knowledge corresponds. This was Plato's assumption—that knowledge must have reality as its object. In challenging the subject-object distinction, the idealist asserts that mind and its object mutually implicate each other and denies that there are objects on one side, thoughts on the other, and some indefinable correspondence between them. He challenges the realist and the man of common sense who say that the truth of a proposition is constituted by its correspondence to some object by asking, "How, on your principles, could you know you have a true proposition?" Or, putting the question in more exact from, "How can you use your *definition* of truth, it being the correspondence between a judgment and its object, as a *criterion* of truth? How can you know when such correspondence actually holds?"

This is an extremely difficult question. Suppose I have an experience that, I believe, authorizes me to say, "Cats love mice." If this statement is true, then it is a fact that cats do love mice. In order to know that the statement is true, according to the principles of the correspondence theory, I should compare my judgment (or the experience that led to the judgment) with the actual state of the relation of cats to mice to see if they correspond. But, according to the idealist, this cannot be done. For how can I know the actual state of the relationship between cats and mice except by having another experience and making another judgment? I cannot step outside my mind to compare a thought in it with something outside it. Here the absolute idealist uses against the realist precisely the fact to which Perry called attention in the egocentric predicament. He says that one can never reach *mere fact* but only other *experienced facts*, and if my experience, "Cats love mice," was in any way wrong, it is quite possible that any fact by which I try to check it may likewise be wrongly experienced or interpreted.

Instead of comparing the judgment, "Cats love mice," with a mere fact to determine whether there is correspondence, I compare one experience and its judgment with another experience and its judgment, and if these judgments are incompatible, then I modify at least one of them. For instance, I have had experiences that lead me to conclude, "Cats love mice"; then I have a perceptual experience of the relationship between a particular cat and a particular mouse that makes me conclude that *this* cat does not love *this* mouse. The judgment based on the latter experience is incompatible with the judgments based on the earlier experience; I do not know which of these judgments corresponds to reality, but I discover an incompatibility between my judgments. Therefore I modify my first judgment to be "Some cats love mice."

If by "fact" one means what is perceived, and if one thinks of the relationship of correspondence between relatively abstract true judgments and relatively concrete particular perceived facts, then the illustration about cats and mice may seem to fit the correspondence theory. This is probably what is meant when one says that he tests his beliefs by reference to the facts. But "fact" is always *experienced fact;* the purported fact may be illusory, and it must be interpreted and judged before it can serve as a test for other judgments. As we know from our earlier studies and from common sense, sometimes we are entirely correct in distrusting the evidence of the senses when it is incompatible with our more abstract, general, theoretical knowledge.

The idealist fully exploits the difficulty of finding a pure case of "correspondence." He says, in effect, that it shows how fruitless is the realist's belief in the independently real object, for when we bring our knowledge to a test, it is not a test before the bar of a Lockean substance, or of a thing that one can claim to know directly, indubitably, and as it actually is. The test in actual cases is precisely what the idealist says it should be: Does more experience corroborate or weaken the conclusion formerly reached on the basis of less experience?

According to this test, a belief is true if it coheres with the systematic whole that we seek as an interpretation of experience. Knowledge grows, as the idealists argue, by bringing the variety and chaos of momentary, fragmentary experiences into a systematic whole. On the very simplest level, we cannot accept contradictory propositions as true, not because we know that metaphysical reality is logically consistent, as the realist might affirm, but because contradictory propositions cannot be brought into a single system of propositions. But coherence is more than mere lack of logical inconsistency;

it means the systematic harmony that we demand of diverse experiences before we accept them all as true. In an ideally coherent system, each judgment is consistent with the others and gives the others positive support.

A coherent system of propositions is "a set of propositions in which each one stands in such a relation to the rest that it is logically necessary that it should be true if all the rest are true, and such that no set of propositions within the whole set is logically independent of all propositions in the remainder of the set." [3]

In using the coherence criterion, the ideal of knowledge by which we judge our less-than-ideal knowledge is that of perfectly integrated experience, in which each part is in harmony with all the others and in which the whole encompasses all experience. If we were omniscient, according to this view, we could see the whole by tracing out the ramifications of any part, as Tennyson suggests in his "Flower in the crannied wall." We are not omniscient, but the surest knowledge possible is knowledge that is systematically supported by the maximum of experience. In making a choice between two beliefs, the reasonable man chooses the belief that is best supported by the whole of his experience—both his present perceptions and his judgments made on grounds of memory and reason as well. The belief he does not choose can then be "explained away" by showing, for instance, that it is a belief one would expect on the level of experience where it actually arose, but a belief seen to be inadequate on a more comprehensive level.

The idealists argue that the coherence criterion is a corollary of the dialectical growth of knowledge. We hold to a belief until it comes into collision with another belief. Then we modify one or both of the beliefs until they are consistent with each other and with the contexts of their origins. We embrace the more comprehensive belief until a new incoherence is found within it or between it and some other parts of our experience. Then the mutual adjustment, choice, or rejection occurs again. All through this process, we are looking for beliefs that we can retain in the face of growing experience. The dialectical correction of any partial experience is founded upon the failure of the partial experience to satisfy the demands of full coherence of experience.

This correction is an endless process. Since we can never have "all experience," we cannot then be sure that any belief is absolutely true. According to the idealist, no belief is incorrigible; even the mathematician is willing to modify his postulates if he finds that a contradiction develops within his system, and it is at least imaginable, as Descartes recognized, that there really is no table here before me. It must not be supposed that the idealist doubts such propositions as, "A straight line is the shortest distance between

---

[3]A. C. Ewing, *Idealism: A Critical Survey* (New York: Humanities Press, 1950), pp. 229f. Quoted by permission of Methuen & Co., Ltd.

two points," or, "I am now reading a sentence in the English language." Rather, he is asserting that our certainty of these propositions does not lie in their self-evident indubitability; it lies in the fact that without these propositions, almost the whole of our systematically organized experience, indeed sanity itself, would be wrecked. But there remains an outside chance, at least theoretically, that these beliefs might someday have to be modified in order to save the systematic order we require of knowledge.

The beliefs we call true are those that have developed in a long and searching criticism of other beliefs and that have held their own in subsequent criticism. Those we are most sure of are those that we least fear will have to be surrendered to new experience. Naturally, then, we can never be absolutely sure that our ideas or beliefs or hypotheses will continue to hold up. "Truth is the whole," said Hegel, but we men can never know the whole, never reach an infinity of experience. Hence, there is always room for error in our firmest beliefs; the coherence criterion is proposed as a way of detecting errors.

The realist and the man of common sense may reply by asking the idealist, "How do you really know that the world itself is a logical whole, so that logically coherent beliefs give knowledge of things as they really are?" He may point out, for instance, that the internal coherence of a novel does not lead us to suppose that the novel is true and may hold that coherence is not a substitute for correspondence as the meaning of truth.

There are two answers to this objection. The first is that coherence means more than consistency within a limited range of experience. We do require consistency or coherence of action and character in a novel, and if we do not find it, we deny that the novel is "true to life" or "realistic." But that internal coherence or consistency does not make the novel true in the usual sense of the word; it remains a novel, however internally coherent it may be. If coherence is supposed to be a mark of truth, how then *do* we distinguish a coherent novel from a history? Not by discovering incoherences *within* it, nor by comparing it with the "actual fact" that we might claim to know directly and without danger of error. Rather, we test it by checking it against broader experience. We find events reported in one book for which there is no documentary evidence; we find that the book is written by a man noted as a novelist and not as a historian; we find that the characters portrayed in the book are different from the characters having the same name that we find described, for instance, in an encyclopedia. How then are we to make our picture of the events in question coherent? We do so by calling some of the books "histories" and others "novels"; the experience reported in the book we call a novel can be rendered coherent with the whole of our experience only if we do not take it at its face value.

The second answer to this objection requires more detailed elaboration because it brings us to the absolute idealist's conception of reality.

The Rational Conception of Reality

We have seen some of the difficulties in attempting to assign priority to either metaphysics or epistemology. To ask the epistemological question "What is knowledge?" prompts the response, "knowledge of what?" which seems to require a metaphysical answer. And the metaphysical question "What is reality?" seems to be a request for knowledge—at least to presuppose that there is such a thing—when it is the province of epistemology to ascertain this. Plato assigned priority to metaphysics over epistemology by requiring that knowledge have *reality* as its object—where reality was characterizable without reference to its being known. The absolute idealist reverses this emphasis. He defines reality by reference to knowledge; by "reality" he *means* "the object of true knowledge." Thus, although they both subscribe to the proposition, "The object of true knowledge is reality," it has a different meaning for each of them. For the idealist, ideal or perfect knowledge is the criterion of reality. No one should assert that anything is real unless he has what he considers to be good and sufficient reasons for it, and good and sufficient reasons are characterized by an internal consistency and a coherence with all the evidence at our disposal. To attribute reality to anything when the belief in it is known to be inconsistent with other beliefs we hold is to be incoherent and self-refuting; such incoherence is the mark of mental imbalance.

Consider a simple example. When I believe, "There are mountains on the moon," I do not infer the existence of mountains on the moon from the mere concept I have of "lunar mountains." The reason I have for believing that there are mountains is not that I can compare my belief with the brute fact and see that they agree; even if I were on the moon, it would still be necessary to believe, think, see, and touch. The reason I believe that mountains are there is that if I did not believe it, I should not know how to bring my other beliefs into any kind of coherent system. I should not know how to interpret the testimony of astronomers, pictures relayed to earth from spacecraft, and what I myself can see through a telescope, if I obstinately persisted in saying "There are no mountains on the moon." This suffices to show me that it is *reasonable* to believe that there are mountains on the moon.

But the realist may still say, "I don't deny that it may be reasonable to interpret your experience in this way; but what makes you think that reality, the real moon, corresponds to your experience?" This is the real force of the objection raised in the preceding section. The answer to it lies in the absolute idealist's conception of reality. Reality for him is not something outside experience that may or may not correspond to its logically coherent structure. Rather, *reality is the name that we give to those aspects of our experience that are most coherent*, and there is no other standard than coherence by which we can justify attributing reality to anything. It is not only "truths" that are coherent and hold their own under dialectical development; reality for us is that maximum sector of our experience that is logically coherent, and reality itself is total, completely coherent, experience. To it we are led and by it we remain in the dialectic of experience.[4]

This is the true meaning in Hegel's oft-repeated statement, "The reasonable is the real, and the real is the reasonable." By that statement, he meant: in the final analysis, the ground that we have for believing that anything is real is the superior reasonableness of the belief in it as compared to disbelief or doubt. He does not mean the absurd statement that whatever is logically possible because not self-contradictory—a unicorn on the moon—is real. A modern idealist (although he happened not to be an absolute idealist) said the same thing in a way less liable to such a misunderstanding: "The question, What is reality? can only be answered by telling how we must think about reality."[5]

In absolute idealism we do not begin with an epistemological dualism, with reality on one side and the data of experience on the other, and then ask what guarantees a correspondence between them. Rather, for absolute idealists there is only experience and its movement from the fragmentary and subjective to what is independent of the particular subjects and centers of consciousness within it. This transition is dialectic, in which the real is able to hold its own in its relation to other aspects of experience. The real is reasonable because only the reasonable is able to preserve itself in dialectical criticism and because we do not persist in attributing the honorific title of "real" to an object of experience unless it is able to stand up to the questioning of reason.

Reality is not something contrasted to experience. Reality is the system of the most comprehensive, coherent, and synoptic experience we can have. Of course, we can and do draw a distinction between "my consciousness" and "things as they really are," and our conception of the latter is the ideal or the norm for judging the adequacy of my own experience. But the distinction is drawn within experience, not between experience and reality. It is drawn between things as I, personally and inadequately, experience them now and as they would be experienced by my mind if it were free from all limitations. My consciousness fluctuates between the trivial and private and a grasp of things freed from the contingent limitations of myself. The Absolute, which is Bosanquet's name for reality, "is simply the high-water

---

[4]Here the absolute idealist develops a modified form of what has been called the "ontological argument" for the existence of God, which says that from the concept of a perfect being the existence of such a being can be inferred. (This argument will be discussed in Chapter 15.) The absolute idealist modifies the argument not for the purpose of proving the existence of God but for the purpose of defending the objective validity of a coherent whole of experience. See Charles Hartshorne, "Ideal Knowledge Defines Reality: What Was True in Idealism," *Journal of Philosophy*, XLIII, No. 21 (October 10, 1946), 573–82; W. E. Hocking, "The Ontological Argument in Royce and Others," in *Contemporary Idealism in America*, ed., Clifford Barrett (New York: The Macmillan Company, 1932), pp. 43–66.

[5]Borden Parker Bowne, *Metaphysics* (1882) (Boston: Boston University Press, 1943), p. 3.

mark of fluctuations in experience, of which, in general, we are daily and normally aware." [6]

Levels of Reality

Plato's theory involved the notion of "levels of reality." It seems evident that if a thing *exists*, it is as existent as anything else; but he said that some things are more *real* than others if they serve as the foundation and explanation of those others. In this sense, Plato's Forms are considered by him to be more real than the phenomenal appearances. Absolute idealists develop the notion of levels of reality as a consequence of their dialectic and their belief that the real is the reasonable. In the coherence criterion, there is a conception of "levels of truth"; beliefs are true according to the wealth of the context of experience with which they cohere. The truer a belief is, the higher its stage in the dialectic. "There is a tree," is true, but in the dialectic it is superseded by another statement, "In 1967 there was a tree at the corner of Fisher's Lane." The second sentence is said to contain "more truth" than the former, because it is less challengeable from variations in the meaning of "there" and "is." When we criticize and modify the first statement, we substitute for it some truth that is more stable and less subject to destructive criticism.

Now consider the objects of our experience. Each thing is related, directly or indirectly, to everything else in the universe, and its character depends upon and is modified by its relationship to other things. Some things are highly contingent upon others, and in an unstable environment they are variable and impermanent. Others have such a broad context of relationships that they preserve themselves through all sorts of vicissitudes. Those that "hold their own" are more real, according to the levels theory, than those that do not. For instance, the tree is "more real" than the leaf on its bough; the queen is "less real" than the British constitutional system; and so on.

If by reality we mean merely physical existence, of course an electron is as "real" as a star, and the queen is more real than the unwritten English constitution. But by real we mean, paradoxically, also the ideal. A thing is real to the degree that it realizes its ideal nature and full potentialities, and the realization of a thing's nature and potentialities occurs only through a dialectical development. In the final analysis, a thing is real to the extent to which it conforms to the widest context of experience and reality, that is, preserves itself through the most comprehensive experience. For this reason, we can say that the only thing that is wholly real is the whole of the universe considered as a self-explanatory system of experience, internally coherent and absolutely comprehensive and synoptic. This is what the absolute idealist

[6]G. Watts Cunningham, *The Idealistic Argument in Recent British and American Philosophy* (New York: The Century Company, 1933), p. 140.

calls The Absolute. Thus he explains things in terms of that which is "higher" than they are:

> ... The basic principle of the theory of reality of all idealism is that we can explain the lower by including it in the higher but that we can never explain the higher by reducing it to the lower, or by developing a metaphysics in terms of a lower level which precludes the possibility of acknowledging the higher. In some form or other this principle is recognized by all idealists and is the central postulate of all idealism. It follows that idealism reaches a single all-inclusive whole as the highest reality.[7]

This all-inclusive reality is The Absolute, a unity in which the manifold diversity of phenomena are but appearances. In this sense absolute idealism marks a sophisticated working-out of the metaphysics of Parmenides.

The proper understanding of the relationship of The Absolute to the things within it, and especially to the human beings who have partial experience of it, is one of the moot points that have split the school of absolute idealism. Sometimes the differences between The Absolute and its appearances are so emphasized that the world of human experience is transcended or abrogated; it is appearance not reality, and to find reality we must have a kind of mystic absorption in The Absolute, in which all distinctions are blurred in the absolute oneness of things.[8]

Other absolute idealists, on the contrary, hold that The Absolute is "with us when we know it not." For these philosophers, The Absolute *is* experience in its highest dialectical development, and at any stage in the evolution of experience, The Absolute is there as its highest point. "When the Absolute falls into the water," wrote Bosanquet, "it becomes a fish." Hegel expressed somewhat the same notion when, after seeing Napoleon, he wrote, "I have seen the World-Spirit on horseback." This interpretation seeks to preserve the individuality of the minds in the world and to maintain the temporal character of reality, even though insisting that we are "all parts of one stupendous whole."

In any event, the absolute idealist carries the emphasis upon mind—a trait of philosophical idealism—to its limit. To Berkeley's theses "To be is to be perceived," and "to perceive is to be," he adds "To be is *to be experience*." Reality itself is a single, all-encompassing, coherent experience. By properly understanding experience and following through the implications of dialectic, we find that we are already out of the egocentric predicament. The very distinction between ego and object, in terms of which it is stated, is transcended in the framing of the problem; it is only within the reality of experience that these terms can be understood. And there is no problem about knowing

[7]D. S. Robinson, *Introduction to Living Philosophy* (New York: The Crowell-Collier Publishing Co., 1932), p. 90. Quoted by permission of the publisher. Actually, the last sentence is a basic principle only of *absolute* idealism.

[8]Hegel, in criticizing this conception of The Absolute that he attributes to Schelling, calls it, "The night in which all cows are black."

a reality beyond experience, because the notion of "reality" itself is understandable only in terms of experience.

The absolute idealist also rejects the Cartesian-Platonic criterion of the infallibility of knowledge. The role of reason in his system is not to provide an infallible organ of knowledge but to provide the model of reality, which in the words of one idealist is "an orderly realm of genuine conscious life, one of whose products, expressions, and examples we find in the mind of Man."[9] The absolute idealist says that the source of knowledge is experience, but his expanded conception of experience makes this mean something very different for him from what it means for traditional empiricists like Locke and Berkeley. When followed through dialectically, the implications of this conception lead to a speculative metaphysics that not even Berkeley would have accepted. Indeed, as we shall see in the next chapter, the absolute idealists' solution to the epistemological problem is at the cost of creating problems that many have considered at least as great in the area of metaphysics. Before elaborating upon this, however, let us complete our picture of idealism by discussing pluralistic or personal idealism.

PLURALISTIC OR PERSONAL IDEALISM

The last of the types of idealism that we shall discuss is pluralistic or personal idealism.[10] Like absolute idealism, it is not a single theory, but a name given to the theories of various philosophers. All personal and pluralistic idealists are more impressed with the plurality of minds in the universe than with the view that there is one single all-embracing Absolute Mind. The pluralist thinks, "Reality may exist in distributive form, in the shape not of an all but of a set of eaches."[11]

The pluralistic idealist holds that the "eaches" are individual selves or minds, comparable to the one that I experience as the context or nucleus in my every experience. He believes that objects must either be ideas in minds or minds themselves or at least mind-like. Reality, for him, is a society or community of minds or selves, appearing from the outside like the familiar world of common sense or science, but understood in its real nature as mental through and through.

Pluralistic idealism has had a long history. Perhaps the first philosopher to defend an explicitly pluralistic idealism was Gottfried Wilhelm Leibniz (1646-1716). In the nineteenth century, the view was further developed by

[9]Royce, *The World and the Individual*, second series, p. 242.

[10]We shall treat "pluralistic" and "personal" as synonymous adjectives when describing this type of idealism. Some idealists prefer one name and some the other, according to which aspect of this idealism they emphasize. But in this general account, we can ignore most of these differences and shall use the two names interchangeably.

[11]William James, *A Pluralistic Universe* (New York: David McKay Co., Inc., 1909), p. 129.

Rudolf Hermann Lotze (1817-1881), who had a strong influence on English and American idealists. In England, pluralistic idealism was elaborated by John McTaggart Ellis McTaggart (1866-1925) and James Ward (1843-1925). The tradition of personal idealism has been carried on in the United States by the disciples of Borden Parker Bowne (1847-1910) and George Holmes Howison (1834-1916), and among them are Edgar Sheffield Brightman (1884-1953) and Ralph Tyler Flewelling (1871-1960).

The Nature and Existence of Minds

Since the ultimate category of idealism is mind itself, we can best see the distinctive traits of pluralistic idealism by comparing its views of the nature of the mind with the views of the two types of idealism we have already studied.

Pluralistic and Berkeleian idealism—If everything that we experience exists only as an idea in the mind, then certainly the mind must be real too. Berkeley, however, was very sparing in his discussion of the nature of the individual mind, and it remained for later idealists to develop this aspect of his theory. We have seen how absolute idealism tended to "explain it away"; we shall now see how the pluralistic idealist emphasizes its irreducible status.

The pluralistic idealist puts awareness of our own minds or selves into the center of discussion. We experience ideas, as Berkeley believed; but I always experience *my* ideas, and you always experience *yours*. Each of us experiences them as ideas of or in his own mind, and each person's experience has himself as a central fact or datum. Berkeley said, "No one ever experiences an object that is not an idea"; the pluralist adds, "and no one ever experiences an idea that is not his own." "The separateness and privacy of each individual," says Brightman, "[is] an ultimate trait of the world."[12]

Berkeley believed that we experience our mind through a specific "notion." The personal idealist says, on the contrary, that awareness of myself is indissolubly given in *every* experience. The mind that Berkeley became aware of in his "notion" was much like the soul of traditional theology. "Soul" is the name generally given to a transcendent entity (existing outside experience) reached only through inference. Psychology, since the time of Hume, has attacked the concept of soul as nonempirical and meaningless; it is, for psychology at least, a poor hypothesis. Berkeley, although he dismissed the unknown material object as a support for ideas, kept a spiritual substratum for them.

For transcendent and nonempirical soul as a spiritual substratum of experience, the personal idealist substitutes the "self." The self is the primary datum *in* experience. All experience is experience by and of a self; it is the individual organic unity of experience, of which each of us is always more

---

[12]Edgar S. Brightman, "The Finite Self," in *Contemporary Idealism in America*, ed., Clifford Barrett (New York: The Macmillan Company, 1932), p. 179.

or less explicitly aware. It has unity in variety, continuity, and purpose; only in relationship to it can anything be known to exist or be experienced or have any meaning or value.

Pluralistic and absolute idealism—The absolute idealist emphasizes a unity of experience not focused in individual centers of consciousness. The unity he seeks is that of a logical whole or system of experience, which he identifies with the reality of things. The consequence is that the absolute idealist derogates from the reality of the individual consciousness. In seeking an Absolute, he reduces the individual mind to a mere organ or aspect of the whole; whatever significance it has is derived from the degree to which it loses its specific nature and privacy in The Absolute. The absolute idealist is therefore a monist in his metaphysics, not a pluralist. When the absolute idealist deals with an idea without considering it in the context of the individual experience in which it arises and functions, the pluralists say he takes "idea" in an abstract and nonempirical sense.

The pluralistic idealists argue that the monist, in trying to find the mind, loses it. He may gain the whole world, but he loses himself in it. Consciousness is ineluctably individual. There are no "floating ideas"; all ideas are anchored in some individual's experience.

Pluralists have objected to the "block universe" or the "totalitarian state" of the absolute idealist. Its monolithic structure, in which each thing has an assigned place in the eternal order of things, they feel, does not allow room for individual spontaneity and freedom. Everything is necessary. It explains evil away as a necessary part of the good or makes it an inevitable part of experience rather than giving man a belief in his own spontaneity that will encourage him to exercise his freedom to eradicate it.

The pluralistic idealist considers the universe as analogous to a democratic community, in which each man can freely choose his own goals and freely cooperate with others, exercise his own initiative, and enlarge his experience without losing his identity. The pluralistic idealist reacts against the monism of absolute idealism because he has a "sentiment" in favor of individualism. But it is not entirely a matter of sentiment; he believes that the monism of absolute idealism is intellectually wrong on at least two counts.

First, he says, absolute idealism is not true to the facts. Although experience is its central fact, absolute idealism deals with only one aspect of experience. It delineates the logical and dialectical structure of experience with immense skill and subtlety; but it ignores the empirical fact that all our experience is individual and personal. However comprehensive experience may become through dialectical development, it is still the experience of some individual. The absolutist rightly recognizes that mind is essential for experience, but for the mind of which we are continuously aware he substitutes a mind that none, except perhaps a few mystics, have ever claimed. Second, the pluralistic idealist says, absolute idealism is wrong in its epistemology. By identifying experience with reality and asserting that reality is only experience understood in all its ramifications, the absolute idealist deprives our "experience" of any meaningful sense. It becomes just a part of experience—nobody's experience, just absolute experience.

The pluralistic idealist rejects the absolutist's view that experience and what is experienced are identical. For if he granted this, he says, "Self would be merged in its world, and a true plurality of selves would be impossible." [13] He goes back to Locke and says that our ideas merely represent reality but are not identical with it. He justifies his distinction between experience and what is experienced, the basis of his preserving plurality of selves, by arguing that the alternative view cannot explain how error can occur or how we are able to know what happened far away and long ago.

Summary—Personal idealists believe with Berkeley and the absolute idealists that the only real things are minds and the contents of experience. They agree with Berkeley (against the absolute idealists) that there are many irreducible and individual minds. But they disagree with both Berkeley and the absolute idealists by drawing a distinction between the contents of consciousness and the real objects of knowledge.

The last sentence leads directly to the central theses of pluralistic idealism. Granting that the only things that are real are minds and their ideas and that there is a difference between ideas and the real objects, only one conclusion is possible: *the objects must themselves be minds or parts of some mind not my own.* In either case he asserts a plurality of minds.

The Existence of External Objects

I am, say personal idealists, directly aware of myself as an active being, and I am directly of my ideas as *my* ideas. Ideas are not independently real things; their being is their being perceived. But how do we know that there are any things besides our ideas? How do I know that there are any independent objects? How do I know that my experience is not just a consistent dream?

The pluralistic idealist points out that ideas have two aspects; their mere being, as psychical events in my mind, brutely given at a particular moment, and their "objective reference," by virtue of which they mean or suggest something other than themselves. We know that one idea can refer to another; there is no reason to doubt that it can refer to other things too. But, a critic may say, the assumption of objective reference begs the question, Are there any objects except ideas?

The pluralistic idealist replies that the assumption is not arbitrarily made but is an empirical aspect of our ideas that ought not be neglected. An open-minded and honest analysis of consciousness, he says, cannot omit the character of objective reference, which is as directly felt a part or aspect of the idea

---

[13]Edgar S. Brightman, "Personalism and Borden Parker Bowne," *Proceedings of the Sixth International Congress of Philosophy* (Boston, 1926), p. 162.

are its secondary or primary qualities. If our analysis deals with the contents of consciousness only as isolated end-products of psychological observation and is interested only in their intensity, color, and the like, our analysis has distorted the facts of experience. Ideas bear the mark of incompleteness as one of their empirical features.

Not only are our ideas felt as incomplete; my experience of myself is incomplete and fragmentary unless I admit its dependence on something else:

> The personalist justifies himself in asserting the existence of this something-beside-me on the ground that I directly experience myself as a limited, hampered self—limited in my perceptual experience to just these special seeings and hearings and limited also in my personal disappointments and in my baffled purposes. But a direct experience of being limited is . . . a direct (not an inferred) knowledge of something existing beyond the limit.[14]

Brightman attempts to answer the charge of solipsism (the belief that only the individual experiencing mind exists) by putting the burden of proof upon the critic of his position:

> The solipsist supposes that whatever is in the mind has no meaning and no explanation beyond the mind in which it is located. But if the solipsist appeals to any meaning, he appeals to reason; and reason is coherence. Now, to suppose that sensations have no explanation beyond the mind in which they are located is to abandon all coherence; for sensations come and go in a most chaotic, formless, and incoherent manner—incoherent, that is, until the reasoning mind takes account of its act of referring beyond itself for its objects and for a rational basis for its existence. The hypothesis that sensations refer to objects of some sort, and that they are produced by some sort of reality other than the mind of the observer, is one that brings order and coherence into the realm of sensation.[15]

Therefore, according to this view, there is an aspect of our consciousness that, when carefully attended to, calls out for explanation. The most plausible explanation is that things exist independently of myself and my ideas and are productive of my ideas. This is only an hypothesis, but it is a more reasonable one than the solipsist's, which leaves the apparent objective reference of consciousness unexplained.

The Nature of Objects

Granting, now, that there is an object, what is it? Here, personal idealists are unanimous in their rejection of materialism. They all deny that the real object is to be understood only as matter under laws of mechanics and charac-

[14]Mary W. Calkins, "The Personalistic Conception of Nature," *Philosophical Review*, XXVIII, No. 2 (March, 1919), 126–27. Quoted with the permission of the Editor of *The Philosophical Review*.

[15]Edgar S. Brightman, *Nature and Values*. (New York and Nashville: Abingdon-Cokesbury Press, 1945), p. 41. Copyright 1945 by Whitmore and Stone. Used by permission of Abingdon Press.

terized only by primary qualities. Although science may understand nature under the materialistic assumption (although most idealists deny the adequacy of this assumption even in science), a metaphysical understanding of nature must be more synoptic and comprehensive. It must conceive nature in a way that is coherent with the most panoramic view of our experience.

Criteria of adequacy of any theory of objects—To satisfy this requirement, a theory of nature and of the objects of science must meet two criteria. First, it must not conflict with any of the established facts of science (although it may disagree with metaphysical theories based upon belief in the adequacy and incorrigible truth of some scientific hypothesis). That is to say, even though science may not give us the whole truth, a theory of the object must be such that the scientific conception of it will be at least a "first approximation." The conception of nature adopted in metaphysics must therefore admit the facts of science, the validity of scientific law, and the presuppositions and results of the impartial study of nature.

Second, it must be consistent with the facts of our immediate experience, which is an experience of a knowing, acting, and valuing self and not of a mechanical aggregate of atoms or material parts with only an epiphenomenal mind. In other words, metaphysical theory, in adapting itself to the results of science, should not explain away the teleological search for values that underlies the scientific enterprise itself. It must be adequate to the one reality we directly experience—ourselves.

No materialistic theory, says the personal idealist, can meet both of these criteria. But not all personal idealists agree as to what theory will best meet them. Some have accepted what I shall call a neo-Berkeleian theory and some a panpsychistic theory of objects.[16]

Neo-Berkeleian theory of objects—What limits our minds and explains the origin and cause of our ideas is another mind that is all-comprehending. The "things" that exist in the physical world are manifestations of the creativity of this supreme mind. Thus Brightman writes:

Every law of nature is a law of God, every energy of nature a deed of God.[17]
Nature is in the Divine Mind; nature is God's working, his activity, his experience. It is nothing external in which he dwells or on which he acts. It is part and parcel of his very being.[18]

Such a conception is quite compatible with positivism as a theory of scientific knowledge, because both oppose the popular materialistic interpretation of

---

[16]It is hard to be entirely sure that any recent personal idealists are neo-Berkeleians; often some of them write as if they were, though occasionally one finds statements by the same writers that are at least seemingly incompatible with this view. But it is a logically possible hypothesis about nature that a pluralistic idealist *could* consistently hold, and therefore we shall describe it briefly; but we would not wish to be interpreted as ascribing this view alone to any particular recent idealist.
[17]Brightman, *Nature and Values*, p. 120.
[18]*Ibid.*, p. 124.

scientific objects. But it goes beyond positivism, because positivism is *only* a theory of science and is not able to meet adequately the second of the criteria mentioned on page 143.[19] When we supplement the positivistic conception of nature with the neo-Berkeleian metaphysical conception, nothing is changed in science itself, so this theory meets the first criterion. The metaphysical supplement of the concept of a divine mind is harmonious with the scientific intepretation of nature and with the facts of our experience of our own mental reality, even though it is a speculation which goes far beyond the needs of science and common sense.

Panpsychistic theory of objects—Panpsychism literally means the view that "all is mind." That is, all reality is psychical and so-called objects are really minds. This view was first developed in modern philosophy by Leibniz and might well be called the "neo-Leibnizian" view. Leibniz defined a substance, a real entity or monad, as "a being that acts," and the only authentic case of action with which I am directly aware is my own activity. Thus Leibniz interpreted both objects and himself as monads, and the differences among them as a difference in the degree to which they had experience of the universe as a whole. A comparable view has been defended by James Ward.

The panpsychist reaches his conception of the object by an analogical argument like that by which Berkeley reached the conception of the mind of God. That is, when I infer beyond my ideas into the world of objects that I do not directly experience, I can interpret them best by analogy to the one reality I know directly: my own mind as a center of experience and action. But the panpsychist, being a pluralist, looks for many realities; everything that exists, he says, is a mind.

No panpsychist means to assert that this book is conscious of you as you are conscious of it. He recognizes that there is a continuous gradation of minds in the animal kingdom, from the subtle consciousness and intelligence of man to the dull restlessness and minimum intelligence of lower animals. He is even willing to argue that consciousness may not be a universal characteristic of minds, for what is called our "unconscious mind" shows teleological processes, and we have no evidence to decide whether a protozoon has any consciousness at all. Believing in the continuity of nature, however, the panpsychist extrapolates beyond the range of evidence of consciousness and posits mind of a very low order in all existing things.

On the face of it, this view may appear silly to most people in our civilization. But it is a common belief in the Orient, and since it has been formulated and defended by some great thinkers—one of whom, Gottfried Wilhelm Leibniz, was one of the most penetrating geniuses who ever lived—it merits careful study. Let us suspend what may be a natural repugnance to this view

[19]See Edgar S. Brightman, *A Philosophy of Ideals* (New York: Holt, Rinehart & Winston, Inc., 1928), Chap. II.

and see how it meets the two criteria that we have placed upon any theory of the object. In this view, what becomes of causality, mechanism, and the laws of nature?

Here the pluralistic idealist draws a useful distinction between the scientific and the metaphysical interpretation of a concept. Consider the two interpretations of the concept of causation and of the concept of substance. (1) By causation, the scientist, since the time of Hume, has meant only regularity in sequences of events. The laws of nature do not state that one event *makes* another event happen but only that events of one specific kind are regularly followed by events of another specific kind.[20] (2) By substance, the scientist, since the time of Locke, has understood only a regular congeries of observable traits or phenomena existing simultaneously in a restricted region of space.

The panpsychist leaves these categories untouched. Even if panpsychism is true, the scientist should continue to seek for regular sequences or statistical correlations and to think of an object as the sum or system of all its observed and observable aspects. Hence, the panpsychistic theory of the object meets the first criterion.

Now consider the metaphysical interpretation of these concepts. (1) Causation, in my own self-experience, does not mean merely the regular sequence of events; it means activity, initiative, agency. I have direct experience of causal efficacy when I "exert myself and *make* something happen." (It does not matter that the psychologist can show that many of the actions I think are free are really effects of what he considers to be physiological conditions. The idealist admits this, but insists that something very important is left out of the full experience of causation when it is replaced by the scientifically useful conception of mere regularity of sequence.) When I interpret causation metaphysically, I should make use of this more adequate, more full-bodied experience of causal efficacy, which is inseparable from the experience of purposing. If the objective connections in the world of nature are to be interpreted metaphysically, then, it will be by analogy to our own experience of purposive causation. Naturally, the object is not supposed to be as free and as purposive in its actions as a higher animal or man is, and hence the laws of nature and of nature's uniformity, expressed in mathematical equations, apply to the relationships among those minds we call physical objects.

(2) Substance does not apply, in my own experience, to a mere aggregate of simultaneously existing qualities, such as intelligence, will, feeling of fatigue, sensation of black, perception of typewriter, and so on. Although psychologists analyze the self, in order to understand a mind or self it must be taken as an organic whole, as an active center of an environment with purposes and causal series radiating from it. The person must be understood organically, by a kind of Bergsonian intuition, as a being that exerts causal

---

[20]This will be discussed at greater length in Chapter 9.

influences and suffers change, yet teleologically perseveres through the changes and preserves itself.

When positivistic scientists speak of objects, they use substance and causality in the restricted senses established by Locke and Hume. If one develops a metaphysics on the basis of these concepts, the metaphysical view is mechanistic. But when the panpsychist speaks of objects, he attributes to them a self-like character for the sake of rendering the facts of science compatible with the rest of this experience.

It is the belief of many panpsychists, moreover, that the development of organismic or holistic theories of the living organism (see p. 256) is in part a scientific vindication of their daring speculation. Most scientists who accept the doctrine of organicism believe that mind is an emergent level based upon the nonmental conditions of matter, but the panpsychist believes that minds or selves are not "late arrivals" in the evolution of the universe but that mind is present throughout. Only after highly integrated organisms with delicately adaptive nervous systems evolved, however, do we find the distinctive traits of mind as we know it.

The Human Person

Mind as it appears on the human level is characterized by the unity-in-variety of its structure, its temporal transcendence, and its appreciation of ideal values. Unity-in-variety means that in mind as we know it, there is an organic interrelation among the parts. The whole is what it is because of the parts, but parts are in turn affected by the whole in which they function. To analyze the mind by removing some part or aspect from the whole and attending to it as if it were an independent thing is not only to deny the integrity of mind but to change the qualities of the parts themselves. This has been discovered empirically in psychology, and many experimentalists in psychology now insist upon taking the organism or the personality as a whole, not as a sum of isolable parts.[21]

Temporal transcendence is the character of mind or of our experience by virtue of which mind is not tied down to its momentary causal reactions to immediately present stimuli. Our consciousness, limited in its existence to the specious present of a few seconds, scans the universe and thinks at one moment of prehistoric days and at the next of tomorrow's breakfast.

> We look before and after,
> And pine for what is not.

Because our consciousness transcends the physiological conditions that vary from moment to moment and integrates our experience from moment to moment, we are able to learn from the past and to plan intelligently for the

---

[21]For the most comprehensive scientific study of this, see William Stern, *General Psychology from the Personalistic Standpoint* (New York: The Macmillan Company, 1938).

future. We not only experience the pushes and pulls of the physical environment, but we can act intelligently upon it. We can transcend the environment itself with all its constraints, and exercise our freedom from its importunities by framing and pursuing ideal values.

The personal idealists call a self or mind that can do this a *person*. Persons are pursuers of ideal values and are themselves objective and ultimate values in the universe. Because they are of infinite value in a teleological universe, which the personal idealist believes is friendly to values, most personal idealists believe in the immortality of persons.

Human and Divine Persons

That which supports the values of the person is not the world of nature. Most personal idealists postulate a higher person than the human as the creator of the world and as the objective support of the highest human purposes. Personal idealists generally take one of three views concerning the relationships that exist among the selves that comprise the universe; the first is very uncommon among them, and most personal idealists accept either the second or the third hypothesis.

Atheistic pluralism—This view, held by McTaggart, is that the universe is a "society of persons" integrated by their relationships but not united into or under a "cosmic personality." McTaggart argued for this view in many extremely subtle ways, but the most obvious ground for his conclusion is the difficulty of conceiving the possibility that one person can be a part of another person, even God. But his argument is so difficult that it cannot be pursued here.

Pluralism combined with theism—This is the answer given by James Ward. A plurality of self-acting minds of "monads" is ontologically incomplete; the unity and regularity of a pluralistically conceived universe is a fact that metaphysics should explain. Furthermore, in a world that is radically pluralistic, there is no ground for the unification of actions and faith in the attainment of this unification, which is a part of our highest moral goal. Hence, for both theoretical and pragmatic or moral reasons (the latter resembling those of Kant [see pp. 384ff.]), Ward was led to "a more fundamental standpoint than [that] of the Many, namely, that of the One that would furnish an ontological unity for their cosmological unity[22] and ensure a teleological unity for their varied ends."[23] This One is God who is immanent in the world yet transcends it. He is not an Absolute, for an Absolute is incompatible with the reality and personality of the individual, which is the most certain fact of all. Ward cannot make clear the exact nature of the relationship between God and man, because it is unlike any that we can experience. But, he says,

---

[22]That is, a metaphysical explanation of the uniformity and unity of nature.

[23]James Ward, *The Realm of Ends or Pluralism and Theism* (Cambridge, Eng.: University Press, 1911), p. 442.

God is "a living God with a living world, not a potter God with a world of illusory clay."[24]

Theistic finitism—This theory, which has been developed chiefly by Brightman, takes the view of Plato and Mill (see pp. 380f.) that God is finite and combines it with personal idealism. Brightman says:

A theistic finitist is one who holds that the eternal will of God faces given conditions which that will did not create . . . . If these conditions . . . are within the divine personality, then the position is a variety of idealistic personalism.[25]

Brightman, as we have seen, sometimes expounds what seems to be a neo-Berkeleian theory of the external world; for Brightman what limits God's will is "the eternal brute facts of [God's] experience."[26] But a more serious ground for attributing finitude of power to God is human personality itself, its freedom, and its irreducible status. Man, says Brightman, "cannot be thought of as a part of God, nor as a rearrangement of matter. . . ."[27] He concludes that God created persons and thereby limited himself. In one sense, God is infinite because there is nothing wholly outside the universe of His creation that limits Him, and He is infinite in value and in His support of human valuations. But in another sense, He is limited by the world of free persons that He created and supports.

CONCLUSIONS

Not only is Berkeleian idealism essential to understanding later developments within realism, which is in large part a reaction against it, but it is pivotal in the development of the idealist tradition itself. Just as the realist tradition eventually swung back to the essentials of the traditional realism of Descartes and Locke, so idealism—following the prosecution of this philosophy to its limits in absolute idealism—returned, with modifications, to the general standpoint of Berkeleian idealism and its recognition of a plurality of individual minds.

The absolute idealist so transfigures the problem of the external world that it ceases to be a problem; he denies the very assumptions necessary to formulating it. However, he follows this through by presenting a metaphysical theory of such proportions that individuality becomes lost in the Absolute. Acceptance of this notion of an absolute experience that is not *anyone's* experience was too high a price for many idealists to pay for a solution to the problem; hence they returned to the Berkeleian conception of

[24]*Ibid.*, p. 444.
[25]Edgar S. Brightman, *A Philosophy of Religion* (Englewood Cliffs, N.J.: Prentice-Hall, Inc., 1945), pp. 313–14. Ward's God is similarly limited.
[26]*Ibid.*, p. 321.
[27]*Ibid.*, p. 333.

ontological plurality. But this, too, was at a cost, for this approach is attended by the same difficulty as Berkeley's—that it must confront the implications of the egocentric predicament. Moreover, it must also meet the objection (brought against Berkeley by the absolute idealist) that although it is an idealistic theory about material objects, it is a realistic theory about minds and (in some of its forms) about God. The problem for it is not how we know that there is an external world of material objects but how we know that there is an external world of individual minds like ourselves. The main problem for both Berkeley and the pluralistic idealist is how to combine epistemological idealism about the material world with realism about minds; for, as the skeptic will be quick to point out, many of the same arguments *against* realism about the material world (for example with regard to verifying a causal connection between ideas and things) can be used against the proposals *for* realism about minds. If, as Brightman argues, the hypothesis that our ideas are caused by a reality independent of the obsever is more plausible than the solipsist's hypothesis, the realist may demand to know why this hypothesis requires that these independent realities be other minds rather than material objects. The pluralist is thus open to attack from both the skeptic and the realist.

It appears that of the later idealists, the absolute idealist presents the most challenging and original proposals concerning the problem of the external world. The main question is whether his metaphysical views, which provide the foundation for his handling of the epistemological problem, can be sustained. Most contemporary philosophers say they cannot.

BIBLIOGRAPHY

General Works

Barrett, Clifford, ed., *Contemporary Idealism in America*. New York: The Macmillan Company, 1932.

Cunningham, G. Watts, *The Idealistic Argument in Recent British and American Philosophy*. New York: Appleton-Century-Crofts, 1933.

Ewing, A. C., *Idealism: A Critical Survey*. New York: The Humanities Press, 1950.

———, ed., *The Idealist Tradition: From Berkeley to Blanshard*. Glencoe, Ill.: The Free Press, 1957.

Harris, Errol E., *Nature, Mind, and Modern Science*. New York: The Macmillan Company, 1954.

Hoernlé, R. F. Alfred, *Idealism as a Philosophy*. New York: George H. Doran Company, 1927.

Muirhead, J. H., *The Platonic Tradition in Anglo-Saxon Philosophy*. New York: The Macmillan Company, 1931.

Robinson, D. S., ed., *Anthology of Recent Philosophy*, Part 2. New York: Thomas Y. Crowell Company, 1929.

Royce, Josiah, *The Spirit of Modern Philosophy*. Boston: Houghton Mifflin Company, 1892.

Absolute Idealism

Blanshard, Brand, *The Nature of Thought.* London: George Allen & Unwin, Ltd., 1939.

Bradley, F. H., *Appearance and Reality* (2nd ed.). New York: The Macmillan Company, 1902.

Findlay, J. N., *Hegel. A Re-Examination.* New York: The Macmillan Company, 1958, 1962.

Hegel, G. W. F., *Hegel Selections*, ed., J. Loewenberg. New York: Charles Scribner's Sons, 1929.

Morris, C. R., *Idealistic Logic.* London: Macmillan and Company, Ltd., 1933.

Royce, Josiah, *The World and the Individual*, I and II. New York: Dover Publications, Inc., 1959.

———, *The Religious Aspect of Philosophy.* New York: Harper Torchbook, 1958.

Schopenhauer, Arthur, *Schopenhauer Selections*, ed., D. H. Parker. New York: Charles Scribner's Sons, 1928.

Walsh, W. H., *Metaphysics.* London: Hutchinson University Library, 1963.

Pluralistic Idealism

Bertocci, Peter A., "Brightman's View of the Self, the Person, and the Body," *Philosophical Forum* (Boston University), VIII, (1950), 21–28.

Flewelling, R. T., *Personalism and the Problems of Philosophy.* New York: Methodist Book Concern, 1915.

Knudson, Albert C., *The Philosophy of Personalism.* New York: Abingdon Press, 1927.

Wahl, Jean, *The Pluralistic Philosophers of England and America.* LaSalle, Ill.: Open Court Publishing Company, 1925.

QUESTIONS FOR REVIEW AND DISCUSSION

1. Evaluate the objection that absolute idealism only puts off and does not avoid the problem of the egocentric predicament; and that by identifying reality with one all-encompassing experience, it is committed to a solipsism "writ large."

2. Compare absolute idealism with the philosophy of Parmenides.

3. In what ways might absolute idealism be considered a suitable metaphysics for a totalitarian ideology? In what ways would it be unsuitable?

4. Evaluate the following criticisms of the coherence theory of truth:

   a. "I know there is a table before me. I do not have to wait for the infinite and unattainable 'totality of experience' before I know it. Hence the coherence theory is wrong."

   b. "What the coherence theory amounts to is this: 'A liar ought to have a good memory.'"

   c. "Coherence is a necessary but not a sufficient condition of truth."

   d. "The idealist assumes that reality is a coherent whole and hence rejects any alleged truth that is not internally and externally coherent. He thereby bases his criterion of truth upon a very shaky metaphysical foundation."

5. Could coherence theory of truth be formulated as a theory and criterion of value?
6. Why do idealists generally insist upon the validity of teleological explanations in science?
7. By what right, if any, is Plato often called an idealist? What are the objections to classifying him in this way?
8. How would an idealist deal with the truths of mathematics and logic? Do they not conflict with his theory of truth?
9. Does the idealist use the word "experience" unambiguously? Or is it a catch-all term that really implies nothing?

7 NEW PERSPECTIVES ON KNOWLEDGE

Although the absolute idealist brought some striking innovations to the philosophical treatment of the problem of the external world, the obstacles to understanding, much less accepting, his metaphysics far outweighed any gains that might be realized. For this reason the idealist's proposals have found little support in recent times. They were rejected, not only on the grounds that they were unacceptable philosophically, but in some cases on the grounds that the very language in which they were couched was meaningless.

This dissatisfaction with absolute idealism was part of a general dissatisfaction with metaphysics, which has been characteristic of a large part of philosophical thinking since the 1930's. We shall, in Chapter 11, cite various grounds upon which metaphysics has been attacked and consider what lines of defense can be made on its behalf. For the moment we shall focus upon just the one underlying the objections of the logical positivists, whose critique of metaphysics is among the most important developments in twentieth-century philosophy. This will set the stage for our discussion of phenomenalism, the final theory to be examined as a possible solution to the problem of the external world.

THE POSITIVIST'S RESTRICTIONS

Positivists argue that all knowledge as it develops tends in the direction of science, which is the perfected stage of knowledge. Metaphysics appears to the positivist to be a stage in the history of thought that we have now transcended. Unlike metaphysics, science, according to this view, has no interest in explaining things; it suffices to describe them. The laws that

152

describe things are only statistical correlations among observed events. The notion of scientific objects, such as atoms, which are commonly thought of as the causes of or realities behind our experiences, is an unfortunate remnant of metaphysical imagery. Value judgments, for the positivist, are expressions of emotive or persuasive meanings and have no cognitive value or truth. The proper attitude to religion, he says, is one of agnosticism or a humanism that emphasizes the human goals previously sought by or disguised in religious activities but now attainable through scientific techniques devoted to human welfare.

Positivism was so named by Auguste Comte in the nineteenth century. But the beliefs, and even the combination of attitudes involved, is much older. Much of it can be found in Protagoras and Hume. But Comte gave it a name and organized its doctrines, which seem negativistic when taken separately, into an affirmative philosophy and program of action. Comte reached his conclusions chiefly from his study of the history of society, science, and technology, but other philosophers after him based their positivism on more strictly epistemological considerations. The leaders of this movement were the Austrian physicist and philosopher Ernst Mach (1838–1916) and the French mathematician and philosopher Henri Poincaré (1854–1912).

About 1920 a group of philosophers in Vienna, known as the "Vienna Circle," revived and brought up to date some of Mach's ideas and put a major emphasis upon the function of language in scientific knowledge. Their school soon scattered throughout the world and became known as "logical positivism," to distinguish it from the earlier positivism of Comte. Although few philosophers today call themselves logical positivists, this movement has been one of the most influential and controversial in twentieth-century philosophy. Whether they have accepted or rejected it, few philosophers have been able to ignore it. We shall first consider its main argument against metaphysics and then examine the theory of phenomenalism as developed by one of its foremost advocates.

Logical positivists say that the proper task of philosophy is the logical analysis of the language we use to record and transmit our knowledge. Philosophy is not concerned with getting facts, for that is the business of science. The proper job of the philosopher is to analyze the methods and the language of the scientists so as to give scientific knowledge a rigorous logical presentation free from the illusions of hidden purposes and alleged, but unknown, realities.

The opposite opinion is that philosophy is the pursuit of synoptic accounts of experience and is thus superior to the departmentalized sciences. The positivist asserts that this view of the task of philosophy has been shown to be unproductive of worthwhile results in the history of philosophy and science. Philosophers have not established any real knowledge. While scientists have been piling up an imposing array of facts and reducing them to simple laws and theories that lead to the discovery of new and useful facts and techniques, philosophers continue to disagree about everything. They still rehash the intellectual fare of ancient Greece, and after 2,400 years, they have not answered the puzzles Socrates put before his disciples. Because philosophy has so notoriously failed to provide any knowledge that is settled and dependable, the positivists think that philosophers, especially in the metaphysical part of their work, have been on the wrong track. They should no longer waste their efforts on trying to get any "speculative" or "synoptic" metaphysical knowledge.

The proper function of philosophy is critical, not speculative.

I believe Science should be defined as the *pursuit of truth*, and Philosophy as the *pursuit of meaning*. . . . It is my opinion that the future of philosophy hinges on this distinction between the discovery of sense and the discovery of truth.[1]

What, then, is "sense" or "meaning," which the philosopher should discover in the statements that scientists make and claim to be true? The positivist's answer to this question is known as the "verification theory of meaning." It is formulated by Schlick:

We know the meaning of a proposition when we are able to indicate exactly the circumstances under which it would be true (or, what amounts to the same thing, the circumstances which would make it false).[2]

The meaning of a proposition is what would be observed if the proposition is true, or what we should expect to observe but fail to observe if the proposition is thought to be true but is actually false. Consider an illustration. There is a proposition in chemistry, "The valence of oxygen is two." What does it mean? We do not see an oxygen atom with anything like two little hooks on its side that grasp other atoms, although some times such a picture as this is used in introductory courses in chemistry. We do not see the outer shell of electrons with its unoccupied positions said by some chemists to "explain" the valence of oxygen. The positivist wants to banish the assumption that such hypothetical, unobservable objects exist as causes of what we observe, even though most positivists will grant that they may be useful fictions in making predictions. What we *do* see, and what the statement *really* means, is a particular quantitative relationship that can be observed and measured in chemical reactions between fairly large volumes

[1]Moritz Schlick, "The Future of Philosophy," in *The University of the Pacific Philosophy Institute Publications in Philosophy* (1932), 54.

[2]*Ibid.*, p. 55.

of oxygen and other elements. The proposition means: A given volume of oxygen will combine with twice its volume of hydrogen. This is what we expect to observe if the proposition, "The valence of oxygen is two," is true.

Consider another example from the biological sciences. "Cancer is caused by a germ." What does it mean? It means what the bacteriologist would observe if the proposition is true, namely, that every cancer would contain some germ. But the observation is not made; therefore the proposition is false, although it does have a meaning.

Now take a third example from traditional metaphysics: "The human will is free." What does it mean? We cannot point out any specific experience that we should have if the proposition is true and that we should not have if it is false. How can we test it? We should have to predict how a person would behave if he did have a free will, and this behavior would have to be recognizably different from the way we should expect him to behave if he did not have a free will. But if we say, "He will behave so and so, under the supposition that he has a free will," we are saying: (1) We know that no amount of knowledge that we could get would suffice to predict his action on the basis of his past history, his nervous system, and the like; and (2) the proposition that he has a free will implies that he will behave in this specific way. The facts of the case, however, are that we know neither 1 nor 2, and 2 seems to be inconsistent with what we ordinarily mean by saying that the will is free—*not* determined. There is therefore no way to test this proposition; it is not false but meaningless.

The so-called problems of the existence of God, the immortality of the soul, the objectivity of value, the "real existence" of scientific objects that are not observed (for example, electrons), the purpose of the universe, the reality of universals, and the like—all traditional problems of metaphysics— are similarly shown to be meaningless. *Any* proposed answers to them are meaningless. They are "nonsense" because they have no counterpart or verification in sense experience. Many questions, such as, "Are values objective or subjective?" *look* like questions, but they are only pseudo-problems and cannot be answered because they have no meaning. They are logically like the question, "Are circles angelic or diabolical?" which does not even *seem* to make sense.

The proper purpose of philosophy is to uncover and expose these pseudo-problems that have troubled philosophers. One positivist has said, "Philosophy is the disease of which it ought to be the cure." If we find that some traditional problem of philosophy is a real problem, it can be turned over to the scientist for solution; if we find that it is not a real problem, it can be handed over to poets and dreamers to whom it may afford "matter for that reverie which is the most delicious pleasure with which man can beguile his idleness."

Thus the fate of all "philosophical problems" is this: Some of them will disappear by being shown to be mistakes and misunderstandings about our language, and the others will be found to be ordinary scientific questions in disguise. These remarks, I think, determine the whole future of philosophy.[3]

The Synthetic A Priori

Let us now examine more closely how these criticisms bear upon the problem we have been discussing. We may do this by noting that although the logical positivist rejects all of the propositions of metaphysics, he does not examine each one, or even a great many of them, individually and try to show that it is meaningless; rather, he argues that there is a certain type of proposition that is *always* meaningless and that metaphysical propositions are of this type. In order to clarify this, some technical distinctions among different types of propositions must be made. In conjunction with earlier distinctions these will enable us to appreciate the force of the positivist's critique.

We distinguished *empirical* from *a priori* propositions—the former being those whose truth or falsity can be ascertained only by experience, the latter being those whose truth or falsity may be ascertained independently of experience. Consider, for example, the following:

1. It is raining outside.
2. All bachelors are unmarried.

The first obviously requires some appeal to experience to determine its truth or falsity, but the second requires only that we understand the meanings of the terms involved. By definition a bachelor is unmarried, hence it would be pointless to try to test the truth of 2 by taking a survey of bachelors to see whether they are all unmarried. No one would qualify as a bachelor in the first place unless he were unmarried. Knowing this, we know a priori that 2 is true.

Notice furthermore that there are two other interesting properties of 1 and 2: To deny 2 would be self-contradictory, but to deny 1 would not. If someone denies that it is raining outside, even if his statement is false it is not self-contradictory. All self-contradictory statements are false, but not vice versa. Consider, on the other hand, the statement,

3. Some bachelors are unmarried.

which is a denial of 2. Anyone who asserts this is denying in the predicate precisely what he has (if only implicitly) asserted in the subject; it is to assert "Bachelors are not bachelors."

Let us call propositions like 2, the denials of which are self-contradictory,

[3]*Ibid.*, p. 60.

analytic propositions, and propositions like 1, the denials of which are not self-contradictory (and which are not themselves self-contradictory) *synthetic* propositions.[4] This gives us the following three categories.

I.	ANALYTIC:	a. A man is a man.
		b. A triangle has 3 sides.
		c. Every effect has a cause.
		d. A quadruped has 4 legs.
		e. What is red is colored.
II.	SELF-CON- TRADICTORY:	(the denials of each of the above)
III.	SYNTHETIC:	a. Children like candy.
		b. All swans are black.
		c. Horses are herbivorous.
		d. Cats bark.
		e. Water boils at 212°.

Returning now to our other set of distinctions, we can see that the propositions in categories I and II are a priori. That each of the analytic propositions is true and each of the self-contradictory propositions false is evident simply from an understanding of the concepts they contain. The conditions making a proposition analytic or self-contradictory suffice to make it also a priori.

Each of the propositions in category III is empirical. Some of them are true and some are false; their being synthetic does not foreclose either possibility. But *whether* they are true or false can be determined only by appeal to experience. Combining these various distinctions, we get the following schematic cross-classification of these categories:

	Empirical	A priori
Analytic	✕✕	I
Self-contradictory	✕✕	II
Synthetic	III	

[4]We are mainly concerned here with propositions of subject-predicate form. Although many propositions are not of this form, being compounded of one or more simpler statements, similar distinctions may be made among them. A proposition like "Either it is raining or it is not raining," for example, although not of subject-predicate form is such that its denial would be self-contradictory. Propositions of this sort are called *tautologies*. Their truth is guaranteed, not by the meanings of their subjects and predicates, but by virtue of their form. Any "either-or" proposition containing exclusive alternatives must be true. Similarly, there are statements compounded of other statements that are self-contradictory and some that are neither self-contradictory nor tautologous. There is little disagreement among philosophers about the analysis of tautologous and self-contradictory statements of this latter type because their truth or falsity can be demonstrated by accepted logical techniques. But there is controversy about the proper analysis of analytic and synthetic statements (or even whether such a distinction can or should be sharply made). We shall have to bypass the subtleties of that controversy and will adopt the above definitions for our purposes.

This conspicuously leaves vacant the category of the synthetic a priori. Are there any such propositions? Some of the most controversial problems in the history of philosophy hinge upon the answer to this question. Indeed, the whole issue between rationalism and empiricism can be framed in terms of it. How?

In addition to being a priori, each proposition in categories I and II deals with conceptual knowledge, that is, knowledge about the meanings and interrelations among concepts. Each of the synthetic propositions, on the other hand, purports to convey factual knowledge of things, events, or states of affairs. But the latter are all empirical propositions. Now the issue between the empiricist and the rationalist, we recall, is whether any factual knowledge is a priori (they are agreed, for the most part, that conceptual knowledge is a priori). Because factual knowledge will be conveyed by synthetic propositions, the issue between them, in linguistic terms, concerns whether there are any synthetic propositions that are known a priori—whether there are any synthetic a priori propositions. The rationalist affirms and the empiricist denies that there are any such propositions.

Among the propositions that either have been, or might be, thought to be synthetic a priori are many from mathematics, metaphysics, religion, and ethics. The following are a few examples:

IV.   SYNTHETIC
      A PRIORI: a. $7 + 5 = 12$.
               b. Every event has a cause.
               c. Pleasure is intrinsically good.
               d. One ought to keep promises.
               e. God exists.

These obviously are not self-contradictory, but it has seemed to many that they are not analytic[5] either and hence that they must be synthetic. Moreover, they do not in any obvious ways require or permit empirical test to determine their truth or falsity,[6] and for this reason it has sometimes been concluded that they must also be a priori.

Now, the logical positivist claims that the only meaningful propositions are those that are either analytic, self-contradictory, or empirical. He does not deny that there are a priori propositions, but he insists that they are all either analytic or self-contradictory. If any proposition is alleged to be both synthetic and a priori, then—because there will be no specifiable observa-

---

[5]Some of them, that is, (a), (d), and (e), have sometimes been thought to be analytic.

[6]There are, however, differences among them on this score. One can certainly test (a) by empirical means, simply by putting together 7 apples and 5 apples and counting up to see if they make 12; but such a procedure, although sufficient to warrant the conclusion, does not seem necessary. We can, for example, ascertain that 7,000,000 plus 5,000,000 equals 12,000,000 without putting together that many objects and counting them up. On the other hand, it is not clear that there are any adequate empirical tests of the truth or falsity of propositions like (d) and (e).

tions expected if it is true—the proposition will be meaningless by the verification criterion. However much they may call up associations or stir the emotions, according to the positivist, synthetic a priori propositions have no literal meaning.

This, he says, is the case with the propositions of metaphysics. They look like other propositions and can easily be mistaken to be significant, but upon closer examination they turn out senseless. The problem with metaphysics is not simply that this or that system happens to be inadequate. It is worse than that. For in order to be true *or* false a proposition must first have meaning, and the propositions of metaphysics fail to meet even this minimal condition.

It is clear why the positivists and their followers rejected the absolute idealist's metaphysics. Citing such statements of the idealist's as "the Absolute enters into, but is itself incapable of, evolution and progress," or "Reality is one system which contains in itself all experience, and . . . itself is experience,"[7] he charges that the idealist is speaking nonsense; such statements are incapable of empirical verification. And if the idealist's metaphysics cannot endure, then the epistemological proposals founded upon it cannot be accepted either.

It is, of course, not only the absolute idealist who is affected by the positivist's attack. Nearly all those philosophers discussed thus far, particularly Plato, Descartes, and Berkeley, subscribe to some metaphysical views about reality or God that turn out to be meaningless by the positivist's criterion.[8] Indeed, if what we said about the egocentric predicament is correct, then according to the positivist the whole dispute between epistemological idealism and realism is a pseudo-dispute, because the basic assertions of neither theory are capable of verification.

If such a view is correct, then what alternatives are left open? One is the theory called phenomenalism. One does not have to be a logical positivist to subscribe to this theory, but one of its most vigorous defenders, A. J. Ayer, was a positivist. It is a statement of his theory that we will discuss.

THE PHENOMENALIST'S RESTRICTIONS

This theory has much in common with Berkeley's epistemological idealism; in fact, it may be regarded as a linguistic refinement of that position without

[7]The first statement is quoted by A. J. Ayer in *Language, Truth and Logic* (New York: Dover Publications, Inc., 1946), p. 36, and said to be "a remark taken at random" from F. H. Bradley, *Appearance and Reality* (Oxford: Clarendon Press, 1959), p. 475.

[8]Not that Berkeley, as an empiricist, would have subscribed to the doctrine of synthetic a priori propositions. Although the positivist argues that all allegedly synthetic a priori propositions are meaningless, he need not say that *only* such propositions are meaningless. There might, for example, be theological propositions that are thought to be empirical but that in fact (according to the positivist) are meaningless.

the metaphysics. Yet, it differs in some important respects from Berkeley's position.

The phenomenalist agrees with Berkeley that sense contents do not exist unperceived; that is, he takes the thesis "to be is to be perceived" to be correct with respect to the immediate data of perception. He further agrees that material things are constituted by sense data. But then he departs from Berkeley and agrees with the realist that material things *do* exist unperceived.[9] These contentions seem prima facie to be incompatible. If sense data do not exist unperceived and physical objects are constituted out of sense data, how can the *latter* exist unperceived? The answer to this, according to Ayer, lies in a proper understanding of the relationship between sense data and objects. It is here, he believes, that Berkeley was wrong.

If a material thing were really the sum of its "sensible qualities"—that is to say, an aggregate of sense-contents, or even a whole composed of sense-contents—then it would follow from the definitions of a material thing and a sense-content that no thing could exist unperceived.[10]

But, according to Ayer, there is another important sense in which objects may be said to be constituted out of sense data, which does not require saying that they are composed of them. They may be regarded as *logical constructions* out of sense data.

The concept of "logical construction" was introduced into philosophy by Bertrand Russell. It is an important concept having far wider application than merely to the problem now before us. For example, the average man is a logical construction; he is not an individual man who can be found by the census to be a member of the population along with Tom, Dick, and Harry. In the sense in which they exist, the average man does not exist, but he is a logical construction from our observations of individual Toms, Dicks, and Harrys. If we know enough about each actual man, we can describe the average man, and this construction may be very useful in organizing our knowledge about particular men. The statement "The average man weighs 150 pounds" is implied by the statements of the weight of each man, but whereas we can weigh and observe each man, we cannot weigh and observe the average man.

The theory that material things are logical constructions from sense data but do not *consist* of them is somewhat analogous. To show this, it will be helpful to distinguish two different classes of propositions: One consists of statements about things, persons, and events in daily life, and the other consists of statements about the immediate data of our sense experience— the sights, sounds, smells, and so forth, of which we are directly aware. The former may be called *physical object statements*, the latter *sense data statements*.

---

[9]See Ayer, *Language, Truth and Logic*, pp. 140f. Quoted by permission of Dover Publications, Inc.

[10]*Ibid.*, p. 140.

Now to say that physical objects are logical constructions out of sense data is, for Ayer, to say that statements about such objects are translatable into sense data statements. To speak of a table as a logical construction, for example, is to say that

... the symbol "table" is definable in terms of certain symbols which stand for sense-contents. . . . And this . . . is tantamount to saying that sentences which contain the symbol "table," . . . can all be translated into sentences of the same language which do not contain that symbol, nor any of its synonyms, but do contain certain symbols which stand for sense-contents; a fact which may be loosely expressed by saying that to say anything about a table is always to say something about sense-contents.[11]

Moreover,

The problem of giving an actual rule for translating sentences about a material thing into sentences about sense-contents, which may be called the problem of the "reduction" of material things to sense-contents, is the main philosophical part of the traditional problem of perception. . . . The question, "What is the nature of a material thing?" is, like any other question of that form, a linguistic question, being a demand for a definition.[12]

Thus the phenomenalist shifts the whole problem of the external world to a linguistic level. It is no longer the problem of showing the relationship between ideas and objects or a knower and the known, but a problem of exhibiting the logical relationships among different types of propositions.

This provides a clue to how the phenomenalist reconciles the claims that although physical objects are constituted by sense data, they nonetheless can exist unperceived. Sentences about unperceived objects can be analyzed into hypothetical sentences about what *would* be perceived if certain conditions were fulfilled. In other words, the "elements" in the construct "material things" are both *actual* and *possible* sense data. That is, physical object statements will be analyzed into sense data statements of two kinds: categorical statements reporting the actual occurrence of sense data, and hypothetical statements asserting that certain sense data would occur if the appropriate conditions were fulfilled.

If, for example, I say that the table in the next room is brown, this does not imply that I am now experiencing any sensations of brownness. Therefore, if this statement is to be analyzed into sense data statements, they must be of a hypothetical nature, such as that "If I were standing in the next room, looking at the table under normal light, and so on, I would be experiencing sensations of brownness." Although I am not now in the next room, such a statement may be true. Thus, to say that physical objects exist unperceived is to say that true statements can be made about them when

[11]*Ibid.*, p. 64.
[12]*Ibid.*

they are unperceived that are translatable into statements about what a suitably situated observer would perceive under certain conditions.

The phenomenalist believes that this enables him to avoid the absurdity of having to say that things cease to exist when unperceived but to do so without appealing, as Berkeley did, to a divine being. Sufficient linguistic and logical ingenuity, he thinks, can handle the problem of perception without resorting to questionable metaphysical assumptions. Extending this line of thinking to the whole of philosophy leads to the positivist's view that philosophy should consist of logical analysis. It cannot, and should not attempt to, tell us anything about nonempirical states of affairs; hence, it is free of metaphysics. But neither is its job to describe empirical states of affairs; for this reason it does not compete with science. Rather, as Ayer says, "the propositions of philosophy are not factual, but linguistic in character . . . they express definitions, or the formal consequences of definitions. Accordingly, we may say that philosophy is a department of logic." [13]

The phenomenalist is an empiricist, but he feels that the efforts of traditional empiricism are inadequate. Empiricism needs to be reinforced by greater logical rigor and closer attention to the problems of meaning. By attempting to carry out his program of analysis thoroughly, he seeks to avoid the problems of both the idealists and the realists. He rejects the assumption characteristic of much of the controversy about knowledge of the external world that there is an irreducible distinction between subject and object. So far, he agrees with the absolute idealists. But whereas their speculations carry them into an abyss of metaphysics, in which both subject and object are absorbed into one all-embracing experience, the phenomenalist holds fast to the essentials of the concept of experience found in Locke and Berkeley, in which experience is analyzed in terms of discrete sense impressions. He departs from the latter by claiming that *both* subject and object must be analyzed in terms of sense data; there is no spiritual self confronted by subjective ideas and hence no problem of how such a self makes contact with an external world. [14] Moreover, there can be no question of whether the world as a whole is mental or physical (the dispute between materialism and ontological idealism), because the sense data constituting the world are themselves neither mental nor physical. [15] The very distinction between mental and physical applies only to logical constructions. It is misleading even to say that sense data exist; they simply "occur" and must be accepted as given.

However, for all the vigor with which phenomenalists attacked this problem, their efforts encountered serious obstacles, two of them in the form of objections to the alleged reduction of physical objects to sense data.

[13]*Ibid.*, p. 57.
[14]On this point he is in close agreement with the third of the great British empiricists, David Hume. See n. 35, p. 116.
[15]Ayer, *Language, Truth and Logic*, p. 123.

Impossibility of the Phenomenalist Reduction

The first objection is that the phenomenalist's reduction can never be carried out, because to define exhaustively a physical object statement would require an infinite set of sense data statements.

Consider the problems that arise as soon as one attempts to analyze a simple statement about an unperceived object, such as that the table in the next room is brown. Since, by hypothesis, no sense data that can be associated with the table are occurring, the statement will have to be analyzed into hypotheticals. Where A stands for an observer, p_1, p_2, p_3, etc. for different locations, and s_1, s_2, s_3, etc. for numerically distinct sense data, these will be of the form:

1. If A were at p_1 under such and such conditions (referring to both physical and mental states), then he would be experiencing s_1.
2. If A were at p_2 under such and such conditions, then he would be experiencing s_2.
3. If A were at p_3 under such and such conditions, then he would be experiencing s_3.

But if we are to have an exhaustive analysis of the original statement, we shall have to specify a sense data statement for each of an infinite number of possible visual experiences that an observer would have under appropriate conditions, and this is impossible to do. And this is not all. The above examples are stated in such a way as to make reference to an observer, specific locations, and specific conditions. This means that in order to carry-out the reduction thoroughly one must also eliminate these in favor of sense data statements. This will require that A and the expressions referring to locations and conditions in turn be translated into sense data statements. The complications here become enormous. How, for example, can one analyze A's being at p_1 without reference to other things and locations in relation to which p_1 can be understood, and without reference to other possible observers whose presence is required for the occurrence of their sense data? And once these are specified, they, too, will have to be eliminated in favor of sense data statements. Such an analysis is impossible. The analysis cannot even be begun without employing the very physical object language that the analysis proposes to eliminate.[16]

The Open Texture of Empirical Concepts

A second objection says that phenomenalism presupposes that empirical concepts are, in principle, completely definable, but in fact, most of them

---

[16]There are also more technical objections, which we cannot go into, concerning the analysis and logical status of the hypothetical required for the translation. These stem from the fact that if the hypotheticals are in the subjunctive, as they are in our examples and as it seems some of them must be in order to account for statements about the distant past or about things that may never be observed, they are incapable of interpretation in the manner of the "if-then" statements typically used in logic.

are not. They are open-textured in such a way that there is always an element of uncertainty about their application.

Suppose I have to verify a statement such as "There is a cat next door"; suppose I go over to the next room, open the door, look into it and actually see a cat. Is this enough to prove my statement? Or must I, in addition to it, touch the cat, pat him and induce him to purr? And supposing that I had done all these things, can I then be absolutely certain that my statement was true? Instantly we come up against the well-known battery of sceptical arguments mustered since ancient times. What, for instance, should I say when that creature later on grew to a gigantic size? Or if it showed some queer behaviour usually not to be found with cats, say, if, under certain conditions, it could be revived from death whereas normal cats could not? Shall I, in such a case, say that a new species has come into being? Or that it was a cat with extraordinary properties? Again, suppose I say "There is my friend over there." What if on drawing closer in order to shake hands with him he suddenly disappeared? "Therefore it was not my friend but some delusion or other." But suppose a few seconds later I saw him again, could grasp his hand, etc. What then? "Therefore my friend was nevertheless there and his disappearance was some delusion or other." But imagine after awhile he disappeared again, or seemed to disappear—what shall I say now? Have we rules ready for all imaginable possibilities?[17]

Thus, this critic concludes, the phenomenalist translation

... would be possible only if the terms of a material object statement were completely definable. For only then could we describe completely all the possible evidences which would make the statement true or false. As this condition is not fulfilled, the programme of phenomenalism falls flat, and in consequence the attempts at analysing chairs and tables into patterns of sense-data—which has become something of a national sport in this country [England]—are doomed to fail.[18]

In short, according to this view the phenomenalist has overlooked an important feature of the very concepts contained in the statements he sets about to analyze. When this is taken account of, it reveals the impossibility of such an analysis ever successfully being carried out. Thus, for all of its sophistication, phenomenalism has, in the eyes of many philosophers, met with no more success in trying to solve this problem than traditional theories have.

NEW BEARINGS IN PHILOSOPHIC INQUIRY

Although phenomenalism modifies significantly some of the assumptions underlying the traditional approaches to the problem of the external world, it still takes the problem seriously and attempts to find a solution to it. In

---

[17]Friedrich Waismann, "Verifiability," in *Logic and Language* (1st series), ed., A. G. N. Flew (Oxford: Basil Blackwell, 1955), p. 119. Quoted by permission of Basil Blackwell.
[18]*Ibid.*, p. 121.

two other twentieth-century developments in philosophy—pragmatism and what has come to be called "linguistic analysis"—the problem is approached in such a way that its basic assumptions and the very foundations of traditional epistemology are challenged.

One of the leading American pragmatists, John Dewey, analyzes the whole tradition of philosophical speculation from the time of ancient Greece to the present in the attempt to explain how some of these mistaken assumptions arose. As we shall see, he urges a departure from this tradition and a "reconstruction" of philosophy as a whole. Two of the leading linguistic analysts of recent years, Gilbert Ryle and John Austin, although they are not particularly influenced by pragmatism, proceed in a manner that complements the work of Dewey. Unlike Dewey, however, they do not undertake quasi-sociological and historical analyses to support their views; rather, they argue that the basic confusions embodied in the problem of the external world derive from philosophers being misled by language. They hold that a scrupulous examination of the proper uses of the various concepts that enter into the formulation of the problem will dispel these confusions and show the problem to be pseudo. We shall first present Dewey's general thesis with some specific criticisms he makes of traditional attempts to solve the problem.

Dewey's Reconstruction in Philosophy

Dewey claims that the misguided attempt to solve the problem of the external world is symptomatic of the mistaken direction that philosophy as a whole acquired in its very beginnings in Western civilization. The problem can be traced to a time in ancient Greece when the rapidly developing body of factual knowledge began to pose a threat to the customs, values, and traditions revered from previous eras. Because the latter lacked the foundation to withstand a decisive clash with the rising scientific knowledge, there developed the dilemma of how to preserve the essentials of these traditional beliefs and at the same time reconcile them with the claims of science.

Speculative philosophy provided the answer. In this way reason was able to rationalize and sanctify what was cherished from the past. It did so by locating it in a realm apart from the factual world of science. Reality thus became partitioned into two separate domains: the absolute and transcendent realm of Forms that we found in Plato, and the immediate, physical, and "less real" world inhabited by man. Because the former constituted a special subject-matter removed from everyday affairs, it, accordingly, required a higher form of knowledge by which to apprehend it; worldly knowledge, mere belief or opinion, was thought suited to little more than meeting commonplace practical needs. Hence a division developed between theory and practice, with the latter relegated to a position of inferiority. No sooner had this speculative philosophy become fledged than it soared high beyond the reach of practical concerns in search of the True, the Beautiful, and the Good.

The distinctive traits of philosophy were determined by the nature of the task to which it was committed: "Reason was to take the place of custom as a guide of life; but it was to furnish rules as final, as unalterable as those of custom."[19] Beliefs previously sanctioned only by custom were to be renovated by the "apparatus of reason and proof." Thus "abstract definition" and "ultra-scientific argumentation" became philosophy's bylaws, as it "bound the once erect form of human endeavor and progress to the chariot wheels of cosmology and theology."[20]

Knowledge of the External World: A Pseudo-problem

Among the resultant misconceptions, according to Dewey, was a mistaken view of what is experience. This in turn set the stage for the problem of the external world. This view was that experience is a subjective phenomenon attached to an ego or subject that is isolated from the world, a private surveying of disconnected sense data. The problem unavoidably arises of how an external world can be inferred, or failing that, constructed, out of such experience. The consequence for epistemology is that the problem of knowledge assumes monstrous proportions, while philosophy as a whole becomes ingrown as it busies itself with philosophers' problems to the neglect of the problems of men.

Dewey rejects this view of experience. He claims that man is from the start involved in the world and that experience in its basic sense is interaction with that world. Consciousness attends this transaction between man and his environment, but it is not the whole of it and cannot be set apart from it. This cuts the ground from under not only the empiricism of Locke and Berkeley, but also the phenomenalism of Ayer. Although phenomenalism rejects the notion of a substantial self to which sense data are directly given, it retains the essentials of the traditional conception of experience—it consists of discrete data that Dewey would say are "outside the course of natural existence." A genuinely empiricistic view of experience, he believes, also undercuts rationalism; for "with the downfall of the traditional notion of experience, the appeal to reason to supplement its defects becomes superfluous."[21]

There are, Dewey says, many particular problems of knowledge, but there is no problem of knowledge *in general* that it is the special business of epistemology to solve. Such a belief derives from the assumption "that there is a knower in general, who is outside of the world to be known, and who is defined in terms antithetical to the traits of the world."[22] The whole discipline of epistemology is on the wrong track when it begins, as Plato did,

---

[19]John Dewey, *The Influence of Darwin on Philosophy and Other Essays in Contemporary Thought* (New York: Holt, Rinehart & Winston, Inc., 1910), p. 48.

[20]*Ibid.*, p. 55.

[21]John Dewey, *et al.*, *Creative Intelligence* (New York: Holt, Rinehart & Winston, Inc., 1917), p. 18.

[22]*Ibid.*, p. 33.

with the question "What is knowledge?" and seeks a general formula in answer to it which will unravel all the problems of knowledge. Similarly, he claims, there is no metaphysical problem of the nature of reality in general. Pragmatism, he says,

... finds that "reality" is a *denotative* term, a word used to designate indifferently everything that happens. Lies, dreams, insanities, deceptions, myths, theories are all of them just the events which they specifically are. Pragmatism is content to take its stand with science; for science finds all such events to be subject matter of description and inquiry—just like stars and fossils, mosquitoes and malaria, circulation and vision. It also takes its stand with daily life, which finds that such things really have to be reckoned with as they occur interwoven in the texture of events. [23]

Once this is recognized, Dewey maintains, traditional empiricism will be seen to be operating with an *un*empirical concept of experience.

The doctrine that sensations and ideas are so many separate existences was not derived from observation nor from experiment. It was a logical deduction from a prior unexamined concept of the nature of experience.

The description of experience has been forced into conformity with this prior conception; it has been primarily a deduction from it, actual empirical facts being poured into the moulds of the deductions. The characteristic feature of this prior notion is the assumption that experience centers in, or gathers about, or proceeds from a center or subject which is outside the course of natural existence, and set over against it—it being of no importance, for present purposes, whether this antithetical subject is termed soul, or spirit, or mind, or ego, or consciousness, or just knower or knowing subject. [24]

Rather than wrestle with unanswerable questions of unlimited scope, philosophers should address themselves to specific problems and the contexts in which they occur. Because they have asked the wrong questions and relied upon unscientific methods, they have been led into a wilderness tract of speculation in which they have lost sight entirely of the urgent and practical problems that need solution—the social, political, and educational problems of the day.

The problem of the external world is not solved by this approach. Rather it is dissolved, because each of the assumptions necessary to formulating it has been rejected. There is, according to Dewey, no sharp distinction between knower and known, no self-enclosing experience of fragmentary sights, smells, sounds, and so forth, and no "external world" on the other side of such experiences. Nothing could be more warranted empirically than that there is a world with which we interact; that there should ever have been thought to be a problem about its existence is one of the "curiosities of orthodox empiricism." [25]

[23] *Ibid.*, p. 55.
[24] *Ibid.*, p. 40.
[25] *Ibid.*, p. 36.

Language Analysis

The expression "language analysis" is somewhat misleading, because there is limited agreement among philosophers about what language analysis is or ought to be. However, the expression is descriptively accurate of the approach to philosophy of some British and Americans influenced by the work of Ludwig Wittgenstein (1889–1951), an Austrian philosopher who taught at Cambridge in England. This approach is sometimes called Ordinary Language Philosophy and sometimes, because certain Oxford philosophers have been among its most noted practitioners, Oxford Philosophy or Oxford Analysis.

This emphasis upon language is not new, of course, even in the twentieth century. The logical positivists, for example, focus upon the analysis of meaning as the pivotal problem of philosophy. We earlier quoted Ayer as saying (p. 162) that the propositions of philosophy are themselves linguistic propositions. What, then, is different about the approach of the language analysts?

This is not easily answered, because practitioners of this method do not adhere to any set program nor is there complete agreement among them as to the exact nature and scope of philosophical analysis. But there are two views that bind them together and set them apart from other philosophers who place an equal, although different, emphasis upon language. The first is that ordinary language is all right as it is and does not need—at least for philosophical purposes—to be replaced or reinforced by technical language (such as the phenomenalist's in his distinction between physical object statements and sense data statements and his account of the logical relationship between the two). Second, in varying degrees they share the conviction that many (if not most or even all) philosophical problems are due to confusions about language. What appear to be factual disputes among philosophers are actually conceptual (or loosely, "logical") confusions. Words like "freedom," "cause," "sensation," and so forth are too often wrenched loose from the contexts in which they are normally used, and from which they derive their meaning, and enlisted in the service of quixotic philosophical causes. The result is a distortion of ordinary language, and the penalty is the generation of insoluble pseudo-problems, perplexing only to their creators and those who follow them. The way out of these confusions and the way to avoid them in the first place is to give careful attention to the correct uses of language. The proper business of the philosopher is to elucidate these uses and to expose the artificiality of problems arising from their neglect.[26]

The work of Oxford philosophers Gilbert Ryle and John Austin bears closely upon the problems we have been discussing. The aspects of their

---

[26]This is not, however, regarded by all advocates of this approach as his sole business. In addition to curing the ills of philosophy, it is thought by some that language analysis is a productive way of *doing* philosophy; that it has a constructive as well as a therapeutic value.

work that we will consider deal specifically with phenomenalism and related problems, but much of what they say is relevant to the whole tradition with which we have dealt.

The Mythical Nature of Sense Data

Ryle is in agreement with Dewey that there is no problem of the external world to be solved in the first place. He believes that the problem owes its origin to certain conceptual confusions, the exposure of which causes the problem to disappear. We shall consider one aspect of his wide-ranging discussion that deals with the language of perception. He argues that there are no such things as sense data and that insofar as the problem of the external world presupposes that there are, it is a pseudo-problem. The following are some of his reasons.

1. In Chapter 4 we considered reasons for supposing that we are directly aware only of subjective impressions. This gave rise to the problem of how we could know that objects exist apart from these impressions, from which it appeared that the only way in which the objects of the world could be known is in terms of (whether by inference or some other means) directly experienced sensations.

Ryle claims that this puts "the cart before the horse." We understand and impart information about our sensations only by reference to what we *already* know about objects. To say that something looks like a haystack, for example, is not to report the occurrence in your mind of a private sense datum about which one can sensibly ask whether it is caused by an actually existing haystack.

> When I say that something looks like a haystack, (though it may actually be a blanket on a clothes-line), I am describing how it looks in terms of what anyone might expect a haystack to look like, when observed from a suitable angle, in a suitable light and against a suitable background. . . . We do not and cannot describe haystacks in terms of this or that set of sensations. We describe our sensations by certain sorts of references to observers and things like haystacks.[27]

2. The Sense Datum Theorist might reply by insisting that sensations *must* be private, because only I can witness my pains, itches, tweaks, and so forth, and only you yours. Ryle answers this by saying that although it is true that you cannot witness my sensations, nor I yours, this is not because sensations are inaccessible to anyone but the person who has them; it is because they are neither witnessable nor unwitnessable by *anyone*. To suppose otherwise is to fall into the conceptual confusion of supposing that to have a sensation is to observe something; of supposing, for example, that the sensation one has when looking through the telescope consists of observing

---

[27]Gilbert Ryle, *The Concept of Mind* (London: Hutchinson & Co., Ltd., 1955), pp. 202f. Quoted by permission of the Hutchinson Publishing Group Ltd. and Barnes & Noble.

a tiny patch of light in one's consciousness. If this were the case, no one else could observe precisely what I am observing (that is, the numerically same patch of light); therefore it is easy to conclude that *what* one observes is subjective and private and from this to think of its connection with the external world.

This assimilation of one concept (having a sensation) to another (observing) leads only to absurdities. It makes good sense, Ryle says, to characterize observings as "careful or careless, cursory or sustained, methodical or haphazard, accurate or inaccurate, expert or amateurish," but it makes no sense to say such things of the having of sensations. "It is nonsense to speak of either making or avoiding mistakes in sensation; sensations can be neither correct nor incorrect, veridical nor nonveridical."[28] Again, properties ascribable to the common objects of observation, such as size, shape, position, and so forth, can neither be affirmed nor denied of sensations.

Sensations do not have sizes, shapes, positions, temperatures, colours or smells. In the sense in which there is always an answer to the question, "Where is?" or "Where was the robin?" there is no answer to the question, "Where is?" or "Where was your glimpse of the robin?" There is indeed a sense in which a tickle is quite properly said to be "in my foot," or a stinging "in my nose," but this is a different sense from that in which bones are in my foot, or pepper-grains are in my nose. So in the muddled sense of "world" in which people say that "the outside world" or "the public world" contains robins and cheeses, the locations and connections of which in that world can be found out, there is not another world, or set of worlds, in which the locations and connections of sensations can be found out; nor does the reputed problem exist of finding out what are the connections between the occupants of the public world and those of any such private worlds.[29]

Ryle is not saying simply that it is too difficult to observe sensations or that with suitable scientific advances we might someday be able to do so. He is saying that sensations are not observable *or* unobservable things; indeed, they are not "things" at all. The whole question whether we can observe them is as confused as the question "How do you spell the first letter of 'London'?" "As letters are neither easy to spell, nor insuperably hard to spell," says Ryle, "so, I argue, sensations are neither observable nor unobservable."[30]

3. Third, Ryle argues that observing (in one sense of the word) entails having sensations. I cannot, for example, observe you do something without having at least one visual sensation. Now if having a sensation were to be observing something, then my having this sensation would entail the having of another, and having it would require having still others, and so on ad infinitum. To insist that we observe sensations is to be led to an infinite

[23]*Ibid.*, p. 204.
[29]*Ibid.*, p. 208.
[30]*Ibid.*, p. 206.

regress. This is the same absurdity that Zeno ascribed to the anti-Parmenidean view that there is motion in the world.

A linguistic consequence of all this argument is that we have no employment for such expressions as "object of sense," "sensible object," "sensum," "sense datum," "sense-content," "sense field," and "sensibilia"; the epistemologist's transitive verb "to sense" and his intimidating "direct awareness" and "acquaintance" can be returned to store.[31]

The Two Languages Doctrine

Dewey rejected a large part of traditional philosophy on the grounds that it represented a misconceived "quest for certainty." Austin claims that a similar quest, what he calls the "pursuit of the incorrigible," characterizes phenomenalism. Speaking specifically of Ayer's position as set forth in *The Foundations of Empirical Knowledge*, he says:

> In a nutshell, the doctrine about knowledge, "empirical" knowledge, is that it has *foundations*. It is a structure the upper tiers of which are reached by inferences, and the foundations are the *data* on which these inferences are based. (So of course—as it appears—there just have to be sense-data.) . . . The way to identify the upper tiers of the structure of knowledge is to ask whether one might be mistaken, whether there is something that one *can doubt*; if the answer is Yes, then one is not at the basement. And conversely, it will be characteristic of the *data* that in their case no doubt is possible, no mistake can be made. So to find the data, the foundations, look for *the incorrigible*.[32]

This suggests that, like Descartes, the phenomenalist is searching for basic knowledge that is absolutely certain and that will provide the foundation for all other knowledge. Such knowledge will be expressible in "basic" propositions that are incapable of being doubted; unlike for Descartes, these propositions will be empirical (the phenomenalist, remember, is an empiricist) rather than a priori. According to this view, if what we know must be verifiable and verification eventuates in direct awareness of sense data, then propositions the truth of which we claim to know must either themselves be, or be analyzable into, propositions about sense data. This is what we called the phenomenalist "reduction" of material things to sense data.

However, according to Austin this problem is contrived from the start. The whole question of whether we "perceive material things" departs from the language of the ordinary man, who has, anyway, little occasion to use such expressions as "perceive" and "material thing." The philosopher's use of "directly perceive" is particularly out of focus. Being said to perceive something directly makes sense only by comparison with cases in which we can be said to perceive things *indirectly*; these are special cases, and the con-

---

[31]*Ibid.*, p. 221.

[32]John Austin, *Sense and Sensibilia* (Oxford, Clarendon Press, 1962), p. 105. Quoted by permission of the Clarendon Press.

cept of indirect perception does not even have the same use in all them. For example, one might,

> ... contrast the man who saw the procession directly with the man who saw it *through a periscope*; or we might contrast the place from which you can watch the door directly with the place from which you can see it only *in the mirror*.[33]

But uses like these lend little support to the view that it makes sense to ask whether we always perceive things directly, for their appropriateness depends upon the special and limited contexts in which they occur. Far from it following that we can sensibly speak of perceiving all things directly or indirectly, it is difficult even to extend these special uses of the notion of indirect perception beyond the visual sense.

> The most natural sense of "hearing indirectly," of course, is that of being *told* something by an intermediary—a quite different matter. But do I hear a shout indirectly, when I hear the echo? If I touch you with a barge-pole, do I touch you indirectly? Or if you offer me a pig in a poke, might I feel the pig indirectly—*through* the poke? And what smelling indirectly might be I have simply no idea. For this reason alone there seems to be something badly wrong with the question, "Do we perceive things directly or not?" where perceiving is evidently intended to cover the employment of *any* of the senses.[34]

From these and similar considerations Austin concludes that "the philosophers' use of 'directly perceive,' whatever it may be, is not the ordinary, or any familiar, use; for in *that* use it is not only false but simply absurd to say that such objects as pens or cigarettes are never perceived directly."[35]

Nor will it do, he contends, to appeal to what has come to be known as the "argument from illusion"—the most common example being the partly submerged stick in the water—the view that what we directly perceive must be different from the object seen.

> Well now: does the stick "look bent" to begin with? I think we can agree that it does, we have no better way of describing it. But of course it does *not* look *exactly* like a bent stick, a bent stick out of water—at most, if may be said to look rather like a bent stick partly immersed *in* water. After all, we can't help seeing the water the stick is partly immersed in. So exactly what in this case is supposed to be *delusive*? What is wrong, what is even faintly surprising, in the idea of a stick's being straight but looking bent sometimes? Does anyone suppose that if something is straight, then it jolly well has to *look* straight at all times and in all circumstances?[36]

To introduce sense data to explain such phenomena is a makeshift solution to an artificial problem. The phenomenalist's Two Languages Theory, Austin says, is without foundation. There simply is no class of statements

---

[33]*Ibid.*, p. 15.
[34]*Ibid.*, pp. 16f.
[35]*Ibid.*, p. 19.
[36]*Ibid.*, p. 29.

that are incorrigible in the way that sense data statements are supposed to be, and there is no set of statements to serve as a criterion of evidence for them.

For even if we were to make the very risky and gratuitous assumption that what some particular person knows at some particular place and time could systematically be sorted out into an arrangement of foundations and super-structure, it would be a mistake in principle to suppose that the same thing could be done for knowledge *in general.* And this is because there *could* be no *general* answer to the questions what is evidence for what, what is certain, what is doubtful, what needs or does not need evidence, can or can't be verified. *If the Theory of Knowledge consists in finding grounds for such an answer, there is no such thing.*[37]

SUMMARY AND CONCLUSIONS

In their respective ways, Dewey, Ryle, and Austin each hold that philosophy has misconceived its proper role and asked the wrong questions. It cannot profitably try to answer such general questions as "What is knowledge?" or "What is reality?" It should not, says Austin, even try to give a general answer to questions of such scope as those in the preceding quotation. Dewey, and probably Ryle, would agree that if "the Theory of Knowledge consists in finding grounds for such an answer, there is no such thing." In this way they level as serious a charge against epistemology as has been brought against metaphysics: that of being mistaken in its very conception. Ryle and Austin see the problem as a result of almost unpardonable confusions about language of a sort that only philosophers could have gotten into, and the solution as lying in careful descriptive analysis designed to untangle these confusions. Dewey views the problem in broader historical and sociological perspective, claiming that it arises from the desire to preserve cherished customs and values from the inexorable tide of scientific and technological progress. His solution is to ride with this tide and to establish what is worth salvaging from tradition on a firmer foundation. To do this requires subjecting it to critical scrutiny from the standpoint of a scientific methodology.

Although they are among the latest words, no one of these views is the last word on the problems we have been discussing. Each is controversial and calls for careful evaluation. Their importance lies not only in the soundness or unsoundness of their arguments, but in the fact that they represent further evolution of the notion of philosophic inquiry itself. Indeed, each major development since Plato has embodied some modification of what has been conceived to be the proper method of philosophy. Socrates, Plato, and the absolute idealists believe that the proper vehicle of philosophic inquiry is some form of dialectic. Descartes adopts a procedure of methodological doubt designed to disclose certainties upon which philosophy can

[37]*Ibid.*, p. 124. Final italics ours.

reconstruct knowledge by a deductive method modeled after mathematics; inquiry for Locke and Berkeley is broadly empiricistic, consisting primarily —for Locke in particular—of psychologistic study aimed at establishing the limits of knowledge. Although we said little about the methods of Perry and Santayana, they were both empiricists—Perry placing particular emphasis upon the importance of a scientific orientation in philosophy. Similarly each of the philosophers discussed in this chapter can be characterized broadly as an empiricist, or at least as a nonrationalist; although Dewey, and perhaps Ryle and Austin as well, would probably resist being classified according to a distinction which, in his view, is associated with so many misconceptions. Ayer's specific method is logical analysis (recall his characterization of philosophy as a branch of logic), whereas Ryle's and Austin's is informal linguistic (conceptual or "logical") analysis. Dewey's pragmatic method, finally, which he calls instrumentalism, is an adaptation of the method of science to the handling of philosophical problems.[38]

The differences among these philosophers might tempt one to say that they do not deal with the same problems. It would be more accurate, however, to say that they approach these problems from different perspectives. Where these perspectives are widely discrepant, it would not be inaccurate to say that they represent wholly different conceptual outlooks or hypotheses about the world; the world, at least viewed philosophically, is simply a very different sort of place for Plato than for Dewey, for Locke than for the absolute idealists, for Parmenides than for Ryle.

At this point philosophic inquiry makes contact with science; for there the notion of hypothesis is central. There is perhaps no area of human thought that has been untouched by the rapid development of science during our century. Indeed, much of the philosophy we have considered in this chapter, representing a break from tradition, has been deeply influenced by science. The logical positivists, in their way, sought to make philosophy scientific, and Dewey, among the pragmatists, was especially concerned to adapt the methodology of science to the handling of philosophical problems.

But if it is true, as Whitehead has written, that "Science and Philosophy are merely different aspects of one great enterprise of the human mind,"[39] it is also true that the differences between the two must not be underestimated. One such difference concerns the role of hypothesis in the two disciplines. One major aim in the next section will be to clarify that role is science. In helping us to understand the distinctive method of science, this will enable us to see both the legitimate bearing and also the limitations of scientific method as applied to philosophy. For although philosophy can profit from close examination of the spirit and temper of scientific methodology, particularly in its employment of hypotheses, it cannot be reduced

---

[38]In discussing naturalism in Part Four, we will see in greater detail the application of such an approach (not specifically Dewey's) to a number of philosophical problems.

[39]Alfred North Whitehead, *Adventures of Ideas* (New York: Mentor Books, 1955), p. 143. Quoted by permission of the Macmillan Company.

to science nor can science solve all its problems. Of particular significance, even the most speculative area of philosophy, metaphysics, need not be abandoned (as the logical positivists claimed) in the light of scientific findings. In Chapter 11 we shall present a defense of metaphysics as hypothesis, one that takes account of the major objections that have been brought against it. This will enable us, in Chapters 12 and 13, to approach the metaphysical theory of naturalism from the standpoint of what we have learned about scientific method.

BIBLIOGRAPHY

Austin, John, *Philosophical Papers*, Chaps. 1 and 2, eds., J. O. Urmson and G. J. Warnock. Oxford: Clarendon Press, 1961.

Ayer, A. J., ed., *Logical Positivism*. New York: The Free Press, 1966.

———, *Philosophical Essays*, Essays 4–6. London: Macmillan & Co., Ltd., 1963.

———, The Problem of Knowledge. Baltimore: Penguin Books, Inc., 1956.

Caton, Charles E., ed., *Philosophy and Ordinary Language*. Urbana: University of Illinois Press, 1963.

Dewey, John, *Experience, Nature and Freedom*, ed., Richard J. Bernstein. New York: The Liberal Arts Press, 1960.

———, *The Quest for Certainty*. New York: G. P. Putnam's Sons, 1960.

———, *Reconstruction in Philosophy*. Boston: Beacon Press, 1962.

Flew, A. G. N., ed., *Essays in Conceptual Analysis*. London: Macmillan & Co., Ltd., 1960.

Marhenke, Paul, "Phenomenalism," in *Philosophical Analysis*, ed., Max Black. Englewood Cliffs, N. J.: Prentice-Hall, Inc., 1963.

Paul, G. A., "Is There a Problem About Sense Data?" in *Logic and Language* (1st series), ed., A. G. N. Flew. Oxford: Basil Blackwell, 1955.

Quine, W. V. O., *From a Logical Point of View*, Chap. 2. Cambridge: Harvard University Press, 1953.

Urmson, J. O., *Philosophical Analysis*, Parts II and III. Oxford: Clarendon Press, 1956.

Warnock, G. J., *English Philosophy Since 1900*. Oxford: Oxford University Press, 1958.

QUESTIONS FOR REVIEW AND DISCUSSION

1. Evaluate the following statements:
   a. "Berkeley, because he denied that there is any hidden material substance behind our sense experiences, is a forerunner of positivism with its theory that the laws of nature are only statements about our experience."
   b. "Berkeley's metaphysics must be denied by any positivist, because the basic thesis of his work, 'To be is to be perceived,' has no verifiable consequences and hence is, to a positivist, meaningless."
2. Evaluate the following objection: The logical positivist asserts that the only meaningful statements are those that are either self-contradictory, analytic, or empirical. But the statement of his own criterion of meaning (that a statement is meaningful if and only if it is verifiable) does not fit

into any of these categories. Hence that criterion is either meaningless or (because it itself constitutes an exception to what it asserts) false.

3. Examine the following sentences and say whether they are synthetic, or analytic, empirical or a priori:

   a. A man is a man for all that.

   b. $s = \frac{1}{2}gt^2$.

   c. If today were Tuesday, tomorrow would be Wednesday.

   d. Business is business.

   e. Yellow is a brighter color than blue.

   f. I cannot experience your toothache; I can only experience my own.

   g. Every effect has a cause.

   h. Every event has a cause.

   i. Every means has an end.

   j. For every end, there is a means.

   It is easy to decide some of these; some are more difficult. In every difficult case, put your finger on the precise source of the difficulty.

4. For each of the following propositions,

   a. Every cube is a cube

   b. Every cube is a solid

   c. Every cube has 12 edges

   explain whether, and for what reasons, it is (1) a priori, (2) analytic. Does this shed any light on the problem of whether there are synthetic a priori propositions? Explain.

5. Read Quine's *From a Logical Point of View*, Chapter 2. What is his objection to the distinction between analytic and synthetic propositions? Suppose you decide that no sharp distinction should be drawn between them; would this mean that the positivists' program for philosophers would fall to the ground?

6. Evaluate the following statement. "For the chemist, 'Water is H_2O' is an analytic statement; for his pupil, it is synthetic." If you agree with this, does it follow that the positivists' program for philosophy falls to the ground?

7. Do you think the phenomenalist avoids the egocentric predicament? Why?

8. Evaluate, with respect to Locke and Berkeley, Dewey's claim that traditional empiricists have operated with an *un*empirical conception of experience.

9. In the previous chapter, the question was raised as to whether the absolute idealists used the word "experience" unambiguously. Do you think Dewey uses it with any less vagueness than the idealists did?

10. Would it be an adequate reply to Ryle and Austin if the epistemological dualist said that he is unconcerned with how expressions like "directly perceive," "sensation," and so forth are *ordinarily* used and that he is *proposing* a terminology that will be useful in discussing problems of which the ordinary person is unaware? Why?

11. Compare and contrast the distinctive methods of philosophic inquiry discussed in Chapters 3–7.

PART THREE THE PHILOSOPHICAL BEARINGS OF SCIENCE

The sciences give us what are perhaps our best examples of knowing. The results of scientific inquiry have profoundly affected philosophical views on all subjects. Therefore, we undertake a study of the processes of inquiry in the sciences and then consider broadly philosophical implications of the world view presented by the successes of science in attaining knowledge.

In Chapter 8 we see scientific knowledge as an extension of the kinds of inquiry occasioned in everyday life when some settled mode of action is frustrated so that our past experience must be reorganized in the light of a new hypothesis. An hypothesis is not known to be true either by reason or by experience; it is only a conjecture, which may or may not be confirmed. A good hypothesis is one that can be either confirmed or disconfirmed—tested; but the tests for an hypothesis about nature are never adequate to establish it beyond a shadow of doubt. At most, we are warranted in asserting tentatively the truth of an hypothesis that has passed the rigorous tests prescribed. The reasons for this tentativeness are found to lie in the important concept of a *family of hypotheses* containing *collateral hypotheses* that serve as basic assumptions in every piece of scientific work.

Chapter 9 discusses one of the goals of science and one of the philosophical problems that are implicated by this goal. The aim is: to discover the laws of nature. Various interpretations of what is meant by "laws of nature" (Plato's, Hume's, Kant's) are described. The problem is: Is it possible for man to act freely in a world "governed by laws of nature"? Several theories—hard and soft determinism, fatalism, compatibilism, and incompatibilism—are examined. It is proposed that free action and scientific explanation require different collateral hypotheses that cannot be members of the same family of hypotheses, and that neither can be established to the exclusion of the other.

Another goal of science is to explain things by means of theories. Two kinds of theories are discussed in Chapter 10: theories that deduce one law from others, and theories that explain what is observed in terms of unobservables. Examples of each type of theory are given from physics, and the special kinds of theories, such as mechanistic and teleological theories, that are required in the biological and social sciences are compared with those used in the physical sciences. The philosophical implications of the fact that human behavior may be explained in terms of two general types of theories, event theories and action theories, are examined.

Chapter 11 raises the question: Is all knowledge actually or at least potentially scientific, or can there be metaphysical knowledge? After various objections to metaphysics are expounded and criticized, it is proposed that *metaphysics as hypothesis*—metaphysics that does not claim to be certain but does claim to continue the method of scientific inquiry beyond the point where confirmation or disconfirmation is possible—is an important and legitimate part of philosophic inquiry.

Chapters 12 and 13 discuss metaphysical theories that profess to be based upon both the methods and the results of science. The first is materialism and the especially important theory, dialectical materialism; the second is critical naturalism. Under critical naturalism we examine a theory of knowledge (objective relativism), a theory of the relationship of mind to body (functionalism), and a theory of religion (humanism).

8 THE ROLE OF HYPOTHESES IN INQUIRY

PROBLEM-SOLVING

To see better the part that making and testing hypotheses plays in getting knowledge, we shall being with several examples of how animals and men solve their problems. We shall begin with a cat, then go on to a man in his morning routine, and finally come to the case of a scientist solving a problem in astronomy.

1. A psychologist puts a cat in a puzzle box and latches the door. The cat gives every indication of confusion, helplessness, and anger; she cries, tries to gnaw her way through the bars, and lashes her tail about. After a while, she accidentally touches the latch on the door and the door flies open and releases her.

The next day the psychologist puts her in the box again. Again she lashes about and eventually lets herself out. Gradually, as the experiment is repeated, she makes the right move sooner and sooner, until in a few days she quickly lets herself out without any random motion or wasted activity. We say that she has learned to solve the problem by "trial and error": she tries this, that, and the other activity until finally, after many errors, she finds the right way.

If we like, we may say she now *knows* something, namely, how to get out of this box. But she knows very little; put her in another box with the latch at a different place, and she is as helpless as before and has to learn again by trial and error.

2. A man awakens in the morning and, while still sleepy, carries out a highly intricate bit of behavior without paying any attention to it: he ties his shoelaces. (That *is* an intricate operation, as anyone can see if he tries to explain how it is done to a person who doesn't know.) He is able to do this because he has learned it so well that his fingers do it almost automatically; he has done it so often that it requires no thought.

Now imagine that some morning his shoelace breaks as he is tying it. This disrupts the routine; suddenly all his attention is directed to the operation that, just a moment before, was below the level of consciousness. His habitual behavior is blocked, just as the puzzle box blocks the cat's habitual behavior.

But the hapless man does not behave as the cat does. To be sure, there may be a moment of nonadaptive floundering around; just as the cat lashes her tail in anger, the man may swear. The man, however, does something the cat cannot do: he thinks.[1]

Thinking is a process of learning by trial and error in which the trials and errors are not made in overt bodily behavior but in imagination. The man's thinking takes the form of trying out certain lines of action or plans without openly committing himself to them. Though his thinking may go so rapidly that it is hard to separate it into stages, probably something like this is going through his head: "I can wear that other pair of shoes, but if I do I mustn't wear this suit; perhaps I can tie this broken string, but no, it is too frayed; I believe there is another pair of brown shoes in that closet; perhaps I can take the laces out of it and use them." In a moment he has thought of three lines of action he might take. He has found out where two of them would lead if he actually followed them (changing his suit, risking another break). He sees nothing against the third, so he overtly acts upon it.

He has solved his problem; he has gained (a little) knowledge in doing so, he has used knowledge he already had about his shoes and clothing, and he has judged each plan in advance of execution in the light of his other knowledge. If he has surveyed all the possibilities and chooses the best, he has used an intelligence that the cat did not possess.

3. John Couch Adams, one of the discovers of Neptune,

... while still an undergraduate ... read of certain unexplained irregularities in the motion of the planet Uranus and determined to investigate them, with a view to ascertaining whether they might not be due to the action of a remote undiscovered planet. Elected a fellow of his college in 1843, he at once attacked the problem. It was this: from the observed [irregularities] of a known planet to deduce by calculation, assuming only Newton's law of gravitation, the mass and orbit of an unknown disturbing body. By September 1845 he obtained his first solution.[2]

Guided by his calculations, astronomers searched for the unknown planet and discovered it by telescopic observations in 1846. "Its mathematical prediction," says the Encyclopedia, "was an unsurpassed intellectual feat."

This "unsurpassed intellectual feat," like the actions of the cat and of the man with the broken string, was a response to a problematical situation. Although no habit was broken by the discovery of the irregularities of Uranus, they gave an intellectual stimulus and aroused a questioning attitude. Pre-

[1]The following analysis of problem-solving is based on John Dewey's now classical *How We Think* (New York: D. C. Heath and Company, 1910, 1933).

[2]Reprinted by permission from *Encyclopaedia Britannica* (14th ed.), I, 155.

dictions as to where Uranus could be seen at specified times had not been verified; what were the reasons for it, which if they could be discovered, would make future predictions of its position more accurate? Many hypotheses about the motions of planets had been held in the history of astronomy. But Adams worked on the basis of one: all the planets go around the sun, and if their velocities are irregular, the irregularity is due to their alternate approach to and recession from some other body that attracts them. His problem, then, was to find out where such an unknown attracting body had to be in order to produce the observed irregularities. Having calculated where it would be if his guess about it was correct, it was a simple matter to look for it with a telescope. When it was found where Adams said it would be, his guess was "verified."

Now let us examine our three examples of problem-solving to see their similarities and differences.

1. *Problem-solving is occasioned by the new, the unexpected, which arouses or thwarts some interest*—If the cat had not wanted to get out of the box, she would not have had a problem to solve; if Adams had not become interested in understanding some aspects of Uranus' motions, he would not have devoted two years to explaining them.

2. *When a problem arises for a thinking man, it appears in an "unsettled area" surrounded by knowledge that is settled*—The man whose shoelace breaks does not at the moment know how to solve the problem it puts to him, but he does not doubt that it is good to wear shoes, that he has other shoes, that shoes and suit ought to match, and the like. Adams did not know how to explain the motions of Uranus, but he did not doubt that planets go around the sun, that planets attract each other, that every event has some cause, that mathematics applies to astronomical facts, and so on.

The more intelligent a man is, the better able he will be to see the problem in the light of the relevant settled facts of his experience. The cat, perhaps, does this little or not at all.

3. *In the light of the relevant settled facts, a guess is made as to the best or only way of solving the problem*—Solving a problem is settling the unsettled. The guess is made about some unknown factor that would bring about this settlement of doubt or frustration. For instance, in the second example, the laces the man believes he can get from another pair of shoes are the object of such a guess, and if they really are there, his problem is solved. In the third example, Neptune at such and such a place in the sky is the object of a guess.

What we suppose (but do not know) to exist so that it will provide a solution to a problem is called a *hypothetical object*, and the guess is called a *hypothesis*. The world "hypothesis" is used in many senses, and it is sometimes advisable to call the hypothesis that is applied to a specific case of this kind a *working hypothesis*.

4. *If a hypothesis helps us to solve a problem, it does so because from assuming the hypothesis we can draw conclusions that will have a bearing on our subsequent experience*—*If* the other shoes are in the closet, then their laces can be used; *if* the planet

exists, then what would previously have been called an "irregularity" can be predicted to have such and such a magnitude in the future.

Acting upon the hypothesis may, of course, not solve the problem. If the other shoes are at the repair shop, acting on the hypothesis by looking for them will not get the man's shoe tied. If Neptune could not be found by aiming the telescope where Adams' hypothesis said it would be found, Adams would not have explained the irregularities of Uranus, could not predict its motions in the future, and would not have solved his problem.

The cat does not have sufficient intelligence to anticipate the results of her actions in a new and strange situation. She therefore has to try out many actions before she hits upon the right one. The men can anticipate and thus avoid the necessity of performing many overt trials, because they can try them out "in their minds" and anticipate what their consequences would be if they actually acted upon them.

THE ORIGIN OF HYPOTHESES

Hypothetical objects are things that we do not observe but that, if real, explain what we do observe. The line between hypothetical object and fact (which we do observe) is often indistinct. Strictly speaking, the legs of the table on which I am now writing are hypothetical; I do not now observe them but I assume that they are still there, and presumably I could observe them again by moving my chair. But an electron is a hypothetical object that we probably can never observe.

Observation alone does not suffice for formulating statements about those kinds of objects. In making hypotheses or guesses about them, we have to go beyond the facts; the hypothetical objects are at first conjured up by a disciplined creative imagination. Probably no rules can be given for this conjuring, although rules can be given for observing facts and drawing inferences from the hypotheses once they have been stated. Native wit, intelligence, lively imagination, a willingness to go out on a limb, and perhaps even genius may be required for making significant hypotheses; the greatest thinkers are not the men who have made new observations or drawn logical conclusions from given axioms, but the men who have made new and unexpected guesses about hypothetical objects—guesses that explain what we observe but do not understand.

But although no rigid rules can be given so that anyone by simply obeying them can be sure to formulate new and valuable hypotheses, a study of the lives and minds of great thinkers does suggest some of the ways in which good guesses about the unknown or unexplained have originated. Graham Wallas[3] believed that he had found a kind of "natural history" of discovery. He said there are four stages that many thinkers have gone through.

[3]Graham Wallas, *The Art of Thought* (New York: Harcourt, Brace & World, Inc., 1926), Chap. IV.

1. *Preparation*—Intelligent guesses about the unknown come only to minds prepared by knowing the available facts. *Examples:* Darwin collected facts about the variations of animals for years before he arrived at the hypothesis of evolution by natural selection; Newton knew many facts of mechanics and astronomy before he formulated his hypothesis of universal gravitation.

2. *Incubation*—The ideas we have must be allowed to incubate or mature. Close and persistent application to learning brute facts may inhibit the imagination; we need to "back away" from them before we can explain and understand them. *Examples:* Poincaré, the French philosopher and mathematician, worked on a problem and then dropped it during his military service, but solved it one day after not having thought of it for years; Helmholtz climbed hills on a sunny day after accumulating the "facts of the case," so that his ideas could mature; we advise our friends, "Sleep on it; it will be clearer tomorrow."

3. *Intimation*—After a period of incubation, we sometimes feel that we can now solve a problem that previously baffled us, although we do not fully know what the solution is. There is a feeling of readiness. *Example:* a famous German philosopher and psychologist, William Stern, said that he collected all the data on a problem, then let them incubate until he felt, "Now I can write it up," although when he began writing, he still did not know in detail what he was going to say.

4. *Illumination*—This is the most dramatic part of thinking, and is variously referred to in such expressions as: "It dawned on me that . . . ," "The idea burst upon me . . . ," "I saw in a flash . . . ," or "I had an inspiration." *Examples:* Archimedes' discovering the principle of specific gravity and dashing naked down the streets of Syracuse shouting, "Eureka!" Darwin's sudden discovery of the principle of natural selection while idly reading Malthus on the human struggle for a diminishing food supply. Kekulé suddenly seeing the ring formula of benzene in the burning soot of his fireplace.

Such illumination, because its occurrence is so dramatic, is sometimes taken as a guarantee of the truth of what seems to have been revealed in it. For this reason it may sometimes seriously mislead us; it must be followed by careful and painstaking efforts at verification, and on further examination, it sometimes turns out that our must brilliant ideas are, unfortunately, not true. False hypotheses come as dramatically as true ones. But because of the liveliness of the experience and because of one's natural love for his own brain-child, we often are not as critical of them as we are of those ideas that come to others or that come to us with less impact. The wise and careful thinker will not give credence to a belief because of its inspirational occurrence; he will still require that it pass the test of verification.

The imagination is a tricky thing. It can be encouraged, it cannot be forced, and it is hard to discipline. So many unconscious and subconscious conditions affect it, and so many apparently trivial experiences and events direct and inhibit it, that it would be silly to say that one ought to do this or that in order to make it work for advancing our knowledge or understanding. One person needs silence in order to do the thinking and dreaming from which his best ideas spring; another may want excitement and noise. Helmholtz said that even the slightest amount of alcohol stopped the process for him; Kekulé, on the other hand, had most of his best ideas over beer and cigars.

Perhaps the only counsel one can give towards improving the imagination for hypotheses—and it is counsel that makes no promises—would be: try to find your own best way of hypothesizing. It involves five bits of advice:

1. Observe yourself; under what conditions—social, emotional, and so on—have your own best ideas come? Then when you need to make a serious attempt to figure something out, try to get yourself into that favorable state.

2. Getting a new idea, formulating some guess or hypothesis, always means going beyond or against some of the ideas you already have. The tenaciously held beliefs we have inhibit our getting new ones; try to examine and suspect the Idols of the Mind so as to give new and unfamiliar imaginings a chance to enter.[4] Brainstorming is the name given to an interesting psychological practice. A group of people faced with an intractable problem force themselves to produce, as rapidly as possible, as many solutions as they can imagine. No self-criticism or criticisms of others is allowed to inhibit the free flow of ideas. The emphasis is simply upon getting a large number of hypotheses out into the open regardless of whether they are fantastic and unfeasible. Most of the ideas can be rejected later, upon critical examination. Criticism and self-criticism introduces a survival of the fittest ideas; but brainstorming is supposed to help the arrival of the fittest. Groups that have participated in brainstorming are often enthusiatic about the fruitfulness of this procedure in opening up many quite unexpected possibilities that would normally have been kept suppressed by the social inhibitions against silliness. It can succeed only in an atmosphere in which these social constraints are temporarily relaxed.

3. Draw a careful distinction between facts and hypotheses. Many so-called facts are really a little factual observation plus a great deal of hypothetical interpretation. Ordinary descriptions of things—and many scientific descriptions—involve the acceptance of hypotheses that may or may not be correct. The physician, for instance, says, "The patient has typhoid fever," but he usually observes only a few symptoms, which might be caused by something else than the typhoid germ. Hence, even here he is not simply reporting a fact but rather making a conjecture, and the conjecture may be wrong although the observation be correct. It is important to remain aware of the hypotheses that we are using; when we remember that they are hypotheses, it is easier to be critical and skeptical of them than if we think they are hard facts. Often, unless we are skeptical of old explanations, it is difficult to formulate new and better ones.

---

[4]Einstein was once asked how he had made one of his discoveries. He is said to have replied, "I challenged an axiom."

4. Give special attention to the unusual facts, the apparent exceptions. These are called "renegade instances,"[5] but they are "renegade" in the light of some accepted hypothesis that they do not fit. Frequently we ignore them. Sometimes we content ourselves with the statement, "Well, the exception proves the rule," as if this statement meant that the rule or hypothesis is proved "true" by the exception. (Actually, this statement means, "It is the apparent exception to a rule that *tests* it, and if the hypothesis cannot apply to the apparent exception, then we should be suspicious of the hypothesis and try to find a better one.") Many a rejected stone has become the keystone of the arch; many a neglected or rejected fact—rejected because "it just couldn't be so"—has given the start to looking for a better hypothesis that will fit *all* the facts. To go back to our illustration: Many men had observed the irregularities in the motions of Uranus, but had neglected them, thinking that they must be the result of observational errors or mistakes in calculation.[6] But Adams took them seriously.

5. Be on the watch for analogies. An analogy is a comparison in which the relationship between two things is said to be the same as the relationship between two others. For instance, "The relationship between a ruler and his people is the same as that between father and children" expresses an analogy. It may be wrong, of course, but frequently an analogy is very revealing even if it is wrong, for it directs us to look for previously unnoticed similarities and differences. In science, we see a good analogy in the work of atomic physicists of a generation ago who thought of the atom as resembling a little solar system: The electrons were to the nucleus as the planets are to the sun. Darwin's theory of evolution is based on an analogy: nature, through the struggle for survival, selects those animals that are to survive and reproduce, as an animal-breeder selects animals for breeding purposes.

An analogy is like a mathematical ratio and proportion. If we know three terms in a proportion, we can calculate the fourth. From $2:4$ as $6:x$, we can determine that x is 12. Outside mathematics, we cannot be so certain of our analogies, but we can be guided by them in looking for some factors we do not now know. For example, if we believe that smallpox can be cured by vaccination, we might reason—correctly—that if we could induce a slight

[5]The name was suggested by V. C. Aldrich (*Philosophy of Science*, III, No. 4 [October, 1936]), but is here used in a broader sense than Aldrich's.

[6]Indeed, one of the most striking examples of missing an important scientific discovery because it just "couldn't be so" is found in the history of the discovery of Neptune. Long before Adams and a French astronomer, Leverrier, had predicted the existence and position of the planet, another French astronomer, LaLande, had actually *observed* Neptune itself telescopically. He was not looking for a planet and had no reason to suspect that a planet was in that part of the sky; hence he disregarded the discovery and attributed his measurements of a change in position of a "star" (as he thought) to an error in observation. James B. Conant, *Science and Common Sense* (New Haven, Conn.: Yale University Press, 1951), pp. 120–21, gives some interesting illustrations from chemistry of discoveries that were missed because the mind of the scientist was not focused upon them when he observed the facts that later served to prove a new hypothesis.

case of still other diseases by inoculation, we could give a person immunity from them; this analogy set scientists to work to find ways of weakening germ-cultures to produce slight attacks of disease and thereby prevent more virulent attacks. A good analogy by itself, of course, proves nothing; but it does open new paths of inquiry.

These bits of advice will not guarantee that new and enlightening ideas will come; but they may improve the chances.

MARKS OF A GOOD HYPOTHESIS

Anybody, of course, can make an indefinitely large number of guesses about anything. What is the cause of cancer? With very little thought, one can guess: a germ, a virus, night air, evil spirits, the wrath of God, something in tobacco smoke, something in beer, the effects of too much study, hereditary factors, and so on. It takes no genius, or even much intelligence, to spin theories if one does not care what sort of hypotheses one is dealing with.

The competent thinker must have a *rich* imagination, or from the list of hypotheses to be considered he may omit precisely the right one. But it is a waste of time just to think of all conceivable hypotheses (as in our list of the possible causes of cancer); the imagination must also be *disciplined*. By a disciplined imagination, we mean one that is able to discover *good* hypotheses,[7] hypotheses that are worth investigating. Good hypotheses have certain specific characteristics, and study of these can save labor by eliminating the necessity of trying to test poor hypotheses.

1. *A good hypothesis is adequate to and consistent with all the relevant known facts*—No matter how attracted we may be to a new hypothesis, we *cannot take it seriously if there are known facts that are inconsistent with it.* For instance, the hypothesis that cancer in general is caused by something in tobacco smoke is clearly a poor one, because men had cancer before tobacco was smoked.

Of course, what we think are facts may not actually be facts at all. For instance, in a detective story it may seem that *X is the murderer of Y* is a poor hypothesis, for it is a "fact" that *X* was *Y's* best friend. But as every reader knows, that may not be a fact at all, although *X* wants the detective to believe it is.

In general, however, we can eliminate many hypotheses as worthless because they are incompatible with what we already know.

2. *A good hypothesis is (usually) consistent with other previously established hypotheses*—For instance, Adams accepted the Newtonian hypothesis that gravitational force was exerted by every body upon every other; he there-

---

[7]A "good" hypothesis is not to be confused with a "true" one. We shall discuss true hypotheses in the next sections.

fore did not have to consider the poor hypothesis that Uranus' motions were independent of other planets and due, say, to sunspots.

As we shall see later, we never establish a hypothesis without making use of other hypotheses that have previously been proposed. It is obvious, then, that we cannot test a hypothesis if it is incompatible with other hypotheses we have to assume in order to test it.

This rule of a good hypothesis is not absolute, for the other hypotheses *may* be wrong. But in general, a hypothesis consistent with other hypotheses that have already been tested is more likely to be correct than one that is not.

3. *A good hypothesis is as simple as possible*—Other things being equal, the simplest among a set of hypotheses that meet the first two requirements is the best. This is known as the *law of parsimony* and sometimes, as "Ockham's razor," after William of Ockham (1290–1349), who is reputed to have said, "Entities [causes] are not to be multiplied beyond what is necessary."

It is very important to understand the meaning of "simple." "Simple" does not necessarily mean "easy to understand." It means *having a minimum of independent assumptions*. For instance, the Newtonian theory of physics is easier to understand than Einstein's, but it is not so good a hypothesis because it includes more independent assumptions. Again, a mathematical theorem may be proved in several ways, and sometimes the one that "goes the long way 'round" is easier to grasp than the proof the mathematician considers most elegant. But it is not the simplest explanation in the present sense for it uses more axioms, postulates, and steps than the shorter, more direct proof.

There is, of course, the danger that a hypothesis may be too simple. For instance, an explanation of human behavior in terms of one drive (sex or egoism, for instance) is simpler than one that uses a long list of "instincts." But it might be too simple in that it might not adequately deal with the variety of human behavior, and thus force the psychologist to supplement it with too many other hypotheses.[8] It is often a matter of dispute whether a very simple hypothesis is adequate, that is, whether it meets Criterion 1. But it is often rather easily decided that some particular hypothesis is more complicated than necessary. For example, astronomers now use only the hypothesis that bodies attract each other instead of the hypothesis suggested in the eighteenth century that they may also repel each other.

Sometimes it is said that the world is not really simple, and hence, the rule of parsimony will mislead us. This, of course, is a valid warning against using hypotheses that are so simple that they are not adequate to deal with the variety of actual facts. But given two hypotheses each of which fits all the known facts, we choose the simpler; we are as cautious as possible. Newton states the rule:

---

[8]Such additional hypotheses for dealing with cases neglected in a major hypothesis, or with renegade instances, are called *ad hoc* hypotheses.

We are to admit no more causes of natural things than such as are both true and sufficient to explain their appearances. To this purpose the philosophers say that Nature does nothing in vain, and more is in vain when less will suffice. For Nature is pleased with simplicity, and affects not the pomp of superfluous causes.

4. *A good hypothesis is fruitful and testable*—By this requirement, we mean that a hypothesis must have consequences at least some of which can be subjected to empirical test. The best hypotheses are those that lead us to expect something that we would not have expected, and presumably would not have found, unless the hypothesis had led us to look for it. In the case of Adams, his hypothesis led him to tell an astronomer where he should look if he wanted to see "a new planet swim into his ken," as Keats puts it. Only if the hypothesis has consequences that we can observe can we find out whether it is true or false. The hypothesis that the moon is a perfect sphere and its apparent hollows are really filled with some invisible glass-like substance is a hypothesis that Galileo could not refute. But it was not worth refuting because it was fruitless and untestable. A hypothesis must make a difference in our expectations about what can be detected in further experience; otherwise it is barren.

As mentioned before, a good hypothesis is not necessarily a true one. Often a hypothesis is good in that it guides us effectively in the discovery of new facts, although the facts that it leads us to observe are not the ones we expected on the assumption that the hypothesis was a true one. Perhaps the most famous illustration of a false hypothesis leading to valuable new facts is Columbus' discovery of America; according to his hypothesis, he should have got to India. Little examples of this fruitfulness of false hypotheses are found every day. A physician believes that a patient has a certain disease. On this hypothesis he predicts what conditions will be found on further examination; the further examination does not show these conditions and thus refutes his hypothesis. But in refuting the original hypothesis, he is not pushed back to his starting point, for the facts he has observed may set going a new line of thought that may lead to a true hypothesis. But without some good hypothesis, he would not know what tests to make or what facts and symptoms to look for.

A poor hypothesis does not have this directing function. The belief that a disease he is treating is due to the will of God may be true, but even if it is, the hypothesis is not a good one, for it does not lead to the discovery of further facts about the disease. Thus Spinoza, who believed that all philosophical explanation eventually takes us back to the ultimate reality he called God, nevertheless said, "The will of God is the refuge of ignorance," because it is the explanation the most ignorant man gives when he has no good hypothesis that will help him understand a particular fact in nature.

A good hypothesis is frequently called a "working hypothesis," for it may guide us to further important observations regardless of whether it is true or not; sometimes an hypothesis that we know quite definitely to be false can be good in this sense and is often used with full consciousness of its falsity.

5. *A good hypothesis must be explanatory*—By explanation is meant relation of apparently unrelated facts to one another in such a way that they can all be seen to have a common cause or to illustrate the same general principle. For instance, we explain the medicinal properties of an organic chemical compound by reference to its structure. Its structure is a hypothetical characteristic that explains both its medicinal and its chemical properties, for from saying, "It has a hydroxyl group in such and such a position," we can compare it to other drugs that *look* quite different but behave the same way in the body or in a test-tube reaction. But a hypothesis that "opium puts people to sleep because of its dormitive power" is not explanatory; reference to its dormitive power explains nothing but only says again what we already knew. When Newton explained the fall of the apple, he did so not by invoking some mysterious power, but by showing that its fall was a special case under the general law that applied also to the motion of the moon around the earth. The hypothesis of gravitation does not explain *why* bodies attract each other, and Newton himself said, "I make no hypothesis." To say gravity is the cause is like saying an animal cares for her young because of the maternal instinct, the *only* evidence for which is that she does care for her young. But Newton's hypothesis does explain the falling apple and the revolution of the moon and the irregularities of Uranus' motion because it shows that whatever law accounts for one of these phenomena also accounts for the others.

An explanatory hypothesis is the focal point of much apparently diverse evidence. So by assuming the hypothesis, we can interrelate what was apparently unrelated and see order and connection where previously we saw only brute fact and confusion. We shall give a fuller account of explanation and its various species in Chapter 10.

THE LOGIC OF HYPOTHESES

Logic is the study of the laws and principles that give validity and correctness to thought, argumentation, and inference. Whenever we draw a valid conclusion from some statement, we follow, usually unconsciously, some law of logic. The laws of logic are for this reason sometimes called laws of thought. They are not laws that tell us how thinking does always proceed, as Kepler's laws tell us how the planets actually do move. They are more like traffic laws, which tell us what we must do if we want to achieve a safe arrival at our destination. In the quest for knowledge, this destination is a true conclusion and the route to it is a sound argument—an argument that is logically valid, with true premises. But they are unlike traffic laws in one important respect. Traffic laws are man-made and are subject to change. The laws of logic—at least the basic ones—are necessary. They are laws describing implications between propositions. Logic tells us the laws by which one proposition *implies* another; and when we know that one proposition implies a second, we can *infer* the truth of the second from the truth of the first.

Each kind of proposition in its implicative relationships to others is under specific laws of logic. Logic is the science that studies these relationships systematically; logicians set up systems of definitions and axioms and prove theorems about these relationships. For an understanding of the methods of science, it is necessary to be familiar with at least one small sector of the extensive field of logic.

In working with hypotheses, our beliefs are generally expressed in *hypothetical propositions* and *hypothetical syllogisms*.

A *syllogism* is an argument with two premises and a conclusion. An example of a syllogism is: "All birds are warm-blooded; a canary is a bird; therefore a canary is warm-blooded." (We do not usually express our thoughts in syllogisms, but frequently omit one of the premises. We should be likely to say, "A canary must be warm-blooded, because all birds are warm-blooded," leaving it unsaid that the canary is a bird. Such an elliptical argument is called an *enthymeme*. However, we can and sometimes do need to complete the argument, especially if we are being very careful, by supplying the missing premise.)

A *categorical proposition* is a statement that does not contain within itself any conditions or alternatives. All the propositions in the syllogism just given are categorical propositions, and that syllogism is called a *categorical syllogism*.

A *hypothetical proposition* is a statement that contains a conditional clause ("if so and so") and a resulting clause ("then so and so"). We call the "if-clause" the *antecedent*, and the "then-clause" the *consequent*. For example, "If germs cause diphtheria, there should be germs in the throat of this patient," is a hypothetical proposition. Its antecedent is "germs cause diphtheria," and its consequent is "there should be germs in the throat of the patient."

Hypothetical propositions are often not expressed in the "if . . . then . . ." form. Rather, we say, "Since the sun is coming out, it will probably stop raining," or "Napoleon lost the battle of Waterloo because he did not have enough men." But for logical exactness, it is better to translate them into strict logical form: "If the sun is coming out, then it will probably stop raining," and "If Napoleon had had enough men, then he would have won the battle of Waterloo." This often sounds artificial, but it improves the clarity of thinking, making it quite explicit what are the stated conditions and what are the consequences if these conditions are or were fulfilled.

A *hypothetical syllogism* is a syllogism whose major premise is a hypothetical proposition and whose minor premise and conclusions are categorical propositions. For instance, "If germs cause typhoid fever, then this water will probably give you typhoid fever; germs do cause typhoid fever; therefore this water will probably give you the disease."

An argument that obeys all the relevant laws of logic is called *valid*. One that does not do so is said to be *invalid*. An argument may have a false premise and still be valid. For example, "All men are Americans" is false, but it validly implies that "Some Americans are men," which is true. "All Americans live two hundred years" is false, but it validly implies, "Some Americans live two hundred years," which is also false. *But true premises and valid arguments always and in every case lead to true conclusions.* Such an argument is said to be *sound*. Only sound arguments let us be sure that our conclusions are true.

It is possible to decide what kinds of hypothetical syllogisms are valid, that is, what combinations of hypothetical and categorical propositions will validly imply a conclusion. We shall, for the purposes of illustration, assume a rather silly major premise and evaluate the various ways in which it might be thought that a conclusion could be drawn.

CASE I:	If wishes were horses, beggars could ride.	Major premise.
	Wishes are horses.	Minor premise, affirming the antecedent of the major premise.
	Therefore beggars can ride.	Conclusion, affirming the consequent of the major premise.

This is valid. The major premise tells us under what condition beggars can ride, and the minor premise tells us that this condition is met. This is known as "affirming the antecedent," or *modus ponens*.

CASE II:	If wishes were horses, beggars could ride.	Major premise.
	Beggars can ride.	Minor premise, affirming the consequent of the major premise.
	Therefore wishes are horses.	Conclusion, affirming the antecedent of the major premise.

This is invalid. There might be, and there are, other reasons why beggars can ride. This is known as the fallacy of "affirming the consequent."

CASE III:	If wishes were horses, beggars could ride.	Major premise.
	Wishes are not horses.	Minor premise, denying the antecedent of the major premise.
	Therefore beggars cannot ride.	Conclusion, denying the consequent of the major premise.

This is invalid, for there might be other reasons why beggars can ride. This is known as the fallacy of "denying the antecedent."

CASE IV:	If wishes were horses, beggars could ride.	Major premise.
	Beggars cannot ride.	Minor premise, denying the consequent of the major premise.
	Therefore wishes are not horses.	Conclusion, denying the antecedent of the major premise.

This is valid, for if the antecedent implies the consequent and the consequent is false, then the antecedent under which the consequent would be true must itself be false. This is known as "denying the consequent," or *modus tollens*.

Thus there are two and only two valid modes of hypothetical syllogisms: that in which the minor premise affirms the antecedent and that in which the minor premise denies the consequent. Any other combination of hypothetical and categorical propositions is not a valid argument.

In science, of course, we are not interested in the type of rather fanciful major premise that we have used in our illustration. We are interested in hypothetical major premises whose antecedents are presumably about some existing things that, if they really do exist, will explain the occurrences we actually or can observe. The antecedent is usually about a hypothetical object, something whose existence is not observed as a fact, but which is thought to exist as the cause or explanation of something we can observe as fact. To take a more serious illustration, Adams said, "If there is another planet at such and such a place, then the irregularities of Uranus' motion would be so and so." The man with the broken shoelace says, "If there is another pair of shoes, then I can use its laces." The chemist says, "If this liquid is acid, it will turn litmus paper red."

If the hypothesis[9] is fruitful and testable, its consequent will be a statement that refers to some observation, so that we can see whether the consequent is true and whether it states an observable fact or not. If we know that the antecedent is true and that the consequent really follows from it, we can be sure of the consequent fact before observing it (method of affirming the antecedent). If we know that the consequent of the hypothetical premise is false by observing the relevant facts—for instance, that in a specific case the litmus paper does not turn red—then we can conclude that the antecedent is also false (method of denying the consequent) and that the liquid was not acid.

---

[9]It is necessary to call attention to the ambiguity of the word "hypothesis." The author cannot make a hard and fast rule as to how the word should be used, as people do use the word in a variety of senses; all he can do is to point out the ambiguity, and put the reader on guard against confusions that may result if the word is used in various senses without attention being called to its exact meaning in each context. The following seem to be denoted by the word "hypothesis":

1. *The entire major premise.* For instance, "It is my hypothesis that if wishes were horses, beggars could ride." "It was Adams' hypothesis that if there were another planet, he could predict the motions of Uranus."

2. *The antecedent of the major premise.* For example, "Adams' hypothesis was that there was another planet."

3. *The object itself referred to in the antecedent*, a real object if the hypothesis (in Sense 2) is true. For instance, "The missing planet was not a known fact, but only a hypothesis, until it was observed telescopically."

I use the name "hypothetical object" instead of "hypothesis" when referring to "hypothesis" in Sense 3. The danger of confusion between Senses 1 and 2 is slight, because the context will usually show which is meant.

It might seem that this little lesson in logic gives us a way of finding out which of our good hypotheses are true and which are false. In simple cases, like that of a man tying his shoe, this is correct. In such a simple example, we can affirm the antecedent by finding the other shoe. In much scientific work we can affirm the antecedent by using some more powerful instrument of observation. An X ray may convert the hypothetical object (say, a stone in the kidney) referred to in a diagnosis or hypothesis into an observed fact. The telescope made visible the existence of a body in the part of the sky where Adams said a new planet would be found. But unfortunately, in most inquiry something more is required than merely observing the object that we have made the antecedent about, and in many cases (for instance, in sub-atomic physics) we cannot do this at all.

A common, but nevertheless erroneous, notion about science is that we verify a hypothesis by observing the consequent. It is often believed that this is the essence of the experimental method—never accept a hypothesis until it is verified by observation. But consider a simple example.

One might say, "If atoms exist, then chemical compounds will illustrate a specific law, say, the law of definite proportions. Dalton showed that chemical compounds follow this law. Therefore atoms exist." This seems to illustrate the process of verifying the hypothesis that atoms exist by referring to a fact of observation. But it breaks the logical laws of the hypothetical syllogism, since it is a case of affirming the consequent (Case II). We can no more logically verify the existence of atoms in this way than we could validly infer (in the example given as Case II) that wishes were horses simply because I have seen beggars ride.

We must conclude either that such scientific work is based on a logical fallacy or that scientific verification is somewhat different from what it appears to be on the surface. Fortunately, the latter is the case.

Scientific verification is a more complex process than simply drawing a conclusion from a hypothesis, observing to see if the conclusion is a fact, and if it is, accepting the hypothesis. There are two processes, both of which must be carried out if a hypothesis is to be verified. The first is the process of drawing a conclusion from a *family of hypotheses*; the second is the process of choosing among rival hypotheses.

Drawing Conclusions from a Family of Hypotheses

One of the requirements of a good hypothesis is that it must be fruitful. It must lead us to search for some observable facts that we would not have expected without the hypothesis. But how does it do so? How does the antecedent, which is about something we do not observe, lead to a consequent about something that we can observe?

The answer to this question appears to be difficult only because we usually think that at any moment we are dealing with only one hypothesis. Actually, we are always dealing with a *family* of related hypotheses that mutually support one another and help to bridge the gap between any one hypothesis and the realm of observable fact. For instance, Adams was using not merely the hypothesis that there was another planet; this hypothesis alone would never have led to the other hypothesis: "If you look at such and such a part of the sky, you will find another planet." Adams was considering at least two hypotheses:

1. A hypothesis that there is between planets an attractive force that varies in the way stated by Newton and accepted by all astronomers.

2. A hypothesis that the irregularities of Uranus can, in the light of 1, be explained by the existence of another planet at the precise place and having the precise mass required to account for these irregular motions.

Notice that Adams was not interested in verifying the former, but used it because it was already sufficiently established. The first is related to the second in somewhat the same way that financial backing is related to a specific business venture, and we can properly call it a *collateral hypothesis*. It is sometimes called a *postulate*, since it is assumed to be true. The collateral hypothesis is a hypothesis about the "settled area of our experience," which is not questioned when the problem calling for Hypothesis 2 occurs.

On the basis of his collateral hypothesis, Adams calculated where the unknown planet would be if the hypothesis about it were true and if the existence of the unknown planet would, under the Newtonian hypothesis, adequately explain the observed motions of Uranus. He told astronomers, "If you point your telescope to such and such a place at such and such a time, you will observe a new planet." Notice that this is a third hypothesis.

This hypothesis, in the form "If you do so and so, you will observe such and such a fact," is an *operational hypothesis*. It is so called because its antecedent is an operation that we can actually do. The operational hypothesis has a peculiar merit: its antecedent *can* be affirmed. The performance of an experiment or the taking of an observation is just this process of actually affirming the operational antecedent to see whether its results are those predicted. But one must be constantly alert to the very real danger that he thinks he has confirmed the antecedent of an operational hypothesis when in fact he has not done so. Suppose an astronomer decides to look at a particular point in the sky, p, at a particular moment, t, in order to find out if the planet can be seen there as predicted. In good faith he writes in his notebook, "At p, t, no planet," But, in fact, his chronometer is incorrect and it was not exactly t when he made his observation. He thought he had affirmed the antecedent, when actually he had not. The failure to affirm an operational antecedent, when not taken into account, is the cause of "experimental errors."

Taking the process of scientific verification of hypotheses as far as we have now pursued it, the scheme is this: If the collateral hypothesis and the hypothesis to be tested are true (and we assume the first is true as a result of earlier inquiries), then if such and such operations are performed, such and such facts will be observed.

Or, to use our former illustration from Adams' work, we can outline the process of verification as far as we have now examined it.

MAJOR PREMISE: Family of hypotheses	If the observations of the positions are correct If the hypotheses about gravitation are true	Collateral hypotheses
	And if the hypothesis about the unknown planet is true	Hypothesis to be tested; "working hypothesis"
	And if a telescope is pointed at Position p at Time t	Antecedent of operational hypothesis
	Then: a new point of light will be seen at p	Consequent
MINOR PREMISE: Experiment	The telescope is pointed at Position p at Time t	Affirming the antecedent of the operational hypothesis
CONCLUSION:	The point of light is seen	Observed fact, and the consequent of the entire family of hypotheses

The process schematically presented here is ordinarily called "testing a hypothesis by a fact," or the "observational or experimental verification of a hypothesis." The question to be considered now is: Does the conclusion, the actual observation of the expected fact, justify the inference that the hypothesis we wanted to test is true? Can we be sure that the point of light that the astronomers did observe indicates the existence of a previously unknown planet and that this planet is the cause of the observed irregularities in the motions of Uranus?

Reluctantly we must admit that we cannot be sure on the basis of the procedure outlined. For we are still affirming the *consequent* of the *family* of hypotheses as a whole. The antecedent we affirmed was merely the antecedent of the *operational* hypothesis, which is only one member of the entire family of hypotheses. We still do not know but that some other hypothesis might be consistent with the operational hypothesis and might better explain the resultant. To make sure that our hypothesis about the unknown planet is true, we must go through still another process, the process of elimination, by which we refute rival hypotheses that might be members of the family or rival families of hypotheses.

The Process of Elimination Considered Logically

First, the process of elimination will be outlined schematically so as to give an over-all, logical picture of it. The next section will show how experiment is used in the process, and the appendix to this chapter will give an actual example of its successful application.

In most problem-solving, there is one set of collateral hypotheses accepted without question, and a few rival, incompatible hypotheses to be tested. Each of these hypotheses we assume to be consistent with the known facts and with the collateral hypothesis, for otherwise we do not bother with them. But they are inconsistent with one another, so our problem is to see how to choose among them if they are equally good.

Let us call the collateral hypothesis or set of collateral hypotheses H_c; the rival hypotheses to be tested, H_1 and H_2; the operational hypotheses O_1, O_2, and so on; and the facts observed as consistent with both H_1 and H_2 by the letters f_1, f_2, f_3, and f_4.

Our present state of knowledge, in which we cannot choose between H_1 and H_2, can be summarized in the following statements:

$$H_c \text{ and } H_1 \text{ and } O_1 \longrightarrow f_1 \text{ and } f_2$$
$$H_c \text{ and } H_2 \text{ and } O_1 \longrightarrow f_1 \text{ and } f_2$$
$$H_c \text{ and } H_1 \text{ and } O_2 \longrightarrow f_3 \text{ and } f_4$$
$$H_c \text{ and } H_2 \text{ and } O_2 \longrightarrow f_3 \text{ and } f_4$$

In other words, the operational hypotheses or experiments we have made do not help us choose between H_1 and H_2. But if H_1 and H_2 are good hypotheses, then they are fruitful, and that means that each should imply some new facts when conjoined to some new operational hypothesis O_3, and some new fact implied by H_1 and O_3 should be observably different from the new fact implied by H_2 and O_3. O_3 is the hypothesis leading to a *crucial experiment,* Then we predict:

$$H_c \text{ and } H_1 \text{ and } O_3 \longrightarrow f_5,$$
$$H_c \text{ and } H_2 \text{ and } O_3 \longrightarrow f_6$$

where f_5 is observably different from f_6. When submitting the two hypotheses to a crucial experiment, we expect one fact if one hypothesis is true, and another fact if the other is true. Only observation will show which of the expected facts actually occurs. Suppose we do the experiment and observe f_5. Now in this case, we are no longer merely affirming the consequent of the family of hypotheses containing H_1 (which alone is invalid ground for affirming its antecedent), but at the same time, we are *denying the consequent* of the family containing H_2. This is a sufficient logical ground for saying that H_2 is refuted. And if H_2 is the only alternative to H_1 in the family of hypotheses consistent with H_c, this is sufficient logical ground for saying that H_1 is true.

It should be noted, however, that we do not usually know for sure that H_2 is the only alternative to H_1; so the most we can say is that so far we know of no other equally good hypothesis against which there is no refuting evidence, and hence we accept H_1.

In verification, therefore, we do not confirm a hypothesis simply by showing that it passes a specific observational test. We must, to be sure, show that it does pass all the tests we put it to, and evidence of widely divergent kinds ought to converge upon it. But we must also show that the other hypotheses do *not* pass all the tests we put to them. Convergence of evidence $(f_1 \ldots f_n)$ and elimination of alternatives, therefore, are the two prerequisites for accepting a hypothesis as true.

THE ROLE OF EXPERIMENT IN ELIMINATING HYPOTHESES

One of the outstanding traits of modern science is its emphasis upon experimentation. "Experimental science" is often taken as a synonym for "modern science," under the erroneous impression that ancient scientists did not perform experiments. Although ancient science was by no means wholly nonexperimental and although there are some highly rigorous modern sciences like astronomy that are not experimental in the ordinary meaning of this word, it is nonetheless true that the laboratory, where experiments are performed, is the typical institution of modern science.

In this section we shall discuss the nature of scientific experimentation to see how experiments are done and why they are so important. All sciences dealing with nature appeal to facts in the verifications of their hypotheses. That is to say, they are observational. Experimentation is only a way of observing things. An experiment is an observation made without having to wait for nature to produce the thing or event we want to observe. It is a technique of forcing nature to answer our questions by setting up artificial conditions (conditions that might not be met with at all in the normal course of nature or at the time and place where they might conveniently be observed). It was in this respect that Bacon compared experimentation to the torture of a witness who might not divulge the information we want unless forced to do so.

We shall briefly compare a scientific study in which experimentation was used with the same scientific study prior to the introduction of experimentation. Physicians had long been interested in the causes of pellagra. By observing many cases, they found that it was a disease of high incidence among the poorer classes of the population but was very rare among the better off. This might be due to any number of causes. Hypotheses about the unsanitary conditions, poor food, wrong diet prevailing among the very poor, or the crowded conditions that might make a disease endemic among the whole population very prevalent among the poor appeared to be good hypotheses, some or all of which might be true. But no one knew which one was correct. It was not possible to find out which was the true cause unless an experiment could be done that would hold some conditions (food, exposure, unsanitary conditions, and so on) constant while varying the condition cited in the remaining hypothesis.

Most people in a society like our own will not voluntarily submit them-selves to the inconvenience and danger of being a guinea pig for a scientist. You will not find the wealthy, who get adequate food, volunteering to eat their good food under unsanitary conditions just to prove some hypothesis about diet. Dr. Joseph Goldberger, of the Rockefeller Institute for Medical Research, however, found an ideal experimental situation: a group of men in prison having a high rate of pellagra-incidence. Their living conditions and diet were more or less identical. He could, therefore, experiment with one of these conditions at a time, while holding the other constant. He found in a very short time that the disease did not spread from person to person, for the solitaries got it as often as the others; improving the sanitary conditions did not lead to lowering the incidence-rate; but changing the diet so as to include fresh fruits and vegetables did cause the number of cases to decline.

Both before and after the situation was subjected to experiment, of course, observations were required. But earlier, the physicians did not really know what they were observing. By simply looking at a man with a disease, you cannot tell whether the important fact is that he is a dirty man or a poorly nourished man or a man who has been exposed to the disease. But with an experiment, in which you can find a man who is clearly an instance of one of these types but not of the others, you can eliminate the false hypotheses.

To normalize and control the possible causal factors and then to vary them one by one is the technique of experiment. In this way, we find relatively "pure" cases that nature and society do not present to us ready-made. The illustration, simple as it is, brings out many important aspects of the experi-mental testing of hypotheses.

1. *An experiment must be planned*—It has been said, "The armchair is migh-tier than the laboratory." Without planning the experiment, setting up pro-per controls, and knowing what factors it is worth while to vary and observe, an experiment is no more than just monkeying around in hopes of stumbling upon an interesting fact. Sometimes this is successful, and there are cases of accidental discoveries in the laboratory. But it is wasteful to count on making them, and when we do get results in this way, we have to repeat the experi-ment under more carefully controlled conditions to learn what our results really mean.

2. *In an experiment, we must know what conditions to hold constant*—The factors to be held constant are those considered in the collateral hypotheses and in the alternative hypotheses we are not now testing. The one to be varied is chosen on the basis of the hypothesis we are interested in testing at the mo-ment. If our collateral hypotheses are wrong, or if we have overlooked some plausible alternative to the hypothesis we are testing, we fail to control a relevant factor. When this happens, the experiment will not mean what it seems to mean. We shall get wholly surprising results that cannot be ob-tained again when we repeat the experiment, or the results will be so vari-able and "scattered" that we shall not know how to account for them.

By what is known as "factor analysis," it is possible for a statistician to design a series of experiments in each of which it is *not* necessary or possible to vary only one of the factors and yet for him to conclude which factor is the decisive one or even to conclude how much each of the variable factors contributes to the end-results that are observed. Even though the logic and mathematics of such experimental designs are complicated and must be learned through the study of statistics, the over-arching features of the use and interpretation of experimental results are not greatly affected by these more complicated and powerful statistical methods.[10]

3. *An experiment must be performed on an isolated system*—By an isolated system is not meant one that is absolutely isolated from everything else. We can never heve isolated systems in this sense. All physical experiments, for instance, are performed in a gravitational field, and we cannot shield our experimental situations from all outside effects. But we do not need that extreme and unattainable degree of isolation. By isolating a system is meant arranging it in such a way that the factors that might affect it but that we are not now interested in testing will remain constant throughout a series of experiments. Which facts are to be held constant throughout a series are determined by the collateral hypotheses. The ones to be held constant in some experiments but altered in others are determined by the set of alternative hypotheses from which the elimination is to be made.

4. *A good experiment usually need not be repeated*—If we have actually controlled all the relevant conditions and have accurately observed the results of carefully controlled variations in the possible causes, there is no need to repeat the experiment. Not all experiments are good in this sense. It is always possible that we are not dealing with an isolated system, and it is always possible that there is some mistake in observation. But a single well-conducted experiment is far more revealing than a large number of uncontrolled observations. We need and have many observations of earthquakes and still do not know very much about their causes; we have only one experiment on the constitution of some chemical compound and no one feels the need to repeat it.

We have here what might appear to be a paradox to those who believe that science is largely inductive, going from many instances to a single generalization. The sciences that collect countless observations do not usually get the neat laws and results obtained in a science that can base its conclusions on a few well-conducted experiments.

5. *An experiment may not mean what it seems to mean*—The facts observed may not actually be relevant to the hypothesis being tested. This happens when the experiment is not properly planned, not carefully performed, or its results not accurately observed. It is, of course, true that some result will be obtained even from a careless or misguided experiment, but the results of such an experiment are not facts that can properly be used as evidence

[10]For a very clear example, as simple as perhaps can be found, of the factor analysis of experiments with several variables, see E. Bright Wilson, *An Introduction to Scientific Research*, Chap. 4 (New York: McGraw-Hill Book Company, 1952).

for or against a hypothesis. We might say that they are facts about some experimenter's work, but not facts that belong to the body of a science as evidence for or against a specific hypothesis. One example of a poor experiment shows the insignificance or misleading character of the results obtained when precautions are not taken.

In a series of experiments in pathology, the purpose was to ascertain whether a certain chemical compound A causes cancer in rats. The experiment seemed to show that A did have this effect, but the observations were so surprising to other investigators that they repeated the experiments. Sometimes they duplicated this result and sometimes they found that the compound did not have this effect. Then it was discovered that in the original experiments, and in some of the subsequent ones, the reagent used had not been pure. The original experimenter had believed that it was a fact that A was a cause of cancer; the real fact was, "These rats, treated with the material in the bottle marked 'A,' developed cancers." It was not a fact that the compound that is *really* A was the cause of the cancers, although this was the conclusion drawn from the experiment; it was suspected and finally rejected because repetitions of the experiment gave different results.

In experiments that cannot be repeated with the same results, we say that there has been some experimental error. Such an error is insidious in its effect on the process of verification because we do not usually know when or in what experiments it occurs. We suspect the existence of experimental error only after some quite unexpected or otherwise unexplained results have been obtained. When an experiment produces results irreconcilable with hypotheses already well established, it is always wise to recheck and, if necessary, to repeat the experiment before saying that the hypothesis has been refuted. In cases where no well-established hypothesis exists to occasion strong expectations of some specific result, it is much more difficult to know when to suspect and how to detect experimental error. Sir Arthur Eddington made a paradoxical turn in a common statement to call attention to the uncertainty of observation and experiment: "Never accept a fact," he said, "until it has been verified by a theory."

This advice is important, and is actually followed. Suppose you do an experiment in a chemistry class and "discover" that the formula for water ought to be H_8O_3 and tell the instructor that you have refuted the textbook's hypothesis that it is H_2O. Without even going over your experiment in detail, he will rightly say that you must have made a mistake. Instead of giving you a good mark for having overturned some ancient error, he will give you a bad mark for being clumsy in the laboratory.

There is always the outside possibility, of course, that you may be right and all the other chemists wrong. Hence Eddington's advice is not quite perfect. If we *never* accepted a fact until it had been verified by theory, we should never have to change any of our hypotheses and would never be able to test any of them. The advice, however, warns us not to be overly confident that anything that seems to be a fact is really the kind of fact that the scientist is interested in—a fact that is decisive for or against some hypothesis or generalization.

6. *Not all problems can be dealt with experimentally*—The astronomer cannot produce an eclipse at will in order to see what causes eclipses; the geologist cannot shift the continents about to see how they fit together; the psychologist cannot bring up a child in complete isolation in order to see how it would react at the age of eighteen to the first sight of another person. Society as a whole does not allow itself to be experimented upon by anthropologists, geneticists, and sociologists.

In such instances as these, we have to work on observations that are given to us in the normal course of events. But in many of these cases, we have a valuable substitute for the controlled single experiment: statistical control. In an experiment we can control or neutralize the irrelevant factors. In a statistical situation, we take as many cases as we can find with the hope that the irrelevant factors will cancel each other out, leaving only the relevant factors or real causes.

To take a simple illustration: You wish to know whether television in the home has any effect on children's school work. There are almost countless factors that probably do affect their school work—their I.Q., their relations to their parents, their affection for their teacher, their diet, their health, and so on. We might suppose, however, that if we take carefully selected groups of children with varying I.Q's, different diets and conditions of health, and differences in other respects that we think may have a bearing on school work, but all of whose parents have television sets, and compare them with other groups of varying I.Q., health conditions, and so forth, whose parents have no television sets, then in each group the high I.Q.'s will statistically cancel out the low I.Q.'s, the good diets and their effects will statistically cancel out the poor diets and their effects, and so on. If the groups have been chosen with proper regard to the rules of statistical inference, the factor that is not canceled out in each group will be the possession of or lack of television sets, and then we can see if the marks of these two groups differ significantly. If they do not, then we can consider the hypothesis that television affects school work as refuted.

Unfortunately, statistical control is seldom as perfect as experimental isolation, so that we are often not able to draw from statistical studies conclusions as definite as we could draw if a laboratory experiment were possible.[11]

7. *It is not always safe to generalize from an experimental to a nonexperimental*

[11]Three other uses of statistics should be mentioned: (1) by studying a small sample, under some conditions it is possible to judge something about the whole group; (2) when experimental results are "scattered" so that the experiment must be repeated, it is possible by use of certain statistical methods to determine which of a set of numerical values is the most acceptable and which are most infected with experimental error; (3) as an experimental shortcut, statistical analysis permits inference from a series of experiments in each of which a *group* of variables (instead of a single one) have been systematically varied in specified ways. (factor analysis).

situation—The cautious scientist will always remember that his inductions and extrapolations are based on the tacit assumption that all important factors in the new situation are the same as those in the experiment. This assumption is known as the *"ceteris paribus* clause" (*ceteris paribus*—other things being equal), and inasmuch as it can seldom be safely eliminated or suppressed, caution requires that the *ceteris paribus* clause be as fully and completely spelled out as possible. This is done by converting from the vague expression, "other things being equal," to a fully explicated family of hypotheses. The other things we tacitly assume will be equal will then appear as factors in the collateral and operational hypotheses; then when an experiment goes wrong, the scientist can redesign his experiment in order to find the assumption that misled him. So long as he is working with only the vague *ceteris paribus* clause, he may not be able to do this, for it is obvious that not *all* other things are ever equal in two experiments. The hazard in such generalization is well known to experimenters trying to determine, for example, the effects of a new drug on man. The original experiments are done on animals, and tentative conclusions are drawn about human beings. When these conclusions are shown to be false, we have not only eliminated a perhaps promising drug but also, through the analysis of the *ceteris paribus* clause, discovered something about the physiological differences between that species and man.

An experiment that does not lead us to expect one thing rather than another in future cases is, of course, utterly worthless. Experiments are not done merely to bring new facts under observation; they are done in order that we may choose among hypotheses so that we can foretell facts that have not yet been observed. But the hypothesis that is confirmed by a series of carefully controlled experiments may not be—indeed, is usually not—the only hypothesis needed for more complex cases where the previously controlled factors are no longer controlled.

CONCLUSION

Bacon, who is sometimes incorrectly considered to be a narrow empiricist, rightly saw how reasoning and observing are connected and how feeble science would be if it depended on either alone. He wrote,

Those who have handled sciences have been either men of experiment [observation] or men of dogmas [reason]. The men of experiment are like the ant: they only collect and use; the reasoners resemble the spiders, who make cobwebs out of their own substance. But the bee takes a middle course, it gathers its material from the flowers of the garden and the field, but transforms and digests it by a power of its own. Not unlike this is the true business of philosophy [science]; for it neither relies solely or chiefly on the powers of the mind, nor does it take the matter which it gathers from natural history and mechanical experiments [brute facts] and lay it up in memory whole, as it finds it; but lays it up in the understanding altered and digested.[12]

Brute facts are rendered intelligible by reason, and reason draws its sustenance and support from experience. To paraphrase a famous statement by Kant, reason without experience is empty, and experience without reason is blind. The method of science, which is by no means restricted to those fields of knowledse we all agree in calling the sciences, is a method of responsible hypothesizing for the sake of rendering intelligible the facts we have and for guiding us to facts as yet unobserved.

Our lengthy study of science has attempted to show two things. The first is the way in which scientific method can be considered quite apart from the techniques of the laboratory; one can use the scientific method whether he ever gathers statistics or works in a laboratory or not. Because this method has reached its highest precision in the sciences and has given us probably the most dependable knowledge we possess or can possess, it is a challenge to us to make use of such a method as far as we can in nonscientific inquiry.

The second thing our study of scientific method has shown is its limits. Science is not an exercise leading to the discovey of absolute and indubitable truths. Science never rises above the level of hypothetical explanation, or explanation based on assumptions, whose only justification is that they enable the scientist to predict future observations in the particular field of experience he claims as his own. Dogmatism is alien to the spirit of science and has no place in its method. We never indubitably know whether a particular hypothesis is true or not. There may always be some better or truer hypothesis waiting to be discovered, some "nasty little fact," as Huxley remarked, "ready to kill the most beautiful hypothesis." In either case we shall have to modify or reject our hypothesis—not because our new knowledge will rest on some foundation that is better than science but because the new hypothesis is called for by more rigorous and extensive use of the scientific method. All that we can ever say about a hypothesis that has been "verified," even one so often "verified" that we think of it as an obvious truth, is this: It has worked better than any other hypothesis we now know; so far we have found nothing against it; and it will probably continue to fit and foretell facts and guide us in our efforts to understand the world. If and when we have to reject or modify it, that will not be an intellectual defeat, for we shall be able to say of the one that takes its place: The new hypothesis is more nearly the truth than was the old one.

Even hypotheses so firmly established that we tend to think of them as being immutable and ultimate—that the earth goes around the sun, that Euclidean geometry applies to astronomical phenomena, that atoms exist—

[12]Francis Bacon, *Novum Organum*, Aphorism 95, in *Bacon Selections*, ed., Mathew Thompson McClure (New York: Charles Scribner's Sons, 1928), p. 341.

are, in the final analysis, only hypotheses that have been gradually confirmed without our finding anything against them. Absolute demonstration, with no if's, and's, and but's, is not the business of science or of any enterprise that makes use of the methods of science.[13]

This fact can make little or no difference to our modest attempts to add a little to the store of knowledge. Acknowledging it is by no means equivalent to skepticism. Recognizing that our best and most dependable knowledge is hypothetical in structure need not make us withhold our judgment that Milton was born in 1608, or that water expands when it freezes, or that the sun will rise tomorrow. It may make some difference, as we shall see in Chapter 11, to the decision we make concerning how much assurance we can properly feel in the philosophers' attempts to "explain everything." But at this stage of our analysis, one task of philosophy with respect to the organization and scope of knowledge is clear. It is to keep us aware of the hypothetical status of the knowledge we have, and to forbid blind dogmatism that this knowledge, or some allegedly better knowledge based on authorities or on our feelings or pure reason, is beyond question and examination. The task is to encourage critical rather than dogmatic use of the conclusions that scientists and others have reached about man and the world, to keep open the path of inquiry, and not to allow inquiry to be stopped at the boundary of present-day science.

APPENDIX TO CHAPTER 8

An Example of Scientific Method in Biology

The preceding sections of this chapter have given a somewhat schematic account of the method of scientific thinking and have illustrated various stages of this method by a variety of examples, each of which was chosen to bring out some specific point. In this appendix we shall use a single example, which has the advantages of being very easily understood in all its details and of illustrating and bringing together all the most important procedures and rules.[1]

---

[13]We certainly do not assert that philosophy has a method that will permit it to give demonstrable certainties beyond the limits of science, as we shall see in Chapter 11; and we have already seen the limits within which mathematics can give demonstrable and indubitable knowledge, in Chapter 4.

[1]The following simplified account is based on three articles: Robert Galambos, "The Avoidance of Obstacles by Flying Bats: Spallanzani's Ideas (1794) and Later Theories," *Isis*, XXXIV, Part 2, No. 94 (Autumn, 1942), 132–40; Robert Galambos, "Flight in the Dark: A Study of Bats," *The Scientific Monthly*, LVI (February, 1943), 155–62; and Robert Galambos and Donald R. Griffin, "Obstacle Avoidance by Flying Bats: The Cries of Bats," *Journal of Experimental Zoology*, LXXXVIII, No. 3 (April, 1942), 475–90. All quotations, unless otherwise noted, are taken from the first of these three articles, by permission of the Editor of *Isis*.

Statement of the facts from common observation and statement of the problem— Galambos writes,

Since ancient times the bat has been an object of interest to biologists and laymen alike. The bat flies at night, and this fact has appealed both to mystics, who saw in its nocturnal wanderings collusion with the powers of evil, and to naturalists, who speculated on how the animal directs itself under conditions where its eyes can be of little or no use.

The first rigorous scientific study of the problem was made by the Italian Lazzarro Spallanzani, who was

. . . thoroughly familiar with the animals and their behavior, and . . . knew at first hand the nature of the dark subterranean passageways in which they lived. Perhaps it was once when his candle flickered out while he was exploring such a passageway that it first occurred to him to wonder how bats avoid obstacles.

Thus arises a problem: in the "settled area" of our experience, where we are at home with what we observe, men and animals usually guide themselves by sight, but this is unlikely to be the case with bats, which fly in the dark. There is thus an "unsettled area" of experience, a problematical area in which we do not know the explanation of what we observe. Our settled experience is that normal men guide themselves by sight, blind men by touch, all of us sometimes by hearing. Our collateral hypothesis, and the one that Spallanzani used, is that there is some sense organ by which the bat guides its motion. The hypotheses to be tested were hypotheses about the specific sense organ required for this behavior.

First hypothesis to be tested (H_1)—Some animals, such as cats, can see in almost complete darkness; perhaps bats can also. If this is so, bats who have been blinded will be unable to guide their flight. Thus the first hypothesis and the operational hypothesis O_1 ("If we destroy the bat's vision, it will be unable to avoid obstacles") led Spallanzani to perform this experiment. Result: "The animals avoided obstacles as well after the operation as before." In other words, the opposite of the predicated fact is observed, and the hypothesis is inferred to be false by the method of denying the consequent of the hypothesis.

Second hypothesis to be tested (H_2)—The bats might be guided by their sense of touch. But they do not come into actual contact with the walls; they avoid them. Hence this hypothesis does not fit the already known facts and requires no further tests.

Modification of second hypothesis, giving a new hypothesis (H_3) *to be tested—* Perhaps the bats have an extraordinarily acute sense of touch, which would be responsive to slight disturbances in the air near walls and obstacles. Such sensitivity is known to exist in many animals with hair. If this is the correct hypothesis, then destroying the alleged sensitivity should make the bats helpless in avoiding obstacles. So Spallanzani coated a bat with a thick varnish (O_2) and predicted that a varnished bat would not avoid obstacles. Yet he observed the opposite; they avoided obstacles as well as unvarnished bats. Thus, H_3 is refuted by denying that its consequent corresponds to the observed facts.

Fourth hypothesis to be tested (H_4)—Taste, in some unexpected way, might be responsible. This is an unlikely hypothesis, for we cannot imagine any mechanism by which the sense of taste could have this effect. But Spallanzani tested it by excising the tongue of a bat (O_3) and observed that the bats retained the ability. Thus this hypothesis is refuted.

Fifth hypothesis to be tested (H_5)—Smell might be responsible. Operational hypothesis O_4: plug the nose of the bat; then if H, is correct, the bat should not be able to avoid obstacles. The experiment was done on several bats, and the results were scattered. Some animals retained the ability, and in others it was lost or reduced. At any rate, the nose was not completely eliminated as a possible causative factor. Spallanzani believed that his experiment had interfered with the bats' breathing,[2] and that this experimental factor might explain his results. In other words, he believed that here there was an experimental error, which would explain the apparent exception or renegade instance. (But remember that a renegade instance may be especially important if properly understood.)

Sixth hypothesis to be tested (H_6)—Hearing may be involved. Operational hypothesis O_5: plug the ears of the bats, and if H_6 is correct, they will not be able to avoid obstacles. Spallanzani performed this experiment, but again his results were not clear-cut. Of eleven bats he used, ten were unaffected by the experiment. In those ten cases, he observed facts inconsistent with H_6, which tended strongly to refute it. The eleventh bat flew "with difficulty," and thus was apparently a case consistent with the hypothesis. But Spallanzani wrote that this was

... an accidental case which, although being negative, does not weaken at all the positive facts advanced and proves only that in our negative decisions we must never abandon ourselves to a single isolated case.

Here again was a renegade instance, which was not further explored.

Seventh hypothesis to be tested (H_7)—A combination of two or more of these organs is required for guided flight. Operational hypothesis O_6: cover all the head organs of the bat with a hood. If H_7 is correct, the bat will not be able to avoid obstacles. The experiment was done by another scientist, Rossi, and he found that the bats lost their ability to avoid hitting the walls.

Now, of course, this does not prove H_7. It is a case of affirming the consequent. Moreover, Spallanzani objected to H_7 on the basis of parsimony or simplicity—he did not think it was a *good* hypothesis. He said:

[2]This is really an *ad hoc* hypothesis, made to explain a specific exceptional event and not taken as applying to all cases.

If these senses, separately considered, are insufficient to this purpose, according to my judgment they will be equally so when used together; for the efficacy or power of the whole is finally to be resolved into the value of its component parts, and if these parts be defective, they will transmit their defect to the union of these senses.

The only hypothesis, then which gives clear-cut results is H_7, but it is poor. How could the bat do something with two or more organs that it cannot do with any of them separately? Spallanzani believed that it could not do so.

Eighth hypothesis to be tested (H_8)—Spallanzani then proposed a new hypothesis on the basis of the following considerations. Since neither eyes, ears, tongue, nose, or touch are separately the condition of guided flight (H_1 ... H_6 are false), and "all taken together" (H_7) is a poor hypothesis, then there might be "some new organ or sense that we do not have and of which, consequently, we can never have any idea." This is obviously a poor hypothesis, for there is no way to test it; it is fruitless, amounting to no more than an admission that bats do guide themselves in darkness by using a power human beings cannot understand.

And there the problem rested for a century and a half. The established facts that we would not have had if Spallanzani had not used good (but false) hypotheses are: (1) that bats without sight, taste, or touch-sense still have the ability to avoid obstacles; (2) that bats with plugged ears or plugged noses sometimes have this ability and sometimes do not; (3) that bats with none of these senses have lost the ability. The explanation of these facts had to await the twentieth century, when scientists had gained more knowledge of the physics of sound.

Ninth hypothesis to be tested (H_9)—An analogy, unthinkable in Spallanzani's time, provided a new hypothesis. Hartridge, an English scientist, "recalled the use of sound-detecting devices used in World War I and proposed that bats hear reflections of their high-pitched cry and thus inform themselves of the location of obstacles," much in the way that a ship can locate a submarine by sending sound-vibrations into the water and picking up their echoes.

This hypothesis fitted all the facts that were consistent with the other hypotheses, and in addition, it fitted the facts that were renegade instances for H_5 and H_6, for both the respiratory organs and the ears are required by this hypothesis—one to be the transmitter of the signals and the other to be the receiver. In addition, this hypothesis is simpler than H_7 because it restricts attention to only two of the five sense organs, and it is better than H_8, for although Spallanzani could not have imagined such a sensory process, the advance of science had taken this kind of explanation out of the realm of mystery.

There was one fact that this hypothesis did not fit: the apparent silence of the bats while flying. But it is known now that there are sounds that are inaudible to the human ear although some other animals can hear them, and such supersonic sounds can be detected by suitable electrical instruments. This objection, therefore, is not serious provided it can be shown that bats do make supersonic sounds that can be detected instrumentally. To test this new hypothesis (H_{10}), which is a modification of Hartridge's, we turn to three experiements of Griffin and Galambos:

O_7: Tie the snout of the bats so that they can emit no sound. This plus H_{10} leads us to expect that the bats will not be able to guide themselves. This is actually observed.

O_8: *Very carefully repeat* the experiment under O_5, plugging the ears of the bats. If great care is taken to prevent any sounds from being heard by the bat, then this experiment with H_{10} would lead us to expect that all bats would behave like the eleventh bat in Spallanzani's experiment. This was observed. (The renegade instance was the significant one.)

O_9: Use an instrument that will convert inaudible supersonic sounds into audible sounds. This with H_{10} leads us to expect that sounds will be heard while the bats are in flight and that no sounds will be heard under the conditions of O_7. This is the crucial experiment. Galambos writes,

We found [supersonic sounds] to be emitted by more than one hundred bats of four different species. . . . The supersonic cries, moreover, usually appear entirely independently of the audible cry and consist of a band of frequencies in the region of fifty thousand cycles.[3]

And under the conditions of O_7, no supersonic sounds are detected.

Conclusion—H_{10} fits all the observed facts and leads to the discovery of new ones. It is the only hypothesis we know that is consistent with all of them. Hence H_{10} is said to be verified by the process of elimination and convergence of evidence.

BIBLIOGRAPHY

Bronowski, Jacob, "Science as Foresight" in *What is Science?*, pp. 385–436, ed., J. R. Newman. New York: Simon and Schuster, Inc., 1955.

Cohen, Morris R., and Ernest Nagel, *Introduction to Logic and Scientific Method*, Chaps. 5 and 11. New York: Harcourt, Brace, & World, Inc., 1934.

Conant, James B., *Science and Common Sense*. New Haven, Conn.: Yale University Press, 1951.

Dewey, John, *How We Think* (1910) (new edition). Boston and New York: D. C. Heath & Company, 1933.

Duhem, Pierre, *The Aim and Structure of Physical Theory*, trans., P. P. Wiener. Princeton, N. J.: Princeton University Press, 1954. (Also New York: Athaneum Press, 1962).

Hadamard, Jacques, *The Psychology of Invention in the Mathematical Field*. Princeton, N. J.: Princeton University Press, 1949.

Hanson, N. R., *Patterns of Discovery*. Cambridge: Cambridge University Press, 1961.

---

[3]Galambos, "Flight in the Dark: A Study of Bats," pp. 155–62, at p. 159. Evidence is presented in this article that bats are able to respond to as well as emit supersonic sounds.

Polya, George, *How to Solve It*. Princeton, N. J.: Princeton University Press, 1945.

Popper, Karl R., *The Logic of Scientific Discovery*. New York: Basic Books, Inc., 1959.

Thomas, Charles Allen, *Creativity in Science*. Cambridge: M. I. T. Press, 1955.

Toulmin, Stephen, *Foresight and Understanding*. Bloomington: Indiana University Press, 1961.

Wallis, W. Allen, and Harry V. Roberts, *The Nature of Statistics*. New York: Collier Books, Inc., 1962.

Wertheimer, Max, *Productive Thinking*. New York: Harper & Row, Publishers, 1959.

Wilson, E. B., Jr., *An Introduction to Scientific Research*. New York: McGraw-Hill Book Company, 1952.

QUESTIONS AND TOPICS FOR DISCUSSION

1. Read selections from Bacon's *Novum Organum*. How does his account of scientific method differ from the one outlined in this chapter?
2. The criticism is made that an experiment affirms a consequent and that science is therefore based upon a logical fallacy.
   a. Show how the argument of the text answers this objection. Do you believe this answer is adequate?
   b. Evaluate the following answer to this criticism: When you say, "If atoms exist, then these and these experimental results will be obtained; and they are obtained; therefore atoms exist," you are indeed affirming a consequent. But that is not what the scientist says. He says, "If you obtain such and such results, then atoms exist, and you do obtain these results; therefore atoms do exist." Therefore he is affirming an antecedent, and this is valid.
3. Comment on the following statements by scientists about their method:
   a. "Others will tell your to try to prove you are right, but I say try to prove you are wrong." Pasteur.
   b. "I make no hypotheses." Newton.
   c. "I didn't think; I investigated." Sir Alexander Fleming, describing his discovery of penicillin.
   d. "Students of the natural sciences . . . possess a healthy disbelief in bare logic. They like to see logical deductions verified by experiment." Gunnar Dahlberg, in *The Scientific American*, CLXXXIV, No. 1 (January, 1951), p. 49.
   e. "As you will see . . . I have sought to arrive at the truth by a succession of facts, by eliminating, as far as possible, reasoning which is often a deceptive instrument, and by following the torch of observation and experiment." Lavoisier, in a letter to Benjamin Franklin.
   f. "Never accept an experiment until it is checked by a theory." Eddington.
   g. "The evidential value of any fact is an unknown quantity until the fact has been explained." W. D. Bancroft.
4. G. B. Brown (*Science, Its Method and Its Philosophy*. New York: W. W. Norton & Company, Inc., 1950) reports that a high correlation was found

between the number of children born in a certain region of Germany and the number of storks in that region. How would a scientist "prove" that this is only a coincidence? What role would hypotheses play in his "proof"?

5. Discuss the obstacles to the use of the method of hypothesis and controlled observation outside the field of the sciences.

6. Explain how it is possible to test a collateral hypothesis. What reorganization of the family of hypotheses is required for such a test?

7. Describe, as carefully as you can, the role of mathematics and logic in a science that must make use of experiment and observation.

8. "Experiment is observation at its best." Discuss. How is it that one of the most accurate of the sciences, astronomy, is not ordinarily considered an experimental science?

9. Comment on the following:
   a. "Knowledge is power." Bacon.
   b. "To know in order to foretell." Comte.
   c. "Ye shall know the truth, and the truth shall make you free." Jesus.

10. It is sometimes objected to evolution and psychoanalysis that they are "just theories." Is this a sound objection? Could the same objection be made to the occurrence of the French Revolution?

9 THE LAWS OF NATURE AND HUMAN FREEDOM

One purpose of the scientist is to discover the laws of nature. He is inspired by the conception that the universe is a cosmos, not a chaos. He has faith that things and events in the world can be comprehended if he can learn some law or set of laws that "govern" them, and he believes that his methods can lead to the discovery of these laws. The greatest triumphs of science are won when a law is discovered that can be illustrated in case after case and used to predict new and otherwise unexpected facts. Historians sometimes look for laws of history, by which the movements of nations and peoples can be understood and foretold. Psychologists sometimes speak as though they had discovered laws that "govern" all human acts. All such quests for laws and the success that these quests have met in many fields raise profound problems concerning the nature of the universe and of man, especially problems touching on human spontaneity, freedom, and fate. It is therefore an important task of the philosopher to examine the presuppositions, methods, results, and implications of the search for the laws of nature.

THE CONCEPT OF LAW

The scientist searches for truths that are illustrated in many cases and is interested in a particular case only to the extent that it is an instance of, or an exception to, some generalization or prediction based upon a hypothesis.

We reach generalizations by abstracting—a process of selection and neglect. "Red," "hot," and "metallic" are abstractions that I can reach beginning from the perception of a poker in a fire. I do not ordinarily experience red by itself; I experience it only as a quality or adjective of a particular thing. But by selecting the color-quality of the thing and neglecting its other qualities, I obtain the abstract quality "red." By combining various abstractions, I can describe particular objects, such as "red, hot, metallic stuff."

As a scientist, I neglect the unique characteristics that an object has and attend to those characteristics that, I believe, apply generally to many other objects. In other words, I am interested in an object as a member of a class of things each of which illustrates the same abstractions.

A description is one type of combination of abstractions. If I wish to describe an ashtray, for instance, each adjective I use (such as "circular," "small," "white") applies to other objects, too. But I hope that the specific combination of them will fit only a few things and, in many instances, I want them to fit one and only one thing. Each time I add an adjective, I narrow my description down so that it describes fewer other things. The adjectives are simply added to one another; from the statement that the ashtray is white, round, and small, I do not determine also that it is shallow or that it is deep. In a description, the abstractions and adjectives I apply to a thing are more or less independent of each other.

It is sometimes said that the "laws of nature describe things and events," but this is not quite true. For a law of nature is a specific kind of combination of abstractions, in which the abstractions are neither *independent* of each other nor *logically dependent* upon each other. On the one side, we have descriptions— the abstractions x, y, and z—from which we cannot infer that the abstraction a applies or does not apply; on the other, we have logical truths in which one term implies another; I know that the abstraction "married" does not apply to a man to whom "bachelor" applies. In between, there are statements like "The atomic number of hydrogen is 1; its valency is 1." I am neither merely describing a sample of hydrogen, nor stating a logical equivalence (that does not exist) between "atomic number" and "valency"; rather, I am saying that whatever has the atomic number 1 has also a valency of 1 and that both these abstract properties fit hydrogen.

A further important difference between a description and a law of nature is that the former applies to an individual thing or to a closed class of things. "This poker is red hot" is a description of an individual thing; "All the people in this room have at least one dime in their pocket" describes a closed or limited class. Laws, however, apply to classes that can be expanded without change in the law. I say, "All metals when heated expand," and I mean to refer not only to the very large class of actual metals that now exist or have existed, but I mean to say that if there *were* a piece of metal in this box, then it *would* expand if it were heated. Statements taken to be laws of nature, therefore, have a broader range than descriptions, in that they also refer, if they are true, to merely *possible* cases.

The most important laws of nature do not merely assert that two abstractions are always present together, or jointly absent; but they say what degree or magnitude of the one is associated with what degree or magnitude of the other. It does not suffice to say "Metals expand when heated"; we want to know what percentage expansion of a unit piece of metal accompanies an increase of its temperature by a specific number of degrees. These are called *functional laws* because they state that the expansion is a (mathematical) function of a change in temperature.

Given a true law of nature and observations indicating that something is an instance of one of the abstractions mentioned in the law, we can predict instances of other abstractions. To take some well-known examples. Newton's law of gravitation mathematically relates the abstract properties of objects denoted by the terms "mass," distance," and "force"; Kepler's laws relate the abstractions "distance from the sun" and "velocity of planet"; Galileo's law of falling bodies relates "distance traversed" and "time elapsed"; the Weber-Fechner law relates "strength of stimulus" and "intensity of sensa-tion"; and the law of supply and demand relates the abstractions we call "supply," "demand," and "price."

The scientist searches for those few abstractions whose instances will be most generally or universally correlated with one another. It may be that instances of all abstractions are related to each other by laws; but if this is so, we are far from knowing it. What we call physical and chemical proper-ties are either universally, or to a very considerable extent, so related, and the physicist and chemist are not interested in properties unless they are so related or unless he thinks he can find such a relationship. Properties like "good" and "bad" and "beautiful" and "ugly"—what we shall later call "value terms"—do not seem, on the other hand, to be related by any simple laws. Indeed, many philosophers have questioned whether there even *are* any such pro-perties. The scientist need not claim that "everything is related to every-thing"; one of his principal tasks is to seek for those properties of things and events that are related to each other so that from instances of some of them he can infer instances of the others, even when he cannot or has not yet observed some of the instances he is talking about.

This task raises one of the principal questions for philosophers interested in the theory of knowledge: Do I know, and if so how do I know, that unob-served cases will be, in specifiable respects, like cases I have observed? Since future cases have not been observed, how do I know that future cases will be like past cases? These are other ways of asking the question: *Why do things obey the laws of nature?*

PRESCRIPTIVE AND DESCRIPTIVE LAWS

This question is based upon a serious ambiguity in the words "obey the law." There are some laws that can be obeyed in the literal meaning of the word, and we call them *prescriptive* laws, whereas other laws can only be *illustrated*. The latter kind of law is called *descriptive* law. So the question must first be answered, "Are the laws of nature prescriptive or descriptive?"

We are all familiar with prescriptive laws, laws that prescribe what we should or should not do. A traffic law is such a prescriptive law. It tells us that we should not exceed fifty-five miles per hour on the highway. It is unfortunately true that such laws are not always obeyed.

Descriptive laws do not tell a thing what it ought to do but tell us what has usually or always been observed to happen. Galileo's law of falling bodies does not tell the ball what it ought to do, that it ought to reach the ground in a certain length of time, but tells us what relationship has been regularly observed between instances of the various abstractions describing its motions. The rolling ball presumably cannot know the law and then decide to obey it, as I can know the traffic law and decide to obey it.

These two types of laws have not always been distinguished. It has sometimes been thought that there must be a law-giver who legislates or dictates the laws to nature, just as government gives law to the citizens. This legislative function has usually been ascribed to God as the Divine Law-Giver. But this inference depends upon the mistake of assuming that because prescriptive laws require a prescriber other general statements also called laws likewise require a law-giver. This mistake is an example of the *fallacy of equivocation*—the error of using one word in two different senses and drawing a conclusion appropriate to one of the senses but inapplicable to the other. Only prescriptive laws are decreed, and only prescriptive laws can be broken; for if a descriptive law is "broken," we have all the evidence we need that what we thought was a law was actually only a generalization that does not apply to all cases. Descriptive laws are not given but are "taken," taken from the facts that illustrate them. We believe them to be illustrated even by events we have not actually observed.

These two kinds of laws are so frequently confused, and so many untenable consequences are drawn from this confusion, that it is worth while to consider how this confusion may have arisen. The French philosopher Auguste Comte (1798-1857) formulated the (descriptive) "Law of the Three Stages" in the development of the human mind. At each stage in the history of thought, he held, a specific kind of explanation is generally considered to be suitable and adequate. In the earliest stage, which he calls the theological, "the human mind, seeking the essential nature of beings . . . supposes all phenomena to be produced by the immediate action of supernatural beings." Such a notion originates from an analogy between nature and the kind of social order in which this type of explanation flourishes, namely, one not governed by unchangeable (prescriptive) laws but by the arbitrary and capricious will of an absolute monarch. In such a society, men get ahead by cajolery and flattery; when their understanding of nature is on this level, they practice magic and intercessory prayer. Nature does not seem to them to be uniform: storms and disease and death occur for no known reason; the best protection against them is to propitiate gods.

The Greeks, so far as we know, were the first people so impressed by the uniformity of nature that they attempted to explain it. Here perhaps their own form of government by law provided the key analogy. Order and harmony in society are brought about through obedience to laws and justice. The order and harmony of nature seem, by this analogy, to require also a natural law or natural justice. This analogy, surely one of the most portentous in the entire history of thought—even though it is a case of the confusion we are now trying to clear up—was drawn by Anaximander, who lived in the sixth century B.C. Another ancient writer, Simplicius, summarized Anaximander's doctrine concerning the events in nature and the changes that things undergo:

And from what source things arise, to that they return of necessity when they are destroyed; for they suffer punishment and make reparation to one another for their injustice according to the order of time, as [Anaximander] says in somewhat poetical language.[1]

Poetical language though it be, it marks a great advance over the more primitive notion that there is no real order in nature and what happens occurs because of the inscrutable will of a god. Anaximander represents the stage of thought that Comte calls "metaphysical," at which "the mind supposes, instead of natural beings, abstract forces, veritable entities [reified abstractions] inherent in all beings, and capable of producing phenomena." We are not entirely beyond this stage of thought when we say, for instance, that an apple falls to the ground "because of gravity" or that the velocity of the earth is nineteen miles per second "because of" Kepler's law.

We reach the third stage, the positive or scientific, when we clearly understand the difference between the two kinds of law and no longer confuse them, and when we do not trouble ourselves about unknown causes of things behind the phenomena we observe and seek only to describe (preferably in mathematical equations) what we do observe. A scientific law reached at this level is only a statement of

. . . invariable relations of succession and resemblance. . . . What is now understood when we speak of an explanation of facts is simply the establishment of a connection between single phenomena and some general facts, the number of which continually diminishes with the progress of science.[2]

According to this conception, a law is only a statement of a "schedule of observations," as one of Comte's followers called it. It is like a railroad timetable that tells us that five minutes after a train arrives from Washington another regularly leaves for Boston, which is all we need to know about trains in order to plan a trip; we do not need to know whether the trains are

[1] Quoted from *Selections from Early Greek Philosophy* (4th ed.), ed., Milton C. Nahm (New York: Appleton-Century-Crofts, 1964), pp. 39f.

[2] Auguste Comte, *The Positive Philosophy* (1830), I, trans., Harriet Martineau (London: John Chapman, 1853), p. 2.

propelled by steam or electricity, nor do we need to know the name of the engineer. Comte believed the same thing to be true of the laws of nature. The schedule of possible observations is all we can know and all we need to know in order to predict and prepare for future events. *Savoir pour prévoir* was the motto of Comte's positivism.

THE STATUS OF LAWS

This clears up the ambiguity in the question, "Why do things 'obey' the laws of nature?" But it does not answer it. We still want an answer to the question, "Why do the specific things in the universe behave the way the general laws of science say they behave?" Laws, we must remember, are statements of specific relationships among classes or instances of abstractions, and we still do not know why things repeatedly illustrate the same relationships among their properties and actions and to other things.

This question has had a long history, and it cannot be said that it has been solved to the satisfaction of many philosophers even today. But we shall consider three possible solutions.

Plato, as we saw in Chapter 3, believed that knowledge is more than perception, which presents only particular objects to the mind. In knowing, Plato believed, we must know how to find and apply and interrelate abstract terms that have many instances presented in perception and not just sense the one unique, ineffable, and irrepeatable object or event before us. The abstract terms, he believed, must also have a denotation. There must be a kind of entity to which they refer but an entity not given to the senses as a particular. These entities he called "Ideas" or "Forms," and later philosophers have called them "universals." "Blue" is a universal term applying to all particular blue things. "Blue" is not just an adjective for *them* but a name for that character by virtue of which blue things are blue and not of some other color. What is named by the word "blue" might be called "the blue" or "blueness." The blue or blueness is a universal, for some philosophers a real being named by the adjective "blue" but not existing as a particular thing at some particular time or place.

According to Plato, the system of universals known by abstraction and reasoning is metaphysically more real than the particular things we know by our senses. The latter change and perish, whereas the universals are permanent or eternal. The system of universals can be known by reason, and with reasonable knowledge of this system we can understand and explain the particular connections among the instances of universals present in the world of sense experience. Plato seems to have believed that the universals stand in necessary mathematical and logical relationship to one another and that God used this world of intelligible universals as a kind of model in creating the world of changing particular things that illustrate their logical connections with one another. Sometimes he goes so far as to suggest that the intelligible world of ideas or universals is the only real world and that the world we see about us is only an illusory reflection or shadow of the real world. Other philosophers, and sometimes Plato himself, did not go this far, but the closest followers of Plato did hold that universals are real and not mere abstractions in our mind, and for that reason they are called "Platonic realists."

It is easy to see that the Platonic realist will take a different attitude toward the status of laws in the universe from those who do not believe that there is any "blue" except the blue of particular blue objects. He holds that the laws of nature are parts of reality, superior to the particular things in nature. He can thus consistently hold that there is a legitimate sense in which we can say that the things in nature *obey* and not merely *illustrate* the laws. Things are what they are because of their participation in the realm of universals; the universals stand in necessary relationships to each other; hence the things we observe must stand in such relationship; the abstractions we make from them must be related to each other necessarily.

Other philosophers, both in Plato's time and since, challenged Platonic realism. They held that it was a poor hypothesis; it "duplicated" nature instead of explaining it. One does not understand the connection between the heat of the poker and its color a bit better when told that in the realm of Platonic forms, "the hot" is related to "the red" universally and necessarily; one should never have known even this if one had not observed specific cases of heated objects beginning to glow. The realm of Platonic universals was attacked by Ockham with his "razor" (see p. 187). (see p. 187) The philosophers who agreed with Ockham said that the only things that exist are particular or individual objects and that universals are only fictions we make by abstraction, for the sake of classifying similar things together. A universal, for those philosophers, is only a name, and they are hence called *nominalists* (from Latin, *nomen* = name). For this school of philosophers, only particulars are real, and a law of nature is only a correlation of abstractions that are shorthand expressions of a great variety of individual similar objects. A law of nature for the nominalist is what Comte said it was—a timetable telling us when one particular perception or instance of an abstraction will occur with respect to other perceptions. Laws are not metaphysically real beings explaining what we observe; they are simply logical or mathematical connections found among particular things and holding more or less generally in similar cases.

Nominalism usually appears to us to be more plausible than Platonic realism, for most people have great difficulty in conceiving how any universal can be objectively real; hence they are easily convinced that nominalism is true, and nominalism is a conviction of our "common sense." But nominalism makes the process of classification and description appear arbitrary and irresponsible, because it does not render intelligible the fact that our perceptions sometimes do and sometimes do not resemble one another. Nominalists cannot even try to explain *why* the relationships among instances of abstractions are constant when the instances themselves vary; they just tell us that they are constant. If the laws are laws connecting universals, and universals are only abstractions in our minds, then the laws seem to be only in our mind, and it becomes rather difficult to see why things outside the mind should even illustrate laws within it.

Philosophers have usually escaped from this quandary by finding some middle ground between Platonic realism and nominalism. The middle ground between an extreme form of Platonism and nominalism was worked out by Aristotle, and his theory is generally called *conceptualism*. According to it, there is no such thing as a bare, unique, and ineffable particular, nor is there any such entity as a real universal standing in splended isolation. Everything that exists is a particular conjunction of content (which Aristotle called "matter") and form or properties. The form does not stand alone, nor is it limited to any particular thing; it may be illustrated in many particular things. A particular thing is a *this*. But with respect to any particular thing, we can always ask *what* it is. The nominalists said that the concrete particularity of a thing (its *thisness*) is all it really is, and everything about it (its *whatness*) is only in our minds. The Platonic realists, on the other hand, said that it is merely an instance of *whatness*, and the *this* is merely a particular manifestation in time of a *what* (or of a form).

Consider how a conceptualist would deal with my dog. There is admittedly something unique and ineffable about my dog. She is precisely the dog she is and not some other dog more or less like her. She has her own history, which is intertwined with my own, and I will accept no substitute for her, however like her that substitute might be. All these unique and particular features are her *thisness*. They are, in fact, what is denoted by the proper name that I have given her and that I do not use for any other dog. But she also has real characteristics that are not unique to her, her *whatness*, the kind of dog she is. She is an animal, in the generic sense that a starfish is also an animal. She is a Dalmatian, in the specific respect that thousands of other dogs are Dalmatians. In order to "understand" her, I must be acquainted with her as a unique individual; I must know her in the way the French call *connaître* and the Germans call *kennen*. But in order to describe her and explain her behavior or treat her when she is injured, this kind of unique knowledge focused directly and exclusively on her as a *this* does not suffice. I must know the universal terms that apply to other dogs as well as to her and see and state their connections in ways that others can understand on the basis of their experience with dogs. I must know about her in the sense of the French *savoir* or the German *wissen*.

When you know she is a Dalmatian, then all your knowledge of other Dalmatians can be brought to bear to determine your expectations of her future behavior; when you know merely that her name is "Braxza," you do not thereby know anything else about her at all. But when you know that she is a Dalmatian—a universal—the conceptualist rightly says that you do not know the universal in complete isolation from all embodiment in particular objects and specific times and places, nor when you know *her* do you know her merely as a brute fact, a mere *this*. In either case, you know some very important universals, and you know them as applying to her. But you do not know anything about a metaphysical world that includes Dalmatianness but, unfortunately, no particular Dalmatians.

The conceptualist answers the question as to how things "obey" laws, then, by saying that there are no absolutely unique, ineffable things, and absolutely universal and transcendent laws that could be impressed upon things perhaps only by an act of God. Rather, a thing, by virtue of being an instance of some specific *kind* of thing, illustrates specific universals and their specific relationships to each other by its very nature. By studying particular things, which are instances of groups of universals embodied in a content, we can state the relationships between things and the properties and actions of things *as if* these relationships held between transcendent real universals and constituted laws that the things must "obey." But, when properly understood, these laws are seen to be what they are because the things behave as they do and regularly evince the same pattern of universals. Far from being isolated from the world of things that it applies to and that it seems to "govern," a law is abstracted from the things that illustrate it.

Laws can, indeed, be stated as definitions of things that "obey" them. To take a simple illustration, consider the notion of force. We have the experience of force when we push on an object, and we notice that the heavier a body is, the more we must push on it to make it move, and that the faster we accelerate it, the more we have to push. There seems to be some rough connection between force, mass, and acceleration. But we may, as the physicist does, *define* force as equal to mass times acceleration $(f = ma)$. Thenceforth no one has to ask whether some future force will vary exactly as mass and acceleration and, if so, why things "obey" this law. The law, as it were, has been "built into" the things by definition. If in some case a physical object seemed not to illustrate the law, we should normally correct our estimate of its mass or acceleration until it did illustrate the law $f = ma$.

INDUCTION AND THE UNIFORMITY OF NATURE

This is all very well, you may say, but we still do not know that future events will be like past cases. Certainly, you may grant, $f = ma$, and if something is not ma, then by definition, it is not f, but that still does not show that we can count on there being future cases of $f = ma$ instead of something different from that. Remember that the laws of nature do not state *logically necessary* relationships between terms or abstractions. We know we shall never find a married bachelor, for "married bachelor" is a self-contradictory expression; but $f \neq ma$ is not self-contradictory. If we measure force with one instrument, mass with another, and acceleration with a third, do we know that—experimental errors aside—we shall never find a case in which the first of these numbers is not the product of the second and the third? We do not. *What gives us reason to believe that the descriptive statements or laws we made on the basis of our past experience are dependable as a basis for predicting future observations?* This is another formulation of the ambiguous question, "Why do things 'obey' the laws of nature?"

It does not suffice simply to define things in such a way that if they do not obey laws, they are "renegade instances." This process of definition does nothing to suggest that our definition of force as equal to mass times acceleration or of a Dalmatian as a dog of such and such a kind will be illustrated in the future and that an equally good definition of a unicorn will have no illustrations. Our problem at this point is not solved by rational definition but by induction.

Bacon reacted perhaps too strongly against the medieval emphasis upon rational thought. He believed that the science of the Middle Ages was long on theory and hypothesis, but short on fact. He proposed, as we have seen, to direct attention to observed facts and to encourage men to gather more and more facts and was confident that when enough facts were available, it would be possible to generalize them into universal laws. This procedure is known as induction—the inference from particular cases to general propositions about all cases. It is illustrated, for instance, by inferring that all crows are black from the observation of many black crows and the failure to observe crows that are not black. In common experience we use such inference at every moment of life whenever we act out of habit; Macaulay said that an infant learns by Baconian induction to expect milk from his mother instead of his father. The rules of sound induction were formulated by Bacon and David Hume and were elaborated by John Stuart Mill in his celebrated *System of Logic* (1843). Recent work on induction has taken the form of studies of the statistical methods by which small samples of a large class can be used as a basis for estimating the composition of the class as a whole. By an induction from a very small number of interviews, for example, highly probable estimates of the national vote can be made.

Induction alone will not, however, lead to scientific knowledge. Merely observing apples falling in his garden would not have led Newton to the law of gravity. He grasped, as a hypothesis, the notion of a universal force of gravity having a specific relationship to mass and distance and found that the motions of the moon illustrated the law just as well as the fall of the apple. But it may be asked "What gave him the confidence that the motions of apples and the moon would *continue* to illustrate the law?" If they do not, labor is wasted in establishing such a "law."

The answer to this question is: the sound application of an inductive method. Newton believed that his observations justified applying his law to events he had not yet observed. We know that he succeeded in doing this; the discovery of Neptune was one of the most impressive consequences of the application of Newtonian laws. We also know that if one is careless in making an induction, as in jumping to a conclusion or neglecting negative instances, he will not get generalizations that will bear up in future experience.

But what justification is there for *any* inductive method, even the most careful? Why, or to what extent, does knowledge about the past justify us in making predictions about the future? David Hume wrote the chief philosophical inquiry into this question.

Hume

David Hume (1711–1776) was a Scottish philosopher, historian, and writer on ethics, politics, and religion. Even before thirty years old, he wrote his *Treatise of Human Nature*, which, as he said, "fell dead born from the press." Later, in 1748 when he had become famous, he wrote his *Inquiry Concerning Human Understanding*, in which he gave a more popular presentation of some of the central doctrines of the earlier and more technical *Treatise*. We shall discuss his examination of the problem of cau ation and induction as he presented it in the *Inquiry*.[3]

Kinds of knowledge—Hume begins by distinguishing two kinds of "objects of human reason or inquiry." They are either *relations of ideas* or *matters of fact*. By the former he means truths "discoverable by the mere operation of thought, without dependence on what is anywhere existent in the universe" (p. 40). Such truths are a priori, known in advance of any particular sense experience. Hume does not mean that these truths would be known to us if we had had no experience at all—then we would not even be conscious. He does mean that the knowledge that we have of such truths is not dependent upon our having made any specific observations of a particular object of sense experience. The truths of mathematics, he believed, are known in this way.[4] We can see by logic that a theorem in geometry is true if the axioms are true and if no error is made in deduction; it must be true. For instance, I know that the interior angles of a triangle are equal to two right angles not because I have ever measured them (if I had, the statement, "All triangles have their interior angles equal to two right angles" would be known as only approximately true) but because, given the postulates of Euclid's geometry, the equality logically follows. Hume thinks that the knowledge we get in this way is only abstract and formal; because it does not *depend* on "what is anywhere existent in the universe," it may not *apply* to

---

[3]The most convenient editions of the *Inquiry* are in *Hume's Theory of Knowledge*, ed., David C. Yalden-Thomson (Edinburgh: Thomas Nelson and Sons, 1951); and *An Inquiry Concerning Human Understanding*, ed., Charles W. Hendel (New York: Library of Liberal Arts, 1955). All page references are to the Hendel edition.

[4]See above, pp. 221ff.

anything in the universe either. There may be no real object corresponding to this kind of knowledge. Reason merely tells us that if the axioms are true, then the theorems are true; it does not tell us that there are things in the actual universe (say, real straight lines) to which the axioms apply. Hence we cannot be sure that this kind of "knowledge" is anything more than an analysis of concepts that are fictional instead of descriptive of things in the actual world.[5]

Matters of fact, on the other hand, are truths that cannot be demonstrated by logic. Our knowledge of them depends upon something more than logic —it depends upon experience. The proposition, "It is now raining," happens at this moment to be true; but it would not be illogical, in the sense of breaking any rule of formal logic, to say, "It is not raining." The way to find out whether it is raining is not to dispute about logic but to look out the window. Now, of course, I may be wrong in saying that it is raining; I may make a mistake in perception and see only water dripping from the trees. But if we take the usual precautions against error, looking is better than reasoning when it is a question of the momentary state of observable affairs or matter of fact at the present moment. Observation does not give us the demonstrative certainty we have of the truths of reason, but it gives us something that knowledge of the truths of reason alone could never give us—evidence about the present actual situation in some part of the real world.

We are never satisfied, however, with knowledge merely of the here and now. Knowledge is useful to us only if it can be generalized so that we can count upon it in the future. We are usually interested in momentary matters of fact only as evidence of what to expect in the future. We must then investigate with Hume some sentences that seem to tell us what *will* happen.

Knowledge of the future—Consider the sentence, "The sun will rise tomorrow." This is probably true; we ordinarily say it is certainly true; neither Hume nor any other sane man, perhaps, has ever seriously doubted it. But we cannot demonstrate it merely by the laws of logic. "The sun will not rise tomorrow," is just as certainly false, but it does not in the least infringe any rule of formal logic. Moreover, it is not a fact of observation either, for our observations are of today, not of tomorrow. How then can we be as sure of it as we seem to be?

Someone might propose to prove it by the following argument:

Events of Kind *a* are always followed by events of Kind *b*.
Sunsets are events of Kind *a*, and sunrises are events of Kind *b*.
Therefore, since the sun has set today, it will rise again.

[5]Hume's argument here is relevant to the conception of law mentioned at the end of the last section—that a law *defines* the object and therefore *must* be illustrated or "obeyed" by it. Thus it was suggested that $f = ma$ will always hold because by f we *mean ma*. Hume would say, "Yes, if there *is* a force in the sense defined, it will, by definition, equal ma; but the definition $f = ma$ does not imply that such forces will actually occur in the real universe."

But how do we know these premises? The first of the premises is a causal law, and the argument does not show how we can be sure, or whether we can be sure, that there are any classes of events such that a member of the first class *is* invariably followed by a member of another specific class.

We also need to understand what ground, if any, there is for asserting the second of the premises. No one doubts that every sunset has, until now, been followed by a sunrise;[6] but the question is whether sunsets are events of one class and sunrises are events of another class such that members of the latter invariably follow the occurrence of members of the first class. I can often be sure that some events are *not* related in this way. By careful observation and induction I can determine, for instance, that full moon and fair weather are not related as *a* and *b*; how can I be sure that sunsets and sunrises are related in this way?

We have, then, two questions: Do we know, and if so how do we know, that there are events of Kind *a* and Kind *b*? Do we know, and how do we know, that sunrises and sunsets are respectively of these kinds?

Analysis of the idea of causation—The first of these sentences involves a law of causation. It states what is ordinarily phrased, "Same cause, same effect." The idea of causation is that of necessary connection of events in time; it is the notion that the prior event has not merely been found in the past to be conjoined to a specific kind of subsequent event but that it is *necessarily* conjoined to it. If this were not so, the idea of causation would not in the least help us to make a transition from the sentence, "Such and such events in the past have always been followed by such and such other events," to the premise that we need for the argument, namely, "Such and such events will be followed by the same kinds of events that have followed them in the past." If a connection is necessary, it will be the same regardless of whether it is in the past, present, or future; and only if it is necessary can we be sure it will apply to the future. The causal principle seems therefore to express a necessary truth, for otherwise we would not feel sure, as we do, that it will apply to future cases.

This is the analysis of the idea of causation as it is involved in the first premise we use in predicting or attempting to demonstrate that the sun will rise. How does this idea come to us? Can the premise be proved? These are Hume's questions. And if Hume's classification of knowledge is correct, there can be only two possible sources and justifications of the causal concept: either reason or experience.

What is the source of this idea?—Hume shows first that it does not arise from and is not justified by pure reason. His argument for this is very simple.

---

[6]We do not say, of course, that the sunset itself is the cause of the sunrise, but because of their invariant sequence, we believe that they are in some way causally related (that is, as effects of a common cause).

If, he says, our knowledge of causation came from reason, we could by reason determine what would be the consequence of any given cause prior to any experience of its particular effect.[7] But we cannot do this:

> Present two smooth pieces of marble to a man who has no tincture of natural philosophy; he will never discover that they will adhere together in such a manner as to require great force to separate them in a direct line, while they make so small a resistance to a lateral pressure.[8]

> Were any object presented to us, and were we required to pronounce concerning the effect, which will result from it without consulting past observation, after what manner, I beseech you, must the mind proceed in this operation? It must invent or imagine some event which it ascribes to the object as its effect; and it is plain that this invention must be entirely arbitrary. The mind can never possibly find the effect in the supposed cause, by the most accurate scrutiny and examination. For the effect is totally different from the cause, and consequently can never be discovered in it.[9]

If this argument is valid (see footnote 7), we are left with only the second alternative. The principle of causation must arise from experience. Following through this alternative, Hume tries to see how experience might have produced it.

But Hume also finds that there is no objective experience that can give us the idea. All that our experience can teach us is that events of a certain kind have usually or always been followed by events of another specific kind. Observe, to take Hume's own example, one billiard ball hit another. We say, "The motion of the first is the cause of the motion of the second." But what do we actually *observe?* Only that the motion of the first billiard ball is followed by the motion of the other when the two come in contact. We do not *see* that the first *makes* the second move. We do not *see* the truth expressed in the subjunctive sentence, "If the first ball had not hit the second, the second would not have moved." We do not *see* that the second *had* to move when the first hit it. We see merely what happens in a given case; we do not see what must invariably or necessarily happen in all cases. We see the conjunction and sequence of events; we do not see causal necessity.

Even common sense tells us that the case we observe might have been simply a coincidence and that we should not make an induction from one event to all events. To prevent an easy error at this point, one says, "Do it again." So we repeat the experiment. Let us suppose that the same thing happens again. It would ordinarily be said, when this had been done a fair

---

[7]Hume has perhaps made an error here. Reason might (in some way Hume did not anticipate) justify the *principle* of causation yet leave the determining of the specific effect of a specific cause to experience. This is, in fact, the conclusion of the German philosopher Immanuel Kant (1724–1804), whose answer to the question of the justification of induction in many respects resembles the one we shall attempt in the next section.

[8]Hume, *op. cit.*, p. 42.

[9]*Ibid.*, p. 43.

number of times with the same result, that we had proved that the first ball caused the second one to move.

Although recognizing that this is what we should do before pronouncing a judgment that one thing is the cause of another, Hume will not allow us to jump to the conclusion that such an induction proves a necessary connection. For if we could not observe causality in the first instance, how can we observe it in the second or the nth instance if the second or the nth is "just like" the first? We obviously could not. And if the succeeding events are *not* "just like" the first, then what is it in the later experiments that makes them different from the first? If there is any objective difference, that is a sign the experiment is not being repeated carefully enough; we should use only repeatable cases in our inductions and generalizations. If they are not alike, we do not make any induction; and if they are alike, we cannot observe anything in the later that we did not also observe in the earlier, and we did not observe causation in the earlier.

Thus we are faced with a dilemma, and we seem blocked in either direction. Yet the fact remains that we do draw the conclusion that one thing causes another when the observations are repeated, even though we might not (and usually ought not) do so from a single case. From this fact, Hume draws one conclusion and asks one question.

The conclusion is this: experiences, no matter how often repeated, cannot give rise to the universal principle necessary for a logical demonstration that the future will be like the past. We cannot empirically justify the inference from, "Up to now this has always happened," to the causal principle, "This will inevitably happen." The causal principle may very well be true, and prudent men like Hume will act as if it is. But experience cannot give us an absolute justification for it.

The question is this: granting that there is no rigorous justification for the belief, why (for what psychological reasons) do we have the belief in the causal principle? In answering this question, Hume points out something that may have been overlooked in saying, "If we cannot infer causation from a single observation, we cannot infer it from a series of observations just like the first." For, he says, the subsequent cases are never *subjectively* just like the first, even if the events observed are as nearly alike as skill in experimentation can make them. Even if the *events* are alike, the *experiences* are not; in fact, the more the events are alike, the less alike are our experiences in one respect—the later experiences include a *difference in expectation*. We see the second case in the light of the first. After several such cases, we fall into the habit of expecting the second billiard ball to move, and the more often we observe this event, the stronger is our habitual or customary expectation. Man, says Hume,

... immediately infers the existence of one object from the appearance of the other, yet he has not, by all his experience, acquired any idea or knowledge of the secret power by which one object produces the other; nor is it by any process of reasoning he is engaged to draw this inference; but still he finds himself determined to draw it, and though he should be convinced that his understanding has no part in the operation, he would nevertheless continue in the same course of thinking. There is some other principle which determines him to form such a conclusion. This principle is *Custom* or *Habit.* . . . . All inferences from experience, therefore, are effects of custom, not of reasoning.[10]

[The belief in causation] is an operation of the soul, when we are so situated, as unavoidable as to feel the passion of love, when we receive benefits; or hatred, when we meet with injuries. All these operations are a species of natural instincts, which no reasoning or process of thought and understanding is able either to produce or prevent.[11]

The Uniformity of Nature as a Hypothesis

"Custom," "faith," "habit," and "instinct" usually connote something emotional. When adduced as a ground of belief, these words suggest that the belief is not quite certain and is held on insufficient grounds. Yet such grounds are those Hume proposes as the only justification for the causal principle and its corollary, the uniformity of nature, and the applicability of scientific laws to cases not yet observed.

The assumptions that we need for rendering induction intelligible and defensible are not propositions that men could have stumbled upon by habit or by watching billiard balls nor can they be demonstrated by formal logic. There are two of these propositions that, taken together, constitute the proposition that nature is uniform. The first is the principle of causation, which may be stated equally well in either of two forms: (1) events of Kind a are usually or always followed by events of Kind b; or (2) any instance of Abstraction a is associated with an instance of Abstraction b. The second is the principle of limited variety: the Kinds of events a and b or Abstractions a and b are limited in unmber but unlimited in scope of application or denotation.

Even if in some way we knew with absolute certainty that the first principle were true, it alone would not permit us to say that nature must present uniformities that could be discovered by induction and formulated as laws applicable to future cases, because it *might* be the case that every class of events had few members or only one member (every event absolutely unique) or that every abstraction had only one illustration. In a world in which that was the case, it might still be true that "same causes produce same effects," but the events in the world would be of such infinite variety that the so-called "same cause" would never recur, even approximately. The second of the principles provides the other condition needed for a justification of

[10]*Ibid.*, pp. 56–57.
[11]*Ibid.*, p. 60.

induction by saying that the classes of events and the classes of properties concerned have many members. Thus the first principle, which states that relations among these classes and properties are constant, has some material for repeated empirical application.

These principles, which constitute the thesis of the uniformity of nature, are not demonstrable by formal logic nor can experience prove them, although experience does illustrate them (or has until now). Let us consider them, therefore, as comparable to the hypotheses we have examined earlier —hypotheses going beyond the facts of experience yet helping us to explain those facts.

We must examine the hypothesis of the uniformity of nature to see whether it is good. Does it fit all the facts we have? Yes, in the sense that we have no facts that demonstrate that nature is not uniform. Whenever there is an apparent lack of uniformity, when what we thought was the "same cause" did not produce the "same effect," the hypothesis that nature is uniform occasions further investigation. In such cases, we usually have found and always expect to find that what appeared to be instances of the same abstraction or "same cause" were not actually alike. At least there are no clear-cut facts against the hypothesis.[12]

Is it consistent with other hypotheses? Yes; without it there is no way to test them by making predictions of what will be observed if they are true. A world that is not at least largely uniform is a world in which no predictions could be made; and a world in which no predictions could be made is one in which no hypothesis could be confirmed.

Is it simple? Simplicity is always relative, never absolute; but it is certainly simpler, both logically and psychologically, to say, "same causes, same effects," than to say that the "same cause" will sometimes produce one effect and sometimes, under identical conditions, produce others.

Is it testable, fruitful, and explanatory? Not in the ordinary sense of these words as examined in Chapter 8. Merely reiterating "Nature is uniform" will not, even if it is true, give explicit guidance toward the discovery of any of nature's more recondite uniformities such as those expressed in the laws of nature. By itself, the uniformity of nature does not explain anything; from it you cannot deduce or predict what uniformiti s may be found. If you tell a scientist who is interested in discovering the cause of sunspots, "Well, you know nature is uniform," you have only told him that there is a cause but have not in the least enlightened him on the question, "What are the conditions under which sunspots are formed?"

The hypothesis of the uniformity of nature, therefore, has some of the marks of a good hypothesis, but by itself it is not testable, fruitful, or explanatory. It is a hypothesis that is not put to the test but one that is eminently

[12]See below, p. 230.

fitted to be a collateral hypothesis. *It is*, in fact, *a member of every family of good hypotheses*, although when isolated neither it nor any other hypothesis is good in the sense of being testable.

No verification of this hypothesis is possible, in the manner that we verified the hypothesis about how bats guide their flight. Evidence for it is indirect and depends upon its position in a system of propositions and a family of hypotheses that we believe represent at least an approximation to the truth.

It is a unique hypothesis. Without it, no hypothesis can be verified. With it, all good hypotheses can be tested, and if it is true, the others that are true can be distinguished from those that are false. If, on the other hand, it is false, no hypothesis can be confirmed. Without it, all hypotheses become poor. There is no way of determining if *it* is false, for whenever it seems to be refuted (that is, whenever some unexpected result occurs under conditions that, we think, would have made an expected result to happen), we modify or reject the hypothesis that the specific expectation of this particular case was true about the specific things in question. To keep inquiry going, we modify or reject the specific hypothesis that led to the false prediction or add some *ad hoc* hypothesis like "experimental error" to explain the apparent lack of uniformity in nature.

Putting the matter succinctly, we cannot experimentally verify or refute the condition without which no experiment is possible. The uniformity of nature is a condition of verification, not an inference from it.

With these unique peculiarities, it does not seem to be merely a matter of "custom" or "instinct" to accept the hypothesis. It appears, on the contrary, to be eminently reasonable even though not required by formal logic. In fact, we have every reason to consider it to be a priori, in the sense that it is necessary for there to be scientific knowledge even though it is itself not derived *from* scientific knowledge. But we must remember that the specific regularities or uniformities we call laws of nature are discovered only a posteriori, by observation.

Some philosophers have regarded the uniformity of nature as a self-evident axiom, indubitable to the natural light of reason or to "common sense." It has been compared to the axioms of geometry, without which nothing in geometry can be demonstrated. There is now reason to believe that not even the axioms of geometry are known by direct intuition but that they are more properly regarded as postulates—assumptions made within a specific body of propositions not all of which can be proved. Modern geometry does not have to start with propositions that everyone can "immediately see" to be true but indemonstrable; it may and does begin with assumptions that are fruitful for the discovery and demonstration of geometrical propositions that might not have been discovered or could not be proved without them.[13]

---

[13]See above, page 90.

The collateral hypothesis of the uniformity of nature resembles the postulates of modern geometry in one respect but differs from them in another. It resembles them in that it is not a logically self-evident proposition; we can imagine a chaotic world in which it does not hold. "Nature is not uniform," is no more logically self-contradictory and absurd, and its contradictory therefore necessarily true, than, "Through a point in a plane external to a straight line, more than one parallel can be drawn," is logically self-contradictory and its opposite therefore necessarily true. And it differs from the postulates of geometry in that they have alternatives that are logically possible and usable in scientific work. There are non-Euclidean geometries in which the well-known postulates of Euclid are not used. Such geometries, as we have seen, are perfectly valid both mathematically and logically, and only experience can tell whether our universe can better be described by one of these geometries or by the better-known Euclidean system. But the hypothesis that nature is uniform appears to have no good alternative. If you try to formulate a science in which nature is not assumed to be largely uniform and regular, it seems that you destroy the chance to verify any hypothesis about it.

If we assume that induction, when carefully conducted, is invalid, we shall not be able to discover, through verification of any specific hypothesis, whatever uniformities there might be. If, on the contrary, we assume that induction is justified, then we might indeed not be able to verify many hypotheses, but we should have at least an even chance of discovering any uniformities that do occur in nature. Induction, therefore, need not be justified by appealing to faith or instinct but simply by indicating that it is a good bet. If you make this bet, you may win some of the time. But if you do not make the bet, you are sure to lose all the time and miss the truths you might discover.

The Principle of Indeterminacy

The conclusion we have just reached may be challenged by those who are acquainted with modern physics. It is said that the motion of a subatomic particle is not uniform; given the same conditions in two different experiments, sometimes a subatomic particle will behave in one way and sometimes in another. Nature is apparently uniform, we are told, only because these chance variations with no inherent uniformity are statistically cancelled out in our observations of aggregates of uncounted billions of these particles.

This is indeed a serious challenge to the doctrine of the a priori character of the assumption of the uniformity of nature. And so far from this being an embarrassment to, or a breakdown in, modern physics under the name of Heisenberg's "principle of indeterminacy," it is one of the fundamental principles of modern physics. But it seems to conflict with the views we have been developing, and it has been used by some incautious thinkers as having widespread and revolutionary implications for parts of philosophy far removed from subatomic physics; for example, it has been said that it over-throws causal theories in science and that it makes way for theories of the freedom of the will, which seemed excluded by the sciences that had been believed to prove the uniformity of nature. Before indulging in such flights of imagination, however, one should take into account one cautionary point.

The theoretical and empirical discovery of the unpredictable behavior of a specific subatomic particle neither refutes the principles underlying induction nor solves the problem of induction. The induction from a set of experimental results to a prediction of the outcome of future experiments is very much the same, although not *exactly* the same, as it would be if one maintained the principle of the uniformity of nature down to the last electron. Consider a small sample of the element radium-228. It consists of many billions of atoms, all, so far as we can tell, exactly alike. Some of these atoms undergo a radioactive decay; others do not. One who believes in the uniformity of nature believes that when all the conditions are the same, the results will be the same; hence there must be some difference between the atoms that decay and those that do not. The physicist who accepts the Heisenberg principle denies it. He asserts that one-half the atoms will disintegrate in 6.7 years but that why some disintegrate and some do not is a meaningless question, theoretically unanswerable. He says nothing about *this* or *that* atom, but only makes a prediction that half of them will disintegrate in 6.7 years; all he can say about an individual atom is that it has a 50–50 probability of disintegrating in the next 6.7 years. In saying this, the physicist is assuming—for very much the same reasons discussed in the previous section—that this prediction will be verified in the future. The problem of justifying inductions and predictions *where they can be made at all* is just like the problem of justifying inductions and predictions elsewhere. It is a question of how fine-grained our predictions are. It was formerly believed that they could be made infinitely finegrained, that there was no theoretical limit on the accuracy of our predictions. Now it is believed that there is a definite, mathematically-fixed limit we can never go beyond; but above that limit, physics is just as predictive, and nature is just as predictable as it was ever thought to be.

HUMAN FREEDOM AND THE LAWS OF NATURE

The view of the universe as a vast mechanism acting according to inexorable laws has aroused the enthusiasm of scientists, philosophers, and some poets and has given them pride in the intellect of man for discovering the pattern of nature. It has given some of them an enthusiasm for the universe or its maker, when they see how well ordered and organized it is. But it has given many men, like Omar Khayyam, the opposite feelings of helplessness, impotence, and unimportance:

And that inverted Bowl they call the Sky,
  Whereunder crawling cooped we live and die,
  Lift not your hands to It for help—for It
As impotently moves as you or I.

With Earth's first Clay they did the Last Man knead,
  And there of the Last Harvest sowed the Seed:
  And the first Morning of Creation wrote
What the Last Dawn of Reckoning shall read.

A world in which everything is caused by something earlier is a world in which human actions are, in principle, as predictable as eclipses of the sun and moon. In such a world, men might believe that they are free only because they do not know the hidden causes of their actions and wishes and choices. In such a world there seems to be no place for human freedom and responsibility, and human choice and effort seem illusory and futile.

This is the reason why so many people once heartily welcomed Heisenberg's principle of indeterminacy, because it seemed to show that not even inanimate nature is as inexorably determined as had been formerly believed. It seemed to reveal a chink in the armor of cold, impartial, inevitable, natural necessity. But more careful inquiry is likely to shatter these hopes.

The Heisenberg principle does not apply to matter consisting of large numbers of these apparently wayward and free particles; large events are still as predictable with the Heisenberg principle as without it.

But, it has been suggested, the human body is not just the statistically evened-out aggregate of all its atomic constituents, as a block of wood presumably is. Rather, it is said, human behavior is controlled by a kind of trigger mechanism in the synapses of the brain, where the unpredictable motion of a single electron might open or close a circuit that would cause an arm or leg to move or not to move; hence the larger motions of the body would be as unpredictable as the subatomic events that trigger the flow of energy to one or another part of the body. Although this may be true, it is hard to get much comfort from it. For mere unpredictable behavior is caprice, not freedom. Such action, due to the entirely fortuitous motion of a particle in my brain, would be an action for which *I* would not be responsible, for such action might just as well be incompatible with my character, responsibility, and will as compatible with them.

Still, it has been argued, the mind or the will might exert the deciding force on the motion of the particle in question, whereas if the particle in question were rigidly determined by prior physical conditions, this would not be possible. Hence, in the small area this principle accords to indeterminacy, the will might step in as the decisive causal factor; therefore, man could be free. In such an explanation as this, one would wonder how what is assumed to be nonphysical could exert a spatial displacement upon what is physical; and if it can do so, there is no reason to think that this displacement could be effected only on particles whose position is previously *undetermined* by that of others. Such a hypothetical superphysical agent could just as well be an *additional* causal factor in a train of events that would *otherwise* have been exhaustively determined by earlier physical conditions.

The essential feature of this argument is really another assumption that has little to do with the mechanism of brain action and nothing to do with the Heisenberg principle. It is the assumption that the mind of man is not itself completely determined by physical or physiological factors and that there is in the universe some center of indeterminacy other than those considered in the Heisenberg principle. That is to say, the Heisenberg principle neither implies nor is implied by the proposition that the will is free. Something other than the motion of subatomic particles must be free if there is to be human freedom.

Of course many philosophers have long agreed with the common belief that the mind is not wholly determined by physical and physiological conditions or at least that it need not be so determined in every instance of action. Beginning with Socrates, they have said that the physical universe, which they grant is largely uniform and determined, is not the whole of reality and that man, in his ultimate nature as a mind or soul, is not really a part of the physical universe and hence not subject to its laws. They see man as only partly natural, and his soul or will as superior to nature. Thus they can conclude that mind is an effective cause that from time to time can intervene in nature and change its course. By learning to control his propensities and passions, which admittedly have a physiological basis and often a compelling influence upon his thought and decision, and perhaps by availing himself of the help of God who is the Author of Nature, man, according to this view, can use and control the natural order without becoming subject to its laws.

In this way these philosophers find an escape from the blind necessity of nature through a metaphysical assumption concerning the essence and dignity of man as being supernatural. Man, they say, is a little island of freedom in a sea of necessity. Man is free because he can break the laws of nature, although at the same time, perhaps, he follows some higher (prescriptive) law. Nature is uniform only in those places where supernatural causes issuing from man or God do not interfere with its course.

In a question of this difficulty and importance, it behooves us to examine with utmost care every link in a chain of argument. For this, it is helpful to have available some technical, emotionally neutral terminology that will permit us to examine the question as dispassionately as possible.

The first word which falls before our effort to achieve an unemotional terminology is *fatalism*. Fatalism suggests an attitude of helplessness and futility because some events are just bound to happen, no matter what I do. All of us, perhaps, have moods of fatalism; we feel that we cannot escape our fate, no matter how much we turn and twist. The turning and the twisting may be under our own wills, but the outcome is fixed, no matter what. When one's number is up, dodging does no good. This view, although it undoubtedly has some emotional appeal when one realizes how little one can foresee and control the future, is about as untenable philosophically as any view can be. It says that there are two kinds of events in the world, those that are fated to occur and those that are not fated to occur. Among the former are such portentous events that befall us as marriage, success and failure, and death; among the latter are human actions and choices. No matter what the latter are, their outcome will issue in predetermined, fated events: I can refrain from crossing a street to avoid being hit by a car, but if it is fated that I shall now die, I will be hit by a bicycle on the sidewalk. But, so far as we know, the causes in reality do not distinguish important from unimportant events. It would be extremely difficult, if not impossible, to give an *unemotional* argument for thinking that only important events are preordained and bound to happen.

For the part of fatalism that has some philosophical merit, let us use the word *determinism*. Determinists say that every event *without exception* happens of necessity. There is no contingency, no chance. An event e will occur if, and only if, there is a sufficient cause for it, d; d will occur if and only if c occurs. If one knew the totality of events occurring at some one moment of time and the causal laws relating them to their effects, in principle one could foretell *all* the future events that will ever occur. Determinism may or may not be correct; but at least it is intelligible and defensible by plausible arguments, and it is commonly believed that, with the exception of the materials covered by the principle of indeterminacy, determinism must be assumed as a fundamental principle in the sciences.

The theory that maintains that nature is determined except insofar as human action freely intervenes in the course of nature, and that human beings are islands of freedom in a sea of necessity, says that determinism and freedom are incompatible with each other. If one holds to a theory of determinism, he must give up the belief in freedom; if one holds to the belief in freedom, he must deny or restrict the scope of determinism. Either such view is called *incompatibilism*. If the incompatibilist is correct, the determinist must deny human freedom, and the believer in freedom, whom we shall call the *libertarian*, must deny determinism. Omar Khayyam and Thomas Hobbes are incompatibilists who deny freedom; Descartes was an incompatibilist who was a libertarian.

The incompatibilist sees the situation as follows:

But there is a missing link in this argument; the logical contradictory of determinism is not libertarianism but *indeterminism*—the denial that nature is completely uniform and predictable. *This* denial says nothing pro or con about freedom. So let us set up a new contrast:

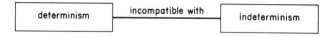

Similarly, we must make still another logical contrast:

Our problem is how to arrange these two pairs in relation to each other. The simplest and most obvious way is:

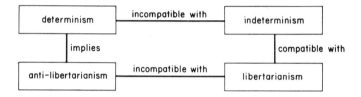

This schema presents the thesis of the incompatibilist in its expanded form. According to this schema, determinism and libertarianism cannot both be true; but instead of saying that one is the contradictory of the other, it says that there is another link in the chain, and besides the obvious incompatibility of determinism and indeterminism, it says that indeterminism permits libertarianism. Our question is: Does it?

Consider the question: Are the actions which I freely do uncaused actions? Are they unpredictable actions? Do they *just happen*? Do I not rather say actions that *just happen* (if there are such) are precisely those actions for which I would *not* claim responsibility, and for which you would not praise or blame me? When I know that my friend John Doe is an honest, hard-working, dependable man, I know with a high degree of assurance what he is going to do in certain situations, and yet I say that he *freely* does those actions in spite of the fact that I know enough about him and his past to be able to predict, inductively, what he will do. It would be acts that *just happen*—so far as I can tell—without any cause that I might be tempted to say he did *not* freely perform. If I cannot be reasonably sure (or "morally certain") how I am going to behave when faced with a serious temptation two minutes hence, I do not exult in my freedom; rather I may feel that this indeterminacy itself is evidence of a lack of self-knowledge and responsibility. The actions that I am most sure about are those I feel most responsible for.

These considerations suggest that we should draw a new schema, which would look like this:

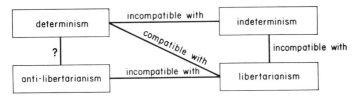

This schema represents the views of those philosophers who are called *compatibilists*, because they think determinism and libertarianism are compatible with each other. But the schema has a question mark on the left side. It was said at first that determinism implied anti-libertarianism; but obviously this implication cannot hold if determinism is compatible with a theory (libertarianism) that is incompatible with anti-libertarianism. How shall we interpret this question mark?

Forget, for the moment, the top line in the schema and concentrate on the bottom line, trying to weigh anti-libertarianism against libertarianism *without reference to the top line*. Looked at in this way, there is no evidence whatsoever that anti-libertarianism is true. Just observing the actions of myself and others, I know very well that my knee-jerk is not a free action, but my writing a letter is; that a man who confesses a crime because he is being beaten is not freely confessing, but a person who deliberately gives himself up to the police is. The difference between free actions and unfree actions is an empirically determinable difference, quite apart from the theory of determinism and indeterminism. Although there are indeed many instances when we do not in fact know whether a man has acted freely or not, there are many cases in which we do know quite well whether he acted freely or not. Hence, *paying attention only to the bottom line*, the case for libertarianism is very strong. The libertarian does not make the extravagant and absurd claim that all human actions are free; but he asserts that some are, and he claims to be able to tell, often, which ones are. Actions are free, he says, that are not the result of coercion by another person, of overwhelming psychological compulsions, of nonculpable ignorance of circumstances and of the quality of the act, of being drugged, hypnotized, tortured, and the like. Actions are free if the causes and reasons for the action lie within oneself and are subject to deliberate rational control. The *compatibilist* argues that man is free not because his actions are uncaused, unpredictable, or capricious, but because and to the extent that his actions follow from his own nature. Freedom, for him, is self-determination under the conditions of the laws of nature, not indeterminacy. He believes that the reign of law seems antithetical to freedom and responsibility only because when we talk about causal laws we ordinarily think of man as merely an effect of alien causes and not also as himself a cause in nature.

We are now prepared to draw a new schema that will represent these somewhat unexpected results in the theory of compatibilism:

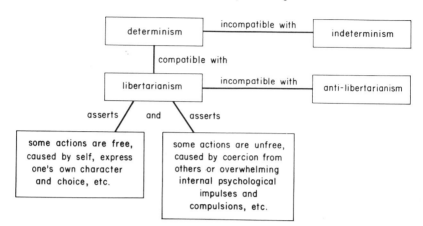

This schema of compatibilism represents the view William James[14] called *soft determinism*. It holds that free actions are determined by causes that are within our personality and under our control; it does not deny that, in principle at least, free actions are as predictable as unfree actions. Now suppose I freely, in this sense, decide to commit a crime and do so. I am caught and charged. Suppose I make the following defense: "I grant," I say, "that another man in a like situation would not have committed the crime I did. But does that show that I, by taking thought of my responsibilities and obligations, could have done otherwise? Perhaps so, but after all, I am not responsible for my character. It was formed before I reached the age of deliberation; it was affected by things my parents did to me, perhaps it all goes back to a defective heredity over which I certainly had no control. It is all very well to *say* I 'freely' did this crime, but if you mean that I am 'a little island of freedom in a sea of necessity' (p. 232), I deny it. Until I can freely choose my parents, the neighborhood in which I was brought up, the psychological quirks and physiological peculiarities I have, I will deny that I could have done otherwise. You say, 'You should have stopped to think before you shot.' All very well, gentlemen of the jury, but why didn't I do so? Because I was not made, I was not brought up by others, to be a man who could stop and think. I did not choose to be the man I am, and therefore I reject the responsibility you impute to me. Bring my parents here and blame them, but not me. And they will, if they are smart, blame it on their parents and so on. 'Of Earth's first Clay they did the Last Man knead . . . .' Don't blame the broken pot; find the potter and blame him!"

[14]"The Dilemma of Determinism," in *The Will to Believe* (New York: Dover Publications, Inc., 1956). The original edition was published in 1897. By "hard determinism" James meant determinism plus incompatibilism.

Rhetoric aside, it seems to us that I would have made a good defense, and the theory of soft determinism does, after all, seem to be incompatible with freedom. By accepting determinism, even in its soft form that permits us, on a common-sense level, to distinguish free from unfree actions, I have tried to show in my imaginary speech to the jury that I was not *really* free but free only in the way the law and common sense understand freedom.

We seem to be faced with a hard decision. If, indeed, determinism is incompatible with libertarianism, which shall we give up? It is an agonizing choice, because science depends upon one and morality upon the other. But do I need to give up either? May not compatibilism still be maintained if we do not assert *either* determinism *or* libertarianism as absolute dogmas?

If we remind ourselves of the conclusions reached in our study of the uniformity and predictability of events in the world, before we took up the problem of freedom, we will recall that we did not there argue that determinism is *true*. We there said that the uniformity of nature is a collateral hypothesis made for the purpose of explaining how things (and people) *do* behave. It is not a prescriptive law, saying that they *must* behave this way. It is not even a descriptive law, saying that they do *always* behave in the same way. It is a hypothesis that we make but cannot demonstrate, and we assume it for the purpose of extending our scientific explanations and for getting along with things practically. Even though not in the least challenging the usefulness and validity of this principle in the explanation of nature, philosophers who hold this view say that outside the field of science we may legitimately make use of other assumptions, such as those of spontaneity and freedom.

It is quite compatible with what we have said about determinism and the uniformity of nature as collateral hypotheses in science to say that—given other purposes than the understanding and prediction of natural events—other collateral hypotheses are permitted. We need to draw a distinction between man as a spectator of nature and man as an agent or actor. When we try to get knowledge of ourselves or other people or natural events, we have to use the collateral hypotheses that make it possible for us to succeed, to the degree that we can succeed, in planning experiments that will have predictive value for future observations. When, however, we are not concerned with predicting what will happen for the purpose of understanding the course of nature but are concerned with our own choices and actions, we have other assumptions without which we could not choose and act. Among these collateral hypotheses is the hypothesis—like any collateral hypothesis, not completely verifiable—that our actions are not causally necessitated by anything that has happened in the past, even in our own personal history.

Perhaps the most typical expression of this view is in the doctrine of Kant, who developed the notion that the uniformity of nature is an a priori postulate of science. Kant held that we organize our sense experience by the use of the hypothesis (or what he called the category) of causation and that the resulting organization of our experience is nature as it can be studied scientifically. Nature is the world of experience, considered as a system of instances of causal laws. But, he held, the world of experience is only a systematic and organized appearance of real things we do not know, and the world of realities may, for all we know, have quite different laws for its own behavior. If this is so, then our entire behavior can be considered from the scientific standpoint as causally necessary in the uniformity of appearances we call nature; yet from another point of view, exactly the same behavior could be considered (although not observed) as a free expression of the reality that is not a part of the system of uniform appearances.

It is thus possible for man to consider himself as a phenomenal part of the realm of nature and thereby subject to its laws, but also as a real being whose appearances only seem to the scientist to be causally determined. In morality and in obedience to the (prescriptive) moral law, Kant held that man is not *re*acting to the things in the world but is manifesting his own spontaneous activity. A man's own activity will appear to the psychologist who examines him as a special case of some uniform law that the psychologist believes the man illustrates; the psychologist will not admit that the man's act is free and spontaneous, because he, like every other scientist, uses the collateral hypothesis of uniformity. But what is good science may not be, in this instance, good morality; for the moral man in making his choice does not act on the assumption, "Whatever I do is simply a response to stimuli over which I have no control." At the moment of moral decision, man feels free. In order to exercise moral choice, he has the right, Kant believed, to make some other postulate or collateral hypothesis than that of the uniformity of nature. He has, in William James' formulation, a right to believe what is necessary if he is to choose and act, just as the scientist has a right to believe the uniformity of nature and any other indemonstrable postulates required in his work.

But this theory of freedom does not contradict the uniformity of nature, nor does it, like the first two theories examined, say that there are *some* events, namely human actions, that occur without natural causes in a world where everything else is determined. Kant himself says,

The illusion about the contradiction [in the notion that the same behavior is both free and naturally necessitated] rests on the fact that we [do not] think of man in a different sense and relationship when we call him free from that in which we consider him as a part of nature and subject to its laws.[15]

Saying this in another way: When we consider man scientifically, we must assume that he illustrates all the relevant laws of nature and therefore that

[15]From Immanuel Kant: *Foundations of the Metaphysics of Morals*, trans. Lewis White Beck, copyright © 1959, by the Liberal Arts Press, Inc., reprinted by permission of The Liberal Arts Press Division of The Bobbs-Merrill Company, Inc. See p. 75.

he is completely determined. Kant himself says that human actions are, in principle, as predictable as eclipses of the sun and moon. Science is one of the ways in which we organize our experience, and the postulate of uniformity and the laws that are established under the assumption of uniformity apply to man only to the extent that we see him in the context of science as an effect of earlier causes. Science, however, is not the only way of organizing our experience. There are other ways, which use prescriptive laws, like the laws of morality, instead of descriptive laws, like those of psychology, as integrating principles in terms of which experience makes sense. Considered in this way, then, man can exercise his freedom in a world that is causally determined, and scientists can seek the putative causes even of the actions for which he takes full responsibility.

BIBLIOGRAPHY

Laws; Induction; Uniformity of Nature

Cohen, Morris R., and Ernest Nagel, *Introduction to Logic and Scientific Method.* New York: Harcourt, Brace & World, Inc., 1934.

Feigl, Herbert, and May Brodbeck, eds., *Readings in the Philosophy of Science*, Part V. New York: Appleton-Century-Crofts, 1953.

Feigl, Herbert, and Wilfrid Sellars, eds., *Readings in Philosophical Analysis*, Parts V and VII. New York: Appleton-Century-Crofts, 1949.

Hempel, Carl G., *Philosophy of the Natural Sciences.* Englewood Cliffs, N.J.: Prentice-Hall, Inc., 1966.

Lewis, C. I., *Mind and the World Order* (1927). New York: Dover Publications, Inc., 1956.

Mill, John Stuart, *Mill's Philosophy of Scientific Method*, ed., Ernest Nagel. New York: Hafner Publishing Co., Inc., 1951.

Nagel, Ernest, *The Structure of Science.* New York: Harcourt, Brace & World, Inc., 1961.

Russell, Bertrand, *Human Knowledge, Its Scope and Limits.* New York: W. W. Norton & Company, Inc., 1948.

Universals and Laws

Aaron, R. I., *The Problem of Universals.* Oxford: Clarendon Press, 1952.

Aristotle, *Metaphysics*, Book 1, Chap. 9; Book 13.

Baylis, Charles F., ed., *Metaphysics.* New York: The Macmillan Company, 1965.

Dewey, John, *Experience and Nature*, Chap. 5. New York: W. W. Norton & Company, Inc., 1929.

Joad, C. E. M., "Plato's Theory of Forms and Modern Physics," *Philosophy*, VIII, No. 30 (April, 1933) 142–54.

Price, H. H., *Thinking and Experience*, London: Hutchinson & Company, Ltd., 1953.

Woozley, A. D., *Theory of Knowledge*, Chap. 5. London: Hutchinson's University Library, 1949.

Laws and Freedom

Compton, Arthur H., *The Freedom of Man*. New Haven, Conn.: Yale University Press, 1935.

Enteman, Willard F., ed., *The Problem of Free Will*. New York: Charles Scribner's Sons, 1967.

Hartmann, Nicolai, *Ethics*, trans., Stanton Coit, Vol. 3. New York: The Macmillan Company, 1932.

Hook, Sidney, ed., *Determinism and Freedom in the Age of Modern Science*. New York: New York University Press, 1958.

James, William, *The Principles of Psychology*, Vol. 2, Chap. 26. New York: Holt, Rinehart & Winston, Inc., 1890.

Lehrer, Keith, ed., *Freedom and Determinism*. New York: Random House, 1966.

Morgenbesser, Sidney, and James Walsh, eds., *Free Will*. Englewood Cliffs, N. J.: Prentice-Hall, Inc., 1962.

Ofstad, Harald, "Recent Work on the Free-will Problem," *American Philosophical Quarterly*, Vol. 4 (July, 1967), 179–207.

Planck, Max, *Where is Science Going?* Chaps. 4 and 5. New York: W. W. Norton & Company, Inc., 1932.

Taylor, Richard, *Action and Purpose*. Englewood Cliffs, N. J.: Prentice-Hall, Inc., 1966.

QUESTIONS AND TOPICS FOR DISCUSSION

1. Read an account of the medieval controversy over universals. What were some of the social and religious forces on each side of this controversy? The Renaissance has been called "the triumph of nominalism over realism." Discuss.

2. Does the notion that the laws of nature are only highly probable instead of certain make the problem of induction easier to solve?

3. Does the notion that the laws of social science are only statements of probabilities make the question of human freedom easier to answer? (Discuss the question: If it is truly a law that 80 per cent of the people with a certain personality trait will commit a crime, is human freedom less restricted than if the law stated truly that 100 per cent of the people with this trait would commit a crime?)

4. Set up a series of criteria that an alleged "law of nature" should meet. How do these criteria resemble those for a "good hypothesis"?

5. Some philosophers reject the postulate of the determinism of nature as a foundation for induction, and attempt to base induction on the theory of probability. One of them says, "We find a certain relative frequency for a series of observed events and assume that the same frequency will hold approximately for further continuation of the series." Is this assumption easier to justify than that of the strict uniformity of nature? How would Hume have attacked this point of view?

6. Discuss the statement, "The Heisenberg principle may be true, but it certainly isn't good."

7. Discuss the following statements:
   a. "The fates guide the willing but drag the unwilling."
   b. "The recognition of necessity is the beginning of freedom."
8. The question, "Why do things obey the laws of nature?" is said in this chapter to be ambiguous. It is analyzed into several other less ambiguous questions. Outline the reasons and results of these various "translations" of the original question.
9. What is meant by "chance"? Does a determinist have any use for the concept of chance? If so, under what conditions?
10. Compare the theory of determinism based upon a theory of causation with determinism based upon the theological theory that an omniscient God would be able to foresee every event and therefore the occurrence of every event must be determined in advance.
11. Compare the theory of freedom said to be compatible with the theory of causal determinism with the theological theory that the freedom of man is compatible with predestination.
12. Does the psychological theory that men have motives and impulses of which they are ignorant have any bearing upon the question of whether they are free or not?
13. Evaluate the following arguments:
    a. Determinism is true. Libertarianism is true. Since true propositions cannot be inconsistent with each other, compatibilism must be true even if we are unable to see *how* determinism and freedom are both possible.
    b. If I were not free to reject an argument, it would be meaningless to say that I *ought* to accept it. But if determinism is true, then if I in fact accept it I have no freedom to reject it. Hence if determinism is true, it cannot be said that I ought to accept it.

10 EXPLANATION AS A GOAL OF INQUIRY

EXPLANATION AND DESCRIPTION

It is sometimes said that science describes how things happen but does not explain why. This statement is often accepted as expressing a limitation of science as if there were some other, nonscientific way of knowing that does tell us why. But this statement is an important half-truth. Both what is true in it and what is false are important. The truth is: There is not a sharp distinction between an explanation and a description. One man's explanation is another man's description. The falsity is: When a statement is offered and accepted as an explanation, it has a very different role from that which it would have if it were offered and accepted as a description. If a sentence is stated and accepted as an answer to the question "Why?" it is labeled an explanation; if it is stated and accepted as an answer to the question "What happened?" it is counted a description. The same sentence, depending upon the intention of the speaker and the attitude of the hearer, can be an explanation or a description. There is no *absolute* difference between an explanation and a description, but the *relative* difference is very important and should not be overlooked.

A description gives us knowledge of what something is or how some event happened, and that is all. An explanation, on the other hand, has the effect, if accepted, of reducing one's puzzlement at what is the case, or what happened. The proper response to true description is: "Now I see better what happened." The proper response to a true explanation is: "Now I understand what I did not understand before." But the sentence that merely adds some bits of information for one person may elicit an "Aha!" response in another.

242

KINDS OF EXPLANATION

There are many kinds of explanation, but we shall discuss only a few of them.[1]

After a freeze, suppose a man finds that a water pipe in his house has burst. He may ask, "Why did the water pipe burst?" For many purposes, it is sufficient to answer, "Usually when a pipe freezes it bursts." This explains the event by reminding the hearer that he had no reason to be surprised or puzzled by this event, that he does not need to accuse his plumber of having sold him a defective pipe, and so on. He is being told: You should have expected it to burst, because this usually happens. He is given an enthymeme, an elliptical syllogism that, when expanded, would read:

If a pipe freezes, it usually bursts.
This pipe froze.
Therefore it was probable that it would burst.

We shall call such an explanation an *inductive* explanation. It is based on an induction from similar cases. Some other examples of inductive explanation are:

"Why was Alfred nervous yesterday?" "He is always nervous the day before an examination."
"Why does the moon look larger than usual?" "It always looks larger when it is near the horizon."
"Why did your headache go away?" "It always goes away when I take aspirin."

A person may not, however, be satisfied with an inductive explanation. He accepts the inductive answer as to why *this* pipe burst, *this* headache went away, the moon *tonight* looks large, and the like. But (to use our first example) he says, "I know that pipes burst when frozen. What I meant was: Why does freezing burst a pipe?" To this question, the answer would be: "Water expands when freezing. If water expands in a closed space, it creates pressure. If the pipe cannot withstand the pressure, it bursts." This answer contains a description of what happens when water freezes and of what happens to pipes under pressure. It explains the class of events "freezing pipes bursting."

This looks quite different from an inductive explanation, even though it is itself based upon an induction from examples of water's freezing. It looks different because it refers to a more abstract general class of events than pipes

[1]We have already discussed explanation by laws and by hypotheses in Chapters 8 and 9. We shall have to mention these again but shall concentrate on other types in this chapter.

bursting when freezing. From this more abstract class of events (the expansion of water upon freezing) an intelligent man could infer cases that have no apparent similarity to bursting pipes. He might say, "Then that will imply that ice has a specific gravity less than 1.0, and therefore ice will float on water." Anyone who knows that pipes burst when freezing will, or at least should, know that ice will float; if he knows one of these facts, he ought not to be puzzled by the other. The explanation tends to reduce his puzzlement about bursting pipes and floating ice. It converts what would otherwise be merely a brute fact in his mind into an understood fact, into a fact he could have, and ought to have, anticipated without observation.

In spelling out the two kinds of explanation of the bursting pipe, there are unstated assumptions that can be made explicit. For the first, it is:

Freezing pipes generally burst; hence it could be expected that this pipe would burst when freezing.

For the second, it is:

If a solid has a lower specific gravity than the liquid from which it forms, then (because of the conservation of matter) it should occupy a greater volume and should (by Archimedes' principle) float in the liquid and create a pressure in the pipe.

It is not stated as a law of nature that freezing pipes generally burst, for reasons already mentioned; but it is a law of nature that substances with a specific gravity less than 1.0 float. The second kind of explanation, therefore, we shall call *nomological* (nomos = Gk. law) *explanation*. A nomological explanation reduces a greater variety of puzzlements than an inductive explanation.

But someone may object, the nomological explanation is still a description; it just describes what happens when water freezes, whether it is in a pipe or a lake. I want to know *why* water expands when it freezes. He is then asking for a more comprehensive nomological explanation, referring to a still more general law that will apply to liquids other than water. The most comprehensive nomological explanation is one that explains an occurrence in terms of a formal system. A formal system is somewhat like a mathematical theory, with axioms (or assumptions), definitions, and theorems that can be proved by deduction from the axioms and definitions and confirmed by observation. It is difficult to give a concrete example of explanation by means of formal system without going into much scientific and logical detail because formal theories have been constructed only in the most exact and intricate sciences. But if one assumes, for example, Newton's laws of motion as if they were axioms, then it is possible to deduce Kepler's laws of planetary motion. If one is surprised to learn that the planets go around the sun in elliptical orbits and wants to know why they do, then Newton provides a formal answer:

If you grant the laws of motion and the existence of a massive sun and less massive moving planets, then it can be proved, like a theorem in geometry, that the path of the planets will be elliptical. To deny that the orbits are elliptical would commit a person to deny the laws of motion that apply not only to planets but to balls rolling down an inclined plane, the rise and fall of the tides, the motion of a pendulum, and the operation of balances.

Another kind of theoretical explanation refers us from what we observe with our eyes and instruments to what cannot be observed in this way. This is explanation in terms of hypothetical objects.[2] The scientist thinks he can explain what is observed by reference to what is not observed but is only inferred to exist. We have seen an example of this (p. 180) in the assumption made by John Couch Adams that the behavior of Uranus could be explained only by reference to an object that had not yet been observed, the planet Neptune.

Many of the unobserved entities used in scientific explanations cannot be observed directly with the telescope or microscope but, if at all, only very indirectly (for example, by means of the cloud-chamber or bubble-chamber that the physicist uses to detect the tracks of subatomic particles). Such indirect observation, of course, already has a great deal of theory presupposed in it; one must *learn to see* by formulating or knowing a theory that regards observables as symptoms of unobservables. The physician who sees an electrocardiogram on a piece of paper must know how to interpret it so that it can function as a symptom of something he does not observe—a defect in the heart. There must be at least an inductive or a nomological explanation of what he sees, such as: Patients with electrocardiograms like this one have been found in autopsy—direct visual observation of the corpse—to have a defective valve in the left ventricle. Such a relation between the electrocardiogram and the heart condition is a *symptom-relation*.

Symptom-relations, however, are not sufficient for explanations and prognosis, for we need to know also the relationship between different inferred entities, each of which has its own symptom-relation. We want to know the nomological explanation of the things we discover through the symptom-relation. A diagram of the situation is given in Figure 1. If the two kinds of relations can be established, then the connection between the unobservable objects serves to explain the inductive or nomological connection between the observations.

For such an explanation to resolve our puzzlement at the inductive connection between observations, however, the connection between the unobservables must, in some way, be clearer and more intelligible to us than the connection between the observations. The connection between the unobservables must be such that when we understand it, we have the "aha!-experi-

[2]See above, page 181.

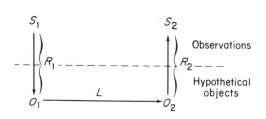

FIG. 1

Hypothetical objects as explanations of observed data. S_1 and S_2 are observations, or symptoms, such as readings on an instrument; O_1 and O_2 are unobserved objects, states of an object, or events; R_1 and R_2 are symptom-relations; and L is a connection between O_1 and O_2 expressed in a law of nature. If we know $O_1R_1S_1$, O_1LO_2, and $O_2R_2S_2$, then knowing S_1 we can predict S_2, or given S_2, we can explain it.

ence" of feeling that we understand the connection between the observations.

Not all inferred objects produce this aha!-experience. We shall examine one case in which they do not and one in which they do.

It has been observed that if a person smokes opium (observation 1), he soon falls asleep (observation 2). This is an inductive explanation of a certain man's falling asleep at a particular time and place. But why does taking opium *in general* cause people to fall asleep? Because, it was once said, there is in opium a *vis dormitiva*, a dormitive power; when one takes opium, one gets also the *vis dormitiva* whose symptom is that the person falls asleep. We rightly say: This "explanation" explains nothing. We know even less about the *vis dormitiva* than we do about opium; I certainly do not know more when I say

Opium, through its dormitive power, puts people to sleep,

than when I say

Opium puts people to sleep.

Fortunately not all theoretical explanations are this fatuous. We shall now consider a splendid example of theoretical explanation in the kinetic theory of gases.

Hiero of Alexandria knew that gases expand when heated, and he used this fact in making many ingenious mechanisms for impressing the gullible public. For instance, by lighting a fire on an altar, he could make the doors of the temple swing open through a series of bellows, wheels, and pullies. In the eighteenth century, the French physicist Charles formulated the exact law of this change and showed exactly how much increase in volume or pressure accompanied each degree of change of temperature (see Figure 2). He could

Apparatus

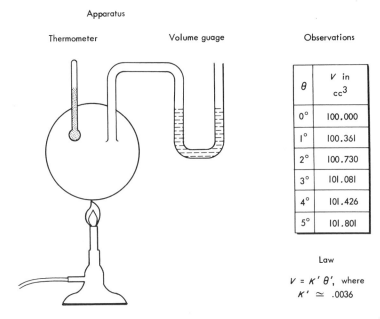

FIG. 2

Schematic diagram for showing Charles' Law as a nomological explanation of the data in the table derived from the experiment at the left. Note that in the table θ is given in degrees Centigrade, while in the statement of Charles' Law θ' refers to degrees on the absolute scale.

give a nomological explanation; but why was Charles' Law itself true? We can explain *it* by use of a theory.

A theoretical explanation by means of a formal system would be something like this.[3] There is a general gas law that we take as an axiom. It reads:

$$K = PV/f(\theta)$$

where K is a constant, P is pressure, V is volume, and θ is temperature. The law say that the pressure of an enclosed gas multiplied by the volume and divided by some function of its temperature is a constant. Now if we keep the pressure constant, by simple algebra we derive

$$V = K'\theta',$$

which is one form of Charles' Law. Thus if we know the general gas law, without an experiment we can derive Charles' Law as a special case: Charles' Law *must* be true because the general gas law is true; thus we explain

[3]Please note that the following account, like most of the scientific examples in this book, is grossly oversimplified. Normally we would not say here that we had given a theoretical explanation unless we had a fuller set of assumptions and a larger number of steps than in our example. But the essential points are illustrated in the example.

Charles' Law. V, P, and θ are observable data, readings on instruments, and K' is a number that depends upon the units in which θ, V, and P have been measured. There is no reference to anything unobservable.

But if we want to explain the general gas law itself, we appeal to the kinetic theory of gases, which says that gases are made up of molecules in rapid motion. We appeal to something we have not seen—molecules—to explain something we have seen—readings on instruments.

In Figure 2 the set-up of the experiment is pictured. We have a flask of gas, a Bunsen burner, and two columns of mercury, one in a closed tube with a vacuum above it (a thermometer) and the other in an open U-tube that measures changes in volume.

Now we must establish some symptom-relations. We say that the thermometer measures heat as follows: The heat of the gas is a measure of the mean velocity of motion of the molecules in the gas, and as this velocity becomes greater the velocity of the molecules in the mercury in the thermometer increases and causes the mercury to expand; the thermometer goes up. This symptom-relation is based on Newton's laws of motion. The symptom-relation tells us that whereas we ordinarily say the thermometer measures the temperature (by definition), this is equivalent to saying that it measures the mean velocity of the molecules in the gas. Second, in the volume-gauge, it is obvious that as the molecules in the gas increase in velocity, they will hit the surface of the mercury in the U-tube with greater force and cause it to sink in proportion to the increase in force. This also is a consequence of one of Newton's laws of motion. If the surface of the mercury sinks, it will rise in the right arm of the U-tube, and the amount of this rise will maintain atmospheric pressure in the flask and measure the increase in volume of the gas. These relations are shown in Figure 3.

Now we are ready to explain Charles' Law. Whereas I previously saw with my eyes that every increase in temperature was accompanied by an increase in volume, I now see, with my mind's eye, why this *must* be so. The thermometer and the volume gauge are, in reality, measuring in two different ways the same unobservable change—the increase in the mean free velocity of the molecules. A table giving temperature and volume readings is simply a table of numbers that the mathematician finds to stand in the nomological relation

$$V = K'\theta'.$$

But the kinetic theory of gases now tells us that we should have been able to expect this prior to any actual observations. The mean free velocity of the molecules, therefore, is related to the results of our experiment in a wholly different way from that in which the theory of *vis dormitiva* was related to people's falling asleep after smoking opium.

Is it not strange, however, that we can understand what we observe by appealing to something we do not observe? How can this be?

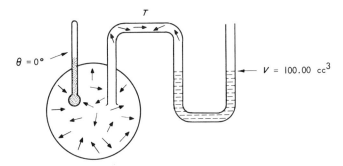

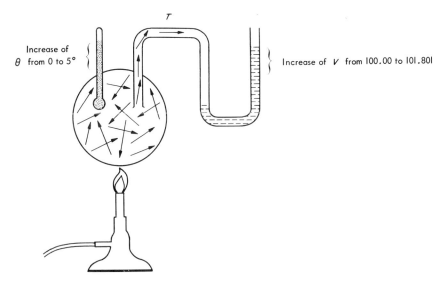

Unheated gas. The mean free velocity of the molecules is small; the mercury does not expand in the thermometer and the air in the chamber and tube *T* does not expand. (The velocity of the molecules is represented by the length of the arrows.)

Heated gas. The greater velocity of gas molecules increases the velocity of the molecules in the mercury in the thermometer, causing a rise in the thermometer; and it increases the momentum of the molecules of the gas hitting the surface of the mercury in tube *T,* causing the mercury to fall in the left part of the tube and to rise in the right part.

FIG. 3

Explanation of Charles' Law by means of a theory with hypothetical objects (unobserved molecules of gas).

At least one way in which we accomplish this strange feat is by the use of a model. Something we can observe is in some important respect like something we cannot observe, but we try to apply the laws that describe the model to the unobservables and test, by means of the symptom-relations, whether the unobservables really behave like the model. We say that if this is confirmed, there is an analogy between the model and the unobservables.

In the kinetic theory of gases, the relationship between the molecules might be guessed at by thinking of the following rather fanciful model. We may think of the molecules in the gas as being in one respect like people at a cocktail party. As long as they are calm and moving around slowly, a large number of people can be accommodated in a room. But as the party heats up and the people become more active, the room becomes too small for them and some of them near the doors will wander into the adjacent rooms. Analogously, as the gas in the chamber (Figure 3) heats up the molecules move about with a greater velocity, more of them will go into the tube T and force the mercury in that tube down, giving a greater volume-reading on the right arm of the U-tube. If this model seems to be too fanciful, there are others that have been meant in dead seriousness. There is much that we can understand about the behavior of light rays by thinking of the model: waves on the surface of water. Thus we get the "wave theory of light"—when no one has ever seen a wave of light. We understand some of the functions of the brain, as shown in overt behavior that does not *resemble* that of the brain, by using the model of a telephone exchange or an electronic computer. At one time, it was thought that we could understand the data of atomic physics by thinking of the atom as if it were a miniature solar system.

When the model is something very familiar to us, explanation in terms of unobservables that are thought to be like the model is one of the most satisfying intellectual experiences an inquirer can have.

A good theory not only helps us to explain what we have already observed; it also leads us to make observations we might not otherwise have made. Although inductive and nomological explanations permit us to anticipate future observations that will be like the past observations, a nomological explanation built into a formal system theory and explanations in terms of hypothetical objects enables us to predict observations of a very different kind that we would never have predicted (and probably would not make) without the theory. We shall give two examples of such predictions, which served both to show fruitfulness and to confirm the theory in question.

First, prediction from a formal system. In the theory of relativity, it was a purely mathematical consequence of its axioms and definitions that the numbers representing mass, energy, and the velocity of light should be related by the formula

$$E = mc^2.$$

At the time Einstein formulated this equation, there was no decisive experimental evidence for it. But because the theory of relativity had explained so many laws of physics, it was believed that $E = mc^2$ was also a law of nature. Direct experimental verification came when experiments on nuclear fission were performed decades later.

Second, prediction from a theory with hypothetical objects. In the kinetic theory of gases it could be asked: If the gas consists of molecules that have kinetic energy, would not gases at a higher temperature (that is, higher mean velocity) penetrate a porous membrane at a higher rate than molecules at a lower velocity?[4] Would there not be a still undiscovered law of nature

$$R = K''\theta$$

where R is the rate of diffusion, θ the temperature, and K'' a constant? Such a law (Graham's Law of Diffusion) could therefore be anticipated on the basis of the unobservable molecules but not by algebraic derivation from the general gas law that says nothing about rates of diffusion.

Summary. We thus see that explanation is not a simple concept. Not all explanations are alike. What is useful in explaining a broken pipe to a little child is very unlike what is useful in explaining the behavior of the brain to a scientifically educated person. But any good explanation reduces someone's puzzlement about some experience that he thinks is not just a brute inexplicable fact but has a reason. Certainly there is a sense in which all the explanations we have discussed are descriptions; even the explanation of phenomena in physics are, in a sense, descriptions of atoms and molecules, fields and forces. But we do not call them descriptions, because what we call descriptions just give added information instead of rendering information more intelligible.

TELEOLOGICAL EXPLANATIONS

Sometimes we think we want explanations that are in no sense descriptions, but which *really* tell us why something happens. What we want might be called an absolute explanation. Teleological explanations seem to approach this type. They explain what happens in a way very much like the way we explain the actions of a person—by telling the reason or purpose of an action. Here are five examples of teleological explanations:

1. Why did Alfred go to the tobacco shop? Because he wanted to buy a cigar.
2. Why do the planets move with marvelous regularity around the sun? Because the Creator wished them to manifest His glory and power to man.
3. Why did the gas rush in when I punched a hole in the can? Because nature abhors a vacuum.
4. Why did the missile change its course? Because it was seeking out the enemy plane in order to destroy it with its warhead.
5. Why does the heart beat? In order to pump blood to the other organs of the body.

[4]A brief but more detailed account of the discovery of Graham's Law is given in H. Feigl and M. Brodbeck, eds., *Readings in the Philosophy of Science* (New York: Appleton-Century-Crofts, 1953), pp. 378–81.

We shall deal with type 1 in the next section and type 2 in Chapter 15. Type 3 is typical of a long list of explanations (for example, "Water always seeks its level," "A body in motion tends to persevere in its motion in a straight line") that were once accepted as good scientific explanations but that are now replaced by one or more of the kinds of explanatory statements discussed in the preceding section. Types 4 and 5 will engage our attention in this section.

Picture the situation referred to in 4. Modern technology has produced machines that act as if they were guided by an indwelling intelligence for the accomplishment of some built-in purpose. As the plane maneuvers to avoid the missile, the missile changes its direction, just as a football tackle changes his direction with every turn the ball carrier makes. We say the tackle wants to intercept the carrier (explanation of type 1), and it is hard to avoid sometimes saying that the missible is trying to intercept the plane. But most of the time we know that this is only a metaphorical way of speaking. The missile sends out radar waves that are reflected back to the missile where they are fed into an on-board computer, which directs the missile to the point where the plane will be in a few seconds. The precision is marvelous, and we can hardly avoid using "information" and "electronic brains" and other metaphors borrowed from biology and psychology. We talk about the missle as if there were an intelligent man in it observing the plane and intentionally correcting his trajectory in order to intercept it. Yet we know that the intelligence lay in the mind of the designers of the missile, and the purpose lies in the intention of the ground crew who fired it in order to destroy the plane. Everything built into the missile—feed-back circuits, servo-mechanisms, information-processing equipment—is machinery built by human beings, using their knowledge of the laws of logic, physics, and chemistry, to accomplish a human purpose. A missile has a purpose in precisely the same sense that a hammer has a purpose; yet the missile seems almost like an animal organism or a human being, whereas a hammer does not.

The apparent similarity of the missile to an animal tracking a prey can be read in two ways. We have noted how animal-like the missile is; but why do we not say, "How like a delicate machine an animal is?" Instead of giving a teleological answer to question 4, why do we not give another type of answer to question 5? Instead of understanding the function of a missile by comparing it to organic behavior, why not try to understand the motion of the heart for example, by comparing it to the behavior of a machine?

We can and do make this comparison. Many advances in our understanding of the heart have come about by the application of the laws of hydrodynamics to the motion of the blood, of the laws of electricity to the control of the heart muscles by nerves, of the laws of chemistry to the understanding of the dull-colored blood in the right auricle and the bright red blood in the left auricle. A machine is often a good model to use in understanding organic behavior, just as an organism (in the missile example) is sometimes an appropriate model for understanding the behavior of a piece of machinery. But neither model is apparently perfect. We do not think that the missile is really acting in order to accomplish a purpose, and we do not think that someone designed the heart (as someone designed the "heart machine" used in surgery) so as to accomplish his purposes. Unless one supposes (with respect to question 2) that God designed the heart as well as the solar system, that analogy between organisms and machines is not perfect. But an analogy does not need to be perfect in order to be useful; it must hold only with respect to the aspects of the phenomena one wishes to explain.

Now there are philosophers and scientists who say: In the important and relevant aspects of machines and organisms, organisms are machines. For this reason, they are called *mechanists*. (Descartes was the first important mechanist with respect to animals, but he held that man was not just a machine; metaphysical materialists [see p. 293] are mechanists even with respect to man.) A mechanist is one who says: All the behavior of a living organism or its individual organs is explicable by the laws, theories, and hypothetical objects used to explain the behavior of inorganic bodies. Biological phenomena are much more complicated than inorganic phenomena, but they do not differ in kind.

Mechanism is, in biological theory, the view that living organisms can be exhaustively explained in terms of the hypotheses and laws of chemistry and physics. No explanation will be regarded by the mechanist as valid and complete so long as there is any term in it (such as life, instinct) that does not belong to chemistry or physics, or any laws (such as the Mendelian laws of heredity) that cannot be seen as special cases of, and derivable from, the laws of chemistry and physics. Sometimes the mechanist expresses rather a hope than an ascertained fact with respect to the laws. He may admit that at present the laws of biology cannot be derived from those of physics and chemistry, but he asserts as the goal of science that they should be derived, and he believes that they can be derived when we have more knowledge.

The mechanist objects to two attitudes frequently taken toward living beings. He rejects, first, the belief that the concept of purpose is valid or useful in biological inquiry. He

. . . warmly denies that there exists any such thing as purpose in the Universe, or that events have any ulterior motive or goal to which they are striving. [He] asserts that all events are due to the interaction of matter and motion acting by blind necessity in accordance with those invariable sequences to which we have given the name of laws.[5]

The teleological view of things (the belief that "there exists any such thing as purpose" or, more accurately, the belief that concepts of purpose have an explanatory and legitimate place in science and phliosophy) is a subjective

[5]Hugh Elliot, *Modern Science and Materialism* (New York: David McKay Co., Inc., 1919), p. 140. Quoted by permission of David McKay Company, Inc.

illusion. It arises from the fact that we generally think of things in relation to ourselves and evaluate them as they affect the accomplishment of what we consider to be our purposes. But we ourselves act, according to mechanists, under the necessity of nature; not only what we do, but what we will to do, is decided by the inexorable laws of nature; as Mephistopheles, in *Faust*, says, "We believe we push; but we are pushed." What appears to us to be purposive in living organisms—for instance, the exquisite mutual adaptation of the parts of an organism to one another—is the mechanical result of the elimination of those organs or organisms that are not physiologically well balanced. We see only the results, and think that the organism was designed or developed itself for the purpose of making such adjustments.

Second, the mechanist rejects the idea that there is

. . . any form of existence other than those envisaged by physics and chemistry, that is to say, other than existences which have some kind of palpable material characteristics and qualities.[6]

The existing universe and all things and events therein may be theoretically expressed in terms of matter and energy, undergoing continuous redistribution in accordance with the ordinary laws of physics and chemistry.[7]

A biological organism, for the mechanist, is simply an extremely complex bundle of chemical compounds, so complicated that it is certainly difficult to resolve it into the simple constituents between which chemical and physical relations can be seen to hold. But analysis is the direction in which the sciences are and ought to be going:

Differences in the forms of organs are accompanied by differences in their chemical composition, and . . . according to the principles of science we have to derive the former from the latter.[8]

We now know a good deal about the physiological processes of the body; we have detailed information about the chemical composition of foods, and we can trace the various changes of food into living tissue without ever coming across a biological fact that is not amenable to chemical explanation; indeed, most of the reactions have been duplicated in the laboratory. The best hypothesis for the biologist, therefore, seems to be that the organism is nothing but an immensely complicated chemical factory or machine. On this assumption, he can discover and has discovered many facts that would otherwise have remained unknown or unexplained. To doubt seriously the truth of this hypothesis in any particular investigation in physiology would block the way of inquiry.

As with all collateral hypotheses that give valid results only when com-

[6]*Ibid.*, p. 142.
[7]*Ibid.*, p. 143.
[8]Jacques Loeb, *The Mechanistic Conception of Life* (Chicago: University of Chicago Press, 1912), p. 104.

bined with other specific hypotheses that can be tested, we do not know whether mechanism is ultimately true or not. But indisputably it is a good hypothesis and may be the best available.

In the past fifty years, such a theory has won triumph after triumph as chemistry and physics have solved more and more obscure biological problems, and among competent biologists it has almost entirely replaced *vitalism*—the theory that there is some irreducible and inexplicable vital element or entelechy in the living body that directs its activities for the accomplishment of biological purposes. For vitalism seemed not to explain anything, but merely to be a polite name for our ignorance of the truly mechanistic, physico-chemical explanation of biological functions.

Yet the fact remains that animals, especially the higher animals like man, do not seem to behave only like machines. They reproduce, they grow, they repair injuries, they seem actively to seek a variety of goals and to turn with ease from one pursuit to another; human organisms laugh, cry, and even philosophize. We shall consider the explanation of exclusively human behavior in the next section; but if we consider only the other animal species, it is very difficult—if not impossible—to avoid using teleological explanations for their behavior in the large, even if we think that every heart beat, every endocrine secretion, every nerve impulse can be explained in terms of the laws and theories of chemistry and physics.

Teleological conceptions are extremely useful, at least in some stages of biological research. They suggest hypotheses about the direction and function of the underlying physico-chemical processes. To take a simple illustration, suppose a biologist investigates the event ordinarily called "cat chasing a mouse." In purely descriptive terms, he would say, "The mouse ran across the floor; five feet behind the mouse the cat ran across the floor in the same direction." He cannot say that the cat chased the mouse, for the word "chase" is teleological, and when we use it we ascribe a purpose to the cat's behavior. The mechanist could no more literally say that the cat chased the mouse than he could say one meteor chased another across the sky, for to him, the cat is a machine and machines do not seek goals. Yet in explaining the cat's behavior, the mechanist does *take into account* what the cat seems to common sense to be doing, namely, trying to achieve a certain purpose by catching the mouse. In the earlier stages of his investigation, at least, the mechanist considers this aspect of the event, for it suggests to him what specific physico-chemical conditions to look for as the explanation of the cat's behavior. For instance, it might suggest to him that the cat is hungry, which will lead him to investigate the chemical conditions in the cat's blood as the *real* cause. In this way the mechanist himself uses the notion of purpose as a *heuristic* hypothesis—as a guiding principle with which to begin but later to be eliminated as a false hypothesis when he profers his mechanistic explanation.

Although one mechanist criticized vitalism by saying that vitalism was "a comfortable couch where reason was lulled to rest on the pillow of mysterious properties," a vitalist properly retorted, "Teleology is a lady without whom no biologist can live, yet he is ashamed to be seen with her in public."

An attempt to reconcile the fact that the biologist uses teleological explanations like 5 with the fact that most biologists are aiming at physico-chemical explanations like 4 has been made by a number of recent biologists and philosophers. We shall consider one such attempt, that by Samuel Alexander (1859–1938), one of the last great speculative metaphysicians in Great Britain. This theory is called the emergentist or holistic or organismic theory.

A central conception of Alexander's philosophy is that of *emergent quality*. An emergent quality is a quality that belongs to a whole but that could not have been predicted from any knowledge of its separate parts. If we could have predicted the quality of a whole from knowledge of the parts (even if we did not actually do so), the property is called a *resultant quality*. Consider water, for example. Water is a whole comprising oxygen and hydrogen. From a knowledge of the weights of oxygen and hydrogen, the weight of their compound could have been predicted; it is their sum. Weight is thus a resultant property and we can have rational and not merely empirical knowledge of it if we have knowledge of its conditions. But from our knowledge of oxygen and hydrogen *alone*, we could not have foretold that their compound would have the properties of wetness, colorlessness, and tastelessness. Such qualities can be learned only a posteriori, by observation. (After we have had one experience that oxygen and hydrogen form a wet compound, we can, of course, predict by induction that they will do so in the future; but the point that Alexander wished to make is that we could not do so without some observation of the properties of the whole itself.)

Knowledge of resultant properties is derivable from knowledge of the conditions. Such properties can be rationally analyzed into the properties of the conditions, of which they are a mere sum or aggregate. With respect to resultant properties, therefore, the whole is equal to the sum of its parts. But Alexander believed that the emergent properties are new, simple qualities that can be learned only by a fresh observation. The wetness of water is a simple property that must be directly experienced, and upon analysis of the whole, it disappears. With respect to emergent properties, it is sometimes said (very ambiguously) that "the whole is greater than the sum of its parts."

For Alexander, nature comprises "immense complexities of elements, hitherto chaotic, now gathering themselves together and as it were flowering into some undreamed simplicity"—a new quality.[9] He believed that there were at least four such critical levels or turning points in the evolution of the universe: matter, emerging from the complexity of space-time; chemical structure, emerging from the complex interrelations of material particles; life; and consciousness.

---

[9]Samuel Alexander, *Philosophical and Literary Pieces*. (London: Macmillan & Company, Ltd., 1939), p. 304. Used by permission of Macmillan & Company, Ltd.

A living body is, according to this conception, a physico-chemical body of a certain degree and kind of complexity, whose actions may severally be viewed as physical or chemical, but taken in their integration or entirety have the quality of life. Life is therefore resoluble without remainder into physico-chemical processes; but it cannot be treated as *merely* physico-chemical. Certain of its functions may be referred to physical or chemical laws, but it is not these separable processes which constitute life. Life exists only when we have that particular collocation of such physico-chemical actions which we know as living. It is the special coordination which conditions the appearance or creation of the new quality of life. . . . But it is not *merely* physico-chemical because merely physico-chemical processes are not alive, and they do not give us life until the requisite complexity of integration is attained. So important is it to remember that besides elements there is their form or combination, and that the form is as much a reality as the elements and gives them their significance.[10]

Against the vitalist, he says, "While there is no new entity life, there is a new quality life, with which certain combinations of matter may be endowed."[11] And against the mechanist: "But the new quality of life which [matter] possesses is neither chemical nor mechanical but something new."[12]

Although perhaps not many biologists have ever read the works of the metaphysician Samuel Alexander, many have developed on their own similar theories of the relation of life to its physico-chemical base. They speak of the importance of understanding the organism "as a whole"; for example, one of them denies that the organism is made up of cells, saying, rather, that it would be more accurate to see cells as arising by the division of the organism. As Aristotle said, "The whole precedes the part," and "A hand cut off is no longer a hand."

But, we must ask, to what extent is it a *good* hypothesis? Like vitalism, it has been fruitful in calling attention to the facts of organization that tend to be played down by mechanists. Unlike vitalism, it does not explain them with just a word like entelechy, for organization or pattern can be observed, modified experimentally, and compared in its diverse manifestations in different organisms. It still asserts, moreover, that every biological phenomenon has a physico-chemical base or substratum, so, unlike a vitalistic hypothesis, it does not have to retreat when the physico-chemical mechanism of some previously unexplained biological process is discovered. Thus it does not block the way of inquiry.

On the other hand, it is probably not as simple as mechanism, for every emergent quality must be accepted as a brute fact, as what Alexander once called a "miracle" accepted with "natural piety." Once a new quality is observed, however, the emergentist, like the mechanist, begins to investigate the conditions under which it has occurred and thus tries to establish physico-chemical laws for the phenomenon. But it may be a more adequate

[10]*Ibid.*, pp. 307–308.
[11]*Ibid.*, p. 309.
[12]*Ibid.*, p. 311.

theory than mechanism, that is, not *too* simple, because it does not minimize the significance of the differences between living and dead matter by saying that the former is only a more complicated case of the latter.

At present there seems to be little to justify a choice between mechanism and the emergent theories to explain life. Some philosophers have, in fact, argued that they are not really two different theories but only two different "languages" reporting the same set of facts, differing from each other only in vocabulary and emphasis. In the future when more adequate knowledge of the parts is available, the mechanist may be able to show that what we call emergent properties, including life itself, are really resultant properties. For the distinction between emergent and resultant may not be an absolute distinction but relative to the state of knowledge available in the simpler science. Such a reduction of emergent to resultant properties has occurred in the past, as we see in the physical explanations that can now be given for chemical phenomena. It is possible, with further advances in physics and chemistry, that all biological phenomena will be so explained. If this happens, purpose and organic wholeness will still be useful as heuristic hypotheses. The real difference between mechanism and the organismic theory of life is probably to be found in the diverse expectations they arouse concerning the future course of biological inquiry and how each fits with philosophical views that concern an even wider realm of phenomena than those of only biology.

EXPLANATIONS OF HUMAN AFFAIRS

On the day of his death, Socrates criticized the natural philosophers like Anaxagoras for wishing to give the same kinds of explanation to human as to natural phenomena. In Plato's words, Socrates told his companions that the natural philosophers would say

that I sit here because my body is made up of bones and muscles; and the bones, as he would say, are hard and have ligaments which divide them, and the muscles are elastic, and they cover the bones, which have also a covering or environment of flesh and skin which contains them; and as the bones are lifted at their joints by the contraction or relaxation of the muscles, I am able to bend my limbs, and this is why I am sitting here in a curved posture: that is what he would say, and he would have a similar explanation of my talking to you, which he would attribute to sound, and air, and hearing, and he would assign ten thousand other causes of the same sort, forgetting to mention the true cause, which is, that the Athenians have thought fit to condemn me, and accordingly I have thought it better and more right to remain here and undergo my sentence; for I am inclined to think that these muscles and bones of mine would have gone off to Megara or Boeotia,—by the dog of Egypt they would, if they had been guided only by their own idea of what was best, and if

I had not chosen as the better and nobler part, instead of playing truant and running away, to undergo any punishment which the state inflicts. There is surely a strange confusion of causes and reasons in all this.[13]

Socrates granted that bodily states are causes of actions, but he said that one could not understand his action in terms of these causes. The natural philosophers offered explanations that were not teleological for actions— his remaining to take the poison when he could have escaped—that he thought must be explained teleologically.

Today, there are philosophers and social scientists who give the kind of explanation the natural philosophers gave in the fifth century B.C., and others who make the same complaints Socrates made on the day of his death in 399 B.C. How justified is the Socratic complaint? Does the voluntary action of a man require teleological explanations, in terms of its reasons, or are teleological explanations only preliminary explanations to be reduced to other types discussed before?

Most of the time when we try to understand an individual's action, we are entirely satisfied with teleological explanations. The following explanation settles the puzzlement that occasioned the question:

1. Why did Alfred go to the tobacconist? Because he wanted to buy a cigar.

This explanation satisfies us and permits us to say, "Now I understand what I did not understand when I asked the question." Most of the time this is the only kind of explanation we can in fact give. I do not know enough about the state of Alfred's muscles and the laws of physiology to give a satisfactory explanation in the form of a complex law of nature or a physiological theory that will show that he crossed the street from physiological necessity. Certainly teleological explanations can be wrong and can be corrected in the light of further evidence or a re-examination of the evidence we have. But in this respect they do not differ at all from other types of explanation.

Now consider three other examples of occurrences for which we desire explanations.

2. Why do social security outlays climb, in the long run, with expenditures for medical research and therapy?
3. Why does an increase in the yield on bonds have a depressing effect on the stock market?
4. What is the child doing? (That is, explain to me what the child is doing.)

In general, answers to these kinds of questions are given by theories, or by laws belonging to theories, of one of two kinds. (a) There are theories that

[13]Plato, *Phaedo*, Steph. 98–99 (Jowett translation). We have changed the fourth word from the end from "conditions" to "reasons."

tend to leave out any explicit mention of the persons and interests involved and tend to take the events to be explained as if they were events under laws and theories about things that do not behave teleologically. Or, (b) they are theories that speak of the meaning of the situation in terms of the interests of the person or persons involved, and they take an explicitly teleological form. The first can be called event-theories and the second, action-theories.[14]

The possibility of these two types of explanation raises the question: Which type of explanation of *this* event is possible, and if both are possible, which one is more suitable? In general, those who wish to assimilate the social to the natural sciences prefer event explanations. They hold that action explanations are only concessions to our ignorance and that the direction of the social sciences will be toward the former replacing the latter.[15] On the other hand, those who wish, in some perhaps poorly defined sense, to have a *human* or a *real* understanding of a puzzling situation will agree with Socrates that the event explanation is "a very careless and idle mode of speaking."

Both types of explanation are often used in explaining some specific human occurrence. Although such hybrid explanations are not intellectually neat and tidy, our ignorance of facts needed to implement one of the types often makes us supplement that type with the other. With this *caveat*, let us now examine cases 2, 3, and 4.

The question in example 2 can be answered without explicit reference to what anyone knows or desires or thinks. The following are the relevant facts of the case.

a. Social security pays out money to people over age sixty-five.
b. Medical research and therapy have, in the long run, the effect of reducing the death rate.
c. Medical research and therapy cost money. Within broad limits, more of them costs more money than less of them.

From these we could construct the following explanation:

The amount spent on medical research determines the amount of medical research.
The amount of medical research is, in the long run, positively correlated with reduction in the death rate.
A reduction in the death rate raises the average age of the population.
As the average age of the population increases, the proportion of aged people will normally increase.
The number of aged people is a positive factor in determining the amount of social security payouts.

[14]This distinction corresponds roughly to that of David Braybrooke, *Philosophical Problems of the Social Sciences* (New York: The Macmillan Company, 1964), who distinguishes between behavior-theories and action-theories. Braybrooke analyzes many interesting examples and discusses the logic of each.

[15]See L. W. Beck, "The 'Natural Science Ideal' in the Social Sciences," *Scientific Monthly*, Vol. 68, No. 6 (June, 1949), 386–94.

Therefore, in the long run, the more money spent upon medical research and therapy, the more money will be paid out in social security benefits.

The conclusion follows "with mathematical certainty," although it is only approximately true, because there are many other factors that determine social security costs, and not all medical research pays off in a reduced death rate. It would not be true in a country that depended upon another country for medical research done at no cost to it, nor of a country that admitted a large number of elderly immigrants, nor if there was an epidemic that struck down mostly aged people, and so on. We have, in giving this explanation, described an *ideal case* that ignores many factual factors but does explain those actual cases in which the correlation holds. If it does not hold, we try to build into the explanation still other factors that will make the ideal case more like the actual. The ideal case has a *ceteris paribus* clause in it, but in real life, other things are often not equal and cannot be made equal. The social scientist at least begins with such ideal cases with their *ceteris paribus* clauses, and then gradually makes them more complicated in order to reduce the discrepancy between the results of the theory and the empirical data. But the most note-worthy feature of this explanation is that it is an event explanation, and it says nothing about people's motives or wishes or purposes. Yet to the extent to which it does in fact explain the facts, it is a good explanation; we do not ask, "Yes, but what was the motive of the medical researchers whose research had this effect?"

The explanation of example 3 is somewhat different. The question pre-supposes an inductive explanation of a specific case of falling stock prices but asks: What is the explanation of this induction? A very elementary an-swer might be as follows:

Money tends to flow into safe and higher-yielding investments rather than into un-safe and lower-yielding investments. Bonds are safer than stocks, but generally do not have so high a yield; hence money flows approximately equally into the bond and into the stock market. When bond interest increases, however, the two factors (safety and yield) work in the same direction, and money goes into bonds that would otherwise have been used to buy stocks. With the decrease in demand for stocks, their prices fall.

Such an explanation can certainly make a situation clear that one might not have understood without the model of money flowing like water into various streams. But money is not water; it does not yield to gravitational forces; it does not, literally, flow. To explain its movements (itself a metaphor), we come up with statements about the needs and wants of human beings gene-rally. We say: The prudent investor prefers safe to unsafe investments when the current yield of the latter is close to that of the former. Most of the time, such human motives as a desire for a safe profit are so obvious that they can be omitted from our explanatory statements; if anyone is interested in the movements of stock prices, he probably does not have to be told basic facts like "Men desire to make profits on their investments." Yet, such basic facts about people (and not just about money) are there as suppressed premises, collateral hypotheses. When there is a great majority of speculators and only a few prudent investors, this "law of economics" does not hold true, and stock prices go higher. The law, in other words, is not actually and accurately descriptive of what invariably happens but only of what happens given certain common human interests and assumptions. If we assume that most human beings wish to maximize profits and minimize hazards, then we can understand this and other facts of economic life. When this explanation does not fit, we add other factors to those we have considered, spelling out the ways in which the *ceteris paribus* clauses in our theory must be modified. We may have to speak of bearish attitudes, excitement, ignorance of market conditions, sunspot cycles, and so on. But even if we do not do this, our event analysis of the fall of stock prices, pushed farther, leads to the kinds of facts that figure in action explanations (general interests, attitudes, hopes, and expectations of human beings).

Example 4 asks: "What is the child doing?" One answer is: "He is sitting at the table making marks on paper with a pen." But this answer does not explain anything; it is just a description. Suppose the answer is: "He is doing his homework. That is why he is sitting at the desk writing with a pen." "Doing homework" is an expression that can be understood only by someone who understands the rules and practices of the institution, the school, that the child attends. To understand the child's unwonted quietness, we must know the rules he knows and know what it means to follow the rules he follows. We should have to know, and would have to explain to another person who does not know, that each person in society acts in a certain role, most of the rules for which are second nature but formulatable as prescriptions for proper behavior. In the example before us there are:

the rule (of the school) that homework must be handed in each day;
the rule (of the teacher) that homework must be written in ink;
the rule (of the parents) that homework must be finished before the child looks at television;
the rule (custom or habit of the child) that this table is the preferred place in the house to work;
the rules of the multiplication table, which he has learned and which he uses in solving the problems assigned;
the rule (of courtesy) that his parents do not interrupt him while he is studying;

and a myriad of other rules that perhaps only an anthropologist or sociologist would be able to express. (Most of the time we do not *know* the rules of our own society as well as we know those of some foreign country, yet we *follow* the rules of our society and we repeatedly break those of other societies.)

It must be noticed that none of these rules is a descriptive law (see p. 213).

For instance, they do not say that it is impossible to do arithmetic with a pencil or that TV sets do not work until both the switch has been turned and the arithmetic problems solved. After all, the child can disobey the rules, but he cannot break a law of nature. To understand the child's behavior, therefore, we must understand the rules he is trying, whether unconsciously or reluctantly, to obey. Even if we believe that we could explain the *events* taking place (his sitting at the table, like Socrates sitting in his cell) by reference to the laws and theories of physiology, they would not explain the "act of doing homework," which is not a term (like "reflex," "glandular secretion," and "response to stimulus") having a place in physiological law or theory. For although physiology has descriptive laws, it does not have a place for prescriptive laws in its theory.

However little we know of physiology, we can still understand the child's sitting at the table when we understand the role the child has in the social community and the rules that are accepted, consciously or unconsciously, as definitive of, or corollary to, this role. We understand the child's sitting at the table by being told he is doing his homework, and by knowing what it means to do homework, we understand what prescriptive rules are adhered to by *anyone* who has the role of the child in a school requiring homework. Because we know these rules about the child, mostly from our own experience, just mentioning the fact that he is doing his homework explains a great deal. If the child were in a society whose rules and roles were alien to us, and we were told, "He is fragellating the mana," we would not have an explanation of his action because we do not know the rules for fragellating mana. Yet we could understand the physiology of that child just as well as we can understand that of our little brother.

Suppose a child was sitting at a desk but not writing when we expected him to be doing so, and we ask, "Why is the child not writing?" Then we might get an event explanation that did not make reference to rules and purposes yet one that was adequately explanatory—"The child's arm is paralyzed." But just as we did not have to be told that investors prefer good to bad investments because it was too obvious to require stating, we do not count it as an explanation of one child's writing that his arm is *not* paralyzed, although we do count it as an explanation of another child's not writing that his arm *is* paralyzed. The reason for it is this: "The child's arm is paralyzed" (event explanation) is adequate to explain the child's not writing, but "The child's arm is not paralyzed" (event explanation) is not adequate to explain that he is actively doing something that can be understood only by recourse to our conception of roles and rules.

Still, the fact that the child's arm is not paralyzed, although not explicitly mentioned, is an important factor, for if it were paralyzed, he could not do his homework. This shows us that in no explanation of human actions do we tell the whole story. We assume a vast amount of common information (and, regrettably, common misinformation) and focus it, without being told to do so, on the specific situation that puzzles us. Most explanatory factors for human actions are, even when known, seldom made explicit. This is one of the principal sources of the difficulty of submitting explanations, laws, and theories about human beings to the rigorous scientific tests we apply when trying to understand inanimate nature. For if the collateral hypothesis that consists of this vast but vague store of information (or misinformation) does contain any unsuspected errors, we know that we cannot be sure when we have confirmed or disconfirmed the substantive hypothesis—the offered explanation.

The Natural and the Social Sciences

There are other reasons why explanations of human behavior as given in the social sciences are usually lacking in the precision and assurance we find in natural scientific explanations. We may mention four of the most important.

a. Bias may enter into the gathering and interpretation of data. The questions dealt with by anyone who inquires into the behavior of human beings are so frought with conceptions of right and wrong, good and bad, desirable and undesirable that it requires the utmost effort to achieve impartiality. Much of the success of the natural sciences has been possible because the abstractions of those sciences are not conceptions of value; the moral values involved in the natural sciences concern the uses to which value-free knowledge can be put, whereas the social sciences in their pursuit of objectivity must deal with human conduct what is guided by the subjects' attitudes toward values and is an object of the social scientists' *own* approvals and disapprovals. The scientist who studies human sexual behavior, for example, may try to be as impartial and objective as the scientist who studies the sexual behavior of insects. He avoids the use of such value terms as "right" and "wrong," "misbehavior" and "bad habits," yet his own value-stance may subtly affect the questions he asks, the assumptions he makes, the material he chooses for study, and the conclusions he draws. Yet bias means a prejudicial estimation of facts, and the social sciences can be truly scientific only when they attain a value-free attitude to value-laden facts of life.

b. The facts of human life and society are so complex that predictions can be only probabilistic, with a wide range of possible error. The range of observations predicted will be generally much more widely dispersed around and average or some other mean than those predicted for a laboratory experiment, and there may be indecisive debate as to whether a certain set of results confirms or disconfirms the hypothesis in question. All predictions in science on the basis of a limited set of hypotheses are predictions *ceteris paribus*. In the natural sciences, the *ceteris paribus* clauses are usually quite precise, and when an experiment goes wrong we usually have considerable confidence in our methods of making the *ceteris paribus* clause of one family of hypotheses into a new substantive hypothesis of a new family of hypotheses.

In the social sciences, the *ceteris paribus* clause usually has a very wide and not well-defined range, and it is almost always possible to spell it out in some way that will save the hypothesis to which one, because of his bias, is already committed.

c. The operational hypotheses in social science are not usually directions for performing controlled experiments. We do not operate in an isolated or closed system, within which all the variables can be controlled. And as we approach the situation in which some important variables are controlled, the enterprise of the experiment itself may affect, in subtle ways, the behavior we are trying to explain. Let a child know that he is being studied by a psychologist; can you be sure he will act as he would if he were not being studied?

d. Lastly, human beings are affected by the results of scientific observation. If people learn, for instance, that rising bond interest depresses the stock market, then when they notice the rising interest rate and *take account of this hypothesis* they may sell stocks that they might have retained had they not been aware of this hypothesis. The hypothesis itself, then, becomes a causative factor in the decline of the stock market, and we have the phenomenon known as the *self-confirming hypothesis*. It may be the acceptance of the hypothesis, not the rise in interest rates itself that causes the decline in stock prices. There are also *self-refuting hypotheses*. If the social scientist lets it be known that according to his hypothesis a man cannot give up smoking if he has smoked c packs of cigarettes for n years, this may be just the added factor that will make many people say "I'll show that psychologist," give up smoking, and thereby refute what would otherwise be a correct hypothesis, *ceteris paribus*.

Yet in spite of all these cautionary remarks, the *logical pattern of explanation of human affairs conforms to the schema given on page* 195. This is certainly true of event explanations, but a little thought will show that it is true also of action explanations. That the little boy is studying in order not to miss a favorite TV show is a teleological explanation quite unlike the astronomical hypothesis that Uranus is attracted by Neptune. But the hypothesis that explains why he is studying is a member of a family of hypotheses for which we have evidence, and we can confirm or disconfirm the hypothesis in much the same way we test the astronomical hypothesis. For instance, tell the child the TV is broken. If he keeps on studying, we can say: The desire to see the TV program was not the only reason, and maybe not the reason at all, why he was studying.

To try to explain human affairs by the use of scientific methods of gathering and evaluating observations perhaps sounds a bit pretentious. But it does not necessarily commit one to reducing the social and the human to the purely physico-chemical or the biological. It does not mean to deny that human actions can, and perhaps must, be understood teleologically. It does mean that teleological and "human" explanations must face tests logically and epistemologically like the tests that have been used with such striking success in the study of nature.

BIBLIOGRAPHY

Explanation and Description; Types of Explanation.

Black, Max, *Models and Metaphors*, pp. 219–43. Ithaca, N. Y.: Cornell University Press, 1962.

Braithewaite, R. B., *Scientific Explanation*, Chap. 4. New York: Harper & Row, Publishers, 1960.

Feigl, Herbert, and May Brodbeck, eds., *Readings in the Philosophy of Science*, Parts 2 and 4. New York: Appleton-Century-Crofts, 1953.

Hempel, Carl G., *Philosophy of Natural Science*. Englewood Cliffs, N. J.: Prentice-Hall, Inc., 1966.

Hesse, Mary, *Models and Analogies in Science*. Notre Dame, Ind. Notre Dame University Press, 1966.

Margenau, Henry, *The Nature of Physical Reality*, Chaps. 3, 4, and 5. New York: McGraw-Hill Book Company, 1950.

Nagel, Ernest, *The Structure of Science*, Chaps. 2–7. New York: Harcourt, Brace & World, Inc., 1961.

Passmore, John, "Explanation in Everyday Life, in Science, and in History," in *Studies in the Philosophy of History*, ed., George H. Nadel. New York: Harper & Row, Publishers, 1965.

Shapere, Dudley, ed., *Philosophical Problems of Natural Science*. New York: The Macmillan Company, 1965.

Turbayne, Colin M., *The Myth of Metaphor*. New Haven: Yale University Press, 1962.

Teleological Explanation

Alexander, Samuel, *Space Time and Deity* (1920), I and II. New York: Humanities Press, 1950.

Braithewaite, R. B., *Scientific Explanation*, Chap. 10. New York: Harper & Row, Publishers, 1960.

Canfield, John V., ed., *Purpose in Nature*. Englewood Cliffs, N. J.: Prentice-Hall, Inc., 1966.

Feigl, Herbert, and May Brodbeck, eds., *Readings in the Philosophy of Science*, Part 6. New York: Appleton-Century-Crofts, 1953.

Goldstein, Kurt, *The Organism. A Holistic Approach to Biology*. New York: American Book Company, 1939.

Nagel, Ernest, *The Structure of Science*, Chap. 12. New York: Harcourt, Brace & World, Inc., 1961.

Taylor, Richard, *Action and Purpose*. Englewood Cliffs, N. J.: Prentice-Hall, Inc., 1965.

Explanations of Human Behavior

Braybrooke, David, ed., *Philosophical Problems of the Social Sciences*. New York: The Macmillan Company, 1965.

Cassirer, Ernest, *The Logic of the Humanities*. New Haven: Yale University Press, 1961.

Donagan, Alan, and Barbara Donagan, *Philosophy of History*. New York: The Macmillan Company, 1965.

Dray, William, *Philosophy of History*. Englewood Cliffs, N.J.: Prentice-Hall, Inc., 1966.

Feigl, Herbert, and May Brodbeck, eds., *Readings in the Philosophy of Science*, Part 7. New York: Appleton-Century-Crofts, 1953.

Marx, Melvin H., ed., *Psychological Theory*. New York: The Macmillan Company, 1951.

Nagel, Ernest, *The Structure of Science.*, Chaps. 13, 14, and 15. New York: Harcourt, Brace & World, Inc., 1961.

Natanson, Maurice, ed., *Philosophy of the Social Sciences*. New York: Random House, 1963.

Popper, Karl, *The Poverty of Historicism*. London: Routledge & Kegan Paul, Ltd., 1957.

Rudner, Richard, *Philosophy of Social Science*. Englewood Cliffs, N.J.: Prentice-Hall, Inc., 1966.

Winch, Peter, *The Idea of a Social Science*. London: Routledge & Kegan Paul, Ltd., 1958.

QUESTIONS FOR REVIEW AND DISCUSSION

1. Look up the etymology of the word *explain*. Does this etymology throw any useful light on the current usage of the word?

2. What is a nomological explanation? How does it differ from an inductive explanation? Does it *really* differ from an inductive explanation?

3. Compare what is said in this chapter about inferred entities and what was said in Chapter 7 about logical constructions. Then comment upon Bertrand Russell's maxim: "Wherever possible, substitute logical constructions for inferred entities."

4. If mathematical truths are logically necessary, does this imply that the formula on page 247, $K = PV/f(\theta)$, is logically necessary?

5. Change the example on page 249 to make it into an explanation of Boyle's Law. Show how Boyle's Law can be derived mathematically from the general gas law. What does this suggest about the relationship between Boyle's and Charles' Laws?

6. Read the little book by Stephen Toulmin, *Foresight and Understanding* (Bloomington: Indiana University Press, 1961). Discuss the relationship between "prediction" and "explanation" as seen by Toulmin.

7. If a chemist should succeed in creating living matter out of inorganic materials, would this affect the philosophical dispute between mechanists, vitalists, and holists?

8. " 'Function' is just the name for whatever an organ does, without any reference to purpose." "Then the function of the heart is to make a thumping sound." Discuss.

9. Show clearly, by several examples, that you understand the difference between an action explanation and an event explanation.

10. What are the principal obstacles in the way of making the social sciences as exact and certain as the natural sciences?
11. Discuss the relationship between the fact that action explanations and event explanations can be given for the same human behavior and the theories of compatibilism and incompatibilism in Chapter 9.
12. Does an event explanation of a human act abrogate the possibility of making a moral judgment about the act?
13. How may a model help and how may it hinder inquiry? Illustrate your answer by reference to the following models:
    a. a map
    b. a structural formula in organic chemistry
    c. a machine as the model of the universe
    d. a computer as a model of the brain
    e. an organism as the model of a society
    f. the eye as a camera
    g. the mind as a blank tablet (see p. 98).
    h. a scientific experiment as a game played by nature and a scientist (see J. Bronowski, "Science as Foresight," in *What is Science?* ed., J. R. Newman (New York: Simon and Schuster, Inc., 1955), pp. 385-436.

11 METAPHYSICS AS HYPOTHESIS

A DEFENSE OF METAPHYSICS

In Chapter 1 philosophy was described as critical, speculative, and synoptic. Later, there were critical inquiries into the nature and limits of knowledge. We saw repeatedly that following through these critical inquiries led to speculative questions about the status of what we know and what we value. It led to questions concerning the most general features of the universe, man, and man's place in the universe. We found that we could not work out the implications of our knowledge of scientific laws without raising questions and suggesting hypotheses about the nature of reality as a whole. Questions and hypotheses of this kind, when explicitly formulated so that they can be discussed rationally, belong to the division of philosophy known as metaphysics.

Such questions and hypotheses, tacitly formulated to meet specific interests in our study of knowledge and value, have occurred so often in the course of this book that there can be no sharp break between our critical and our speculative inquiries. A "persistent attempt to think things through" has its critical and speculative stages, however, and one merges into the other.

The word *metaphysics* has an unusual history. Aristotle wrote a work that dealt with the basic concepts of the sciences of nature, which he called *Physics*. After his death, editors who compiled his writings collected a group of short and more or less independent treatises and put them, in their edition, after the treatise on *Physics*. They therefore called them the treatises "after physics," which in Greek is *meta ta physika*. But Aristotle, who is one of the most important of all writers in the field that *we* call "metaphysics," was innocent of the word.

The treatises collected under the name of *Metaphysics* were not greatly dependent on one another, and they were probably never intended to be regarded as a single work. But so strong was the influence of the work of

Aristotle on later thinkers that it is almost correct to say, "Metaphysics is the part of philosophy that deals with all the problems discussed in Aristotle's *Metaphysics*." In that book, Aristotle studies the organization of knowledge, the meaning of explanation, the nature of "being as being," the relationship of universals and particulars, the nature of mathematics, causation, the existence of God, the purpose of the world, the unity of nature—all of which have continued to be regarded as parts of the metaphysician's province.

Metaphysics may be roughly described as a serious intellectual attempt to describe the general features of reality, to see them in their relation to our knowledge and experience of values, and to apply inquiry, which is usually directed to particular kinds of events and things, to the whole of everything.

Somerset Maugham, with a passion for philosophy, wrote of it:

Metaphysics never lets you down. You can never come to the end of it. It is as various as the soul of man. It has greatness, for it deals with nothing less than the whole of knowledge. It treats of the universe, of God and immortality, of the properties of the human reason and the end and purpose of life, of the power and limitations of man, and if it cannot answer the questions that assail him on his journey through this dark and mysterious world it persuades him to support his ignorance with good humour.... It appeals to the imagination as well as to the intelligence, and to the amateur, much more, I suppose, than to the professional it affords matter for that reverie which is the most delicious pleasure with which man can beguile his idleness.[1]

THE DISTRUST OF METAPHYSICS

In spite of this deserved praise, over the years metaphysics has been attacked from many sides. We remarked in Chapter 1 about its reputation for obscurity and saw in Chapter 7 the logical positivist's charge that it is meaningless. Let us now examine some other serious objections to metaphysics and consider whether it can be defended against them.

Common Sense Objections to Metaphysics

The man of "healthy common sense" is likely to be impatient with what he calls metaphysics, although many of his own beliefs (in free will or against free will, for instance) belong to the subject-matter of metaphysics. Ignoring the metaphysical content of his own uncritical beliefs, he is likely to consider metaphysics fruitless speculation that is foolish and a waste of time.

Certainly metaphysics is a waste of time for one who thinks that time is well spent only in building houses, making money, fighting wars, curing disease, or "wine, women, and song." So also, according to this standard, operas, novels, churches, history, and higher mathematics are ways of

---

[1]From *The Summing Up* by W. Somerset Maugham. Copyright, 1938, by W. Somerset Maugham. Reprinted by permission of Doubleday & Company, Inc., W. Somerset Maugham's literary executor, and William Heinemann, Ltd.

wasting time. But it might well be argued that the value judgment that metaphysics and these other pursuits are wastes of time is too narrow. It may be very important to an individual (and if he has a superior mind, to society) to formulate defensible notions about the whole of things and man's place in it. There are, fortunately, some men like Dmitri Karamazov who, as Dostoevski tells us, "did not care about making a million dollars, but did want an answer to his questions."

Metaphysicians are sometimes said to be blind men looking for a black cat at midnight when there's no cat there. Or they are compared to the blind men who felt of an elephant and disputed whether it was more like a rope, a tree, or a wall. The man of common sense is likely to be skeptical of the alleged power of the human mind to understand reality as a whole, especially when it seems to lead to conclusions about reality that are opposed to his own common-sense view of things.

And he may well be skeptical. There is no guarantee that we can discover truth about reality as a whole. Of course, in the beginning there was no guarantee that we could discover the truth about anything; but men tried to learn, and they did learn much about the weather, molecules, stars, germs, and themselves. The common-sense attitude, which we have called the dogmatism of ignorant minds, would always block the way of inquiry if it were taken as the final judge of what we can know.

The wisest conclusion would seem to be: use whatever abilities we have for understanding the world, but do not be overconfident that the answers we get are true. Dogmatism has no more place in metaphysics than it has in science, but a narrow skepticism would prevent us from pursuing any kind of inquiry.

Psychological Objections to Metaphysics

According to one view of psychology, the higher thought processes are merely rationalizations of our instinctive needs. F. H. Bradley, one of the greatest metaphysicians, said, "Metaphysics is the giving of bad reasons for what we believe upon instinct." The Freudians say that a metaphysical belief like the belief in God is only the persistence of the infantile need for the love of a father.[2] Some men sublimate their sexual urges by writing poetry; others do so by writing books on metaphysics.[3] There is no more reason to expect the latter to be true than the former.

Sociological Objections to Metaphysics

Metaphysics, according to many sociologists and anthropologists, is a reflection of the social or cultural conditions under which it develops. Men

[2]Sigmund Freud, *The Future of an Illusion* (London: H. Liveright and the Institute of Psychoanalysis, 1928), p. 34.

[3]See Morris Lazerowitz, *Studies in Metaphilosophy* (London: Routledge & Kegan Paul, Ltd., 1964).

project into their pictures of ultimate reality the kind of laws and structures they find in their society (see p. 215 for an example) because their thought about the unknown is conditioned by their conventional beliefs about the world around them. It is said, the intellectual climate within which metaphysical speculation occurs is not determined by considerations germane to the truth or falsity of a metaphysical theory but by the political ideologies, religious outlook, and technological situation of the society. Just as an individual cannot see things except from a point of view determined by his own psychological make-up, so also, it is said, the social situation still further restricts his perspective.

Such an objection can be illustrated by reference to the way a language may incline those who speak it to accept tacitly a certain kind of metaphysics. The European languages, including Greek, have what is known as a subject-predicate syntax. Sentences in these languages typically take the form, "The tree is green," "Der Baum ist grün," "L'arbre est vert." In such sentences we verbally separate a thing (tree) from its quality (green), which seems to be a "universal" that applies to many things (see p. 216). This peculiarity of our languages raises a question we have already discussed, the solution of which belongs to the study of metaphysics. The question is: What sort of "being" does the universal possess, and how is the universal related to the particulars it qualifies? This has been one of the central problems of European metaphysics since the time of Plato.

But, according to those who object to metaphysics, it is a "pseudo-problem" that has arisen only because of the peculiarity of the language spoken. Peoples who speak other languages with a different syntactical structure (for instance, Chinese) have developed other metaphysical theories with quite different questions to be answered. "Reality," the critic says, "is indifferent to our grammatical distinctions; metaphysical questions arise from a confusion of such grammatical distinctions with categories of reality."

If we generalize this objection, it comes to the general statement that all metaphysical problems are pseudo-problems arising from the confusion of the linguistic or other peculiarities of a culture with alleged characteristics of "ultimate reality."

Linguistic Objections to Metaphysics

Generalized in this way, this objection encompasses the view of many linguistic analysts that traditional metaphysical problems arise through the abuse of language. Earlier we saw this charge leveled against the traditional handling of the epistemological problem of knowledge of the external world. Let us now consider a similar argument directed against the metaphysical problem of the nature of mind. Although this argument is not intended to refute the whole of metaphysics as a discipline, it typifies the strategy used by many contemporary philosophers against specific doctrines. The argument is developed by Gilbert Ryle in his book *The Concept of Mind.* His critique of the notion of sense data, which we examined in Chapter 7, is part of a broader attack upon the particular conception of mind held by Descartes, which says that the mind is an immaterial substance residing in a material body. Ryle variously caricatures this view—sometimes called Cartesian dualism—as The Official Doctrine, the "dogma of the Ghost in the Machine," and the paramechanical hypothesis.

Cartesian Dualism

According to this view, which Ryle says is held by many laymen, philosophers, and religious teachers,[4] everyone possesses a body and a mind, and the two, although different, are somehow linked. But whereas the body exists in space and is observable and subject to mechanical laws, the mind is non-spatial, unobservable, and subject to special nonmechanical laws. The events that take place in a person's mind are private episodes knowable only to himself.

When someone is described as knowing, believing or guessing something, as hoping, dreading, intending or shirking something, as designing this or being amused at that, these verbs are supposed to denote the occurrence of specific modifications in his (to us) occult stream of consciousness. Only his own privileged access to this stream in direct awareness and introspection could provide authentic testimony that these mental-conduct verbs were correctly or incorrectly applied.[5]

This doctrine, Ryle contends, is mistaken in principle. It commits what he calls a category mistake by representing "the facts of mental life as if they belonged to one logical type or category (or range of types or categories), when they actually belong to another."[6] The consequence is that the whole doctrine is a "philosopher's myth." To rectify this mistake one need not deny any accepted facts; he need only clarify the logic of mental-conduct concepts. For the basis of the doctrine lies in a misunderstanding of the "logic" of that area of our language dealing with mental concepts. In short, the problem is not factual but conceptual, the clarification of which calls for greater sensitivity to the proper and improper uses of language.

Category Mistakes

In order to understand better what Ryle means by a category mistake, it will be necessary to introduce some technical notions.

The first is that of a "sentence-factor," which Ryle characterizes as a word,

[4]Gilbert Ryle, *The Concept of Mind* (London: Hutchinson & Company, 1955), p. 11. Quoted by permission of the Hutchinson Publishing Group, Ltd., and Barnes and Noble, Inc.
[5]*Ibid.,* p. 15.
[6]*Ibid.,* p. 16.

phrase, or clause that can enter into otherwise dissimilar sentences.[7] Consider, for example, the sentence:

1. I am the man who wrote this paper.

Each of the bracketed portions indicates a sentence-factor; although each is a "part" of sentence 1, it may also enter into many other sentences.

The second notion is that of a "sentence-frame"—an incomplete sentence that requires for its completion the introduction of sentence-factors in the appropriate places.[8] For example, the sentence-frame

2. I am the man who . . . ,

can be completed in many ways (in addition to that represented in 1), such as by adding "wrote this exam," "delivered this lecture," and so forth. But it cannot be completed in just *any* way, for its completion by such sentence-factors as "is the square root of 4" or "has a valency of 2" yields absurdities.

In order for meaningful propositions to result, the gaps in sentence-frames must be completed by sentence-factors that (a) are of certain grammatical types and (b) express proposition-factors of certain *logical* types.[9] The important requirement philosophically is b, for the deceptive cases are likely to be those in which a sentence is grammatically correct but fails to express a meaningful proposition. "To say that a given proposition-factor is of a certain category or type," Ryle asserts, "is to say that its expression could complete certain sentence-frames without absurdity."[10] For example, "desk" and "chair" express proposition-factors of the same type, because they can both be used to complete such sentence-frames as ". . . is in my office," or ". . . is a piece of furniture," in a manner consonant with requirements a and b. On the other hand,

Two proposition-factors are of different categories or types, if there are sentence-frames such that when the expressions for those factors are imported as alternative complements to the same gap-signs, the resultant sentences are significant in the one case and absurd in the other.[11]

For example, consider the sentence-frame

3. . . . is in my office.

---

[7]Gilbert Ryle, "Categories," in *Logic and Language* (2nd series), ed., A. G. N. Flew (Oxford: Basil Blackwell, 1955), p. 68. Quoted by permission of Basil Blackwell.

[8]*Ibid.*, p. 69.

[9]Notice that we have shifted from talking about sentences to talking about propositions. Ryle's reason for this is the following: "Now sentences and sentence-factors are English or German, pencilled or whispered or shouted, slangy or pedantic, and so on. What logic is concerned with is something which is indifferent to these differences—namely (it is convenient though often misleading to say), propositions and the parts or factors of propositions. When two sentences of different languages, idioms, authors or dates say the same thing, what they say can be considered in abstraction from the several sayings of it. . . . And, just as we distinguish propositions from the sentences which propound them, so we must distinguish proposition-factors from the sentence-factors which express them." *Ibid.*, p. 69.

[10]*Ibid.*, p. 70.

[11]*Ibid.*, pp. 77f.

It makes good sense to complete 3 with "Jones" or "the department secretary," but it makes no sense to complete it with "Saturday" or "the number
2." For even though the resultant *sentences* would be grammatically correct,
they would not express meaningful *propositions*. Thus "Jones" and "the
department secretary," on the one hand, are of different logical types from
"Saturday" and "the number 2" (not that the latter two are of the *same*
type).

We can now characterize a category mistake as the combining of proposition-factors of incompatible types in such a way as to create an absurdity.
To use an illustration of Ryle's, if a foreign visitor to a university were shown
the various buildings, laboratories, dormitories, and so forth, and he then
asked "But where is the university?" he would be committing a category
mistake. He would be assuming that the university is another *thing* of the
same type (category) as the various structures he has just been shown. But
whereas one can show someone a university by showing him its various
buildings, facilities, and so forth, there is no "thing" over and above all of
these that can be said to be the university. Anyone who supposes that there
is has not yet learned the correct use of the concept of a university.

The same type of confusion, Ryle contends, gave rise initially to the
Official Doctrine.

> The differences between the physical and the mental were thus represented as dif-
> ferences inside the common framework of the categories of "thing," "stuff," "at-
> tribute," "state," "process," "change," "cause" and "effect." Minds are things, but
> different sorts of things from bodies; mental processes are causes and effects, but
> different sorts of causes and effects from bodily movements. And so on. Somewhat
> as the foreigner expected the University to be an extra edifice, rather like a college
> but also considerably different, so the repudiators of mechanism represented minds
> as extra centres of causal processes, rather like machines but also considerably
> different from them.[12]

In such a view, the world is divided into the inner and the outer, the subjective and the objective. In this manner this conception of the mind contributes to the creation of the problem of our knowledge of the external world.
The confusion in this thinking is to suppose that when we talk about minds
(which we can sensibly do) and when we talk about objects (which we can
sensibly do) we are talking about things belonging to the same logical type
or category.

> It is perfectly proper to say, in one logical tone of voice, that there exist minds and to
> say, in another logical tone of voice, that there exist bodies. But these expressions do
> not indicate two different species of existence, for "existence" is not a generic word
> like "coloured" or "sexed." They indicate two different senses of "exist," somewhat
> as "rising" has different senses in "the tide is rising," "hopes are rising," and "the
> average age of death is rising." A man would be thought to be making a poor joke

[12] *The Concept of Mind*, p. 19.

who said that three things are now rising, namely the tide, hopes and the average age of death. It would be just as good or bad a joke to say that there exist prime numbers and Wednesdays and public opinions and navies; or that there exist both minds and bodies.[13]

In short, subscribers to the Official Doctrine have been beguiled into asserting things that not only are untrue but that are not even meaningful.

What lines of defense can be offered on behalf of metaphysics against the various objections to it? We shall begin by taking closer account of the logical positivist's objection as discussed in Chapter 7. This was, we recall, that metaphysical statements are senseless, because they fail to meet the verificationist's criterion of meaning.

An Answer to the Logical Positivist's Objections

Metaphysics, at least since the time of Hume and Kant, has not been subjected to so subtle and thorough a criticism as this one formulated by the logical positivists. Can metaphysics meet the attack?

Certainly much of metaphysics cannot, and we should be glad to have it so thoroughly eradicated. If one who is familiar with modern positivism and its analytical methods reads some ordinary (but perhaps not the best) metaphysical books of sixty years ago, he will be annoyed by the lack of precision and the general fuzziness of argument it shows. The positivists have shown how justly we can ignore much of the tedious lucubrations that have appeared under the title of speculative metaphysics. They tempt us to exclaim, with Hume:

When we run over libraries, persuaded of these principles, what havoc must we make? If we take in our hand any volume—of divinity or school metaphysics, for instance—let us ask, *Does it contain any abstract reasoning concerning quantity or number?* No. *Does it contain any experimental reasoning concerning matter of fact and existence?* No. Commit it then to the flames for it can contain nothing but sophistry and illusion.[14]

But a little more examination may make the careful thinker suspicious of the great victory claimed by positivism. We shall examine two grounds of suspicion.

1. Is the verification theory of meaning valid? What does *it* mean? It is a decision freely taken by the positivist, announcing that he will use the word "meaning" in a *specific* way. What justifies him in this? No dictionary defines meaning in this way; this is not what most people *mean* by "meaning." Can we test the meaning of the sentence by itself, so that its "meaning" is what would be observed if the sentence is true? Hardly, for its meaning in this sense is nothing but the observed fact that the positivists behave in a certain way when they investigate the meaning of any other sentence.

---

[13]*Ibid.*, p. 23.

[14]David Hume, *An Enquiry Concerning Human Understanding*, ed., Charles W. Hendel (New York: The Library of Liberal Arts, 1955), p. 173.

Yet what we want to know is whether this belief of the positivist is true, and the behavior of the positivist, who already believes it, is not a fair test.

The positivist may say that the sentence setting forth his criterion of meaning is not intended to be *true* but is rather a stipulation or an assumption he makes. It expresses a decision of how he will act not a discovery of some already existing state of affairs. But seen in this way, it is clear that if someone else prefers to use some other criterion of meaning, the positivist cannot legitimately object, although he may not *like* the behavior of the other person who insists on using some other "rule of the game." This, however, is a value judgment, which, according to the positivist, can express only a subjective preference.

At some stage in every theory, of course, a decision must be made, and the decision expresses a preference. But conclusions based on such decisions are not valid objections to conclusions made on the basis of other decisions. Thus one may say that, with the positivist's decision concerning meaning, he cannot consistently say anything that is metaphysical; but that is by itself no criticism of metaphysics, nor does it demonstrate that metaphysics is *per se* impossible.

2. It is not certain that the positivist, in attacking metaphysics, has not fallen into metaphysics himself. We saw earlier that many people object to metaphysics in general when they ought to be arguing only against some specific metaphysical theory, for they themselves make universal judgments about man and the world and the limits of knowledge and the status of values—every one being a judgment in metaphysics. Although the positivist is careful not to call any of his judgments metaphysical, the discerning reader can often detect the predilections of a positivist author that when consistently worked out, would be a full-fledged metaphysical system.[15]

If metaphysics is considered as the inquiry into ultimate presuppositions or as a comparative study of presuppositions taken as ultimate by some "person or group of persons, on this or that occasion or group of occasions, in the course of this or that piece of thinking," then it is clear that positivism can be considered metaphysically, just as metaphysics is considered critically by the positivist.

An Answer to the Psychological and Sociological Objections

These two objections are, in principle, the same. They agree that metaphysical beliefs are caused by conditions that we cannot control and of which we are generally ignorant. The purpose of intelligent inquiry should be to uncover these hidden causes of belief, not to defend the speculations that flow from them.

There are three responses to these objections. First, they properly put us on guard against an easy dogmatism in metaphysics. If their premises are

[15]Several works pointing out metaphysical assumptions involved in positivism are listed in the bibliography.

correct, as they undoubtedly are to some extent, they warn us against formulating metaphysical theories with the headlong confidence we might feel if we believed that our desires and our social environment had no influence on our beliefs. In Chapter 10 we have seen how difficult it is to eliminate bias and the "personal equation" in studies of society. Some of these biases are personal, and some are dependent upon our culture. It is not possible or even desirable to eliminate the personal commitment to some values, although this commitment has its psychological and social causes. It is, however, possible to become aware of biases and to take precautions so that they will not mislead us like a blind man's evil guide. What is true of bias in those fields is even truer in metaphysics proper. It is exceedingly difficult to be sure what our most deep-rooted convictions are. But one of the best ways of finding out what they are is to see what reasonable alternatives have been held by others (see p. 35). Perhaps our own stock of bias may prevent us from getting to an objective, impersonal truth in metaphysics; but a good dose of metaphysics can often do much to purge us of our bias. What Bertrand Russell says of philosophy in general is especially applicable to metaphysics:

The man who has no tincture of philosophy goes through life imprisoned in the prejudices derived from common sense, from the habitual beliefs of his age or his nation, and from convictions which have grown up in his mind without the co-operation or consent of his deliberate reason. . . . While diminishing our feeling of certainty as to what things are, it greatly increases our knowledge as to what they may be; it removes the somewhat arrogant dogmatism of those who have never travelled into the region of liberating doubt and it keeps alive our sense of wonder by showing familiar things in an unfamiliar aspect.[16]

The second response to these objections is that they clearly indicate the great importance, personal and social, of metaphysical thinking at the same time that they claim that it cannot be conclusive or valid. The quotation made earlier from F. H. Bradley, about metaphysics being the giving of bad reasons for what we believe by instinct, continues: "but the giving of these bad reasons is itself a matter of instinct." Even if it sometimes seems that man is not a rational animal, it does appear that he is a "metaphysical animal." He wants answers to the question that his mind puts to him about his place in the world as a whole. This need in many men and women is so strong that they *will* have an answer to it in spite of all objections; they *will* have a metaphysics, even if they are ignorant of the very name of this study.

The present generation of men want answers just as their less skeptical and critical ancestors did. The arguments of psychologists and sociologists have convinced many of the best minds that metaphysics is impossible, a waste of time, or a sign of neurosis, so that they have turned their talents to

[16]From *Problems of Philosophy* by Bertrand Russell (Oxford: Home University Library, Oxford University Press, 1912), pp. 156–57. Quoted by permission of Oxford University Press.

science (or, if they are philosophers, to the "critical" rather than "speculative" problems). They leave the ordinary person without the benefit of philosophy that was supplied to their ancestors by such metaphysicians as Thomas Aquinas, Thomas Hobbes, Hegel, or Herbert Spencer.

But the consequence is not that the ordinary layman gives up his interest in metaphysics. Rather, it is catered by uncritical second-rate writers with press-agents. Our age may not be favorable to the development of metaphysics, but it is favorable to the large sale of books on peace of mind, the destiny of man, the origin of the universe, and the purpose of existence. In spite of the sociological and psychological objection to the possibility of metaphysics, there is a metaphysical vacuum that, if not filled by competent philosophical thinkers, will be filled by still more unsatisfactory thinkers— among them those who proclaim the death of philosophy at the hands of its critical practitioners—who do not even know of the valid objections that have been made to metaphysical speculation.

The third reply to these objections is more in the spirit of critical philosophy. The objections are based upon conclusions derived, or believed to have been derived, from a study of science. For instance, it is proposed as a *law* that the higher mental functions of a man are what they are because of his position in a culture or because of repression and subsequent sublimation of his sexual drive. But we have repeatedly seen that science itself, in its doctrine of law, makes use of some metaphysical hypothesis about universals. To be sure, the psychologist and sociologist do not usually call their basic assumptions metaphysical; they may not even be aware that they have any such basic principles, so blinding is the effect of shared belief. The psychologist and sociologist usually make objections *only* to those metaphysical theories that they do not like and that are not presupposed in their own scientific work—such as the belief in the objectivity of values. But the assumptions they themselves make are not less metaphysical. Hence their objection should be directed to some specific metaphysical theory instead of to metaphysical inquiry itself.

But even if we grant that the individual's personality and the culture in which it develops determine in part the metaphysical views that will be put forward by one philosopher and accepted by others, it still would not follow that metaphysical speculation and study would be useless. Even if the study of metaphysics does not lead to results that can be established with certainty, its pursuit has been and still is significant in understanding the organization of the knowledge we do have. The study of metaphysical speculation can be valuable for the light it throws on the science, art, religion, morals, and ideology of the culture from which it grows. This is because every search for value or knowledge depends upon presuppositions that implicitly guide it but that might guide it better if they were better understood. The study of metaphysics includes the elaboration and criticism of such presuppositions, which are made explicit only in philosophic inquiry.

In earlier chapters we examined the presuppositions of science, such as the various theories of the uniformity of nature, of the status of natural laws, of the relation of life to inanimate matter, and the like. If we had oriented our study toward religion, we should have had to deal with some of these presuppositions and with still others. Had we been writing a thousand years earlier, certainly the presuppositions we would have unearthed would have been different. The highest claim of metaphysics might be to uncover and examine the "presuppositions presupposed in all presuppositions," and they would be formulated in a conceptual scheme that would be a theory about "ultimate reality." But the more cautious metaphysician, who takes seriously the sociologist's and the psychologist's objection, will not stake such a vast claim. He may, however, accomplish more by trying to discern the hidden presuppositions that have been or are now *taken* to be ultimate but may be superseded by still further developments of knowledge and of our ability to analyze it.

This conception of the role of metaphysics is immune to the sociological and psychological objections. In fact, this kind of work in metaphysics continues the work of the sociologists and psychologists who are interested in the analysis of the intellectual activities of men in the context of the psychological and social factors influencing it. It is the "attempt to find out what absolute presuppositions have been made by this or that person or group of persons, on this or that occasion or group of occasions, in the course of this or that piece of thinking." [17]

An Answer to the Linguistic Objections

We shall confine our comments here to Ryle's specific charge that advocates of a Cartesian theory of the mind have committed a category mistake. Can this be substantiated?

Ryle emphasizes that one cannot tell by the grammar of a sentence whether a category mistake has been committed, since such a mistake may be committed even though the language in which it is expressed is grammatically correct. By what criterion, then, can one tell? The test, in Ryle's view, seems to be whether the proposition in question (assuming that it is grammatically correct, employs conventional vocabulary, and so on) is absurd. For a category mistake is said to have been committed when one conjoins proposition-factors of incompatible types; and we have seen that "to say that a given proposition-factor is of a certain category or type, is to say that its expression could complete certain sentence-frames without absurdity." [18] If so, then one cannot first claim that a category mistake has been committed and *then* conclude that a certain proposition is absurd; rather, one must *first* show that the proposition in question is absurd.

In the example of the visitor to the university, who surveys the buildings and grounds and then asks where the university is, the absurdity is clear.

---

[17]R. G. Collingwood, *An Essay on Metaphysics* (Oxford: Clarendon Press, 1940), p. 47.
[18]Ryle, "Categories," *Logic and Language*, p. 70.

But is it equally clear that the statement that the mind is an immaterial substance in which private events take place is absurd? Obviously, to many people it is not. Indeed, if Ryle is correct that this doctrine is prevalent among many theorists and laymen and that "most philosophers, psychologists and religious teachers subscribe, with minor reservations, to its main articles,"[19] then it may even be that it is not absurd to *most* people. If so, then the accusation that this view commits a category mistake looks dubious.

It might be replied—unlike in the example of the university—that the requirement here is only that the doctrine appear absurd to a certain group of persons, say, linguistic philosophers. But then we must ask why their opinion should be privileged over the opinions of many others—including other philosophers who may be followers of Descartes, theologians who believe that the immaterial-substance theory is dictated by the tenets of their theology, and many ordinary people for whom the belief is an integral part of their religious convictions. It is possible, of course, that after reading Ryle these people would agree that their beliefs are absurd and promptly relinquish them. (We should remember that Ryle presents a book-length argument in support of his contention that the doctrine is full of absurdities; we have considered only a part of that argument.) But even granting that not all absurdities are readily apparent and that they often require painstaking argument for their disclosure, it would be incautious to expect large-scale conversions to result from reflection upon Ryle's arguments. Not even all philosophers who are equally familiar with the issues are prepared to endorse his assessment; it seems even less likely that those ordinary people for whom the belief is interwoven with their most cherished convictions would do so either.

This points up a serious difficulty for Ryle's line of attack. For if an appeal to absurdity is to be the criterion for identifying category mistakes, and thereby for determining what is meaningful, then careful specification of the persons to whom something must seem absurd in order to qualify as a category mistake must be made and defended. If this is not the criterion, then we must ask what is. Once we exclude purely formal features of sentences and range beyond simple cases like that of the visitor to the university, we are at a loss for guidelines. And it is at just those times that we encounter the philosophically interesting and controversial problems.

METAPHYSICS AS HYPOTHESIS

These objections to metaphysics do not destroy either its possibility or its value. But they do make us skeptical of any claims that in metaphysics we can expect to demonstrate final answers to the ultimate problems of human life. This would once have sufficed to make metaphysics seem worthless,

---

[19] *The Concept of Mind*, p. 11.

for many philosophers (for example, some rationalists) have believed that metaphysics is the most certain kind of knowledge.

Our previous studies, however, have shown that the sciences neither claim nor give ultimate knowledge; yet they give nonetheless valuable knowledge. In view of this, perhaps the metaphysician should not despair when he concludes that metaphysics, too, does not give absolute certainty about the whole of things. He should be more than satisfied if he could get even as much certainty in metaphysics as he has in science; in fact, he has to be satisfied with much less.

When metaphysicians claimed to have some special way of knowing, such as intuition or a priori reasoning, they strove for absolute certainty and ended in disagreements and polemics with others who likewise claimed absolute knowledge. If metaphysicians can make use of the method of hypothesis, however, then their claims may be somewhat less extravagant and their accomplishments somewhat more substantial. Our present task is to see how the method of hypothesis can be exported from the field of science to the field of metaphysics.

Here our hypotheses will be extremely abstract and general. They will have as their subject-matter nothing less than the whole of existence about which they make a conjecture. Cicero tells us that Democritus began one of his books with the modest statement, "I shall discourse about everything." Stephen C. Pepper has called metaphysical propositions "world hypotheses":

> The peculiarity of world hypotheses is that they cannot reject anything as irrelevant. When certain inconvenient matters are brought to a mathematician, he can always say, "These are psychological [or physical, or historical] matters. I do not have to deal with them." Similarly with other students of restricted fields. But students of world hypotheses can never have that way out. Every consideration is relevant to a world hypothesis, and no facts lie outside it.[20]

A metaphysical or world hypothesis is in the form, "Reality is such that . . ." and the "such that . . ." must include shoes and ships and sealing wax, cabbages and kings, facts and values, scientific hypotheses and feelings—literally everything.

Of course no man can know everything, so the metaphysical hypotheses will always be based on a small number of the things that are relevant to them. But by observing the work of some of the great metaphysicians, we can see how they went about the job of making their hypotheses on the basis of their experience, which, if small compared with the standard of all that is, was large and broad by human standards. Some philosophers have formulated their hypotheses out of the received tradition of their church or the ideology of their government or have taken the facts of science as their raw material or have had a mystical experience in which they "saw" the truth.

[20]Stephen C. Pepper, *World Hypotheses* (Berkeley and Los Angeles: University of California Press, 1942), p. 1. Quoted by permission of the publisher.

In spite of great differences of technique and disposition, however, all the great systems of metaphysical hypotheses seem to owe their birth to a procedure that, when properly understood, is seen to be that of formulating and elaborating a hypothesis.

Let us look at several different descriptions of how metaphysical hypotheses originate and are used. The first is from Dorothy Emmett:

Metaphysics is an analogical way of thinking. . . . It takes concepts drawn from some form of experience or some relation within experience, and extends them either so as to say something about the nature of "reality," or so as to suggest a possible mode of coordinating other experiences of different types from that from which the concept was originally derived.[21]

The second is from Pepper:

A man desiring to understand the world looks about for a clue to its comprehension. He pitches upon some area of common-sense fact, and tries if he cannot understand other areas in terms of this one.

This original area becomes then his basic analogy or *root metaphor*. He describes as best he can the characteristics of this area or . . . discriminates its structure. A list of its structural characteristics becomes his basic concepts of explanation and description. We call them a set of categories. . . . Since the basic analogy or root metaphor normally (and probably at least in part necessarily) arises out of common sense, a great deal of development and refinement of a set of categories is required if they are to prove adequate for a hypothesis of unlimited scope.[22]

The third is from an English philosopher, Bernard Bosanquet. He describes the method of philosophy in general, but what he says has primary reference to metaphysics:

What philosophy needs as its material is the sort of thing that is in a sense obvious, and yet is hard to make plain and distinct. The very greatest things are of this kind—simple examples are, what the painter perceives when he represents a wood, and not merely a number of trees, or the sociologist, when he understands a crowd and not merely a number of persons—both late in being learnt, though the things are so obvious. The *central facts* should be in the centre. This needs a continuous arduous effort, as opposed to resting upon fixed points here and there.[23]

Our last quotation is from Whitehead:

The true method of discovery is like the flight of an aeroplane. It starts from the ground of particular observation; it makes a flight in the thin air of imaginative

---

[21]Dorothy Emmett, *The Nature of Metaphysical Thinking* (London: Macmillan and Company, Ltd., 1949), p. 5. Used by permission of The Macmillan Company, Publishers, and St. Martin's Press, Inc.

[22]Pepper, *op cit.*, p. 91 (italics supplied).

[23]Bernard Bosanquet, *The Principle of Individuality and Value* (1912) (London: Macmillan and Company, Ltd., 1927), p. xvii (italics supplied). Used by permission of The Macmillan Company, Publishers.

generalization; and it again lands for renewed observation rendered acute by rational interpretation.[24]

One might think that this is Whitehead's account of scientific method; it is, in fact, his description of his philosophical or metaphysical procedure.

What stands out clearly in all these accounts is that metaphysics begins by our taking something in the world seriously, regarding it as a synecdoche or analogy for the whole or as a microcosm that reflects the macrocosm and using it as a metaphor for the whole. These central facts are generally highly charged with value; hence a system of metaphysics will to some extent carry to the end the marks of its birth in a particular personality and cultural milieu. A metaphysical hypothesis is like a great work of art, which is the whole world seen from a particular artist's point of view and fashioned by his genius working within, or slightly beyond, the style of his culture.

Unlike a work of art, however, a metaphysical hypothesis is supposed to be factually true. It must pass some tests that we do not usually apply to a poem. It must justify itself not by its beauty or style but more in the way in which a scientific theory is justified: by comprehending, explaining, and rendering integral and intelligible a mass of otherwise chaotic experiences.

Metaphysical hypotheses, however, cannot be verified by scientific test. We cannot search for the purpose of the universe in order to verify a teleological metaphysics by looking for it through a telescope or microscope. The hypotheses of metaphysics are so general that they do not have specific consequences that can be predicted in detail and tested in the laboratory. This was the reason the logical positivists said they had no meaning at all. Moreover, when, as is often the case, metaphysical theories spring from metaphors that provide models for the whole of reality, there is no longer a completely neutral criterion for determining what the "facts" are. How then do we adjudicate between rival theories? It has been said that

... the deeper-level answer to this question is in part that we cannot answer the question, because we can never be sure what the facts are ... a new metaphor changes our attitudes to the facts. Once we see the world from the point of view of one metaphor, the face of it is changed. But when do we become aware of all the metaphors so that at last we know we are confronted with the unmade-up face of the truth?[25]

Our inability to answer this question prevents us from verifying metaphysical hypotheses in the same manner in which we verify those of science. This inability, moreover, is precisely what led many men beyond the bounds of

[24]Alfred North Whitehead, *Process and Reality* (New York: The Macmillan Company, 1929), p. 7. Quoted by permission of The Macmillan Company (copyright renewed 1957 by Evelyn Whitehead).

[25]Colin Murray Turbayne, *The Myth of Metaphor* (New Haven, Conn.: Yale University Press, 1962), p. 214. Quoted by permission.

science into metaphysical speculation in the first place. Greater sensitivity to it may even be part of a healthy scientific attitude; for, as Dewey asserts,

As long as we worship science and are afraid of philosophy we shall have no great science; we shall have a lagging and halting continuation of what is thought and said elsewhere. As far as any plea is implicit in what has been said, it is . . . a plea for the casting off of that intellectual timidity which hampers the wings of imagination, a plea for speculative audacity, for more faith in ideas, sloughing off a cowardly reliance upon those partial ideas to which we are wont to give the name of facts.[26]

But if metaphysical theories cannot be verified by scientific test, there is another test: that of dialectic. Given a metaphysical hypothesis, apply it again and again to the broader and ever-widening reaches of experience to see if it "holds its own" or to see what modifications must be introduced in it to enable it to integrate experience and make experience intelligible. The process is essentially like the Platonic dialectic (p. 55), but it will lead to Platonic conclusions only if it begins with the root metaphors with which Plato began.

Just as a scientific hypothesis is judged by the degree to which diverse evidence converges around it, a metaphysical hypothesis must be judged by the degree to which all our experiences—and not just those in a certain sector of science—point to and converge around it. It may be that no metaphysical hypothesis can serve to bring all our experience into this kind of focus. It is possible that there is some truth about "everything," but that it is so obscure that it cannot be discovered by the human mind; in this case, the best we can do is to try to get a hypothesis that will fit as much of our experience as possible. Or it may indeed be true that the universe is not all of a piece— that the most penetrating analysis will discover contradictions and incongruities in existence that no synthesis can overcome.

Although a philosopher may conceivably be forced to some such conclusion as one of these, they are conclusions to which he should adhere only after he has done his best to discern whatever intelligible order there is. And although he may confess that he cannot find a final answer that is demonstrable and wholly adequate to all parts of experience, he must also acknowledge that the metaphysical theories we have are not all *equally* impotent and inadequate. Some metaphysical theories break down under comparatively little critical inquiry. Others hold their own much better under dialectical scrutiny. Some metaphysicians believe that they have found the one hypothesis that requires no revision. But alternative metaphysical hypotheses cannot be tested so as to eliminate all but one, leaving that one perfect hypothesis standing.

The consequence of this is that metaphysical hypotheses that start from

[26]John Dewey, *Philosophy and Civilization* (New York: Capricorn Books, 1963), p. 12. Quoted by permission of G. P. Putnam's Sons.

a pregnant root metaphor or a rich central fact or analogy may be developed side by side with other theories that have their origin in different metaphors and analogies. No one of them may be strong enough to eliminate all the others. For this reason, dogmatism about final answers is unjustified in metaphysics.

BIBLIOGRAPHY

Ayer, A. J., ed., *Logical Positivism*. Glencoe, Ill.: The Free Press, 1959.

————, *Language, Truth and Logic*. New York: Dover Publications, Inc., 1946.

Ballard, Edward G., "Metaphysics and Metaphor," *Journal of Philosophy*, XLV, No. 8, (April 8, 1948) 208–14.

Barnes, Winston H. F., *The Philosophical Predicament*. London: Adam & Charles Black, 1950.

Baylis, Charles A., ed., *Metaphysics*. New York: The Macmillan Company, 1965.

Bergson, Henri, *An Introduction to Metaphysics* (1903), trans., T. E. Hulme, with an introduction by T. A. Goudge. New York: Liberal Arts Press, 1949. (The Little Library of Liberal Arts, No. 10.)

Burtt, E. A., *The Metaphysical Foundations of Modern Science* (revised edition). Garden City, N.Y.: Doubleday & Company, Inc., 1954.

Carnap, Rudolf, "On the Character of Philosophical Problems," *Philosophy of Science*, I, No. 1 (January, 1934), 5–19.

Emmet, Dorothy, *The Nature of Metaphysical Thinking*. London: Macmillan & Co., Ltd., 1949.

Hawkins, D. J. B., *Being and Becoming*. New York: Sheed & Ward, 1954. A Thomistic defense of metaphysics.

Hocking, W. E., Sterling P. Lamprecht, and John Herman Randall, Jr., "Metaphysics, its Function, Consequences, and Criteria," *Journal of Philosophy*, XLIII, No. 14 (July 4, 1946), 365–78, and No. 15 (July 18, 1946), 393–412.

Lazerowitz, Morris, *The Structure of Metaphysics*. London: Routledge & Kegan Paul, Ltd., 1955.

Lee, Harold N., "Metaphysics as Hypothesis," *Journal of Philosophy*, XLIV, No. 13 (June 19, 1947), 344–52.

Mannheim, Karl, *Ideology and Utopia. An Introduction to the Sociology of Knowledge*. New York: Harcourt, Brace & World, Inc., 1936.

Taylor, Richard, *Metaphysics*. Englewood Cliffs, N.J.: Prentice-Hall, Inc., 1963.

Turbayne, Colin Murray, *The Myth of Metaphor*. New Haven, Conn.: Yale University Press, 1962.

Walsh, W. H., *Metaphysics*. New York: Hillary House, 1962.

Werkmeister, W. H., "Seven Theses of Logical Positivism Critically Examined," *Philosophical Review*, XLVI, No. 3 (May, 1947), 276–97, and No. 4 (July, 1947), 357–76.

QUESTIONS FOR REVIEW AND DISCUSSION

1. Explain what is meant by: metaphor, root metaphor, synecdoche, analogy, and central experience. Compare their use in metaphysics with the use of models in science, as described in Chapter 10.

2. How is an analogy related to a hypothesis? Compare the use of analogies and hypotheses in the sciences and in metaphysics.

3. What characteristics of a good hypothesis are lacking in metaphysical hypotheses?

4. A frequent objection to metaphysics is that metaphysicians cannot agree with one another. Evaluate this objection.

5. What are some of the assumptions underlying the various objections to metaphysics. Are these assumptions themselves metaphysical?

6. "By the very word, metaphysics has to come after physics. Until the physicists get answers to all their questions, metaphysics is premature." Discuss.

7. What are some of the ways in which one metaphysical theory might be judged to be better than another?

8. Evaluate the claim that every science has an underlying metaphysics.

9. Evaluate the charge that Plato (in his doctrine of Forms), Berkeley (in his conception of the relationship between ideas and things), and the absolute idealists (in their conception of experience) have all committed category mistakes.

10. It has been argued that metaphysical theories should be compared not to scientific theories of the universe but to intellectual myths. What features of metaphysics neglected in one of these comparisons is made salient by the other comparison?

11. How is the word "metaphysics" used (or abused) in advertisements by quacks who promise to teach you to "unlock your secret powers"? How do you think the word came to be thus abused?

12 NATURALISM I—
MATERIALISM

INTRODUCTION

During the course of our discussion in Parts Two and Three, we had occasion to examine certain metaphysical theses of a generally speculative sort, the most notable of which were the doctrines of absolute idealism and pluralistic idealism. Having now the advantage of our discussion of science, we shall concentrate upon a more critical approach to metaphysics, one that attempts to adapt the methodology of science to the handling of philosophical problems. This approach, which encompasses a variety of different but related positions, is called naturalism. One of its key objectives is to combat supernaturalism—the view that there is a higher dimension to reality than that which can be investigated by science—which is usually associated with the divine. In subsequent references to this view, we shall have in mind theological supernaturalism as found in orthodox Christainity. Naturalism is the approach prescribed by John Dewey for carrying through the reconstruction that he urged for philosophy as a whole (see Chap. 7).

A naturalist is a philosopher who takes nature as his central fact. Things usually distinguished from nature he interprets as manifestations of nature. Nature is his basic category; belief that some value or experience or object is contrasted to nature he takes to be evidence of ignorance of the manifold character and complexity of nature itself. Art, religion, science, society, culture, and morality, he believes, have their roots in the world of nature and are to be understood in its terms.

"Nature" is a name for the ultimate reality or totality of things, both human and subhuman, organic and inorganic. "Nature" thus serves a function for the naturalist like that of "mind" for the idealist and "God and the world" for the supernaturalist. They are all names given to the whole of reality. It might seem, accordingly, to be utterly trivial to dispute about naturalism and idealism, for such a dispute seems to be about the "best name" to call the universe. If a rose by any other name would smell as sweet, it is reasonable to think that the universe will "smell as sweet" whether we call it "mind" or "God's creation" or "nature."

This is a very superficial criticism, however, for each of the names is used in a metaphorical sense, and each metaphor has its own peculiar suggestive value. The idealist who calls the world a mind does so because he takes as his central fact those things within it that everyone calls a mind, and then from this central fact, he attempts to read off the significant characteristics of the whole. He sees the world as a whole by analogy to the minds within it, which he takes as preeminent instances of those qualities and relationships that he believes are most fundamental in the universe itself. He regards mind as being especially typical of the ultimate character of the universe, and hence he does not think that "mind" is merely an empty name for something that would "smell as sweet" if it were called "nature".

Similarly, the naturalist would deny that "nature" is simply an empty name for something that might equally well be called "mind" or "God's creation." He holds that those parts of the universe that everyone agrees to call nature have a central position within experience and illuminate all the rest. Nature, in the naive, common-sense use of this world, suggests the analogy by which he interprets everything; accordingly, he attributes to reality a very different character and structure from that given to it by other metaphysicians.

The Theses of Naturalism

The characteristics the naturalist attributes to reality are given in three theses:

1. *The anti-dualistic thesis*—The naturalist says, "Everything in the universe is to be understood as parts of or manifestations of nature." Reality does not consist of nature *plus* minds, as Descartes believed, nor does it consist of nature *plus* God, as the supernaturalists believe. According to the naturalist, "Nature is considered as the domain in which both knowledge and happiness are pursued." It is "the familiar setting of human history . . . the primary subject matter of all human inquiry."[1] The naturalist believes that the urge many people feel to accept some supernatural entity like God or some extranatural realm of entities like objective values, springs from a narrow conception of nature that includes only the colorless, odorless, tasteless, and valueless entities of physics. He also believes that a sufficiently broad and comprehensive conception of nature can make room for the sights and sounds and aspirations and ideals that men experience.

Many naturalists admit that there are strata of reality or emergent levels within nature, but they do not sharply segregate the levels they distinguish,

---

[1]Reprinted from Frederick J. E. Woodbridge, *An Essay on Nature* (New York: Columbia University Press, 1937), pp. v, 3, 4. Copyright 1937 by Columbia University Press.

as the supernaturalist does; they say that the various levels are all aspects of one complex reality, which they call nature in the broadest sense.

2. *The anti-idealistic thesis*—This is the thesis that minds and their experiences are to be explained in terms of nature. The naturalist holds that the things we know or can discover by the use of the mind are more explanatory than the fact that we know them. Minds and their acts are in some sense real for the naturalist; they are observable facts that cannot be explained away. But, says the naturalist, they can be explained if we learn enough about the nature in which they arise and to which they are directed. To be sure, if there were no minds, there could be no process of explanation; but the premises of our explanation, he says, are to be found in the facts we know, not in some transcendental mind whose eternal existence must be presupposed.

Minds, the naturalists usually assert, are relatively late arrivals in the evolutionary process, and we can understand how they evolved and how they now function in much the same way that we understand other complex phenomena of nature and life. Although the process of knowing is undoubtedly the most complex of all the known processes of nature, in principle this process is to be explained in terms of nature instead of being taken as a *prius* in the explanation of nature itself. The naturalist feels that the young sciences of psychology, cultural anthropology, and sociology can be scientific, empirical studies of the conditions and processes of consciousness.

3. *The scientific thesis*—The naturalist says: "The best or only sure method of getting knowledge is the method of carefully observing, formulating explanatory hypotheses, and empirically testing them to eliminate the false hypotheses, followed by systematic attempts to generalize observations into laws and hypotheses into theories." This is the method that has worked best in the scientific study of what is ordinarily called "nature," and for this reason it is called the scientific method. In stating that everything real is natural, the naturalist is announcing a *methodological* program, which lays reality open to the careful and strict kind of empirical and rational investigation associated with scientific work. The naturalist does not propose that the philosopher should go into the laboratory or observatory, nor does he think that philosophy can be experimental in the way that physics is; but he does believe that the essential traits of scientific method can be used not only in science but also in history, in practical affairs, and in constructing a metaphysical world-view. In this way he repudiates any appeals to revelation, authority, and intuitive self-evident truths. These have been eliminated from scientific knowledge but are still practiced in some philosophies, and the naturalist proposes to eliminate them from philosophy, too.

The Relation of Naturalism to Science

The scientific thesis is sometimes expressed in a different form. It is said, "The results of scientific study are the surest knowledge we have; therefore, metaphysics should be based upon the results of science." This interpretation of the scientific thesis expresses a very important half-truth, and we should carefully examine its meaning and validity.

Consider first the premise: "The results of science are the surest knowledge we have." Athough many supernaturalists and idealists would not accept this statement, as responsible thinkers they would not challenge, on speculative philosophical grounds, any of the established facts of science (although they might challenge some hypotheses that most scientists would consider well established). One task of the philosopher is to integrate and synthesize facts, and the facts of science must be especially respected because of the meticulous care that has gone into their observation. No responsible thinker, therefore, will profess disrespect for the facts of science; and no competent thinker who loves truth will disregard them. He may have what others consider very peculiar ways of interpreting them, but he accepts them as facts. It is therefore unfair to nonnaturalists to say, ". . . The naturalist is one who has respect for the conclusion of natural science."[2]

But "respect for natural science" means one or more of three attitudes. (1) The first we have just described. One can regard scientific facts as facts that must be taken into account in philosophical thinking, so that the philosopher does not make himself ridiculous by challenging the observations and well-founded hypotheses of competent scientists about the facts of nature. Whether a philosopher likes it or not, and however he chooses to interpret it, he must believe that light travels at approximately 186,000 miles a second, that the earth is not in the center of the galaxy, that the earth did not suddenly appear out of nothing in 4004 B.C., that feelings of guilt can frequently be relieved by psychoanalysis, that things that happen in the brain influence a man's thinking and behavior, and so on.

(2) One can take the facts of science as *metaphysically* true. That is, one can take the established results of science as an adequate foundation for metaphysical hypotheses or as "building blocks" in the metaphysical mansion one builds for oneself. If the psychologist says that only the brain can influence consciousness in such and such a way, then that is a fact that will be taken into metaphysics and destroy idealism; if the physicist says that everything in nature is a form of energy, that will be taken over into metaphysics as a modification of strict materialism.

(3) One can recognize that even though scientific facts and generalizations about them are the surest knowledge we have, none of them is "eternally true," and the hypotheses they support may have to be modified in the course of further work. But instead of this attitude being one of distrust of science, it entails acknowledging that beliefs based on science will be corrected and augmented only by a more extensive application of the very same method by which they were established. In this case, the deepest respect is reserved

for the procedures of science and is not given to the present-day results of science as if they were "eternally true,"

The first type of respect for science is not the peculiar prerogative of any school of philosophers. The second type of respect, however, is very widespread among naturalists, especially in the past, but its effect on their work has almost always been unfortunate. If a philosopher builds a metaphysical theory in which the latest results to science are used as his foundation, new scientific discovery can suddenly outmode his entire metaphysics. This happened, for instance, in the case of Herbert Spencer, who at the end of the nineteenth century wrote a system of "synthetic philosophy" in which he aimed to integrate and synoptize all the facts of science; yet the facts of science and the best scientific thinking changed so rapidly that he was regarded as old-fashioned even before his death. Because it dogmatizes on the momentary results of science without realizing that more scientific discoveries will be made and will force a revision in the premises of the metaphysician's work, such respect for science is false to the very spirit of science. Metaphysics based on this kind of respect for science can last only until the next fundamental discovery is made.

This kind of respect for science has another drawback in philosophy. The fields of science are so immense now that no one scientist or philosopher can survey them or keep up with all the latest discoveries. Aristotle could do this; to some extent, Leibniz was able to do so; but Spencer failed, and few today even attempt such a gigantic task. But that does not mean that science is now regarded as irrelevant to metaphysics; we still have to consider the third type of respect for science.

The third kind of respect for science is that which characterizes naturalism at its best. Although not challenging the specific results of science—that is the business of the scientist himself—or dogmatizing about them, the naturalist seeks to understand the world by following a method in philosophy that is continuous with and essentially like that of the scientist. What unites all naturalists, says Sidney Hook, "is the whole-hearted acceptance of scientific method as the only reliable way of reaching truths about the world of nature, society, and man." [3]

A philosopher, although unable to know all the facts of science, can and should learn and practice the method that has made science preeminent as a study of fact. Then the philosopher can apply this method in those fields of value, practical affairs, and metaphysics where Idols of the Mind and powerful forces and ideologies have previously banned open-minded and impartial inquiry. In this respect, the philosopher's admiration for science is an admiration for what has made science a pre-eminent way of knowing and not a parasitical and futile attempt to gather the results of science into

[3]Reprinted from Sidney Hook, "Naturalism and Democracy," in *Naturalism and the Human Spirit*, ed., Yervant H. Krikorian (New York: Columbia University Press, 1944), p. 45. Copyright 1944 by Columbia University Press.

some kind of metaphysical theory with a little psychology here, a bit of chemistry there, and a summary of a second-hand report on the latest discoveries in endocrinology or astrophysics.

Both the second and the third kinds of respect for science have been current in naturalistic philosophy; sometimes one and sometimes the other has been uppermost. When respect for the facts of science has been predominant, metaphysical theories have usually been speculative and dogmatic materialisms. When respect for the procedures of science has been most prominent, there is usually less dogmatism about answers to metaphysical questions, but a strong intention to break down the barriers erected around a narrow conception of nature by belief in the impenetrable mysteries of religion and undisciplined speculation of all sorts.

In this and the following chapter, we shall discuss briefly two types of naturalistic philosophy. In the first, materialism, we shall see the acceptance of the results of science as having basic metaphysical significance; in the second, critical naturalism, we shall see the acceptance of the procedures of scientific inquiry applied to the problems of metaphysics.

MATERIALISM

Materialism is the naturalistic metaphysics that regards nature as consisting of matter in motion. Whatever is apparently not matter in motion is to be regarded as "mere appearance" of what is matter in motion. All explanation, therefore, in philosophy as well as in science, is to be phrased in terms of the laws now known or yet to be discovered concerning the relationships among the different kinds of matter and the laws of their motion with respect to each other.

At the beginning of one of the classical expressions of the materialistic philosophy, *Of the Nature of Things*, the Roman poet Lucretius expresses the indebtedness men should feel toward Democritus, the founder of atomistic materialism:

> Whilst human kind
> Throughout the lands lay miserably crushed
> Before all eyes beneath Religion—who
> Would show her head along the region skies,
> Glowering on mortals with her hideous face—
> A Greek it was who first opposing dared
> Raise mortal eyes that terror to withstand,
> Whom nor the fame of Gods nor lightning's stroke
> Nor threatening thunder of the ominous sky
> Abashed; but rather chafed to angry zest
> His dauntless heart to be the first to rend
> The crossbars at the gates of Nature old.

And thus his will and hardy wisdom won;
And forward thus he fared afar, beyond
The flaming ramparts of the world, until
He wandered the unmeasurable All.
Whence he comes to us, a conqueror, reports
What things can rise to being, what cannot,
And by what law to each its scope prescribed,
Its boundary stone that clings so deep in Time.
Wherefore religion now is under foot,
And us his victory now exalts to heaven.[4]

The discovery of Democritus, which is said to have emancipated the mind from superstition, was this: reality consists of nothing but empty space and indestructible, minute particles of matter. These particles he called "atoms," from the Greek word meaning "indivisible." The purported effect of this discovery, Lucretius proclaimed, was to free men from religious hopes and fears, which they feel only because they do not know that nature is infinite in space and time and that all happenings in nature are to be explained in terms of other happenings in nature, according to inexorable laws discovered by patient observation. With this discovery, they can see that in order to understand nature they do not need to know the ways of the inscrutable gods. This discovery encourages them to learn the secrets of nature and not to live in ignorant fear of the caprice and wrath of the gods.

Materialists for the past two millennia have accepted this as a fair statement of the effect their philosophy can have upon human affairs. But the particular characteristics that they attribute to the world of matter have changed with every advance of scientific knowledge. In spite of the variations in detail, however, there are certain common beliefs found among materialists of all ages.

The Theses of Materialism

1. *The atomistic thesis*—All materialists think of nature as comprising a large or infinite number of irreducible realities, the nature of each of them being independent of the rest, although the behavior of each is determined by the motion of the others. In ancient philosophy, the atoms were thought of as minute particles differing from each other in size, shape, and (sometimes) mass. Even then, long before the development of modern science, matter—that is, reality—was thought of as having only the primary qualities. But as scientific knowledge grew, the details of this conception changed. Now a materialist would say that the atoms of physics and chemistry are not the ultimate building blocks of the universe but that they consist of more elementary entities having electrical charges, spin, and other physical proper-

---

[4]Lucretius, *Of the Nature of Things*, trans., William Ellery Leonard (New York: E. P. Dutton & Co., Inc; Everyman's Library edition, 1950), pp. 4–5. Quoted by permission of E. P. Dutton & Co., Inc., and J. M. Dent & Sons, Ltd.

ties. But they still hold that everything that exists consist of various combinations of relatively few different kinds of things. So although at various stages of science there are different beliefs about the ultimate constituents of things, materialists have always believed that the way to understand anything is to analyze it until one comes to what is simple, elementary, and unanalyzable and then to see how these elements can be put together to make up the world's manifold variety.

2. *The reductionistic thesis*—It follows from this that the number of kinds of real things in the world is far less than the number of kinds of apparent realities.[5] Just as millions of different kinds of molecules consist of different arrangements and proportions of about 100 different kinds of atoms, and the different kinds of atoms are merely different complexes of a smaller number of more elementary entities (electrons, protons, neutrons, and so on), so also

> . . . the world, which seems
> To lie before us like a land of dreams,
> So various, so beautiful, so new. . . .

is only a reshuffled hand, the same old particles, hurrying hither and yon, reacting chemically with each other or pushing each other about according to the laws of physics. There is nothing new under the sun:

The irresistible passion that draws Edward to the sympathetic Ottilia, or Paris to Helen, and leaps over all bounds of reason and morality, is the same powerful "unconscious" attractive force which impels the living spermatozoon to force an entrance into the ovum in the fertilization of the egg of the animal or plant—the same impetuous movement which unites two atoms of hydrogen to one atom of oxygen for the formation of a molecule of water.[6]

Explanation, therefore, must take the form of reducing the variety of things apparently real to relationships and patterns of relationships among the elementary constituents of matter. No explanation is ultimate and satisfying unless it shows the thing explained to be a conjunction of the very simple elementary facts of physics and chemistry.

3. *The mechanistic thesis*—A philosophical theory is called *determinism* if it holds that whatever happens does so of necessity. Determinism is the view that events do not occur by chance. Determinism can be based upon the laws of the mind in idealism or upon the predestination by God in supernaturalism. But in either case, it is the belief that whatever happens does so because of the necessity that the same kind of effect will invariably and inevitably result from the same kind of cause. The special from of deter-

---

[5]See Iredell Jenkins, "The Postulate of an Impoverished Reality," *Journal of Philosophy*, XXXIX, No. 20 (September 24, 1942), 533–47.

[6]Ernst Haeckel, *The Riddle of the Universe* (New York: Harper & Row, Publishers, 1900), p. 224.

minism held by the materialist is called *mechanism*.[7] Mechanism is the deterministic theory that whatever occurs happens because of the *preceding physical events*.

Because the materialist it usually a mechanist, it is sometimes said that he conceives of the universe according to the root metaphor of a billiard table. Imagine a billiard table with perfectly elastic balls and no friction. By hypothesis, a ball rolling on this table will collide with other balls and set them in motion, and these will hit still others and set them in motion. Although this motion would continue without end, we could, theoretically, predict where all the balls would be at any time if we knew where they are and the force with which they are moving at any instant. Of course we cannot actually do so for any actual billiard table, because the mathematical complexity of the problem is too great and the billiard table is not an isolated system (see p. 199). But the materialist believes that the material universe is a closed, isolated system, with nothing outside it (minds or gods) to interfere with its motions. Hence, only the complexity of the calculation prevents us from being able to foretell in the minutest detail every event in the future—not only eclipses of the sun and moon, but also the fall of every sparrow and the rise and decline of cultures and empires:

If an intelligence should for a given instant be acquainted with all the forces by which nature is animated and with the positions of the beings composing it, and if this intelligence should be vast enough to submit these data to analysis, it would include in one and the same formula the movements of the largest bodies in the universe and those of the lightest atom. Nothing would be uncertain for it; the future as well as the past would be present to its eyes.

Laplace, the great astronomer who wrote these words, is said to have been asked by Napoleon why in his writings in astronomy he did not mention God. He replied, "Sire, I have no need for that hypothesis." The story may be apocryphal, but the answer is the only one that a consistent materialist could have given; everything is to be explained in terms of what occurs in nature, according to the laws of physics.

This conception specifically denies the use and validity of the concept of purpose and design. Whatever happens happens because it must; and it must happen because of what happened just before it. Although men think they act for the sake of purposes, their illusion that they do is itself caused by the nature of their bodies and events that have befallen them in the past. Men attribute purpose and design to the world (and therefore feel impelled to imagine a designer) only because they do not see into the causal necessity of physical things and events.

---

[7]There are a few materialists who deny mechanism; Lucretius, for instance, does so. See also page 229 for a discussion of the principle of indeterminacy in modern physics. For the materialistic or mechanistic theory in biology, see above, page 253.

Materialistic Theories of the Mind

One of the most difficult questions for the materialist to answer is: What are mind and consciousness? Awareness is indubitably one of the characteristic aspects of human beings, and it is extremely likely that all the higher animals are consciously aware of some things in their surroundings to which they adjust. But if it is true, as the materialist holds, that everything in the world, including human beings, consists only of matter in motion, how can they acknowledge even the existence of "states of mind," awareness, consciousness, feelings, and other so-called mental phenomena? Because of the difficulty of this question for the materialists, they have attempted to answer it in almost every conceivable way that is at all consistent with their basic theses—and sometimes in ways that are not consistent with their ultimate theory.

As to the nature of mind, we may mention five theories held by various materialists: Mind is a particular kind of matter (Lucretius); mind is a form of internal motion (Hobbes, some behaviorists); mind is a property of matter (Diderot, Lenin); mind is a property of certain organizations of matter;[8] mind is a collective name we give to certain appearances of bodily events, events in the nervous system; and mind is a byproduct or epiphenomenon of the body.

It is questionable whether the first three of these views really make sense. Certainly they do not if "matter" means what it is ordinarily taken to mean or what the physicist means by it, for such matter is stuff characterized by the primary qualities alone. If the materialist does not use the word "matter" in the scientific sense, then he has to give up his claims that his is a philosophy supported by science and in need of no other support. The fourth theory—that mind is a property not of matter itself but of certain organizations of matter—is hardly consistent with the materialists' emphasis upon the atomistic and reductionistic theses. It is rather hard to see the justification for calling this theory materialistic, and we shall find it easier to explain and evaluate in our discussion of another type of naturalism;[9] we call attention here only to the fact that some contemporary philosophers accept this view of mind *and* call themselves materialists.

Materialists are more inclined now to accept one of the last two theories mentioned: that conscious events (for example sensations, feelings, and thoughts) are identical with bodily events or that they are nonbodily events caused by bodily events but are not themselves causes of other bodily events. The first is called "the identity theory" and the second is called "epiphenomenalism."

The identity theory is now attracting a great deal of attention from philosophers, and in recent years it has been given a number of very technical and

[8]R. W. Sellars, Marvin Farber, and V. J. McGill, eds., *Philosophy for the Future. The Quest of Modern Materialism* (New York: The Macmillan Company, 1949), p. viii.

[9]See below, pages 326ff.

sophisticated expositions and defenses. In its simplest form, it holds that a sensation is related to a physiological process in a nervous system in the same way that what we see as lightning (that is, a brilliant flash of light) is related to a physical process (namely, a sudden discharge of electricity from one cloud to another). Lightning seems to be very different from a flux of electrons; if for no other reason, one sees lightning, and one does not see electrons. But, the identity theorist argues, we *do* see the electrons—for lightning is just the way in which we see what is in fact nothing but a flux of electrons. That is what is meant by saying that lightning is the appearance of the electric event. Physicists talk about it in words like "electron," which do not directly denote anything we can see *as* electrons; and we nonphysicists talk about it in terms of brightness and color, which are of little interest to physicists. But the physicists' technical explanation and our descriptions all refer to the same thing—the physical process.

Similarly, the identity theory holds that the sensation of red that I experience under certain circumstances (for example, when I introspect on my perception of a poppy) is only an appearance of the brain process stimulated by the light from the poppy as it affects the retina of my eye. The neurophysiologist describes it in physical terminology; I describe it in terms of "how it looks." But we are said to be describing the same thing. "Red" is just another name for this brain process; red is the appearance of my brain process to me.

There is, however, an obvious difference between the lightning-electricity and the sensation-brain connection. For given the first of these combinations, we can answer the question, "Lightning is an appearance of an electron flux *to whom* or *to what*?" by saying that it is an appearance to me, or to my consciousness. In the latter, we have no consciousness left over to which the brain process is to appear. What might be true of data in consciousness, namely that they might be appearances of brain processes to consciousness, can hardly be said of consciousness itself; because the very word "appearance" requires not only reference to what appears but also reference to that *to which* the thing appears. To make the analogy between lightning-electron flux and consciousness-brain hold, we should have to have another consciousness *to which* the first consciousness was an *appearance of* the brain. Then we would abandon the theory or have to imagine still another consciousness to which the second consciousness was an appearance, and so on without end.

We do not need to criticize this theory in detail, however, because the arguments for and against the last theory, epiphenomenalism, apply with about equal weight to the identity theory. Since epiphenomenalism is easier to explain and to evaluate, we shall now consider it in more detail.

Epiphenomenalism is the theory that admits that mind *is not* matter or energy and is not even an appearance of it, but it teaches that it is a byproduct of some activity of a nervous system. We can understand what is most important in this theory by comparing it with the more common-sense view called psychophysical interactionism or—named for one of its chief defenders, Descartes—Cartesian dualism, a theory we have already examined (p. 273).

According to this widely held view, there are two kinds of reality, minds and bodies. The body is affected by physical stimuli from its environment, and the influences of these stimuli are carried to the brain by nerves. This process can be understood in physical or physiological terms. But somewhere along the line, the nervous excitation affects the mind, which is not a physical entity at all, and produces in it a sensation. The mind decides on some line of action and affects the body through the mechanism of the brain. A "message" goes out from the brain to the appropriate organ of the body, which "executes the command." The process from the sense organ to the brain, and the process from the brain to the muscle or gland, can be understood exactly as the materialist says. But the dualist holds that this account is incomplete, for there is a point in this series at which there is interaction between the physical and the mental.

In the other theory, epiphenomenalism, consciousness exists as an effect of a physiological process but not as a cause of anything, neither of subsequent bodily behavior nor of subsequent states of consciousness. If exactly the same physiological processes that cause it and cause subsequent behavior were able to cause only the latter, nothing in the latter would thereby be different. The same acts could be done, the same words spoken, whether there was consciousness or not. Consciousness does occur, however, so we are conscious automata, but nonetheless automata. We can explain everything a man does without needing to mention his consciousness as an explanatory fact or hypothetical object. It could cease to exist and nobody would miss it—the man himself would not miss it because he would be unconscious, and no one else would miss it because his behavior would not be any different from what it was before. "Mind," said Santayana, "is a lyric cry in the midst of business."

This theory may seem on its face to be preposterous, but it is not. It does not imply the false conclusion that conscious or intelligent behavior is just like unconscious and unintelligent behavior. It does not imply that human action is automatic and mechanical in the sense that some jerky physical mechanism is automatic and mechanical. The theory admits and insists upon the complexity, adaptability, and plasticity of human behavior; it admits that it seems to be goal-directed and self-governing; it does not imply that men cannot do any of the things we know they can do, from tying their shoes to writing symphonies. It does not even deny that men can think. It only says that an organism with a sufficiently complex nervous system and the past training sufficient to produce intelligent behavior attended with consciousness would produce identical behavior even if consciousness were not present. Consciousness is an effect of what is going on, but it is not a cause.

A simple design will show the difference between Cartesian dualism and epiphenomenalism and bring out some at least apparent superiorities of the latter.

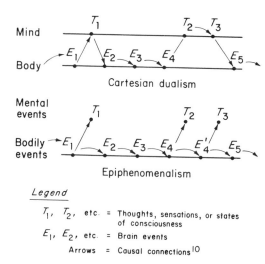

Cartesian dualism

Epiphenomenalism

Legend

T_1, T_2, etc. = Thoughts, sensations, or states of consciousness

E_1, E_2, etc. = Brain events

Arrows = Causal connections[10]

These diagrams show that epiphenomenalism fits the empirical facts as well as the Cartesian theory does. In both theories, T_1 is followed by E_2, but it is described in different ways. The Cartesian says that T_1 is a cause, or part of the cause, of E_2. The epiphenomenalist says that E_1 is the cause of E_2, and the relation of T_1 to E_2 is simply one of regular sequence. In both theories, the observable facts are exactly the same, namely the sequence of events E_1, T_1, E_2, E_3, and so on. Hence, neither theory can be refuted by any observable test, as it could be if one were able to predict an event that would not occur if the other were the true theory.

How, then, shall we choose between them? The Cartesian theory seems to accord better with our common-sense beliefs and ordinary language, as when I say, "I moved my hand because I wanted to pick up my pencil". But the epiphenomenalist theory enjoys the advantage of scientific economy. All the laws of behavior can be expressed in terms of bodily events, either observed or hypothesized. The sequence we must understand is E_1, E_2, E_3, E_4 . . . , for from it alone we can predict, if epiphenomenalism is true, any subsequent event E_n. We can do this, if epiphenomenalism is true, without paying the least attention to the T_1, T_2, and so on, which were in the observable sequence mentioned in the previous paragraph. Introspection is not required for us to get the data needed for physiological explanation, and we need not fear that a law that says "Events of type E_1 will always be followed by events of type E_2" will be abrogated sometimes by the presence of an objectively undetectable nonphysical event T_1', which might cause E_2' instead of E_2. We are now, of course, far from being able to do so in fact, but that is a consequence of our ignorance of the total physiological situation and the

---

[10]If the symbol ⟋ is interpreted as "appears as" instead of "causes," then the second diagram illustrates the identity theory.

relevant physiological laws. But, in principle, we should have no reason to try to do so if we believed that the antecedent physiological conditions were not sufficient to determine the subsequent physiological responses. The theses of reductionism and mechanism and the theory of epiphenomenalism, therefore, seem to be highly advantageous collateral hypotheses for the understanding of human behavior.

It is sometimes objected that this theory and the program of investigation that it underlies degrade man and rob him of his freedom and moral significance. To this the epiphenomenalist simply replies that he is not denying any facts and certainly not denying that there are interesting and important differences between good men and bad men, intelligent men and stupid men, men of good taste and men of poor taste. Instead of degrading men by taking away their souls, he might say that he is elevating the worth of their bodies. Indeed, he might point out how valuable discoveries might be made under his hypothesis that would make it possible for men to avoid not only physical but also "psychical" and moral ills to which, in a very literal sense, the flesh is heir.

A weightier objection to epiphenomenalism is that it is involved in a self-stultifying paradox. Suppose one man says, "Epiphenomenalism is true," and another asks him, "Why do you say that?" If epiphenomenalism is true, the only true answer would be, "Because my brain-state produced the belief that it is true and caused my larynx to move in such a way that I pronounced the words, 'Epiphenomenalism is true.' " But if the second man is to be rationally persuaded to believe in epiphenomenalism, however, this answer will not do. The first speaker must explain why he said the words, "Epiphenomenalism is true," but he must also be able to defend the statement and any other statements having the same meaning, such as "*Der Epiphenomenalismus ist wahr.*" Defense of the statement, like defense of any statement, requires reference to evidence, reasons, grounds, inferences, logical principles, and the like. But the epiphenomenalist cannot, in good faith, adduce them. For if epiphenomenalism is true, the reasons he gives for it and the reasons that are meant to appeal to the other person cannot be truly claimed to be the sufficient reason for his accepting the theory or for the decision of those whom he is trying to convince.

The paradox is this: If epiphenomenalism is true, we cannot rationally argue for it. If epiphenomenalism is false, however, we can. That is why we call it self-stultifying.

Self-stultification of the kind exemplified here is not a fallacy of formal logic. There is nothing self-contradictory in the statement, "My brain-state completely determines my state of consciousness and what I believe and say," and arguments of impeccable validity in logic may be formulated with this as their conclusion. To see that we are not accusing the epiphenomenalist of an error in logic and to discover what is really wrong with the statement, let us imagine an experiment.

Take several thousand white cards and on each one write a sentence taken from, say, this morning's newspaper and the latest issue of *The Philosophical Review*. Take several hundred gray cards, and on each one write either "Therefore," or "Therefore it is false that." Now put these cards into a card-shuffling machine and thoroughly shuffle them. Then withdraw the cards from the pack, following this procedure: Run through the pack until you come to a gray card, then take the two preceding and the one succeeding white cards, and read them off. You will, from time to time, get perfectly valid arguments. Moreover, if the first two cards have true sentences written on them and the argument is valid, the sentence on the third card will be true too. One might thus get the following argument: White card 1: "Pope Paul appeared on the balcony of St. Peter's this morning and blessed the crowd in St. Peter's Square." White card 2: "A crowd of thousands of pilgrims was in St. Peter's Square this morning." Gray card: "Therefore." White card 3: "Pope Paul blessed thousands of pilgrims in St. Peter's Square this morning."

This little experiment shows that a machine can produce not only valid but also sound arguments. Naturally it produces many more sequence of four cards that will read like arguments but that are neither valid nor sound. But if a machine can produce sound arguments, then obviously a living human organism with an epiphenomenal consciousness can do so, too.

Does not this experiment show that it is incorrect to say that epiphenomenalism is self-stultifying? No, because "self-stultifying" does not mean "never producing sound arguments." Rather, it means: The conditions under which an argument is taken as contributing to a proof are incompatible with the causal conditions that explain why the argument was given. In every case, of course, the conditions under which an argument is taken as proof are different from the conditions that produced it, for the former belong to logic and the realm of evidence whereas the latter (according to any theory) belong to psychology and physiology or (in our experiment) to machine technology.[11] Mere difference of the two sets of conditions is not sufficient to stultify an argument. Incompatibility is necessary and sufficient to do so. We shall attempt to explain what we mean by "incompatibility," but in order to do so we must first define still another term, "probative value."

An argument has probative value if it constitutes, in the mind of a rational man, a ground for rational credulity in the conclusion of the argument. An argument with probative value increases the rational credibility of its conclusion.

An argument known to be sound is maximally probative. If a rational man knows that an argument is sound—that the premises are true and the inference is valid—he cannot ask for a more decisive reason why he should accept the conclusion; he knows all he needs to know in order to be sure that the conclusion is true. If T and T' are the premises, there is no other

---

[11]See the quotation from Socrates (p. 259) on the difference between the causes and the reasons of a human act.

true proposition U that, conjoined with T and T', will increase or decrease the rational credibility of the conclusion. Any other proposition U' that would decrease it would be inconsistent with T and/or T' and would therefore be known to be false. On the other hand, an unsound argument has no probative value even if its conclusion should in fact be true.

But often, especially in philosophy, we do not enjoy the luxury of knowing whether our arguments are sound or not; there is far more debate about premises than there is about conclusions. Even though we can tell that an argument is valid because we have in logic definite tests for validity, we often only believe that the premises of an argument are true. We may believe it on evidence that is sufficient for a rational man. But a rational man may have sufficient evidence for believing a proposition B and in fact believe it when, as a matter of fact, B is false. Now a valid argument from such premises, let us call them B and B', may not be sound or be known to be sound and yet have probative value in the sense that it raises the rational credibility of its conclusion C. It would be irrational for him to accept B and B', as he does, and not accept C as rationally credible; and if he had previously doubted C, the argument would have probative value in that it would, for him as a rational man, raise the credibility of C. He would then say that the argument had probative value even if he could not be certain that it was actually sound.

In the case of a sound argument, we have seen that there is no true proposition U that added to the premises makes a sound argument unsound. But in the case of an argument of less than maximal probative value, there can be some other proposition U known, or rationally believed, to be true that, when added to B and B', reduces that probative value of the argument even if U should be logically consistent with B and/or B'. For instance, a rational man might know or believe that the person who gives him the argument "B and B' imply C" is his enemy who is anxious to trap him in some way. Now this proposition, "The author of this argument is my enemy" added to the argument does not affect its validity or its soundness if it is sound, but it may properly reduce the credence the hearer gives the premises and therefore the conclusion, or the conclusion and therefore the premises. A man who has the reputation of being a malicious liar might find his arguments rendered ineffective by the very fact that *he* preferred them. Someone might say, "I believed the stock market was going to fall until I heard that man arguing that it would."

It is our thesis that (1) no one knows epiphenomenalism to be true and no one knows that there is a sound argument that proves it; (2) for any argument in its favor there is a U that cancels its probative value; and (3) the proposition U that does so is a corollary of epiphenomenalism itself. Because of (3), the argument for epiphenomenalism is not only stultified by U but is self-stultified. U is: The conclusion of the argument is not reached because of the premises.

Let us now suppose that I am presented with an argument in favor of epiphenomenalism. It consists of two premises and a conclusion. It is valid;

but we do not know whether the premises are true or not although they look very plausible, and hence the argument has some probative value for me as a rational man. If I believe that the argument was presented by a rational man who found the premises credible to him, the argument will be more probative to me than if I believe the argument was manufactured by a machine that happened by chance to pick out cards in an order that constituted a valid argument. Although in either case I have to evaluate the argument and make my own decision about it, the argument of a rational man comes to me with a credential lacking in an argument that issues from a card-shuffling machine. In my ignorance of whether the argument is sound, the credential gives it a claim to probative value, whereas the machine-produced argument has no antecedent credential at all.

We can see this easily if we imagine another experiment. Suppose the machine produces the following cards in order: (1) "This is a card shuffling machine that produces cards in random order." (2) "The second card after this one will be produced without choice, i.e., randomly." (3) "Therefore." (4) "This card is ejected from the machine at random." Now this happens to be a sound argument;[12] *but it does not prove what is in fact true*—that the fourth card was produced randomly; for if we tried to use the argument for this purpose, assigning it some probative value, we would be saying that there was a good reason for card 4, and then premise 2 would be false.

Turn now to an argument produced by a rational man. Here I have, or seem to have, a reason for accepting the conclusion; that is, in fact, precisely what we ordinarily mean by calling what he says an argument. The proposition U in the case of the machine argument was: The fourth card was not produced because of the first three cards. In the case of an argument produced by a rational man, U is supposed to be false.

But now consider the argument produced by the man under the assumption that epiphenomenalism is true. The situation then is exactly the same as that of the machine-produced argument. The same U that canceled the probative value of the machine-produced argument is present in the man-produced argument: The conclusion was not reached because of the premises. (In the machine, it was produced by vacuum tubes, transistors, relays, and wheels; in the man, it was produced by nerves, synapses, and ganglia.) Then if epiphenomenalism is true, an argument from an apparently rational man should be accorded no more probative value than the machine-produced argument.

---

[12]In this experiment, an argument known to be sound lacks probative value. We have previously said (p. 302) that an argument known to be sound has maximum probative value. We were there speaking of sound arguments for conclusions not antecedently known to be true. In the present experiment, we know independently of the machine-produced argument that the conclusion is true and cannot cite the sequence of cards produced by the machine as constituting a proof for it. If we did so, we would have to assume that there was a reason why card 4 was produced and this is not only false but also inconsistent with the premises and the conclusion.

The defender of epiphenomenalism, however, might well challenge this argument as based upon a false analogy. No epiphenomenalist has ever said that a rational man is like a card-shuffling machine and produces sentences at random. That a card-shuffling machine produces arguments that do not increase the rational credibility of the conclusions does not say that a brain cannot do so. Brains attached to bodies do produce arguments with probative value; hence they cannot be like card-shuffling machines, which do not. Brains may, however, be like computing machines, sometimes called "electronic brains," which are sometimes said, more than half seriously, to be able to think. Such a machine can produce new theorems in mathematics, which I accept with confidence. Does not this strengthen the case for saying that a human brain, which if epiphenomenalism is true is only a computing machine, can produce an argument for epiphenomenalism that has probative value?

This analogy of brain with epiphenomenal consciousness to a computing machine is better than the analogy of the brain with epiphenomenal consciousness to a card-shuffling machine. But it is not perfect, and the differences between a brain and a computing machine are significant. For how does the computing machine produce arguments that do have probative value? It does so because it was designed the way it was by someone who knew the laws of logic and used this knowledge in designing the circuitry. He arranged it so that when, for instance, relay A, which corresponds to a true proposition P, is in the state we decide it should be in when the statement P is a part of the input, relay B will be in the state that corresponds to the proposition Q (that is, "Q is true") if and only if P implies Q. For me, as a thinking being, the truth of P, if the argument "P implies Q" is valid, implies Q is true, or my belief in P and "P implies Q" increases the rational credibility of Q. I accept the output of the machine, namely, "Q is true" because I not only believe that the machine is not working at random but because I believe the design of its circuits reflects the logical connection between "P," "P implies Q," and "Q is true." Leave out this confidence in its rational design, and then even if the machine is not running at random its output will have no rational credibility. The designer of the machine can put in a myriad of connections, one after another, so that the machine might print out "Z is true" in a fraction of a second whereas it would take me, unaided, many minutes to solve the logical problem. For these long computations and inferences, I depend upon the machine. I do not depend upon it because I think it is conscious and knows logic but because I believe that someone who knew logic designed its circuitry in such a manner that if true propositions are fed into it, only true propositions will be printed out. It is my belief that there was effective thinking and skillful design by the designer and programmer. This belief keeps me from having to think that this machine produces self-stultifying arguments.

Machine technology has advanced so far that now machines can design and program other machines more efficiently sometimes than people can do it. But the grandfather of all machines cannot be said to be another machine. If it were, no machine-produced argument would lend rational credibility to its conclusion. The originator of all the machines, however, cannot be said to be simply a machine-brain acting under physiological laws and without regard to logical laws. For if we say this we stultify the whole argument.

Two lines of argument might be developed to avoid this stultification by showing that brains, though machines, are so organized as to produce non-stultifying arguments. The first of them is so speculative that it is unlikely to appeal to anyone who is attracted to epiphenomenalism by its apparently fixed scientific status. It is that there is a designer of all things in the world, namely, God, who devised human brains so that they can do what computing machines are designed by men to do. A theory not wholly unlike this was promulgated by the German philosopher Gottfried Wilhelm Leibniz (1646–1716) who was not an epiphenomenalist in his metaphysics but who held that "bodies act as if . . . there were no souls at all, and souls act as if there were no bodies, and yet both body and soul act as if the one were influencing the other."[13] This conclusion is a part of a much more general argument, the so-called argument from design, which we shall evaluate later (see p. 375). At the moment it suffices to say that no naturalist who is attracted to epiphenomenalism would be likely to jettison his naturalism by accepting the desperate expedient of the theory of a harmony between mind and body pre-established by God.

Another hypothesis, much more in keeping with a naturalistic world view, argues that brains have undergone a process of evolution in which, under the pressure of natural selection, brains that handle information about the environment in ways that favor the organism survive and predominate over brains or more primitive nervous systems that do not lead to adaptive behavior. It is as if machines that do not produce sound arguments tend to break down more frequently than machines that do, and those that do not break down reproduce and pass on their superior circuitry to still other machines. Natural selection and the survival of the fittest are believed to explain the effectiveness of other widespread modes of behavior in organisms; why should they not explain the information-processing that goes on in the brain?

The theory of evolution by natural selection is certainly consistent with the epiphenomenalist theory, and it suggests ways in which the apparently purposive design of the nervous system could have originated without having to assume some transcendent designer. Yet the theory of evolution is equally compatible with the opposing theory. An organ or function has developed perhaps by chance, but it has been passed on only because it was advan-

---

[13]*Monadology* (1716), §81.

tageous to the organism that possessed it and gave that organism an advantage in the struggle for survival. Organs and functions do not persist over thousand and millions of generations unless they do provide some advantage, however slight, to their possessors. A superior nervous system certainly endows its successors with advantages and gives them some cumulative advantages over others less well endowed. But why are superior nervous systems found to be associated with consciousness? We do not know whether a jelly fish with a primitive nervous system is conscious or not; we know that we are, and in general it seems to be a safe assumption even for the epiphenomenalist that superior brains are correlated with higher forms of consciousness (for example, better memories, a wider range of emotional response, more penetrating foresight, and the like). Now if these phenomena that belong to consciousness did not give some advantage to their possessors over competing organisms that had the same neural endowment but lacked consciousness, the theory of evolution suggests that consciousness itself would not have survived. But if consciousness does make a difference that would be to the advantage of conscious organisms, then epiphenomenalism, which says that consciousness does not make a difference, is less likely to be correct.

This argument is certainly not decisive. It might be that efficient brains just cannot help producing useless consciousness. But we mention this argument simply in order to show that the theory of evolution does not speak with one voice, either for or against epiphenomenalism. This is contrary to the views of some who have regarded evolutionary biological theories as decisive for one or the other of the theories of the relation of mind to body.

DIALECTICAL MATERIALISM

Dialectical materialism, as developed by Karl Marx (1818–1883), Frederick Engels (1820–1895), and Vladimir Ilyitch Lenin (1870–1924), is the official philosophy of the communist movement; it is the philosophy professed by a sizeable portion of the human race. Therefore, we should understand some of its principal tenets. We shall not consider the political and economic consequences of this set of beliefs known as Marxism. This restriction is made because we are here interested in metaphysical theories *as such* and not as patterns of life or ideologies.

The "Materialism" of Dialectical Materialism

The dialectical materialists profess to be strict materialists, although in many respects they resemble critical naturalists more than the materialists we have been studying.[14]

[14]Sidney Hook, in his *Toward an Understanding of Karl Marx* (New York: The John Day Company, Inc., 1933), p. 31, calls Marx an "activistic naturalist."

Materialism in full agreement with natural science takes matter as the *prius*, regarding consciousness, reason, and sensation as derivative, because in a well-expressed form it is connected only with the higher forms of matter (organic matter).[15]

The basic reality of the world is matter in motion (or whatever substitute for it is established by detailed scientific work of physicists). Those aspects of reality that are not apparently matter in motion are said to be "directly interwoven with material activity."[16] There is in nature a continuous development of quality through quantitative change: Vibrations of a certain frequency give rise to heat, and vibrations of a higher frequency appear as visible color; complexity of chemical organization may reach such a degree of elaborateness that the phenomenal quality of life may appear. Thus the dialectical materialist *is* a materialist in his assertion of the fundamental and irreducible character of matter, although he admits something like the process of the emergence of quality (he does not use the word "emergence") from quantitative changes in the levels of integration of material elements.

The Marxist is a materialist also in a more common-sense use of the word. Although the Marxist does not argue—as is commonly believed—that only economic or biological values are real and that the so-called higher values are to be neglected, denied, or reduced to the pursuit of economic goods, the Marxist does believe that, in the final analysis, the determining factor in human behavior is to be found in men's relations to the material productive system of their society. Men stand to each other in a context that is organized with respect to the means of production and distribution of goods. What they believe and aspire to, or at least those beliefs and aspirations that are more than individual vagaries and are able to play a determining role in social change, are subtly determined by their social and cultural organization. Social organization is, at its root, a growth from the material needs of men, and the pattern of their thought and action is impressed upon them by the economic system in which they live. Thus, an agricultural economy will have not only a different form of government from that of an industrial economy but also different art forms, moral ideals, religious beliefs, and philosophical speculation. Feudalism as an economic institution developed its own ideology or rationalization of the arrangement of power in a feudal community; mercantilism had its peculiar ideology or rationalization; capitalistic nationalism has its own; and all will differ from that of a communistic culture.

This does not imply that men always react automatically and mechanically to the economic arrangements. There are unusual individuals in every social group, and the desires and interests of men cannot be neglected in any study

[15]V. I. Lenin, *Materialism and Empirio-Criticism* (1909), from *Selected Works*, Vol. XI (New York: International Publishers, 1943), pp. 112–13.
[16]From *The German Ideology*, by Karl Marx and Frederick Engels, ed., R. Pascal (New York: International Publishers, 1947), p. 13. By permission of International Publishers Co., Inc.

of social organization or historical change. But according to Marx, the economic organization does *largely* determine which ideas and interests will be considered normal and acceptable at any given time and which ones will be only curiosities without historical efficacy.

Philosophy is a "rationalization" of an economic system. The ruling ideas in philosophy, as in art, morality, and religion, says Marx, are the ideas of the ruling class; and the philosophy that appears to us to be best supported intellectually is actually the one that is most fitting to our place in a social system. Philosophizing may be a protest against the ruling ideas that have tended to dignify a given economic system as "eternally justified," or it may be a defense mechanism by which we justify the *status quo*; but in neither case can philosophy be mere contemplation of reality. Philosophy is a weapon in the economic conflict between classes; and for this reason, the dialectical materialist prefers to call both technical philosophy and "philosophy of life" by the name of "ideology."

Life is not determined by consciousness, but consciousness by life. . . . Where speculation ends—in real life—, there real, positive science begins: the representation of practical activity, of the practical process of development of men. Empty talk about consciousness ceases, and real knowledge has to take its place. . . . Philosophy as an independent branch of activity loses its medium of existence.[17]
The philosophers have only *interpreted* the world in various ways; the point, however, is to *change* it.[18]

In the ideal of an independent philosophy, which shall "survey all time and all existence," there is either conscious or unconscious deception; the notion of a completely objective knowledge is an empty and unattainable ideal. Self-deception is present even in an ideology, but the dialectical materialist recognizes this also as a necessary consequence of man's nature as a creature of material needs:

If in all ideology men and their relations appear upside down, as in a camera obscura, this phenomenon arises just as much from their historical life-process as the reversal of objects on the retina does from their directly physical life-process.[19]

The "Dialectic" of Dialectical Materialism

In our discussion of absolute idealism, we examined the notion of dialectic as developed by Hegel (see p. 129). In Hegel's dialectic, the dynamics of historical change lie in the logical instability of any partial scheme of ideas (thesis) that gives rise to another partial scheme (antithesis) until some reconciliation or synthesis of the opposition is produced.

[17]*Ibid.*, p. 15.
[18]From *Ludwig Feuerbach and the Outcome of Classical German Philosophy*, by Frederick Engels (New York: International Publishers, 1941), p. 84. By permission of International Publishers Co., Inc.
[19]From *The German Ideology*, by Marx and Engels, p. 14.

Marx accepted the Hegelian dialectic, but "stood it on its head." That is, in the Marxian dialectic, it is, first, nature as a material order that undergoes dialectical development, and then society and social institutions carry on a dialectical conflict because of their inimical economic (material) conditions. Dialectic is carried on at the ideological level as a conflict between opposing ideas, but these only reflect the opposing material interests that give practical relevance to ideological conflict. In dialectic and history, Engels said, "Hegel confused the driving forces [ideologies or philosophical ideas] with the driving forces *behind* the driving forces [the material or economic factors]." ". . . In direct contrast to German philosophy [Hegelianism], which descends from heaven to earth, here [in dialectical materialism] the ascent is made from earth to heaven."[20]

The dialectical process in nature and society introduces new levels of integration and provides the stage on which qualitative novelty is produced by quantitative changes in the relations of matter. Marx was led to this dialectical consideration through Hegel's philosophy of history, and this, he held, was an entirely new line of departure for materialism. Materialism before this time had been metaphysical and dogmatic, having its origin in a natural science not yet seriously affected by the idea of evolutionary change. Hence, materialism prior to Marx was static. But Engels says,

With each epoch-making discovery even in the sphere of natural science, [materialism] has to change its form; and after history also was subjected to materialistic treatment, here also a new avenue of development was opened.[21]

In eighteenth-century science, man was still regarded as a machine because of the poorly developed status of chemistry as compared with mechanics; but the development of the biological sciences—especially the idea of evolution—and the development of chemistry with its emphasis upon the variety of properties of matter prepared the way for a more comprehensive and activistic materialism that could account for a greater variety of facts than a simple, reductive materialism could.

In fact, Engels traces the development of Marx's materialism from the simple form of earlier metaphysical materialism and idealism as itself an example of dialectic:

The philosophy of antiquity was primitive, natural materialism. As such, it was incapable of clearing up the relation between thought and matter.[22] But the need to get clarity on this question led to the doctrine of a soul separable from the body [psychophysical interactionism], then to the assertion of the immortality of this soul, and finally to monotheism. The old materialism was therefore negated by idealism. But in the course of the further development of philosophy, idealism too became untenable and was negated by modern materialism. This modern materi-

[20]*Ibid.*
[21]From Engels, *Ludwig Feuerbach,* p. 26.
[22]See Lucretius for an example of this difficulty.

alism, the negation of the negation [that is, the dialectical synthesis] is not the mere re-establishment of the old, but adds to the permanent foundations of this old materialism the whole thought-content of two thousand years of development of philosophy and natural science, as well as of the historical development of these two thousand years.[23]

The Materialistic Philosophy of History

The most important contribution of Marx to theoretical philosophy was his view of history. His theory of history has had wide influence upon historians, even among those who are neither Marxists in their general philosophical outlook nor political communists. There had been materialistic philosophies of history before Marx, as in the writings of the historians who emphasized the role of climate and other natural factors in historical change. But Marx combined Hegel's dialectical conception of history with an emphasis upon the material conditions of social life and movement.

The essentials of his view are very simple. History is a struggle between classes, and classes are defined by the relationships of their members to the productive system. History is thus the story of the struggles between masters and slaves, feudal lords and serfs, capitalists and proletarians. Each of these classes develops its own ideology, on the basis of its needs and its relationship to the wealth of the society, and the ruling ideas of any period are the ideas of its ruling class. The ideas of the privileged ruling class are defenses of its favored position in society, which the rulers and the intelligentsia who support them seek to defend by interpreting the whole of reality from a standpoint that will make their exploitation and rule over others appear just and natural.

But opposed to any ruling ideology, there is the ideology of the exploited majority, who are economically motivated to reject the ruling ideas and who attempt to justify their dissatisfaction and to correct its causes by appeal to another set of principles, which constitute an antithesis to the ruling philosophy. Reconciliation between the two, according to Marx, is not effected by a mere logical dialectic that brings out the truth of each and synthesizes them into some higher truth. Rather, the struggle is on the material level, although it is a struggle in which ideas are weapons along with more direct and violent action.

Consider one stage in the dialectic, the one that the Marxist holds exists in a capitalistic society. In such a society, there are two important classes— the owners of the means of production and the workers who "own" only their labor. They sell their labor for wages to the capitalist and use these wages to buy the goods they have themselves produced. (The middle class, in a pinch, has to side with one or the other of these two classes.) For various economic reasons that we cannot here inquire into, Marx believes that such a society is inherently unstable; it cannot prevent unemployment, depression, and

[23]From Frederick Engels, *Anti-Dühring* (*Herr Eugen Dühring's Revolution in Science*) (New York: International Publishers, 1939), p. 152. By permission of International Publishers Co., Inc.

war. Gradually, the lot of the proletariat becomes intolerable, and debate between the capitalistic and the working class ceases to be a war of words and becomes actual revolution. Thus we have:

THESIS: capitalists expropriating the working class.
ANTITHESIS: proletarian reaction through organizations for protection of workers' interests.
SYNTHESIS: a classless society, in which the expropriators are expropriated ("negation of the negation") and every man not only works, but owns the means of production.

In this dialectic, the power of the state is originally controlled by the capitalist and is used for the control of the masses; similarly, ethical ideals, patriotism, and the ruling philosophical and religious[24] ideologies are instruments of oppression and control. But after the revolution, these means of exploitation and control are no longer needed. After a short transition period, the state will be expected to "wither away," religion will no longer be needed as a means of social control, and each man will enjoy complete independence and freedom. The goods of such a society will be distributed to each according to his need, and labor will be freely given by each according to his ability.

Needless to say, things have not worked out in the way Marx envisaged, and the countries under communist domination are not the Utopias he anticipated. Historians and economists have found many flaws in the details of his argument. In spite of this, Marx's emphasis upon the dialectical structure of social movements and upon the necessity of tracing each social force back to the economic and material conditions that engender and favor it has done much to take the writing of history out of the realm of chronology and chronicles of courtly intrigue and to show that many facts previously ignored by historians are relevant to the understanding of historical change.

CRITICISM AND CONCLUSION

There are several points to the credit of materialism. First, materialism is the metaphysical theory that has perhaps been most favorable to the development of rigorous scientific knowledge of reality. It combats any tendency to draw a line anywhere in reality and to say, "Beyond this, science cannot go." These lines have been drawn time and again; but each time it has been crossed, and obscurantists have had to retreat still further to draw the next line. Materialists believe that the main obstacle to the advancement of science is not the insufficiency of science itself but the opposition to science by those who wish to have some sheltered refuge from its progress.

Second, and a corollary to this, is the hard-headedness of the materialists. From the earliest times, they have been the philosophical debunkers who will not be put off with high-flown ideas and inspirations. They assert, often with

---

[24]See Marx's statement, "Religion is the opium of the people."

acerbity, that the unsolved questions of philosophy are in principle like the solved problems of science and that only time, effort, and courage are required to reduce speculative answers to scientific test.

Opponents of materialism hold that these attitudes of favoring and fostering scientific work are not the exclusive prerogative of materialism and that the same attitudes can be fostered by a metaphysical theory that is less susceptible to destructive criticism.

Moreover, they argue that materialism is not in step with science itself because physics today has energy, not matter, as its basic category. Even though opponents of materialism have drawn comfort from this, it seems quite unjustified. The essential thesis of materialism is not that the world consists only of little hard bits of matter but that reality is composed of irreducible and identical, or almost identical, elements that can be studied by scientific analysis and found to follow the laws of physics. That these elements are quanta of energy instead of hard matter is a detail without great metaphysical significance outside of cosmology and the philosophy of science. No more weight should be given to the common accusation that materialism is dogmatic. Critics of Marxism have bitterly attacked the Russian scientific community for espousing, under political pressure, untenable scientific hypotheses in genetics. But although it is tragic to see a philosophy that calls itself a science, as dialectical materialism does, actually going against scientific evidence to support an ideology, such regrettable falling away from objectivity can neither be blamed on nor confined to systems of philosophy that are materialistic.

Much more embittered criticisms of materialism are made by those who hold that it is inherent in the theory—not just a political accident—that materialism neglects or even is antithetical to human values. Supernaturalists and some idealists seem to place a higher premium upon human values by interpreting them as depending upon some transcendental spiritual foundation. Materialists and naturalists deny that this is necessary, but it does not lead them to deny that these spiritual values are important. It is not true that materialists in philosophy always, or even usually, are materialists in the common connotation of the word—men devoted to the indulgence of the flesh or the lust for money or power. And the materialist rejects the charge because he says that only through increasing our knowledge of the material conditions of life can we take the pursuit and criticism of value out of the obscurity to which it has been relegated by idealists and theologians. By studying the material conditions of the experience and pursuit of value, they rightly say, we may be able to use scientific knowledge to further the pursuit of ideals more successfully than we can in a society where some men devote themselves to the "higher spiritual values" with such assiduity that other people starve to death.

These objections to materialism seem to be both ill-informed and superficial, but there are three objections to materialism that are more weighty.

1. *The error of pseudo-simplicity.* One of the strongest points in favor of

materialism is its simplicity; the world consists of only one kind of thing, and there is only one kind of law in the world. But, it is argued, the simplicity that the materialist finds in matter is spurious; for having defined simple matter as a basic category, the materialist must endow it with indefinite potentiality to be, or to appear to be, all the various things that we find in the world. Thus matter in the ordinary sense has only the primary qualities and the physical and chemical properties that the scientist ascribes to it; but the world is full of colored things, for instance, so the materialist must attribute to his matter the potentiality of producing color under certain psychological conditions. Some of the materialists even attribute the potentiality of consciousness directly to matter. Hence to matter, simple *in name*, is attributed indefinite complexity and potentiality, so that matter as it is ordinarily understood in science is not adequate as a basis for the explanations predicated upon it.

2. *The error of misplaced concreteness.* The adjective "abstract" refers to some aspect or character or part of a thing that cannot exist or be found in isolation from it; thus, "red" is abstract. "Concrete," on the other hand, refers to a thing having many properties and capable of existing in itself. For example, a living animal is concrete, whereas life is abstract. Whitehead says that the fallacy of misplaced concreteness occurs whenever a philosopher takes some abstract characteristic of a thing and treats it as the concrete reality.

This occurs in materialism. What I see before me is a table, with primary and secondary qualities, sentimental and economic value, aesthetic qualities, and molecular constitution. But the materialist makes an abstraction from this, and considers only its primary physical and chemical properties, which exist as properties of the concrete object, as being the *real* properties of the *real* table. All the other properties are banished from reality. This is an example of misplaced concreteness, just as damaging in its philosophical consequences as if one were to make the color of the table ultimately real and to say its shape was only an illusory appearance.

Because the world does have, prima facie, a great many characteristics that matter, by hypothesis, does not have, the materialist must find some limbo for the unreal appearances of things. This is usually found in the realm of the mind, which is regarded as an epiphenomenon of a low degree of reality. The real world is impoverished, because all values and sensuous qualities are extruded from it. Even though this impoverishment of reality has been of use in tidying up nature so that it can be studied by the parsimonious methods of science, it has produced a metaphysics that does justice to only one part of reality. For in this metaphysics, what appears is not real, and what is real does not appear. The realm of phenomena becomes a kind of limbo containing everything reality lacks. Instead of explaining away the phenomena in question—after all, they will not vanish regardless of how little they are understood—materialism leaves them unexplained.

3. *The error of self-stultification.* Materialism normally leads to epiphenomenalism—the theory that the mind is not an effective agent in behavior.

We have argued epiphenomenalism cannot be established as a general metaphysical hypothesis, however useful it may be as a collateral hypothesis in psychology and physiology. For we argued that if epiphenomenalism is true, no argument to establish its truth has probative value. Moreover, epiphenomenalism destroys the probative value of arguments for other conclusions, even the conclusion that materialism is true. Hence, although we cannot be sure that materialism is in fact false, we believe that no argument rightly persuasive of its truth can be given.

We have attempted a fair evaluation of materialism. We have mentioned its most attractive features, rejected three widespread but, in our opinion, unfair criticisms of it, and explained three errors that, we believe, are fatal to materialism. Materialism is a theory attractive because of its simplicity; but materialism promised much, only to disappoint us in the end. Just as some forms of idealism were designed to overcome the weak points and to preserve the strong points in supernaturalism, there is another form of naturalism that aims to avoid the crucial objections to materialism while retaining the undoubted strengths that a materialistic metaphysics has. This form of naturalism is the topic of the next chapter.

BIBLIOGRAPHY

Materialism

Broad, C. D., *The Mind and its Place in Nature*, Chap. 1. New York: Harcourt, Brace & World, Inc., 1925.

Büchner, Ludwig, *Force and Matter* (1855). New York: Eckler, 1920.

Burnet, John, *Early Greek Philosophy*, Chaps. 5, 6, and 9. London: Black, 1920.

Elliot, Hugh, *Modern Science and Materialism*. New York: David McKay Co., Inc., 1915.

Hobbes, Thomas, *Hobbes Selections*, ed., Frederick J. E. Woodbridge. New York: Charles Scribner's Sons, 1928.

La Mettrie, Julien de, *Man a Machine* (1748). La Salle, Ill. Open Court Publishing Co., 1927.

Lange, Friedrich Albert, *History of Materialism* (1866) (3rd ed.). New York: Harcourt, Brace & World, Inc., 1915.

Montague, William Pepperell, *The Ways of Things*, Chaps. 13 and 15. Englewood Cliffs, N. J.: Prentice-Hall, Inc., 1940.

Perry, Ralph Barton, *Present Philosophical Tendencies*, pp. 57–84. New York: David McKay Co., Inc., 1912.

Sellars, Roy Wood, Marvin Farber, and V. J. McGill, eds., *Philosophy for the Future. The Quest of Modern Materialism*. New York: The Macmillan Company, 1949.

The Relation Between Mind and Body

Anderson, A. R., ed., *Minds and Machines*. Englewood Cliffs, N.J.: Prentice-Hall, Inc., 1964.

Beck, Lewis White, "Agent, Actor, Spectator, and Critic," *The Monist*, Vol. 49 (1965), 167–82.

Broad, C. D., *The Mind and Its Place in Nature*, Chaps. 1 and 3. London: Routledge & Kegan Paul, Ltd., 1923.

Cornman, James W., *Metaphysics, Reference and Language*. New Haven, Conn.: Yale University Press, 1967.

Descartes, René, *Meditations*, Parts II and VI. Many editions and translations.

Feigl, Herbert, "The 'Mental' and the 'Physical,' " *Minnesota Studies in the Philosophy of Science*, pp. 370–498. Minneapolis: University of Minnesota Press, 1957.

Hook, Sidney, ed., *Dimensions of Mind*. New York: New York University Press, 1960.

Shaffer, Jerome, "Mind-Body Problem," *Encyclopedia of Philosophy*, Vol. 5, pp. 336–46. New York: The Macmillan Company, 1967.

Smart, J. J. C., *Philosophy and Scientific Realism*, Chaps. 5 and 6. London: Routledge & Kegan Paul, Ltd., 1963.

Young, J. Z., *Doubt and Certainty in Science. A Biologist's Reflections on the Brain*. New York: Oxford University Press, Inc., 1951.

Dialectical Materialism

Acton, H. B., "Dialectical Materialism," *The Encyclopedia of Philosophy*, Vol. 2, pp. 389–97. New York: The Macmillan Company, 1967.

Dewey, John, *Freedom and Culture*. New York: G. P. Putnam's Sons, 1939.

Haldane, J. B. S., *The Marxist Philosophy and the Sciences*. New York: Random House, 1939.

Hook, Sidney, *Towards an Understanding of Karl Marx*. New York: The John Day Company, Inc., 1933.

Laski, Harold J., *Communism*. New York: Holt, Rinehart & Winston, Inc., 1927.

Marx, Karl, *Selected Writings in Sociology and Social Philosophy*, ed. and trans., T. B. Bottomore. New York: McGraw-Hill Book Company, 1964.

————, and Frederick Engels, *Basic Writings on Politics and Philosophy*, ed., Lewis S. Feuer. Garden City, N.Y.: Doubleday & Company, Inc., 1959.

Somerville, John, *Soviet Philosophy. A Study in Theory and Practice*. New York: Philosophical Library, Inc., 1946.

Venable, Vernon, *Human Nature, The Marxist View*. New York: Alfred A. Knopf, Inc., 1945.

QUESTIONS AND TOPICS FOR DISCUSSION

1. Discuss some of the ways in which modern materialism differs from ancient materialism. Ought we to use the same word to describe the Greek belief in material atoms and that of modern philosophers who base their work on modern science?

2. Can an epistemological *skeptic* be a materialist?

3. Compare mechanism in biology (Chap. 10) with materialism. Could a biologist be a mechanist, yet reject materialism as a system of philosophy?

4. Some antimaterialists have rejoiced that "materialism is dead" because the physicists now explain matter in terms of energy. Is this rejoicing justified?

5. Many people complain that we live in a "materialistic age." What does this mean? Do you think that they could "reform" the "materialists" by criticizing the metaphysical theory of materialism?

6. If a philosopher believes that the sensation of blue is identical with a state of the brain, how does he explain the fact that a neurosurgeon does not see any part of a patient's brain to be blue when the patient says that he sees something blue?

7. If all that you observe in another person is his bodily behavior, how do you know that he is conscious at all? (Consider Scheler's argument, below, pp. 392f.)

8. It is said in the text that no empirical evidence can decide between epiphenomenalism and psychophysical dualism. If the occurrence of telepathic communication were to be established as a fact, would this serve to confirm one and to refute the other?

9. Compare the argument in this chapter against epiphenomenalism with the argument in Chapter 8 against "hard determinism." Could you apply the charge of "self-stultification" to arguments for the latter?

10. Dialectical materialists have claimed that their theory is really a science; others have said that both it and communism are more like theology and religion. Discuss.

11. "Communism is a Christian heresy." Evaluate.

12. Can the present situation in communist nations—assuming that it is as commonly pictured—properly be interpreted as an "indictment of the theory of dialectical materialism"?

13. Can a man be a Marxist in philosophy and not be a communist in politics?

14. Read one of the following books and point out the human relevance of some of the philosophical theories stated or implied:
    a. Turgenev's *Fathers and Sons*.
    b. Hauptmann's *Lonesome Lives*.
    c. Koestler's *Arrival and Departure*.
    d. Koestler's *Darkness at Noon*.
    e. Skinner's *Walden Two*.

15. Can a machine think? Assuming that you answer this affirmatively, what would you say to the question: Can a machine feel?

16. Suppose you answer both questions in the negative. Now suppose upon approaching another planet in a space-ship, human beings from earth picked up radio messages (news broadcasts, music, soap operas) from this planet; however, upon disembarking on the planet, they found that the beings sending and receiving the programs were made of wheels, levers, and electric circuits. They were found to move about much as human beings do and carry on most activities very much as men do. Would you wish to change your answer to question 15? Why, or why not?

13 NATURALISM II—
CRITICAL NATURALISM

ONE TREND IN RECENT THOUGHT

About sixty years ago there were forces, both social and intellectual, that brought about the demand for what Dewey calls a "Reconstruction in Philosophy."

Supernaturalism with its tendency to exempt certain areas of experience, such as the religious and the moral, from scientific examination, was challenged by the growing strength of sciences that invaded the precincts of religious thought. The Darwinian theory of evolution, first announced in 1859 and widely accepted by the end of the nineteenth century, not only impugned the accuracy of the Biblical account of creation but also made many thinkers give up the religious answer to the question, "What is man?" The stability of the religious doctrines that had been the constant ballast for European and American thought for centuries was upset by a growing secularism in all phases of life, and optimism was soon shattered in the cataclysm of war.

Idealism, which had been one of the dominant movements, was challenged and eclipsed by a variety of new interests and doctrines. Its theory of knowledge was attacked by many philosophers, and its belief in the ultimate status of mind seemed unable to cope with new views of mind coming from Darwinian biology and from behaviorism and Freudianism in psychology. Idealism, rightly or wrongly, seemed unable to adjust itself to the empirical discoveries of science and the practical exigencies of a technological civilization. "Ideals are all very well," the representatives of the new century seemed to say, "but we are more interested in realities—in hard facts discovered but not created by mind."

Materialism, however, was unable to exploit the situation brought about by the decline of its old rivals. Had idealism done nothing else, it was important because it had exposed the epistemological superficiality of materialism. Materialism put its own interpretation upon the facts of science and called it metaphysics; but the work of scientists like Einstein and Planck made the materialistic interpretation seem superficial even in its account of the results of science.

Although none of these attacks and counterattacks were sufficient to refute the metaphysical theories, they did show a general dissatisfaction with the kind of conclusions that metaphysicians had traditionally drawn. Philosophy is always responsive to much more than the demands of professional philosophers for consistency of system and elegance of argument. It is responsive to the needs of men who are not primarily philosophers but thinkers sensitive to the intellectual and moral currents of their time. The twentieth century, with its confusion and hurry and horrors mixed with stupendous advances in science and technology, has not been wholly satisfied with the thoughts of earlier generations. It has required a new philosophy, or at least a new emphasis in philosophy, that would take account of its peculiar problems.

Any philosophy responsive to the temper of our period must be thought to be scientific yet sensitive to the claims of the implicit religious, moral, and political ideals of our culture.[1] It must be tentative in its conclusions and not too sweeping in its claim to have apprehended the ultimate truths and values. It must not be Utopian but fully cognizant of the confusions of our life and patient in its inquiry into their sources and into ways of resolving them. It must, in the common-sense meaning of these words, be realistic and practical.

That they are formulating such a *Weltanschauung* is the claim of the philosophers called critical naturalists.

NATURE AS THE ULTIMATE CATEGORY

Critical naturalism (frequently called simply "naturalism") is based upon a broader conception of nature than that found in materialism. Materialists begin with a conception of nature as essentially the subject-matter of the natural sciences and contrast nature to the realm of value, spirit, culture, and mind; then they "reduce" the latter realm to the former and say that the world is ultimately only what it is found to be in physics. Critical naturalists, on the other hand, do not begin with a distinction between what is natural and what belongs allegedly to some other realm of being; they say that the distinction between what is natural and what is not is predicated upon too thin and homogeneous a conception of nature.

If by nature we mean only what is studied in the natural sciences, then, of course, distinctions between nature and society, fact and value, body and mind, the secular and the sacred, and the like, must be drawn. For the natural

[1] See Joseph Wood Krutch, *The Modern Temper* (New York: Harcourt, Brace & World, Inc., 1929).

sciences do not study culture or value or the more complex human affairs and interests. But, say the naturalists, all of these phases of experience arise in the course of nature and have a legitimate claim to be considered natural. A conception that identified nature with matter in motion is not synoptic enough to deal fairly with those parts of experience not already mastered by scientific experimentation. So while the materialist denies their significance or tries to force them into the mold of material nature, the critical naturalist attempts to broaden the concept of nature so that it will contain them without doing violence to their difference from mere matter in motion.

Shakespeare recognized the unjustified narrowness of the term "nature" as usually employed. He clearly brought out the need for a more panoramic conception. His characters in *A Winter's Tale* (IV, iv) are discussing some flowers that had been cultivated by the art of grafting, and one of them objects to these flowers as being "unnatural," that is, as not arising in the course of nature understood to be alien to man and his works. But another says,

> Yet nature is made better by no mean
> But nature makes that mean; so, over that art
> Which you say adds to nature, is an art
> Which nature makes.
>   . . . This is an art
> Which does mend nature, change it rather, but
> The art itself is nature.

Generalizing on this kind of consideration, the critical naturalist says that we ought not to ascribe to nature merely material, savage, animal, or brutish parts of man only to have to find some supernatural explanation for his culture, art, science, and religion. Man and all his works appear in nature and are to be best understood as all one piece, although this is not just a piece of matter in motion.

We can see the contrast between the naturalist and the anti-naturalist best, perhaps, in regard to the question of the origin and status of morals. The anti-naturalists, from the earliest times, have held that nature is too brutely factual, too indifferent from the standpoint of value, to explain men's experiences of value. Their thesis is summed up in Matthew Arnold's verses "To an Independent Preacher":

> Know, man hath all which Nature hath, but more,
> And in that *more* lie all his hopes of good.

Their only disagreement turns on what this "more" really is. It might be a revelation of God or reason or some transcendental moral sense or the like. But the naturalist replies,

Moral feelings are not innate but acquired, [but] they are not for that reason less natural. It is natural for man to speak, to reason, to build cities, to cultivate the ground, though these are acquired faculties. The moral feelings are not indeed a part of our nature, in the sense of being in any perceptible degree present in all of us; but this, unhappily, is a fact admitted by those who believe the most strenuously in their transcendental origin. Like the other acquired faculties above referred to, the moral faculty, if not a part of our nature, is a *natural* outgrowth from it.[2]

Thus the naturalist agrees with the materialist in opposing any division between a realm of nature and a realm of mind, value, or God. But he agrees with the supernaturalist that "matter in motion" is not an adequate metaphor for "reality." So he takes the monism of the materialist and combines it with the frank acknowledgment of diversity and value that was insisted upon by idealist and supernaturalist. In this way he conceives of nature in the broadest possible sense: It is whatever really is, and this is more than matter in motion.

Why, then, call reality by the name "nature"? The reason for this metaphor we have already seen: The naturalist asserts that the whole of reality is subject to the same kind of study that has already gone far toward mastering that part of reality that everyone agrees in calling nature. The critical naturalist says whatever is claimed as knowledge must be justified by careful empirical inquiry, like that to which the natural sciences are devoted. Whatever any experience offers as insight into reality must be tested before it is accepted; no credence is to be given to intuitions or a priori insights. They are, at most, kinds of experiences that must be tested to see if what they suggest is true. As valuable kinds of experience, and as possible sources of knowledge, the naturalist is interested in cultivating, enjoying, and examining them. He does not dogmatically pronounce them absurd, as the materialists tend to do.

Many beliefs incompatible with strict materialism are able to pass such an empirical test, and the critical naturalist accepts them. For instance, he accepts the reality of purposes in living organisms, even though denying that nature is designed "for a purpose." He finds that he can best explain biological phenomena on the hypothesis that animal behavior is goal-seeking. He therefore refuses to reject, on the basis of a metaphysical dogma of materialism, the evidence of purposes in behavior. Without becoming a vitalist, he broadens the conception of nature to include the phenomena that the vitalist had interpreted as evidence for some supernatural agency. Already, in Chapter 10, we have discussed the theory that life is an emergent within nature from physico-chemical processes. This theory, or others very much like it, would be accepted by most critical naturalists but, of course, denied by materialists.

To consider another example of belief held by naturalists but not by most materialists, take the difference between their conceptions of value. The

[2]John Stuart Mill, *Utilitarianism* (1863), ed., Oskar Piest (New York: Liberal Arts Press, 1948. The Little Library of Liberal Arts, No. 1), p. 32 (italics supplied).

materialist regards man as merely a complex animal, and his actions as mere reactions to stimuli. Most of the higher value experiences are reduced to the subjective pleasures of physiological responses. Whereas the idealist and the supernaturalist denature values and place them in some realm above that of nature understood scientifically, the naturalist considers men's pursuit of values as perfectly natural, growing our of their natural environment and context. But the naturalist does not reduce value experience to mere physiological response to physical stimuli; he holds, on the contrary, that value experience shows that men have potentialities that are neglected or denied if man is understood merely as a reactive mechanism. The critical naturalist seeks to render the ideals and moral rules of men intelligible by interpreting them as empirically established habits or rules that have been found relatively successful in guiding men in their quest for deep and abiding satisfactions.

The remainder of this chapter is devoted to a brief examination of the views of some naturalists concerning knowledge and its objects, the nature of mind, and the nature and value of religion.

NATURALISTIC THEORIES OF PERCEPTION

A naturalist rejects any theory of knowledge and perception, like that of Berkeley and other idealists, that implies that the objects we perceive depend upon the mind or upon consciousness of them. The naturalist has a realistic theory of perception according to which the objects perceived exist whether perceived or not and have the properties they are perceived to have.

In previous discussions of the problem of perception we encountered three realistic theories of perception. The first was the theory of Locke and Descartes. It is generally called representative realism, because it holds that there is a real object (substance) represented by ideas that it causes; we directly experience ideas and indirectly know the objects that they represent and, in part, resemble. The second was the theory known as neorealism, whose thesis is that we directly know an object as it really is and that the object we directly know is not an idea dependent upon any mind—human or divine. The third was critical realism, which holds that objects and the immediate data of perception are nonidentical but that our knowledge of objects is nonetheless direct.

We shall now discuss yet another theory of perception, one which is particularly suitable to a naturalistic metaphysics. It is the theory known as objective relativism. John Dewey, presented in Chapter 7, was one of its principal advocates.

Objective relativism—According to objective relativism, a thing is what it is in a context of relationships to other things. To consider it to be what it is in only one of its contexts is to commit the fallacy of misplaced concreteness, to confuse an abstract conception of it with its actual being, which is what it is in the totality of its relationships. Indeed, nothing, so far as we know, exists in isolation. Certainly, when we know an object, we know it not only in relation to us but in relation to other objects that environ and affect it. An object is heavy only in a gravitational field that includes other objects attracting it; how heavy it is depends upon its mass in relation to the masses of other things, and an absolutely isolated object would have neither mass nor weight. How large an object is depends upon the ratio of its dimensions to those of some other object; an absolutely isolated object could not be said to be of any particular size. The color we attribute to an object depends not only on the functioning of the eye that sees it but also on the composition of the light that falls upon its surface, and so on through all the qualities we ascribe to objects.

Theaetetus (see p. 56) was saying something like this when he recognized that what we perceive depends not only on *it* but also on *ourselves in relation to it*. But Theaetetus, as we have seen, relativized all perceptual experience to such an extent that he could not account for the difference between accurate and illusory perception. The modern relativist wishes not to fall into this kind of skepticism, and he points out a very important distinction that Theaetetus neglected. It is the distinction between the relation of an object to the perceiving person and its relation to other objects. Although Theaetetus was correct in noticing that the object of perception is related to the perceiver, he did not see that the object's qualities depend not only on this highly variable relation, but also upon its more stable relations to other objects in its context. It is the emphasis upon these relations, a relativity among objects, that gives this theory its name, *objective* relativism.

All the qualities attributed to an object depend upon its relation to its context of other objects. Some depend upon the context that includes the nervous system and mind of the organism that responds to it. The former qualities are the qualities called primary, and because they do not depend upon the relation of an object to a particular organism's nervous system, with all the peculiarities that distinguish it from that of other organisms, they are the qualities about which there can be considerable agreement among individuals. They are the qualities we adduce when we give a scientific explanation of the behavior of objects, the qualities we usually think belong to the object intrinsically, as it really is. But they do not belong intrinsically to the object. They are relational properties in a context of objects that is so easily agreed upon, so easily standardized, so comprehensive in its scope, that its effect is commonly ignored. That is why we ordinarily think of weight as belonging to an object intrinsically and do not add that its weight is dependent upon the earth and would be different on another planet. We say, "This book weighs a pound"; we do not say, "On the earth, at this latitude, this book weighs a pound." We take for granted the context in which primary qualities are determined; but we should not, in philosophical analysis, allow this to hide the fact that even the primary qualities are contextually determined.

The secondary qualities are more obviously determined by context, because the context in which they appear includes human beings with all their variability. The secondary qualities emerge in relation to a sentient organism, but they do not emerge in a realm of mind set over against the realm of nature. According to the objective relativist, a secondary quality is no more "in the mind" than the weight of an object is "in the earth," although the mind is necessary to the emergence of the former just as the earth is necessary to the phenomenon we call the weight of the object.

For theoretical accuracy, we ought to say, "This book weighs a pound in relation to the earth," and, "This apple is red in relation to me." In each case, there is a context that ought to be stated when we attribute a property to an object. When that context includes ourselves, it is especially important to indicate this, for the personal context varies from individual to individual. In all cases of perception, of course, there is a personal context, but often its effect can be minimized so that social agreement on perception can be reached. Thus, for instance, there is no need to say, "This book weighs a pound in relation to the earth and to me," for the "to me" is probably not a significant factor in determining what the weight of the book is. Everyone on earth can agree on its weight. For this reason, therefore, objective relativists believe that they can escape the skeptical conclusions Theaetetus was made to infer from his relativism. The objective relativist asserts that the most important kind of relativity in establishing the properties of an object is the relativity of one object to another and not its relativity to us.

Proponents of objective relativism believe that their theory meets the objections brought against the other realistic theories of perception. As against Locke, it does not take secondary qualities into the mind in such a way that the real object outside of consciousness becomes a dubious hypothesis. And against neorealism, objective relativists believe they have a simple and plausible theory of error.

When I look at a straight stick in water and it appears bent, the theory tells us that this is what should be expected in this context. Visual straightness is a property of tactually straight sticks in a context in which rays of light going from it to the eyes or a camera are not distorted by passing from one medium to another. Visual bentness, on the other hand, is a property of tactually straight sticks in a context in which the rays of light going from it to the eyes are refracted by passing from one medium to another. I would be in error if I said that the physical, tactual stick is bent by being put into water; water, fortunately, does not have the property of bending physical sticks when they are put into it at an angle. But I am not in any error if I say that under the conditions of visual observation, it *appears* to be bent, or that the stick in the visual context *is* bent.

It is not that there is a straight stick "in the world" and a bent stick "in my mind" or "in the realm of subsistent entities." Rather, "the shape of the stick" is an ambiguous term, and we must specify the context in which we are speaking of shape. The shape of the stick as a tactual, physical object, in a context of straightedges and compasses, is not affected by its being put into water. But the shape of the stick as a visual object, in the context of light rays and eyes or cameras, is affected by this context.

COMPARISON OF FIVE IMPORTANT THEORIES OF PERCEPTION

Philosopher or Type of View	What is Directly Experienced	Status of Objects in External World	Status of Illusions	Theory of Mind
Locke, representative realism (pp. 97–101)	Ideas of sensation and ideas of reflection (ideas of activity of mind)	Substances, unknown causes of sensation, with primary qualities and power to produce ideas of color, odor, and so on	Complex ideas in the mind not corresponding to substance	Mind as thinking substance; Cartesian dualism
Berkeley, idealism (pp. 103–20)	Ideas, and notions of spirit or mind	Ideas in God's mind	Ideas in my mind, but not in God's; ideas that are not organized and regular	Mind as active, creative, and ultimate reality
Neorealism (pp. 120f.)	Real objects selected by attention and behavior of organism	Existent objects having all properties they are perceived to have, and spatio-temporal and causal relations to others	Subsistent entities without location in objective space or causal relations	Mind as a relation between objects and organism; "searchlight theory"
Critical realism (pp. 121ff.)	According to different accounts, either ideas (particulars) or essences (universals), thought to reveal and causally mediate objects	Independent existents, directly known or judged to exist through instinct, faith, or interpretation of sense contents	Sense contents thought in error to reveal actual structures of objects	Various views, including epiphenomenalism, dualism and panpsychism
Objective relativism (pp. 322–26)	Objects in a context including other objects and organisms, thereby having both primary and secondary qualities	Objects, considered without reference to the context of the perceiving organism, and thereby having only primary qualities	Objects in a context including the organism or medium of perception as a determining condition, but interpreted without reference to this condition	Mind as emergent from organism and its purposive relation to environment; mind as functional, or a "way of acting"

We cannot say what the shape of the stick is apart from every context. We are usually interested in how the stick behaves as a tactual, physical object in causal relation to other sticks, the pressure of the water, and so on. There is, therefore, good practical reason for saying that the stick is really straight and only seems bent. But this is only a statement of a very natural and justified preference for dealing with the stick in those contexts in which its behavior and properties are uniform, simple, and permanent, in which it does not physically bend as it is put into water and straighten out when it is withdrawn or grow smaller as it recedes from my eyes.

There is a pragmatic or practical element involved in perception, in choosing among the various contexts in which we describe objects, and in choosing which of the various appearances of things (that is, visual rather than tactual) we shall call illusory. We normally say that an object *really* is what it seems to be in the context in which we use it practically or refer to it as a cause of changes in other physical objects. But it would be an error of misplaced concreteness if we regarded its properties in that context as being metaphysically real and all its other properties as subjective or illusory.

THE NATURALISTS' THEORY OF THE MIND

Most of the theories of mind examined thus far deal with mind as though it were either a thing (in technical philosophical language, a substance) or a property of a thing, and they disagree only about the nature of this thing (is it mental? or physical?) or about the relation of one of its properties to another. In Chapter 11 we considered Ryle's objections to this concept of mind. The naturalist agrees that these theories are mistaken and develops in their place a theory that is consistent with the implications of Ryle's critique. The mind, he says, is not a thing or substance but a way of acting. Mind is not an occult agency that makes us act in certain ways; it is the name we give to a way of acting. Mind is mind*ing*. This view of mind is frequently called the "functional theory."

At first glance, this theory seems either obscure or absurd or both. We are so in the habit of using "mind" as a noun—as a name for something that is "in our heads" and causally related to our brain—that it takes some effort at reorienting our ways of thinking to grasp the point of this theory. But the naturalist believes it is worth the effort; for although our common language suggests and almost forces us to think of mind as a kind of thing, mind as a thing or substance has never been observed. "Its" workings are all that we observe. "Its" workings are the conscious and intelligent behavior of ourselves or others. The naturalist therefore proposes that we use the word to denote what we *do* observe in intelligent, conscious behavior of ourselves and others and not speculate about a hidden entity supposed to be the cause of this behavior.

This way of looking at mind is, in fact, very old, but it was displaced first by the Christian theory of the soul as a substance created by God and then by the Cartesian theory of two kinds of beings, extended objects and minds. Aristotle, however, had a functional theory of mind, and compared the relationship of body and mind to the relationship between an axe and cutting or between an eye and seeing: "If the eye were an animal, eyesight would be its soul."[3] The seeing eye is not an unseeing anatomical entity plus something else existing as a different kind of being—sight; a cutting axe is not a piece of metal plus another being whose faculty is only to cut. Rather, cutting and seeing are functions of the substances in question and not properties of something else hidden within them. Similarly, Aristotle holds that "mind" or "soul" as applied to human beings is simply a name for certain faculties of action. They are names for potentialities that are manifested in specific ways in specific circumstances. For instance, I have the power to digest food even when I am not doing so, but the evidence that I have this potentiality is that under specific circumstances I do actually digest it. Aristotle, then, quite consistently (although it sounds strange to modern ears) says that I have a "nutritive soul"—not a *thing* in my stomach that in some way interacts with my body so as to digest food but a potentiality for action that is actualized when I eat.

In modern times, we use the words "soul" or "mind" in a more specific sense to refer to what we commonly believe *makes* us think, feel, will, be aware, and act more or less intelligently. We do not use the word "soul" to refer to our digestive powers, but according to the critical naturalist, what Aristotle says about the nutritive soul suggests what modern philosophers and psychologists should say about what is ordinarily called "the mind." Mind is not a thing but a way of acting. James succinctly describes the kind of action in question: "The pursuance of future ends and the choice of means for their attainment are ... the mark and criterion for the presence of mentality in a phenomenon."[4]

The mark of intelligent behavior, which is possible only through the integrative action of the nervous system, is the organism's ability to adjust to stimuli impinging upon it in the light of the needs and conditions existing in the body and built up there through past actions and reactions. One of the most obvious differences between the behavior of a machine and that of an organism is that a machine reacts in an automatic way to the forces acting upon it.[5] An organism, on the contrary, responds sometimes in one way and sometimes in another to objectively identical stimuli. How it reacts depends not only on the stimulus itself but also on what is going on in various parts of the organism's body as a consequence of past experience that arouses

[3]Aristotle, *De Anima*, trans., R. D. Hicks (Cambridge: Cambridge University Press, 1907), p. 412b.
[4]William James, *The Principles of Psychology*, Vol. I (New York: Holt, Rinehart & Winston), p. 8.
[5]See above, pages 252f.

memories and expectations. Animals differ greatly in their abilities to choose means for the pursuit of future ends; man has this ability to a pre-eminent degree.

The difference between the behavior of an intelligent organism like man and one that is merely trained or whose reflexes are thoroughly conditioned is almost as great as that between a machine and an organism. The intelligent organism has a much greater capacity for variable adaptive responses to identical stimuli. My dog "Blue Tooth," who has been conditioned to walk with me, becomes excited whenever he sees me pick up his leash; he will do this as readily in the middle of a stormy night when his master is wearing pajamas as on a sunny spring day. An intelligent person, on the other hand, reacts in one way to a stimulus under one set of conditions and in another way under other conditions, and all these conditions need not be physically acting upon him at the moment. The mark of intelligence is that the person responds to stimuli and their meanings. Their meanings are not physical properties of the stimuli but are their interpreted implications for what is not physically present.

An animal can be trained to react to a stimulus in the same way that he has formerly reacted to what follows it. Such a stimulus we call a *signal.* Pavlov's dogs reacted to the sound of a buzzer by salivating, for through training, a connection had been established between hearing the buzzer and the response to the granting of food. Intelligent behavior, however, although undoubtedly dependent in part upon the conditioning of reflexes, is not automatic response to a stimulus. It is response that depends upon an appraisal of a total situation. It may vary greatly even though the overt stimuli are identical from case to case. A stimulus subject to this kind of appraisal is called a *symbol,* and intelligence is response to the symbolic, rather than to the signal, characteristics of stimuli. Both signal and symbolic responses are preparatory to what is coming; but symbolic responses are those in which the organism takes account of alternative possibilities instead of responding automatically to a stimulus.

Consider a simple illustration. I am quietly reading in my home when suddenly the doorbell rings. My immediate reaction may be the typical startled response—I give a slight jump; this is a case of mere unconditioned reflex. Blue Tooth jumps up and runs to the door; this is a conditioned reflex, for in the past, when the bell has sounded he has found someone there to bark at or to welcome. His response in this case is anticipatory and preparatory for what is coming, whereas mine is neither.

Then compare these actions with those in another similar case. I have been reading a newspaper account about a dangerous criminal who has come to several houses in the neighborhood, rung the doorbell, and attacked the person who opened the door. Now my doorbell rings. On this occasion, I do not simply react to it as a physical stimulus affecting my ear. I react in the light of the conditions reported in the newspaper. I cautiously approach the door and try to see who it is that has rung the bell. On still another occasion, when I am expecting a friend, I respond to the same physical stimulus in the light of that expectation with almost as much alacrity as the dog and quickly go to open the door. In the latter two instances, I am responding to absent and future events in the light of past events, acting so as to prepare for them—reacting to identical physical stimuli in different ways according to their different meanings. The dog, however, reacts in the same way to the same stimulus regardless of the differences in their meaning, of which I am aware.

Such anticipatory or preparatory responsiveness to stimuli is a function of the organism made possible by the complex action of its nervous system. By distant receptors my nervous system enables me to deal with an event before it is in physical contact with me and by its integrative action, to respond to stimuli according to their promised meanings for my needs and tendencies. Therefore, the nervous system is, as it were, the cutting edge of the organism. Although an axe may be used as a hammer and a human organism as ballast in a boat, the proper function of the one is to cut and of the other is to respond intelligently and teleologically to stimuli that bear upon its needs. Only if the axe can cut does it have the specific function we ascribe to it; only if a human being can respond to the symbolic aspects of its environment do we ascribe mind and intelligence to it.

The mind is the body's perfected operation and achievement, as Aristotle taught us long ago. . . . [The naturalist] would find it difficult to take the problem of interaction [between mind and body] seriously. For to him it is quite evident that conscious bodies are more efficient than those that are not [conscious]. . . . No one doubts that beings become more efficient by becoming conscious, any more than one doubts that a live man is more efficient than a dead one.[6]

Mind is not a *thing* having efficacious power, something that makes or permits a man to act symbolically. It is, says the naturalist, this way of acting itself. "Mind may be defined as response to the meanings of stimuli . . . as the control of behavior by anticipation."[7]

In Chapter 8 intelligent problem-solving was contrasted to trial and error solutions to problems. Intelligent problem-solving involves acting on a hypothesis that has been tried out symbolically—through anticipation—before it is put into overt practice. A hypothesis is a plan of action. In the case of the dog who runs to the door when the bell rings, the hypothesis has been "built into the nervous system" by training and habit; he not only leaps before he looks, but he runs before he "thinks." I do neither when I am

[6]Reprinted from Frederick J. E. Woodbridge, *Nature and Mind* (New York: Columbia University Press, 1937), p. 333. Copyright 1937 by Columbia University Press.

[7]Reprinted from Yervant H. Krikorian, "A Naturalistic Theory of Mind," in *Naturalism and the Human Spirit*, ed., Yervant H. Krikorian (New York: Columbia University Press, 1944), p. 252. Copyright 1944 by Columbia University Press.

responding intelligently. Although certainly there are physiological conditions and past training that affect the way I act, the hypotheses I use in intelligent problem-solving are not built-in habits. In responding to the symbolic aspects of a stimulus, I suspend action until more stimuli arrive to clarify the problematic and unsettled aspects of the situation. The substitute for the overt action is the consciousness of the hypothesis; "To have an idea is to be ready to respond in a specific way to a stimulus; to reason is to rehearse various anticipatory responses in relation to a problem."[8]

Conscious appraisal of a situation, which is reasoning about the meanings of the stimuli, occurs in the period of tension between the occurrence of an unexpected stimulus and overt response to it. My dog does not pause to consider; he acts but does not reason. My organism does not respond automatically. The stimulus arouses in me various alternative reaction patterns that are possible plans for action. Observation of the facts of the situation, followed by anticipatory tracing out of their probable consequences, occurs in me because my nervous system has built into in *many* possible plans of action that can be tried out before being put into practice. Reasoning is the process of comparing and interpreting symbols before responding to them overtly.

Reasoning, therefore, need not be interpreted as a transcendental function of an other-worldly entity called mind or pure reason. It is rather a way of acting under the guidance of alternative sets of symbolic interpretations of the stimulus, each of which promises its own anticipated consequences for the future behavior of the organism. Reasoning reaches the highest degree of abstractness or distance from the determinative role of the merely physical characteristics of the stimulus in the use of words and mathematical symbols, which owe little of their meaning for behavior to their specific and unique physical characteristics. Logic, mathematics, and grammar are concerned with the symbolic interrelations among stimuli and concern only their meanings; but they are meanings of stimuli that arise in the natural interaction between a delicately balanced organism and the environment.

Awareness of the symbolical relations constitutes knowledge if the circumstances they imply or suggest are actually met with in the future experience of the organism. In this respect the pragmatic theory of truth fits in with the functional theory of mind.

PRAGMATISM

The naturalist, as we have just seen, asserts that the mind is a natural phenomenon, not something above or beyond nature. Mind is a mode of behavior, in which the organism seeks goals and anticipates the future.

[8]*Ibid.*, p. 257.

Mind as functionally understood is no epiphenomenon but an agent in the struggle for survival. The biological theory of evolution, applied to the theory of mind and knowledge, leads to an important conclusion: The test of the value of mental workings is not whether they produce beliefs that in some way correspond to reality but whether they facilitate the adjustment of the organism to its environment or help to resolve the problems presented by the environment. "Knowledge is power," said Bacon; the modern naturalist says, "Knowledge is the fruit of undertakings that transform a problematic situation into a resolved one."[9]

Elaboration of this naturalistic doctrine is the work of the American school of philosophers known as pragmatists. Pragmatism, according to one of its leaders, John Dewey, is "the theory that the processes and materials of knowledge are determined by practical or purposive considerations—that there is no such thing as knowledge determined by exclusively theoretical, speculative, or abstract intellectual considerations."[10] For these philosophers, a meaningful judgment is one that has consequences for our practical experience, one whose truth or falsity makes a difference within experience. A true judgment is one that is useful in meeting the practical situation that calls forth the belief as a preparation for dealing with the situation. The true is the useful. The doctrine is not that a true belief is subsequently discovered also to be true but rather that the criteria of truth can be shown upon analysis to involve only questions of usefulness in adjustment.

Just as intelligence is a response to a practical situation that is problematical and threatens the on-going of life and inquiry, the criterion of intelligent response guided by a belief and the criterion of the belief itself is the degree to which the belief and the action based upon it resolve the problem that elicited it. If a belief aids us in adjusting ourselves to a situation or resolves the problems presented by the situation, it is useful. The pragmatists said that this is what we mean when we call a belief true; this is how we discover that it is true, in the only sense of "true" that actually matters. A true belief is one that works, one that brings about the response that resolves the problem:

The ultimate test for us of what a truth means is . . . the conduct it dictates or inspires. But it inspires that conduct because it first foretells some particular turn to our experience which shall call forth just that conduct from us.[11]

This test of meaning has been illustrated again and again in our study of hypotheses. An idea, a judgment, a concept, or a hypothesis is not primarily a copy of reality, judged by its correspondence to reality. It is rather a plan

[9]John Dewey, *The Quest for Certainty* (New York: Minton Balch, 1929), pp. 242–43.

[10]*The Century Dictionary Supplement* (New York: Appleton-Century-Crofts, 1909), II, 1050; cf. I, viii.

[11]William James, *Collected Essays and Reviews* (New York: David McKay Co., Inc., 1920), p. 412.

of action, a foresight toward future adjustment. Not the origin but the application determines its value or truth. The criterion of its value and truth is whether it produces actions that bring foreseen results.

Pragmatists have differed among themselves in the ways they assess the usefulness and, hence, the truth of a judgment. Peirce, for instance, emphasized the usefulness of general or abstract concepts in simplifying and ordering experience. Ideas, according to him, must be tested by their application to, and usefulness in, all conceivable experience, without regard to particular personal interests of the believer. Usefulness meant to him primarily intellectual simplification and integration, and the pragmatic criterion, as he interpreted it, had much in common with the universal coherence sought by the idealists.

William James appealed to two criteria of usefulness. For judgments that could be tested in future experience, James' theory has much in common with Peirce's. He called truth the "cash value of an idea," comparing an idea to a check, which is valueless in itself but valuable if it can be cashed. An idea is "cashed" at the bank of future experience; if it is "honored" by having our expectations from it fulfilled, we call it true. What was new and distinctive in James' version of pragmatism, however, was his insistence upon the relation of some beliefs to our irrational or "passional" nature. When the facts of the case are not sufficient to decide the truth or falsity of a hypothesis and when the hypothesis is about such an urgent human problem that one must take a stand for or against it, James emphasized that the consequences of *believing* the hypothesis take the place of the consequences of the hypothesis itself. The consequence of the act of belief bears upon our passional nature as acting, desiring human beings. Our passional nature is and, James believed, should be decisive for or against belief in the hypothesis. Thus, for instance, the proposition "God exists" does not itself have any testable consequences; but the *belief* that God exists does have consequences for our conduct, and these consequences are and should be the determining reasons for choosing whether to believe in God's existence.[12]

John Dewey thinks more in terms of the social consequences of beliefs. The conflicts that most concern him are social in origin, and he insists upon the fact that warranted beliefs are those that release the potentialities of men and institutions for further free inquiry and growth unhampered by authoritarianism and dogmatism, which derive the value of beliefs from their origin rather than their application.

Each of these philosophers is saying, in his own way, that the true is the useful. Each of them is perhaps inadvertently illustrating the pragmatic principle that interests determine outlook. Peirce was a mathematician and scientist and could be expected to emphasize universality as characteristic of true and useful beliefs; James was a psychologist with a strong bias

---

[12]For James' use of this as an argument to justify belief in God, see pages 394–96.

toward religion; Dewey's thought was oriented largely toward the social setting of intelligent action, and he was devoted to educational reform.

Even though the doctrine that a true belief is a useful belief is treated differently by each of these men, those outside the pragmatic movement have criticized it on the basis of the assumption of still another meaning of "useful." They have objected to it because they think of "useful" as meaning the technologically or economically useful. On that basis, of course, the doctrine can appear absurd. A lie is not true, however much it helps a man to get out of a scrape, nor is a false statement in advertising made true by the fact that such a statement sometimes pays. The writings of the pragmatists have not always been sufficiently lucid to prevent this kind of misinterpretation, but the careful reader of the pragmatists, especially of Peirce and Dewey, can readily see that it is a misinterpretation.

Usefulness is not to be interpreted in a narrow sense, as the personally advantageous in a particular situation. *The kind of usefulness relevant to the establishment of any truth is determined by the kind of problem that engenders the belief to be tested.* One would not ordinarily call the proposition, "Caesar crossed the Rubicon," a useful bit of knowledge, for one generally thinks of the useful as having close relation to overt practical behavior. But precisely why does anyone think it worthwhile to say, "Caesar crossed the Rubicon"? It would ordinarily be in response to a problematic situation facing a historian who wishes to understand the events of Roman history, and it is a useful belief to the extent that it foretells what he will find if he consults other books or what he and other historians will conclude if they weigh all the evidence at hand. It is entirely irrelevant whether making this statement is a help or a hindrance in furthering his reputation. But the kind of usefulness required for the judgment is usefulness determined by the problem itself. Following out the plan of action (research) dictated by his belief that Caesar crossed the Rubicon and his need for understanding other events in history, this belief shows its usefulness in preparing him for further experiences and in simplifying and integrating the evidence that this action leads him to uncover.

Because usefulness was thus interpreted by the pragmatists, at least when they were writing most carefully, it is unfair of their opponents to say that pragmatism was just a manifestation of American commercialism masquerading as epistemology or a corollary of the American "philosophy of getting ahead." It might be fairer criticism to go to the opposite extreme, in fact, and to say that the pragmatist has to interpret usefulness in such a way that it ceases to have any distinctive meaning other than what everyone has heretofore always meant by "truth," for a true belief is one that satisfies doubt and answers the question that led to it. In other words, it might be said that the pragmatists trivialized the concept of usefulness so that "the useful" denoted primarily what met empirical tests and the requirement of coherence.

Be that as it may, however, pragmatism is an important doctrine because it at least shows how a naturalistic theory of mind, unlike epiphenomenalism, can account for the occurrence and testing of true beliefs. Pragmatism did more than any other movement in modern philosophy to bridge the gap that had opened between behavior and thought, practice and theory, value and fact, interest and objective truth. For doing so, it deserves a prominent place both in modern philosophy and in educational reform.

A NATURALISTIC THEORY OF FREEDOM

Pragmatism and the naturalistic or functional theory of the mind have thrown new light on the old problem of freedom and responsibility. If their theory of the bearing of foresight upon present behavior is correct, it is not possible to assume that the future is wholly determined by the past. It is not necessary to believe that the world is wound up like a clock and that man is but a passive spectator of a process that he cannot control. The universe, for the naturalist who is not a materialist, is still "in the making," and among the makers of the universe are the acting human beings whose behavior is guided by their foresight into what might occur but can be prevented or what might not occur but can be produced. For this to be possible, moreover, it is unnecessary to think of mind as something above nature, intervening in it, as the Cartesian dualist does. Intelligence guiding interest is a factor within nature that introduces novelty, teleology, and new departures.

When it is supposed that the mind is a substance existing outside nature, there is always the troublesome problem of how it acts. If it does not interfere with the processes in the body that would have occurred without it, mind seems a useless epiphenomenon. In such a case, it is supposed that the organism is but a machine and that the will (as an alleged faculty of the mind) is not free. On the other hand, if it is supposed that the will is free and that the mind is thus able to interfere with and redirect the activity of the body, there is the problem of the uniformity of nature; for this theory seems to deny the possibility of indefinitely extending our understanding of the human body in scientific terms by the discovery of laws describing its behavior.

The functional theory of mind, with its pragmatic emphasis upon the anticipatory and teleological character of mental behavior, is believed by its adherents to provide a way out of this dilemma and to make man's claim to be free compatible with the discoveries and postulates of psychology. The functional theory makes the will the active, executive aspect of mind.

Before using the word "will" as the name for a kind of thing in our minds that might be thought to be free or necessitated, the functionalist asks that we analyze the concept of will just as we have previously analyzed that of mind. On what occasions do we say that a person acted voluntarily, that is, as a consequence of an "act of willing"? Not on occasions when he acted capriciously, unpredictably, perhaps inexplicably. If that were the kind of action we call voluntary, "will" would be incompatible with morality and responsibility, for moral actions result from a disposition to act in accordance with some principle rather than from the variable impulses that cannot be foreseen from moment to moment. When a man we regard as morally good suddenly does some quite unexpected action, some action that we could not anticipate from our knowledge of his character, we tend *not* to consider this action as one that he has "freely willed" but to interpret it as due to some uncontrollable psychological quirk or overpowering urge for which he is not wholly responsible.

When we say that a man has acted voluntarily or freely and we hold him responsible for his action, we mean that he has not been coerced by another person. No one is twisting his arm when he does a free action. We mean also that he is not acting out of ignorance of the true state of affairs. A man is not freely committing suicide when he takes poison from a bottle marked "For headache." And lastly we mean that the action he performs is one that, to use a rather vague expression, "follows from the kind of man he is." A free action, in some sense, expresses a man's character.

What, then, is character? Character is more than reflex. It is a settled disposition to react to circumstances and needs with due regard to the symbolic value and implications of the stimuli and occasions of the action. A man's character cannot be manifested when he is under overpowering compulsion or coercion, nor is it expressed when he is laboring in ignorance of the important facts that he would be disposed to consider in making his decision. Only those actions that the person performs as a result of insight into the symbolic significance of the occasion are the actions for which he is held responsible; all other actions are his responses to coercion, either overt or subtle (from another person, from fear, from ignorance, and so forth). A free and responsible action is one that flows not from the momentary push of circumstances, but from his settled character based on insight into himself and his situation. Settled character is the moral corollary of insight into the potential ways of responding, combined with a disposition to prefer one kind of outcome to another.

A *good* character is one that is most responsive to the value-implications of each possible line of action, so that its choice is guided by intelligent comprehension of alternative values and a habitual preference for those lines of action that will most probably lead to approved values.

The actions for which men are rightly held responsible are the actions that could have been otherwise. This does not mean that we cannot find sufficient causal reasons for the acts that took place; for the moral conduct of men may be as determined as any other psychological behavior, and naturalists believe that it is. But the actions are free in the sense that the man who does them is not just a reacting victim of circumstance. Rather, through his insight into the whole situation and himself, integrated through a concept he has of what sort of being he is and hopes to become, he himself becomes one of the effective factors in the decision as to what his action will be. And because human acts are initiators of new causal chains in nonhuman nature and society, the free man is one of the determinants of the future.[13]

IMPLICATIONS FOR PSYCHIATRY AND MEDICINE

The theory that mind is a purely natural function to be understood by the methods of science has definite and fruitful implications for psychiatry and medicine. In studying mind, philosophers have frequently thought that they were leaving the world of nature behind them, and they drew a distinction between the natural sciences and the sciences of mind. A comparable distinction was drawn, in the medical sciences, between those parts of the art of healing that were concerned with men's bodies and those parts concerned with their minds. But with the development of the theory that mind is a mode of behavior, the naturalist bridges the gap between these two kinds of medical research and therapy.

The naturalist's functional theory enables us to look upon so-called mental illness in a new light. Instead of thinking that there is a sick or abnormal mind and that it is just a pity there is no drug that we can give to cure it as some medicines cure illnesses of the body, the psychiatrist now sees the patient as a single complex unity, not a compound of a physiological body and an immaterial, psychical entity called mind. Abnormal behavior, attributed long ago to possession by evil spirits and later to warped or diseased minds, is now thought of as simply a pattern of behavior gone wrong and not effectively adaptive and truly anticipatory. Mental illness is interpreted literally as behavior disorder, instead of the disordered behavior being looked upon as only a symptom of something wrong in a hidden mind or soul. This revised view has called scientific attention to the physiological conditions of so-called mental illness to a much greater degree than would be justified if it were thought that the body is merely the vehicle or prison of the mind. Psychosomatic medicine, even in its name, indicates this new outlook.

This theory has rich suggestions to make concerning the physiological basis of abnormal behavior, which was formerly attributed only to a diseased mind; it also renders intelligible some of the physiological effects of behavior disorders (such as anxiety). And it suggests new lines of therapy for pathological conditions that were once thought of as purely organic in origin. The physician often deals with physiological conditions that are results of behavior that has gone wrong, and frequently, these conditions and symp-

[13]This theory of freedom has been compared with others and evaluated in our discussion of freedom and the laws of nature; see page 235.

toms can be righted through aiding the patient to reconstruct the attitudes, habits, and expectations that have issued in this maladjustment. The organismic theory of life (see pp. 256ff.), when applied to human beings, provides a basis for understanding these bodily conditions due to states of mind without suggesting that the mind is a kind of diseased organ.

NATURALISM AND HUMANISM IN RELIGION

At first glance it might seem that a naturalistic system of metaphysics would be able to provide little or no place for religious values. It might seem that the naturalist, for whom science is the central fact, would have to derogate religion in the manner of Lucretius, who equated it with superstition. Because the religious emphasize the supremacy of faith over critical inquiry and because Christian orthodoxy has emphasized the conception of a God who stands at least in part above nature, it might be expected that the naturalistic metaphysics would be incompatible with any religious commitment.

Supernaturalism and naturalism are indeed incompatible. But the belief that there is *necessary* opposition between religion and science or between a metaphysics based on religion and a metaphysics based on science as the central fact, overlooks a very important consideration—that neither religion nor science is an eternal and unchanging attitude or set of dogmas. Although there are naturalists who are agnostics or atheists and religiously oriented people and societies who think of religion as simply a way of propitiating a capricious and petulant anthropomorphic god, neither of these narrow views is characteristic of, or essential to, the religious or the scientific philosophy of life:

The warfare which has been waged between science and religion at certain periods of history has been due to the fact that a premature naturalism or an antiquated religion or both have been current.[14]

Consider these two terms: "antiquated religion" and "premature naturalism." By the former, Lamprecht means religion that has not kept step with knowledge and enlightenment in the pursuit of value. By the latter, he means a naturalism that, like materialism, is too thin and dogmatic in its own way to do full justice to religious values.

Religious conceptions and attitudes, as we have seen, continuously change over long periods of time. Thus they take account of the insights gradually acquired in fields originally quite irrelevant to men's dealing with whatever they consider to be sacred. A narrow anthropomorphism is intellectually dead, but modern religious thinkers do not regard its demise as a loss to

[14]Lamprecht, "Naturalism and Religion," in *Naturalism and the Human Spirit*, p. 17.

religion—it is rather a sign that religion is intellectually responsible and responsive to the facts of life. However, naturalism and the scientific attitude also change and grow to take account of whole areas of fact and value that were formerly either denied or regarded as transcending nature and the scope of scientific investigation. It is therefore very unrealistic to speak of an opposition between them as though naturalism meant a narrow materialism and religion meant a narrow anthropomorphism. Redefinition of both is required before a meaningful analysis of their interrelations can be made.

In this chapter, the concept of nature has been redefined, just as the concept of science and scientific knowledge was broadened to make it more generally applicable. It remains to show how naturalistic philosophers modify some common conceptions of religion so that the alleged opposition between them and naturalistic views can be replaced by fruitful cooperation.

The naturalist, as we have seen, is interested in many kinds of experience that the materialist is likely to ignore or to deride as mere illusion and wasted effort. Among the experiences that naturalists have analyzed in recent years is the religious experience. Analyzing and being interested in a specific kind of experience, however, are very different from accepting the experience in question as a source of *truth*. The naturalist is committed to a method of constructing and testing hypotheses, a method that makes him unwilling to accept the truth of a religious dogma simply because he has an experience he calls religious. Having any experience is only the first stage of knowledge. Knowledge is a verified interpretation of experience.

No experience, the naturalist says, is necessarily to be taken at its face value. Just as an observation in a laboratory does not explain itself or guarantee its own truth apart from all hypothesis concerning its foundations, validity, and consequences, so also the religious experience—whose existence and value as lifting up the human spirit is not denied—must be investigated before its claim to *truth* is granted.

The naturalist decides that any alleged empirical vindication of supernaturalistic beliefs on the basis of the religious experience is invalid. He holds that the religious experience is not really an empirical test for the hypothesis of supernaturalism. In spite of that, he admits the *value* of the religious experience just as the supernaturalist does; and whereas the latter proposes one hypothesis to account for the characteristics and value of the experience, the naturalist proposes another. Let us compare them briefly.

The supernaturalist finds in the religious experience an awareness of a value transcending the ordinarily narrow values that the individual experiences in his daily life. In the religious experience, he truly says, man feels that he is in personal contact with a being greater than man that (or Who) supports his highest aspirations and saves him from triviality of purpose. In interpreting this experience, the supernaturalist asserts that this experience reveals, and is unintelligible without the belief in, a being that metaphysically embodies perfection. The values we experience in religious devotion are held to be mere appearances of another value, eternally realized and fully actual, whose antecedent existence supports man's religious and moral values and guarantees their final triumph in the world.

The belief in the complete antecedent embodiment of religious value in a perfect and eternal God is said by the naturalist to be an unwarranted interpretation of the experience. This belief, in Santayana's language, is merely comforting poetic imagery to rationalize and dignify the experience itself. Religion is a

... symbolic rendering of that moral experience which it springs out of and which it seeks to elucidate. Its falsehood comes from the insidious misunderstanding that clings to it, to the effect that these poetic conceptions are not merely representations of experience as it is or should be, but are rather information about experience or reality elsewhere.[15]

Dewey says essentially the same thing: the values experienced in religion do not

... depend upon some prior complete embodiment—as if the efforts of human beings in behalf of justice, or knowledge, or beauty, depended for their effectiveness and validity upon assurance that there already existed in some supernal region a place where criminals are humanely treated, where there is no serfdom or slavery, where all facts and truths are already discovered and possessed, and all beauty is eternally displayed in actualized form.[16]

If such dualistic, perfectionistic hypotheses are rejected, as the naturalist does reject them, what is there in the religious experience that gives it its value? Not the cognitive claim the theologian makes but the emotional and moral significance of the experience itself. If the experience has any informative value, the valuable information we get from it is information about ourselves, our potentialities and ideals. The religious experience, says Dewey, is not a foundation for faith in a specific kind of metaphysical truth called theological. It is the experience of a faith valuable in itself as

... the unification of the self through allegiance to inclusive ideal ends, which imagination presents to us and to which the human will responds as worthy of controlling our desires and choices.[17]

This kind of experience need not be induced by prayers and fasting or by the act of worship, although it may be. The value of the experience is its consequences for our attitude toward ourselves and others. The religious experience lifts us out of narrow concern with ourselves and vividly presents

[15]George Santayana, *Reason in Religion* (New York: The Crowell-Collier Publishing Co., 1962), p. 14.
[16]John Dewey, *A Common Faith* (New Haven, Conn.: Yale University Press, 1934), p. 49. Quoted by permission.
[17]*Ibid.*, p. 33.

ideals and undreamed-of possibilities. The integration and harmonization of our otherwise divisive and dispersive concerns around some central goal of aspiration is its justification and warrant. Because the values that are relevant in the evaluation of the experience are social and human, this view of what is essential in religion is commonly called "humanism."

But why, one may ask, should humanism be thought of as a religion, or why should the experience as the humanist interprets it be considered a religious experience? Anti-religious naturalists, as well as philosophers with a more affirmative appreciation of the usual and typical forms of religion, say that humanists misuse the word "religion" when they apply it to an entirely different kind of activity and experience having different psychological characteristics, metaphysical presuppositions, and emotional consequences. If by "religious" we refer to an attitude toward transcendent perfect reality, as distinguished from concern with ideals to be achieved by men's working together in nature, it is not religious. Humanism makes no claim that there is a God who supports our aspirations or rewards our efforts. *God*, says Dewey, is a name for a system of values, not a name for a person or thing. The word *God* "denotes the unity of all ideal ends arousing us to desire and actions."[18]

We are in the presence neither of ideals completely embodied in existence nor yet of ideals that are mere rootless ideals, fantasies, utopias. For there are forces in nature and society that generate and support the ideals. They are further unified by the action that gives them coherence and solidarity. It is this *active* relation between ideal and actual to which I would give the name "God."[19]

Dewey admits that many people will not wish to use the word "God" in this way, and few humanists have followed his usage. Some humanists who join Dewey in rejecting the notion of a transcendent God do not follow him in discerning forces in nature that support man's ideals. For them, nature is utterly indifferent to men's aspirations and men should defiantly assert human values without any theological or metaphysical corollaries at all.

Matthew Arnold and Bertrand Russell have pointed out the "indifference" and even "enmity" of nature to man's highest aspirations. Russell sees man as an accident of nature that has, in some unknown way, risen above its source in value and dignity but not in power. Russell calls on man not to slavishly deify the power of nature and worship it as a god or to project his yearnings into an imagined god who, he might wish to believe, can secure his triumph over the ruthless natural forces that will destroy him. Russell calls on man "to sustain alone, a weary but unyielding Atlas, the world that his own ideals have fashioned despite the march of unconscious power."[20]

[18]*Ibid.*, p. 42.
[19]*Ibid.*, pp. 50–51.
[20]Bertrand Russell, "A Free Man's Worship," in *Mysticism and Logic* (New York: David McKay Co., Inc., 1918), p. 57. Used by permission of George Allen & Unwin, Ltd.

Thomas Henry Huxley, who, a generation earlier, had been one of the men most responsible for the acceptance of Darwin's theory of evolution, likewise rejected the belief that nature supports our highest aspirations; but he also criticized those philosophers who urged a revision of our moral ideas into such a form that they could be promoted by the "blind forces of nature." Many evolutionists believed not only that the theory of evolution could explain the origin of moral codes in the social struggle for survival but also that in the theory of evolution they could find moral guidance. They argued that right action is action that leads to survival or that helps to prepare the way for a being (such as Nietzsche's Superman) in some way better than man. Adapt and survive, they said, or make way for those who can. Huxley, on the other hand, believed that this was really an excuse for immorality. Instead of the Golden Rule and the ideal of being one's brother's keeper, it leads to the Nietzschean commandment, "That which falleth, that shalt thou also push." He so opposed the ethical implications drawn from the study of nature that he wrote:

Let us understand, once for all, that the ethical progress of society depends, not on imitating the cosmic process, still less in running away from it, but in combatting it.[21]

Russell and Huxley do not appeal to a being outside of nature—a transcendent God—for help in finding the right and in securing human values, and their essays leave him an orphan in the universe. Nature produced him, but nothing in nature cares for him, and there is nothing in nature that will sustain him. Man is absolutely alone.

This, according to other naturalists who combine a broader conception of nature with modernism in religion (see p. 351), is too narrow a conception of both nature and moral value. Man is a part of nature, and it would be unintelligible, they say, to suppose that nature had produced a being with interests and needs wholly unsupported in the natural process in the broadest sense, which includes both the minds of men and their society and culture.

They therefore attempt to formulate metaphysical theories through which they can see man as more at home in nature than Russell and Huxley were willing to concede. For this purpose, they have proposed metaphysical interpretations of religion without supernaturalism, insisting rather on the immanence of the divine in nature. Perhaps the most typical of these is the belief that the words "god" or "deity" can be responsibly used for a tendency, a process, or a goal in nature, which is evolving, reaching higher levels of integration on which new and higher values and consciousness of new ideals can emerge. For such a philosophy, God is—as in Dewey's usage—the name given to the tension between the ideal that can come to be and the actual.

---

[21]Thomas Henry Huxley, "Evolution and Ethics" (1893), in *Selections from the Essays of T. H. Huxley*, ed., Alburey Castell (New York: Appleton-Century-Crofts, 1947), p. 109.

BIBLIOGRAPHY

General Works

Dewey, John, *Experience and Nature*. New York: W. W. Norton & Company, Inc., 1929.

————, *Reconstruction in Philosophy* (1921). New York: New American Library, Mentor Books, 1950.

Krikorian, Yervant H., ed., *Naturalism and the Human Spirit*. New York: Columbia University Press, 1944.

McCarthy, John W., *The Naturalism of Samuel Alexander*. New York: King's Crown Press, 1948.

Murphy, Arthur E., "Naturalism and Philosophic Wisdom," in *Reason and the Common Good*, eds., W. H. Hay, M. G. Singer, and A. E. Murphy. Englewood Cliffs, N. J.: Prentice-Hall, Inc., 1963.

Pratt, James B., *Naturalism*. New Haven, Conn.: Yale University Press, 1945.

Sellars, Roy Wood, *Evolutionary Naturalism*. La Salle, Ill.: Open Court Publishing Company, 1922.

On Perception

Hahn, Lewis E., *A Contextualistic Theory of Perception*. Berkeley: University of California Press, 1942.

Miller, David L., "The Nature of the Physical Object," *Journal of Philosophy*, XLIV, No. 13 (June 19, 1947), 352–59.

Murphy, Arthur E., "Objective Relativism in Dewey and Whitehead," and, "What Happened to Objective Relativism," in *Reason and the Common Good*, eds., W. H. Hay, M. G. Singer, and A. E. Murphy. Englewood Cliffs, N. J.: Prentice-Hall, Inc., 1963.

Oliver, W. Donald, "The Logic of Perspective Realism," *Journal of Philosophy*, XXXV, No. 8 (April 14, 1938), 197–208.

Robinson, Daniel S., ed., *Anthology of Recent Philosophy*, Part 3. New York: Thomas Y. Crowell Company, 1929.

Robischon, Thomas, "What Is Objective Relativism?" *Journal of Philosophy*, Vol. 55 (1958), 1117–32.

Naturalistic Theory of Mind

Hook, Sidney, ed., *Dimensions of Mind*. New York: The Crowell-Collier Publishing Co., 1961.

Mead, George Herbert, *Mind, Self, and Society*. Chicago: University of Chicago Press, 1934.

Morris, Charles W., *Six Theories of Mind*. Chicago: University of Chicago Press, 1932.

Santayana, George, *Reason in Common Sense*, Chap. 5. New York: The Crowell-Collier Publishing Co., 1962.

Pragmatism

Alston, William P., "Pragmatism and the Verifiability Theory of Meaning," *Philosophical Studies*, VI, No. 5 (October, 1955), 65–71.

Dewey, John, et al., *Creative Intelligence, Essays in the Pragmatistic Attitude*. New York: Holt, Rinehart & Winston, Inc., 1917.

Fisch, M. H., ed., *Classical American Philosophers*, Parts 1, 2, and 5. New York: Appleton-Century-Crofts, 1950.

Gallie, W. B., *Peirce and Pragmatism*. Baltimore: Penguin Books, Inc., 1952.

James, William, *Pragmatism*. New York: David McKay Co., Inc., 1907.

———, *The Meaning of Truth*. New York: David McKay Co., Inc., 1909.

Leonard, Henry S., "The Pragmatism and Scientific Metaphysics of C. S. Peirce," *Philosophy of Science*, IV, No. 1 (January, 1937), 109–21.

Lewis, C. I., *Mind and the World Order* (1929). New York: Dover Publications, Inc., 1956.

Peirce, Charles S., *Chance, Love, and Logic*, ed., Morris R. Cohen. New York: Harcourt, Brace & World, Inc., 1923.

Robinson, Daniel S., ed., *Anthology of Recent Philosophy*, Part 3. New York: Thomas Y. Crowell Company, 1929.

Theory of Value; Philosophy of Religion

Beck, Lewis White, *Six Secular Philosophers*. New York: The Free Press, 1966.

Burtt, Edwin A., *Types of Religious Philosophy*, Chap. 11 (2nd ed.). New York: Harper & Row, Publishers, 1951.

Dewey, John, *Human Nature and Conduct* (1922). New York: Random House, Modern Library Edition, 1930.

Huxley, Julian, *Religion Without Revelation*. New York: Mentor Books, 1958.

Lamont, Corliss, *Humanism as a Philosophy*. New York: Philosophical Library, 1950.

Lippmann, Walter, *A Preface to Morals*. New York: The Macmillan Company, 1929.

Quillian, William F., *The Moral Theory of Evolutionary Naturalism*. New Haven, Conn.: Yale University Press, 1945.

QUESTIONS AND TOPICS FOR DISCUSSION

1. A prominent naturalist has said, "Nature produces spirit, just as soil produces flowers." Do you find this a good analogy?

2. Many naturalists claim that their philosophy is the best foundation for a democratic philosophy of life. Compare it, in this respect, with pluralistic idealism.

3. Is the naturalist, with his functional theory of mind, able to meet the criticisms in Chapter 12 of epiphenomenalism? Is the functional theory merely a disguised form of epiphenomalism? Can the functional theory meet Ryle's criticisms in Chapter 11?

4. "The naturalist's theory of nature is more like that of the pluralistic idealist than like that of the materialist." Discuss.

5. Materialists deny that naturalists have any right to claim science as a support for their metaphysics, because naturalists use teleological explanations. Discuss.

7. A hunter sees a tree trunk and shoots at it, having mistaken it for a bear. Does the objective relativist have to say, "It *was* a bear in relation to the hunter at that moment"? If he does have to say this to remain consistent with his theory, does not this constitute a *reductio ad absurdum* of objective relativism?

8. It is sometimes said that the theory of relativity in modern physics is a scientific corollary of objective relativism in philosophy. Point out the analogies between the two, and evaluate the comparison.

9. Discuss the naturalist's theory of freedom in the light of the argument of Chapter 9.

10. Does the naturalist have any legitimate right to use the word "God" to denote a natural process?

11. Santayana is said to have stated, "There is no God, and the Virgin Mary is His mother." Why should a naturalist like Santayana wish to preserve the ritual and liturgical aspects of a religion whose metaphysics he has rejected?

12. Compare naturalism and Cartesian dualism with respect to their use in the theory of mental hygiene and psychiatry.

13. An idealist might say: "I have been treated very unfairly in this book. The authors discussed my theory and dismissed it. Then they discussed scientific method, and then gave an exposition of naturalism as if it were in some way more 'scientific' than idealism. I insist, on the contrary, that my theory is as consonant with scientific method and with the results of science as naturalism is. The position of the chapters on naturalism in the book gives the naturalist an unfair advantage over the idealist." Evaluate this argument and complaint.

14. Of the types of metaphysical theory thus far discussed, which one seems to you to be most nearly satisfactory? Why?

PART FOUR

FAITH,

INQUIRY,

AND

CONDUCT

Our study thus far has dealt principally with metaphysics and epistemology—attempts to understand the nature of man and reality and the bases of our knowledge of them. There is yet a third concern of philosophy that—from the standpoint of man's most vital interests —is more urgent than these. It is to understand man's place in the overall scheme of things and to try to establish proper guidelines for his conduct. Although this concern cannot be divorced from the other two, philosophic inquiry here acquires a more direct relevance to the concerns of everyday life. This brings us to the areas of religion and conduct.

Chapters 14 and 15 deal with the problems of religion. In Chapter 14 we shall examine the main theses of traditional religion, consider the conflict between religion and science, and note the relationship between theology and philosophy. We shall then take account of the challenge to supernaturalistic religion from atheistic existentialism. This challenge, we shall see, is countered by recent developments in radical theology (which presents its own challenge to orthodox religion), the most controversial being the Death of God movement.

Chapter 15 undertakes an examination of the main arguments for the existence of God, ranging from attempted proofs of His existence (the ontological argument) to appeals to the nature of religious experience (mysticism). Although serious objections can be brought against all these arguments, we find in William James' discussion of the "will to believe" a forceful defense of the right to accept religious beliefs on faith, under carefully specified circumstances.

In Chapter 16 we turn to the discussion of types of value, the relationship of values to facts, and the relationship of value theory to ethics. Our central concern is to determine whether disciplined inquiry has a legitimate role to play in these latter two areas. Two issues in particular require discussion: (a) the question of the ontological status of values, and (b) the question of the linguistic status of judgments of value. Evaluation of the main objections to objectivism (Plato) and cognitivism (ethical naturalism and intuitionism) leads us to the conclusion that although there are important differences between the subject-matters of science and value theory, the method of hypothesis does have an important role to play in the fields of value and ethics.

14 THE RELIGIOUS HYPOTHESIS

THE "CENTRAL FACT"

The central fact for the supernaturalistic theist (henceforth, supernaturalist) is the religious experience. His basic analogy is that there is a being who stands to the entire universe in a relation like that in which man stands to some parts of it that he cares for and controls. The fundamental thesis of supernaturalism is that in order to understand the world of nature and man and history, it is necessary to see them in relation to what is higher than nature or man or history.

The doctrines of religion, therefore, have pre-eminent significance in the thinking of supernaturalists. Experience as a whole can be understood, they say, only when interpreted in a context of metaphysical principles that a religious person accepts on faith. It follows that there may be various metaphysical theories that are species supernaturalism, depending upon the specific religious doctrines that are accepted and elaborated as metaphysical theses. We shall be concerned primarily with the kind of supernaturalism that grows from the conviction that some form of Christian theology is true and that the truths of this theology are truths that any adequate metaphysics must accept and elaborate.

The basic *philosophic* beliefs of orthodox Christianity are:

1. There are some experiences of great and permanent value that cannot be fully understood if seen only as results of physiological, psychological, or social causes. Their understanding requires an acknowledgment that they are evidence of a being above or beyond the realm that can be understood scientifically, that is, nature.

2. What is above nature and is the cause of nature and the object of man's religious experience is God, a personal being who created the world. Evidence for the existence of God is to be found in the study of both nature and human nature and in the interpretation of religious experience considered as a revelation of God.

3. Man, in addition to his animal nature, is also a spiritual being. Man is

to be understood both in his relation to other natural beings and in his relation to God. God's purpose in human existence is more fundamental than the individual's purposes, which are often vain, but God sustains man's ethical and religious conduct.

4. Man's spiritual being makes him superior to his position in the natural course of events in time. This suggests that the essential spiritual element in man, his soul, is immortal.

5. Man's spiritual being is not completely determined by events in the course of nature, whether physical, psychological, or social. Man is more than "the sum of his yesterdays" and is not wholly a victim of natural circumstance. He has real freedom to seek out and to fulfill the pu poses of God, which are implicit in his creation. Man can make use of this freedom in a religiously significant way, however, only with the help or grace of God.

6. Values, especially moral values, are inherent and central characteristics of reality. In acting morally or in pursuing the higher values, man attunes himself to the ultimate reality in things, but in acting selfishly or immorally, he alienates himself from God and falls below his proper status in reality.

7. Man's growth in the experience of values is incomplete if it is restricted to secular values, even if it includes the highest moral, aesthetic, and intellectual values. There is a positive value in religious activity itself, in which man comes to acknowledge God as the supreme value of existence and to see that whatever worth he and his concerns have is derived ultimately from the supreme value of God.

8. There is justifiable faith that God as the maker of the universe and as its moral governor will establish His Kingdom in which the earnest pursuit of the supreme value will be made consonant with felicity or blessedness.

It is readily seen that these beliefs are incompatible with naturalism. They have been formulated in many ways. In the form just given, they are not restricted to Christianity or even to the Judaeo-Christian tradition. Theologians of some of the other higher religions could subscribe to them; they do not state what is *specifically* Christian in religion. In order to distinguish the theological from the philosophical content of Christianity and Christianity from other religions that have many of the same philosophical foundations it is necessary to add to these philosophical statements some other statements having a more explicitly doctrinal content. Such statements of the dogmas of the Christian churches concerning the divinity of Christ and His mission in the world are formulated in various creeds, confessions, and articles of faith, which most sects take as the foundation of their specific religious rites.

DEVELOPMENT OF THE THESES OF RELIGION

Unlike specifically religious beliefs, philosophical theses expressing in full generality the basic tenets of a philosophical world view based on religion were slow in arising in the history of thought. Religious beliefs, although accepted as referring to something eternal, "the same yesterday, today, and forever," do change with the changes in the intellectual and moral atmosphere of a society. The earliest conceptions of God and of His relation to man are very different from the refined metaphysical doctrine just listed.

In primitive religions, man's belief in the *numinous*, or the sacred, included belief in impersonal power, such as *mana*, individual personal spirits in things, such as *anima*, and individual personal beings who transcend natural objects, or *gods*.[1] The activity of the divine or numinous reality was evidenced chiefly in unusual events, which men feared, or in any portentous events (such as birth and death, war, harvesting) where men felt their own impotence. Men believed that the divine reality could be coerced by magic as well as solicited and propitiated by prayers and religious rites. Many anthropologists believe that both religion and science, as we know them, descended from primitive man's concern with the numinous, the control of it by magic being gradually replaced by control through the techniques of applied science; and the solicitation and persuasion of it by prayer and ritual was the germ of the later development of religions as we know them.

The numinous was originally thought of as a superior natural force, frequently inimical to man or at least indifferent to his aspirations. Evidence for the divine was found in storm and earthquake, famine and plague. The gods, which were only one species of the numinous reality, were thought of as having human form (the doctrine of *anthropomorphism*). They were originally distinguished from man by their superhuman power. They were regarded as having both human vices and virtues in a magnified degree.

Only later did this narrow anthropomorphism give way to the notion that God has only the highest human characteristics in a magnified degree, without the baser human characteristics of anger, lust, and caprice. In the later parts of the Old Testament, we see this change in the conception of God from that of a rather irresponsible and jealous oriental potentate to that of God as the wise and just father of the human family; and in the New Testament, this refinement is carried still further until it is said, simply, that "God is love."

Primitive gods were not only capricious and often inimical to man but also strictly limited in scope. Each place had its own god (*numen loci*), and each tribe its own tutelary deity. Belief in these local, tribal gods is known as *henotheism*. (Henotheism differs from monotheism in that the former refers to a group's belief in the god supreme *for it*, whereas the latter refers to a group's belief in a god supreme for it and for all men. *Polytheism* denotes the belief in more than one god.) Under henotheism, each god was a deity whose care was limited to a very small portion of the human race. When the Old Testament says, "Thou shalt have no other gods before me," it does not mean that Jehovah is the only god; it does not assert monotheism so much as henotheism,

---

[1]For the meaning of some of these terms, see V. F. Calverton, ed., *The Making of Man*, Part V (New York: Random House, Modern Library edition, 1931).

warning the Children of Israel to remain true to *their* god and not to worship the gods of the surrounding tribes.

As the narrowly anthropomorphic aspects of the primitive conception of gods were gradually replaced by a more elevated spiritual conception, henotheism and polytheism gave way to monotheism, the belief that there is only one god. Monotheism is the basis of two important characteristics of higher religions. First, it frees the conception of God from any narrow limitation to a particular social group or geographical region. It thus brings an element of universalism into religion, inspiring the belief that "our God" is the real God of all men and that it is our religious duty to spread His gospel to all men. Thus, tribal religion is replaced gradually by an ideal of one religion for all mankind. And second, in freeing the conception of God from tribal limitation, monotheism makes the conception of the individual's relation to God more direct and personal. God is not the god of this or that tribe or even of all tribes, but is the god of *each person*, who can and ought to seek him individually so as to comprehend his own religious and moral duty.

This pattern of change from physical anthropomorphism to the conception of God as a divine personality without human form—from polytheism to monotheism, from tribal to universal religion, and from the religion of social group-activity to religion of the individual—can be traced through most of the higher religions. Although men think of their gods as eternal, their thoughts about gods reflect their time and circumstance. The give up one conception of God for a better one. In Whitehead's words, "The progress of religion is defined by the denunciation of gods. The keynote of idolatry is contentment with the prevalent gods."[2]

If the existence of God is thought of as a hypothesis for metaphysics, this continuous change in details of the conception is precisely what we should expect. Although men do not begin to philosophize about God until fairly late in the history of a religion, philosophy then refines and clarifies the conception in two ways. First, it performs a critical examination of the religious practices current in a society. One can see this in Plato's criticism in the *Republic* of the popular religious myths and practices of his day. Second, it integrates the concept of God with other concepts of metaphysics, so that the concept of God becomes a category for metaphysics as a whole, not just a conception restricted to the language and outlook of religion itself. This can be seen in many philosophical systems that use the concept of God as an explanatory principle without any religious overtones except the name itself.

One instance of a widespread religious doctrine holding that a conception of God as traditionally formulated is the ultimate and final truth is sometimes called *fundamentalism*. This is the belief that the Bible is the true and final

[2]Alfred North Whitehead, *Adventures of Ideas* (New York: New American Library, Mentor Book, 1955), p. 18. By permission of The Macmillan Company, copyright 1933.

revelation of God to man, that the Bible is the divinely inspired and dictated word of God, that the Bible is equally and uniformly inspired in all its parts, and that any revision or modification of the conception of God presented in the Bible is sacrilegious, blasphemous, and heretical. Diametrically opposed to fundamentalism is the doctrine of *modernism*. It holds that the conception of God is subject to interpretation, because whatever knowledge of God man possesses is mediated through the changing forms of human experience. As our experience grows, says the modernist, we become cognizant of the limitations of the formulas and doctrines of theology that an earlier period has passed down to us. We can then improve more primitive conceptions so as to render theological hypotheses more adequate and significant for our own experience.

The development of modernism has been favored by the comparative study of religions. Comparison of the religious beliefs of different peoples shows that each people forms its own conception of God, suitable to the social and cultural conditions prevalent in that society or suitable to specific directions determined by the aspirations of the seers and prophets of that people. Comparison of the various conceptions of God and of the religious cultus of each people also reveals which elements of belief appear in all, or almost all, religions, and this provides some basis for the discovery of the philosophical content implicit in the specific religious content that distinguishes one sect from another.

These two conclusions of the comparative study of religion—the specificity of each people's conception of God and the generality of certain fundamental traits in various conceptions of deity—suggest to the modernist that the wise attitude to our own and to other religions is to see each of them as a partial, but to some extent distorted, view of what God really is. Thus modernists hold that Christianity is the most adequate of the various representations of God, but they believe that Christians can learn much of value about the nature of God and about valid religious practices from seeing what aspects of man's relation to Him have been emphasized and perfected in other religions.

Fundamentalists, of course, cannot take this attitude of tolerance, because they hold that they possess a view of God that is directly and infallibly given them by a special dispensation of God Himself. Thus their view cannot and need not be corrected in any detail.

THE "CONFLICT OF SCIENCE AND RELIGION"

Another factor favoring the development of modernism is the interaction of science and religion. What is often referred to as the "conflict of science and religion" is to a great extent misnamed. There is, undoubtedly, a conflict between science and fundamentalism, just as there is a conflict between sci-

ence and any body of doctrine claimed to be final truth. Science thrives on
the conviction that man does not have final knowledge about anything,
and that any doctrine, no matter what its credentials, should be subject to
inquiry and correction. When the fundamentalist insists that the world was
created in six days, for instance, there is a head-on collision with both the
attitude and the conclusions of science. There are many statements in the
Bible that are not consistent with the findings of modern science; and because
fundamentalism has so often been identified with religion as a whole, it has
seemed that there is a conflict between religion itself and science. This belief
has been very widespread, especially since Darwin's *Origin of Species* was
published in 1859; but similar beliefs in irreconcilable conflict are traceable
to early Greek religion and science.

Fundamentalism, however, is not equivalent to religion. It is one among
various hypotheses. The modernist holds that the concept of God and the
hypothesis of His existence must be made harmonious with the greatest
possible extent of our experience, and this experience includes science. Consider the following analogy. The Greek scientists and philosophers had a
conception of the atom, which they thought of as a hard little pebble of
matter. One can imagine a kind of "fundamentalist" in science who would
say that the modern conception of the atom is wrong because it does not
conform to that presented in the writings of Democritus. The "modernist"
in science, on the other hand, would say that the ancient conception of the
atom was adequate to the knowledge of nature that the Greeks had, but
since our knowledge of chemical and physical phenomena has grown, we
must either give up the hypothesis altogether or change it to be adequate to
our experience. Similarly with the concept of God. In earlier times men
thought of God as a tribal deity with anthropomorphic characteristics, and
this represented the most adequate conception available to them. But we
now have, or believe we have, a wider knowledge of nature and man. We
need a concept that will do the same intellectual and religious "job" for us
today that the concept of Jehovah did for the Hebrews. We shall call whatever
is competent to do that job by the name "God," although it will now be
represented in a somewhat different concept and hypothesis from what was
represented by the concept of Jehovah for them. We can, on this basis, expect
that the concept of God will undergo still further changes as our experience
and knowledge continue to change.

There is no conflict between the facts of science and religion. The sciences
and religion deal with different things. Science studies the connections of
one fact with another; religion is the appreciation of the relation in which
men believe they and the whole world stand to something above and beyond nature—a relation transcending those studied in the sciences.

Nevertheless, there may be a conflict between a metaphysics or philosophy
based on religion and one based solely on science. A fundamental belief of
the philosopher who takes science as his central fact and nature as his root

metaphor is that everything in the universe (or above it, if that notion is allowed) can be subjected to scientific study. Such a philosophy does not admit that there is any dualism in the universe, with the facts of science on one side and the objects of religious faith on the other.[3] Such a dichotomy is claimed in the metaphysics of supernaturalism. Hence there is a dispute concerning the relative adequacy of a metaphysics based on religion and of a metaphysics based on science.

Metaphysical theories based primarily upon a religious outlook, however, usually do make room for science, just as those based upon science frequently acknowledge the values embodied in religion. But they dispute about the structure of the metaphysical system. Those with the religious experience as central explain science in the light of supernaturalism, generally holding that science deals with a "lower order" of reality than the divine and that the study of science contributes at least indirectly to man's awareness of his relation to what is above the facts of nature. Those who take scientific experience as central attempt to account for the facts and values of the religious experience without appealing to a metaphysical dualism of God and nature as its foundation.

PHILOSOPHY AND THEOLOGY

Religion is an attitude of mind and a mode of conduct predicated upon the acceptance of theses or dogmas. Religion is not an intellectualistic attitude of inquiry and tentative acceptance of hypotheses; it is an attitude of active faith, showing itself in willingness to act with enthusiasm in accordance with this faith. Because philosophy is primarily inquiry, questioning, and investigation, the philosophical attitude is quite different from the religious attitude, even though a man can entertain the articles of faith as metaphysical hypotheses when he is deliberately philosophizing and accept them on faith as dogmas of his religion when he is carrying out his religious devotions and practices.

Religion is quite distinct from theology. Theology is the study or inquiry into the existence and attributes of God and into His relation to man. Theology is an intellectual exposition and defense of theses accepted as articles of faith in religion. Theology is thus much more like philosophy than religion is. To the extent that the theologian is an open-minded investigator of God who does not commit himself irrevocably to drawing certain conclusions set before him by a religious institution, the theologian *is* a philosopher.

Theology is divided into at least two parts: natural and revealed. *Natural theology* is concerned with evidence of God's existence and attributes found in a study of nature. It argues that the best explanation of nature is to be

[3] This is the thesis of naturalism. See Chapters 12 and 13, especially pages 289ff.

found in the hypothesis of the existence of God. *Revealed theology* is an elaboration of articles of religious faith in the light of the religious experience and religious texts regarded as God's special revelation to man.

If the evidence for the existence of God is drawn largely or exclusively from natural theology, the supernaturalism reached is usually some form of *deism*—the belief that God is the creator or designer of the world but not a personal agent who shows His care for man by revealing Himself or intervening in the course of nature or human affairs. If the evidence for the existence of God is found in revealed theology, the theological conclusion most generally reached is *theism*—the belief that God is a personal being in part immanent in the world and in part transcending it, caring for man and revealing Himself to man in religious experience, scripture, miracles, or incarnation in human form. Deism regards God as the Author of the world, as a kind of "constitutional monarch" of the world, or as an "absentee landlord" for the world; theism considers Him as more adequately represented in the symbol of a loving Father who instructs and guides man.

Natural and revealed theology are usually thought to be consistent with each other, but revealed theology is considered to go further than natural theology in the detail of its conception of God. This view of their relations to each other can be seen best in the philosophy of St. Thomas Aquinas (1226–1275). According to him, the human intellect, by its own powers and without aid of supernatural revelation, can logically assure itself of the existence of God. (In the next section we shall see some of the ways in which Aquinas believed it could do so.) It leads us to sure knowledge of the existence and the metaphysical attributes of God—His omnipotence, omniscience, omnipresence, perfection, and infinity. But only faith and its elaboration in revealed theology can lead to certainty about the theological attributes of God, such as His grace, His trinitarian personality, and the other specific characteristics by which the Christian conception of God differs from those of other religions. The function of philosophy is to be a handmaiden for theology (*ancilla theologiae*) and to prepare the way for faith (to be *praeambula fidei*), which is made perfect only by the acceptance of the revelation God gives to man. What we learn from one is perfectly consistent with what we learn from the other:

The knowledge of naturally known principles is instilled into us by God, since God Himself is the author of our nature. Therefore the divine wisdom also contains these principles. Consequently whatever is contrary to these principles, is contrary to the divine Wisdom; wherefore it cannot be from God. Therefore those things which are received by faith from divine revelation cannot be contrary to our natural knowledge.[4]

[4]From the *Summa Theologica* of St. Thomas Aquinas, Part I, trans., the English Dominican Fathers (London: Burns, Oates & Washbourne, Ltd., 1924), p. 14. Used by permission of the publisher and of Benziger Brothers, Inc., New York, American publishers and copyright owners.

But suppose that the conclusions of philosophy are inconsistent with faith claiming to be justified by revelation. Here we have a conflict of theology and philosophy. There are two ways in which such a conflict could be resolved. The Catholic theory, based on St. Thomas Aquinas, would hold that the philosophy was spurious; the theology of modernism would be more likely to conclude that the revelation was spurious. Let us consider each possibility.

According to Catholic theory, reason (as expressed in philosophy) is consistent with revelation, but if in any case it seems to be inconsistent with it, then that is evidence that what claims to be reason is not reason but error. This means, then, that there is only one true philosophy. Consider this statement by Pope Pius XII:

It is well known how highly the Church regards human reason, for it falls to reason to demonstrate with certainty the existence of God, personal and one; to prove beyond doubt from divine signs the very foundations of the Christian faith; to express properly the law which the Creator has imprinted in the hearts of men; and finally to attain to some notion, indeed a very fruitful notion, of mysteries. But reason can perform these functions safely and well, only when properly trained, that is, when imbued with that sound philosophy which has long been, as it were, a patrimony handed down by earlier Christian ages, and which moreover possesses an authority of even higher order, since the Teaching Authority of the Church, in the light of divine revelation itself, has weighed its fundamental tenets, which have been elaborated and defined little by little by men of great genius. For this philosophy, acknowledged and accepted by the Church, safeguards the genuine validity of human knowledge, the unshakable metaphysical principles of sufficient reason, causality, and finality [teleology], and finally the mind's ability to attain certain and unchangeable truth.

Of course this philosophy deals with much that neither directly nor indirectly touches faith or morals, and which consequently the Church leaves to the free discussion of experts. But this does not hold for many other things, especially those principles and fundamental tenets to which We have just referred. However, even in these fundamental questions, we may clothe our philosophy in a more convenient and richer dress, make it more vigorous with a more effective terminology, divest it of certain scholastic aids found less useful, prudently enrich it with the fruits of progress of the human mind. But never may we overthrow it, or contaminate it with false principles, or regard it as a great, but obsolete, relic. For truth and its philosophic expression cannot change from day to day, least of all where there is question of self-evident principles of the human mind or of those propositions which are supported by the wisdom of the ages and by divine revelation. Whatever new truth the sincere human mind is able to find, certainly cannot be opposed to truth already acquired, since God, the highest Truth, has created and guides the human intellect, not that it may daily oppose new truths to rightly established ones, but rather that, having eliminated errors which may have crept in, it may build truth upon truth in the same order and structure that exist in reality, the source of truth. Let no Christian, therefore, whether philosopher or theologian, embrace eagerly and lightly whatever novelty happens to be thought up from day to day, but rather let him weigh it with painstaking care and a balanced judgment, lest he lose or corrupt the truth he already has, with grave danger and damage to his faith.

If one considers all this well, he will easily see why the Church demands that future priests be instructed in philosophy "according to the method, doctrine, and principles of the Angelic Doctor [Thomas Aquinas]," since, as we well know from the experience of centuries, the method of Aquinas is singularly pre-eminent both for teaching students and for bringing truth to light; his doctrine is in harmony with divine revelation, and is most effective both for safeguarding the foundation of the faith, and for reaping, safely and usefully, the fruits of sound progress.[5]

The Catholic theologian thus holds that philosophy and theology are consistent with each other, but should there be a conflict between what is claimed to be sound philosophy and theology, the philosophy is spurious:

As the superior science, theology *judges* philosophy. . . . It therefore exercises in respect of the latter a function of guidance or government, though a negative government, which consists in rejecting as false any philosophic affirmation which contradicts a theological truth. In this sense, theology controls and exercises jurisdiction over the conclusions maintained by philosophers.[6]

The ground for this conclusion is the central position occupied by religion in this system of thought:

The premises of theology are the truths formally revealed by God (*dogmas* or articles of faith) and its primary criterion of truth the authority of God who reveals it. . . . Though, as St. Thomas points out, the argument from authority is the weakest of all, where human authority is concerned, the argument from authority of God, the revealer, is more solid and powerful than any other.[7]

The opposite course would be followed by modernism. It would hold that although religion is an attitude of faith rather than of inquiry, it is the business of the theologian to proceed like the philosopher in attempting to formulate a hypothesis that will cover all the facts and values in the most adequate and parsimonious way. Because of the variety of revelations to which different religions appeal, it would prefer to make philosophical reasoning the criterion by which the alleged revelations should be judged. It does not deny that God can and does reveal Himself; but it holds that no alleged revelation is self-supporting or self-evidently valid. Consider the modernist's attitude toward the Bible as the medium of God's revelation to man. Modern critical studies have shown inconsistencies among its various parts; historical scholarship and scientific study have shown inconsistencies between it and other facts established by sound historiographical and scientific procedures. This means to the modernist that we cannot reasonably accept the entire Bible as the dictated word of God. On the other hand, however, this does not mean to the modernist that we must reject the Bible's religious message

[5]Pius XII, *Humani Generis*, §§29–31. From the English translation published by the National Catholic Welfare Conference (Washington, D. C., 1950).

[6]Jacques Maritain, *An Introduction to Philosophy* (New York: David McKay Co., Inc., 1931), p. 126. Quoted by permission of David McKay Company, Inc.

[7]*Ibid.*, p. 125.

because of its factual inaccuracies. He takes a middle course; he maintains that the Bible contains an authentic "deposit of faith" but that men must use their God-given reason to judge and weigh its authenticity. Usually he comes out with a quite different conclusion from that of the fundamentalist, so different that it is sometimes disputed whether modernism in theology is Christian in anything but name.[8]

IMPLICATIONS FOR VALUE THEORY

According to the supernaturalist, the world cannot be adequately understood as only a physical world, the values of which are subjective responses of the human organism. The perfection of God necessarily implies that His work will not be mere brute fact but will have meaning and value. Thus, the supernaturalist is likely to be an objectivist in the theory of values—to hold that values have objective metaphysical being.

The objectivism based on this theory holds that values and the laws of value are divinely instituted. The moral law, for instance, is not to be inferred from men's mundane experience of how best to get along with their fellows, nor is it to be deduced from pure reason. The moral law is revealed to man (as in the Ten Commandments), and it ought to be obeyed because it is the World of God. Whereas primitive religions put much emphasis upon God's rewarding virtue and punishing vice, conceptions of heaven and hell are not absolutely essential parts of religious belief, and many religions do not have them. These religions tend to emphasize rather the harmony of the world of fact and value, so that the man who loves God and does His will has the Kingdom of God within him.

Primitive religions generally emphasize the arbitrariness and power of God, so that their adherents usually think right is right *because* God commands it. This doctrine seems to underly many of the tabus in the earliest parts of the Old Testament, and is effectively criticized by Plato in the *Euthyphro* (see p. 13). In the more subtle metaphysical theories of the nature of God, as found in later parts of the Old Testament, in the New Testament, and in Greek philosophy—whence it later passed into the Christian tradition —the doctrine is reversed. Instead of an action being right because God commands it, God commands it because it is right, and God is by nature the moral governor and the font of all value.

Supernaturalists further hold that the highest values are not the values of morality and beauty and intellect but that there is a specifically religious

---

[8]Fundamentalism and modernism are prominent opposing movements in Protestantism, Catholic modernism having been condemned by the Papacy toward the end of the nineteenth century. The official Catholic view, however, is not that the *simplest* and *most direct* interpretation of all parts of scripture is necessarily the correct one; see the Encyclical letter *Humani Generis*, just quoted, §§38 and 39, for the Catholic doctrine on free and literal interpretation of scripture.

value that can be appreciated only through living a life in which one feels himself to be sustained by God in seeking eternal values. The theological moralist says that the love of God will be evidenced in one's moral conduct and in the inward joy of his life; but these moral and hedonistic consequences are not the essential and ultimate values by which religion is to be justified and judged. The ultimate values are above our lives and circumstances, and man must free himself from his involvement in the things of this world in order to reach them. This may end in monasticism and asceticism; but it may also be a stage in our experience that enriches and deepens our appreciation of the world itself and of others who are then regarded as our brothers because all are children of God.

IMPLICATIONS FOR THE PHILOSOPHY OF HISTORY

Human life, according to the supernaturalist, must be understood in the light of what is above nature and not merely as a product of blind natural forces. Organic evolution is thought of as manifesting a divine purpose; to an even greater degree, from the dawn of religions, human history has been interpreted as due in large measure to the plans and acts of God in His relation to man. Every religion has its own account of the creation and subsequent history of man. Each account manifests the particular relationship in which human affairs are thought by that religion to stand to God's plan. In the earlier anthropomorphic stages of tribal religion, the agency of God in human affairs was seen in extraordinary and miraculous events and prophecies, in which God was supposed to express His wrath or vengeance or care for some particular man or His chosen people. Primitive history usually takes the form of myth, in which gods and men fight alongside one another or fight against each other.

As the religious conception is refined in the direction of a more spiritual, universalistic theology, the agency of God in history comes to expression in subtle philosophies of history. Christian theology is associated with the philosophy of history formulated by St. Augustine (354-430) in his *City of God*. For Augustine, there are really two histories—one, the history of the city of earth, dealing with man as a natural political organism, and the other, the history of the City of God, dealing with man as a spiritual being who has fallen from God's grace by sin and who is predestined to find his way back to the grace of God. The former is secular history, and a study of it will show, according to Augustine, that it is not self-explanatory. It requires interpretation in accordance with the pattern of man's spiritual history of the Fall and Redemption. The destiny of man lies in his discovering that he is pre-eminently a citizen of the City of God. Men seek false and unworthy purposes in striving for status as citizens of the city of the earth; it matters not whether Rome or Carthage wins, for both are doomed to decay in time.

Despite Augustine's occasionally generous estimates of the achievements of paganism, only the coming of the Kingdom of God has genuine religious significance and historical value for him.

Many diverse philosophies of history are associated with the theology and metaphysics of Christianity, but all have some features common to this Augustinian doctrine. They all see in secular history a higher plan and destiny than can be explained in terms of geography, economics, or politics. The greatest evidence of the contact between mundane history and a theological superhistory (*Heilgeschichte*) is found in the revelation God gives man in the supernatural and superhistorical teachings of Jesus. Reinhold Niebuhr, who is perhaps the leading philosopher of history in the Christian church today, says,

There are elements in the "behaviour" of history which point to a "hidden" source of its life. It is in that sense that history is meaningful but pointing beyond itself.[9] History after Christ [is] an interim between the disclosure of its true meaning and the fulfillment of that meaning.[10]

The fulfillment of that meaning is not to be found, according to Niebuhr, in some future historical event, such as the establishment of a temporal Kingdom of God on earth; the goal and meaning of history are outside the processes of time. The *Pilgrim's Progress* is only an allegory of man's fall and redemption in history; the man who fully understands the implications of his history does not await "some far-off divine event" or expect that Christ will return to earth at some future date, to set up His Kingdom. The world of superhistory is eternal and not in temporal passage at all. Man achieves the fulfillment of the meaning of history and thereby transcends time and history, by seeing it *sub specie aeternitatis*.

Niebuhr believes that the fulfillment of the meaning of history—even though it transcends the complexities and ambiguities of all historical processes—is relevant to the processes of historical change. But a more temporalistic interpretation of history, also from a Christian point of view, is found in the works of the English historian Arnold Toynbee. After surveying the rise and fall of societies, Toynbee believes he finds evidence that justifies the faith that there has been a gradual spiritual progress in mankind, the continuation of which is the only hope of civilization. This, he believes, can be secured only with the help of God:

. . . In the classic version of the myth [*Pilgrim's Progress*] we are told that the human protagonist was not left entirely to his own resources in the decisive hour. According to John Bunyan, Christian was saved by his encounter with Evangelist. And, inas-

---

[9]Reinhold Niebuhr, *The Nature and Destiny of Man*, Part II (New York: Charles Scribner's Sons, 1943), p. 67. Quoted by permission of Charles Scribner's Sons and James Nesbit & Co., Ltd.

[10]*Ibid.*, p. 49.

much as it cannot be supposed that God's nature is less constant than Man's, we may and must pray that a reprieve which God has granted to our society once [in the incarnation of God in Christ] will not be refused if we ask for it again in a humble spirit and with a contrite heart.[11]

THE EXISTENTIALIST'S CHALLENGE

Existentialism is a vast and amorphous position having ill-defined boundaries and doctrines. In some of its forms it is more an attitude of brooding despair than it is a philosophical theory. Although its darker regions are perhaps best left to the novelist and playwright to explore, there are problems of genuine philosophical interest and import discernible in that penumbral area. We shall comment upon just one aspect of the atheistic existentialism of Jean-Paul Sartre, in order to see what alternative it proposes to supernaturalism. (There are also theistic forms of existentialism, but we shall not consider them.)

The importance of existentialism in the present discussion will be clear if set against the background of the theory that religion arises from, and expresses itself in answer to, human needs. It has been argued, for example, by Freud and Henri Bergson, that religion originates as a defense against those mysterious and frightening aspects of the world that man does not understand. Helplessness before the forces of nature and the inevitability of death lead him to place a construction upon the universe that will assuage these fears and render him more secure. As Freud puts it:

. . . when the child grows up and finds that he is destined to remain a child for ever, and that he can never do without protection against unknown and mighty powers, he invests these with the traits of the father-figure; he creates for himself the gods, of whom he is afraid, whom he seeks to propitiate, and to whom he nevertheless entrusts the task of protecting him.[12]

An account of the origin of religious beliefs does not, of course, settle whether or not they are sound. Whether one concludes from such a theory with Freud that religion is an illusion or with Bergson[13] that religion needs a more reliable foundation, the important point is that critics and defenders alike have often agreed that religion answers to a human need to depend upon something higher and more powerful than man.

Now, a central theme of Sartre's existentialism is that man must face squarely the fact that there is no God and hence no higher power to depend

[11]A. J. Toynbee, *A Study of History*, abridged, D. C. Somervell (New York: Oxford University Press, Inc., 1946), p. 554. Quoted by permission of the publisher.

[12]From *The Future of an Illusion* by Sigmund Freud (New York: Liveright Publishing Corp., 1953), p. 42. By permission of Liveright, Publishers, New York.

[13]See Henri Bergson, *The Two Sources of Morality and Religion* (New York: Holt, Rinehart & Winston, Inc., 1935).

upon and that only by so doing can he lead an authentic existence free of self-deception. Man is alone in the universe, and each man is totally responsible for his personality. One cannot even appeal to objective values for guidance, for in the absence of God man is the sole creator of values. He is completely free—indeed, because he cannot choose to be otherwise, he is "condemned to be free." In this realization is the source of dread.

This is the import of the doctrine most often associated with Sartre's existentialism—*existence* precedes *essence*. According to the supernaturalist, who asserts the existence of a perfect being who creates all things, man's *essence* precedes his *existence*. Just as the artisan has a conception of an object before he fashions it, so, in this view, God had a conception of man's nature or essence before he created man.

But, Sartre argues, *this* view deprives man of total freedom. For it means that even if he has it within his power to make choices within a certain area, he does not have it within his power to determine what type of person he is. This is determined in advance by God. Man's essence is fixed before he comes into existence.

Sartre illustrates this by reference to the story of Adam and his eating of the apple. Adam's essence, he says,

. . . is not chosen by Adam himself but by God. Thus it is true that the act committed by Adam necessarily derives from Adam's essence and that it thereby depends on Adam himself and on no other, which, to be sure, is one condition of freedom. But Adam's essence is for Adam himself a *given;* Adam has not chosen it; he could not choose to be Adam. Consequently he does not support the responsibility for his being. Hence once he himself has been given, it is of little importance that one can attribute to him the relative responsibility for his act.[14]

In Chapter 9 we considered an example of a person exculpating himself for a criminal act on the grounds that being the type of person he was, he could not have done otherwise. He could not have chosen to do otherwise because his very character, from which his choices issue, was determined by causes external to him. To say that he (or Adam) could have done otherwise is to say in effect that he could have been a different person. But according to Sartre, if God created man, then man is not free to determine his own nature or essence. That has been predetermined by God. However, God does not exist; hence man's existence precedes his essence.[15] Men create their essence through their free choices and decisions—the ends they adopt and the goals they pursue. For this reason, each man alone bears full responsibility for being the person he becomes.

It is true, of course, that even if all this should be correct, it does not show

[14]Jean-Paul Sartre, *Being and Nothingness*, trans., Hazel E. Barnes (New York: Philosophical Library, 1956), p. 468. By permission of the publisher.

[15]See Jean-Paul Sartre, *Existentialism*, trans., Bernard Frechtman (New York: Philosophical Library, 1947).

that God does *not* exist. It may be that man is not completely free and that it is self-deception not to realize this. Sartre does present arguments specifically against the existence of God, but these arguments are philosophical and have little to do directly with existentialism per se. The following chapter will be devoted to evaluating arguments for the existence of God; therefore, we shall not comment upon them except to note that the soundness of the views we have been considering depends upon their soundness. Our concern has been to exhibit the challenge presented by existentialism: a challenge to man to overthrow his dependence upon fictitious higher powers and to rely upon his own resources and freedom in his engagement with the world. This challenge is found in one form or another in naturalism, humanism and existentialism. Whatever the merits of these positions, this challenge cannot be ignored.

NEW BEARINGS IN THEOLOGY. IS GOD DEAD ?

Santayana once caricatured Christanity as "one of these domesticated evils or tonic poisons, like the army [and] the government . . . all of them traditional crutches with which, though limping, we manage to walk."[16] He had in mind a conception of Christianity of the sort the existentialists rejected; a religion of myth, illusion, and self-deception in which emotional security is purchased at the expense of intellectual integrity. Radical or secular theology takes up the challenge of the existentialists directly[17] and denies the need for man to depend upon God. It frankly concedes that

. . . the whole schema of a supernatural Being coming down from heaven to "save" mankind from sin, in the way that a man might put his finger into a glass of water to rescue a struggling insect, is frankly incredible to man "come of age," who no longer believes in such a *deus ex machina.*[18]

It stresses that human resources and intelligence must be relied upon to solve man's problems:

God must not be asked to do what the world is fully capable of doing: offer forgiveness, overcome loneliness, provide a way out of despair, break pride, assuage the fear of death. These are worldly problems for those who live in this world, and the world itself can provide the structures to meet them.[19]

[16]Quoted from *Dialogues in Limbo*, 1948 edition, p. 158, by George Santayana, by permission of Charles Scribner's Sons.

[17]We shall in the next chapter consider another response to this criticism in William James' defense of the right to believe, in which he maintains that faith and intellectual integrity can go hand in hand.

[18]From *Honest to God*, by John A. T. Robinson, p. 780, © 1963, SCM Press Ltd. Published U. S. A., The Westminster Press, 1963. Used by permission of both publishers.

[19]William Hamilton, "Dietrich Bonhoeffer," *The Nation*, April 1965. From *Radical Theology and the Death of God*, copyright © 1966 by Thomas J. J. Altizer and William Hamilton, reprinted by permission of the publishers, The Bobbs-Merrill Company, Inc., p. 116.

Really to travel along this road of radical theology means that we trust the world, not God, to be our need fulfiller and problem solver, and God, if he is to be for us at all, must come in some other role.[20]

Radical theology does not simply modify the religious hypothesis in point of detail as modernism does (p. 356), it radically restructures it to fit the facts of what it calls a modern world "come of age."

As with existentialism, much of the thought and direction of this movement has roots in the anti-Naziism of World War II. For the existentialists, these roots lie in the resistance movement in France; for the radical theologians, they spring from the thought of a young German theologian, Dietrich Bonhoeffer, who was imprisoned by the Nazis and executed shortly before the war's end. But despite this continental influence and some important British contributions, there is a distinctly American character to one part of the movement—the death of God theology. Its place in theology might be likened to that of pragmatism within philosophy. For it, the religious hypothesis must not only be restructured but replaced with a new hypothesis—one that dispenses with God altogether. Following Bonhoeffer, it holds that God must not even enter as a "working hypothesis."

There are significant differences among those associated with radical theology, which has its moderate and extreme elements. But they are agreed on several points. One of them is the rejection of the traditional conception of God and the traditional arguments for his existence. Paul Tillich, whose work has been influential in this regard, sees this rejection owing in part to the rise of science.

Both the theological and the scientific critics of the belief that religion is an aspect of the human spirit define religion as man's relation to divine beings, whose existence the theological critics assert and the scientific critics deny. But it is just this idea of religion which makes any understanding of religion impossible. . . . A God about whose existence or nonexistence you can argue is a thing beside others within the universe of existing things. . . . It is regrettable that scientists believe that they have refuted religion when they rightly have shown that there is no evidence whatsoever for the assumption that such a being exists. Actually, they have not only not refuted religion, but they have done it a considerable service. They have forced it to reconsider and to restate the meaning of the tremendous word *God*.[21]

Hand in hand with this rejection of God as a being who answers to human needs in the manner of a cosmic father goes the categorical rejection of supernaturalism. As John A. T. Robinson says, supernaturalism

. . . can be the greatest obstacle to an intelligent faith—and indeed will progressively be so to all except the "religious" few. We shall eventually be no more able to

---

[20]William Hamilton, "The Death of God Theologies Today," *The Christian Scholar* (Spring, 1965). Also reprinted in *Radical Theology and the Death of God*, pp. 40f.

[21]Paul Tillich, *Man's Right to Knowledge* (2nd ser.) (New York: Columbia University Press, 1954). Reprinted as Chap. I of *Theology and Culture* (New York: Oxford University Press, Inc., 1954), pp. 4f. Quoted by permission of Oxford University Press.

convince men of the existence of a God "out there" whom they must call in to order their lives than persuade them to take seriously the gods of Olympus. If Christianity is to survive . . . there is no time to lose in detaching it from this scheme of thought. For, as supernaturalism becomes less and less credible, to tie the action of God to such a way of thinking is to banish it for increasing numbers into the preserve of the pagan myths and thereby to sever it from any real connection with history. As Christmas becomes a pretty story, naturalism . . . is left in possession of the field as the only alternative with any claim to the allegiance of intelligent men.[22]

In short, the denial of man's dependence upon God as traditionally conceived requires the overthrow of the whole supernaturalistic metaphysical structure of which that conception is a part.

But the death of god theologians, the radicals in the movement, do not stop here. They feel that the defection from orthodoxy, in order to be complete, must not merely shift to a different conception of God; it must completely dispense with God.

We have insisted all along that "death of God" must not be taken as symbolic rhetoric for something else. There really is a sense of not-having, of not-believing, of having lost, not just the idols or the gods of religion, but God himself. And this is an experience that is not peculiar to a neurotic few, nor is it private or inward. Death of God is a public event in our history. . . . This means that we refuse to consent to that traditional interpretation of the world as a shadow-screen of unreality, masking or concealing the eternal which is the only true reality.[23]

Despite this, they represent themselves as Christians and claim to be theologians. The obvious objection to this is that they are trying to have their cake and eat it too, trying to be Christians while denying Christianity.

This is a damaging objection, and it has not yet been directly met by these writers. Nonetheless, a clue to a possible reply to it is found in the claim by one advocate of this view that what distinguishes this position from atheistic humanism is expectation and hope.

Our waiting for God, our godlessness, is partly a search for a language and a style by which we might be enabled to stand before him once again, delighting in his presence.
But we do more than play the waiting game. We concentrate our energy and passion on the specific, the concrete, the personal. We turn from the problems of faith to the reality of love.[24]

Traditionally, the Christian virtues, including hope and love, spring from faith; this suggests that the death of God theologians seek faith through hope and love. If so, their movement, at heart, is less an abandonment of the

[22]Robinson, *Honest to God*, pp. 43 and 68, respectively.
[23]Hamilton, "The Death of God Theologies Today," *Radical Theologies and the Death of God*, pp. 46f.
[24]*Ibid.*, pp. 48 and 47, respectively.

Christian religion than a reversal—however far-reaching in its implications—of the priorities of its virtues. On the other hand, if one equates religion with theism, then their movement is (as they claim) a nonreligious Christianity, for it not only rejects the institution of the church and its forms but the belief in God that is the core of that institution. Its Christianity seeks expression not in faith and worship but in the spheres of ethics and the world.

In all this one can discern the influences of naturalism, humanism, and existentialism. Like the naturalists they reject the partitioning of reality into two separate domains; like the humanists they exhibit optimism about the possibilities of a successful encounter with the world's problems; like the existentialists they seek the meaning of life in, or at least through, man's existence. Unlike naturalists, however, they remain theologians; unlike humanists they reject atheism; unlike the existentialists they reject the pessimism of anxiety and dread. Their over-all position might be likened to Americanized existentialism. For all its paradoxes, it represents a vigorous response to many of the traditional objections to theology.

BIBLIOGRAPHY

Beck, Lewis W., *Six Secular Philosophers* (1960). New York: The Crowell-Collier Publishing Co., 1966.

Brightman, Edgar S., "An Empirical Approach to God," *Philosophical Review*, XLVI, No. 2 (March, 1937), 147–69.

Burtt, Edwin Arthur, *Types of Religious Philosophy* (2nd ed.). New York: Harper & Row, Publishers, 1951.

Grene, Marjorie, *An Introduction to Existentialism*. Chicago: University of Chicago Press, 1948.

Kaufmann, Walter, ed., *Existentialism from Dostoevsky to Sartre*. New York: Meridian Books, 1957.

————, *Critique of Religion and Philosophy*. New York: Harper & Row, Publishers, 1961.

Macintosh, Douglas Clyde, ed., *Religious Realism*. New York: The Macmillan Company, 1931.

Martin, J. A., *Empirical Philosophies of Religion*. New York: King's Crown Press, 1945.

Murchland, Bernard, ed., *The Meaning of the Death of God*. New York: Vintage Books, 1967.

Niebuhr, Reinhold, *Faith in History*. New York: Charles Scribner's Sons, 1949.

Santayana, George, *Reason in Religion*. New York: Charles Scribner's Sons, 1905.

————, *The Idea of Christ in the Gospels*. New York: Charles Scribner's Sons, 1946.

Smith, J. D., *The Teachings of the Catholic Church*. New York: The Macmillan Company, 1940.

Smith, John E. ed., *Philosophy of Religion*. New York: The Macmillan Company, 1965.

Stace, Walter, *Religion and the Modern Mind*. New York: J. P. Lippincott Co., 1960.

Wieman, Henry N., *Religious Experience and Scientific Method*. New York: The Macmillan Company, 1926.

QUESTIONS FOR REVIEW AND DISCUSSION

1. Comment on the following quotations:
   a. "He that takes away reason to make way for revelation puts out the light of both." Locke.
   b. "It is absolutely necessary that one be convinced of the existence of God; but it is not so essential that one demonstrate it." Kant.
   c. "For Him [Jesus] there was nothing supernatural, because for Him there was nothing natural." Renan.
   d. "Faith is the substance of things hoped for, the evidence of things not seen." St. Paul.
   e. "Religion is man's acute awareness of the realm of unattained possibility and the behavior that results from this awareness." H. N. Wieman.
   f. "Religion is the feeling of absolute dependence." Schleiermacher.
2. Compare the religious beliefs and practices found to be typical in an American city in 1925 with those of 1936. (See Robert S. Lynd and Helen M. Lynd, *Middletown* and *Middletown in Transition.* New York: Harcourt, Brace & World, Inc., 1929, 1937.) What do you think such a study would reveal today?
3. Describe the relationship between reason and faith in the Catholic philosophy. Comment on Bishop Sheen's statement, "The Church is in love with reason."
4. Why does religious argument so readily tend to use the appeal to authority? Must it do so?
5. Assess the following argument: The value of a scientific hypothesis has little to do with how it was arrived at (whether, for example, by deliberation, conjecture, or guesswork.) Similarly, the value of the religious hypothesis is undiminished by the fact that it evolved from superstition and myth.
6. What implications does the existentialist's conception of freedom have for our judgments of responsibility?
7. Does the expression "death of God" contain a category mistake? Explain.
8. Read a famous classic of nineteenth-century religious controversy, *The Essence of Christianity,* by Ludwig Feuerbach (New York: Harper Torchbook, 1957). How does Feuerbach's conception of "man is the God of man" (p. 83) resemble the views of modern radical theologians?
9. Read Nietzsche's *Thus Spake Zarathustra* (in any of several translations), especially Prologue, section 2; and Part 4, section 46. Compare what Nietzsche means by "God is dead" with the views of more recent radical theologians.
10. A reader might say: "The authors of this book make a great show of being 'fair' to religion, but they really show an antireligious bias by the very title of this chapter, viz., 'The Religious Hypothesis.' Anyone who speaks of the religious *hypothesis* shows either that he does not understand what religion is or that he despises it." Is this a just criticism?

15 CAN THE EXISTENCE OF GOD BE PROVED?

IS RELIGIOUS LANGUAGE MEANINGFUL?

It should be readily apparent that the objections the logical positivists brought against metaphysics can equally well be brought against the claims of theology. Similarly, the replies we made to these objections (Chap. 11) can also be made on behalf of these claims. Still, if the claim that religious language is devoid of significance could be made valid, it would vitiate *any* hypothesis about God's existence, his attributes, and his relation to the world.

A contemporary philosopher, A. G. N. Flew, arguing on grounds somewhat similar to the logical positivist's, challenges the significance of religious statements by a test of meaning, which he thinks they fail to meet.[1] The test consists of asking of a putatively meaningful assertion what would count against its truth. If nothing counters it, then it is not a genuine assertion. In other words, to assert that something is the case is equivalent to denying that something else is not the case (to assert, for example, that *it is* raining outside is equivalent to denying that it is the case that *it is not* raining outside). Thus if a given assertion can be shown not to rule anything out, that is, if it is compatible with any state of affairs, then it will have been shown not really to assert anything at all.

To illustrate his point, Flew relates a parable about two jungle explorers who come upon a clearing where flowers are growing. One of them asserts, and the other denies, that there must be a gardener who tends the flowers, so they set about to determine who is right. They watch closely, but no gardener appears, whereupon the "believer" qualifies his assertion to say that the gardener is invisible. They then enclose the plot with an electric

[1]A. G. N. Flew and A. MacIntyre, eds., "Theology and Falsification," in *New Essays in Philosophical Theology* (London: SCM Press, Ltd., 1955), pp. 96f. Reprinted with permission of SCM Press, Ltd., and The Macmillan Company, New York.

fence, patrol it with dogs, and so forth, and still there is no evidence of intrusion. The believer then qualifies his assertion further by claiming that the gardener is not only invisible but "intangible, insensible to electric shocks ... has no scent and makes no sound."[2] As this procedure continues, the initial assertion eventually dies a "death by a thousand qualifications"; for there is no longer anything that the believer will count against the assertion and hence no longer anything that it literally asserts.

Is the same true of theological assertions? Do statements like "God exists" and "God is good" really assert nothing at all? According to Flew, the way to answer this is to ask whether they rule anything out. The answer to this question is that they obviously do, because a person who asserts

1. God exists

will say that he thereby denies that it is the case that God does not exist. So there is one (nonempirical) state of affairs ruled out by his assertion. However, the critic is unlikely to be satisfied with this. He will insist that there must be something *else* ruled out by the assertion other than its strict negation. To this the theist may reply that the only states of affairs *necessarily* ruled out are those reported by propositions the denials of which are entailed by the initial assertion (a statement, which *must* be true if a given statement is true, is said to be entailed by that statement). Are there, first of all, any propositions entailed by 1? The supernaturalistic theist might hold that 1 entails such propositions as

2. Nature is purposive
3. Man has an immaterial and immortal soul
4. There is a higher order of reality than that known to science.

Therefore, 2 through 4 are the denials, respectively, of mechanism, materialism, and naturalism, so that if 1 is true, it rules out the states of affairs represented by each of these theories. The hypothesis that God exists would, in this view, be incompatible with the hypotheses of mechanism, materialism, and naturalism.

But now the statements formulating these theories are of such a degree of generality that—for purposes of settling the dispute between the supernaturalist and his critic—they are likely to be as problematic as the initial assertion that God exists. Each of them asserts a metaphysical thesis, and if one puts them to the same test as 1, their status as assertions can be questioned on the same grounds as 1 was. If the critic presses his case still further, it appears that now he will have to begin qualifying *his* assertion; he will require not only that a genuine assertion rule out its negation and the negations of any statements entailed by it but also that it rule out some *empirical*

2*Ibid.*, p. 96.

states of affairs. To be meaningful, he would have to say, a statement must at least be empirically falsifiable.

At this point several lines of reply are open to the supernaturalist. First, he may argue that because his assertions report nonempirical facts, their truth or falsity and evidence relating thereto must be established a priori—that to make a requirement that they be testable (at least in the sense of being falsifiable) by empirical means is to beg the question against him. Such a reply would open up all the issues dividing empiricism and rationalism, particularly those centering about the status of synthetic a priori assertions. This in itself would by no means establish the correctness of the supernaturalist's initial assertion; but it would mean that the issue between him and his critic (concerning the meaningfulness of 1) could not be settled without prior (or simultaneous) settlement of some of the most controversial problems in the history of philosophy.

Second, he might grant that empirical evidence is relevant to testing his hypothesis, in the sense that there are some empirical states of affairs that we should expect to be nonexistent if his hypothesis is correct, and insist that those states of affairs *are* nonexistent. What these are would have to be specified (one might be that there is continuous and unmitigated suffering in the world) and the relevant inquiries undertaken to see whether in fact they exist; but if this were done, the theist would be accepting his critic's challenge and contending that it can be met. Settlement of the issue between them would them have to await evaluation of the evidence.

Third, he might grant that empirical evidence is relevant but claim that the evidence is inconclusive and that so long as it is he is justified in holding to his belief. A person might, for example, count the existence of evil as evidence against the existence of God. He might furthermore be willing to abandon his belief in God if he were convinced that the world is more evil than good. But he might argue that at present the evidence is inconclusive and although it is unclear that there is a balance of good over evil in the world, it is equally unclear that the reverse is the case. Such a person would be in the position of holding the nonrationalist thesis 2 on page 386.

He might grant, as a fourth alternative, that empirical evidence is relevant (that is, that there are verifiable empirical states of affairs that the truth of 1 excludes) and furthermore that the evidence weighs *against* his assertion, but he might still defend the assertion on the grounds that is it part of the burden of faith to "believe the absurd." If he takes this line, his standpoint will be that of what we called irrationalism. Because this alternative removes the question of God's existence entirely from the realm of rational inquiry, we shall not discuss it in what follows.

Each argument discussed in the following sections develops along one or the other of these lines of inquiry. The first alternative is represented most clearly by the ontological argument, the second by the cosmological and teleological arguments, and the third by William James' defense of the right to believe. The moral argument, although it does not attempt to prove God's existence, is an a priori argument and thus fits best into the first category. The argument from miracles and those from religious experience, even though they are not all easily classifiable, appeal in different ways to verifiable experiences.

PHILOSOPHICAL ARGUMENTS FOR THE EXISTENCE OF GOD

In order to examine the metaphysical theory of supernaturalism, one must take an attitude quite different from that of religious faith. It is necessary, for such an examination, to suspend the normal belief in God's existence that perhaps most people in our society have, to regard the existence of God as a hypothesis, and then to weigh the evidence for and against the hypothesis. Such an attitude is difficult for many people who feel that true religious fervor and faith are incompatible with such a cold attitude of suspended judgment.

The religious attitude of faith—"the substance of things hoped for, the evidence of things not seen"—is utterly different from that of philosophical inquiry. Yet many of the greatest theologians, such as St. Thomas Aquinas, have recommended impartial philosophical investigation as a propædeutic or preamble to a still deeper religious faith. They believe that a thorough philosophical appraisal of the doctrine of the existence of God will prevent later doubts that might trouble the serenity of direct religious faith. Most of the classical arguments for the existence of God have been proposed by theologians and religious philosophers who did not require an intellectual proof to convince them that God exists. Most of them have held that the human intellect is capable of attaining theoretical certainty, by philosophical arguments, that God does exist; and they have held also that faith is compatible with the conclusions reached philosophically. They usually believed that faith also goes beyond the truths that can be established philosophically and that theology is thus more than sound philosophy but perfectly harmonious with it.

Philosophers and theologians have proposed arguments of the existence of God. It should be noted in advance that most of these arguments have usually been thought of as *proofs*. Most of them originated in an intellectual atmosphere favorable to the notion that it is possible to get metaphysical conclusions with as much certainty as rewards our efforts to arrive at scientific knowledge.

Chapter 11 pointed out reasons for concluding that what is ordinarily called proof is nowhere possible in a speculative field like metaphysics. Every metaphysical theory depends upon some particular interpretation of the broad reaches of our experience. No interpretation is the *only possible* one. Whether the arguments that follow or the criticisms of them are the more convincing turns upon the evidence cited and the logical validity of the inference and also upon answers to the question: Is the general intellectual framework of the philosophy in which the given hypothesis is proposed more acceptable than its alternatives? For example, in the case before us, does a given argument for God's existence, taken in conjunction with the general philosophical system of which it is a part, make our experience as a whole more intelligible than any other hypothesis?

Whether one's answer to these questions is affirmative or negative may depend to a great extent upon one's prior religious orientation and general philosophical outlook. It has been said, probably correctly, that no believer has ever been made an atheist by an argument against the existence of God and that no atheist has ever been convinced by logic that God exists. Nevertheless, if one does try to suspend faith in God, or predilections against the belief in God, one can then examine, with some fair degree of impartiality, the arguments that have been proposed and evaluate supernaturalism as a metaphysical theory.

The Ontological Argument

This is one of the most intriguing arguments in the history of philosophy. Lively controversy over its merits continues even today. It is a rationalistic argument designed to demonstrate God's existence a priori. It holds that there is at least one factual judgment that is a priori: God exists. It is called "ontological" because it proceeds from an analysis of the concept of God's being or nature. If the soundness of such an argument could be established, it would vindicate the whole rationalist enterprise against its empiricist critics.

The version of the argument we shall discuss[3] was set forth in the seventeenth century by Descartes, whose attempted proof of the existence of an external world we considered in Chapter 4. That proof presupposed God's existence, which means that if Descartes' arguments for God's existence fail, he has no way to establish the existence of the external world. One of his arguments for God was presented earlier (p. 86); this one differs from it because this argument does not involve the notion of causality.

According to Descartes, we ordinarily make a distinction between the existence of a thing and its essence or definition. I can define a mountain, for instance, without knowing or caring whether there is actually such a thing, because the essence of a mountain (that is, what any geological formation *would* be if it *were* a mountain) is independent of the existence of this particular kind of geological structure. But

I find it manifest that we can no more separate the existence of God from his essence than we can separate from the essence of a [rectilinear] triangle the fact that the size

---

[3]See the appendix of this chapter for a discussion of the two other main traditional versions of the argument.

of its three angles equals two right angles, or from the idea of a mountain the idea of a valley. Thus it is no less self-contradictory to conceive of a God, a supremely perfect Being, who lacks existence—that is, who lacks some perfection—than it is to conceive of a mountain for which there is no valley.[4]

The argument defines God as a perfect being, and a perfect being is one that possesses all perfections or positive qualities. These include the property of being real. Hence it follows that reality pertains to the definition of God. To say, "God does not exist," is as self-contradictory as to say, "Mountains exist, but no valley exists." As the contradictory of a self-contradictory proposition is necessarily true, it follows that "God exists" is a necessary truth, demonstrated by logic from the definition or essence of God.

The classical objection to the ontological argument was made by Kant, who rejected the claim that pure reason can give metaphysical truths. According to Kant, "exists" ("is real" or "has being") is not a predicate and hence cannot be part of the definition of anything.[5] If so, it cannot be part of the definition of God; therefore one cannot infer from the definition of God that he exists.

To say that existence is not a predicate is to say that although it may function *grammatically* like other predicates—such as "red," "heavy," and "soluble"—it does not function *logically*, as they do, to ascribe a property to things. That, for example, the sentences

1. Dogs bark
2. Dogs exist

function differently can be brought out by showing that they are not susceptible to the same analysis.[6] For 1 may be interpreted as saying either of the following:

1a. If there are any dogs, they bark
1b. There are dogs, and they bark

each of which is a synthetic statement and purports to convey an item of information about dogs. The two differ in that 1a leaves open the question whether there are any dogs whereas 1b does not. But we encounter problems if we try to analyze 2 in analogous fashion:

[4]From René Descartes: *Meditations*, p. 59, trans., Laurence J. LaFleur, © 1950, 1956, by The Liberal Arts Press, Inc., reprinted by permission of the Liberal Arts Press Division of The Bobbs-Merrill Company, Inc.

[5]Immanuel Kant, *Critique of Pure Reason* (1781), trans., Norman Kemp Smith (New York: St. Martin's Press; and London: Macmillan & Co., Ltd.), p. 505. Quoted by permission of the publishers.

[6]This analysis is patterned after that of C. D. Broad, *Religion, Philosophy and Psychical Research* (New York: Harcourt, Brace & World, Inc., 1953), pp. 177–83.

2a. If there are any dogs, they exist
2b. There are dogs, and they exist

because 2a is not an accurate translation of 2, since to say that dogs exist does not, like 2a, leave open the question whether there are any dogs. Moreover, whereas 2 is a factual assertion, 2a is a tautology and is true irrespective of what the facts are with respect to the existence of dogs. On the other hand, 2b consists of two statements that say the same thing. Unlike when we say that there are dogs *and they bark* (as in 1b), we are not conveying any new information when we say that there are dogs and then add *and they exist*. The "predicates" in 1 and 2, therefore, function differently. The first ascribes a property to dogs, the second merely signifies that there are dogs—not that there are dogs and additionally that they exist. Hence "exists," unlike "barks," is not a predicate.

But if existence is not a predicate, then it cannot be included in a definition (for a definition specifies a thing's essential properties). And if existence is not part of the definition of God, then there is no contradiction in denying that God exists and hence no reason to suppose that "God exists" is a necessary truth. In short, the fact that

3. God is perfect

may be interpreted as either

3a. If there is a God, he is perfect

or

3b. There is a God, and he is perfect,

which means that 3 *leaves open* the question whether there is a God. Therefore one cannot deduce, purely a priori from a statement of the nature of God as a perfect being, that he exists.

Arguments from the Impossibility of an Infinite Series of Conditions

A group of more common arguments for the existence of God depends upon the notion that because everything in the world is dependent upon other things, these upon still others, and so on, there must be one thing above the world that is not dependent upon anything else but is the condition of all others.

This argument has several types. One may argue from the existence of motion in the world to the concept of a Prime Mover, from the existence of contingent things to the concept of a Necessary Being, and from the existence of causes and effects to a First Cause. The logic of the three arguments is identical, so we shall discuss only one of the three. We shall take the last one, which is the most commonly used. It is usually called the "cosmological argument," because it assumes the existence of the cosmos, or world.

The argument is this. Everything that occurs has a condition that precedes it in time and is called its efficient cause.[7] And the cause has a cause; and the cause of the cause has a cause, and so on. The question is, how far can this series be continued?

In efficient causes it is not possible to go on to infinity, because in all efficient causes following in order, the first is the cause of the intermediate cause, and the intermediate is the cause of the ultimate cause, whether the intermediate cause be several, or one only. Now to take away the cause is to take away the effect. Therefore if there be no first cause among the efficient causes, there will be no ultimate, nor any intermediate cause. But if in efficient causes it is possible to go on to infinity, there will be no first efficient cause, neither will there be an ultimate effect, nor any intermediate efficient causes; all of which is plainly false.[8]

Therefore the series of causes cannot be infinite, and the series of causes must have a first cause, "to which everyone gives the name of God."

Let us put the same argument in a different form. No event can occur unless there is a sufficient reason for it. The sufficient reason for an event is the sum of all its causes, and the causes of the causes, and so on. If the series of causes of causes of causes is infinite, there is no *sum* of causes, and we could not say that *all* the causes of an event had occurred; for the infinite series is one without a first member and thus without a sum or totality. Therefore, if the series is infinite, there is no sufficient reason for anything; hence nothing will occur. But this is false; therefore the series cannot be infinite. Hence, there must be a first cause.

It should be noted that this argument assumes the objective reality and metaphysical validity of the principle of causation; causation is not here understood as simply regularity in sequences of events. This argument, therefore, cannot be employed by anyone who accepts the Humean analysis of causation (see pp. 223f.). This is not said in criticism of the argument, however, for it is quite possible to argue, and the followers of Aquinas do argue, that Hume is wrong. It is mentioned merely to call attention to the fact that the argument is not innocent of metaphysical assumptions. The argument is not a proof based *only* on the admitted fact that something happens.

Let it be granted that the concept of cause implies the concept of first cause. Then a serious objection, raised by Kant, can be brought against the

---

[7]Contemporary philosophers interpret the argument as implying, not temporal priority, but only ontological priority. See F. C. Copleston, *Aquinas* (Baltimore: Penguin Books, Inc., 1955), p. 118; and Richard Taylor, *Metaphysics* (Englewood Cliffs N. J.: Prentice-Hall, Inc., 1963), p. 94.

[8]From the *Summa Theologica* of St. Thomas Aquinas, trans., the English Dominican Fathers, Part I (London: Burns, Oates & Washbourne, Ltd., 1924), p. 25. Used by permission of the publisher and of Benziger Brothers, Inc., New York, American publishers and copyright owners.

argument. It says that the first cause is a being that must be assumed to be a cause of itself, for by definition, it is dependent upon nothing else for its being. Hence its being depends only upon its own essence or definition. That is, the concept of *first cause* is equivalent to the concept of *necessary being*, the existence of which follows from its definition. But unless the ontological argument is valid, we cannot infer *real* existence from the *concept* of a necessary being. Hence the crucial step in this argument is an ontological argument, and if the ontological argument fails, so also does any argument that includes it as an essential step.[9]

Still, one may say, "There's *got* to be a cause for things!" This is an entirely natural and understandable response. It seems that the human mind cannot form a conception of causes ad infinitum. But can we really succeed any better in trying to form a conception of an absolutely first beginning? Both conceptions are so far removed from the sure ground of experience that we cannot be certain that we have any clearer conception of a first cause than we have of an infinite series of causes.

In spite of this, most persons probably do find it easier to think of a first cause than to think of an infinite series of causes. We shall tentatively suggest two reasons for this: First, each of us is familiar with the experience of feeling our own activity, of at least seeming to be the cause of our own actions. I seem to myself to be a free agent, a cause of subsequent events but not the effect of previous events. Therefore I seem to myself to be a kind of first cause, and it is relatively easy to suppose that if there is a God, this is the way in which He acts. (That decisions may have causes is true but irrelevant here, for we are not attempting to discover whether the concept of a first cause is valid, but only why it seems clearer and more acceptable than the concept of an infinite series of causes.) Second, each of us is familiar with the symbolism of religion. Through it, we have a *name* for the uncaused cause. Although the *concept* of an uncaused cause is difficult to comprehend, the name "God" is easy to pronounce and to surround with the imagery of our religion. But there is no emotionally colored and traditionally accepted name for an infinite series of causes, nothing to obscure its logical complexity and difficulty. By having a proper name and imagery for the one but no proper name and imagery for the other, it is psychologically easier to accept the concept of an uncaused cause than to accept the concept of an infinite series of causes. It is possible that, by the rich imagery of the name of God, men have been blinded to the logical difficulties of the concept.

The Teleological Argument, or The Argument from Design

This argument, unlike the cosmological argument, is based upon the *particular kinds* and *organizations* of things found in the cosmos. It begins with the observation that things in the world seem to be designed for some purpose

[9]Kant, *Critique of Pure Reason*, p. 509.

and argues from that to the existence of a designer or artificer. Thomas Aquinas writes:

The fifth way [to prove the existence of God] is taken from the governance of the world. We see that things which lack intelligence, such as natural bodies, act for an end, and this is evident from their acting always, or nearly always, in the same way, so as to obtain the best result. Hence it is plain that not fortuitously, but designedly, do they achieve their end. Now whatever lacks intelligence cannot move towards an end, unless it be directed by some being endowed with knowledge and intelligence; as the arrow is shot to its mark by the archer. Therefore some intelligent being exists by whom all natural things are directed to their end; and this being we call God.[10]

Or consider the argument of the eighteenth-century British theologian Bishop Paley. Paley asks us to imagine a man walking in a desert and suddenly coming upon a watch. He will conclude rightly that some man must have devised the instrument; its parts would not have come together in this purposive form without some plan or design. Then he proposes an analogy: The universe itself is like a vast clockwork, and we must infer that it also was designed and planned by a supreme intelligence.

Kant, although not convinced by this argument, respected it:

This proof always deserves to be mentioned with respect. It is the oldest, the clearest, and the most accordant with the common reason of mankind. It enlivens the study of nature, just as it itself derives its existence and gains ever new vigour from that source. It suggests ends and purposes, where our observation would not have detected them by itself, and extends our knowledge of nature by means of the guiding-concept of a special unity, the principle of which is outside nature. This knowledge again reacts on its cause, namely, upon the idea which has led to it, and so strengthens the belief in a supreme Author [of nature] that the belief acquires the force of an irresistible conviction.[11]

With this recommendation, the argument requires more detailed study than we have had space to give to the others. The most thoroughgoing examination of the argument is by David Hume, in his *Dialogues Concerning Natural Religion* (1776), and some of the points to be mentioned are discussed in detail by him. We must ask four related questions about the argument. (1) Is the analogy a good one? (2) Is there really evidence of purpose in the universe? (3) What does the argument do with the evidence of lack of purpose in some parts of the universe? (4) Does purpose, if it is real, require an intelligent designer for its explanation?

Examination of the analogy—An analogical argument is one in which, from the relationship known to exist between two things, we infer a like relationship from one known thing to another, unknown thing. Thus $2:4 = 6:x$

[10]From the *Summa Theologica* of St. Thomas Aquinas, trans., the English Dominican Fathers, Part I (London: Burns, Oates & Washbourne, Ltd., 1924), pp. 26–27. Used by permission of the publisher and of Benziger Brothers, Inc., New York, American publishers and copyright owners.
[11]Kant, *op. cit.*, p. 520.

is an analogy; from it we can infer $x = 12$. In doing so, we do not have to raise the question of the degree of similarity between the 2 and the 6. In a nonmathematical analogy, like Paley's, we do have to raise this question. Is the world sufficiently similar to a watch, so that we can infer the existence of a being comparable to a watchmaker as its creator? From the world's similarity to a house, can we infer a Divine Architect? From its mathematical order, can we infer, as many have, that "God is a great mathematician"? A fertile imagination can see similarities amidst many differences. Shall we think of the world by analogy to an organism and then infer that it originated sexually? Or that it is like a work of art, so that there must be a Supreme Artist?

We may, or we may not. Whether we do so or not depends upon our prior faith that our particular analogy is a good one, and this depends upon what our central fact is. Each of us sees so little of the universe that we cannot be sure that any part of the universe—a watch, a house, an organism, a painting, a mathematical equation—is really a typical part of the universe as a whole. If the blind man who felt of the elephant's tail and inferred that the elephant was like a rope had used an analogical argument, he would have supposed that the cause of the elephant was not another elephant but a human ropemaker.

In spite of objections like these, and many more, Hume does not assert that the analogy is worthless. Hume's chief work on religion is in the form of a dialogue, and it is sometimes difficult to decide which of the speakers presents Hume's own point of view. Scholars disagree on what Hume's real attitude was, but there is evidence that he did believe that there was a being that bore a "remote analogy" to mind as we know it in man. But Hume remained critical of any specific analogy by which theologians might try to infer anything in detail concerning the nature and purposes of God.

Is there really purpose in the universe?—It may be argued that the evidence for purposive design in nature is overwhelming, whatever particular sector of it you examine. No one seriously argues, it will be said, that God is *really* an artist or an architect or a watchmaker; but because of the manifold evidences of design throughout the universe it may reasonably be inferred that there is an intelligent creative being. The evidence of purpose in the universe is of three kinds: (1) the rational intelligibility of things, (2) their adaptation to each other; and (3) their suitability to human purposes. We shall examine each.

1. *Intelligibility as evidence of purpose*—Things seem to be intelligently designed because they "fit" the way the mind works. Nature does nothing in vain—this fits the mind's law of parsimony. Everything that happens does have a cause—this fits the mind's law of causality. Nature is measurable—this fits the mind's mathematical abilities. The laws of nature can be expressed in elegant mathematical formulas, and highly complex computations give us knowledge of facts that have not been observed.

This argument is impressive. We should note, however, that it depends upon a realistic conception of laws—that there are laws that things obey and hence there must be a law-giver. We have seen earlier (pp. 213f.) that the words "law" and "obey" are ambiguous, and it might be that the admitted harmony of nature is due to the success we have in eliciting statistical generalities from a much larger mass of data that are not dependent upon or obedient to any realistically conceived law. The proponent of this argument will be quite willing to accept the realistic conception of scientific law and to reject the alternative conception just mentioned. But pointing out his assumption about laws does serve to show that his argument is dependent upon certain debatable metaphysical conceptions and is not a proof dependent merely upon the admitted fact that nature is regular and intelligible.

Another objection can be made to this view. The argument seems to suppose that there is a kind of Procrustean bed of unchangeable laws of thought, which exist eternally in the human mind, and that if things fit them, it is because they were designed and made so as to fit them. But it is at least as plausible to argue that the mind and its functions developed in a long evolutionary course along with our bodies, which evolved in such a way as to fit them to the conditions of the environment. If one takes this evolutionary argument seriously, then it appears that the intelligibility of things is a consequence of the mind's slow adaptation to things, rather than to the prior design of things so that they will be suitable to mental comprehension.

2. *Mutual adaptation as evidence of purpose*—There is much mutual adaptation of things. One need consider only our example of how bats guide their flight in darkness (pp. 205–8) to be impressed with the way different parts of a single organism are integrated with all the others; and a balanced aquarium is an example of the mutual adaptation of different organisms to each other.

Nevertheless, there is another hypothesis that will explain the adaptation of part to part and organism to environment. This is the hypothesis of evolution. According to Darwin's theory, animals and plants vary accidentally and spontaneously, or at least in random and unforeseen ways. There then ensues a struggle for survival among these organisms, and those whose variations facilitate their adjustment, including the adjustment to each other, will tend to survive and pass on their variations to their offspring, whereas those less well-adapted will be eliminated. This process, repeated generation after generation, leads to flowers and bees perfectly adapted to each other's needs, or plants and animals in a lake living in balanced harmony with each other. We can discern a direction in evolution toward increase in an animal's control over the environment, increase of interdependence of parts on whole, and increase of internal coordination.[12] But when we understand the process,

---

[12]See Julian Huxley, *Evolution: The Modern Synthesis* (New York: Harper & Row, Publishers, 1942), p. 576.

we do not need the concept of purpose or design in order to account for it.

It is sometimes said, against the sufficiency of this hypothesis, that it explains the "survival of the fittest," but not the "arrival of the fittest." That is, it does not explain how fortunate variations occur or how they are preserved during the earliest stages when their contribution to survival must have been insignificant. It is therefore argued that there must be a purposive agent responsible for the occurrence and perseverance of fortunate variations and that this shows itself in evolutionary progress.

The theory of evolution, it must be admitted, does not explain and does not even attempt to explain the origin of variations. Even so, however, the case for design is not very convincing. One bit of evidence against it must suffice: The great majority of mutations (distinct and inheritable variations of significant magnitude to function as factors in the struggle for survival) are deleterious to the survival of their possessors, whereas on the theory that they are designed or planned, we should reasonably expect the opposite.[13]

3. *Suitability to human purpose as evidence of design*—There is the common belief that nature is designed especially for human purposes. This view of purposes was more popular in the optimistic eighteenth century than it is today, but nonetheless, men sometimes still argue that all things were put on earth for their benefit. It we think of man as the goal of all things, then we may find much evidence in nature that all things suit his purposes—grass was made for cows to eat, and cows were made to give man milk, butter, and leather.[14] But if we look upon man as himself the product of evolution, we can easily argue that man survived because he took better advantage of the environment and adapted to what he found until he began to use his intelligence in adapting things to himself. It must be said again that such a counterargument does not rule out the hypothesis of design in nature. But it does suggest another good hypothesis, so that we cannot consider the argument from design as *proved* by the natural fitness of the environment to human needs and purposes.

Is everything designed? The problem of evil—Although most men prefer to look upon nature's marvelous organization, there is also much evidence of lack of organization. There is not only survival of the few relatively fit; there is extinction of the many less fit. There is degeneration as well as progress. There are things in the world that do not seem rationally explicable by men's minds, constituted as they are. There are mosquitoes and germs, rattle snakes and poison ivy, poverty and pain, which do not seem prima facie to indicate that nature was perfectly adapted to be man's home. There are evil purposes to which human beings subjugate the forces of nature, and one might sometimes wish, for instance, that nature were not so organized that atom bombs

---

[13]*Ibid.*, p. 465.

[14]For some amusing eighteenth-century examples of such arguments, see Ernest Cassirer, *Rousseau Kant Goethe*, trans., James Gutmann, Paul Oskar Kristeller, and John Herman Randall, Jr. (Princeton, N. J.: Princeton University Press, 1947), pp. 66f.

could work. There are rivalries and aggressions among men that show that they are far from being a happy and harmonious family.

How does the argument from design deal with these undisputed facts? Two ways have been proposed.

First, it is sometimes denied that these so-called evils really are evil. They are parts of a larger system of things of which Pope could say, "Whatever is, is right," and Leibniz could say, "This is the best of all possible worlds." Optimists have shown great ingenuity in explaining evil away. They say that we could not appreciate the good in the world unless there were evil with which to contrast it; that men are made better by having to struggle against evil; that wars are good because they promote national vigor. They are right in saying that at least some evils are disguised goods, and could we but see the whole of things, many other evils might appear to us to be necessary for some greater good that we do not suspect. We might even say, with F. H. Bradley, "This is the best of all possible worlds, for everything in it is a *necessary* evil."

Such optimism, even if justified, does not really meet the logical issue. *If* there is a god, then we might feel some assurance that the evil in the world would be set right in some "far off, divine event, to which the whole creation moves," as Tennyson expressed the optimistic sentiment. But in the argument for the existence of God, emphasis was first placed upon the salient goods and purposes in the world in order to show that the world was designed. Until we show that the design *does* exist, we have no right to discount or neglect the evidence of lack of design or to try to show that it must be interpreted as a part of God's hidden design; we must know that the design exists before we can avail ourselves of these *ad hoc* hypotheses. Whatever may be the recommendations provided by religious faith, we have no logical right to argue from only *part* of the evidence (the part that seem to show design), to conclude from this that the *whole* was designed, and only then to look at the other part of the evidence in order to explain it away.[15]

Second, a more daring and logically more cogent argument has been formulated by some recent philosophers, acting on a suggestion of Plato's. It is an attempt to resolve the paradox involved in the notion that an omnipotent and perfect God has created less than a perfect world, by denying the omnipotence of God. John Stuart Mill proposed to account for the evidences of design and purpose in the world by the hypothesis of a Designer and then to take the evidence of lack of perfect design as indicating that the Designer is limited or finite. Mill felt that infinite benevolence joined with infinite power is incompatible with the real evil in the world, and rather than give up the belief in the benevolence of God or close his eyes to the evil in the world, he denied His infinite power. Even though his hypothesis detracts from the

---

[15]Hume, in a speech he attributes to Epicurus (*Inquiry Concerning Human Understanding*, XI), gives the most effective version of this criticism of the use of the concept of God in answering questions about evil and disorganization.

power of God, it need not detract from His infinite worth; he regarded the
the requirement that what is worthy of worship must be omnipotent as a
vestige of a primitive worship of mere power—an attitude that grows out of
fear, not love.

This hypothesis, Mill believed, does not detract from the seriousness with
which one can take the religious outlook upon the world. Mill's conception
is not dogmatically optimistic, like the previously suggested solutions to the
problem of evil, and his view is sometimes called *meliorism*—the belief that the
world has a tendency to become better and that man ought to participate in
its betterment. This, Mill believed, strengthened the moral content of religious activity and faith.

One elevated feeling this form of religious idea admits of, which is not open to those
who believe in the omnipotence of the good principle in the universe: the feeling of
helping God—of requiting the good he has given by a voluntary cooperation which
he, not being omnipotent, really needs, and by which a somewhat nearer approach
may be made to the fulfilment of his purposes. . . . To do something during life, on
even the humblest scale if nothing more is within reach, towards bringing this
consummation ever so little nearer, is the most animating and invigorating thought
which can inspire a human creature.[16]

Does purpose imply design?—If it be granted that there are purposes in the
universe and that the universe itself has a purpose, does this imply that there
is a being that designed the universe? This is one of the most conjectural of
all questions in metaphysics, and no sure answer can be given to it. We have
evidence in our own experience to indicate that some purposes do imply
intelligent design, for the intelligent design in attaining purposes is often our
own careful plans. We do not have any absolute evidence, however, that the
purposive behavior of animals and even of plants is not due to at least a
very low order of consciousness and intelligence on *their* part. But this belief
is so speculative that it will not be acceptable to most people, especially when
extended to plants and the lower animals.

The more difficult question, however, is whether purposive behavior in
every case requires intelligence. Unless we assume that it does, then even
admitting purposes in nature will not suffice to guarantee that there is a
designer above nature. It might well be that purposiveness requires intelligence and consciousness only in the case of the higher animals and man.
Have we any right to regard human purposiveness, at least some of which
is predicated upon intelligence and design, as typical of *all* purposiveness that
we may believe exists anywhere in the universe?

Here is a question on which all intellectualistic argument must founder.
Those who accept the root metaphor or central fact on which religious philosophies are based will justify an affirmative answer by their faith that man is

---

[16]John Stuart Mill, *Theism* (1874), ed., Richard Taylor (New York, Liberal Arts Press,
1957), pp. 86–87.

a key to understanding the universe. Those who do not have this orientation will be more inclined to think that if there really are purposes in the universe apart from men's freely chosen purposes, they may be explained without the assumption that natural purposes always presuppose intelligent design. In either case, it is not a matter to be settled by argument so much as a question of basic orientation or faith.

The Argument from Miracles

Another common and popular argument for the existence of God is based upon the belief that there are events that occur against the law of nature and give evidence of a power above nature. Just as human beings occasionally break a law in order to do some good, the argument runs, God also breaks the law that He has ordained in order to reward or punish man or in order to give man a vivid awareness of His existence, power, and goodness.

Few things so excite men as the report of a miracle. For this reason, alleged miracles are not uncommon, and they provide a rich field for charlatans to prey upon the gullible. For this reason also, responsible theologians and religious institutions are very skeptical of reports of miracles,[17] and many an alleged miracle has been declared spurious by ecclesiastical authorities, even in cases where the alleged miracle had turned men's minds to religious matters and convinced them of the existence of God. David Hume, in his *Inquiry Concerning Human Understanding*, prescribed tests (like those used by a lawyer in determining the credibility of a witness) that a report of an alleged miracle must meet before it will be accepted by cautious and mature minds. He asks of every alleged miracle:

[Is it] attested by a sufficient number of men, of such unquestioned good-sense, education, and learning, as to secure us against all delusion in themselves; of such undoubted integrity, as to place them beyond all suspicion of any design to deceive others; of such credit and reputation in the eyes of mankind as to have a great deal to lose in case of their being detected in any falsehood; and, at the same time, attesting facts performed in such a public manner and in so celebrated a part of the world, as to render detection unavoidable[?][18]

Hume believed that no report of a miracle can pass these tests. But for the sake of argument, let it be granted that some reports of alleged miracles can do so. We still have to raise two questions. The first is the question of the miraculous nature of the unusual and unexplained event *called* a miracle. For an event to deserve this name, it is necessary that it should be inexplicable by the laws of nature. This does not mean that we are not able to explain it with our present knowledge; most events are miraculous, if that is all we

---

[17]Morris West, *The Devil's Advocate* (New York: William Morrow & Co., Inc., 1959) is an interesting account, in the form of a novel, of such skepticism and the inquiry it occasions.

[18]David Hume, *An Inquiry Concerning Human Understanding* (1748), Section 10 (New York, Liberal Arts Press, 1955), p. 124.

mean, and the more ignorant we are, the larger will be the store of miracles. No, the miraculous event is one that is *in principle* inexplicable, *except* on the assumption that its cause is outside the order of nature. It must be an event of such a character that the most complete knowledge of nature will *never* suffice to explain it. Only if we can eliminate the *possibility* of any natural explanation can we be content with the miraculous interpretation of the event, that is, with the belief that the event transcends all laws of nature both known *and unknown* and is due directly to the intervention of God.

Many events that once seemed miraculous are now understood scientifically. Many of the most stupendous and impressive miracles performed in perfect good faith by holy men and reported accurately by honest people can now be explained in terms of the principles of psychosomatic medicine, which regards a person's emotional attitude, including his faith, as one of the scientifically relevant conditions for understanding his bodily state. Even in cases where specific explanations of this kind have not been found, most scientifically oriented thinkers would not care to go so far as to say that they will never be discovered; they do not wish to block the way of inquiry.

We have here a conflict between faiths—the faith in a God who can break the laws of nature and the faith in science, which says that whatever happens can eventually be explained in terms of laws of nature. One might say that unless a man already believes in God, he cannot believe in miracles. The occurrence of events called miraculous is not evidence for the existence of God, but the belief in the existence of God *is* the reason why the unusual events are called miraculous.

Our second question turns upon the religious significance of the belief in miracles. A person who accepts the argument from design, taking as his premise the grand order of nature, cannot argue that evidence for God's existence is found in cases which seem *not* to be under the inexorable laws and beneficent plan of nature. If God's design is real and perfect, then an event that is not consonant with the laws of nature's design is impossible; if the evidence of God's existence is found in the unusual and extraordinary events, then the argument from design is weakened:

> You bring down Heaven to vulgar Earth;
>   your Maker like yourselves you make,
> You quake to own a reign of Law, you
>   pray the Law its laws to break.[19]

There is one way in which the argument from design might be reconciled with the argument from miracles. It might be said (and it is true) that the appeal of the argument from design presupposes a good bit of intelligence, and the inquiring mind is more likely to be impressed by evidences of design

---

[19]The Kasîdah of Hâjî Abdû el-Yezdî, *nom de plume* of Sir Richard Francis Burton (Portland, Maine: Thomas B. Mosher, 1908), pp. iv, 14.

than by alleged miracles. And it might be said (and it is true) that miracles are more likely to impress and arouse the wonder and awe of the man who is ignorant of the subtlety of nature's intricate workings. Hence it has been suggested that God could and would reveal Himself in many ways, adapting His revelation to the mind of the beholder—a miracle here, a law there.

This argument might be a convincing one in theology if we assume as its premise that God exists; then one would expect that "God fulfills himself in many ways." But the purpose of the argument from design and of the argument from miracles is to *prove* the existence of God, not to *assume* it in order to show that there is design or that there are miracles in the world. If neither argument alone can prove it, it might be supposed that each of them would strengthen the other. But this is not true here, because the two arguments start out with incompatible assumptions—one, that nature as a whole is designed, and the other, that it is not.

The Moral Argument

This argument states that the existence of God is a necessary, or at least a justified, assumption for understanding and supporting moral experience. We shall examine the form of the argument defended by Kant.

If the existence of God is connected in any way with moral experience, Kant believed that it had to be a logical rather than an emotional connection. Yet we also know that Kant rejected the doctrine that the existence of God could be proved by natural theology. Having rejected the ontological, cosmological, and teleological arguments, Kant devised a moral argument based on reason, not on emotion.

Morality, he held, requires man to strive for the highest good, which is the perfect proportion of happiness to virtue.[20] Man alone cannot attain this highest good, yet it is his duty to strive for it. If we are to take seriously our obligation to try to achieve it and not explain obligation away as a mere chimera, the highest good must be at least possible of attainment, although not necessarily by man's unaided efforts; it therefore implies that for imperfect man, there is some power superior to man that can effect it. The only agency that could make it actual, Kant believed, is God, regarded as the moral governor of the universe. Therefore, if the moral obligation under which man lives is not illusory and if he accepts it, he must accept its corollary of God's existence.[21]

Our acceptance of this postulate of morality, Kant continues, does not give us any right to claim that we have knowledge of the existence, nature, purposes, and attributes of God. Indeed, it is not knowledge of any kind. God's existence is a matter of faith but of rational faith rather than an

---

[20]The argument is given in Immanuel Kant, *Critique of Practical Reason*, trans., Lewis W. Beck (New York: Liberal Arts Press, 1956), pp. 128–36, 150.

[21]*Ibid.*, p. 150; see L. W. Beck, *A Commentary on Kant's Critique of Practical Reason* (Chicago: University of Chicago Press, 1960), p. 253.

emotional faith. For this reason, although Kant presents his argument in an a priori rational form, he writes in a skeptical vein about all metaphysical theories based upon, or directed toward proving, the existence of God. *Knowledge* that God exists is not available to man; Kant does not even regard such knowledge as desirable from the point of view of the effects it would have on our conduct, for it would make our morality merely a calculation of likely consequences (for instance, the consequences of an action in getting us to heaven) and not a ready obedience to what we see as our duty, wherever it may lead.[22] But on the other hand, the postulate that God exists is not the product of wishful thinking with all its subjectivity and variability from man to man.

Kant was unwilling to admit that hypotheses, as we have described them, have a legitimate place in metaphysics; because metaphysical knowledge is not a priori, with demonstrative certainty, he believed that there is no metaphysical knowledge at all and that our a priori knowledge does not and can not extend farther than our knowledge of the world of appearances. For this reason, he surrendered all claim to speculative metaphysics considered as a kind of knowledge. Because he believed that no logical proof of God's existence is possible, he concluded that belief in it could not be admitted as a truth into theoretical metaphysics but could at most be taken as a postulate of a practical metaphysics of the moral life.

Most recent philosophers agree that metaphysical propositions cannot be demonstrated, but those who believe in the possibility of metaphysics nevertheless hold that metaphysical hypotheses are useful for rendering our experience as a whole intelligible, just as scientific hypotheses cannot be demonstrated yet render parts of our experience intelligible and manageable. Morality is just as much in need of intellectual explanation and defense as any other kind of experience. And if the hypothesis of the existence of God renders moral experience intelligible, that is precisely the kind of credential we require for any metaphysical hypothesis. Kant's rigorous demands on metaphysics, perhaps, made him more skeptical of its results than was warranted.

This last point provides a way of summarizing the discussion of the moral argument. If metaphysics is to throw intelligible light on our experience, the moral experience is certainly a sector of the whole that must be rendered intelligible by suitable metaphysical hypotheses concerning the nature of things in general. It is an important and central experience, and the understanding of it is as important as that of any other kind of experience. If analysis of moral experience shows—as Pascal, James, and Kant believed—that the hypothesis that God exists is required or indicated in any validation of moral experience, then morality is evidence for the hypothesis that God exists.

---

[22]Kant, *Critique of Practical Reason*, pp. 151–53.

The Argument from Religious Experience

Earlier we distinguished rationalism and empiricism according to their views about the origin of knowledge. But *both* rationalists and empiricists are "rationalists" in a broader sense; they think that rational or intellectual processes—the making of inferences, generalizations, and so forth (whether as part of an a priori deductive method like Descartes' or as part of the scientific method of the empiricist)—are essential to the acquisition of knowledge. Rationalism in this broader sense is contrasted, not with empiricism, but with *nonrationalism*, which asserts either or both of the following:

1. that some things can be *known* independently of the intellect,
2. that some things may justifiably be *believed* in the absence of a favorable balance of evidence gathered by the intellect.

Both rationalism and nonrationalism in this broad sense may be distinguished from *irrationalism*, which asserts that some things ought to be believed even in the face of countervailing evidence afforded by the intellect.

Thus far we have dealt with attempts to establish God's existence as the conclusion of an argument, that is, through the use of the intellect. However, many philosophers, both historical and contemporary, who believe that God exists, reject all such arguments. They agree with the agnostic and atheist that one cannot prove or demonstrate God's existence. Still, they maintain that God's existence can be known or justifiably believed. They base this claim upon an appeal to religious experience. Insofar as they take this line, they are nonrationalists. (There also are and have been irrationalists, who concede that the evidence weighs against the hypothesis that God exists but who nonetheless profess belief). Mysticism provides an example of a defense of 1; William James, in an argument defending the right to believe upon insufficient evidence, provides an example of a defense of 2.

By religious experience, one means such experiences as mysticism, prayer, devotion, and worship. Mysticism claims that there is an experience that is direct and intuitive evidence of a God in whom the mystic and perhaps the whole world merge; there is unification into the perfection and oneness and splendor of a supreme and eternal God. Such an experience can be brought on by religious ritual and ceremony or by fasting and ascetic practices; sometimes it seems to come without any deliberate preparation and simply to overwhelm the person who has it. The latter was the case, for example, with the experience of Arthur Koestler, which occurred while he was imprisoned awaiting possible execution during the Spanish Civil War. The experience occurred as he was scratching mathematical formulas on the wall of his cell. There suddenly came to him, as he contemplated Euclid's proof that the number of primes is infinite, an understanding of the enchantment that he had always felt for the proof.

The scribbled symbols on the wall represented one of the rare cases where a meaningful and comprehensive statement about the infinite is arrived at by precise and finite means. The infinite is a mystical mass shrouded in a haze; and yet it was possible to gain some knowledge of it without losing oneself in treacly ambiguities. The significance of this swept over me like a wave. The wave had originated in an articulate verbal insight; but this evaporated at once, leaving in its wake only a wordless essence, a fragrance of eternity, a quiver of the arrow in the blue. I must have stood there for some minutes, entranced, with a wordless awareness that "this is perfect—perfect." . . . Then I was floating on my back in a river of peace, under bridges of silence. It came from nowhere and flowed nowhere. Then there was no river and no I. The I had ceased to exist.

It is extremely embarrassing to write down a phrase like that when one has read *The Meaning of Meaning* and nibbled at logical positivism and aims at verbal precision and dislikes nebulous gushings. Yet, "mystical" experiences, as we dubiously call them, are not nebulous, vague or maudlin—they only become so when we debase them by verbalisation. However, to communicate what is incommunicable by its nature, one must somehow put it into words, and so one moves in a vicious circle. When I say "the I had ceased to exist," I refer to a concrete experience that is verbally as incommunicable as the feeling aroused by a piano concerto, yet just as real—only much more real. In fact, its primary mark is the sensation that this state is more real than any other one has experience before—that for the first time the veil has fallen and one is in touch with "real reality," the hidden order of things, the X-ray texture of the world, normally obscured by layers of irrelevancy.[23]

When such experiences occur, they are usually considered by the person who has them to be a revelation of God and to be the most worthwhile experiences; but not always. Koestler characterizes his experience more in metaphysical than in religious terms. But such experiences are generally considered to be the most worthwhile that man is capable of and they are often followed by a complete revolution in one's mode of life, so that one says he has been "born again."

Psychologists have often proposed explanations of these experiences.[24] They point out similarities between them and some of the symptoms of hysteria found in the psychiatric patient. Anxiety, a strong but not entirely successful repression, and, perhaps, a lively imagination tending toward hallucination, play a part in both the hysterical and religious experience. It has also long been recognized that drug-induced experiences are often akin to those reported by mystics. Some users of "consciousness-expanding" hallucinatory drugs characterize their experiences in decidedly religious terms: but any such experience can also be characterized in purely descriptive terms, by reference to the effect of various chemicals upon the neurological system. However, all such explanations of why people have religious experiences, even if true, are irrelevant to the main question: Are the experiences sources of knowledge? It does not matter really whether the people who have them are "normal and healthy" or "hysterical" or "saintly." All

[23]Arthur Koestler, *The Invisible Writing* (New York: The Macmillan Company, 1954), pp. 351f.

[24]See, for instance, J. H. Leuba, *The Psychology of Religious Mysticism* (New York: Harcourt, Brace & World, Inc., 1926).

that matters is the answer to the question: Does the experience give knowledge of the existence and attributes of God?

The psychologist who discusses and investigates these experiences is interested in their causes and not in what they mean, except as an index about the personality of the religious person. The philosopher, however, cannot ignore the fact that *every* experience has its psychological causes, whereas at least some experiences supposedly also have reference to something objectively real outside the person. Certainly, then, psychological conditions can be found for religious experience; but the philosopher wants to know whether the religious experience *also* has any validity with respect to what it seems to reveal, not about man but about God. The philosophical question is: Is the religious experience of such a kind that it can be more plausibly interpreted, in a system of metaphysics, as evidence of the reality of the *object* of the experience (God) or only as evidence of some abnormal psychological state?

We must be careful not to beg this question by making an assumption that will require us to interpret the religious experience as merely a psychiatric symptom. If we assume, for example, that there is no God, then obviously it will be easy to interpret the religious experience as hallucinatory. But the question is precisely whether there is a God or not, and the proponent of this argument asserts that the best evidence for an affirmative answer is found in the religious experience. The religious experience may be hallucinatory; but we cannot say that it *must* be unless we already know on some other ground that what is said to be revealed in it, God, is unreal.

The argument from religious experience may take several forms; we shall examine three.

Argument from the individual religious experience—This argument is based upon the claim that in experiences otherwise similar to Koestler's, one is in direct communication with God. It says that such experiences can adequately be explained only on a theistic hypothesis. C. C. J. Webb says that in the religious experience there is felt to be

... an excitation in our souls by the Reality by which we find ourselves confronted and environed, of perceptions and sentiments which, apart from such an object as Theism assigns to them, must be regarded as essentially illusory and incapable of satisfaction.[25]

This experience is of a Person who, as it were, meets us "half-way." The experience is felt to be ultimate and intimate to a higher degree than our ordinary experiences of other persons.

By itself, of course, the experience proves nothing; but it is sufficiently impressive evidence to convince the person who has the experience that

[25]C. C. J. Webb, *Religion and Theism* (London: George Allen & Unwin, Ltd., 1934), p. 134. Quoted by permission of the publisher.

there is a God. Then, the person who accepts this evidence as sufficient for himself says, "You do such and such things and you will have the experience I am speaking of; then you will see that what I said is true. But you have to have the experience yourself." The experience is incommunicable, although it may be suggested by symbols, art, and imagery. But the way to have such an experience can be communicated and taught; the proponent of this argument therefore invites us to have the experience he has had and to see if we do not find it most reasonable to interpret it the way he does.

Certainly no one will challenge the efficacy of this procedure. The best way to know God—assuming He exists—is to have the experience in which He is supposed uniquely to reveal Himself. The absence of the experience of the "vision of God" cannot be made up for by any amount of intellectual argument. Nevertheless, the skeptic may not be convinced. Suppose that the skeptic goes through the preparatory exercises and tries to have the "vision of God" but that it does not come. What can be done about this apparent failure of the empirical test? There might be two replies, but neither quite suffices. (a) It might be argued that the preparation for the experience does not "force the hand of God." The vision of God is not a purely human achievement to be attained by rigorous adherence to minute prescriptions but essentially a gift of God, which God gives or withholds. This is the usual theological position, but it does not meet the logical issue. It begs the question, for it presupposes the existence of God. (b) It might also be said, "You did not get yourself in the proper frame of mind; there is some lurking skepticism that shuts you off from God." Perhaps the typical answer to the person who says that he does not "get anything out of" the experience of worship or devotion is, "you did not completely surrender yourself." But this answer reveals a question-begging definition of the religious experience. It defines the religious experience not in terms of religious practices that can be observed impartially but as one that does reveal God; any experience that does not do so is, by definition, not a religious experience. Such an argument decides in advance which of men's experiences are to be considered evidence for the existence of God and ignores the negative result of any experience that does not seem to reveal the existence of God. Hence, it falls into the fallacy of neglect of negative instances.

Sometimes this kind of proof is called an "empirical argument" for God, because it appeals to experience. But it is different from the kind of empirical argument that would be used elsewhere in science and philosophy, because here the experience is defined in such a way that, by definition, it must lead to a certain conclusion. Any other experience that does not lead to that conclusion is declared spurious. A valid empirical argument would say that we should put ourselves in such and such a condition to observe, and then *whatever* we observe would have equal worth in deciding questions of fact. At the same time, it is doubtful that many religious skeptics have ever prepared themselves in the circumspect manner of the mystics; for this reason, reliable empirical findings, insofar as they are relevant to settling the basic issue, are not in abundance.

Argument from comparative studies of religious experience—This argument recognizes that each individual has his own form of experience, which depends not only upon his personality but also upon the religious tradition in which he is trained. It has therefore been proposed that we should compare various experiences called religious to determine if there is some common core that seems to be independent of the individual circumstances. The comparative study of various religions, William James believed, does reveal such a core, which appears in different forms in different religions. But stripping away the accidental and variable, James found a nucleus of religious experience, consisting of two parts:

1. An uneasiness; and 2. Its solution.

1. The uneasiness, reduced to its simplest terms, is a sense that there is *something wrong about us* as we naturally stand.
2. The solution is a sense that *we are saved from the wrongness* by making proper connection with the higher powers.[26]

James reached this nucleus by inductively comparing a great many reports of religious experiences. Other philosophers have made comparable studies and have reached more or less the same conclusions as to the essence of the religious experience. It is not a question "Do men have experiences that they take as evidence of their contact with God?" for the answer to this question is obvious. It is the question "Does this common nucleus of religious experience show us something about the metaphysical status of the *object* of the religious experience, or does it only show us something universal (or at least widespread) about *human nature*?"

If we remember the conclusions reached in our earlier study of hypotheses, we shall readily see that no final answer can be satisfactory to everyone. In science, after the observations are made and everyone agrees about what they are, we still must ask what they mean. That is, we still must ask what hypothesis best accounts for them. We must do likewise with the observations that James has summarized. Can they be better interpreted as evidence of the existence of the "higher powers," or God, who saves us "from the wrongness," or as evidence merely that most men feel that they *need* some higher power to support them and that they believe that they find it in religious experience?

Nothing compels us to adopt either hypothesis; an indefinite number of hypotheses will always be consistent with the same set of facts. From the standpoint of a purely scientific inquiry it may well be sufficient to explain the facts of religious experience as expressions of verifiable human needs. But if one's prior orientation and sense of values, or philosophy of life, leads

---

[26]William James, *The Varieties of Religious Experience* (London: Longmans, Green & Company, Ltd., 1902), p. 508.

him to regard the facts of religious experience as more central than those of scientific experience, then there may be no satisfactory explanation of these facts short of a hypothesis that postulates the existence of God. This means, in a sense, that one's criteria for judging between two hypotheses springs ultimately from his character, purposes, and values. This does not mean that neither hypothesis is correct but only that insofar as one restricts himself to a purely empirical examination of the facts of religious experience, these facts will not provide a conclusive resolution of the problem whether God exists.

A nonmystical direct awareness of God—We should mention yet another way in which it has been claimed that God can be known. This is by a kind of direct perception that does not require the occurrence of a unique experience like those that occur in mysticism.

It will be helpful in explaining this to recall what we said earlier (p. 262) about human behavior. We can describe what human beings do from one or the other of two standpoints. We can give a purely descriptive account of their bodily movements, or we can characterize their performance of intelligent, purposive actions. Although one may have to make reference to bodily movements in characterizing an action, to do *only* the former is not equivalent to doing the latter. No description, however detailed, of the movements of Jones' arm, the successive positions of his bones and muscles, and the marks made on a paper by the pen secured in his hand is equivalent to saying that he is signing his name. In Ryle's terminology (p. 274), descriptions of bodily movements and descriptions of actions belong to different categories. Yet a person might describe the same event in one or the other of these aspects, depending upon his interests and purposes. In one sense, nothing changes when we shift from one perspective to the other; but in another sense, the whole situation changes. For what a person does can be understood as the performance of an action only in a broader context of purposes, language, and institutions.

The difference between these perspectives has a distant kinship with what Wittgenstein characterizes as "seeing-as," a phenomenon notably manifest in optical illusions. In a simple but relevant example, he points out that we can alternately see the following configuration either as a duck or a rabbit.[27]

[27]Ludwig Wittgenstein, *Philosophical Investigations* (2nd ed.), trans., G. E. M. Anscombe (Oxford: Basil Blackwell, 1958), p. 194.

The configuration itself remains precisely the same in each case, so that a person describing how the lines lie on the page would report no change. Yet the figure's significance changes as we move from one perspective to the other. Similarly, one and the same behavior may be viewed either as a sequence of bodily movements or as the performance of an action. In the case of our earlier example from Plato (p. 258), it is seen merely as the movements of bones and tissues; in the other, it is viewed as an expression of purpose and intention.

The German philosopher Max Scheler (1874–1928) finds in such phenomena a clue to the understanding of personality. He calls attention to a phenomenon on the human scale similar to that cited above:

One may look at the face of a yelling child as a merely physical object, or one may look at it (in the normal way) as an expression of pain, hunger, etc. . . . the two things are utterly different.[28]

He then adapts this to an account of how we may be directly aware of other persons through what he calls expressive phenomena:

. . . that "experiences" occur there [in others] is given for us *in* expressive phenomena . . . not by inference, but directly, as a sort of primary "perception." It is *in* the blush that we perceive shame, *in* the laughter joy. To say that "our only initial datum is the body" is completely erroneous. This is true only for the doctor or the scientist, i.e., for a man in so far as he abstracts *artificially* from the expressive phenomena, which have an altogether primary givenness. It is rather that the same basic sense-data which go to make up the body for outward perception, can also construe, for the act of insight, the expressive phenomena which then appear, so to speak, as the "outcome" of experiences within. For the relation here referred to is a *symbolic*, not a causal one. We can thus have insight into others, in so far as we treat their bodies as a *field of expression* for their experiences.[29]

This provides the beginning of an interpretation of persons that avoids the problems of Cartesian dualism. That view, as we have seen, conceives of the self as an immaterial substance enclosed in a material body—a "ghost in the machine," as Ryle calls it—of which we do not, and cannot, have direct awareness. This creates a problem analogous to that of our knowledge of the external world—that of how we can know that other minds exist when we cannot perceive them. Scheler is claiming that we do have a direct and immediate awareness of other persons through what he calls the "act of insight," which consists of seeing persons in a certain aspect or from a certain perspective. He maintains that this is the normal way of perceiving them; it is only by abstraction that their bodies as such become the primary object of perception. If so, then there is no problem of how to construct an argu-

---

[28]Max Scheler, *The Nature of Sympathy*, trans., Peter Heath (New Haven, Conn.: Yale University Press, 1954), p. 8. Quoted by permission of Yale University Press and Routledge & Kegan Paul, Ltd.
[29]*Ibid.*, p. 10.

ment to prove that other persons (or minds) exist; we are directly in contact with them in our ordinary experience.

Peirce, who agrees that we have direct knowledge of other persons, claims furthermore that if God is known, our knowledge of him must also be direct.[30] His reasons for believing that we have such knowledge are complicated, and we can only outline them briefly. His strategy is to argue that personality involves such traits as growth, the projection and development of ends, consistency, feeling, and temporal extension. These are manifest in one's actions, language, habits, and so forth, and all are invested with significance. One's life is like a train of thought. Thought requires language, and the language of personality includes what one does as well as what one says. In this broad sense of language, "my language is the sum total of myself."[31]

But now, Peirce argues, the traits ingredient in personality are also found in the universe as a whole. We can directly apprehend personality in nature no less than in our dealings with our fellow men. If a person's thoughts, actions, purposes, and so on are all signs of him (hence a kind of language, hence the statement that one is the sum total of his language), so it may be that the events and processes of nature are God's language and that he is the sum total of his language. If, and as Peirce also suggests, the laws of nature are God's ideas,[32] then there is no incompatibility between religion and science because the advances of science are simply revelatory of God.

Scheler finds the essence of this view represented in St. Francis, whose conception of the relationships among man, God, and Nature, he says, is unparalleled in the history of Western Christianity.

A natural object, for St. Francis, is a symbol, a mark, a signpost, a significant pointer to the spirit and person of God. . . . He thinks of Nature as a living whole, whose relation to its visible manifestations is rather like that of a man's countenance to the various expressions it may betray. There is a *single* divine life embodied in the forms of Nature, and "expressed" in her aspects and incidents. Nature is a *single* field of expression for this same surging life which finds a continuous embodiment of itself in the plenitude of natural forms.[33]

In this view one may be directly aware of God, but in a manner that does not require as a vehicle an unusual experience such as those found in mysticism. God is not identical with the universe any more than a person is identical with his physical body; but God is revealed in the universe in the same way in which a person is revealed in his conduct. To know God, as to know a person, one must apprehend the "facts" from a certain perspective.

Experiences allegedly involving such awareness of God would be difficult

[30]Charles S. Peirce, *Collected Papers of Charles Sanders Peirce*, eds., Charles Hartshorne and Paul Weiss (Cambridge, Mass.: The Belknap Press of Harvard University Press, 1960), 6.162. Quoted by permission of the publisher.

[31]*Ibid.*, 5.314.

[32]*Ibid.*, 5.107.

[33]Scheler, *The Nature of Sympathy*, p. 90.

to evaluate as evidence of the hypothesis that God exists. Although some of our comments about mystical experience would be relevant here, a main difference between the two—one that would call for careful assessment—is that this approach stresses the similarity rather than the dissimilarity of the experience of God with ordinary experiences. The skeptic, of course, is unlikely to be convinced. For just as you could never convince him that another person was performing a purposive action if he persisted in saying that all he sees are various muscles and tendons moving, so the theist would be unlikely to convince him that the universe expresses the personality of God if he can see nature only as consisting of sequences of events and the operation of purposeless forces. The value of such an approach, therefore, is less in providing neutral evidence for the existence of God than in showing how God is known *if* he is known.[34]

THE RIGHT TO BELIEVE

We have mostly been weighing the pros and cons of the religious hypothesis. But what if, as the third alternative (p. 369) suggests, the evidence for or against that hypothesis is inconclusive? This possibility was envisioned by William James, who developed an argument designed to justify religious faith under carefully defined conditions. We have already seen (p. 332) that although James agrees in general that to be meaningful a statement must make a difference to experience, he interprets this to allow that a statement (or hypothesis) is meaningful if *believing* it has experiential consequences, where these consequences may be of a personal, emotional type.

His argument bears some similarity to, but differs in important respects from, the well-known argument of Blaise Pascal (1632–1662), the famous mathematician who contributed to the mathematical theory of probability. Pascal could find no scientific proof of the existence of God, but he believed that the hypothesis that God existed was justified by considerations of probability when we take into account our human concern with our future happiness. It is logically as reasonable to suppose that God exists as that He does not; but it is morally more reasonable to assume that He does. Therefore Pascal makes a wager that God exists, just as a player takes a chance that his partner will do such and such things—not because he can prove that his partner will do so but because his chances of winning are improved by a line of play predicated upon this assumption:

Your reason is no more shocked in choosing one rather than the other [hypothesis about the existence or nonexistence of God], since you must of necessity choose. This is one point settled. But your happiness? Let us weigh the gain and loss in

[34]This possibility is suggested by John Hick, who develops a view somewhat similar to the one presented above. See his *Faith and Knowledge*, Chap. VI (Ithaca, N.Y.: Cornell University Press, 1957).

wagering that God is. Let us estimate these two chances. If you gain, you gain all; if you lose, you lose nothing. Wager, then, without hesitation, that He is.[35]

It was James' view that God, if he exists, would take a dim view of someone's believing in him on such grounds. Thus James set about to show that only when much more specific conditions were met was one justified in believing in God. His argument is as follows.

Hypotheses can be assessed from the standpoint of one's willingness to act upon them.[36] Where one has some tendency to act upon an hypothesis, it is said to be a live hypothesis; where no such tendency exists, the hypothesis is dead. James next characterizes a decision between two hypotheses as an option. When both hypotheses are live, the option is a live one; when the hypotheses are dead, so is the option. Moreover, if the situation is such that one *must* accept one or the other hypothesis, the option is said to be forced ("believe *X* or do not believe it" presents a forced option; "believe *X* or believe *Y*" does not). Finally, if an option promises to have lasting significance for one's life as a whole, it is said to be momentous. When an option is live, forced, and momentous, it is said to be a *genuine option.*

Now James holds that when a person is confronted with a genuine option that cannot be settled on intellectual grounds—on the basis of evidence and rational inquiry—he may justifiably believe whatever he wants. For some people, the religious hypothesis fits this description. The option it presents cannot be settled on intellectual grounds; you can neither demonstrate rationally nor produce convincing empirical evidence for, the hypothesis that God exists. Moreover, for some the option is a genuine one.

That the religious hypothesis is live and momentous for many people is indisputable. But does it present a *forced* option? Ordinarily we distinguish among theism, agnosticism, and atheism, as though agnosticism (the suspension of judgment) were an alternative to belief or disbelief. James argues, however, that from a practical standpoint there is no middle ground; to withhold judgment is practically equivalent to disbelief.

We cannot escape the issue by remaining sceptical and waiting for more light, because, although we do avoid error in that way *if religion be untrue,* we lose the good, *if it be true,* just as certainly as if we positively chose to disbelieve. It is as if a man should hesitate indefinitely to ask a certain woman to marry him because he was not perfectly sure that she would prove an angel after he brought her home. Would he not cut himself off from that particular angel-possibility as decisively as if he went and married someone else? Scepticism, then, is not avoidance of option; it is option of a certain particular kind of risk.[37]

[35]Blaise Pascal, *Pensées,* trans., W. F. Potter, §233 (New York: E. P. Dutton & Co., Inc., Everyman's Edition, 1931). Quoted by permission of E. P. Dutton & Co., Inc., and J. M. Dent & Sons, Ltd.
[36]See William James, "The Will to Believe" (1896) in *The Will to Believe and Human Immortality* (New York: Dover Publications, Inc., 1956).
[37]*Ibid.,* p. 26.

Thus he concluded that the religious hypothesis is a forced—hence for some people a genuine—option that cannot be settled on intellectual grounds. Therefore, they see nothing unreasonable about believing in God. This does not settle, or purport to settle, the question whether that hypothesis is correct; that is, whether God does in fact exist.[38] Rather, it purports to provide a justification for belief in God when evidence for that belief is incomplete. James is trying to show by intellectual means that sometimes (and his argument applies to any area of belief, not just religion) we are justified in holding a belief for which the intellect cannot provide adequate evidence. He is not saying that one should or must believe in God or that there is anything unreasonable or irrational about disbelieving in God.

APPENDIX TO CHAPTER 15

St. Anselm's Two Ontological Arguments

It is generally agreed that Descartes' version of the ontological argument presupposes that existence is a predicate (because it says that God has all perfections; existence is a perfection, hence God has existence along with the other attributes constituting perfection). Thus if our reasoning above (pp. 371–73) is sound, it vitiates Descartes' argument.

There are, however, two other important (and more difficult) traditional versions of the argument. They were set forth by the eleventh-century theologian St. Anselm (1033–1109). Addressing his arguments to the Fool, who "hath said in his heart, there is no God" (Psalms XIV: 1), he first characterizes God as a being "than which nothing greater can be conceived." He then reasons, in his first argument as follows:

Even the fool is convinced that something exists in the understanding, at least, than which nothing greater can be conceived. For, when he hears of this, he understands it. And whatever is understood, exists in the understanding. And assuredly that, than which nothing greater can be conceived, cannot exist in the understanding alone. For, suppose it exists in the understanding alone: then it can be conceived to exist in reality; which is greater.

Therefore, if that, than which nothing greater can be conceived, exists in the understanding alone, the very being, than which nothing greater can be conceived, is one, than which a greater can be conceived. But obviously this is impossible. Hence,

---

[38]*Ibid.*, pp. xi-xii. James did think, however, that if God exists, evidence for his existence might be forthcoming only if people do believe. As he says, "I have preached the right of the individual to indulge his personal faith at his personal risk. . . . If religious hypotheses about the universe be in order at all [that is, if there is no logically clinching evidence against them] then the active faiths of individuals in them, freely expressing themselves in life, are the experimental tests by which they are verified, and the only means by which their truth or falsehood can be wrought out."

there is no doubt that there exists a being, than which nothing greater can be conceived, and it exists both in the understanding and in reality.[1]

Many people have thought this argument also presupposes that existence is a predicate. We can assess this claim and simultaneously achieve a better understanding of the complexity of the argument by outlining its structure in nontechnical terms. We shall interpret it as an *ad hominem* argument against anyone who grants that a certain conception of God (as a being than which nothing greater can be conceived) is meaningful but who then denies that God exists. Conceived in this way, it is also what we earlier (p. 51) called a *reductio ad absurdum* argument.

The argument may conveniently be broken down into three parts: the first establishes the common ground between Anselm and the Fool, the second details the absurdity, and the third draws the conclusion. The Fool, it is assumed, grants that he understands what it means to speak of a being than which nothing greater can be conceived, but he denies that there exists any such being. This claim of his, which Anselm sets about to disprove by exposing the absurdity to which it supposedly leads, we shall call thesis *T*. It is assumed at the outset of Part II of the argument. We may now reconstruct the argument as follows (changing the order of some of the premises and adding some of the more obviously required premises):

I. 1. What is understood exists in the understanding.
    2. That than which nothing greater can be conceived is understood.
    3. Therefore: that than which nothing greater can be conceived exists in the understanding.
II. Fool's claim (*T*): That than which nothing greater can be conceived exists in the understanding *alone* (hence not in reality).
    1. That than which nothing greater can be conceived can also be conceived to exist in reality.
    2. To exist in reality is greater (than to exist in the understanding alone).
    3. Therefore: the very being than which nothing greater can be conceived is one than which a greater *can* be conceived.
III. 1. But this is impossible.
    2. Therefore: *T* must be rejected.
    3. Therefore: that than which nothing greater can be conceived exists in reality as well as in the understanding.
    4. Therefore: God exists.

Now the Fool, if he has his wits about him, will sense that Anselm has misrepresented his position. He will point out that Part I of the argument, the part to which he assents, obscures some important distinctions. In the interest of brevity in bringing these out, let us substitute "God" for the

[1]*St. Anselm: Basic Writings*, trans., S. N. Deane (La Salle, Ill.: The Open Court Publishing Company, 1962), p. 8. Quoted by permission of the publisher.

cumbersome expression "that than which nothing greater can be conceived." Let us furthermore distinguish references to the *concept* represented by these expressions from references to *what the concept represents* by enclosing the expression in single quotation marks when the former is intended and in italics when the latter is intended. (Thus we would say "*God* is omniscient" but "'God' [the concept] is understood differently in different cultures.")

With this in mind, the Fool will point out that what he intends to say in premise I(2) is that the concept 'God' is understood and in premise I(3) that the concept 'God' exists in the understanding. He is not saying that *God himself* exists in the understanding (as though he were somehow trapped in our minds). This would be absurd. Similarly, in *T* he is not saying that *God* exists in the understanding alone; rather he is saying that there is nothing in reality to which the concept 'God' refers (or there is nothing in reality answering to the description 'God'). Indeed, he may object to the whole distinction between "existence in the understanding" and "existence in reality" on the grounds that it implies that there are different *kinds* of existence. Although we sometimes speak this way, he may argue that in the case at hand it should be understood as a simple way of distinguishing references to the concept 'God' from references to a possibly existing *God*.

In view of this, Part II of the argument, in which Anselm attempts to exhibit the absurdity of the Fool's position, encounters serious difficulties. For the only interpretation of premise II(1) that the Fool will accept is one that says something like: that it is conceivable that there exists in reality a being to which the concept 'God' corresponds. He will not, for reasons given above, assent to any interpretation that implies that *God* can also be conceived to exist in reality, as though *God* already has one kind of existence (in the understanding) and the only question is whether he has the other kind. Given the Fool's understanding of II(1) and granting for the moment premise II(2), what follows? That it is conceivable that there exists in reality a being greater than . . . what? The problem is how to complete this. It is tempting to say that what follows is: that it is conceivable that there exists in reality a being greater than any being identical with it in every respect except that it exists only in the understanding.[2] But to say this would be to perpetuate the very confusion just disclosed. For it implies that it is *God* that exists in the understanding, and the Fool denies that *God* exists at all. He concedes only that the concept of 'God' is understood (and, if we are to speak of "existing in the understanding" at all, only that the concept of 'God' has such existence). In his view there is no *being* that exists in the understanding and that can be compared with a possibly existing (and hence, according to II(2), a greater) being in reality. There is only the concept 'God' and the possibility of there existing an actual being to which it refers. If so, then III(3), which

---

[2]The other possibility is that the conceivably existing being is greater than the *concept* of it that exists only in the understanding; but such a comparison of a possible being with a concept would be peculiar and would not, in any event, yield II(3).

says that *the very being* than which nothing greater can be conceived is one than which a greater *can* be conceived, does not follow. And without III(3) no absurdity has been shown to follow from the Fool's position.

Thus either the argument begs the question against the Fool, by presupposing that *God* already exists (if only in a shadowy way in the understanding), or it fails to derive an absurdity from *T*. Either way, it fails to prove that God exists.

But suppose the Fool is less perspicacious than we have been supposing; what if he grants that there are two kinds of existence and that *God* does indeed enjoy the funny kind that locates him in the understanding? Would Anselm's argument then reduce his position to absurdity? Not necessarily. For we can now see that even with this concession the argument presupposes that existence (or, in Anselm's terminology, "existence in reality") is a predicate. For it designates a property that a thing (existing in the understanding) might or might not have and that enhances (in the sense of making greater) what possesses it. Thus, in answer to our original question, the argument as here formulated does indeed presuppose that existence is a predicate. But even if it did not, it is faulty on the grounds that it either begs the question or fails to establish one of its essential premises.

Anselm's second argument is even briefer than the first. It is as follows:

It is possible to conceive of a being which cannot be conceived not to exist; and this is greater than one which can be conceived not to exist. Hence, if that, than which nothing greater can be conceived, can be conceived not to exist, it is not that, than which nothing greater can be conceived. But this is an irreconcilable contradiction. There is, then, so truly a being than which nothing greater can be conceived to exist, that it cannot even be conceived not to exist; and this being thou art, O Lord, our God.[3]

It has been contended that this argument is stronger than Descartes' and Anselm's first argument, because it does not presuppose that existence is a predicate. It presupposes, rather, only that *necessary existence* is a predicate.[4] But what is meant by necessary existence? A clue to this is provided by the first premise of the argument, which asserts that it is possible to conceive of a being whose nonexistence is inconceivable. A being that not only exists but whose nonexistence is inconceivable, is said to have necessary existence. It is clear that this differs from saying simply *that* a being exists, because most beings (and in Anselm's view all beings except God) are such that their nonexistence is easily conceivable. We can say, for example, of any given person that he might never have come into existence (say, if his parents had never met) and that, being mortal, he will someday cease to exist. Thus a

---

[3]Deane, *St. Anselm: Basic Writings.*
[4]See discussions by Charles Hartshorne, *The Logic of Perfection* (LaSalle, Ill.: The Open Court Publishing Co., 1962), and Norman Malcolm, "Anselm's Ontological Arguments," *The Philosophical Review*, LXIX (1960), 41–62.

being might very well exist and yet not have the additional characteristic that his nonexistence is inconceivable.

Now if God's nonexistence is inconceivable, then according to the argument, it is impossible that he not exist. For to say that God (so conceived) does not exist would be to contradict oneself; it would be to say that the nonexistence of a being whose nonexistence is inconceivable *is* conceivable. Hence, if God's nonexistence is inconceivable, then God exists.

But even granting that necessary existence is a predicate and that God is defined in such a way that reference to such existence is part of the concept of God, this argument can still be shown to be inconclusive. For before a thing can have *any* properties at all, it must already exist; this is one of the reasons why existence cannot sensibly be considered a property. If this is correct, then it is no less true of necessary existence than of any other property. So that in order to predicate necessary existence of *God* (as against merely including the concept of necessary existence in the concept of 'God'), we must presuppose that *God* already exists, else there is nothing to which 'God' refers over which it can sensibly be debated whether or not it has this property. If so, then the same argument used to show that existence is not a predicate, even though it does not suffice to show that necessary existence is *not* a predicate, suffices to show that one cannot demonstrate the existence of anything from the attribution to it of necessary existence—unless, of course, that thing already exists.

Although the last word is far from having been said on the ontological argument, the foregoing considerations suggest that, for all its deserved admiration and respect, it cannot yet claim to be a conclusive proof of God's existence.

BIBLIOGRAPHY

Alston, William P., ed., *Religious Belief and Philosophical Thought*. New York: Harcourt, Brace & World, Inc., 1953.

Ayer, A. J., *Language, Truth and Logic*, Chap. VI. New York: Dover Publications, Inc., 1946.

Broad, C. D., *Religion, Philosophy and Psychical Research*, Section II. New York: Harcourt, Brace & World, Inc., 1953.

Hick, John, ed., *Classical and Contemporary Readings in the Philosophy of Religion*. Englewood Cliffs, N. J.: Prentice-Hall, Inc., 1964.

———, *Philosophy of Religion*. Englewood Cliffs, N. J.: Prentice-Hall, Inc., 1963.

———, ed., *The Existence of God*. New York: The Macmillan Company, 1964.

Hume, David, *Dialogues Concerning Natural Religion* (1776). Many editions.

Lewis, H. D., *Our Experience of God*. London: George Allen & Unwin, Ltd., 1959.

Matson, Wallace I., *The Existence of God*. Ithaca, N.Y.: Cornell University Press, 1965.

Moore, G. E., "Is Existence a Predicate?" in *Logic and Language* (2nd series), ed., A. G. N. Flew, pp. 82–94. Oxford: Basil Blackwell, 1955.

Pike, Nelson, ed., *God and Evil*. Englewood Cliffs, N. J.: Prentice-Hall, Inc., 1964.

Plantinga, Alvin, ed., *Faith and Philosophy*. Grand Rapids, Mich.: William B. Eerdmans Publishing Co., 1964.

———, ed., *The Ontological Argument*. Garden City, N. Y.: Anchor Books, 1965.

Ramsey, Ian, *Religious Language*. New York: The Macmillan Company, 1963.

Smith, John E., ed., *Philosophy of Religion*. New York: The Macmillan Company, 1965.

Stace, W. T., ed., *The Teachings of the Mystics*. New York: Mentor Books, 1960.

Taylor, Richard, *Metaphysics*. Englewood Cliffs, N.J.: Prentice-Hall, Inc., 1963.

Webb, C. C. J., *Kant's Philosophy of Religion*. Oxford: The Clarendon Press, 1926.

QUESTIONS FOR REVIEW AND DISCUSSION

1. Using the diagram on page 195 as a model, see if it is possible to analyze one or more of the arguments for the existence of God into different kinds of hypotheses and projected tests of the substantive hypothesis that God exists. What major differences and similarities do you discern in the argument you analyze and Adams' argument for the existence of an unobserved planet?

2. Consider the following two arguments:

   Round-squares cannot be conceived to exist.
   Therefore, round-squares do not exist.

   God cannot be conceived *not* to exist.
   Therefore, God exists.

   If the first is a good argument, why isn't the second?

3. In the first form of Anselm's ontological argument, there is the statement: "For, suppose it [that than which nothing greater can be conceived] exists in the understanding alone: then it can be conceived to exist in reality, which is greater." In the appendix to this chapter, we have interpreted this to assert that *to exist* in reality is greater; whereas it may mean that *to be conceived to exist in reality* is greater. On the latter interpretation, existence does not have to be intepreted as a predicate. How, then, would you state Anselm's argument on this interpretation?

4. A mathematician might say, "There necessarily exists one and only one even integer between any two consecutive odd integers." Since necessary existence in mathematics can be demonstrated, a philosopher might think that the ontological argument that attempts to prove the necessary existence of God has a model in mathematics. Do you agree?

5. Do psychological explanations of religious beliefs have any value as evidence for or against their truth?

6. Which of the various arguments for the existence of God seems to be the strongest? Why? How would you attempt to answer criticisms made of it?

7. Discuss the view that if the soul is not immortal and if God does not reward or punish men, there is no reason for being moral if one can get away with immorality. Do you think that most religious people actually hold this?

8. It has been said that our rational beliefs are based upon precisely the same type of evidence as the mystic's beliefs. Explain and comment.
9. Evaluate the objection that William James' defense of the right to believe is merely an invitation to take wishful thinking seriously.
10. In an earlier chapter, Berkeley's argument for the existence of God was explained. Which of the "standard" arguments outlined in this chapter does Berkeley's resemble most closely? What are the principal differences between his argument and the ones given here?

16 INQUIRY IN THE CHOICE OF VALUES

FACTS AND VALUES

The world we see around us seems very different from the world described by the sciences. The scientific world is one of "cold fact," discovered by the most rigorous attempt to eliminate the personal element from observing and thinking. The facts of science are just what they are, and our liking or disliking them seems to be an impertinence in the face of their impartial truth. The onward march of science constricts the area of ignorance and illusion; it also sometimes seems to make man himself merely accidental, his interests superficial, and his ideals imaginary:

> Science! true daughter of Old Time thou art!
> Who alterest all things with thy peering eyes.
> Why preyest thou upon the poet's heart,
> Vulture, whose wings are dull realities?
>
> How should he love thee? or how deem thee wise,
> Who wouldst not leave him in his wandering
> To seek for treasure in the jewelled skies,
> Albeit he soared with an undaunted wing?
>
> Hast thou not dragged Diana from her car?
> And driven the Hamadryad from the wood
> To seek a shelter in some happier star?
> Hast thou not torn the Naiad from her flood,
> The elfin from the green grass, and from me
> The summer dream beneath the tamarind tree?[1]

Yet the world we see does not seem to be composed of just cold facts. Some parts of the world are suffused with beauty; some actions of men are not mere conditioned reflexes but are moral actions. The aspects of the world

[1]Edgar Allan Poe, *Sonnet to Science*.

we value *seem* as real as the aspect we try to know in an objective, impartial way.

Moreover, the world we see does not seem to be put together out of cold facts plus something *else* we call values. The world seems to be one world, with values appearing to be at least as inherent in the things we experience as are the facts and laws that the scientist discovers by analyzing them. Primitive man and the ordinary man of today do not first experience a world of brute and valueless facts and then wonder how it comes about that a world consisting of colorless, odorless, and tasteless molecules seems to have all the beauties and gratifications he can find in enjoying it or all the evils that beset him as if the world were planned for his woe. He sees the world originally as the site of things that he appreciates or rejects, long before he understands it as a realm of fact and law.

The facts of science are reached by abstraction and logical construction from the variegated world of experience. Long ago, men learned that in order to understand, explain, and control things, they had to center their attention on those aspects of things about which they could agree with one another. Judgments of the beauty, pleasantness, goodness, or desirability of things vary from individual to individual; hence these judgments were banished from the organization of the knowledge of "things as they are." Primitive men learned how to mix pigments and fight wars; their discoveries were probably the ancestors of the kind of knowledge we now call the natural and the social sciences. But they did not learn, and we have not learned, how to get real agreement on whether a specific painting made with these pigments is beautiful or whether a war fought according to good scientific strategy is morally just. We have established sciences of chemistry and optics and strategy. We have no rigorous science of aesthetics and ethics.

In the early seventeenth century, a resolute attempt was made to banish all thought of the values of things from scientific attention and to concentrate on the measurable, the geometrical, the mechanical aspects of things. Science was to become impartial with respect to value; the facts of science were to be "value-free" facts. When this was accomplished in the physical sciences and purposes and values were relegated to some not-quite-real world of human desires and fancies, men achieved unprecedented success in discovering laws relating one cold fact to another. From then on, it was natural that the world understood by scientists should seem quite different from the world loved or feared. At the very time when the decision to disregard purpose and to investigate only mechanical causes put into men's hands almost unlimited power to achieve their purpose of controlling nature, the concept of purpose and value was declared illusory and subjective.

Thus, whereas in antiquity the bifurcation of reality assigned a privileged place to values and relegated empirical facts to a secondary position,[2] scien-

---

[2]Recall Dewey's characterization of this as part of the quest for certainty. See above, pages 165f.

tific progress reversed this emphasis. It nurtured the view that there is no realm of the eternal in which values reside. Because it was thought that values have no objective status in a world of hard facts, they were judged to spring from the vagaries of feeling and emotion; it was they, and not empirical facts, that were deemed to lack stability and foundation.

In our study of science we have already examined one consequence of this bifurcation of experience. It was the rapid advance of science in the study of nature, the conception of which was greatly simplified by the vigorous use of Ockham's razor for the elimination of values, purposes, and ideals in the study of fact. We have also seen (in Chapter 13) some of the difficulties in the scientific study of society, where such an elimination of value is more difficult to perform and where it is still a debatable question whether it ought to be attempted.

In this chapter we are to see some other effects of this bifurcation, the effects it has had on our understanding, choosing, and pursuing values. One of these effects has been to strengthen the notion that disciplined inquiry is out of place in our experience of values. This means that inquiry is limited to "fact" and hence that evaluating the experience of values, especially in aesthetics and ethics, must be left to "instinct," feeling, or desire. It is the correctness or incorrectness of this point of view that we must carefully weigh.

STATEMENTS OF FACT AND JUDGMENTS OF VALUE

For the reasons given, it is convenient to draw a distinction between factual statements and judgments of value. Factual statements are either true or false and purport to convey information about things, events, or states of affairs.[3] Usually we know how to confirm or refute them, even though we rarely trouble to do so (we generally rely upon the creditability of those who make the statements, as, for example, when we accept what we read in a reliable newspaper). Although factual statements may be uttered or written in such a way as to convey approval or disapproval of the facts they report, to express approval or disapproval is not their primary function. Their main function is a cognitive one—to inform or convey knowledge. Below are examples of factual statements.

A. 1. Beethoven wrote nine symphonies.
   2. There are no brick houses on Elm Street.
   3. Sodium cyanide is a poison.
   4. He is a tall man.
   5. Higher taxes are under consideration.

[3]Depending upon whether the facts they purport to convey are empirical or nonempirical, factual statements may be either empirical or a priori. Throughout this section, unless otherwise specified, by "facts" and "factual statements" we shall mean empirical facts and empirical statements.

Each of these statements is informative, and there are fairly standardized procedures by which to determine their truth or falsity.

Judgments of value, on the other hand, differ from the above in some important respects. Consider, for example, the following.

B. 1. Beethoven's symphonies are the best ever written.
   2. Elm Street would be prettier if it had some brick houses.
   3. It would be bad to serve sodium cyanide to one's guests.
   4. He is a good man.
   5. Higher taxes are desirable.

The most conspicuous difference between these sentences and the preceding is the occurrence in them of words like "good," "bad," and "desirable." These (and similar words like "worthwhile," "valuable," "praiseworthy," and so on) are called value words, because they are part of the vocabulary we use to evaluate things. Judgments of this sort, unlike those of fact, generally express the feelings and attitudes of those who make them; they indicate whether the person approves or disapproves of those things about which he is judging. Moreover, they are characteristically made with a view to influencing the feelings and attitudes of others and to guiding their future conduct and choices; that is, they have a pronounced *noncognitive* function. And finally, there is much less agreement about how to determine whether such judgments are correct or incorrect than there is in the case of those in group A. That Beethoven wrote nine symphonies, for example, is a matter of historical fact that can be established by generally accepted procedures. That they are the best ever written is a matter of taste, which no amount of scientific or historical inquiry can settle.

Few philosophers have denied these differences between factual statements and value judgments. But philosophers have differed radically over how far-reaching these differences are, particularly whether value judgments are essentially different in *kind* from factual statements or whether they are themselves basically factual statements of a particular kind—hence a species of cognitive statement. Are value judgments true or false and informative, or are they principally noncognitive in their function, serving only secondarily, if at all, to convey information?

It *may* be true that while the distinction between the two kinds of proposition is useful and valid, judgments of both kinds are quite proper and intellectually defensible. In other words, it may be that if I say, "Every man has some inalienable rights," I am stating a true or false judgment just as surely as if I say, "Every man has some iodine in his body," although the first is correctly called a value judgement.

The obvious fact that we cannot test the former by anything comparable to a chemical analysis or a public opinion poll does not necessarily mean that it is not really a statement. It may mean only that the methods of scientific observation are not directly applicable to all kinds of statements. There is nothing in the useful distinction between two kinds of judgment or in the commitment scientists have made to consider only the factual judgments, that implies that only valueless facts are real and that values are to be reduced to them or thrown out altogether. There might be other things in the world besides facts subject to scientific inquiry; if so, they could be studied by some inquiry other than the scientific. At all events, many philosophers believe this, and we should not deafen ourselves to their arguments in advance by equating reality with scientific fact.

Before weighing some opposing theories about the status of values, it will be useful to introduce some distinctions.

EXTRINSIC AND INTRINSIC VALUE

As the above examples suggest, anything whatever may be the subject of a value judgment, and virtually anything whatever may have value under appropriate circumstances. But not all things are of equal value. For this reason it is important to distinguish some of the relevant considerations in determining what value should be assigned to a given thing.

First, notice that many things derive their value from their relationships to other things. The value, for example, of taking bitter medicine, saving regularly, and studying hard consists in their being means to good health, a secure future, and a college education. It derives, in other words, from the value of the end that can be accomplished by them. And many things that from one standpoint are ends may be means when viewed from another standpoint. For example, although a college education is an end with respect to the activity of studying and taking examinations it itself is a means with respect to getting a good job, enjoying a fuller life, and so forth. Virtually all our thoughts and activities involve means and ends with interrelated values.

Those things whose value derives from their relationships to other things are said to have *extrinsic value*; their value, so to speak, lies outside them. On the other hand, things that have value in themselves, apart from their relations to other things, are said to have *intrinsic value*. They may also have extrinsic value, but at least a part of their overall value consists simply in their being just the sort of thing that they are.

Among the things that have sometimes been held to have intrinsic value are pleasure, aesthetic experiences, knowledge, and happiness.[4] Consider the enjoyment of a concert or the contemplation of a work of art. It seems that such *experiences* have a clear, intrinsic value; they are worthwhile just in themselves, quite apart from their role in leading to other values. Indeed,

---

[4]One of the main traditional disputes in value theory is between those who say that pleasure and pleasure alone has intrinsic value (the doctrine called *hedonism*) and those who say that other things besides (although usually including) pleasure have intrinsic value.

it may well be that the only intrinsic values are the values of certain experiences, because it is doubtful that anything else has value in complete independence of its relationship to other things. We sometimes speak as if works of art have intrinsic value, but upon reflection it seems that their value consists in their capacity to produce experiences having intrinsic value. Their relationship to such experiences, however, differs from the relationship of means to ends in the examples cited above; hence, it is misleading to think of art objects as having purely extrinsic value. For this reason it is helpful to introduce a third category, that of inherent value. A thing is said to have *inherent value* if the experience of it is intrinsically valuable. Thus we may say that a work of art has inherent value, as the locus of beauty; but the experience in which its beauty is appreciated has intrinsic value. Similarly truth has inherent value (as well as extrinsic), while the knowledge of truth is intrinsically valuable.

Some experiences, of course, have both intrinsic and extrinsic value. The experience of enjoying a concert may also contribute to one's education or eventually to a happy life. There are many cases, too, that illustrate what has been called the "Law of Preponderance of Means over Ends." According to this, there is a tendency for means, which borrow their value from the ends they serve, to become ends in themselves. Most people, for example, value money simply as a means to the things that can be got with it; but the miser values the money *itself* as an end; for him it acquires intrinsic (or probably more accurately, inherent) value. Men who enjoy their work are happier illustrations of this same principle. The principle has such wide application that it is sometimes difficult in specific cases to decide whether "the end justifies the means" or "the means justifies the end."

Although everything that is valued as a means will have extrinsic value, not everything that is valued as an end has intrinsic value; for some ends are also means. An end with respect to a given activity *may*, in other words, have only extrinsic value (a completed workbench may be an end with respect to the activity of constructing one, but the workbench itself has only extrinsic value). The conviction that the series of means and ends must somewhere terminate is what led many philosophers to suppose that there must be something that has intrinsic value to a pre-eminent degree—something that is valued apart from being a means to anything else.

Now, many judgments of extrinsic value can be confirmed or disconfirmed in the manner of factual statements. In science we may ask, for instance, "Does mandelic acid kill such and such germs?" This is a factual question about cause and effect and can be answerd by empirical inquiry. But we can transform this into a question about extrinsic value by asking "Is mandelic acid good (extrinsically) as a remedy for such and such a disease?" This also can be answered empirically. The more we know about the causal conditions of the things we desire, the more able we are to achieve our ends. It is chiefly because of this fact that science is useful in the pursuit of values.

But can *all* judgments of value be verified or disconfirmed empirically? If they can, then the problems of value will be capable of resolution by scientific means and value theory will be an empirical discipline. If they cannot, then value theory will not lend itself to purely scientific treatment. If the latter, then two main alternatives present themselves: (a) that judgments of value are statements of *nonempirical fact*, the truth or falsity of which must be settled by a priori means, or (b) that judgments of value are not genuine judgments at all and cannot properly be said to be either true or false in any literal sense. This highlights the importance of the question of the status of values in reality, because the answer to the question as to whether value judgments can be verified depends in large measure upon the answer to this question.

A CLASSIFICATION OF VALUES

Although the following values overlap in part and do not exhaust all possible values, they do cover the most important species of value:

1. *Biological values.* Values attached to aspects of life as a biological fact. Examples: food, drink, sex, health, survival.
2. *Economic values.* Values attached to material things used or exchanged for other goods and services (other types of value, or other economic values). Examples: money, property, tools, "credit."
3. *Affective values.* Values experienced in sensuously pleasant experiences. Examples: play, sex, delight in food and drink, excitement, comfort.
4. *Social values.* Values experienced in social intercourse, cooperation, and competition. Examples: friendship, power, status, a "good name."
5. *Intellectual values.* Values experienced in the satisfaction of disinterested[5] curiosity and the intellectual use of the mind. Examples: knowledge, truth.
6. *Aesthetic values.* Values experienced in the disinterested appreciation of natural and artistic beauty. Examples: beauty, the sublime, the comic, the tragic, genius and talent, "good taste."
7. *Moral values.* Values experienced in social or individual conduct with respect to their rightness, goodness, or ideal development. Examples: values of character and good will, virtues.
8. *Religious values.* Values experienced in or aspired to in religious devotion and worship; values based on what is interpreted to be man's relationship to God. Examples: the holy, the sacred.

Several points stand out immediately upon examining this list or other comparable lists proposed by various writers.[6] It would be difficult to segre-

---

[5]Disinterested in the sense of not being a means to the satisfaction of some other interest. Knowledge, of course, has also an economic, biological, and social value.

[6]See W. G. Everett, *Moral Values* (New York: Holt, Rinehart & Winston, Inc., 1918); Eduard Spranger, *Types of Men* (Halle: Max Niemeyer Verlag, 1928); and Stephen Pepper, *Ethics* (New York: Appleton-Century-Crofts, 1960).

gate the religious from the moral; the biological and the affective certainly involve each other; the economic values may be a subclass of the social.

Second, conflicts may occur between values of the various classes. Certainly the pursuit of moral values may conflict with the cultivation of the economic; there is often an antithesis between the moral and the aesthetic; the intellectual is often thought to conflict with the religious, and so on.

Third, there is a complicated relationship of dependence among the various classes of values. Some of them depend upon others. Few values can be attained unless some of the biological values are available, and one would be rightly suspicious of a religious value if it were dissociated from moral values. In general, some degree of achievement of one or more of the first four types seems to be a condition of achievement of most of the last four.

There have been attempts to set up such a listing as this as a scale or standard of value, calling the first four the lower values and the last four the higher values. This is itself a value judgment, and it would be difficult to vindicate it in any detail, although something can be said for it if it is not pushed too far. Although it is perhaps true that any value can be used as a means to some other end (for example, piety can be a means to achieve social values; intelligence, a means for economic advancement) and probably true that any value can be intrinsic (as in the case of the miser), the higher human cultures, and not merely our own, have most often professed to regard the last four types as values that make life "worth living," whereas the first four make it possible simply "to live."[7]

Furthermore, the last four types of value afford a broader base for distinctively human personality to develop. The first, third, and fourth types, and rudiments of the second, are sought by animals as well as man; and the first and third are perhaps achieved more fully by animals than by men. The last four are pre-eminently or exclusively human and depend upon the "higher powers" of the human being. Moreover, the last five types are more genuinely social than the first three; pursuit of the first three tends to separate and segregate men, for they are not values that are multiplied by sharing, while the latter types reach their fullest fruition in a community of like-minded persons.

Such considerations as these occupy a central position in one of the most important books on values, Aristotle's *Nicomachaean Ethics*. Aristotle thinks that each being in the world has its own end or good, which depends upon its own specific nature. The proper purpose of anything, its prime good, is what it can do best or what it alone can do. For instance, a good saw is one that can cut well; a good harpist is a person who can play the harp well; it is not necessary in addition that the good saw be beautiful or that the good harpist be also a kind person. "Let the cobbler stick to his last," expresses the Aristotelian notion. But what is *man's* last? According to Aristotle, man is

---

[7]See W. T. Stace, *What are Our Values?* (Lincoln: University of Nebraska Press, 1950).

an animal, but he is unique among animals in being a "rational animal" and a "political animal." Hence by analogy to the answer to the question, "What is a good harpist?" Aristotle is able to answer that a good man is one who has perfected the rational and the political (social) aspects of his personality; he is one who lives with his fellows and uses his reason in choosing and accomplishing social and political values.

VALUE JUDGMENTS AND PRESCRIPTIVE JUDGMENTS

We have been discussing what is good, worthwhile, and desirable and distinguishing value judgments from statements of fact. But what is the relationship between value judgments and judgments about rightness, wrongness, and obligation? And what is the relationship between these latter judgments and statements of fact? Let us try to answer these questions by first considering examples of sentences typically used to make such judgments.

C. 1. You ought to keep your promise to Jones.
   2. That's the wrong way to hold a golf club.
   3. He did the right thing in repaying his debt.
   4. You should have moved your queen instead of your bishop.
   5. One ought not to eat with his fingers.

First notice that these differ from factual statements in many of the same ways as value judgments. They usually express some pro or con attitude of the speaker toward the action or activity in question, and they frequently are used to influence the feelings and attitudes of others. In these respects they, too, have definite noncognitive functions. Also, there is much less likely to be agreement than in the case of factual statements about whether such judgments are correct and less agreement about how to determine *whether* they are correct or incorrect. On the other hand, they differ from value judgments in that whereas the former may have virtually anything as their subject matter, the above deal primarily with actions. Specifically, they prescribe what is correct or incorrect in the way of conduct; in this respect they are even more directly action-guiding than value judgments. For this reason, they are sometimes called *prescriptive judgments*.

The features that value judgments and prescriptive judgments share and that set them apart from factual statements are sufficiently striking to warrant calling them both *normative* judgments. They either set forth, prescribe, or presuppose norms for guiding conduct and choices. Factual statements of the type considered earlier are nonnormative because they do not (explicitly) do any of these things. In certain well-understood contexts, of course, what looks like a factual statement may function like a normative judgment. Thus, "Sodium cyanide is a poison!" may not merely inform someone of a property of sodium cyanide; it may tell him that he should **not** taste it. The question still remains open, however, whether normative judgments of either type can ultimately be reduced to factual statements.

VALUE AND OBLIGATION

A review of the various normative judgments in categories B and C reveals that not all normative judgments are *moral* judgments. Judgment B-2, for example, that Elm Street would be prettier if it had some brick houses on it is clearly a value judgment but it is not a moral judgment; rather, it is what we call an aesthetic judgment. Similarly judgment C-5, that one ought not to eat with his fingers, although clearly prescriptive of how one should act, is not a moral judgment; no one is *morally* culpable (even though he may be guilty of bad manners) for eating with his fingers. On the other hand, judgments B-3 and B-4, and C-1 and C-3 are moral judgments (or would be in most contexts in which they are likely to be made). In the case of B-3 and B-4 they express evaluations based upon moral grounds; and in C-1 and C-3 they refer to the performance or nonperformance of actions that would be grounds for holding a person morally, and perhaps also legally, responsible.

This means that two important distinctions must be recognized under the heading of normative judgments: first, between value judgments and prescriptive judgments, and second, between moral judgments and nonmoral judgments.

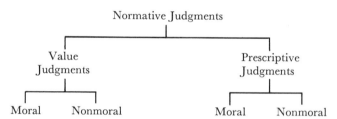

Even though morality is, or should be, our primary concern, we do much evaluating and prescribing that is not distinctively moral in character.

It should be clear from this that value theory is not identical with ethics. Ethics is concerned with morality and the grounds, analysis, and justification of moral judgments, whereas value theory has a much broader interest in the elucidation of values of all sorts, nonmoral as well as moral. Although our primary concern here is with value theory, it is important that we consider briefly the relationship between it and ethics; that is, between what is good and what is (morally) right or obligatory.

There are two main views about the relationship between moral judgments and value judgements. The first says that what is morally right or obligatory is dependent upon what will promote value in the world; the second says that what is right or obligatory is not dependent solely upon what brings about value in the world. Each of these positions embodies a family of possible theories, classifiable as:

TELEOLOGICAL THEORIES: An act is morally *right* if and only if it realizes at least as great a balance of nonmoral good over evil as any other, and *obligatory* if it realizes a greater balance of nonmoral good over evil than any other.

DEONTOLOGICAL THEORIES: What is *right* and what is *obligatory* are not dependent solely, if at all, upon the consequences of actions for the balance of nonmoral good over evil in the world.

In short, the teleologist says that moral judgments should always be based upon an estimate of the value to be brought about by actions; the deontologist says that, sometimes at least, other considerations are relevant and may be overriding.

Suppose, for example, that we could measure value (say human pleasure) to such a fine degree that we could say in a particular instance that one course of action would result in 1000 units of goodness (and no evil) and an alternative course in 1001 units (and no evil).[8] Suppose furthermore that there is no other action open to us that equals or surpasses these in balance of good over evil produced. Now the teleologist is committed to saying that we should perform the second action and that it would be morally wrong not to. But suppose, the deontologist says, that performing the second action would involve breaking a solemn promise, whereas the first would involve keeping the promise. Should we break the promise in order to realize a (slightly) greater nonmoral value? The deontologist claims that it is at least an open question what we should do and that sometimes the keeping of a promise is of greater importance from a moral standpoint than maximizing value. Sometimes, he says, one may be required to foresake a greater good in order to perform an action that, like keeping a premise, has other relevant moral features.[9] For him, but not for the teleologist, not all questions of ethics can be settled by answering the questions about value; ethics, for him, is not simply a branch of value theory.

In what follows we shall be speaking specifically about values, although much of what we say will be applicable to rightness and obligation as well.

---

[8]This example is adapted from W. D. Ross, *The Right and the Good* (Oxford: Clarendon Press, 1930), p. 38. Ross is a deontologist and also (see below, p. 424) an intuitionist.

[9]Deontologists differ about what the relevant features are. Ross cites, as obligation-creating facts, such considerations as that one has wronged another (giving rise to duties of reparation), that one has been done a service by another (giving rise to duties of gratitude), or that one is in a position to distribute pleasure or happiness in accordance with merit, giving rise to duties of justice (*ibid.*, 21f.). The Stoics thought of duties as rooted in the very nature of the various relationships that hold among individuals, for example, father to son, husband to wife, and so on.

VALUES AND PHILOSOPHIC INQUIRY

Let us now return to the question we raised earlier concerning the possibility of rational inquiry having a place in the field of values. Arguments against this possibility generally assume one of two forms. Either they challenge the ontological status of values, charging that values simply are unreal and not on a par with the properties investigated by science, or they challenge the view that value judgments are genuine judgments at all, arguing that instead of conveying factual information or having a clear cognitive function, they simply perform various noncognitive functions. If either of these charges can be sustained, it seriously undercuts the ground for saying that rational inquiry has a legitimate place in the field of values. Let us examine these objections and consider what replies can be made to them.

The Ontological Status of Values

The theory that values are objective properties of objects or actions is certainly the view that is prima facie most plausible. We generally—even when we think we know better—take the beauty of a sunset, the goodness of an act of courage, and the agreeableness of a cup of coffee as though they were qualities of these things. In our ordinary experience, we speak as if the values were properties that we experience as being in the *things* and not just in *us*.

It is only after a certain degree of sophistication is reached that one begins to have doubts about this. If we decide that not even the color is really in the sunset or the sweetness in the coffee but that these are psychological responses to physico-chemical conditions we do not directly experience, it is almost inevitable that we also conclude that values are dependent upon ourselves.

And once we have decided to attribute to objects only those characteristics about which men generally agree or those characteristics that can be adduced as bases for predicting their future behavior—a decision long ago made by science—the ground for regarding value as an objective property is surrendered, for men quickly find that they often disagree with one another about value judgments. Even if they can agree about the facts relevant to works of art, for instance, they often cannot agree about their values; psychologists often agree about what motives a man has, but as men they disagree about whether the man's action was praiseworthy or blameworthy.

Troubled by these disagreements among value judgments, philosophers have usually taken one of two courses. Either they agree with Plato and say that the values we seem to experience as qualities or adjectives of things are mere appearances or instances of real values about which we can come to agreement by intellectual inquiry into our diverse experiences; or they agree with Protagoras that each man is the measure and ground and locus of every value. Thus, from the difficulties in the naive belief that we know values directly by a kind of value-sense arise objectivism and subjectivism as value theories.

Plato's Theory: Objectivism

It was variability and dependence upon circumstances that led Plato (Chap. 3) to argue that the true realities of the world are not the things and their qualities that we perceive by our senses. They change and conflict, as Theaetetus saw, and men cannot agree on them sufficiently to derive any general conclusions or laws.

The same lead is followed here. The Socratic method, which begins with the things of the senses and rises to the contemplation of Ideas, can start from either the factually described qualities of things or from their values. Things that we perceive as valuable will be transcended in the search for the essences of these values. These essences themselves will be real values—absolute, eternal, unchanging—and the condition of the lesser values that we perceive but dimly and variably in the things of the world. Professor Gilbert writes:

Beauty Itself is stable. The many beauties come into being and pass out again. No concrete object, either physical or spiritual, which we might praise by calling it beautiful, could satisfy the test of Beauty's permanence. Bodies and ornaments, laws, customs, and sciences, however good, fine, or appropriate, are limited and perishable. The contrast for Plato between the ideas or essences and the particular existences or instances always implies the opposition between an unchanging one and the changing many.[10]

As before, the search begins with these particular and perishable values, and by comparing them, discovers their idea, then discovers relationships among the ideas until it finally arrives at a supreme Idea that is the ultimate source of all the values that things can have.

We may follow Plato's ascent to the idea of value in several ways. For instance, we can see what it is that valuable things, such as good characters, well-governed states, and beautiful works of art, have in common. Plato finds the common principle in a certain harmony or proportion—a balance of function in which each part plays its proper role and all are taken up into some unity-in-complexity.[11] In morality, or what Plato calls justice, he finds the essence to be the proper balance of the various levels of the soul or personality, with the lower levels (the passions and desires) ruled for the sake of the whole by the higher faculty of reason. In works of art, similarly, there is a natural order and articulation that must be preserved; a good state is one in which each social class fulfills its proper role in the commonwealth. In fact, as Plato in various works develops these diverse themes in a common

[10]Katherine Gilbert and Helmut Kuhn, *A History of Esthetics* (New York: The Macmillan Company, 1939), p. 49. Quoted by permission of Professor Alan H. Gilbert.
[11]See Aristotle's closely related view, page 410.

direction, the Good and the Beautiful seem to merge with the Form of Truth. Hence arises the Platonic trinity of "the Good, the True, and the Beautiful."

But the dialectic leading to knowledge of the Ideas of the Good and the Beautiful is not coldly analytical; at crucial stages of its presentation, Plato turns from argument to parable and allegory. We shall consider two passages in which this occurs; although lacking in logical precision, they seem eminently suited to the high theme on which he is discoursing.

The first passage occurs in the *Symposium*. After several men at the banquet have discussed love and lovers, Socrates tells how the love of the eternally beautiful can lead men beyond the transient world. Most men, he says, love but the appearance of the beautiful and the good; they try to hold on to them amidst the transience of life, but they fail; even their love of children is but a futile desire for a little longer life and immortality in a world of continuous flux. Socrates says that he has been taught the true way to the love and enjoyment of the good and the beautiful, the Forms that will not be destroyed by time and circumstance:

He who would proceed rightly in this matter should begin in youth to turn to beautiful forms; and first, if his instructor guide him rightly, he should learn to love one such form only—out of that he should create fair thoughts; and soon he will perceive that the beauty of one form is truly related to the beauty of another; and then if beauty in general is his pursuit, how foolish would he be not to recognize that the beauty in every form is one and the same! And when he perceives this he will abate his violent love of the one, which he will despise and deem a small thing, and will become a lover of all beautiful forms; this will lead him on to consider that the beauty of the mind is more honorable than the beauty of the outward form.

On this "ladder of love" he will rise to contemplate the beauty of laws and institutions and sciences, until "at length he grows and waxes strong, and at last the vision is revealed to him of a single science, which is the science of beauty everywhere."

This brings him to the final goal:

When he comes toward the end [he] will suddenly perceive a nature of wondrous beauty—and this . . . is that final cause of all our former toils, which in the first place is everlasting—not growing and decaying, or waxing and waning; in the next place not fair in one point of view and foul in another, or at one time or in one relation or at one place fair, at another time or in another relation or at another place foul, as if fair to some and foul to others, or in the likeness of a face or hands or any other part of the bodily frame, or in any form of speech or knowledge, nor existing in any other being . . . but beauty only, absolute, separate, simple, and everlasting, which without diminution and without decrease, or any change, is imparted to the ever-growing and perishing beauties of all other things. . . . The divine beauty [is] pure and clear and unalloyed, not clogged with the pollutions of mortality.[12]

[12]Plato, *Symposium*, trans., Benjamin Jowett (New York: The Liberal Arts Press, 1948); Steph. pagination pp. 210, 211. (The Little Library of Liberal Arts, no. 7.)

The second passage occurs in the *Republic*. Socrates says that he cannot answer the question of what is the real nature of the Good, but he will try to elucidate it by an analogy. He calls the sun the "offspring which the Good has created in the visible world, to stand there in the same relation to vision and visible things as that which the Good itself bears in the intelligible world to intelligence and to intelligible objects [Forms]."[13] The sun is not only the source of the visibility of things like animals and plants but is also the source of their life and existence. By analogy, then, the Idea of the Good is the source of the goodness of all other things, of their being known, and of their very existence.

From this we can gather several general features of the most important argument for objectivism that has ever been presented. Objectivism argues for the complete intelligibility of our experience of value; there is, as Plato says, a "science" (true knowledge) of values just as there is science or true knowledge of reality. It argues that value is a basic category in the world and that the world cannot be understood in terms of mere fact. The things around us must be understood as vehicles or revealers of value underlying their existence. Nature itself, and especially human beings, strive to realize the values that are only dimly adumbrated in the mundane concerns of men; the wise man will model his life after his vision of the ultimate values in reality itself. The disputes about values are due to ignorance of true values, to the variability and dependence of the appearances of value upon variable human circumstances. But to know the good is to do it. Reason, then, is or should be the guide of life, for it can enable us to know what the ideals themselves really are. Philosophy, which is the perfection of this kind of reasoning, is or can become a true and rigorous science of the proper goals of mankind.

The appeal of Platonic philosophy has been one of the leading motifs in the history of Western thought. It was congenial to Christianity, which personalized the process by which the supreme values were made to bear upon the world, holding that they were revealed to man in the person of Christ. In the history of literature, later poets found in Platonism an elevation above the kind of despair Poe expressed in finding that scientific knowledge led only to dull fact. The classical tradition in art—painting the ideal rather than imitating the observable with all its blemishes and imperfections—has its philosophical root in Plato's philosophy, which says that such classicism is not an escape from reality but is the only true realism. And in their political life, men have always found inspiration in the notion of a value that is dignified above the variable laws of states and that has held up to them the standard of a "law of nature" that is unchanging and abiding.

The same arguments can be brought against this theory of value as against

---

[13]Plato, *Republic*, trans., F. M. Cornford (New York: Oxford University Press, 1945); Steph. pagination p. 508. Quoted by permission of Oxford University Press.

the doctrine of Forms in general (see p. 67). Insofar as the theory of Forms is rendered dubious by metaphysical and epistemological considerations, the theory of value based upon it is also rendered dubious.

Critics of this objectivist view first make effective appeal to the principle of parsimony. A value not experienced, they say, is merely an empty hypothesis. Everything important that we can say about value is really said about the *experience* of value. What we are really interested in, they say, is not what things have value but what experiences have value; and they complain that the objectivist applies the word value to something that has value only in the context of valuable experience. Indeed, they say, it makes no sense to speak of values apart from sentient beings. As William James says:

> How can one physical fact, considered simply as a physical fact, be "better" than another? . . . Physical facts simply *are* or are *not*. . . . Goodness, badness, and obligation must be *realized* somewhere in order really to exist; and the first step in ethical philosophy is to see that no merely inorganic "nature of things" can realize them. Neither moral relations nor the moral law can swing *in vacuo*. Their only habitat can be a mind which feels them; and no world composed of merely physical facts can possibly be a world to which ethical propositions apply. . . . Nothing can be good or right except so far as some consciousness feels it to be good or thinks it to be right.[14]

Plato, of course, does not think of the world as consisting simply of "physical" facts. But James's objection can easily be extended to nonempirical facts as well. His point is that without conscious beings, who are capable of having feelings, attitudes, desires, and aversions, there can be no values at all.

Subjectivism

This viewpoint is carried to its extreme in the position called *subjectivism*. Subjectivistic theories of values are held by those who are impressed with the variety and apparent irresolvability of conflicting value judgments and who are convinced, on metaphysical or epistemological grounds, that the world of actual existence has only the properties attributed to it by the sciences. From this they conclude: (1) that value is only a name that we give to certain kinds of experiences; (2) that the specific kinds of experience called valuable differ from person to person; (3) that there is nothing outside or above the individual's experience that can be considered valuable; and (4) that no specific objective standard binding on all men can be found or appealed to as a basis for evaluating their value judgments. Subjectivists differ among themselves about what kinds of experiences (experiences of pleasure, or power, or self-expression, or satisfied interests?) are to be called valuable. But they all recognize that, underlying value judgments, there is always the experience of desire or interest, an experience of "taking sides" with or against some kind of occurrence.

[14]William James, *Essays in Pragmatism*, ed., Alburey Castell (New York: Hafner Publishing Co., Inc., 1948), pp. 69–71.

Suppose that the critics of Plato are right that there are no values apart from conscious beings—that, at least in one sense, Protagoras is right that "man is the measure" of values. Does it then follow that the subjectivist is right and that each person is equally the measure of what is good or right, in the sense that whatever each person judges to be good or right is so? Does it follow that what we call values are nothing more than arbitrary and impulsive desires, liking, dislikings, and so on? If so, then the rejection of objectivism does indeed seem to have the consequence that rational inquiry is out of place in matters pertaining to value.

However, even if one grants that values presuppose the existence of conscious beings, it does not follow that they may not yet have objective status. For Plato's is not the only form of objectivism. Let us now consider a reply to the subjectivist that concedes values to be relative to human beings but nonetheless insists they have objective status.

Objective Relativism as a Theory of Value

Objective relativism is a theory claimed by its proponents to synthesize the positive insights of both objectivism and subjectivism. Objective relativists assert that any property of an object is at least in part dependent upon its relations to other things. The weight of an object, for instance, depends not only on its own mass but on the gravitational field of the earth; its color depends not only on its chemical structure but also on the composition of the light that falls upon it and the functioning of the eye that responds to the light it reflects. Properties of objects are not intrinsic but relational or relative. This does not imply, however, that properties are subjective, even if one of the entities in the relationship within which qualities or properties emerge is a subject or person.[15] "Relational" does not mean "subjective." A quality belongs to an object only in a context or relationship—hence, it is relational.

According to this theory, values are relational properties. They emerge in the object (or in the action) that is judged to be valuable, in its relationship to the person who has an interest in it or appreciates it. The values of the object or action are in part dependent upon the person's attitude, but they are not values *of* the attitude or *in* the person.

Because this theory insists that values are at least in part dependent upon the person's directing his interest or appreciation to the object said to be valuable, it is in agreement with subjectivism. Human need or interest is a necessary condition for anything to have value. But holders of this theory do not go so far as to say that the value is exclusively subjective and can be considered in isolation from the factual conditions surrounding the experiencing person. Value depends also upon the nature of the thing to which the

---

[15]The theory of objective relativism has also been discussed in connection with the problem of perception. See above, pages 322–26.

organism is related, and value is properly attributed to *it* in the context of its bearing upon our conduct.

Because it says that the values are values of the object or of the real action and not just values of states of mind or attitude, the theory of objective relativism does not belie the adjective "objective." Those who adhere to objective relativism agree with the objectivists that values are not exclusively private or personal but have objective bases and conditions independent of the person. They dispute only the belief of the objectivists that the things we experience as having value do have value apart from our experience.

What recommends a philosophical theory, like a scientific hypothesis, is its ability to meet problems that other theories have failed to resolve. Compromise between opposing views is philosophically sound only if it permits us to solve divergent problems by means of a single theory instead of by means of shifting from one theoretical base to another as problems shift and change. Compromise, in the sense of merely borrowing a little from this theory and a little from that, is not fruitful in philosophy because it results in a theory that is more complex than any of the views from which it borrows and that has less internal integrity than they do.

Objective relativists assert that their theory is not a compromise in the pejorative sense of this word. They do not, they say, take objectivism from one philosopher and subjectivism from another and mix them together. Rather, objectivism and subjectivism are themselves simply extremes or exaggerations of aspects found within our dealing with values. Objective relativism does not ignore the interrelatedness of all the factors in this experience. For that reason, objective relativists propose their theory as a single answer to two quite different questions that trouble the objectivists and subjectivists, respectively.

The questions are: How shall we account for the diversity of value judgments or beliefs about values if value is a simple property of real beings, open to discovery by intuition and dialectical reasoning? How shall we account for the agreement and near-unanimity on some value judgments, if value judgments are merely expressions of the likes and dislikes of highly variable individuals? Objective relativists claim to have a theory that answers both questions on the basis of the same definition of, and hypothesis about, value and therefore claim that their theory is logically simpler than its alternatives, which have to appeal to *ad hoc* hypotheses to answer one or the other of these questions. Objectivists have difficulty in answering the first of the questions, and they have to explain disagreement as due to ignorance or "value blindness" or "bad taste." Subjectivists have difficulty in answering the second and can only regard such agreements as really occur as due only to a fortunate, but by no means expected, similarity in the physiological and psychological make-up of individuals. But if values have two conditions—one subjective and one objective—and if one of these conditions (the subjective) varies, then obviously the value will vary also. These variations, however, will not be so broad, radical, and irreconcilable as they would be if subjectivism were the whole truth, that is, if the subjective condition were the sole condition of value. For the objective relativist recognizes and insists upon the permanent and uniform objective pole and condition of experiences of value.

Objective relativism is able to further a rapprochement between the social sciences and the theory of value. Even though psychology and sociology attempt to be purely descriptive sciences, dealing with facts as if they were value-free and being concerned only in establishing hypotheses and laws about how human beings actually behave, the human situations they deal with are by no means value-free. Descriptive sciences are not competent to establish criteria of the values by reference to which these situations are considered desirable or undesirable; usually, scientific workers in the fields of sociology and psychology accept the common-sense decisions of their society on questions of value and do not evaluate the standards the society itself professes to accept.

The theory of value, which is concerned with these criteria as its chief problem for investigation, is sometimes called a *normative science*, in order to distinguish its function from the descriptive functions of sciences like psychology and sociology. Although it is true that psychology and sociology do not have the task of establishing and evaluating criteria for judgments of value, they are certainly interested in and informative about the conditions under which individuals and social groups make their choices among values. For that reason, these sciences can make practically important contributions to value theory if the value theory is so organized as to take into account the personal and social factors as relevant not only to the *facts* of value experience but also to the *standards* of value judgment.

The social sciences, as descriptive, are interested in the facts about the experience of value—the conditions of success or failure in striving for values to which an individual or social group is committed. If one reads the Lynds' study of Middletown or the Kinsey reports on sexual behavior, for instance, one finds how much in the center of scientific interest is the comparative study of the standards of value prevalent in different social classes in America. However, each of these books is a factual study and does not pass value judgments on the experiences and on the value judgments of the people they describe. But in the normative study of values, we need such facts about the actual needs, interests, experiences, and judgments of people, and the scientific study of human motivation and society supplies this important set of facts.

It would be incorrect to say that we can learn from sociology and psychology what is really valuable; it is not the task of the descriptive sciences to give such answers to questions about value. But we too readily make value judgments on what would be good or desirable for men in disregard of the facts of human personality and social organization; all too frequently in our value judgments of ourselves and others, we are ignorant of the facts that would render the value-seeking of ourselves and others intelligible and comprehensible to us. If objective relativists are correct in saying that values are dependent in part upon human motives, then what we can learn from psychology and sociology about these motives and how they actually are expressed and brought to fruition or frustration can rank with the most important practical knowledge we can obtain.

This theory may be able to provide some reasonable criterion of values. It might be argued, in line with this theory, that whatever is truly valuable is not what actually satisfies me or what I actually desire but what *would* satisfy me or what I *would* desire *if* I had more knowledge about myself and the action or the thing in question and could see the implications of this knowledge for my present and future concerns. In this way we could make use of scientific knowledge as one of the most important factors in deciding questions of value. This theory does not relativize values as much as subjectivism does, for it does not equate what I actually enjoy or desire with the valuable; it says that what is valuable or desirable is what I *would* desire if I knew my deep-lying interest and the full facts of the case. On the other hand, it does not absolutize values, as objectivism does; objectivism tends toward dogmatism about what one's own values are and what the values of others ought to be, frequently without sound scientific knowledge of what are the needs and circumstances involved in the pursuit of values.

Thus the argument that inquiry is out of place in matters of value, on the grounds that values are not real properties is inconclusive. For the fact that values are dependent upon human nature does not mean that they are unreal. Like many of the properties investigated by science, they may be relational.

THE STATUS OF VALUE JUDGMENTS

Let us consider the related objection that value judgments are not cognitive assertions. This focuses on the question of the linguistic status of judgments about values, not on the question of the ontological status of values. The two objections are closely related, however, in that the person who believes that there are real value properties in the universe is likely to be a cognitivist about value judgments, and the person who takes an extremely subjectivistic view about the nature of values is likely to a be noncognitivist about value judgments.[16] Let us begin by considering in more detail what it is that the cognitivist says. The two forms of cognitivism that we shall consider are called ethical naturalism and ethical intuitionism.

Ethical Naturalism

The ethical naturalist claims that value judgments are a species of statement about empirical fact, and he usually claims that the value words

---

[16]There are qualifications to this, as we shall see, because the ethical naturalist both denies that there are distinctive value properties and affirms that value judgments have cognitive status. In what follows, we should bear in mind that one may be a naturalist in his ethics without being a naturalist in his metaphysics, and vice versa.

contained in such judgments are definable in terms of concepts that refer only to empirically verifiable properties. One of the chief advocates of a naturalistic value theory, R. B. Perry, defines value in the following way.

According to the definition of value here proposed, *a thing—any thing—has value, or is valuable, in the original and generic sense when it is the object of an interest—any interest.* Or, *whatever is an object of interest is ipso facto valuable.*[17]

"Interest" here is broadly defined to include desire, approval, liking, loving, and so forth. Because it is an empirical question whether a given thing has an interest taken in it in these senses, it is an empirical question whether any given thing has value. Hence value judgments are empirical statements, confirmable or refutable in principle by the same means as scientific statements.

If ethical naturalism is correct, then the differences cited earlier between value judgments and factual statements (and between normative and non-normative propositions generally) are not basic differences. For in this view, value judgments (and for most naturalists, prescriptive judgments as well) are ultimately reducible to statements of empirical fact, and their primary function is to convey empirical knowledge.

The ethical naturalist therefore makes value theory an empirical discipline. And he accounts for the legitimacy of rational inquiry of values without committing himself to an objectivist theory about the ontological status of values. He denies that there are any unique value properties in the universe. There are, he says (at least with respect to values), only empirical properties. Although words like "good," "desirable," "worthwhile," and the like are definable in terms of words that refer to empirical properties, there is no property of goodness over and above the empirically verifiable properties of being desired, liked, approved, and so forth.

The major objection to this position has been that it commits the "naturalistic fallacy"; that by defining value words in terms of empirical-property words, it confuses empirical properties with value properties and mistakenly supposes that from a purely factual non-normative statement (like "*x* is desired") one can legitimately infer a value judgment (like "*x* is desirable").

A test designed to expose this alleged fallacy has come to be called the open-question test.[18] It says that whenever confronted with a proposed definition of "good" (and the same may be said of other normative words) in terms of some nonvalue property, one should consider whether it makes sense to ask if a thing possessing this latter property *is* good. If this question makes sense—that is, if it is an *open-question* (debatable) whether what possesses the empirical property in question is good—then the proposed definition is incorrect.

---

[17]R. B. Perry, *Realms of Value* (Cambridge, Mass.: Harvard University Press, 1954), pp. 2–3. Quoted by permission of Harvard University Press.
[18]For discussions of this and the naturalistic fallacy, see G. E. Moore, *Principia Ethica* (Cambridge, Eng.: Cambridge University Press, 1903), Chaps. 1 and 2.

To illustrate, in Perry's view "*x* is good" means "*x* is an object of interest." Therefore, if we once establish that a thing is an object of interest, it should be pointless to ask further whether it is also good. For to say

1. *X* is an object of interest, but is it good?

would then be simply to say

2. *X* is an object of interest, but is it an object of interest?

But now, the critic says, it makes perfectly good sense to ask of anything that is an object of interest whether or not it is also good. Therefore, "good" and "is an object of interest" do not mean the same. Because this will prove true of any naturalistic definition, ethical naturalism is false.

The naturalist may, of course, deny that such questions are open-questions in the way his critic supposes. Or he may argue that they are open-questions only insofar as one ignores ambiguities of the value words in question. For example, if "good" should mean "is an object of interest" in some contexts and "is an object of reflective interest" in others, then to ask of something that is an object of interest whether it is also good *will* be an open-question until the relevant sense of "good" is specified. Both possibilities must be explored before the test can become effective.

Because there has yet to be a searching appraisal of naturalistic definitions in the light of these (and other) possibilities, this line of attack remains inconclusive. Yet it has been extremely influential, and with the belief that the more difficult questions about value cannot be answered by scientific means, it has led to a general decline of naturalism among contemporary philosophers.

Intuitionism

The second major defense of a cognitivist theory of value attempts to revive the essentials of Platonism. We shall consider only its view of intrinsic goodness. It says that intrinsic goodness is a real property different in kind from empirical properties. Whereas the latter are *natural* properties investigatable by science, goodness is a *non-natural* property undiscoverable by the senses. It must be apprehended by an act of intuition.[19]

Goodness is a simple and unanalyzable property, which means that it is not susceptible to analysis into constituent properties. This means furthermore, the intuitionist maintains, that attempts to define goodness, either in terms of empirical (natural) properties or even in terms of complex nonempirical properties (like "is commanded by God"), are doomed to failure. What is ultimately and irreducibly simple, he says, cannot be analysed in terms of anything else.

---

[19]One may be an intuitionist either about value or obligation or both. We are here considering an intuitionist theory about value of the type defended by Moore, *Principia Ethica*.

However, the intuitionist agrees with the naturalist that value judgments are factual statements; but in his view what they report are nonempirical facts of a special, non-natural sort. Hence their truth or falsity must be established a priori. Value judgments for him are synthetic a priori propositions. If the intuitionist is correct, value theory is indeed a cognitive discipline. Whereas for the naturalist it is an empirical science, for him it is a priori.

Many of the same considerations that led to the abandonment of Platonism have cast serious doubts upon intuitionism. Epistemologically, philosophers are skeptical of theories based upon an appeal to synthetic a priori propositions, because there has yet to be a convincing explanation of how such judgments are known. Metaphysically, the notion of non-natural properties has proved puzzling in the same ways Plato's doctrine of the Forms is puzzling. Exactly what are they, and how are they known? Many people who introspect when making judgments of intrinsic value claim no awareness of a simple, unanalyzable non-natural property. For such reasons, intuitionism—as a hypothesis about the nature of value and the analysis of judgments of value—has been unable to sustain widespread support.

Noncognitivism

The noncognitivist rejects both the ontological and the linguistic theses about value. He denies that there are any such things as value properties, and he denies that value judgments are (primarily at least) cognitive assertions. He agrees with the naturalist that natural properties are the only properties; but he also agrees with the intuitionist that it is impossible to define value words in terms of these properties. Value judgments, in his view, are not cognitive assertions at all—either empirical or a priori. Their main function is noncognitive.

Emotivism

One of the most important and controversial noncognitivist theories is emotivism. It was held by many philosophers associated with positivism and has had a marked effect upon the direction of ethical philosophy in the last thirty years.[20] According to the emotivist, it is incorrect (or at best misleading) to call value judgments real judgments or propositions. One characteristic usually attributed to a judgment is that it must convey information, and another is that it must be *either* true *or* false. But, they say, the sentence, "This picture is better than that," really conveys no information about the picture, and there is no way in which we can verify or refute it. According to them, the sentence is not so much a judgment like, "This bottle holds more than that," as it is like the Oh's and Ah's of a person walking through

---

[20]The most complete statement and defense of emotivism is found in C. L. Stevenson, *Ethics and Language* (New Haven, Conn.: Yale University Press, 1944).

a gallery and expressing his personal emotional reaction to the pictures he sees.

These philosophers draw a distinction between the assertive and the expressive functions of language and hold that value judgments illustrate the latter. I can say, "I like Beethoven more than I like Humperdinck," and this assertion is either true or false. But I can express my liking Beethoven more than I like Humperdinck by my gestures, by my habit of going to concerts in which Beethoven is played and avoiding those in which Humperdinck is played, or by making the value judgment, "Beethoven is a greater composer than Humperdinck." Just as facial expression cannot be true or false because it does not assert anything, a value judgment cannot be true or false because it does not assert anything—either about myself and my likings or about what it is that I like or dislike. Just as a facial expression may be sincere or insincere, a value judgment may be an honest or a deceptive expression of my emotions. But there is an important distinction between saying I like Beethoven and making a value judgment about Beethoven, and the latter, which makes no true or false assertion, cannot be translated into the former, which does.

If we do not give due weight to this distinction between assertion and expression, emotivism cannot be properly distinguished from mere subjectivism—the theory that value judgments are true or false assertions about my private attitude. Subjectivism is a cognitivist theory because value judgments for it can be translated into sentences that convey cognitive information and are true or false. Emotivism is a noncognitivist theory because value judgments for it cannot be translated into sentences that convey cognitive information even about my own state of mind.

Nevertheless, a value judgment that is made with sincerity permits us to infer something about the state of mind of the person who makes the judgment. I would not say, "Tea with milk is better than tea with lemon," unless it were true that I preferred tea with milk, although I am not *asserting* that I do have this preference. Why, then, it might be asked, do people make value judgments instead of just asserting that they, in fact, have certain attitudes? Here the emotivist points to the different functions of factual statements about one's attitude and value judgments. A value judgment functions persuasively, emotively, in a way in which a factual judgment about my emotions does not. "I prefer tea with milk to tea with lemon" is just a statement about myself that happens to be true. "Tea with milk is better than tea with lemon," however, *seems to be* about tea, *seems to say* something true about tea with milk—to wit, that it is better than tea with lemon. The value judgment is a recommendation. It may influence another's conduct in a way in which the bare statement of my own preference would not.

Consider another example. When I say, "Lying is wrong," I am not asserting the true statement, "I disapprove of lying," although I would be hypocritical and insincere if I said the former and if the latter were not true. When I say "Lying is wrong," I am expressing the hope that you will not tell lies, or I am expressing my own resolution not to tell lies. In important ethical matters, I am much more interested in affecting the future behavior of myself and others than I am in influencing people to take milk instead of lemon in their tea. Hence, for practical purposes, the factual and the value judgments about tea are just about on the same level, whereas the socially important features of ethical conduct are so portentous that the persuasive or emotive meaning predominates. Hence, we fall into the error (which we would not make in the judgment about tea) of thinking that the ethical judgment is a true statement about the objective wrongness of lying.

Most recent noncognitivists, however, think that language is richer and more flexible than the emotivist and the cognitivist recognize. They believe it serves a plurality of functions, other than conveying information and expressing and evoking feelings—a fact that must be accounted for in one's analysis of the linguistic status of value judgments. Thus, they argue, in addition to having emotive meaning (which most of them concede), normative judgments (now including prescriptive judgments) acquire their distinctive meaning in the performance of such acts as commending, praising, prescribing, commanding, and recommending. Not only do these writers object to reducing normative judgments to factual statements, but they also oppose the reduction of the uses of normative judgments to some one use.

Summary of Metaethical Theories

Before proceeding, it may be helpful to set in perspective the major theories about the status of value judgments. These are sometimes called *metaethical* theories to distinguish them from *normative* theories, which are theories about what sorts of things have value and what sorts of actions are right or wrong. Although proponents of these theories sometimes take different stands on the analyses of value judgments and prescriptive judgments, we shall, for simplicity, state them as theories about normative judgments generally.

COGNITIVIST THEORIES

Ethical Naturalism	*Ethical Intuitionism*	*Theological Ethics* (See pp. 13 and 357)
Normative judgments are empirical assertions; normative terms are definable by reference to natural properties.	Normative judgments are synthetic a priori assertions; basic normative terms are indefinable and refer to non-natural properties.	Normative judgments are synthetic a priori assertions; normative terms are definable by reference to supernatural properties (e.g., being commanded or willed by God)

NONCOGNITIVIST THEORIES

Emotivism	*Postemotivist theories*
Normative judgments are not (primarily, at least) cognitive assertions; main functions are (a) expressive, and (b) evocative (of feelings, emotions, attitudes). Normative terms not property-referring.	Normative judgments are not (primarily, at least) cognitive assertions; main uses (in addition to, or instead of, emotive) for commending, grading, prescribing, recommending, etc. Normative terms not property-referring.

REASONS AND RATIONAL INQUIRY

Let us suppose that the noncognitivist is right that value properties have no ontological status and that value judgments are not primarily cognitive assertions, although they may in some measure impart information. This would lend considerable support to the Protagorean thesis that man is the measure of all things pertaining to value. Would it then follow that rational inquiry has no place in the theory of value? Not at all, says the "postemotivist." Let us consider why.

First, if a person intends his value judgments to be taken seriously, he must be prepared to support them with *reasons*. A person who is unable or unwilling to do this will soon be ignored, and it is doubtful that his judgments should even be regarded as genuine value judgments. Many philosophers have thought that the distinctive function of value judgments is to guide conduct, and this function often cannot be discharged unless one is prepared to provide the requisite supporting reasons. In this view, even though a value judgment (as opposed to a factual statement) is not literally true or false and does not impart knowledge, it nonetheless must admit of justification by the adducing of reasons. This provides an opening whereby rational inquiry can become operative in value matter, even if value judgments are not themselves cognitive assertions.

The emotivist exploits this possibility by claiming that the important cognitive element in discussions of value is not contained in the value judgments themselves but is contained in the *reasons* offered in support of them. For these reasons will often themselves be cognitive, factual assertions and as such will be verifiable by the methods of science. Questions about their truth or falsity will, in principle, be answerable in the same way as similar questions about scientific statements.

If, for example, two men are disputing over the value of a given automobile, each will introduce a cognitive element into the discussion by citing various facts about it. These may cover a whole range of considerations, but each person will concentrate upon those that he thinks the other person is most likely to respond to—those that are most likely to effect a change in the attitude of approval or disapproval expressed in the other person's initial judgment. One person might be impressed by new safety features, another by the results of road tests, and another by stylistic innovations. The range of relevant considerations will vary with individual differences and hence from one context to another. But purely factual considerations will be drawn into the discussion, thereby injecting definite cognitive content into the dispute.

A similar process can take place in any dispute over values or in any dispute over the rightness or wrongness of actions. Thus whereas the cognitivist, so to speak, builds the cognitive element in value discussions into value judgment itself, the emotivist locates it in the reasons offered in support of the judgment. Because these reasons, insofar as they themselves are factual assertions, are amenable to rigorous scientific test, rational inquiry acquires a clear, if limited, relevance to value discussions.

It may be objected here that even if the emotivist's analysis allows the *possibility* of rational inquiry being used in value discussions, it provides no assurance that it will, or even that it always *ought*, to be so used. There is nothing in the emotivist's analysis to rule out the legitimacy of purely persuasive, propagandistic, and rhetorical means of altering the attitudes of other persons—nothing to rule out nonrational and even irrational methods. If the uppermost consideration is to employ techniques that will alter the feelings and attitudes of one's audience, then it must be recognized that often— perhaps more often than one likes to admit—people are more responsive to propaganda than to an objective presentation of facts.

Recent discussions have sought to find a rational basis for ethics that will avoid this objection to emotivism. We shall consider one such attempt, which marks a step in the direction of adapting the methods of science to the areas of value and ethics. This view introduces a rational element into value discussions by following through the implications of what it takes to be one of the logical features of value judgments, that is, that they are universalizable.

According to this view, to say that value judgments (and normative judgments generally) are universalizable, is to say that when one makes such a judgment, he is committing himself to a similar judgment about any similar thing in similar circumstances. If I judge that this car is good because it possesses features P, Q, and R, I am saying, implicitly, that *any* car that possesses these features is also good. I am committing myself to a standard of value (and in a particular prescriptive judgment like "you ought to do x" to a principle of conduct like "Everyone in similar situations ought to do x"). In short, a feature of normative judgments (which, incidentally, they share with factual statements) is that when one makes such a judgment, he is not judging simply about the *particular* thing that is the subject of his judgment but about a class of things that are similar to it. This creates interesting possibilities for rational discussion about values.

To illustrate, consider an example designed to show how a person can be brought to withdraw or modify a judgment when the implications of the judgment's universalizability are drawn out.

The example is adapted from a well-known parable [Matthew XVIII: 23]. *A* owes money to *B*, and *B* owes money to *C*, and it is the law that creditors may exact their debts by putting their debtors into prison. *B* asks himself, "Can I say that I ought to take this measure against *A* in order to make him pay?" He is no doubt *inclined* to do this, or *wants* to do it. Therefore, if there were no question of universalizing his prescriptions, he would assent readily to the *singular* prescription "Let me put *A* into prison." . . . But when he seeks to turn this prescription into a moral judgement, and say, "I *ought* to put *A* into prison because he will not pay me what he owes," he reflects that this would involve accepting the principle "Anyone who is in my position ought to put his debtor into prison if he does not pay." But then he reflects that *C* is in the same position of unpaid creditor with regard to himself (*B*), and that the cases are otherwise identical; and that if anyone in this position ought to put his debtors into prison, then so ought *C* to put him (*B*) into prison. And to accept the moral prescription "*C* ought to put me into prison" would commit him (since, as we have seen, he must be using the word "ought" prescriptively) to accepting the singular prescription "Let *C* put me into prison"; and this he is not ready to accept. But if he is not, then neither can he accept the original judgment that he (*B*) ought to put *A* into prison for debt.[21]

Although the person in this example is represented as uncovering the inconsistency by himself through private deliberation, it is easy to see how such a disclosure could be achieved in an interpersonal discussion involving two or more persons.

Recognition of this feature of normative judgments provides a means by which a person can be brought to withdraw or modify a previous judgment because of unwillingness to accept the full implications of his commitment in making the judgment; and it also shows how, sometimes at least, one may be brought to accept a new judgment by being shown that it accords with a standard or principle to which he is committed.

Suppose, for example, that you were attempting to convince someone that he should enroll in medical school. If in his previous judgments he had committed himself to a standard like "If an action has such and such characteristics, it is desirable," and you could argue convincingly that for such a person as himself studying medicine has these characteristics, you could lead him to accept the judgment that studying medicine is desirable for him. Your reasoning would then take the form of supplying a factual premise from which, in conjunction with a general value premise, a specific value judgment follows:

1. If an action has such and such characteristics, it is desirable (value premise)
2. Studying medicine for a person like yourself has these characteristics (factual premise)
3. Therefore, studying medicine for a person like yourself is desirable (value conclusion).

[21]R. M. Hare, *Freedom and Reason* (Oxford: Clarendon Press, 1963), pp. 90f. It is also presupposed in this example that to call an "ought" judgment prescriptive means that in making such a judgment one commits himself to assenting to an imperative which is entailed by it (what, in the example, is called a "singular prescription").

Not that in everyday discourse we set out our reasoning in nice, neat syllogistic form; but given a person's acceptance of a standard of value, one effective way of guiding his conduct is to bring him to realize that certain things or actions (that he might not previously have realized) indeed possess just those features he regards as value conferring.[22]

This mode of inquiry, as we have suggested, bears an analogy to that employed in science.

Just as science, seriously pursued, is the search for hypotheses and the testing of them by the attempt to falsify their particular consequences, so morals and value theory, we would add . . . consists in the search for principles and the testing of them against particular cases. Any rational activity has its discipline, and this is the discipline of moral thought: to test the moral principles that suggest themselves to us by following out their consequences and seeing whether we can accept *them*.[23]

A value hypothesis, we shall therefore propose, *can be considered validated to the extent that it does not lead the individual who holds it to conclusions that he is unwilling to accept as valuable or right and to the extent that it does lead to conclusions that he is willing to accept as valuable and right even when they do not accord with his momentary interest.* Unless inquiry leads to hypotheses that do not require continual modification and are fruitful for rendering choices intelligible and defensible to individuals who could not at the beginning agree on them, then there is no way for inquiry to settle disputes about values. Experience shows, however, that in most cases, agreement on underlying hypotheses or value judgments can be obtained even in the midst of disagreements about particular instances. Many "disagreements about values" are really disagreements about the facts of the case, that is, about the second premise; and we know that, in principle at least, disputes about facts can be settled by investigation and cooperation.

There is no guarantee that such a method will resolve all disputes about values; such a belief would be naive. But then it is doubtful that any method of inquiry in any reasonably large area whatsoever, whether it be in science, mathematics, economics, or politics, guarantees the resolution of all the problems of that area. This is true if only because *some* of the problems in virtually all but the most abstract of disciplines are problems of value. And we should be mindful here of Aristotle's cautionary observation that in dealing with questions of value we must be satisfied with as much certainty as the subject matter allows.[24] That rational inquiry has an important place in the field of value does not require that there be a fool-proof formula for solving all the problems of value.

Although the methodological analogy between science and value theory

[22]We are assuming, in this example, that the person also accepts the principle that one ought to do what is desirable.

[23]Hare, *op. cit.*, p. 92.

[24]Aristotle, *Nicomachaean Ethics*, 1098a.

is fruitful in the above respects, we must emphasize that it is a limited one. Whereas in science the considerations that lead us to modify or abandon an hypothesis will usually be formulable in verifiable statements of fact—those that lead us to modify a value hypothesis may be other value judgments (or, as in the above example, other prescriptive judgments and the singular prescriptions entailed by them). A specific value judgment that conflicts with a general hypothesis about value may be wrong itself, so that the specific value judgment in the particular case ought to be modified and the hypothesis reasserted; or the specific value judgment or decision in the particular case may be right, so that the hypothesis about values ought to be modified and rejected. In other words, the argument brings out a conflict of judgments that can be made consistent only if *either* the conclusion *or* the premise is changed; but we have no supersyllogism by which, in cases of such conflict, we can decide where the truth lies.

There does not, therefore, seem to be any way by which a value judgment, either a specific one applicable only to a given case or a general hypothesis about the kinds of things and actions that have value, can be *proved*. Although we know that the common notion that science proves its hypotheses is generally exaggerated and that science only shows that up to now such and such a hypothesis is superior to any known alternative, not even this limited degree of proof is available in an inquiry into what values may be absolute.

Science gets along very well without being able to reach the stage of proof. Yet because most people desire the comfort of assurance that they are absolutely right and feel dissatisfied with any inquiry concluding that such a degree of certainty in value judgments is unwarranted, they overlook the positive advantages that flow from recognizing that value principles are hypotheses. By searching out from the myriad of often conflicting desires and interests the common and underlying purposes and fundamental value judgments that we blindly and gropingly sought before, we may uncover a few ideals of great generality—ideals that would make a fundamental and ultimate appeal to us and to others. These fundamental principles, when acknowledged, become a standard by which our less fundamental and less well integrated desires are to be judged and disciplined. The unity of character is made more intelligible, and the settled disposition in our choices is made more intelligent when we orient our seeking for values around some critically examined principle. Even if the principle cannot be proved, it can be critically elaborated so that its implications can be applied to new and unexpected situations for which training and tradition have not adequately prepared us.

But a meeting of minds can be reached, if at all, only by the use of reason, by examining and weighing the conflicting commitments and choices we are pressed into making. Certainly such an exercise of reason in inquiry does not guarantee any individual's or institution's scale of values, nor can it promise that some scale of values can be found that will bring peace and harmony among now conflicting interests. But it may do two things, neither of which can be accomplished by any substitute for inquiry.

First, the use of reason in conjunction with the facts about our diverse experiences may reveal that the apparent diversity of value judgments is not so great as it seems. There will always be those whose value hypotheses are so deeply rooted in prejudice or dogmatism that they will persistently distort, misinterpret, or ignore facts that should lead them to revise their hypotheses. Moreover, there will always be legitimate (and indeed desirable) differences among the more particular values to which various persons subscribe. It is a good thing, for example, that some individuals value the study of medicine more than that of law or prefer carpentry to plumbing or truck driving to teaching. But on a more abstract level we might find that all or most men do fundamentally desire some of the same sorts of things and actions and states of mind, even though some seek them in one form and others in other ways. If this is so (and only the future progress of investigations in the psychology and sociology of value experience can show whether it is), then the conflicts among values may be found to lie on a relatively superficial level and appear to be fundamental and radical only because no deeper level of agreement and cooperation has been suspected or found. In this way, the French proverb *tout comprendre c'est tout pardonner*, so often cited as a basis for moral cynicism, indifferentism, and do-nothing-ism, might be found to contain a profoundly significant moral insight of quite another kind.

Whether this level of agreement can be attained is in the realm of conjecture and hope. If it is reached, it will be reached by a serious inquiry into what men do desire and consider valuable and by a reasonable attempt to discover among their desires some common core of what they *would* desire were they more reasonable, impartial, and wise. It will never be found by appealing to intuitions and revelations and authorities, which, because of their own divergencies, tend to divide instead of unite men.

Second, the exercise of reason in tolerant inquiry into conflicts of value is itself a value, perhaps one of the highest. Quite apart from whether it can eventually produce peace among men—of which one must have serious doubts—the attitude of inquiring, questioning, and cutting the suit of belief to fit the cloth of evidence seems to us to be good. A society that permits and encourages it is a more fit place for the development of the distinctive human talents of intellect and good will than a society that buys peace of mind by thwarting the quest for reasonable understanding and criticism of its values. Peace of mind brought about by a dominant ideology and enforced by propaganda and the sword might produce agreement and peace and harmony among men (although it has not done so in the past). But that peace would not be as valuable as the faltering and uncertain steps of men who are trying to understand what is right and to choose it by their own reason, even if they should never agree.

Even if one assumes that values do not have ontological status on a par with the properties investigated by science and that value judgments do not enjoy the cognitive status of empirical statements (both of which are issues that are far from settled), this in no way forces the conclusion that the fields of value and morality are off-limits to disciplined inquiry. It means only that the challenge to clarify and implement viable techniques of inquiry in these areas is that much greater. For there is a vast middle ground yet to be explored between the positions of Plato and Protagoras. Indeed, it is in this area that the justification of philosophic inquiry itself is to be found, for the question "Why Philosophy?" is a demand for a justification of the judgment that studying and doing philosophy are worthwhile ventures. We have tried to answer this by revealing some of what philosophy is and letting it speak for itself. However, it is not only the justification of philosophy but in the last analysis the justification of every purposeful human activity—from the commonplace matters of daily life to the most sophisticated efforts of the scientist—that calls for a judgment of value. It is only at risk of leaving unexamined the whole of man's theoretical and practical life that values can be exempted from inquiry.

BIBLIOGRAPHY

Ayer, A. J., *Language, Truth and Logic*, Chap. 6. New York: Dover Publications, Inc., 1952.

Baier, Kurt, *The Moral Point of View*. Ithaca, N.Y.: Cornell University Press, 1958.

Brandt, Richard B., *Ethical Theory*. Englewood Cliffs, N. J.: Prentice-Hall, Inc., 1959.

———, "The Significance of Differences of Ethical Opinion for Ethical Rationalism," *Philosophy and Phenomenological Research*, IV, No. 4 (June, 1944), 469–94.

Dewey, John, *Theory of the Moral Life*. New York: Holt, Rinehart & Winston, Inc., 1960.

———, "Theory of Valuation," *International Encyclopedia of Unified Science*, II, No. 4. Chicago: University of Chicago Press, 1939.

Frankena, William K., *Ethics*. Englewood Cliffs, N.J.: Prentice-Hall, Inc., 1963.

Hare, R. M., *The Language of Morals*. Oxford: Clarendon Press, 1952.

Kant, Immanuel, *Foundations of the Metaphysics of Morals* (1785), trans., Lewis W. Beck. New York: Liberal Arts Press, 1959.

Lafferty, T. T., "Empiricism and Objective Relativism in Value Theory," *Journal of Philosophy*, XLVI, No. 6 (March 17, 1949), 141–56.

Lewis, C. I., *An Analysis of Knowledge and Valuation*. Lasalle, Ill: Open Court Publishing Co., 1946.

Mothersill, Mary, ed., *Ethics*. New York: The Macmillan Company, 1965.

Otto, Max C., *Science and the Moral Life*. New York: New American Library, Mentor Books, 1950.

Parker, Dewitt H., *Human Values*. New York: Harper & Row, Publishers, 1931.

Pepper, Stephen C., *Ethics*. New York: Appleton-Century-Crofts, Inc., 1960.

———, *The Sources of Value*. Berkeley: University of California Press, 1958.

Perry, Ralph Barton, *General Theory of Value*. Cambridge, Mass.: Harvard University Press, 1926.

Plato, *Gorgias, Republic, Protagoras, Euthyphro, Crito*. Many editions.

Rice, Philip Blair, *On the Knowledge of Good and Evil*. New York: Random House, 1955.

Stevenson, Charles L., *Ethics and Language*. New Haven, Conn.: Yale University Press, 1944.

———, *Facts and Values*. New Haven, Conn.: Yale University Press, 1963.

Taylor, Paul W., *Normative Discourse*. Englewood Cliffs, N.J.: Prentice-Hall, Inc., 1961.

Toulmin, Stephen E., *An Examination of the Place of Reason in Ethics*. Cambridge, Eng.: Cambridge University Press, 1950.

QUESTIONS FOR REVIEW AND DISCUSSION

1. Review the account given in Chapter 1 of the ethical view presented by Euthyphro. Classify Euthyphro's theory according to the rubrics presented in the table on page 427.

2. Do you believe that psychological studies of human nature and anthropological studies of the various cultures can help us solve our own ethical problems?

3. It is sometimes thought that because different cultures have different values and different ethical practices there are no universal values or moral principles. Evaluate the objection that this view confuses descriptive laws of sociology with the prescriptive laws of ethics.

4. What influences has the theory of organic evolution had on ethical beliefs?

5. Review the theories of freedom presented earlier in this book on pages 230–39 and 334–36. What ethical theory or theories do these conceptions best accord with?

6. "To view the world as consisting only of physical facts and no values is like viewing human behavior as consisting only of bodily movements and no actions." Discuss.

7. "Take any action allowed to be vicious [wrong]: Willful murder, for instance. Examine it in all lights, and see if you can find that matter of fact, or real existence, which you call *vice* [wrongness]. In whichever way you take it, you find only certain passions, motives, volitions and thoughts. There is no other matter of fact in the case." Hume.
   If Hume is correct, does it follow that there is no such thing as right and wrong, hence no such thing as morality? Explain.

8. Plato believes that value concepts stand for eternal realities, whereas many positivists believe that they are pseudo-concepts and do not stand for anything at all. If a person subscribed to Plato's view would he be any more (or less) likely to pursue what he thinks is good than if he subscribed to the positivists' view? If so, why? If not, does it make any difference which view is more nearly right? Explain.

9. Ayer is one of the principal proponents of noncognitivism in ethics. He holds that value judgments are expressions of "certain moral sentiments." (*Language, Truth, and Logic*, p. 107). Is this singling out of *moral*

sentiments as a special kind of emotion consistent with the noncognitivists' denial that "moral" is a concept having empirical meaning?

10. Suppose that on his deathbed a close friend exacts from you a solemn promise to see that his fortune is spent improving the recreation facilities of the private club for millionaires to which he belongs; and that immediately after his death you receive an urgent request for just that sum of money from a research laboratory that is on the verge of discovering a cure for cancer. Suppose further (a) that you alone are entrusted to dispose of the money, and that in the law's view it now belongs to you; (b) that no one else knows of the promise; and (c) that you don't believe in God or an after life. What should you do and why? Does your answer to this make you a teleologist or a deontologist?

11. Using the model on page 195, try to analyze some moral decision as if it were an hypothesis to guide action. What are the collateral hypotheses involved? What takes the place of observation in the verification shown in that schema? What are the principal similarities and differences between a scientific hypothesis and your "decision as hypothesis" as indicated by a comparison of the two structures?

12. What are some of the historical and cultural consequences of the distinction between fact and value? Which have been good and which have been bad? Could science dispense with this distinction? Could philosophy?

INDEX